Television Program Master Index
Second Edition

Television Program Master Index

Access to Critical and Historical Information on 1,927 Shows in 925 Books, Dissertations, and Journal Articles

SECOND EDITION

Charles V. Dintrone

McFarland & Company, Inc., Publishers
Jefferson, North Carolina, and London

ISBN 0-7864-1492-8 (softcover : 50# alkaline paper) 

Library of Congress cataloguing data are available

British Library cataloguing data are available

Manufactured in the United States of America

McFarland & Company, Inc., Publishers
Box 611, Jefferson, North Carolina 28640
www.mcfarlandpub.com

To my wife, Pat,
for her assistance and encouragement

Acknowledgments

The origins of the first edition of this index begin with a student (Natalie Van Doren) who was doing research for a class taught by Dr. Michael Real at San Diego State University. I thank them both. Typing for the first edition was done by Sharon Dillon. Some of the typing for the second edition was done by Maria Canedo. My wife, Pat, also contributed with both ideas and hard work for both editions.

Enhancements for this edition required obtaining books and dissertations from other libraries. For this, I thank Kelly Martin and her Interlibrary Loan staff at San Diego State. I also thank the Circulation Desk under the supervision of Wendy Schmidt and her student assistants, who processed and checked out the books to me. I especially want to acknowledge Jenny Wilson, who seemed most often to be the one hauling books to the desk for me and who always did so in a cheerful manner.

Finally I thank everyone at San Diego State University Library who put up with me in the last stages of preparing the book.

Contents

Introduction

The first edition of this book came about when a student was referred to me for help on a paper she was doing on the show *60 Minutes*. I am a reference librarian at San Diego State University, and one of my subject areas is film and television. As a member of the first generation to grow up with television, I have always been fascinated by its influence and impact. While previewing the new books received by the library, I often see books about television, many of which have information on individual programs.

Television has become a major area of study. Television criticism began in the early days of television but in recent years has become more sophisticated, scholarly, and prolific. This is especially true since the first edition of this book was published in 1996. Television, because of its great presence and popularity, is an excellent subject for analysis and critical thinking. When writing and thinking about television programs from a critical viewpoint, it is important to have sources that tell you what others have said about these programs.

Libraries carry a wealth of material in this area, but useful references can be hard to find—especially references to specific shows that may be contained inside books on broader subjects. A book about situation comedies or westerns might contain valuable material related to specific programs such as *I Love Lucy* or *Gunsmoke*.

In order to make such material more accessible, I began a card-file index of references to television programs contained in books on television, communication, the media, and related topics. That index grew until it became the first edition of this book.

In this new edition I have expanded the number and types of sources indexed. The 1996 first edition indexed 341 sources containing references to 1,002 television programs. This new edition indexes 925 sources referring to 1,927 shows.

The index includes references to television programs (I use "show" and "program" interchangeably) found in the following kinds of sources:

Books on broad subjects but containing references to specific shows (as in the original edition), with many new books.
Books about one show.
Books covering many shows listed alphabetically.
Dissertations.
Major journal articles.

Whether or not to include a particular reference hinged on three factors: the source, the nature of the program, and the value of the reference.

Types of Sources Indexed

The vast majority of the books (and some dissertations and major journal articles) indexed are those that deal with television itself. However, books about communication and media are included, as are biographies and autobiographies of individuals who were influential in television. Congressional hearings on television violence, quiz show scandals, and so forth are also indexed.

Most of the books included are scholarly, but there are also many of a more popular nature, including memoirs, books meant for fans, and non-critical descriptive listings of shows. Books that consist mostly of photographs with very little text are not included. In some cases, a book is indexed only for its references to groups (see Appendix B) and not for any references to individual programs.

The earliest book indexed was published in 1956. It is Steve Allen's *The Funny Men*, which discusses the comedians of early television (Milton Berle, Sid Caesar, and others). There are several 2002 titles.

I searched for dissertations via DAI online and included them only if I could obtain them through Interlibrary Loan, since this means they would be available to others.

Journal articles are included if they are scholarly and with a few exceptions, at least four pages long or more (some of only three pages are included if noteworthy). To find the articles, I did a search via Ebscohost. I used Ebscohost because it is easy to search, allows for important limits (such as type of article and number of pages), and includes many journals that one could expect to have references to television programs.

Programs Included

The basic rule for a show to be included is that it appeared on a network, which for purposes of this book means ABC, CBS, FOX, NBC, UPN, or WB. Exceptions are noted below. Although most shows were broadcast during prime time, this is not a criterion. Network programs shown during the daytime (such as talk shows, soap operas, and game shows) and those shown late at night (such as *The Tonight Show* and *Saturday Night Live*) are also included. Generally, PBS shows are not included, but *Sesame Street* and *Mister Rogers' Neighborhood* are indexed because of the great number of references and the importance of these shows.

Syndicated or cable shows are generally excluded, but some exceptions seemed necessary. When I was uncertain whether to add a syndicated program, I generally referred to the seventh edition of Tim Brooks and Earle Marsh's standard work *The Complete Directory to Prime Time Network and Cable TV Shows, 1946–Present* (New York: Ballantine, 1999). Despite its title, it does include some syndicated shows, and some of those shows are indexed here. Some syndicated programs not in Brooks and Marsh were also included.

Another criterion for a show to be indexed is that it must be a series. Specials, television movies, and other one-time productions are excluded. Generally, miniseries are excluded, but a few (e.g., *Roots*) are indexed because of their importance and length.

In all cases, decisions as to what programs to include are, though based on the criteria enumerated above, the subjective judgment of the author.

The earliest program included in the listings is *Kraft Television Theater* from 1947. Other early shows are *Toast of the Town* (Ed Sullivan) and *Texaco Star Theater* (Milton Berle). The latest shows are *Normal, Ohio* and *City of Angels* (the medical one). Thanks to *The X-Files* and *Xena*, there are programs listed under every letter of the alphabet. The show with the most references is *Star Trek* (not including all variations but just the main entry, which includes the original series and general references). Next is *All in the Family* (the "winner" in the first edition), followed by *The Cosby Show*. These are the only three shows that have over 100 references.

Nature of References

The final determination that needed to be made, as I perused the books for mentions of programs, was what constituted a reference worth indexing. I settled on the guideline of citing only those show references that were important enough to be used for referencing in a paper. Mere mentions of the show (for example, in the midst of a listing of many shows) are not included. The rule of thumb was that there had to be at least two, or preferably three, sentences about the show in question. However, there are instances in which the show is mentioned as an example of a type or there is only one sentence but that one sentence, in my judgment, says something worthwhile (and worth quoting). In these cases, despite its brevity, the reference is indexed.

Books about one program were included if they were more than pictorials or trivia books. Books with shows in alphabetical order were added if they included episode guides or substantive descriptions of the show.

Organization of the Book

This book consists of two major sections with three appendices. The first part of the book contains all the television programs (alphabetically), each with a list of references (to works listed in Sources Used) in alphabetical order by author. The shows are alphabetized in a word-by-word (and not letter-by-letter) arrangement: For example, *I Spy* comes before *Incredible Hulk* and *Star Trek* before *Starsky and Hutch*. Dr., Mr., and St. are alphabetized as if spelled out as Doctor, Mister, and Saint. Numbers are also alphabetized as if spelled out. Articles (the, a, an) are put at the end of the show's title. Shows whose names begin with or consist of strings of letters are alphabetized as though the letters make up a single word. This is true regardless of any punctuation between the letters. Hence *N.Y.P.D. Blue* follows *Nutt House*; *M*A*S*H* follows *The Mary Tyler Moore Show*; and *WKRP in Cincinnati* follows *Wizards and Warriors*. For clarification, programs with the same title have appropriate notations to distinguish them.

The references show only author, year and page number; full publication information is found in the list of Sources Used beginning on page 000 (the second of the two major sections). More than one reference to the same last name and the same year are differentiated by letters after the year (1995a, 1995b). There is one exception to the author-year method: books that list shows alphabetically (i.e., page numbers are unnecessary) are given at the end of the references with the notation "Also in" (unless the program's only reference is from that book, in which case the notation is just "IN"). Specific page numbers are generally not given as well for dissertations and journal articles.

An asterisk (*) following a reference indicates that the information is substantial (usually at least two pages); two asterisks (**) mean that the source offers very substantial information (usually five or more pages) on the show.

Following the main sequence of the book—the programs, alphabetically—are three appendices. The first is a list of websites that lead you to information about programs. The second is an index to references on television to groups or classes of people—ethnic groups, occupations, demographic categories, and other identifiable population segments that are referred to collectively in the books. I tried to identify individual ethnic groups and other groups by the most widely accepted term. Under the names of these groups, references are given to works in the Sources Used listing in the same manner as for the television programs. Some titles appear in the Sources Used solely because they contain references to one or more groups in Appendix B.

The third appendix is a grouping of television programs by type or genre (situation comedy, Western, etc.). This allows researchers to locate references to that genre as well as to specific shows that can be used as examples of it. The genre with most shows listed is, not surprisingly, situation comedy.

The final section of the book is the bibliographical Sources Used. Arranged by author, then date, most entries include a descriptive annotation along with the bibliographic information. When the title makes it obvious what the book, dissertation, or journal article is about, there is no annotation. All works by one author come before works by that main author with coauthors. Works by one main author with different coauthors, are alphabetized by the second author. Multiple works by the same author or authors are listed chronologically (oldest first). Journal articles are listed with the first page only and then the number of pages. The year is repeated later in the entry if the date is more specific (for example, June 99).

I have written all of the annotations except where they were taken from the abstracts in Ebscohost for the journal articles. In those cases, a note is given at the end of the annotation: [Copyright Ebscohost].

It is my hope that this new and greatly expanded edition will be a valuable element for any reference collection (library or personal), allowing for a greatly enhanced and speeded-up ability to conduct research on television programs. I invite readers to write me to propose other sources for possible inclusion in any future edition.

Charles V. Dintrone
San Diego State University Library
5500 Campanile Drive
San Diego, CA 92182-8050
charles.dintrone @sdsu.edu

The Index
(by Television Show)

** = Substantial Information*
*** = Very Substantial Information*

1983, pp. 379–389**; Lichter, Lichter, & Rothman, 1991, pp. 186, 239; Lichter, Lichter, & Rothman, 1994, pp. 277, 342; Marc & Thompson, 1992 (Ch. 12 on Jack Webb), pp. 132–139; Martindale, 1991, pp. 1–15 (episode summaries); Meyers, 1981, pp. 141–142; Miles, 1975, pp. 44–46 (Nov. 21, 1973 show); Moyer & Alvarez, 2001, pp. 162–170**; Neuman, 1991, p. 112; Pearl & Pearl, 1999, pp. 125–126; Rovin, 1977b, p. 121; Rushkoff, 1994, pp. 47–48; Sackett, 1993, pp. 188–189; Turow, 1989, p. 166

Adam's Rib
Jarvis & Joseph, 1998, p. 172; Lichter, Lichter, & Rothman, 1991, pp. 40, 73–74; Lichter, Lichter, & Rothman, 1994, pp. 97, 140; Miles, 1975, pp. 63–64 (Dec. 21, 1974 show)

Addams Family, The
Bennett, 1996, pp. 71–74; Castleman & Podrazik, 1982, p. 173; Javna, 1985, pp. 40–43*; Jones, 1992, pp. 175–176; Mitz, 1980, pp. 211–215*; Penley, et al., 1991, p. 220; Skal, 1993, pp. 281–284; Spigel, 2001, p. 124; Stark, 1997, p. 117; Stempel, 1992, pp. 99–100; Story, 1993, pp. 81–97**; Van Hise, 1991, whole book**; Waldrep, 2000, pp. 196, 202; Wittebols, 1998, p. 4; Also in Bianculli, 1996, Eisner & Krinsky, 1984, Terrace, 1993

Admiral Broadway Revue
Castleman & Podrazik, 1982, pp. 39–40

Adventure
Gianakos, 1980, pp. 369–370

Adventures in Paradise
Castleman & Podrazik, 1982, pp. 131–132; Gianakos, 1978, pp. 239–242*; Hamamoto, 1994, p. 20; Rovin, 1977b, p. 74; Also in Terrace, 1993

Adventures of Brisco County, Jr., The
Aquila, 1996, p. 183; Capsuto, 2000, pp. 309–310; Jackson, 1994, pp. 218–219; Yoggy, 1995, pp. 625–629*; Also in Lentz, 1997

Adventures of Champion, The
Davis, 1995, pp. 211–212; Lichter, Lichter, & Rothman, 1994, p. 279; Yoggy, 1995, pp. 28–29; Also in Lentz, 1997

Adventures of Ellery Queen *see* **Ellery Queen**

Adventures of Jim Bowie, The
Davis, 1995, pp. 219–220; Gianakos, 1981, pp. 365–368; Jackson, 1994, pp. 73–74; Lichter, Lichter, & Rothman, 1991, pp. 262–263; Lichter, Lichter, & Rothman, 1994, p. 372; Rovin, 1977b, p. 49; Also in Lentz, 1997, West, 1987

Adventures of Kit Carson, The
Davis, 1995, p. 220; Jarvis & Joseph, 1998, pp. 192–193; Yoggy, 1995, p. 41; Also in Lentz, 1997, West, 1987

Adventures of Ozzie and Harriet, The
Bryant & Bryant, 2001, pp. 165–166; Castleman & Podrazik, 1982, pp. 17, 76–77; Cavallo, 1999, p. 36; Crotty, 1995; Davis, 2001, pp. 4–5; Fultz, 1998, p. 145; Gianakos, 1992, pp. 426–428*; Guida, 2000, pp. 184–185; Hawes, 2002, pp. 77–78; Himmelstein, 1994, p. 125; Jones, 1992, pp. 92–95, 123*; Kulzer, 1992, pp. 132–134; Leibman, 1995, pp. 7–9, 22, 28,

34, 37, 38, 41, 47, 51, 65–66, 89–90, 126–127, 133–135, 155, 205, 237, 238, 267**; Marc, 1989, p. 22; Marc, 1989, p. 92; Marc, 1997, pp. 18, 76–77; Meehan, 1983, pp. 35–38, 151–152, 164*; Mehling, 1962, pp. 153–155; Mitz, 1980, pp. 63–67*; Panati, 1991, pp. 304–305; Penley, et al., 1991, pp. 213–214; Putterman, 1995, p. 19; Silverblatt, Ferry, & Finan, 1999, p. 176; Spigel, 1992, pp. 60, 65, 131, 158–159, 167–168, 171, 177–178*; Spigel, 2001, pp. 44, 116, 196; Spigel & Mann, 1992, pp. 21–24*; Also in Bianculli, 1996, Eisner & Krinsky, 1984

Adventures of Rin Tin Tin, The
Castleman & Podrazik, 1982, p. 95; Davis, 1995, pp. 226–227; Fagen, 1996, pp. 9–15 (interview with Lee Aaker)**; Gianakos, 1981, pp. 313–318**; Hawes, 2002, p. 126; Jackson, 1994, pp. 54–56; McDonald, 1987, p. 38; Rovin, 1977b, p. 39; Yoggy, 1995, pp. 43–45*; Also in Lentz, 1997, West, 1987

Adventures of Robin Hood *see* Robin Hood

Adventures of Sir Francis Drake, The
Gianakos, 1983, pp. 352–353

Adventures of Sir Lancelot, The
Miller, 2000, pp. 21–22, 22–23

Adventures of Superboy *see* Superboy

Adventures of Superman, The
Bifulco, 1998, whole book**; Daniels, 1995, pp. 108–112*; Davis, 1995, pp. 37–41**; Fitzgerald & Magers, 2002, pp. 32–34, 196–199*; Gerani, 1977, pp. 13–23**; Harmon, 1992, p. 213; Heldenfels, 1994, pp. 148, 153; Javna, 1985, pp. 32–35*; Klobas, 1988, pp. 13–14; Rose, 1985, p. 93; Rovin, 1977b, pp. 11, 21–24*; Also in Bianculli, 1996

Adventures of Wild Bill Hickock, The
Davis, 1995, pp. 231–233*; Gianakos, 1983, pp. 263–269**; Jackson, 1994, pp. 49–50; Jarvis & Joseph, 1998, p. 194; McDonald, 1987, pp. 26, 29–30, 33; Rainey, 1998, pp. 205–210; Yoggy, 1995, pp. 39–41*; Also in Lentz, 1997, Terrace, 1993, West, 1987

A.E.S. Hudson Street
Kalisch, Kalisch, & Scobey, 1983, pp. 98–100; Paietta & Kauppila, 1999, p. 321; Turow, 1989, pp. 219–220

After M.A.S.H.
Hamamoto, 1994, pp. 25–26; Klobas, 1988, pp. 254–255, 301–302; Lichter, Lichter, & Rothman, 1991, pp. 121–122; Lichter, Lichter, & Rothman, 1994, pp. 198–199; Paietta & Kauppila, 1999, p. 321; Pegg, 2002, p. 105; Turow, 1989, pp. 224–228*; U.S. Congress, 1985, p. 170

Against the Grain
Suman, 1997, pp. 77, 114

Against the Law
Leonard, 1997, p. 140

Airwolf
Gianakos, 1987, pp. 338–339; Gianakos, 1992, pp. 267–269*; Klobas, 1988, pp. 178–179, 189–190, 262–263, 335–336; Lichter, Lichter, & Rothman, 1991, pp. 39, 266–267; Lichter,

Lichter, & Rothman, 1994, p. 97; Pearl & Pearl, 1999, p. 178; Also in Terrace, 1993

A.K.A. Pablo
Rodriguez, 1997, pp. 66, 67

Alan Young Show, The
Kulzer, 1992, pp. 201–203

Alaskans, The
Castleman & Podrazik, 1982, p. 131; Fitzgerald & Magers, 2002, pp. 138–139; Gianakos, 1978, pp. 237–238; Jackson, 1994, pp. 135–136; Yoggy, 1995, p. 243; Also in Lentz, 1997, West, 1987

Alcoa Premiere
Gianakos, 1978, pp. 352–355*

Alcoa Presents
Gianakos, 1978, pp. 198–200*

Alcoa Theatre
Gianakos, 1978, pp. 167–169

Aldrich Family, The
Castleman & Podrazik, 1982, p. 53; Hawes, 2002, p. 78; Mitz, 1980, p. 22

ALF
Jones, 1992, p. 262; Klobas, 1988, pp. 109–111; Owen, 1997, pp. 55–56; Putterman, 1995, pp. 102–106*; Sackett, 1993, pp. 318–319; White, 1992, pp. 1–6, 10**; Also in Bianculli, 1996, Terrace, 1993

Alfred Hitchcock Presents
Abelman, 1998, p. 394; Bogle, 2001, pp. 58–59; Buxton, 1990, pp. 24–26; Gianakos, 1978, pp. 63–76**; Gianakos, 1992, pp. 398–400*; Hawes 2002, pp. 194–196*; Javna, 1985, pp. 126–129*; Kapsis, 1992, pp. 30–34, 37–42**; Klobas, 1988, pp. 266–267; Lichter, Lichter, & Rothman, 1991, pp. 146–147; Lichter, Lichter, & Rothman, 1994, pp. 230–231*; Martin, 1980**; Muir, 2001a, pp. 139–160**; Muir, 2001b, pp. 219–220; Nelson & Gaonkar, 1996, p. 334; Sackett, 1993, pp. 64–65; Spoto, 1983, pp. 369–375, 377, 403–404, 409, 415, 446–448**; Taylor, 1978, pp. 226–232**; Also in Bianculli, 1996

Alias Smith and Jones
Creeber, 2001, p. 16; Gianakos, 1981, pp. 412–415*; Jackson, 1994, pp. 190–193; Marc & Thompson, 1992, pp. 171–178; Rovin, 1977b, p. 130; Yoggy, 1995, pp. 471–484**; Also in Lentz, 1997, West, 1987

Alice
Coakley, 1977, pp. 35–36, 137, 139, 156; Guida, 2000, pp. 208–209; Jones, 1992, pp. 246–247; Klobas, 1988, pp. 77–78, 176–177; Lichter, Lichter, & Rothman, 1994, pp. 136, 196–197; Meehan, 1983, pp. 92–94, 178; Mitz, 1980, pp. 383–386*; Panati, 1991, pp. 427–428; Pegg, 2002, p. 220; Pitrone, 1999, p. 180; Press, 1991, pp. 37, 117–120, 128–129*; Puette, 1992, p. 179; Rafkin, 1998, pp. 95–96; Sackett, 1993, pp. 248–249; Schwartz, 1999, p. 134; Shaheen, 1984, pp. 64–67; Also in Eisner & Krinsky, 1984, Terrace, 1993

Alien Nation
Jarvis & Joseph, 1998, p. 296 (n. 22); Leonard, 1997, pp. 120–122*; Parenti, 1991, pp. 34–35; Also in Terrace, 1993

Aliens in the Family
Owen, 1997, p. 23

All-American Girl

Cotter, 1997, pp. 461–463; Holtzman, 2000, pp. 223–224; Kamalipour & Carrilli, 1998, pp. 128–134**; Owen, 1997, pp. 122–123; Patton, 2001

All in the Family

Abelman, 1998, p. 327; Abt & Mustazza, 1997, pp. 44–45; Adler, 1976, pp. 59–75**; Adler, 1979, whole book**; Adler, 1981, pp. 66–67; Agee, Ault, & Emery, 1982, pp. 192–195; Alley, 1977, pp. 33, 41, 46, 133–137; Andrews, 1986, pp. 135–136; Atwan, Orton, & Vesterman, 1978, p. 383; Barnouw, 1990, pp. 432–434; Batra, 1987, pp. 115–117*; Bedell, 1981, pp. 39–50**; Bennett, 1996, pp. 95–96; Blum & Lindheim, 1987, pp. 16, 144; Burks, 1990; Caldwell, 1995, p. 43; Cantor & Cantor, 1992, p. 29; Capsuto, 2000, pp. 71–73, 135–137**; Carey, 1988, pp. 128–130; Castleman & Podrazik, 1982, pp. 226–227, 237–239**; Cater, 1975, pp. 52–58**; Chunovic, 2000, pp. 12, 13, 61–65, 73**; Coakley, 1977, pp. 35, 43–47 (passim), 92–93, 137, 141–142, 235–237, 263; Combs, 1993, p. 37; Cortes, 2000, pp. 80–81; Croteau & Hoynes, 2000, pp. 177, 217, 250–251*; Crotty, 1995; Crown, 1999, pp. 37, 49; Cuklanz, 2000, pp. 128–129, 139–141*; Dates & Barlow, 1990, p. 268; Dates & Barlow, 1993, pp. 290–291; Davis, 2001, pp. 10–11, 97; Dow, 1996, p. 149; Erickson, 2000, pp. 194, 241; Everitt, 2001, p. 205; Freeman, 1980, pp. 93–95; Gabler, Rich & Antler, 2000, pp. 37–38; Gauntlett & Hill, 1999, p. 214; Gelbart, 1998, p. 117; Gitlin, 1983, see index, especially pp. 211–217*; Goethals, 1981, pp. 41–46**; Goldenson, 1991, pp. 321–322; Griffin, 1980, p. 265; Gross, 2001, pp. 81, 163; Hamamoto, 1989, pp. 103–104; Hawes, 2002, p. 197; Heldenfels, 1994, pp. 56–57; Hiebert & Reuss, 1985, pp. 468–472; Himmelstein, 1984, pp. 121–131**; Himmelstein, 1994, pp. 117, 165–173**; Holtzman, 2000, p 124; Howitt, 1982, pp. 65–67; Jackson, 1997, p. 258; Jarvik, 1997, p. 266; Javna, 1985, p. 22; Jones, 1992, pp. 204–213, 221, 222–223**; Kassel 1993, p. 77; Kuney, 1990, pp. 79–85*; Kutulas, 1998; Lazere, 1987, pp. 247, 249; Leibman, 1995, p. 262; Lester, 1996, pp. 61–62, 153; Lichter, Lichter, & Rothman, 1991, pp. 92–93, 153–154, 240–242, 256–257, 276, also see index*; Lichter, Lichter, & Rothman, 1994, pp. 92–93, 95, 164–165, 237–239, 343–345, 361, 364**; Luke, 1990, pp. 227–228; Mankiewicz & Swerdlow, 1978, pp. 97–100; Marc & Thompson, 1992 (Ch. 4 on Norman Lear), pp. 49–60, especially pp. 51–53; Marc, 1989, pp. 25–26, 174–184, 185–187**; Marc, 1996, p. 13; Marc, 1997, pp. 21–22, 137, 144–152, 153–155, 190–191**; Marsh, 1975, whole book**; Marsh, 1977, whole book**; Martin, 1980**; McCrohan, 1990, pp. 7, 208–224**; McDonald, 1983, pp. 178–181*; McDonald, 1992, pp. 181–185*; Meehan, 1983, pp. 46–49, 130, 152, 175*; Miles, 1975, pp. 65–67 (Nov. 10, 1973); Miller, 1980, pp. 35, 37–38, 67, 94, 128, 152, 181, 191, 192, 194, 200*; Miller, 2000, pp. 141–150, 151, 155–156, 157–158, 161**; Mitz, 1980, pp. 253–259**; Newcomb, 1976, pp. 11–13, 26–34, 35–42**; Newcomb, 1979, pp. 26–28, 55–58, 266, 311, 351–352, 428, 528*; Newcomb, 1982, pp. 18–20, 374–375; Newcomb, 1987, pp. 26–27, 180–193, 337, 462, 497–498, 514, 618, 626**; Newcomb, 1994, pp. 88–98, 509, 522**; Newcomb, 2000, pp. 170–181, 579–580**; Newcomb & Alley, 1983, pp. 174–195 (passim)*; Orlik, 1994, p. 113; Oskamp, 1988, p. 115; Panati, 1991, pp. 416–418; Parenti, 1991, pp. 71–73; Pearl & Pearl, 1999, pp. 5, 26, 40, 53, 91, 96, 109*; Puette, 1992, pp. 51–52, 174–175; Real, 1977, pp. 33–36; Rodriguez, 1997, p. 62; Rose, 1985, pp. 110–112, 120*; Rubin, 1980, p. 192; Sackett, 1993, pp. 182–183; Schwartz, 1999, p. 130; Selnow & Gilbert, 1993, p. 6; Shaheen, 1984, pp. 61–62; Shales, 1982, pp. 78–80; Silverblatt, Ferry, & Finan, 1999, p. 121; Smith, 1997a; Staiger, 2000, pp. 47, 81–111, 119, 161, 162, 163; Stark, 1997, pp. 162–167**; Stempel, 1992, pp. 144–148*; Suman & Rossman, 2000, p. 117; Tabarlet, 1993; Taylor, 1989, pp. 46, 57, 66–77**; Thompson, 1996, pp. 29, 54–55; Tinker & Rukeyser, 1994, p. 103; Toll, 1982, pp. 240–241; Turow, 1984, pp. 178, 180–182; U.S. Department of Health..., 1982, pp. 268–269; Vane & Gross, 1994, p. 104; Waldrep, 2000, pp. 195, 201; Walters, 2001, p. 60; Weimann, 2000, p. 238; Williams, 1982, pp. 135–136; Wilson & Gutierrez, 1985, pp. 47–51*; Witney, 1981, pp. 274–279 (passim); Wittebols, 1998, pp. 5–7, 8, 9*; Wolff, 1996, p. 11; Woll & Miller, 1987, pp. 80–81; Also in Bianculli, 1996, Eisner & Krinsky, 1984, Terrace, 1993

All My Children

Abelman, 1998, pp. 360–263*; Allen, 1992, pp. 225–237**; Allen, 1995, pp. 175, 190–192*; Alley & Brown, 2001, p. 27; Berry & Manning-Miller, 1996, pp. 154, 156; Broughton, 1986, pp. 181–182; Brown, 1994, p. 69; Bryant, 1990, pp. 115–118, 121–122; Buckman, 1984, pp. 139, 190; Capsuto, 2000, pp. 181–182, 190; Cross, 1983, pp. 125–126, 127, 133–134, 135, 138; Fiske, 1987, p. 123; Gilbert, 1976, pp. 132–151*; Gitlin, 1986, pp. 43, 44, 46, 49; Greenberg & Busselle, 1996; Gross, 2001, pp. 86, 217, 219–220; Gross & Woods, 1999, p. 294; Harris, 1998, pp. 115–126 (passim); James, 1991**; Jenrette, McIntosh, & Winterberger, 1999; Kalisch, Kalisch, & Scobey, 1983, pp. 172–174; Kaminsky, 1985, pp. 89–91, 94, 96–97, 99, 100, 101–103, 105, 107–108*; Kaplan, 1983, pp. 104–105; Kuney, 1990, pp. 124–126 (passim); Lechner, 2000, pp. 68–71, 98–99, 130–131, 167–169, 207–209**; Lembo, 2000, pp. 186–187, 188; Matelski, 1988, pp. 8, 20, 22, 44, 50–59**; Matelski, 1999, pp. 23, 40; Nelson, 1995, pp. 57, 58–59; Newcomb, 1982, pp. 136–143**; Newcomb, 1987, pp. 166–173**; Parenti, 1991, p. 99; Press, 1991, pp. 88–90; Raymond, 1990, pp. 112–118**; Rose, 1985, p. 142; Rouverol, 1984, pp. 23, 140, 152–153, 157–158; Rouverol, 1992, pp. 253, 280; Stark, 1997, pp. 204, 206–208; Suman & Rossman, 2000, p. 16; Wakefield, 1976, whole book**; Walters, 2001, pp. 102–103; Warner, 1994, whole book**; Warrick, 1980, whole book**; Williams, 1992, pp. 30, 32, 45–47, 53, 56–59, 82–83, 84, 87, 88, 99–100, 101–102, 106, 114–115, 131–132, 135, 146, 153–155, 163–164, 174, 176**; Also in Bianculli, 1996

All Star Revue *see* **Jimmy Durante Show**

All's Fair

Capsuto, 2000, pp. 347–348; Coakley, 1977, pp. 31, 34, 105, 188–189, 237–238; Puette, 1992, pp. 52, 176

Ally

Lechner, 2000, pp. 112–113

Ally McBeal
Capsuto, 2000, p. 410; Castarphen & Zavoina, 1999, p. 284; Chunovic, 2000, pp. 21–22, 150–151, 173; Cortes, 2000, pp. 23, 136; Creeber, 2001, p. 45; Davis, 2001, pp. 20, 82–94, 310**; Entman & Rojecki, 2000, p. 220; Gross, 2001, p. 93; Helford, 2000, pp. 6, 165; Hollows, 2000, p. 198; Isaacs, 1999, pp. 9, 110–111, 112–113, 129*; Jarvis & Joseph, 1998, pp. 177–178, 248; Johnston, 2000, p. 74; Longworth, 2000, pp. 61, 63; Marek, 1999; Nochimson, 2000; Patton, 2001; Schwartz, 1999, p. 135; Suman & Rossman, 2000, p. 119; Walters, 2001, pp. 119–120

Almost Grown
Lichter, Lichter, & Rothman, 1994, p. 158

Almost Home
Cotter, 1997, pp. 429–432*; Also in Terrace, 2000

Aloha Paradise
Gianakos, 1983, p. 192; Also in Terrace, 1993

Alright Already
IN Terrace, 2000

Alvin Show, The
Davis, 1995, pp. 46–47; Also in Eisner & Krinsky, 1984

A.M. America
Hack, pp. 89–90

Amazing Spider-Man
Gianakos, 1981, p. 250; Also in Terrace, 1993

Amazing Stories
Edelman & Kupferberg, 1996, p. 224; Gianakos, 1992, pp. 395–397*; Muir, 2001a, pp. 569–573*; Also in Bianculli, 1996

Amen
Bogle, 2001, pp. 312–315; Dates & Barlow, 1990, pp. 278–279; Dates & Barlow, 1993, pp. 300–301; Hamamoto, 1989, pp. 137–138; Jarvis & Joseph, 1998, p. 175; Suman, 1997, p. 80; Also in Terrace, 1993, Terrace, 2000

American Bandstand
Castleman & Podrazik, 1982, pp. 121–122; Davis, 1995, pp. 123–126**; Goldenson, 1991, pp. 161–165; Jackson, 1997, almost whole book**; McDonald, 1983, p. 79; McDonald, 1992, p. 89; Panati, 1991, pp. 275–277; Shore, 1985, whole book**; Stark, 1997, pp. 68–73**; Also in Bianculli, 1996

American Chronicles
Caldwell, 1995, pp. 233–236*; Woods, 1997, pp. 132–133

American Dreamer
IN Terrace, 1993, Terrace, 2000

American Girls, The
Gianakos, 1981, p. 257; Meyers, 1981, p. 251; Schwartz, 1999, p. 140; Also in Terrace, 1993

American Gothic
Muir, 2001a, pp. 397–409**; Paietta & Kauppila, 1999, pp. 321–322

American Parade, The (Later Crossroads)
Joyce, 1988, pp. 273–280, 287–288, 336–337, 344–347, 396–397**

American Scene *see* **Jackie Gleason Show**

Americans, The
Gianakos, 1978, p. 320; Also in West, 1987

America's Funniest Home Videos
Dienst, 1994, p. 91; Munson, 1993, pp. 149–151; Sackett, 1993, pp. 329–330; Also in Bianculli, 1996

America's Most Wanted
Abelman, 1998, p. 419; Block, 1990, pp. 246–256**; Boylan, 2000, pp. 297–304, 307–311**; Caldwell, 1995, p. 259; Fishman, 1999; Friedman, 2002, pp. 18, 236–255**; Gross, 2001, pp. 164–166; Munson, 1993, see index; Roman, 1996, p. 73; Tulloch, 2000, p. 74; Walsh, 1998, whole book**; Walsh, 2001, whole book**; Also in Bianculli, 1996

Amos Burke, Secret Agent *see* **Burke's Law**

Amos 'n' Andy
Abelman, 1998, pp. 38, 329; Andrews, 1986, pp. 46–64, 67–103, 107–108, 113–116, 148–181**; Barker, 1999, pp. 78–79; Bernardi, 1998, p. 32; Bogle, 2001, pp. 26–41, 48**; Castleman & Podrazik, 1982, pp. 42–43, 57–59, 77*; Cortes, 2000, pp. 41–42; Dates & Barlow, 1990, pp. 264–265; Dates & Barlow, 1993, pp. 286–288*; Davis, 2001, pp. 2–3; Davis & Baran, 1981, pp. 85–86; Ely, 1991, pp. 6–9, 203–254**; Entman & Rojecki, 2000, p. 160; Fox, 2001, pp. 41–42; Hamamoto, 1989, pp. 42–43; Harris, 1989, p. 32; Harris, 1994, p. 37; Hawes, 2002, pp. 71–72, 171–172; Heldenfels, 1994, pp. 33–34; Hiebert & Reuss, p. 386; Holtzman, 2000, p 248; Jackson, 1982*; Jarvis & Joseph, 1998, pp. 167–168; Jones, 1992, pp. 40, 50–61, 127, 216–217**; Kalisch, Kalisch, & Scobey, 1983, p. 15; Kamalipour & Carrilli, 1998, pp. 81–82, 83; Lichter, Lichter, & Rothman, 1991, pp. 233–237; Lichter, Lichter, & Rothman, 1994, pp. 336–337*; McDonald, 1983, pp. 26–33**; McDonald, 1992, pp. 27–35**; Means Coleman, 2000, pp. 60–65, 84, 104, 124**; Means Coleman, 2002, pp. 52–54*; Mitz, 1980, pp. 27–31*; Montgomery, 1989, pp. 14–15; Newcomb, 2000, pp. 57–58, 286; O'Connor, 1983, pp. 33–50**; Pounds, 1999, p. 50; Roman, 1996, p. 56; Rubin, 1980, pp. 127–129; Smith, 1997a; Spigel, 1992, pp. 129–130, 156; Spigel & Mann, 1992, pp. 78, 80, 92, 94–97*; Staiger, 2000, pp. 146–147; Turner, 1994, pp. 121–122*; Wagner & Lundeen, 1998, p. 4; Wilson & Gutierrez, 1985, p. 98; Woll & Miller, 1987, pp. 70–71; Also in Bianculli, 1996, Eisner & Krinsky, 1984, Terrace, 1993

Amy Prentiss
Alley & Brown, 2001, p. 100

Andros Targets, The
Daniel, 1996, pp. 16–17; Gianakos, 1981, pp. 220–221

Andy Griffith Show, The
Bennett, 1996, pp. 35–42; Castleman & Podrazik, 1982, p. 144; Craig, 1992, pp. 100–101; Freeman, 1980, pp. 89–90; Guida, 2000, pp. 188–189; Hamamoto, 1989, pp. 53–54; Himmelstein, 1984, pp. 102–106*; Himmelstein, 1994, pp. 142–146**; Javna,

1985, pp. 210–213*; Jones, 1992, pp. 136–140*; McCrohan, 1990, pp. 161–168**; McDonald, 1992, pp. 89–90; Mitz, 1980, pp. 163–167*; Newcomb & Alley, 1983, p. 28; Panati, 1991, p. 351; Pegg, 2002, pp. 13, 174–182, 198, 201–204**; Pfeiffer, 1994, whole book**; Rafkin, 1998, pp. 36–41*; Robinson & Fernandes, 1996, whole book**; Sackett, 1993, pp. 100–101; Spignelli, 1987, whole book**; Stempel, 1992, pp. 95–96; Story, 1993, pp. 15–34**; Thomas, 1991, p. 213; Thompson, 1996, p. 27; Also in Bianculli, 1996, Eisner & Krinsky, 1984, Terrace, 1993

Andy Williams Show, The
Mott, 2000, pp. 149–151

Andy's Gang
IN Terrace, 1993

Angel
Kaveney, 2001**; Muir, 2001a, pp. 564–566*

Angel Street
Lichter, Lichter, & Rothman, 1994, p. 72; Also in Terrace, 1993

Angie
Paietta & Kauppila, 1999, p. 322; Sackett, 1993, pp. 252–253; Also in Terrace, 1993

Ann Jillian
IN Terrace, 2000

Ann Sothern Show, The
Hawes, 2002, p. 95; Meehan, 1983, p. 166; Sanders & Gilbert, 1993, pp. 158–160; Schultz, 1990, pp. 11–12, 136–148 (episode guides)*; Seger, 1996, p. 33; Also in Eisner & Krinsky, 1984, Terrace, 1993

Annie McGuire
Also in Terrace, 1993

Annie Oakley
Davis, 1995, p. 209; Gianakos, 1983, pp. 299–301; Hamamoto, 1994, pp. 57–58; Heldenfels, 1994, p. 39; Holtzman, 2000, p. 223; Jackson, 1994, pp. 52–54; McDonald, 1987, pp. 27, 32–33; Rovin, 1977b, pp. 38–39; Yoggy, 1995, pp. 25–28*; Also in Lentz, 1997, Terrace, 1993 , West, 1987

Another World
Berry & Manning-Miller, 1996, p. 146; Broughton, 1986, pp. 183–184; Buckman, 1984, pp. 49–51, 152, 154–155*; Cross, 1983, pp. 129, 135; Edmondson & Rounds, 1973, pp. 167, 171–173; Edmondson & Rounds, 1976, pp. 151, 155–156; Fowles, 1982, p. 152; Gilbert, 1976, pp. 80–107**; James, 1991**; Kalisch, Kalisch, & Scobey, 1983, pp. 170–172, 174*; Lemay, whole book**; Matelski, 1988, pp. 23, 44, 59–70**; Matelski, 1999, pp. 40–41; Nelson, 1995, p. 59; Newcomb, 1976, pp. 57–58, 59–62*; Newcomb, 1979, pp. 78–79, 80–83*; O'Dell, 1997, p. 189; Parenti, 1991, p. 98; Schultz, 2000, p. 123; Weimann, 2000, p. 174; Williams, 1992, p. 84; Also in Bianculli, 1996

Antagonists, The
Jarvis & Joseph, 1998, p. 234

Anything But Love
Pearl & Pearl, 1999, pp. 43, 44–45, 46, 197–198*; Sackett, 1993, p. 327; Steenland, 1990, p. 15; Also in Terrace, 1993

Apple Pie
IN Terrace, 1993

Apple's Way
Bedell, 1981, p. 88; Gianakos, 1978, pp. 751–752; Lichter, Lichter, & Rothman, 1991, pp. 95–96; Lichter, Lichter, & Rothman, 1994, p. 168

Appointment with Adventure
Gianakos, 1980, pp. 418–419

Aquanuts *see* Malibu Run

Archer
Gianakos, 1978, p. 771

Archie Bunker's Place
Hiebert & Reuss, 1985, pp. 468–472; Marc, 1989, p. 186; Marc, 1997, pp. 153–154; Pearl & Pearl, 1999, pp. 21–22, 48, 115–116, 130–131, 217, 219*; Puette, 1992, pp. 52, 185; Williams, 1982, pp. 135–136

Armstrong Circle Theatre
Gianakos, 1978, pp. 83–105**; Gianakos, 1980, pp. 254–260, 473, 475**; Hawes, 2001, pp. 137–139

Arnie
Jones, 1992, p. 193; Marc, 1989, p. 179; Marc, 1997, p. 148; Tinker & Rukeyser, 1994, p. 85; Also in Terrace, 1993

Arrest and Trial
Gianakos, 1978, pp. 406–408*; Lichter, Lichter, & Rothman, 1994, p. 276; Meyers, 1981, pp. 91–92; Rovin, 1977b, p. 87

Arsenio Hall Show, The
Bogle, 2001, p. 358; Capsuto, 2000, p. 267; Carter, 1994, pp. 84–86, plus see index; McDonald, 1992, p. 288; Also in Bianculli, 1996

Arthur Godfrey
Castleman & Podrazik, 1982, pp. 18–19, 39, 47, 61, 86*; Heldenfels, 1994, pp. 17–18; Jackson, 1982; Lewis & Lewis, 1979, pp. 149–154; McCrohan, 1990, pp. 38–46**; Putterman, 1995, pp. 12–14*; Rafkin, 1998, pp. 23–25*; Sackett, 1993, pp. 18–19, 29; Singer, 2000, pp. 88–89, 90–91, 92–123, 124–155, 163–175 (passim); Spigel & Mann, 1992, p. 51; Stark, 1997, p. 324; Wilk, 1976, pp. 153–158*; Also in Bianculli, 1996

As the World Turns
Adams, 1980, whole book**; Allen, 1985, p. 57; Allen, 1995, pp. 145, 149, 153; Blumler, 1992, pp. 97–114*; Broughton, 1986, p. 186; Buckman, 1984, pp. 71, 76; Burks, 1990; Edmondson & Rounds, 1973, p. 167; Edmondson & Rounds, 1976, p. 152; Fowles, 1982, p. 151; Fowles, 1992, pp. 167–168; Fulton, 1995, whole book**; Gilbert, 1976, pp. 58–79**; James, 1991**; Kassel, 1993, p. 20; Matelski, 1988, pp. 23, 44, 70–86**; Matelski, 1999, p. 41; Nelson, 1995, pp. 59–60; Nochimson, 1992, pp. 15–18, 59–63, 174–178**; O'Dell, 1997, pp. 187, 188, 189; Rouverol, 1984, pp. 42, 55–63, 93–101, 151*; Rouverol, 1992, pp. 34–35, 249, 257–274**; Williams, 1992, pp. 30, 38, 84–85, 88, 102, 108, 132, 155–156, 173–174, 180*; Also in Bianculli, 1996

Asphalt Jungle, The
Gianakos, 1978, pp. 322–323

Assignment: Foreign Legion
Gianakos, 1981, p. 371

Automan
Gianakos, 1987, pp. 333–334

Autry, Gene *see* **Gene Autry Show**

Avengers, The
Aldgate, 2000, pp. 37–69, 185**; Buxton, 1990, pp. 96, 98–107**; Castleman & Podrazik, 1982, pp. 169, 184, 202; Chunovic, 2000, pp. 51–54*; Creeber, 2001, pp. 20–21; Gamman & Marshment, 1988, P. 10; Gianakos, 1978, pp. 527–532**; Gianakos, 1981, pp. 268–269; Gregory, 2000, p. 6; Inness, 1999, pp. 31–32, 33–37, 49**; Javna, 1985, pp. 62–65*; Kidd-Hewitt & Osborne, 1995, p. 166; Lichter, Lichter, & Rothman, 1994, p. 261; Lisanti & Paul, 2002, pp. 24, 69–71, 257–259, 288–289**; Meyers, 1981, pp. 126–131*; Miller, 1997, whole book**; Miller, 2000, pp. 51, 53–60, 63–74, 93, 179–180**; Newcomb, 1976, pp. 99–101 (passim); Osgerby & Gough-Yates, 2001, pp. 3, 7–8, 25, 84–85, 197–198, 221–235**; Seger, 1996, p. 155; Smith, 1989, pp. 165–169, 174; Soter, 2002, pp. 64–97, 127–148, 157–189**; Spigel & Curtin, 1997, pp. 87, 89; Story, 1993, pp. 211–223**; Also in Bianculli, 1996, Terrace, 1993

Baa Baa Black Sheep
Gianakos, 1981, pp. 204–206*; Kalisch, Kalisch, & Scobey, 1983, pp. 109–113*; Lichter, Lichter, & Rothman, 1991, pp. 273, 275–276; Lichter, Lichter, & Rothman, 1994, pp. 385–386; Paietta & Kauppila, 1999, p. 322; Thompson, 1990, pp. 74–79*; U.S. Congress, 1977b, p. 435

Babes
Haralovich & Rabinovitz, 1999, pp. 194–197*; Also in Terrace, 1993, Terrace, 2000

Baby Boom
Bryant, 1990, p. 42; Also in Terrace, 1993

Baby, I'm Back
Berry & Mitchell-Kernan, 1982, pp. 77, 125; McDonald, 1983, p. 226; McDonald, 1992, pp. 226–227; Also in Terrace, 1993

Baby Talk
IN Terrace, 1993, Terrace, 2000

Bachelor Father
Bernardi, 1998, p. 32; Caldwell, 1995, p. 71; Hamamoto, 1989, pp. 33–34; Hamamoto, 1994, p. 7; Hawes, 2002, p. 89; Jarvis & Joseph, 1998, p. 169; Jones, 1992, pp. 128, 130; Lichter, Lichter, & Rothman, 1991, p. 91; Lichter, Lichter, & Rothman, 1994, p. 163; Mitz, 1980, p. 145; Also in Eisner & Krinsky, 1984, Terrace, 1993

B.A.D. Cats
Spelling, 1996, pp. 198–199; Also in Terrace, 1993

Bagdad Café
IN Terrace, 1993

Baileys of Balboa, The
Andrews, 1980, pp. 1–6*; Story, 1993, pp. 136, 139

Bakersfield, P.D.
Cotter, 1997, pp. 439–441

Banacek
Martindale, 1991, pp. 24–27; Meyers, 1981, p. 176; Also in Terrace, 1993

Banyon
Gianakos, 1978, pp. 730–731; Martindale, 1991, pp. 27–28; Meyers, 1981, p. 180; Rovin, 1977b, p. 134

Barbara Stanwyck Show, The
Gianakos, 1978, pp. 297–298

Barbary Coast, The
Gianakos, 1981, pp. 172–175*; Jackson, 1994, p. 200; Also in Lentz, 1997, Terrace, 1993 , West, 1987

Bare Essence
Gianakos, 1987, pp. 315–316; Also in Terrace, 1993

Barefoot in the Park
Andrews, 1986, p. 133; Bogle, 2001, pp. 174–175

Baretta
Alley, 1977, pp. 92–96*; Berger, 1987, p. 217; Castleman & Podrazik, 1982, p. 260; Collins & Javna, 1989, pp. 86–88; Cuklanz, 1998; Cuklanz, 2000, pp. 55–59, 77–78, 104, 114, 121**; Gianakos, 1978, pp. 770–771; Gianakos, 1981, pp. 128–131*; Klobas, 1988, pp. 129–132, 207*; Lichter, Lichter, & Rothman, 1991, p. 31; Lichter, Lichter, & Rothman, 1994, pp. 86–87; Marc & Thompson, 1992 (Ch. 13 on Roy Huggins), pp. 141–151; Martindale, 1991, pp. 28–37; McDonald, 1983, p. 201; McDonald, 1992, p. 203; Meyers, 1981, pp. 194–196; Newcomb, 1979, pp. 131–133*; Newcomb, 1982, pp. 102–104*; Newcomb, 1987, p. 484; Rose, 1985, pp. 20–21; Rovin, 1977b, p. 147; Sackett, 1993, pp. 238–239; Also in Bianculli, 1996, Terrace, 1993

Barnaby Jones
Alley, 1977, p. 91; Cuklanz, 1998; Cuklanz, 2000, pp. 32–33, 70, 71–72, 89, 104; Gianakos, 1978, pp. 731–734*; Gianakos, 1981, pp. 152–158**; Klobas, 1988, pp. 30–31, 63; Marc & Thompson, 1992 (Ch. 14 on Quinn Martin), pp. 153–161; Marc, 1996, pp. 81–82; Martindale, 1991, pp. 37–54; Meyers, 1981, pp. 191–192; Newcomb, 1979, p. 130; Sumser, 1996, pp. 118–119, 121; U.S. Congress, 1977b, pp. 346–347, 360–362, 366–367

Barney Miller
Bedell, 1981, pp. 116–117; Berry & Mitchell-Kernan, 1982, p. 156; Capsuto, 2000, pp. 122–123, 148–149; Castleman & Podrazik, 1982, p. 258; Chunovic, 2000, p. 73; Collins & Javna, 1989, pp. 125–127; Craig, 1992, pp. 107–108; Cuklanz, 2000, pp. 129–132**; Gabler, Rich & Antler, 2000, p. 37; Greenburg, 1980, p. 10; Hamamoto, 1989, p. 97; Javna, 1985, pp. 148–151*; Jones, 1992, pp. 245–246, 247; Klobas, 1988, pp. 45–46, 227–228; Lichter, Lichter, & Rothman, 1991, p. 29, also see index; Lichter, Lichter, & Rothman, 1994, p. 83; Marc, 1996, p. 93; Meyers, 1981, pp. 228–231*; Miller, 1980, p. 192; Mitz, 1980, pp. 331–336**; Newcomb, 1987, p. 447; Panati, 1991, pp. 425–426; Pearl & Pearl, 1999, pp. 50, 95, 184–185; Pegg, 2002, pp. 135–137, 138; Puette, 1992, pp. 178–179; Rodriguez, 1997, p. 65; Rose, 1985, p. 20; Schneider, 2001, p. 95; Sklar, 1980, pp. 62–63; Suman & Rossman, 2000, p. 135; Surette, 1984, p. 117; Taylor, 1989, pp. 137–138, 143–145*; Thompson, 1996, p. 61; Wahl, 1995, p. 9; Also in Bianculli, 1996, Eisner & Krinsky, 1984, Terrace, 1993

Baron, The
Gianakos, 1978, p. 527

Bat Masterson
Fitzgerald & Magers, 2002, pp. 138, 291; Gianakos, 1978, pp. 207–209*; Jackson, 1994, p. 115; Magers & Fitzgerald, 1999, p. 184; McDonald, 1987, p. 52; Rainey, 1998, pp. 166–167, 236–263**; Rovin, 1977b, pp. 61–62; Yoggy, 1995, pp. 143–144, 146–147*; Also in Bianculli, 1996, Lentz, 1997, West, 1987

Batman
Collins & Javna, 1989, pp. 131–133; Fitzgerald & Magers, 2002, pp. 138, 291; Gerani, 1977, pp. 89–99**; Gianakos, 1978, pp. 207–209*; Goldenson, 1991, pp. 245–247; Harmon, 1992, p. 48; Javna, 1985, pp. 142–145*; Kulzer, 1992, pp. 83, 87–91; Magers & Fitzgerald, 1999, p. 184; Rainey, 1998, pp. 166–167, 236–263**; Rovin, 1977b, pp. 99–101; Sackett, 1993, pp. 136–137; Smith, 1989, pp. 123–124; Vane & Gross, 1994, p. 104; Also in Bianculli, 1996

Batman: The Animated Series
Daniels, 1995, pp. 220–221

Battlestar Galactica
Castleman & Podrazik, 1982, p. 287; Gianakos, 1981, pp. 259–259; Jarvis & Joseph, 1998, pp. 156, 160, 163; Marc & Thompson, 1992 (Ch. 16 on Glen Larson), pp. 171–178; Miller, 1980, pp. 107–109, 133–135*; Muir, 1999, whole book**; Also in Terrace, 1993

Bay City Blues, The
Chunovic, 2000, p. 145; Gianakos, 1987, p. 329; Stempel, 1992, pp. 239–240

Baywatch
Pitrone, 1999, pp. 95–135**; Also in Bianculli, 1996, Terrace, 1993

Beacon Hill
Andrews, 1980, pp. 7–14*; Edmondson & Rounds, 1976, pp. 236–237; Gianakos, 1981, pp. 178–179; Miller, 2000, pp. 163–164; Also in Morris, 1997

Bearcats
IN Lentz, 1997, Terrace, 1993

Beat, The
Longworth, 2000, pp. 186–187

Beat the Clock
DeLong, 1991, pp. 146–148*; Rafkin, 1998, p. 18; Also in Bianculli, 1996

Beautiful Phyllis Diller Show, The
Edgerton, Marsden & Nachbar, 1997, p. 29

Beauty and the Beast
Bacon-Smith, 1992, pp. 197–198; Barr, 2000, p. 295; Burks, 1990; Caldwell, 1995, pp. 32, 89–91, 108–109*; Gross, 1988, whole book**; Henderson & Mazzeo, 1990, pp. 62–65*; Leonard, 1997, pp. 123–124; Lichter, Lichter, & Rothman, 1991, pp. 145–146; Lichter, Lichter, & Rothman, 1994, p. 229; Swanson, 2000, pp. 98–103**; Also in Terrace, 1993

Beavis and Butthead
Caldwell, 1995, p. 23; Guida, 2000, p. 227; Hendershot, 1998, pp. 14, 18; Kellner, 1995, pp. 107, 139, 143–152**; Miller, 1994, p. 251; Newcomb, 2000, pp. 239, 319–329**; Rushkoff, 1994, pp. 153–157*; Also in Bianculli, 1996

Becker
Paietta & Kauppila, 1999, p. 322

Behind Closed Doors
Hamamoto, 1994, pp. 113–114

Believe It or Not
Gianakos, 1980, pp. 206–207

Ben Casey
Adler, 1976, pp. 96–98, 103*; Adler, 1981, pp. 233–234, 238; Alley, 1977, pp. 59–64, 68–69*; Bogle, 2001, p. 106; Caldwell, 1995, pp. 40–42; Castleman & Podrazik, 1982, p. 149; Gianakos, 1978, pp. 341–347**; Himmelstein, 1994, pp. 212–213; Javna, 1985, p. 18; Kalisch, Kalisch, & Scobey, 1983, pp. 18–22, 39–40, 192–193*; Lichter, Lichter, & Rothman, 1991, pp. 75, 126, 127, 156–161 (passim)*; Lichter, Lichter, & Rothman, 1994, pp. 142–143, 204, 206, 244–245, 251*; McDonald, 1992, p. 113; Newcomb, 1976, pp. 75–77*; Paietta & Kauppila, 1999, pp. 322–323; Pearl & Pearl, 1999, pp. 181, 204, 230; Rose, 1985, pp. 76–78; Rovin, 1977b, p. 80; Sackett, 1993, p. 119; Spigel & Curtin, 1997, pp. 191–194*; Stempel, 1992, p. 91; Turow, 1989, pp. 45–52, 59–66, 67–79, 104, 105, 176**; Williams, 1982, p. 44; Also in Bianculli, 1996

Benny, Jack *see* **Jack Benny Show**

Benson
Andrews, 1986, pp. 144–145; Dates & Barlow, 1990, p. 273; Dates & Barlow, 1993, pp. 295–296; Davis, 2001, p. 13; Jones, 1992, pp. 253–255; Lichter, Lichter, & Rothman, 1991, p. 126; Lichter, Lichter, & Rothman, 1994, p. 205; Marc & Thompson, 1992 (Ch. 7 on Susan Harris), pp. 84–92; Means Coleman, 2000, p. 94; Puette, 1992, p. 190; Schultz, 2000, pp. 110, 120–121; Shaheen, 1984, p. 68; Wolff, 1996, p. 25; Also in Terrace, 1993

Berle, Milton *see* **Texaco Star Theatre**

Berrenger's
Gianakos, 1992, pp. 380–381; Also in Morris, 1997

Bert D'Angelo, Superstar
Gianakos, 1981, pp. 190–191

Best of Broadway
Gianakos, 1980, pp. 400–401; Hawes, 2002, pp. 22–23

Best of the West
Yoggy, 1995, pp. 437–438; Also in Lentz, 1997, Terrace, 1993

Best Times, The
Gianakos, 1992, p. 391

Better Days
Hamamoto, 1989, p. 138

Betty Hutton Show, The
IN Terrace, 1993

Betty White Show, The
Castleman & Podrazik, 1982, pp. 281–282; Newcomb, 1987, pp. 73–74; O'Dell, 1997, pp. 213–214

Between Brothers
IN Terrace, 2000

Beulah
Andrews, 1986, pp. 66, 103; Bogle, 2001, pp. 3, 9, 19–26, 34, 41**; Caldwell, 1995, pp. 48, 68–69; Castleman

& Podrazik, 1982, p. 59; Dates & Barlow, 1990, pp. 262–263; Dates & Barlow, 1993, pp. 284–286*; Entman & Rojecki, 2000, p. 160; Hamamoto, 1989, pp. 41–42; Hawes, 2002, pp. 71–72; Jackson, 1982; Kamalipour & Carrilli, 1998, pp. 82–83; McDonald, 1983, pp. 22–23; McDonald, 1992, pp. 23–24; Means Coleman, 2000, pp. 59–62, 65; Mitz, 1980, p. 38; Smith, 1997; Sochen, 1987, p. 80; Turner, 1994, pp. 53, 60–61

Beverly Hillbillies, The
Allen, 1987, pp. 124–125; Allen, 1992, pp. 149–150; Batra, 1987, pp. 107–108; Bedell, 1981, pp. 306–307; Bennett, 1996, pp. 63–66; Castleman & Podrazik, 1982, pp. 161–162, 171*; Cortes, 2000, p. 62; Hamamoto, 1989, pp. 52–53; Himmelstein, 1984, pp. 106–110*; Himmelstein, 1994, pp. 146–150**; Jones, 1992, pp. 163, 165–167*; Lichter, Lichter, & Rothman, 1991, pp. 81–82, 140; Lichter, Lichter, & Rothman, 1994, p. 222; Lisanti & Paul, 2002, p. 232; Marc & Thompson, 1992 (Ch. 2 on Paul Henning), pp. 30–37; Marc, 1984, pp. 39–63, especially pp. 44–58**; Marc, 1989, p. 78; Marc, 1996, pp. 39–63, esp. pp. 44–58**; Marc, 1997, pp. 64–65, 67; McCrohan, pp. 127–139**; Meehan, 1983, pp. 27–29, 50, 168–169; Mitz, 1980, pp. 195–199*; Newcomb, 1976, p. 227; Newcomb, 1979, p. 293; Newcomb, 1987, p. 223; Newcomb & Alley, 1983, pp. 27–28; Panati, 1991, pp. 355–356; Pegg, 2002, pp. 8–15**; Penley, et al., 1991, pp. 220–221; Putterman, 1995, p. 38; Rowland & Watkins, 1984, pp. 22–26, 237–240, 245–248*; Sackett, 1993, pp. 114–115; Smith, 1989, pp. 13–21*; Smith, 1997a; Spigel, 2001, pp. 124–125; Staiger, 2000, pp. 54–80, 160, 162, 163, 165**; Stark, 1997, pp. 107–111**; Story, 1993, pp. 45–56**; Winship, 1988, pp. 62–63; Also in Bianculli, 1996, Eisner & Krinsky, 1984

Beverly Hills 90210
Capsuto, 2000, pp. 294–296, 367*; Davis, 2001, pp. 155–169**; Gabler, Rich & Antler, 2000, p. 61; Gross, 2001, pp. 176–177; Hollows, 2000, p. 101; Johnston, 2000, p. 95; Lichter, Lichter, & Rothman, 1994, p. 40; Meyers, 1999, pp. 274–275; Owen, 1997, pp. 10, 72–77, 79–82, 102, 130, 131, 136, 184, 205: Pearl & Pearl, 1999, pp. 83, 118, 199; Rapping, 1994, p. 158; Roberts, 1993; Schwartz, 1999, p. 132; Silverblatt, 1995, pp. 32–33; Spelling, 1996, pp. 166–175, 176–177, 178–181, 198–199**; Tulloch, 2000, pp. 202–218, 220, 242**; Vane & Gross, 1994, p. 57; Ward, 1995; Wild, 1999, pp. x, xvi; Also in Bianculli, 1996, Terrace, 1993

Bewitched
Bennett, 1996, pp. 79–82; Crotty, 1995; Dow, 1996, p. xvii; Fagen, 1996, p. 209; Guida, 2000, pp. 194–195; Hamamoto, 1989, p. 63; Helford, 2000, pp. 2, 15; Inness, 1999, p. 49; Javna, 1985, pp. 116–119*; Javna, 1988, p. 17; Jones, 1992, pp. 177–180*; Kulzer, 1992, pp. 115–120, 196–199*; Lichter, Lichter, & Rothman, 1991, pp. 51–52, 110, 140–141; Lichter, Lichter, & Rothman, 1994, pp. 222–223; Marc, 1989, pp. 134–141**; Marc, 1997, pp. 110–116, 190**; McCrohan, pp. 145–151**; Meehan, 1983, pp. 96–98, 112, 169–170*; Miller, 2000, pp. 62–63; Mitz, 1980, pp. 217–219*; Newcomb, 1987, p. 338; Penley, et al., 1991, pp. 205–224 (passim), esp. pp. 216, 219, 224–225, 226–227*; Pilato,

1996, whole book**; Press, 1991, pp. 102–105*; Putterman, 1995, pp. 95–101**; Sackett, 1993, pp. 126–127; Smith, 1989, pp. 63–71*; Spigel, 2001, pp. 119–120, 122–123, 128–130, 132–133*; Spigel & Curtin, 1997, pp. 58–59; Stark, 1997, p. 118; Story, 1993, pp. 64–80**; Waldrep, 2000, pp. 7, 196–202**; Also in Bianculli, 1996, Eisner & Krinsky, 1984, Terrace, 1993

Beyond Westworld
Gianakos, 1981, p. 290

Big Brother
Chunovic, 2000, p. 189

Big Easy, The
Jarvis & Joseph, 1998, pp. 237–238

Big Eddie
IN Terrace, 1993

Big Event, The
Castleman & Podrazik, 1982, pp. 273–274

Big Hawaii
Cuklanz, 2000, pp. 48–49*; Gianakos, 1981, p. 238; Hamamoto, 1994, p. 19; Also in Lentz, 1997

Big Party, The
Andrews, 1980, pp. 15–21*

Big Shamus, Little Shamus
Gianakos, 1981, pp. 280–281

Big Story, The
Daniel, 1996, pp. 3–4; Gianakos, 1983, pp. 236–249**; Lichter, Lichter, & Rothman, 1994, p. 265; Rovin, 1977b, p. 37

Big Surprise, The
Anderson, 1978, pp. 30–33, 84, 88–90*; DeLong, 1991, pp. 200–201

Big Top
Davis, 1995, pp. 94–95

Big Town
Daniel, 1996, pp. 4, 6–7; Gianakos, 1983, pp. 256–263**; Meehan, 1983, pp. 40–41, 103–105, 161*; Rovin, 1977b, p. 45

Big Valley, The
Alley & Brown, 2001, p. 219; Aquila, 1996, pp. 178–179; Bennett, 1996, pp. 43–46; Brauer, 1975, pp. 120–121, 128–129, 131–132, 135*; Diorio, 1983, pp. 201–207*; Fagen, 1996, pp. 213–214; Gianakos, 1978, pp. 499–504*; Himmelstein, 1994, p. 214; Isaacs, 1999, p. 73; Jackson, 1994, pp. 165–167; Jarvis & Joseph, 1998, pp. 213–214; Magers & Fitzgerald, 1999, p. 66; McDonald, 1987, p. 95; Meehan, 1983, pp. 67, 86–87, 169; Rovin, 1977b, p. 98; Smith, 1974, pp. 293–304*; Yoggy, 1995, pp. 323–338**; Yoggy, 1998, pp. 122–125*; Also in Lentz, 1997, Terrace, 1993, West, 1987

Big Wave Dave's
IN Terrace, 2000

Bilko *see* **Phil Silvers Show**

Bill and Ted's Excellent Adventures
IN Terrace, 1993

Bill Cosby Show, The
Andrews, 1986, p. 132; Bogle, 2001, pp. 165–170**; Dates & Barlow, 1990,

p. 281; Dates & Barlow, 1993, pp. 305–306; McDonald, 1983, pp. 117–119; McDonald, 1992, pp. 126–127; Means Coleman, 2000, pp. 86–87; Pearl & Pearl, 1999, p. 50; Smith, 1986, pp. 90–100*; Smith, 1997b, pp. 87–95**; Zook, 1999, p. 9; Also in Eisner & Krinsky, 1984

Bill Dana Show, The
Holtzman, 2000, p 229; Spigel & Curtin, 1997, p. 71 (n. 41); Wilson & Gutierrez, 1985, p. 100

Billy
IN Terrace, 2000

Billy Daniels Show, The
McDonald, 1983, p. 18; McDonald, 1992, pp. 19–20

Bing Crosby Show, The
IN Terrace, 1993

Bionic Woman, The
Castleman & Podrazik, 1982, p. 268; Edelman & Kupferberg, 1996, p. 219; Fiske & Hartley, 1978, pp. 192–193; Gianakos, 1981, pp. 193–196*; Inness, 1999, pp. 31–32, 45–48, 49, 162, 167**; Lichter, Lichter, & Rothman, 1991, pp. 147, 173–174; Lichter, Lichter, & Rothman, 1994, pp. 262–263*; Paietta & Kauppila, 1999, p. 323; Sackett, 1993, p. 223; Sochen, 1987, p. 100; Also in Bianculli, 1996, Terrace, 1993

Birdland
Paietta & Kauppila, 1999, p. 323

B.J. and the Bear
Gianakos, 1981, pp. 270–272*; Gianakos, 1983, pp. 148–149; Lichter, Lichter, & Rothman, 1991, p. 43; Lichter, Lichter, & Rothman, 1994, p. 102; Marc & Thompson, 1992 (Ch. 16 on Glen Larson), pp. 171–178; Also in Terrace, 1993

B.L. Stryker
Also in Terrace, 1993

Black Saddle
Gianakos, 1983, pp. 344–345; Jackson, 1994, pp. 139–140; Jarvis & Joseph, 1998, pp. 204–205; Yoggy, 1995, pp. 182–183; Also in Lentz, 1997, West, 1987

Black Tie Affair
Muse, 1994, whole book**; Also in Terrace, 2000

Blacke's Magic
Gianakos, 1992, pp. 416–417

Blansky's Beauties
IN Terrace, 1993

Bless This House
IN Terrace, 2000

Blondie
Fagen, 1996, p. 120; Also in Terrace, 1993

Blossom
Capsuto, 2000, p. 301; Cotter, 1997, pp. 383–392**; Ward, 1995; Also in Terrace, 1993, Terrace, 2000

Blue Knight, The
Castleman & Podrazik, 1982, p. 249; Gianakos, 1981, pp. 196–197; Martindale, 1991, pp. 57–60; Meyers, 1981, p. 219; Sklar, 1980, pp. 30–31; U.S. Congress, 1977b, pp. 352–354

Blue Light
Gianakos, 1978, pp. 526–527

Blue Skies
IN Terrace, 1993

Blue Thunder
Gianakos, 1987, pp. 343–344

Bob
IN Terrace, 1993, Terrace, 2000

Bob Crane Show, The
Kalisch, Kalisch, & Scobey, 1983, pp. 85–86; Paietta & Kauppila, 1999, p. 324; Turow, 1989, p. 218

Bob Cummings Show, The (and Love That Bob)
Alley & Brown, 2001, p. 23; Fitzgerald & Magers, 2002, p. 66; Hamamoto, 1989, pp. 33–34; Jones, 1992, p. 129; Marc, 1984, p. 43; Marc, 1989, pp. 78–80; Marc, 1996, p. 43; Marc, 1997, pp. 65–67*; Marc & Thompson, 1992 (Ch. 2 on Paul Henning), pp. 30–37; Mitz, 1980, pp. 113–114; Pegg, 2002, pp. 84–86, 88–89*; Putterman, 1995, p. 34; Also in Eisner & Krinsky, 1984, Terrace, 1993

Bob Newhart Show, The
Alley, 1977, pp. 47, 147, 150–152*; Castleman & Podrazik, 1982, p. 281; DiMaggio, 1990, pp. 63, 45–46, 62–83 (script)*; Himmelstein, 1984, pp. 113–116 (passim); Jones, 1992, pp. 227–228; Leibman, 1995, p. 262; Marc, 1989, p. 172; Marc, 1997, pp. 142–143; Mitz, 1980, pp. 289–295**; Newcomb, 1987, pp. 71, 81; Paietta & Kauppila, 1999, p. 324; Pegg, 2002, pp. 75–79, 261, 286, 293–296*; Press, 1991, pp. 80–81, 166; Putterman, 1995, pp. 42–46, 102, 103**; Rafkin, 1998, pp. 76–79; Stark, 1997, pp. 248–249 (passim); Taylor, 1989, pp. 131, 147; Tinker & Rukeyser, 1994, pp. 99, 101; U.S. Congress, 1977a, p. 97; Also in Bianculli, 1996, Eisner & Krinsky, 1984, Terrace, 1993

Bodies of Evidence
IN Terrace, 1993

Bold and the Beautiful, The
Caldwell, 1995, p. 149; James, 1991; Matelski, 1999, pp. 5, 41, 46–47; Nelson, 1995, p. 60; Rouverol, 1992, pp. 221–246**; Williams, 1992, pp. 47–48, 84, 103, 114, 137, 141–142, 148–150*

Bold Ones, The (*see also* Lawyers, The)
Adler, 1976, p. 99; Adler, 1981, p. 235; Alley, 1977, p. 63; Capsuto, 2000, p. 65; Gianakos, 1978, pp. 641–647**; Hamamoto, 1989, pp. 101–102; Kalisch, Kalisch, & Scobey, 1983, pp. 42–43, 58; Lichter, Lichter, & Rothman, 1991, pp. 97, 279–280; Lichter, Lichter, & Rothman, 1994, pp. 170, 307, 393; Meyers, 1981, pp. 149–150; Rovin, 1977b, p. 126; Turow, 1989, pp. 135, 138–143, 158**; Also in Bianculli, 1996

Bonanza
Aquila, 1996, p. 178; Berry, 1993, pp. 208–210; Berry & Asamen, 1993, pp. 208–210; Bodroghkozy, 2001, pp. 88–89; Brauer, 1975, pp. 106–107, 114, 115, 121–126, 130, 131, 132–136, 179, 183–184, 193–194**; Buxton, 1990, pp. 30–36, 109*; Castleman & Podrazik, 1982, p. 137; Fagen, 1996, pp. 72, 139–140, 213; Fitzgerald & Magers, 2002, pp. 75, 136–137, 215, 264; Gianakos, 1978, pp. 213–228**; Guida, 2000, p. 76; Hamamoto, 1994, pp. 33–39**; Hawes, 2002, pp. 144–145; Himmelstein, 1984, pp. 173–174; Himmelstein, 1994, pp. 213–214;

Jackson, 1994, pp. 126–130; Joshel, Malamud & McGuire, 2001, p. 133; Klobas, 1988, pp. 15–18, 120–123, 200–201, 342–344*; Leiby & Leiby, 2001, whole book**; Lichter, Lichter, & Rothman, 1991, pp. 136, 264; Lichter, Lichter, & Rothman, 1994, pp. 217, 374; Magers & Fitzgerald, 1999, pp. 18, 39, 79–80, 195; Martin, 1980**; McCrohan, 1990, pp. 111–116**; McDonald, 1987, pp. 96–98*; Meehan, 1983, pp. 29–30, 86, 105, 166–167; Newcomb, 1976, p. 226; Newcomb, 1979, pp. 292–293; Parks, 1982, pp. 130–141 (passim), 146–151*; Pearl & Pearl, 1999, pp. 70, 74, 113, 205; Rose, 1985, p. 63; Rovin, 1977b, p. 73; Sackett, 1993, pp. 108–109; Spigel & Curtin, 1997, pp. 309–310, 313–320*; Staiger, 2000, p. 20; Stark, 1997, pp. 66–67; Stempel, 1992, p. 81; Taylor, 1989, p. 37; Toll, 1982, p. 93; Yoggy, 1995, pp. 294–303, 305–323, 370–371**; Also in Bianculli, 1996, Lentz, 1997, Terrace, 1993, West, 1987

Bonino
Javna, 1988, pp. 34–35*; Krampner, 1997, pp. 86–87

Boone
Gianakos, 1987, pp. 326–327

Born Free
Gianakos, 1978, pp. 754–755

Born to the Wind
Yoggy, 1995, pp. 363–365

Bosom Buddies
Craig, 1992, p. 108; Crown, 1999, pp. 82–84*; Javna, 1988, p. 106; Also in Terrace, 1993

Bourbon Street Beat
Anderson, 1994, p. 268; Castleman & Podrazik, 1982, p. 131; Gianakos, 1978, pp. 238–239; Meyers, 1981, p. 59; Rovin, 1977b, p. 71; Also in Terrace, 1993

Boy Meets World
Cotter, 1997, pp. 444–449*

Boys of Twilight, The
IN Terrace, 1993

Bracken's World
Bodroghkozy, 2001, pp. 91–92, 211–213*; Castleman & Podrazik, 1982, pp. 214–215; Gianakos, 1978, pp. 663–664

Brady Brides *see* **Brady Bunch**

Brady Bunch, The
Bennett, 1996, pp. 83–86; Bryant & Bryant, 2001, pp. 166–168; Chunovic, 2000, p. 12; Davis, 1995, pp. 105–106; Inness, 1999, p. 49; Jones, 1992, pp. 190–191; Kottak, 1990, pp. 5–6; Lechner, 2000, pp. 36–37, 105; Lichter, Lichter, & Rothman, 1994, p. 82; Marc & Thompson, 1992 (Ch. 3 on Sherwood Schwartz), pp. 38–48; Miles, 1975, pp. 60–61 (Dec. 7, 1973 show); Mitz, 1980, p. 249; Moody, 1980, p. 122; Newcomb, 1987, p. 462; Newcomb, 1994, p. 508; Newcomb, 2000, p. 566; Owen, 1997, pp. 17–29, 44; Pegg, 2002, pp. 89–94*; Press, 1991, pp. 160, 162–163, 164; Stark, 1997, pp. 160–162; Torres, 1998, p. 75; Also in Bianculli, 1996, Eisner & Krinsky, 1984, Terrace, 1993

Brady Bunch Hour *see* **Brady Bunch**

Bradys *see* **Brady Bunch**

Brand New Life
IN Terrace, 1993

Branded
Gianakos, 1978, pp. 470–472*; Jackson, 1994, p. 169; McDonald, 1987, p. 69; Rovin, 1977b, p. 94; Yoggy, 1995, pp. 222–224*; Also in Bianculli, 1996, Lentz, 1997, Terrace, 1993, West, 1987

Brave Eagle
Buscombe & Pearson, 1998, p. 13; Davis, 1995, p. 210; Hawes, 2002, pp. 133–134; Jackson, 1994, pp. 67–68; McDonald, 1987, pp. 34, 36; Wilson & Gutierrez, 1985, p. 96; Yoggy, 1995, p. 353; Also in Lentz, 1997, Terrace, 1993, West, 1987

Breaking Away
Gianakos, 1983, p. 177

Breaking Point
Gianakos, 1978, pp. 411–412; Kalisch, Kalisch, & Scobey, 1983, pp. 25–27; Lichter, Lichter, & Rothman, 1994, p. 245; Paietta & Kauppila, 1999, p. 324; Schneider, 2001, p. 13; Turow, 1989, pp. 91–92

Brenner
Castleman & Podrazik, 1982, p. 128; Meyers, 1981, p. 65; Rovin, 1977b, p. 72

Bret Maverick
Gianakos, 1983, pp. 206–207; Heil, 2001, pp. 33–34, 43–44; Jackson, 1994, pp. 209–210; Robertson, 1994, pp. 173–176, 184–193**; Also in Lentz, 1997

Brewster Place
Bogle, 2001, pp. 368–369

Brian Keith Show *see* **Little People**

Bridges to Cross
Gianakos, 1992, p. 417

Bridget Loves Bernie
Gabler, Rich & Antler, 2000, p. 37; Lichter, Lichter, & Rothman, 1991, p. 244; Lichter, Lichter, & Rothman, 1994, p. 348; Montgomery, 1989, pp. 39–40; Pearl & Pearl, 1999, pp. 105, 180–181, 209–210, 218*; Sackett, 1993, p. 197; Suman & Rossman, 2000, p. 125

Bright Promise
Matelski, 1999, p. 43

Brighter Day
Matelski, 1999, p. 43

Brimstone
Muir, 2001a, pp. 541–551**

Bring 'Em Back Alive
Gianakos, 1987, pp. 290–291

Bringing Up Buddy
IN Eisner & Krinsky, 1984, Terrace, 1993

Broadway Open House
Abelman, 1998, p. 205; Castleman & Podrazik, 1982, p.p. 48, 92; Chunovic, 2000, pp. 28–29; Corkery, 1987, pp. 87–88; Marc, 1996, pp. 23, 140–141; Also in Bianculli, 1996

Broken Arrow
Buscombe & Pearson, 1998, p. 13; Gianakos, 1981, pp. 362–365*; Jackson,

1994, pp. 74–77; Lichter, Lichter, & Rothman, 1991, pp. 252–253; Lichter, Lichter, & Rothman, 1994, p. 359; Magers & Fitzgerald, 1999, p. 60; Rico, 1990, p. 151; Rovin, 1977b, p. 49; Wilson & Gutierrez, 1985, p. 96; Yoggy, 1995, pp. 353–356*; Also in Lentz, 1997

Broken Badges
Paietta & Kauppila, 1999, p. 324; Also in Terrace, 1993, West, 1987

Bronco
Gianakos, 1978, pp. 248–249; Jackson, 1994, pp. 123–124; Yoggy, 1995, pp. 194–196*; Also in Lentz, 1997, Terrace, 1993, West, 1987

Bronk
Gianakos, 1981, pp. 170–171; Martindale, 1991, pp. 60–64; Meyers, 1981, p. 221

Bronx Zoo, The
Cuklanz, 2000, pp. 53–54; Lichter, Lichter, & Rothman, 1994, p. 258; Pearl & Pearl, 1999, pp. 29–30, 95; Puette, 1992, pp. 191–192

Brooklyn Bridge
Gabler, Rich & Antler, 2000, pp. 47–48, 63; Pearl & Pearl, 1999, pp. 46, 49–50, 162, 210–211*; Swanson, 2000, pp. 122–128**; Also in Terrace, 1993

Brooklyn South
Bryant & Bryant, 2001, p. 190

Brotherly Love
Cotter, 1997, pp. 472–474

Buccaneers, The
Davis, 1995, pp. 11–12; Rovin, 1977b, p. 50

Buck James
Paietta & Kauppila, 1999, p. 324; Pearl & Pearl, 1999, pp. 47–48, 80, 82, 215–216*; Turow, 1989, p. 262

Buck Rogers in the 25th Century
Gianakos, 1981, pp. 285–287; Gianakos, 1983, pp. 161–162; Goethals, 1981, pp. 79–81; Klobas, 1988, pp. 351–353, 418–420; Lichter, Lichter, & Rothman, 1994, pp. 136, 260; Marc & Thompson, 1992 (Ch. 16 on Glen Larson), pp. 171–178; Newcomb & Alley, 1983, pp. 101, 102, 121–124; Rose, 1985, p. 100; Also in Terrace, 1993

Buckskin
Jackson, 1994, pp. 120–121; Also in Lentz, 1997, West, 1987

Buddies
Cotter, 1997, pp. 477–478; Owen, 1997, p. 116

Buffalo Bill
Alley & Brown, 2001, p. 192; Miller, 1994, p. 232; Newcomb, 1987, pp. 76–80*; Putterman, 1995, p. 103; Thomas & Evans, 1990, p. 287; Vane & Gross, 1994, p. 114; Also in Bianculli, 1996, Terrace, 1993, West, 1987

Buffalo Bill, Jr.
Davis, 1995, pp. 210–211; Fitzgerald & Magers, 2002, p. 16; Jackson, 1994, pp. 60–61; McDonald, 1987, p. 29; Yoggy, 1995, p. 28; Also in Lentz, 1997

Buffy, the Vampire Slayer
Braun, 2000; Chunovic, 2000, p. 160; Creeber, 2001, p. 42; Golden &

Holder, 1998, whole book**; Helford, 2000, pp. 15, 163–186**; Hiebert, 1999, p. 372; Isaacs, 1999, pp. 133–134*; Kaveney, 2001**, Longworth, 2000, p. xx; Muir, 2001a, pp. 497–518**; Osgerby & Gough-Yates, 2001, p. 1; Owen, 1999; Schwartz, 1999, pp. 193–194; Walters, 2001, p. 116; Wilcox, 1999; Wilcox & Lavery, 2002, whole book**

Bullwinkle Show, The *see* **Rocky and His Friends**

Burke's Law
Buxton, 1990, p. 96; Gianakos, 1978, pp. 432–436*; Lisanti & Paul, 2002, pp. 24–25, 195, 229, 232; Meyers, 1981, pp. 90–91; Rovin, 1977b, p. 87; Spelling, 1996, pp. 46–49, 53*; Spigel & Curtin, 1997, p. 82; Also in Bianculli, 1996, Terrace, 1993

Burnett, Carol *see* **Carol Burnett Show**

Burning Zone, The
Muir, 2001a, pp. 455–466

Burns and Allen *see* **George Burns and Gracie Allen**

Burns and Schreiber Comedy Hour
Edgerton, Marsden & Nachbar, 1997, p. 33

Bus Stop
Castleman & Podrazik, 1982, p. 152; Gianakos, 1978, pp. 334–336; Lichter, Lichter, & Rothman, 1994, p. 273; Schneider, 2001, p. 12; Spigel & Curtin, 1997, p. 171; Also in Terrace, 1993

Busting Loose
IN Terrace, 1993

Buttons, Red *see* **Red Buttons Show**

Byrds of Paradise
Lester, 1996, pp. 36–37; Swanson, 2000, pp. 200–201

Cade's County
Gianakos, 1983, pp. 400–402*; Martindale, 1991, pp. 66–67; Meyers, 1981, p. 157; Yoggy, 1995, pp. 174–177*; Also in Lentz, 1997

Caesar, Sid *see* **Caesar's Hour, Your Show of Shows**

Caesar's Hour
Adir, 1988, pp. 72–88 (passim)*; Caesar, 1982, pp. 141–146, 150–160, 162–168**; Gelbart, 1998, pp. 19–24, 172–173*; Holtzman, 1979, pp. 111–127**; Joshel, Malamud, & McGuire, 2001, pp. 193, 198; Putterman, 1995, pp. 71–72, 78–79*; Stempel, 1992, pp. 39–41; Wilk, 1976, pp. 159–175 (passim)

Café Americain
IN Terrace, 2000

Cagney & Lacey
Allen, 1987, pp. 153–159**; Allen, 1992, pp. 181–186 (similar)**; Alley & Brown, 2001, p. 42, 202; Avery & Eason, 1991, pp. 367–374, 378, 381–382**; Baehr & Dyer, 1987, pp. 203–223**; Bodroghkozy, 2001, p. 292 (n. 13); Brown, 1990, pp. 58, 75, 82–88 (passim), 117–133**; Caldwell, 1995, pp. 88–89; Capsuto, 2000, pp. 193–195; Collins & Javna, 1989, pp. 83–85;

Cruz & Lewis, 1994, pp. 60–61, 64; Cuklanz, 2000, pp. 42, 117–118, 119, 121–126, 132–135**; D'Acci, 1994, whole book**; Davis, 2001, p. 123; Dow, 1996, pp. 101–104*; Edelman & Kupferberg, 1996, p. 219; Field, 1989, pp. 148–149; Fiske, 1987, pp. 27–33, 47, 52–53, 112, 113, 155–168, 177–178, 214, 216–227**; Fiske, 1994, p. 54; Gamman & Marshment, 1988, pp. 8, 12, 13–26**; Gianakos, 1983, pp. 215–216; Gianakos, 1987, pp. 227–228; Gianakos, 1992, pp. 299–303*; Goethals, 1990, pp. 113–115; Gross, 2001, p. 86; Henderson & Mazzeo, 1990, pp. 25–27*; Holtzman, 2000, pp. 78–79; Inness, 1999, p. 162; Jarvis & Joseph, 1998, pp. 229–230; Javna, 1985, p. 239; Kendall, 1989*; Kidd-Hewitt & Osborne, 1995, pp. 167, 172; Klobas, 1988, pp. 161–163, 307–309*; Leonard, 1997, p. 65; Lewis, 1991, pp. 65–66; Lichter, Lichter, & Rothman, 1991, pp. 34, 38, 47–48, 69, 77, 87, 123, 281, 290; Lichter, Lichter, & Rothman, 1994, pp. 95, 107, 135, 144–145, 157, 200–210; MacDonald, 1995, pp. 11, 155–156; Marris & Thornham, 2000, pp. 341–353**; Montgomery, 1989, pp. 194, 201–215**; Moorti, 2001, pp. 122–123; Nelson, 1994, p. 23; Newcomb, 1987, p. 108; Newcomb, 1994, pp. 428–436, 439–443**; Newcomb, 2000, pp. 100–102, 105–134**; Oskamp, 1988, p. 116; Parenti, 1991, pp. 124–125; Pearl & Pearl, 1999, pp. 45–46, 156, 184, 215; Press, 1991, pp. 40, 146–150*; Raymond, 1990, pp. 193–194, 196; Riggs, 1996; Ringer, 1994, p. 119; Sackett, 1993, pp. 290–291; Seger, 1996, pp. 155, 233, 250–251*; Shaheen, 1984, pp. 51–52; Sochen, 1987, pp. 101–102; Spigel & Curtin, 1997, p. 89; Spigel & Mann, 1992, pp. x–xi, 169–194**; Stempel, 1992, pp. 253–254; Swanson, 2000, pp. 2–21, 51–52, 177, 180**; Tasker, 1998, pp. 91, 94–97*; Thomas & Evans, 1990, pp. 295–296; Thompson, 1996, pp. 13, 98–109, 126, 142**; Tulloch, 2000, p. 65; U.S. Congress, 1985, pp. 150, 155–156; Winship, 1988, pp. 117–120; Also in Bianculli, 1996, Terrace, 1993

Cain's Hundred
Bogle, 2001, pp. 98–100*; Gianakos, 1978, pp. 351–352; Meyers, 1981, pp. 81–83; Rovin, 1977b, p. 82

California Dreams
IN Terrace, 1993, Terrace, 2000

California Fever
IN Terrace, 1993

Californians, The
Fitzgerald & Magers, 2002, pp. 162–163; Gianakos, 1983, pp. 323–326*; Jackson, 1994, pp. 96–98; McDonald, 1987, p. 67; Rovin, 1977b, p. 54; Also in Lentz, 1997, Terrace, 1993, West, 1987

Call to Glory
Gianakos, 1992, pp. 366–368*; Kellner, 1990, pp. 62–63; Lichter, Lichter, & Rothman, 1991, p. 274

Cameo Theatre
Gianakos, 1980, pp. 252–254*

Camp Runamuck
Erickson, 2000, p. 157; Pegg, 2002, pp. 212–213; Putterman, 1995, pp. 55–58, 59, 66*; Also in Eisner & Krinsky, 1984, Terrace, 1993

Camp Wilder
IN Terrace, 1993, Terrace, 2000

Candid Camera
Fiske, 1987, p. 242; Lechner, 2000, pp. 222–223; McCrohan, 1990, pp. 140–145**; Sackett, 1993, pp. 104–105; Scheider, 1997, p. 178; Also in Bianculli, 1996

Cannon
Alley, 1977, p. 91; Bedell, 1981, pp. 55–59; Gianakos, 1978, pp. 691–696**; Gianakos, 1981, pp. 126–128*; Marc & Thompson, 1992 (Ch. 14 on Quinn Martin), pp. 153–161; Martindale, 1991, pp. 67–78; Meyers, 1981, pp. 162–164; Miles, 1975, pp. 52–55 (Feb. 13, 1974 show)*; Newcomb, 1979, p. 130; Orlik, 1994, p. 43; Rose, 1985, p. 42; Rovin, 1977b, p. 130; Sackett, 1993, pp. 208–209; Shaheen, 1984, pp. 40–42; Sumser, 1996, pp. 112–113, 120

Can't Hurry Love
IN Terrace, 2000

Capitol
Matelski, 1988, pp. 45, 86–90*; Matelski, 1999, p. 43; Rouverol, 1984, pp. 108–117*

Capitol News
Longworth, 2000, pp. 91–92

Captain and Tennille, The
Bedell, 1981, pp. 144–145

Captain Kangaroo
Davis, 1995, pp. 135–138**; Mott, 2000, pp. 43, 113–116*; Also in Bianculli, 1996

Captain Nice
Rovin, 1977b, pp. 118–119; Also in Eisner & Krinsky, 1984, Terrace, 1993

Captain Video
Alexander, 1994, p. 119; Caldwell, 1995, p. 48; Heldenfels, 1994, p. 190; Rose, 1985, pp. 92–93; Rovin, 1977b, pp. 19–20; Also in Bianculli, 1996, Terrace, 1993

Car 54, Where Are You?
Bogle, 2001, p. 94; Castleman & Podrazik, 1982, p. 151; Collins & Javna, 1989, pp. 134–136; Everitt, 2001, pp. 79, 149–176**; Jones, 1992, pp. 169–170; Meyers, 1981, pp. 84–86; Mitz, 1980, pp. 177–179*; Pearl & Pearl, 1999, pp. 19, 86–87, 180, 184; Pegg, 2002, pp. 238–239; Also in Bianculli, 1996, Eisner & Krinsky, 1984, Terrace, 1993

Cara Williams Show
Rafkin, 1998, pp. 45–46; Also in Terrace, 1993

Caribe
Gianakos, 1978, pp. 771–772; Martindale, 1991, pp. 78–80

Carol & Company
Capsuto, 2000, p. 305; Cotter, 1997, pp. 374–378*

Carol Burnett Show, The
Adir, 1988, pp. 56–60, 111–115*; Alley, 1977, pp. 48, 135; Horowitz, 1997, pp. 3, 74–82, 128**; Marc, 1989, pp. 220–222; Marc, 1997, pp. 183–185*; Newcomb, 1982, pp. 68–69, 87–88; Pegg, 2002, pp. 63–65; Putterman, 1995, pp. 80–85**; Sklar, 1980, pp. 25–26; Sochen, 1987, pp. 86–87; Sochen, 1999, pp. 157–158.; U.S. Congress, 1977c, pp. 28–29, 32–33; Also in Bianculli, 1996

Carol Burnett Show (New)
Cotter, 1997, pp. 378–381

Caroline in the City
Gabler, Rich & Antler, 2000, p. 47; Owen, 1997, p. 6; Smith, 1999, pp. 149–150; Also in Terrace, 2000

Carson, Johnny *see* **Tonight Show**

Carter Country
Puette, 1992, p. 179; Also in Eisner & Krinsky, 1984

Casablanca
Anderson, 1994, pp. 182–183, 186, 198, 199–201, 207–209**; Gianakos, 1987, p. 312

Cases of Eddie Drake, The
IN Terrace, 1993

Casey Jones
Gianakos, 1992, pp. 453–454

Cassie and Company
Gianakos, 1983, pp. 221–222

Cavalcade of America
Gianakos, 1980, pp. 338–343*

Cavalcade of Stars
Adir, 1988, pp. 125–127; Bacon, 1985, pp. 87–92*; Castleman & Podrazik, 1982, p. 39; Henry, 1992, pp. 92–113, 120–121**; Pegg, 2002, pp. 39, 326–328; Starr, 1997, pp. 58–60, 64–65, 66–69*; Weatherby, 1992, pp. 66–70, 73–78*; Also in Bianculli, 1996

Cavanaughs, The
Starr, 1997, pp. 217–218; Also in Terrace, 1993

CBS Morning News
Hack, 1999, pp. 73–75, 79–81, 110, 119–120, 122–124, 133, 138, 141, 144, 149**; McCabe, 1987, whole book**

CBS Reports
Buzenberg & Buzenberg, 1999, pp. 50–51, 167, 265–267*; Kendrick, 1969, pp. 445–459 (passim); Sperber, 1986, pp. 555–569 (passim)*

CBS This Morning
Hack, 1999, pp. 156–157, 198–199, 203–204, 207, 209, 210, 218, 224, 226–227*; Lechner, 2000, p. 55

Celanese Theatre
Gianakos, 1980, pp. 292–293; Hawes, 2001, pp. 127–131*

Centennial
Yoggy, 1995, pp. 419–424*; Also in Lentz, 1997

Center Stage
Gianakos, 1980, pp. 390–391

Central Park West
Heil, 2001, p. 155; Owen, 1997, pp. 152–153

Champions, The
Gianakos, 1978, pp. 615–616; Lisanti & Paul, 2002, 54

Channing
Gianakos, 1978, pp. 425–426

Charles in Charge
Harris, 1989, p. 43; Harris, 1994, p. 45; Rafkin, 1998, p. 117; Also in Terrace, 1993

Charlie & Co.
Rafkin, 1998, pp. 120–122

Charlie Hoover
IN Terrace, 1993

Charlie's Angels

Bedell, 1981, pp. 135–139*; Berger, 1987, p. 216; Caldwell, 1995, p. 58; Castleman & Podrazik, 1982, p. 271; Chunovic, 2000, pp. 79–80; Coakley, 1977, pp. 107, 113, 191–192, 231–232; Condon, 2000, whole book**; Conrad, 1982, pp. 152–154; Cuklanz, 1998; Cullingford, 1984, pp. 91, 93; Fiske, 1987, pp. 45, 189; Fowles, 1982, pp. 39–41; Fowles, 1992, pp. 46–47; Geraghty, 1991, pp. 81–91; Gianakos, 1981, pp. 207–211**; Gianakos, 1983, pp. 128–129; Gitlin, 1983, see index, especially pp. 71–73; Helford, 2000, p. 2; Inness, 1999, pp. 31–32, 37–45, 49**; Kassel 1993, p. 55; Kidd-Hewitt & Osborne, 1995, p. 166; Lazere, 1987, p. 252; Leonard, 1997, p. 68; Lester, 1996, p. 83; Lichter, Lichter, & Rothman, 1991, pp. 8, 55–56, 70; Marc, 1984, p. 89; Marc, 1996, p. 89; Marc & Thompson, 1992 (Ch. 15 on Aaron Spelling), pp. 163–169; Martin, 1981; Meehan, 1983, pp. 80–82, 105–106, 177–178*; Meyers, 1981, pp. 233–235*; Miller, 2000, p. 159; Monaco, 2000, p. 490; Newcomb, 1976, pp. 27–29*; Newcomb, 1979, pp. 35–37; Newcomb, 1987, pp. 34–36, 465, 483; Newcomb, 1994, p. 511; Newcomb, 2000, pp. 105, 569, 581; Osgerby & Gough-Yates, 2001, pp. 6, 83–99**; Oskamp, 1988, p. 108; Press, 1991, pp. 35–36, 148–151*; Rose, 1985, pp. 44–45; Rovin, 1977b, pp. 153, 162; Rubin, 1980, pp. 203–204; Sackett, 1993, pp. 232–233; Schneider, 2001, p. 35; Schwartz, 1999, pp. 134–135; Shales, pp. 37–42 (passim); Sklar, 1980, pp. 54–55, 57–59*; Spelling, 1996, pp. 100–113, 114–116, 199**; Spigel & Curtin, 1997, p. 89; Thompson, 1996, p. 100; Toll, 1982, p. 209; Voort, 1986, p. 147; Wahl, 1995, p. 8; Weimann, 2000, p. 154; Also in Bianculli, 1996, Terrace, 1993

Charmed

Muir, 2001a, pp. 530–540**; Wild, 1999, p. 9

Charmings, The

IN Terrace, 1993

Chase

Gianakos, 1978, pp. 741–742; Martindale, 1991, pp. 91–94; Thompson, 1990, p. 54; Also in Terrace, 1993

Checkmate

Gianakos, 1978, pp. 287–290*; Meyers, 1981, pp. 79–80; Rovin, 1977b, p. 78

Cheers

Allen, 1987, p. 129; Allen, 1992, pp. 154–155; Auletta, 1991, see index; Bianculli, 1992, pp. 266–268; Bignell, 1997, p. 142; Bjorklund, 1997, whole book**; Blum 1995, pp. 104–105; Burks, 1990**; Burns & Thompson, 1989, pp. 89–101**; Carey, 1988, pp. 95–96; Carter 1995, p. 257; Chunovic, 2000, pp. 104–106, 121*; Davis, 2001, p. 16; Edgerton, Marsden & Nachbar, 1997, pp. 61–62; Fallows, 2000; Field, 1989, pp. 158–159, 161–162; Grammer, 1995, pp. 3, 5–11, 174–180, 207–208**; Henderson & Mazzeo, 1990, pp. 66–67; Javna, 1985, p. 240; Jones, 1992, pp. 263–265; Lichter, Lichter, & Rothman, 1991, p. 33; Lichter, Lichter, & Rothman, 1994, p. 89; McCrohan, 1990, p. 3; Neale & Krutnik, 1990, pp. 91–92; Orlik, 1994, pp. 176–177; Paietta & Kauppila, 1999, p. 325; Panati, 1991, pp. 478–479; Pearl & Pearl, 1999, pp. 31, 222; Putterman, 1995, pp. 120–121;

Roman, 1996, p. 29; Rowland & Watkins, 1984, p. 261; Sackett, 1993, pp. 302–303; Silverblatt, 1995, p. 80; Silverblatt, Ferry, & Finan, 1999, p. 108; Stark, 1997, p. 285; Steenland, 1990, p. 15; Thomas & Evans, 1990, pp. 285, 287; Thompson, 1996, pp. 34–35; Tinker & Rukeyser, 1994, pp. 138–139, 169; Van Hise, 1992, whole book**; Vande Berg & Trujillo, 1989, pp. 221–225; Vande Berg & Wenner, 1991, pp. 48–57**; Vane & Gross, 1994, pp. 119–120; Also in Bianculli, 1996

Cher
Abelman, 1998, p. 313

Chevrolet Tele-Theatre, The
Gianakos, 1980, pp. 168–170*

Chevy Chase Show, The
IN Bianculli, 1996

Chevy Show, The
Erickson, 2000, pp. 51, 63

Cheyenne
Anderson, 1994, pp. 182–187, 198, 203–207, 210–214, 229, 237–240**; Aquila, 1996, p. 169; Barnouw, 1990, pp. 194–195; Buscombe & Pearson, 1998, pp. 128, 132; Cavallo, 1999, p. 38; Fagen, 1996, pp. 216–228 (interview with Clint Walker)**; Fitzgerald & Magers, 2002, pp. 68, 170; Gianakos, 1978, pp. 200–205*; Gianakos, 1980, pp. 469–473*; Jackson, 1994, pp. 69–71; Magers & Fitzgerald, 1999, pp. 17, 186; Marc & Thompson, 1992 (Ch. 13 on Roy Huggins), pp. 141–151; McDonald, 1987, p. 51; Osgerby & Gough-Yates, 2001, p. 148; Rovin, 1977b, pp. 48–49; Stempel, 1992, pp. 63–64; Yoggy, 1995, pp. 186–194, 368–369**; Also in Lentz, 1997, Terrace, 1993, West, 1987

Chicago Hope
Abelman, 1998, p. 74; Capsuto, 2000, pp. 304, 347; Diem & Lantos, 1996; Lechner, 2000, pp. 184–187*; Longworth, 2000, p. 123; Owen, 1997, p. 94; Paietta & Kauppila, 1999, p. 325; Silverblatt, Ferry, & Finan, 1999, pp. 187, 226; Thompson, 1996, pp. 187–188; Weimann, 2000, pp. 176–178

Chicago Story
Gianakos, 1983, pp. 199–200; Paietta & Kauppila, 1999, p. 325

Chicken Soup
Alley & Brown, 2001, p. 73; Lester, 1996, pp. 51–52; Pearl & Pearl, 1999, pp. 44, 87, 110, 216, 218; Rafkin, 1998, pp. 129–130; Also in Terrace, 1993

Chico and the Man
Alley, 1977, p. 47; Castleman & Podrazik, 1982, p. 257; Greenberg, 1980, pp. 9–10; Holtzman, 2000, p 229; Jones, 1992, pp. 221–223, 225–226; Lichter, Lichter, & Rothman, 1991, pp. 141–142, 254; Lichter, Lichter, & Rothman, 1994, p. 361; Miles, 1975, pp. 61–63 (Nov. 8, 1974 show); Miller, 2000, p. 157; Mitz, 1980, pp. 337–341*; Montgomery, 1989, pp. 62–63; Rannow, 1999, p. 159; Rodriguez, 1997, pp. 63–64; Sackett, 1993, pp. 210–211; Also in Eisner & Krinsky, 1984

China Beach
Ballard-Reisch, 1991; Caldwell, 1995, pp. 91–92; Field, 1989, pp. 155–156; Friedman, 2002, pp. 267–268, 284; Hamamoto, 1994, pp. 133–140**;

Hanson, 1990; Leonard, 1997, pp. 12–13; Lichter, Lichter, & Rothman, 1991, p. 274; Lichter, Lichter, & Rothman, 1994, pp. 386–387; Longworth, 2000, pp. 122, 127; Paietta & Kauppila, 1999, p. 325–326; Steenland, 1990, pp. 41, 47; Stempel, 1992, pp. 269–277**; Swanson, 2000, pp. xiii, 54–57, 107–111**; Thompson, 1996, pp. 142–148**; Also in Bianculli, 1996, Terrace, 1993

CHiPS
Caldwell, 1995, p. 58; Greenberg, 1980, pp. 10–11; Klobas, 1988, pp. 149–150, 234–235, 320–325, 350–351*; Martindale, 1991, pp. 94–106; Meyers, 1981, p. 244; Puette, 1992, pp. 54–55, 183; Rodriguez, 1997, p. 65; Rose, 1985, pp. 74–75; Also in Terrace, 1993

Chisholms, The
Yoggy, 1995, pp. 371–372; Also in Lentz, 1997

Christy
Heldenfels, 1994, pp. 81–82; Suman, 1997, pp. 11, 52, 112, 116

Cimarron City
Guida, 2000, p. 187; Jackson, 1994, pp. 113–114; Magers & Fitzgerald, 1999, pp. 242, 244; Also in Lentz, 1997, West, 1987

Cimarron Strip
Fagen, 1996, p. 41; Gianakos, 1978, pp. 595–596; Jackson, 1994, pp. 182–183; Stempel, 1992, pp. 82–83; Yoggy, 1995, pp. 416–417; Also in Lentz, 1997, West, 1987

Circle of Fear *see* **Ghost Story**

Circus Boy
Davis, 1995, pp. 212–213; Gianakos, 1987, pp. 377–378; Also in Lentz, 1997

Circus Time
Davis, 1995, pp. 95–96

Cisco Kid, The
Brauer, 1975, pp. 27, 39, 43–51 (passim)*; Davis, 1995, pp. 213–214; Gianakos, 1987, pp. 399–408**; Heldenfels, 1994, p. 35; Holtzman, 2000, p 228; Jackson, 1994, pp. 38–41; Jarvis & Joseph, 1998, pp. 191–192; Magers & Fitzgerald, 1999, pp. 107, 137–138; McDonald, 1987, pp. 30–31; Rovin, 1977b, pp. 29, 38; Wilson & Gutierrez, 1985, p. 99; Yoggy, 1995, pp. 35, 37–39*; Also in Bianculli, 1996, Lentz, 1997, West, 1987

City, The
Abelman, 1998, pp. 378–379; Also in Terrace, 1993

City Hospital
Kalisch, Kalisch, & Scobey, 1983, pp. 8–9; Paietta & Kauppila, 1999, p. 326; Sconce, 2000, p. 1

City of Angels (detective)
Collins & Javna, 1989, pp. 23–25; Gianakos, 1981, pp. 192–193; Meyers, 1981, pp. 232–233

City of Angels (medical)
Bogle, 2001, p. 452

Civil Wars
Jarvis & Joseph, 1998, pp. 219–221, 230*; Marc & Thompson, 1992 (Ch. 20 on Steven Bocho), pp. 218–229; Also in Terrace, 1993

Class of '96
Gabler, Rich & Antler, 2000, pp. 63-64; Owen, 1997, pp. 86-87, 136-137; Pearl & Pearl, 1999, pp. 87-88, 91, 118-119*

Cleghorne!
Means Coleman, 2000, p. 122

Cliffhangers
Gianakos, 1981, pp. 273-274; Muir, 2001a, pp. 91-95*; Also in Lentz, 1997, Morris, 1997

Climax!
Gianakos, 1980, pp. 403-413**; Hawes, 2002, pp. 23-24

Clock, The
Gianakos, 1980, p. 227-229

Clueless
IN Terrace, 2000

Coach
Blum, 1995, pp. 12-13, 36, 87-96, 110, 127-128, 165-180**; Kutulas, 1998; Lindheim & Blum, 1991, pp. 57-121, 217-249**; Rafkin, 1998, pp. 142-146*; Sackett, 1993, p. 339; Also in Terrace, 1993, Terrace, 2000

Code Name: Foxfire
Gianakos, 1992, pp. 390-391; Also in Terrace, 1993

Code R
IN Terrace, 1993

Code Red
Gianakos, 1983, pp. 200-201; Klobas, 1988, pp. 420-421; Also in Terrace, 1993

Colbys, The
Gianakos, 1992, pp. 407-409*; Hollows, 2000, p. 93; Spelling, 1996, p. 158; Also in Morris, 1997

Colgate Comedy Hour, The
Bakish, 1995, pp. 144-145; Caldwell, 1995, pp. 47-48; Castleman & Podrazik, 1982, pp. 55, 68-69, 85, 93*; Cornes, 2001, p. 226; Everitt, 2001, pp. 63-64, 69-70, 117*; Heldenfels, 1994, p. 17; Levy, 1996, pp. 126-128, 130-133, 159-160, 172-174, 193-201 (passim)**; Robbins, 1991, pp. 144-147*; Sackett, 1993, pp. 12-13; Scheider, 1997, pp. 50-51; Also in Bianculli, 1996

Colgate Theatre
Hawes, 2001, p. 28

Colgate Western Theater
IN West, 1987

Colonel Humphrey Flack
IN Eisner & Krinsky, 1984

Colt .45
Anderson, 1994, pp. 229, 245; Brauer, 1975, pp. 56, 57, 63-64; Fitzgerald & Magers, 2002, p. 17; Gianakos, 1981, pp. 383-386*; Jackson, 1994, pp. 98-102; Magers & Fitzgerald, 1999, p. 17; Yoggy, 1995, pp. 197-200*; Also in Lentz, 1997, Terrace, 1993, West, 1987

Columbo
Alley, 1977, pp. 91-92; Bedell, 1981, p. 194; Bounds, 1996, pp. 49, 118-119; Castleman & Podrazik, 1982, p. 233; Collins & Javna, 1989, pp. 68-70, especially pp. 184-187*; Dawidziak, 1989, whole book**; Delamater & Prigozy, 1998, pp. 124, 126-127; Freeman,

1980, pp. 140–142; Gottfried, 1999, p 255; Himmelstein, 1984, p. 181; Leonard, 1997, pp. 150–151; Levinson & Link, 1981, pp. 85–101**; Lichter, Lichter, & Rothman, 1994, pp. 201–202, 381; Marc & Thompson, 1992 (Ch. 17 on Richard Levinson & Wm. Link) pp. 180–192; Martindale, 1991, pp. 111–117; Meyers, 1981, pp. 169–173*; Newcomb, 1979, pp. 130–131, 547–548; Newcomb, 1982, pp. 101–102; Newcomb, 1987, pp. 637–638; Newcomb, 2000, p. 602; Newcomb & Alley, 1983, pp. 133–134, 146–153 (passim); Pearl & Pearl, 1999, p. 177; Root, 1979, p. 38; Rose, 1985, p. 42; Rovin, 1977b, p. 129; Sackett, 1993, p. 198; Seger, 1996, p. 36; Sklar, 1980, p. 14; Stempel, 1992, pp. 176–177; Also in Bianculli, 1996, Terrace, 1993

Combat
Castleman & Podrazik, 1982, p. 159; Gianakos, 1978, pp. 373–378**; Lichter, Lichter, & Rothman, 1991, pp. 123–124, 278; Lichter, Lichter, & Rothman, 1994, pp. 201–202, 381; Rovin, 1977b, pp. 83–84; Sackett, 1993, pp. 134–135; Worland, 1989; Also in Bianculli, 1996

Combat Sergeant
Gianakos, 1980, p. 487; Rovin, 1977b, p. 51

Coming of Age
IN Terrace, 1993

Commando Cody, Sky Marshal
Gianakos, 1987, pp. 372–273; Also in Terrace, 1993

Commish, The
Hamamoto, 1994, pp. 188–191*; Lichter, Lichter, & Rothman, 1994, p. 42; Marc & Thompson, 1992 (Ch. 19 on Stephen J. Cannell), pp. 205–216; Pearl & Pearl, 1999, pp. 17–18, 222; Also in Terrace, 1993

Common Law
Jarvis & Joseph, 1998, p. 177

Como, Perry *see* **Perry Como Show**

Concrete Cowboys, The
Gianakos, 1983, p. 179

Continental, The
Caldwell, 1995, pp. 34, 48; Castleman & Podrazik, 1982, p. 70

Convoy
Gianakos, 1978, pp. 518–519

Cop Rock
Abelman, 1998, pp. 30, 93–94; Caldwell, 1995, pp. 284–285; Leonard, 1997, pp. 145–146; Monaco, 2000, p. 498; Tabarlet, 1993; Thompson, 1996, p. 130; Also in Bianculli, 1996

Cops
Abelman, 1998, pp. 419–421*; Block, 1990, pp. 279–280; Fishman, 1999; Lechner, 2000, pp. 253–254; Lester, 1996, p. 178; Orlik, 1994, p. 148; Orlik, 2001, pp. 26–27; Rushkoff, 1994, pp. 52–55*; Sharrett, 1999, pp. 256–270**; Slade, 2002, p. 208; Smith, 1997; Also in Bianculli, 1996

Corner Bar, The
Capsuto, 2000, pp. 75–78

Coronet Blue
Gianakos, 1978, p. 574

Cos
Smith, 1986, pp. 149–152; Smith, 1997, pp. 138–140

Cosby
Alley & Brown, 2001, pp. 49, 72, 75; Bogle, 2001, pp. 449–451; Means Coleman, 2000, pp. 127–128; Smith, 1997, pp. 225–230*; Spigel, 2001, p. 373

Cosby Mysteries, The
Bogle, 2001, pp. 448–449; Smith, 1997, pp. 218–221*

Cosby Show, The
Abelman, 1998, p. 339; Allen, 1987, pp. 32–39**; Andrews, 1986, p. 146; Avery & Eason, 1991, pp. 302–304; Barker, 1999, pp. 80–81; Batra, 1987, pp. 118–120*; Berry & Manning-Miller, 1996, pp. 131, 140–144, 150*; Bignell, 1997, pp. 156–157*; Bogle, 2001, pp. 5, 286, 290–303, 317, 318**; Bryant, 1990, pp. 44–45; Bryant & Bryant, 2001, pp. 170–171, 209, 342–343; Burks, 1990**; Caldwell, 1995, p. 20; Chunovic, 2000, pp. 49–50, 103–104; Cortes, 2000, pp. 85–96, 88; Cottle, 2000, p. 120; Craig, 1992, pp. 111–123**; Croteau & Hoynes, 2000, pp. 267–268; Crotty, 1995; Cruz & Lewis, 1994, pp. 28–30, 36; Dates & Barlow, 1990, pp. 282–284, 457–458*; Dates & Barlow, 1993, pp. 306–308; Davies, 1997, pp. 30, 75, 101–104, 107–188, 195–196, 202–203, 212, 224–225**; Davis, 2001, pp. 14–15, 57; Dow, 1996, p. 100; Ely, 1991, p. 250; Entman & Rojecki, 2000, pp. 39, 71, 222; Fiske, 1994, pp. 48, 66, 97–123**; Frazer & Frazer, 1993; Fuller, 1992, whole book**; Gitlin, 1986, pp. 207–215**; Goethals, 1990, pp. 111–113, 115, 150*; Hamamoto, 1989, pp. 136–137; Harris, 1989, p. 48; Harris, 1994, pp. 47, 51, 53; Hendershot, 1998, pp. 105, 207; Henderson & Mazzeo, 1990, pp. 121–125*; Hiebert, 1999, pp. 250, 374; Himmelstein, 1994, pp. 156, 158–159; Holtzman, 2000, pp. 125–128, 249–251**; Inniss & Feagin, 1995; James, 1991; Jarvis & Joseph, 1998, pp. 175, 226, 235; Johnston, 2000, pp. 25, 66–67; Jones, 1992, pp. 3–4, 250–251, 259–261*; Kamalipour & Carrilli, 1998, pp. 52–53, 54, 85; Kendall, 1989**; Kottak, 1990, p. 63; Lechner, 2000, p. 270; Lembo, 2000, pp. 171, 172, 173, 175, 176, 187, 188–189, 197*; Leonard, 1997, pp. 4, 61; Levinson & Link, 1986, pp. 123–131 (Jay Sandrich interview)**; Lewis, 1991, pp. 110–115, 159–202, 205**; Lichter, Lichter, & Rothman, 1991, pp. 94, 246–247; Lichter, Lichter, & Rothman, 1994, pp. 53, 58–59, 351–352; Lusane, 1999; Marc, 1997, pp. 182–183; 191; Marc & Thompson, 1992 (Ch. 9 on Carsey & Werner), pp. 99–107, especially pp. 101–103*; Mayerle, 1991; McDonald, 1992, pp. 269–273, 293–294*; Means Coleman, 2000, pp. 95–98, 99, 105, 133, 173, 189–198, 255**; Means Coleman, 2002, pp. 159–204**; Mendoza, 1986; Miller, 1988, pp. 69–78**; Monaco, 2000, p. 498; Neuman, 1991, p. 167; Newcomb, 1994, pp. 184–185; Newcomb, 2000, p. 66, 290–294, 298, 299*; Orlik, 1994, pp. 188, 209–210, 228–229, 290–314 (script); Orlik, 2001, pp. 185, 301–325 (script); Oskamp, 1988, pp. 98, 109; Owen, 1997, p. 44; Paietta & Kauppila, 1999, p. 326; Panati, 1991, pp. 480–482; Parenti, 1991, pp. 140–141; Patton, 2001; Payne, 1994; Pounds, 1999, p. 72; Press, 1991, pp. 44–46, 80, 84–86, 105–111, 115–116,

134–135, 106–168**; Putterman, 1995, p. 102; Raymond, 1990, p. 128; Real, 1989, pp. 106–131**; Rodriguez, 1997, pp. 67–68; Roman, 1996, pp. 29, 66; Sackett, 1993, pp. 292–293; Schwartz, 1999, p. 140; Silverblatt, Ferry, & Finan, 1999, p 21; Sklar, 1980, pp. 324–335**; Smith, 1986, pp. 175–197**; Smith, 1997a*; Smith, 1997b, pp. 162–184, 194–195, 198–201, 202–207, 213–214**; Spigel & Curtin, 1997, pp. 352–353; Staiger, 2000, pp. 6, 45, 110, 141–159, 161–162, 163, 164–165**; Stark, 1997, pp. 28, 254–258, 295*; Steenland, 1990, p. 24; Sut & Lewis, 1992, whole book**; Tartikoff, 1992, pp. 3–18**; Taylor, 1989, pp. 160–164*; Thomas & Evans, 1990, p. 295; Torres, 1998, p. 79 (n. 6); Tulloch, 2000, pp. 157–158, 160–165, 168–175, 176–177**; Turner, 1994, pp. 132–136**; Turow, 1989, pp. 260–261; Twitchell, 1992, p. 223; U.S. Congress, 1985, pp. 176–177; Vande Berg & Wenner, 1991, pp. 58–84 (reprint of Chapter from Real, 1989)**; Wagner & Lundeen, 1998, p. 4; Walters, 2001, pp. 12–13; Weimann, 2000, pp. 79–80, 127, 222, 223, 237; Woll & Miller, 1987, pp. 84–85; Zook, 1999, pp. 8, 29; Also in Bianculli, 1996, Terrace, 1993

Cosmopolitan Theatre
Gianakos, 1980, p. 292

Court Martial
Gianakos, 1978, pp. 532–533

Court of Last Resort, The
Gianakos, 1981, pp. 377–378

Courtship of Eddie's Father, The
Hamamoto, 1989, pp. 95–97; Hamamoto, 1994, pp. 11–12; Lichter, Lichter, & Rothman, 1991, pp. 83, 242; Lichter, Lichter, & Rothman, 1994, p. 152; Rafkin, 1998, pp. 66–67; Also in Eisner & Krinsky, 1984, Terrace, 1993

Covington Cross
Caldwell, 1995, p. 89; Lichter, Lichter, & Rothman, 1994, p. 50

Cowboy G-Men
Davis, 1995, pp. 214–215; Hamamoto, 1994, pp. 53–54; Jarvis & Joseph, 1998, p. 195; Rovin, 1977b, pp. 36–37; Yoggy, 1995, p. 50; Also in Lentz, 1997

Cowboy in Africa
Gianakos, 1978, pp. 589–590; Also in Lentz, 1997, Terrace, 1993, West, 1987

Cowboy Theater
IN West, 1987

Cowboys, The
IN Lentz, 1997, West, 1987

Cracker
Cortes, 2000, p. 104

Crazy Like a Fox
Gianakos, 1992, pp. 381–383; Klobas, 1988, pp. 96, 358–359; Sackett, 1993, pp. 300–301; Sumser, 1996, pp. 67–68, 71, 72, 100, 109, 112, 115–117, 122–123, 152–153*

Crew, The
Gross & Woods, 1999, pp. 337–338; Owen, 1997, p. 116

Crime and Punishment
Longworth, 2000, pp. 7–8

Crime Photographer
Daniel, 1996, p. 7; Also in Terrace, 1993

Crime Story
Collins & Javna, 1989, pp. 77–79; Cuklanz, 2000, pp. 36, 74; Dienst, 1994, pp. 70–78**; Himmelstein, 1994, pp. 229–230

Critic, The
Capsuto, 2000, p. 370; Owen, 1997, p. 66; Also in Terrace, 2000

Crossroads (anthology)
Gianakos, 1980, pp. 480–483*; Lichter, Lichter, & Rothman, 1991, p. 277; Pearl & Pearl, 1999, pp. 18–19, 24, 66–67

Crossroads (news magazine) *see* **American Parade**

Crusader
Gianakos, 1983, pp. 317–319*; Lichter, Lichter, & Rothman, 1991, pp. 175, 207

Cupid
Paietta & Kauppila, 1999, p. 326; Wild, 1999, pp. 37–40, 43–45, 65–66, 100–104, 136, 145–149, 166, 209**

Current Affair, A
Mellencamp, 1992, pp. 208–211; Orlik, 1994, p. 137; Vane & Gross, 1994, p. 235; Also in Bianculli, 1996

Current Edition
Stark, 1997, p. 252

Custer
Gianakos, 1978, pp. 593–594; Jackson, 1994, pp. 184–186; McDonald, 1987, pp. 118–119; Rovin, 1977b, pp. 115–116; Spigel & Curtin, 1997, pp. 327–346**; Yoggy, 1995, pp. 360–361; Also in Lentz, 1997, West, 1987

Cutter to Houston
Gianakos, 1987, pp. 319–320; Paietta & Kauppila, 1999, p. 326

Cutters
Capsuto, 2000, p. 293; Cotter, 1997, p. 437

Cybill
Barr, 2000, p. 71; Capsuto, 2000, pp. 349–350; Dow, 1996, p. 208; Isaacs, 1999, p. 97; Lechner, 2000, pp. 194–195

D.A., The
Gianakos, 1978, pp. 705–706; Lichter, Lichter, & Rothman, 1991, pp. 139, 196; Lichter, Lichter, & Rothman, 1994, pp. 220–221, 289–290; Martindale, 1991, pp. 119–122; Meyers, 1981, pp. 159–160; Moyer & Alvarez, 2001, pp. 178–180

D. A.'s Man, The
Gianakos, 1983, p. 343

Daddy Dearest
Paietta & Kauppila, 1999, p. 326; Suman, 1997, p. 77

Daddy's Girls
Wild, 1999, p. 111

Dakotas, The
Andrews, 1980, pp. 22–26*; Fagen, 1996, p. 191; Gianakos, 1978, p. 403; Jackson, 1994, pp. 155–156; Also in Lentz, 1997, West, 1987

Daktari
Andrews, 1986, pp. 123–124; Bogle,

Dallas

pp. 65–66; U.S. Congress, 1985, pp. 47, 111, 160; Vande Berg & Trujillo, 1989, pp. 145–146, 166, 169–170, 213–218**; Vande Berg & Wenner, 1991, pp. 166–175 (passim)*; Vane & Gross, 1994, p. 176; Weimann, 2000, pp. 241, 368; Williams, 1992, pp. 47, 105, 179–180 (passim); Also in Bianculli, 1996, Morris, 1997

Damon Runyon Theatre
Gianakos, 1980, pp. 416–418*

Dan August
Gianakos, 1978, pp. 676–677; Martindale, 1991, pp. 122–124; Meyers, 1981, pp. 150–151

Dan Raven
Gianakos, 1978, p. 312

Dana Carvey Show, The
Abelman, 1998, p. 312

Danger
Gianakos, 1980, pp. 277–283**

Danger Agent *see* **Secret Agent**

Danger Man *see* **Secret Agent**

Dangerous Assignment
Gianakos, 1987, p. 363

Dangerous Curves
IN Terrace, 1993

Dangerous Minds
Abelman, 1998, pp. 416–417

Daniel Boone
Fitzgerald & Magers, 2002, p. 129; Gianakos, 1978, pp. 460–466**; Jackson, 1994, pp. 157–159; Lichter, Lichter, & Rothman, 1994, pp. 9–10; Magers & Fitzgerald, 1999, pp. 35–39, 139, 253–254*; Newcomb, 1976, pp. 198–200*; Rovin, 1977b, pp. 77, 93–94; Wagner & Lundeen, 1998, p. 177; Yoggy, 1995, pp. 358–360*; Also in Bianculli, 1996, Lentz, 1997, West, 1987

Danny Thomas Hour, The
Gianakos, 1987, pp. 394–396

Danny Thomas Show, The *see* **Make Room for Daddy**

Dante's Inferno
Gianakos, 1978, pp. 296–297; Meyers, 1981, p. 75; Also in Terrace, 1993

Dark Justice
IN Terrace, 1993

Dark Shadows
Harris, 1998, pp. 199–201, 204–218**; Matelski, 1999, p. 43; Morris, 1971, pp. 33–34; Muir, 2001a, pp. 292–301; Paietta & Kauppila, 1999, p. 327; Rouverol, 1984, p. 13; Story, 1993, pp. 224–239**; Williams, 1992, pp. 28–29; Also in Bianculli, 1996, Morris, 1997, Terrace, 1993

Dark Skies
Muir, 2001a, pp. 441–454**

Darkroom
Gianakos, 1983, pp. 217–218; Muir, 2001a, pp. 96–102**

Date with Judy, A
IN Terrace, 1993

Date with the Angels
O'Dell, 1997, p. 211

Dateline NBC
Christians, Fackler, & Rotzoll, 1995, pp. 48–51; Crossen, 1994, p. 31; Johnston, 2000, p. 106; Kovach & Rosenstiel, 1999, pp. 4, 113, 134; Orlik, 2001, p. 22; Roman, 1996, pp. 102–103; Spragens, 1995, pp. 22, 99–100, 133**; Winch, 1997, pp. 95–112**; Also in Bianculli, 1996

Dating Game, The
Castleman & Podrazik, 1982, p. 211; Also in Bianculli, 1996

Dave's World
Paietta & Kauppila, 1999, p. 327; Also in Terrace, 2000

David Letterman
Abelman, 1998, pp. 210, 216–220*; Blum, 1995, pp. 189–190; Carter, 1994, entire book (passim), pp. 51–69, 151–165, 184–191, 208–211**; Carter, 1995, entire book (passim), pp. 24–25, 45–47, 51–69, 157–168, 187–193, 208–211, 250–256, 269–274, 280–282, 286–291, 295–297**; Chunovic, 2000, p. 144; Himmelstein, 1984, pp. 286–287; Himmelstein, 1994, pp. 344–345; Javna, 1985, p. 242; Lechner, 2000, pp. 154, 155–156; Leonard, 1997, pp. 257–258; Newcomb, 1994, pp. 270–271; Newcomb, 2000, pp. 356–358*; Owen, 1997, p. 54; Putterman, 1995, pp. 102, 144; Rose, 1985, p. 340; Rose, 1999, pp. 119–134**; Scott, 1996, pp. 262–270*; Shattuc, 1997, p. 5; Stark, 1997, pp. 186–188; Tartikoff, 1992, pp. 104–110**; Tinker & Rukeyser, 1994, pp. 251–252; Vande Berg & Wenner, 1991, pp. 416–423 (passim)*; Zehme, 1999, pp. 309, 315–318; Also in Bianculli, 1996

Davis Rules
Alley & Brown, 2001, p. 75; Hamamoto, 1994, p. 13; Also in Terrace, 1993

Dawson's Creek
Capsuto, 2000, pp. 407–408; Helford, 2000, p. 183 (n. 12); Lechner, 2000, pp. 142–144*; Slade, 2002, p. 27; Wild, 1999, p. 44

Day by Day
Caldwell, 1995, p. 91

Days and Nights of Molly Dodd, The
Abelman, 1998, p. 342; Haralovich & Rabinovitz, 1999, pp. 163–164 (n. 2); Leonard, 1997, p. 63; Pearl & Pearl, 1999, p. 207; Also in Bianculli, 1996, Terrace, 2000

Days of Our Lives
Allen, 1995, p. 182; Berry & Manning-Miller, 1996, pp 151, 153–154; Blumenthal, 1997, pp. 55–56, 69, 79, 96*; Brown, 1990, pp. 194–198*; Brown, 1994, pp. 57, 80–89, 105–111, 119–123, 137–139, 144**; Chunovic, 2000, p. 69; Cross, 1983, p. 136; Edmondson & Rounds, 1973, pp. 175–176; Edmondson & Rounds, 1976, p. 160; Fiske, 1987, p. 193; Gilbert, 1976, pp. 108–131**; Greenberg & Busselle, 1996; James, 1991**; Lembo, 2000, p. 182; Matelski, 1988, pp. 45, 90–103**; Matelski, 1999, pp. 4, 41; McDonald, 1983, p. 164; McDonald, 1992, pp. 169–170; Modleski, 1982, pp. 93–94; Nelson, 1995, p. 60; Newcomb, 1976, pp. 62–63; Newcomb, 1979, pp. 83–84; Nochimson, 1992, pp. 7, 28, 85–104, 154–155, 161, 164–174, 195, 196**; O'Dell, 1997, p. 189; Ornellas, 1987**; Parenti, 1991, p. 98; Rouverol, 1984, pp. 21, 30–32, 41–42, 140; Rouverol, 1992, pp. 27, 60–78, 248**; Russell,

1995**; Schultz, 2000, pp. 123–124; Vande Berg & Wenner, 1991, pp. 182–185, 187–196**; Williams, 1992, pp. 27–28, 82, 84, 96–97, 109–110, 137; Also in Bianculli, 1996

Deadline
Daniel, 1996, p. 10

Dean Martin Show, The
Capsuto, 2000, p. 353; Erickson, 2000, pp. 56–57; Martin, 1980**; Sackett, 1993, pp. 150–151; Also in Bianculli, 1996

Dean Martin Summer Show, The
Erickson, 2000, pp. 57, 59–61*

Dear Detective
Gianakos, 1981, pp. 274–275

Dear John
Capsuto, 2000, pp. 357–358; Also in Terrace, 1993, Terrace, 2000

Dear Phoebe
Guida, 2000, p. 183; Also in Terrace, 1993

Death Valley Days
Aquila, 1996, p. 168; Broughton, 1986, pp. 33–34; Fitzgerald & Magers, 2002, pp. 68, 70; Gianakos, 1987, pp. 350–362**; Jackson, 1994, pp. 50–53; Magers & Fitzgerald, 1999, pp. 102, 189; Yoggy, 1995, pp. 78–82*; Also in Bianculli, 1996, Lentz, 1997, West, 1987

December Bride
Harris, 1991, pp. 209–210; Hawes, 2002, p. 84; Jones, 1992, pp. 85–86; Mitz, 1980, pp. 103–105*; Sackett, 1993, p. 55; Sanders & Gilbert, 1993, pp. 85–86; Also in Eisner & Krinsky, 1984, Terrace, 1993

Decoy
Meehan, 1983, pp. 67, 69, 73–74, 165

Deep Space Nine *see* **Star Trek: Deep Space Nine**

Defenders, The
Bogle, 2001, pp. 100–102*; Caldwell, 1995, p. 40; Castleman & Podrazik, 1982, pp. 147–148*; Everitt, 2001, p. 181; Gianakos, 1978, pp. 328–332*; Hawes, 2002, p 119; Himmelstein, 1984, pp. 171–172; Himmelstein, 1994, p. 212; Jackson, 1982; Jarvis & Joseph, 1998, pp. ix–x, 3–15, 251–253**; Lichter, Lichter, & Rothman, 1991, pp. 41–43, 45, 215*; Lichter, Lichter, & Rothman, 1994, pp. 99–101, 314*; McDonald, 1983, p. 103; McDonald, 1992, p. 113; Mehling, 1962, p. 151; Meyers, 1981, pp. 86–87; Newcomb, 1976, pp. 75, 77–82, 227**; Pearl & Pearl, 1999, pp. 158–159, 165, 209; Rovin, 1977b, pp. 80, 82; Schneider, 2001, p. xi; Stempel, 1992, pp. 87–89*; Thompson, 1996, p. 27; Turow, 1989, p. 95; Williams, 1982, pp. 37–38; Also in Bianculli, 1996

Delphi Bureau
IN Terrace, 1993

Delta
IN Terrace, 1993

Delta House
IN Terrace, 1993

Delvecchio
Coakley, 1977, pp. 159, 160; Gianakos, 1981, pp. 202–203; Gitlin, 1983, pp.

276–279; Heil, 2001, pp. 290–292, 317–320, 323–330**; Lichter, Lichter, & Rothman, 1991, p. 223; Lichter, Lichter, & Rothman, 1994, p. 323; Longworth, 2000, pp. 197–198; Marc & Thompson, 1992 (Ch. 20 on Steven Bochco), pp. 218–229; Martindale, 1991, pp. 127–131; Meyers, 1981, pp. 235–237

Dennis the Menace
Davis, 1995, pp. 106–107; Jones, 1992, pp. 120–121; Kulzer, 1992, p. 44; Martin, 1980**; Spigel & Curtin, 1997, pp. 119–135**; Also in Bianculli, 1996, Eisner & Krinsky, 1984, Terrace, 1993

Deputy, The
Gianakos, 1978, pp. 229–231; Jackson, 1994, p. 131; Rovin, 1977b, p. 72; Yoggy, 1995, pp. 168, 170–171; Also in Lentz, 1997, West, 1987

Designing Women
Berlant, 1997, pp. 239–242*; Bogle, 2001, pp. 343–344; Capsuto, 2000, pp. 221–222; Doty, 1993, pp. 41–43, 57–61, 122 (n. 27), 125 (n. 37)*; Dow, 1996, pp. xxiv, 104–134, 137, 209**; Fiske, 1994, pp. 38–39, 77–78, 81, 87, 89*; Haralovich & Rabinovitz, 1999, pp. 148, 149–156, 160, 227; Jones, 1992, p. 262; Kim, 1999; Lichter, Lichter, & Rothman, 1991, p. 296; Lichter, Lichter, & Rothman, 1994, p. 42; Marc, 1989, pp. 45–46; Means Coleman, 2000, pp. 178–179; Newcomb, 2000, p. 295; Puette, 1992, pp. 56–57, 58, 192; Ringer, 1994, pp. 96–97, 98–99, 109; Sackett, 1993, pp. 334–335; Schwartz, 1999, p. 135; Seger, 1996, p. 159; Selnow & Gilbert, 1993, p. 53; Smith, 1997a; Steenland, 1990, pp. 15, 48; Stempel, 1992, pp. 255–256; Swanson, 2000, pp. 22–31, 46, 49–50, 108–109**; Weiner, 1992, p. 33; Also in Bianculli, 1996, Terrace, 1993, Terrace, 2000

Desilu Playhouse
Gianakos, 1978, pp. 169–171; Harris, 1991, pp. 13–14, 237–241, 245–247*; Sanders & Gilbert, 1993, pp. 149–153, 169, 189–193**

Destry
Gianakos, 1978, pp. 440–441; Also in Lentz, 1997, Terrace, 1993, West, 1987

Detective in the House
Gianakos, 1992, pp. 389–390

Detective School
Pegg, 2002, p. 137

Detectives, The
Gianakos, 1978, pp. 269–272*; Meyers, 1981, pp. 65–66; Rovin, 1977b, p. 70

Devlin Connection
Gianakos, 1987, p. 291; Also in Terrace, 1993

Dharma & Greg
Isaacs, 1999, p. 47; Rannow, 1999, pp. 76–79*; Schultz, 2000, pp. 126–128*; Smith, 1999, p. 22; Also in Terrace, 2000

Diagnosis: Murder
Paietta & Kauppila, 1999, p. 327

Diagnosis: Unknown
Gianakos, 1983, p. 347; Paietta & Kauppila, 1999, p. 327

Diana
Miles, 1975, pp. 38–40 (Nov. 5, 1973, show); Smith, 1989, pp. 171–172; Story, 1993, p. 216; Also in Terrace, 1993

Dick Cavett Show, The
IN Bianculli, 1996

Dick Clark Presents the Rock 'n' Roll Years
Jackson, 1997, p. 262

Dick Clark Show, The
Jackson, 1997, pp. 104–123, 131, 140, 173, 174, 175, 194, 199**

Dick Clark's Live Wednesday
Jackson, 1997, p. 269

Dick Clark's World of Talent
Jackson, 1997, pp. 159, 167, 174

Dick Powell Show, The
Gianakos, 1978, pp. 348–351*; Pearl & Pearl, 1999, p. 20; Spelling, 1996, pp. 46–47

Dick Powell's Zane Grey Theater
Bogle, 2001, pp. 86–88; Fagen, 1996, p. 31; Gianakos, 1978, pp. 134–138*; Hawes, 2002, p. 136; Jackson, 1994, pp. 72–73; Jarvis & Joseph, 1998, pp. 203–204; Magers & Fitzgerald, 1999, pp. 136–137; Spelling, 1996, pp. 23–26, 28–42**; Yoggy, 1995, pp. 83–84, 149, 155, 219, 286; Also in Lentz, 1997, West, 1987

Dick Tracy
Castleman & Podrazik, 1982, p. 60; Also in Terrace, 1993

Dick Van Dyke Show, The
Abelman, 1998, p. 131; Adir, 1988, pp. 221–222; Alley & Brown, 2001, p. 118; Bedell, 1981, pp. 62–63; Bennett, 1996, pp. 75–78; Bogle, 2001, pp. 118–119; Caldwell, 1995, p. 72; Capsuto, 2000, p. 49; Castleman & Podrazik, 1982, p. 150; Crotty, 1995; Davis, 2001, p. 8; Freeman, 1980, p. 17; Gabler, Rich & Antler, 2000, pp. 15, 35; Javna, 1985, pp. 58–61*; Jones, 1992, pp. 140–147, 197**; Kulzer, 1992, pp. 123–128*; Kutulas, 1998; Lichter, Lichter, & Rothman, 1991, pp. 70–71, 98–99, 110, 119; Lichter, Lichter, & Rothman, 1994, pp. 136–137, 171–172, 196*; Marc, 1989, pp. 86, 90–91, 93–118**; Marc, 1997, pp. 70, 72–76, 77–98**; Meehan, 1983, pp. 42–45, 168*; Mitz, 1980, pp. 181–186**; Newcomb, 1987, p. 57; Paietta & Kauppila, 1999, p. 327; Panati, 1991, pp. 354–355; Pearl & Pearl, 1999, p. 18; Pegg, 2002, pp. 100, 312, 314–317*; Putterman, 1995, p. 96; Rafkin, 1998, pp. 35–36; Sackett, 1993, pp. 120–121; Smith, 1986, pp. 60–61; Smith, 1989, pp. 43, 45–47; Sochen, 1987, pp. 80–81; Sochen, 1999, p. 147; Stark, 1997, pp. 100–103*; Stempel, 1992, pp. 96–98; Taylor, 1989, pp. 31–32; Thomas, 1991, pp. 216–219; Thompson, 1996, pp. 26–27, 51–52; Tinker & Rukeyser, 1994, pp. 48–49, 57–61*; Waldron, 1994, whole book**; Weissman & Sanders, 1993, whole book**; Williams, 1982, pp. 51–52, 107–113, 143–144**; Wylie, 1970, pp. 192–230**; Also in Bianculli, 1996, Eisner & Krinsky, 1984, Terrace, 1993

Different World, A
Abelman, 1998, p. 131; Bogle, 2001, pp. 316–322**; Caldwell, 1995, pp. 326–327, 330; Cuklanz, 2000, pp. 42, 43, 116–117; Dates & Barlow, 1990, p. 279; Dates & Barlow, 1993, pp.

303–304; Entman & Rojecki, 2000, p. 161; Guida, 2000, pp. 221–222; Kamalipour & Carrilli, 1998, pp. 85, 86; Lichter, Lichter, & Rothman, 1994, pp. 28, 60; Marc & Thompson, 1992 (Ch. 9 on Carsey and Werner), pp. 99–107; McCrohan, 1990, pp. 344–349*; Means Coleman, 2000, pp. 98, 102, 103, 160, 254; Means Coleman, 2002, p. 190; Neuman, 1991, p. 168; Sackett, 1993, pp. 316–317; Smith, 1997b, p. 195; Smith, 1997a; Steenland, 1990, pp. 28–29; Turner, 1994, pp. 143–145*; Vane & Gross, 1994, pp. 146, 171; Zook, 1999, pp. 9–10, 29, 89; Also in Terrace, 1993

Diff'rent Strokes
Andrews, 1986, pp. 143–144; Bedell, 1981, pp. 243–246; Fiske, 1987, p. 70; Hamamoto, 1989, p. 127; Jones, 1992, pp. 223–224; Kassel 1993, pp. 120–121; Klobas, 1988, pp. 174–176, 398–399; Lichter, Lichter, & Rothman, 1991, pp. 88–89, 155, 255; Lichter, Lichter, & Rothman, 1994, pp. 159, 160, 240, 362; McDonald, 1983, pp. 198–199; McDonald, 1992, p. 201; Pearl & Pearl, 1999, p. 20; Puette, 1992, p. 191; Raymond, 1990, pp. 124, 125; Rose, 1985, p. 121; Staiger, 2000, p. 154; Turner, 1994, pp. 125–130**; Also in Bianculli, 1996, Eisner & Krinsky, 1984, Terrace, 1993

Dilbert
Wild, 1999, pp. 119, 125–127, 143–145, 202–203*

Dinah Shore Chevy Show, The
IN Bianculli, 1996

Dinah's Place
Lewis & Lewis, 1979, pp. 249–256*; Sochen, 1987, p. 113; Sochen, 1999, pp. 20, 168, 169–177**

Dinosaurs
Cotter, 1997, pp. 397–403**; Lichter, Lichter, & Rothman, 1994, p. 40–41; Also in Terrace, 1993, Terrace, 2000

Dirty Sally
IN Lentz, 1997, West, 1987

Disney Presents the 100 Lives of Black Jack Savage
Cotter, 1997, pp. 394–396*

Disneyland (Also Walt Disney Presents and Walt Disney's Wonderful World of Color)
Abelman, 1998, p. 397; Anderson, 1994, pp. 4, 10, 133–155, 163, 214–215, 279–280**; Aquila, 1996, p. 165; Capsuto, 2000, pp. 37–38; Castleman & Podrazik, 1982, pp. 95, 102; Cotter, 1997, pp. 57–74, 75–178 (passim)**; Davis, 1995, pp. 42–44*; Friedman, 2002, pp. 54–62**; Gianakos, 1978, pp. 105–126**; Gianakos, 1980, pp. 401–403*; Gianakos, 1981, pp. 85–92**; Gianakos, 1987, pp. 201–203; Hawes, 2002, pp. 57–59, 129–130; Heldenfels, 1994, pp. 154, 158–161*; Hollis & Sibley, 1988, pp. 67–72, 79*; Marling, 1994, pp. 121–125*; McDonald, 1987, pp. 39–43; Newcomb, 1994, pp. 70–84**; Newcomb, 2000, pp. 17–33**; Sackett, 1993, pp. 50–51, 164–165; Stark, 1997, pp. 52–55*; Stempel, 1992, pp. 62–63; Yoggy, 1995, pp. 52–61, 66–76, 557–558**; Also in Bianculli, 1996

Divorce Court
Klobas, 1988, pp. 94–95; Orlik, 1994, p. 145; White, 1992, pp. 72–75*

Dobie Gillis *see* **Many Loves of Dobie Gillis**

Doc
Kalisch, Kalisch, & Scobey, 1983, pp. 86–90, 93*; Paietta & Kauppila, 1999, p. 328; Tinker & Rukeyser, 1994, p. 105; Turow, 1989, pp. 217–219

Doc Corkle
Jones, 1992, p. 77; Paietta & Kauppila, 1999, p. 328

Doc Elliot
Gianakos, 1978, pp. 746–747; Kalisch, Kalisch, & Scobey, 1983, pp. 63–64; Paietta & Kauppila, 1999, p. 328

Doctor, The
Gianakos, 1983, pp. 292–294*; Kalisch, Kalisch, & Scobey, 1983, p. 9; Paietta & Kauppila, 1999, p. 328

Doctor, Doctor
Capsuto, 2000, p. 245; Paietta & Kauppila, 1999, p. 328; Pearl & Pearl, 1999, pp. 41, 105; Tabarlet, 1993; Also in Terrace, 1993

Dr. Kildare
Adler, 1976, pp. 96–98*; Adler, 1981, pp. 233–234; Alley, 1977, pp. 59–64*; Caldwell, 1995, p. 40; Castleman & Podrazik, 1982, pp. 148–149; Chunovic, 2000, pp. 48–49; Creeber, 2001, pp. 24–25; Gianakos, 1978, pp. 356–362**; Javna, 1985, p. 17; Kalisch, Kalisch, & Scobey, 1983, pp. 18–19, 23–25, 39–40, 192–193*; Lichter, Lichter, & Rothman, 1991, pp. 156–162 (passim); Lichter, Lichter, & Rothman, 1994, pp. 244–245, 248, 251*; Lisanti & Paul, 2002, p. 65; Martin, 1980**; Meehan, 1983, pp. 167–168; Newcomb, 1976, pp. 76, 78, 83; Newcomb & Alley, 1983, pp. 82–96 (passim); Paietta & Kauppila, 1999, p. 329; Pearl & Pearl, 1999, pp. 43–44; Rose, 1985, pp. 76–78; Rovin, 1977b, p. 80; Sackett, 1993, p. 113; Spigel & Curtin, 1997, pp. 190, 191–194*; Stempel, 1992, pp. 90–91; Thompson, 1996, p. 26; Turow, 1989, pp. 51, 52–66, 67–79, 80–82, 104, 105, 110, 112, 175**; Williams, 1982, pp. 43–44; Also in Bianculli, 1996

Dr. Quinn, Medicine Woman
Alley & Brown, 2001, pp. 199, 203–206, 209–214**; Aquila, 1996, p. 183; Buscombe & Pearson, 1998, pp. 200, 201, 205, 209, 211*; Dow, 1996, pp. xxii, xxiv–xxv, 164–202, 210; Harrison, et al., 1996, p. 236; Isaacs, 1999, pp. 73–74*; Jackson, 1994, pp. 216–218; Lisanti & Paul, 2002, p. 269; Meyers, 1999, pp. 99–101, 105, 106*; Paietta & Kauppila, 1999, p. 329; Rainey, 1998, pp. 109, 143; Seger, 1996, pp. 226–230**; Spigel & Curtin, 1997, p. 343; Suman, 1997, p. 76; Yoggy, 1995, pp. 607–617, 621**; Also in Lentz, 1997, Terrace, 1993

Dr. Six-Gun
McDonald, 1987, p. 55

Doctors, The
Buckman, 1984, pp. 77–86**; Kalisch, Kalisch, & Scobey, 1983, pp. 160–161, 169–170, 174; Matelski, 1988, p. 18; Matelski, 1999, p. 43; Mayer, 1972, pp. 123–124; Newcomb, 1976, pp. 63–64; Newcomb, 1979, pp. 75–76; Also in Bianculli, 1996

Doctors and the Nurses, The
see **Nurses, The**

Doctors' Hospital
Alley, 1977, p. 73; Gianakos, 1981, p. 181; Kalisch, Kalisch, & Scobey,

1983, pp. 66–69*; Paietta & Kauppila, 1999, p. 330; Turow, 1989, p. 178

Doctors' Private Lives
Gianakos, 1981, pp. 276–277; Kalisch, Kalisch, & Scobey, 1983, p. 79; Lichter, Lichter, & Rothman, 1991, p. 165; Lichter, Lichter, & Rothman, 1994, p. 252; Paietta & Kauppila, 1999, p. 330; Turow, 1989, pp. 180–181

Dog and Cat
Cuklanz, 1998; Cuklanz, 2000, pp. 35, 80, 101; Gianakos, 1981, pp. 217–218; Also in Terrace, 1993

Dolphin Cove
IN Terrace, 1993

Domestic Life
IN Terrace, 1993

Donahue
Abelman, 1998, pp. 212–215*; Abt & Mustazza, 1997, pp. 60–64, 66–67*; Abt & Seesholtz, 1994; Barnouw, 1990, p. 521; Capsuto, 2000, p. 357; Conrad, 1982, pp. 55–56; Daniel, 1996, p. 141; Diamond, 1982, p. 45; Donahue, 1979, pp. 62–244**; Gross, 2001, pp. 185–187; Hamamoto, 1994, pp. 230–232; Haralovich & Rabinovitz, 1999, pp. 172–173, 175; Himmelstein, 1994, pp. 359–362*; Keyes, 1997**; Mellencamp, 1992, pp. 213–214; Moorti, 1995; Moorti, 2001, pp. 152, 153–154, 172–182, 214–215**; Munson, 1993, see index; Rapping, 1987, p. 136; Rapping, 1994, pp. 192–196; Rose, 1985, pp. 338–339; Rose, 1999, pp. 31–35*; Rushkoff, 1994, pp. 34, 61–63; Scott, 73, 75–76, 79–83, 94, 124–125**; Stark, 1997, pp. 278–279, 280; Tulloch, 2000, pp. 239–240, 242; Twitchell, 1992, pp. 239–240; Winch, 1997, pp. 87–90; Also in Bianculli, 1996

Donna Reed Show, The
Abt & Mustazza, 1997, pp. 43–44; Bennett, 1996, pp. 13–16; Caldwell, 1995, pp. 39–40, 72; Cavallo, 1999, p. 38; Fultz, 1998, pp. 117–156**; Hawes, 2002, pp. 87–88; Jones, 1992, pp. 154–156; Kalisch, Kalisch, & Scobey, 1983, pp. 12–13, 16; Kulzer, 1992, p. 105–112, 134; Leibman, 1995, pp. 1, 22–23, 29, 33, 37, 38, 47, 52, 76, 90, 123, 125, 148–149, 154, 156–157, 164, 168, 175–176, 182, 191–193, 199–201, 211–212, 225, 227, 237, 238, 242–243, 248, 268**; Mitz, 1980, pp. 149–152*; Paietta & Kauppila, 1999, p. 330; Penley, et al., 1991, pp. 215, 224; Rafkin, 1998, p. 47; Schwartz, 1999, p. 138; Spigel & Mann, 1992, pp. 178–179; Stark, 1997, p. 72 Also in Bianculli, 1996, Eisner & Krinsky, 1984, Terrace, 1993, Turow, 1989, p. 198

Doogie Howser, M.D.
Caldwell, 1995, p. 325; Capsuto, 2000, p. 299; Marc & Thompson, 1992 (Ch. 20 on Steven Bochco), pp. 218–229; McAllister, 1992; Paietta & Kauppila, 1999, p. 330; Steenland, 1990, pp. 26–27; Also in Terrace, 1993

Doris Day Show, The
Lichter, Lichter, & Rothman, 1994, pp. 124–125; Sackett, 1993, pp. 166–167; Schwartz, 1999, p. 133; Also in Eisner & Krinsky, 1984, Terrace, 1993

Double Dare
Bogle, 2001, p. 303; Gianakos, 1992, p. 387

Double Life of Henry Phyfe, The
Lisanti & Paul, 2002, pp. 27, 233

Double Trouble
IN Terrace, 1993

Down and Out in Beverly Hills
Cotter, 1997, pp. 335–336*

Down Home
Hamamoto, 1994, pp. 29–30; Also in Terrace, 1993

Down the Shore
IN Terrace, 1993

Down You Go
Castleman & Podrazik, 1982, pp. 59–60

Downey, Morton *see* **Morton Downey, Jr. Show**

Downtown
IN Terrace, 1993

Dracula: The Series
IN Terrace, 1993

Dragnet
Alexander, 1994, pp. 121–124; Anderson, 1994, pp. 67, 68; Bodroghkozy, 2001, pp. 76–80*; Bogle, 2001, p. 57; Bounds, 1996, p. 10; Carlson, 1985, p. 42; Castleman & Podrazik, 1982, pp. 67–68, 201–202; Collins & Javna, 1989, pp. 61–64*; D'Acci, 1994, p. 109; Davis, 2001, pp. 106, 116–117; Fitzgerald & Magers, 2002, p. 186; Gianakos, 1983, pp. 274–287**; Hawes, 2002, pp. 104–106; Heldenfels, 1994, pp. 71–72, 148; Javna, 1985, pp. 120–124*; Lane, 2001; Lazere, 1987, p. 253; Lichter, Lichter, & Rothman, 1991, pp. 124, 202, 226–227, 257; Lichter, Lichter, & Rothman, 1994, pp. 202, 296, 297, 306–307, 327–328, 364–365*; Marc, 1984, pp. 74–79*; Marc, 1996, pp. 74–79*; Marc & Thompson, 1992 (Ch. 12 on Jack Webb), pp. 132–139, especially pp. 134–136*; Martin, 1980**; Martindale, 1991, pp. 132–142; McCrohan, 1990, pp. 62–66*; Meehan, 1983, pp. 38, 57–58, 163; Meyers, 1981, pp. 18–21; Monaco, 2000, p. 483; Moyer & Alvarez, 2001, pp. 80–104, 135, 136–139, 146–155**; Newcomb, 1994, p. 193; Rose, 1985, pp. 13–14; Rovin, 1977b, pp. 27, 33; Rushkoff, 1994, p. 46; Sackett, 1993, pp. 34–35; Sharrett, 1999, p. 252; Spelling, 1996, pp. 15–17, 20, 67; Stark, 1997, pp. 2, 31–35*; Sumser, 1996, pp. 158–159; Taylor, 1989, p. 35; Toll, 1982, pp. 171–172; Turow, 1989, p. 30; Weiner, 1992, pp. 152–153; Williams, 1982, pp. 122–125*; Also in Bianculli, 1996

Dream On
Wild, 1999, p. 15; Also in Bianculli, 1996

Dream Street
Auletta, 1991, pp. 512–513, 522–525

Drew Carey Show, The
Smith, 1999, pp. 28, 53–54, 55–56, 63, 87, 152*; Wild, 1999, pp. 49–50, 54–55; Also in Terrace, 2000

Drexell's Class
IN Terrace, 1993

Duck Factory, The
IN Terrace, 1993

Due South
Lechner, 2000, p. 78

Duet
IN Terrace, 1993

Duffy's Tavern
IN Terrace, 1993

Duke, The
Gianakos, 1981, pp. 278–279

Dukes of Hazzard, The
Castleman & Podrazik, 1982, pp. 297, 298; Freeman, 1980, p. 82; Gianakos, 1981, pp. 277–278; Gianakos, 1983, pp. 166–169*; Gianakos, 1987, pp. 275–278*; Gianakos, 1992, pp. 345–346; Goethals, 1981, pp. 78–79; Guida, 2000, pp. 206–207; Hofstede, 1998, whole book**; Lichter, Lichter, & Rothman, 1991, p. 265; Lichter, Lichter, & Rothman, 1994, p. 375; McCrohan, 1990, pp. 303–311**; Owen, 1997, p. 43; Sackett, 1993, pp. 264–265; Schultz, 2000, pp. 124–125; Also in Bianculli, 1996, Terrace, 1993

Dumplings, The
IN Eisner & Krinsky, 1984

Dundee and the Culhane
Gianakos, 1978, p. 594; Jarvis & Joseph, 1998, pp. 214, 250; Also in Lentz, 1997, West, 1987

Dupont Show of the Week
Gianakos, 1978, pp. 336–339*

Dusty's Trail
Yoggy, 1995, pp. 436–437; Also in Lentz, 1997, Terrace, 1993

Dweebs
Owen, 1997, p. 184

Dynasty
Abelman, 1998, p. 101; Allen, 1995, pp. 246–249; Andrews, 1986, pp. 146–147; Baehr & Dyer, 1987, p. 13; Batra, 1987, pp. 94–96; Blumler, 1992, pp. 105–106; Bogle, 2001, pp. 262–264; Brown, 1990, pp. 158–180**; Buerkel-Rothfuss, 1993, pp. 36–38, 40–41; Capsuto, 2000, pp. 132–133, 154, 177–182, 206–207**; Chunovic, 2000, pp. 23, 92; Dates & Barlow, 1993, p. 319; Dow, 1996, p. 97; Drummond & Peterson, 1988, pp. 61–80**; Fiske, 1987, pp. 71, 190, 193; Gamman & Marshment, 1988, pp. 53, 102, 105–111**; Gaunt, 1993, p. 36; Geraghty, 1991, pp. 23, 27–29, 30, 49–63 (passim), 64–66, 70–74, 121, 132, 136, 141–142, 154–157, 158–159, 163–165, 168–169, 181*; Gianakos, 1983, pp. 184–186*; Gianakos, 1987, pp. 246–249*; Gianakos, 1992, pp. 315–319*; Gregory, 2000, pp. 6, 118, 149; Gripsrud, 1995, whole book**; Gross, 2001, pp. 84–85; Hagen & Wasko, 2000, p. 195; Haralovich & Rabinovitz, 1999, p. 6; Harris, 1989, p. 41; Harris, 1994, p. 43; Himmelstein, 1994, p. 226; Hollows, 2000, pp. 91, 92–93, 94–95, 103, 105; Holtzman, 2000, p 303; Javna, 1985, p. 244; Johnston, 2000, p. 59; Joshel, Malamud, & McGuire, 2001, pp. 139, 146; Lembo, 2000, pp. 183, 189, 190; Lichter, Lichter, & Rothman, 1991, p. 87; Lisanti & Paul, 2002, p. 101; Livingstone, 1990, p. 22; Livingstone, 1998, p. 25; Marc & Thompson, 1992 (Ch. 15 on Aaron Spelling), pp. 163–169; Matelski, 1988, p. 178; McCrohan, 1990, pp. 311–319**; Modleski, 1986, p. 170; Newcomb, 1994, pp. 552–561*; Newcomb, 2000, pp. 508, 531–553**; Oskamp, 1988, p. 321; Owen, 1997, pp. 95–96; Panati, 1991, pp. 474–476; Press, 1991, pp. 67–70, 73–75, 84, 90–94, 111–115**; Sackett, 1993, pp. 276–277; Spelling, 1996,

pp. 143–154, 155–158, 159**; Taylor, 1989, pp. 159–160; Vande Berg & Wenner, 1991, pp. 168–175 (passim)*; Walters, 2001, pp. 63–65; Weimann, 2000, p. 261; Williams, 1992, pp. 179–180 (passim); Also in Bianculli, 1996, Morris, 1997

Dynasty II: The Colbys *see* **Colbys, The**

E.A.R.T.H. Force
IN Terrace, 1993

Earth 2
Paietta & Kauppila, 1999, p. 331; Suman, 1997, pp. 76–77

East Side/West Side
Bogle, 2001, pp. 108–113**; Castleman & Podrazik, 1982, p. 165–166; Dates & Barlow, 1990, p. 255; Gianakos, 1978, pp. 412–414*; Himmelstein, 1984, pp. 172–173; Jackson, 1982; Lichter, Lichter, & Rothman, 1991, pp. 32, 73, 92; Lichter, Lichter, & Rothman, 1994, pp. 87, 139–140, 163–164; McDonald, 1983, pp. 104–106; McDonald, 1992, pp. 114–116; Rovin, 1977b, pp. 87–88; Williams, 1982, pp. 80–82*

Easy Street
IN Terrace, 1993

Ed
Keller, 2002, p. 179

Ed Sullivan *see* **Toast of the Town**

Ed Wynn Show
Burns, 1990, pp. 263–264, 267, 289; Castleman & Podrazik, 1982, p. 50

Eddie Capra Mysteries, The
Gianakos, 1981, pp. 267–268; Also in Terrace, 1993

Eddie Dodd
IN Terrace, 1993

Edge of Night, The
Kaminsky, 1985, p. 93; Matelski, 1999, pp. 22, 43; Nelson, 1995, p. 61; Also in Bianculli,1996

Eerie, Indiana
IN Terrace, 1993

Egg and I, The
IN Terrace, 1993

Eight Is Enough
Goethals, 1981, pp. 46–48*; Lembo, 2000, p. 161; Lichter, Lichter, & Rothman, 1991, pp. 69, 71; Lichter, Lichter, & Rothman, 1994, pp. 135, 137; Marc & Thompson, 1992 (Ch. 18 on Lee Rich, Lorimar), pp. 195–202; Pearl & Pearl, 1999, p. 200; Press, 1991, pp. 162–163; Puette, 1992, pp. 178, 184–185; Sklar, 1980, pp. 60–61; Also in Terrace, 1993

87th Precinct
Castleman & Podrazik, 1982, p. 152; Gianakos, 1978, pp. 339–340; Meyers, 1981, pp. 83–84; Rovin, 1977b, p. 82

Eischeid
Martindale, 1991, pp. 146–149; Gianakos, 1981, pp. 287–288

Electra Woman and Dyna Girl
IN Terrace, 1993

Eleventh Hour, The
Bogle, 2001, p. 103; Capsuto, 2000,

pp. 44–45; Castleman & Podrazik, 1982, p. 160; Gianakos, 1978, pp. 393–396; Kalisch, Kalisch, & Scobey, 1983, pp. 25–27; Paietta & Kauppila, 1999, p. 331; Spigel & Curtin, 1997, pp. 194–195, 197; Stempel, 1992, pp. 91–92; Turow, 1989, pp. 81–92**; U.S. Congress, 1977a, p. 300

Elgin TV House, The

Gianakos, 1980, pp. 392–393

Ellen

Abelman, 1998, p. 52; Barr, 2000, p. 71; Capsuto, 2000, pp. 363, 378–403**; Carstarphen & Zavoina, 1999, pp. 185–195**; Cotter, 1997, pp. 454–460**; Cortes, 2000, pp. 41, 66–67, 105, 107–109, 117, 127–128; Croteau & Hoynes, 2000, pp. 223–224; Davis, 2001, pp. 19–20, 75, 76; Dow, 1996, p. 208; Dow, 2001; Erickson, 2000, p. 17; Gross, 2001, pp. 156–163, 178–179**; Gross & Woods, 1999, pp. 9, 294–295; Helford, 2000, pp. 140–141; Holtzman, 2000, pp. 303–304; Hubert, 1999; Isaacs, 1999, pp. 130–131; Johnston, 2000, p. 139; Keller, 2002, pp. 122–123; Owen, 1997, p. 122; Schwartz, 1999, pp. 130, 151; Silverblatt, Ferry, & Finan, 1999, p 6; Smith, 1999, pp. 66, 149; Suman & Rossman, 2000, pp. 24–27, 94–95, 106, 109*; Walters, 2001, pp. xiv–xvi, 81–94, 126–127**; Also in Terrace, 2000

Ellen Burstyn Show

Cotter, 1997, pp. 330–332*

Ellery Queen

Collins & Javna, 1989, pp. 100–102; Gianakos, 1981, pp. 187–188; Gianakos, 1992, pp. 421–426**; Martindale, 1991, pp. 149–153; Meyers, 1981, pp. 4–9*; Rose, 1985, pp. 33, 36, 38; Rovin, 1977b, p. 26; Also in Terrace, 1993

Emerald Point, N.A.S.

Gianakos, 1987, pp. 327–328; Also in Morris, 1997

Emergency

Castleman & Podrazik, 1982, p. 231; Gianakos, 1992, pp. 457–462**; Kalisch, Kalisch, & Scobey, 1983, pp. 101, 105–109, 113*; Marc & Thompson, 1992 (Ch. 12 on Jack Webb), pp. 132–139; Moyer & Alvarez, 2001, pp. 177–189**; Paietta & Kauppila, 1999, p. 331; Rovin, 1977b, pp. 132–133; Turow, 1989, pp. 166–169*

Empire

Gianakos, 1978, pp. 380–382*; Jackson, 1994, pp. 152–153; Lichter, Lichter, & Rothman, 1991, pp. 118–119, 136–137; Lichter, Lichter, & Rothman, 1994, pp. 195, 217; Puette, 1992, p. 190; Root, 1979, pp. 154–156; Rovin, 1977b, p. 85; Yoggy, 1995, p. 338; Also in Lentz, 1997, Terrace, 1993, West, 1987

Empty Nest

Cotter, 1997, pp. 357–371**; Marc & Thompson, 1992 (Ch. 7 on Susan Harris), pp. 84–92; Paietta & Kauppila, 1999, pp. 331–332; Sackett, 1993, pp. 324–325; Also in Terrace, 1993, Terrace, 2000

Enos

Gianakos, 1983, pp. 189–190; Hofstede, 1998, pp. 329–330

Ensign O'Toole

Lichter, Lichter, & Rothman, 1991, pp. 74–75; Lichter, Lichter, & Rothman,

1994, p. 142; Also in Eisner & Krinsky, 1984

Entertainment Tonight
Caldwell, 1995, p. 6; Lechner, 2000, pp. 108–109; Mellencamp, 1992, pp. 207–208; Rapping, 1987, pp. 139–140; Stark, 1997, pp. 249–252; Swanson, 2000, pp. 7, 17; Winch, 1997, pp. 90–91; Also in Bianculli, 1996

Equal Justice
Bogle, 2001, pp. 373–376; Hamamoto, 1994, pp. 175–178; Jarvis & Joseph, 1998, pp. 244–245, 247–248; Leonard, 1997, pp. 158–159; Steenland, 1990, pp. 16, 40–41

Equalizer, The
Cuklanz, 2000, pp. 66–68, 88; Cumberbatch & Negrine, 1992, p. 49; Gauntlett & Hill, 1999, p. 50 (note 1); Gianakos, 1992, pp. 404–405; Gunter & Wober, 1988, pp. 26–30 (passim), 42–44*; Klobas, 1988, pp. 107–108, 111–112; Leonard, 1997, p. 61; Lichter, Lichter, & Rothman, 1991, p. 219; Lichter, Lichter, & Rothman, 1994, pp. 318–319; Sumser, 1996, pp. 69–70, 105; Thomas & Evans, 1990, p. 288; White, 1992, pp. 157–162, 167–172 (passim)**; Also in Terrace, 1993

E/R
Hamamoto, 1994, p. 15; Paietta & Kauppila, 1999, pp. 330–331; Turow, 1989, p. 257; U.S. Congress, 1985, p. 156

E.R.
Bogle, 2001, pp. 442–447**; Buresh & Gordon, 1995; Capsuto, 2000, pp. 304, 371; Carter, 1995, pp. 289–290; Creeber, 2001, p. 24; Davis, 2001, pp. 137–146, 142–154**; Diem & Lantos, 1996; Entman & Rojecki, 2000, pp. 149, 150, 152–153, 154, 156–159, 220, 222*; Friedman, 2002, pp. 277–279, 284*; Hollows, 2000, p. 198; Jarvis & Joseph, 1998, p. 31; Kalat 1998, pp. 265–267; Lechner, 2000, pp. 187–190*; Longworth, 2000, pp. xii, 44, 97–98, 122–124, 127–128, 130–134*; Newcomb, 2000, pp. 246–247, 250–251; Newitz, 1998; Owen, 1997, pp. 14, 61, 93–95*; Paietta & Kauppila, 1999, p. 331; Pearl & Pearl, 1999, p. 164; Pourroy, 1995, whole book**; Ross & Gibbs, 1996, whole book**; Schwartz, 1999, p. 163; Stark, 1997, pp. 291–294*; Swanson, 2000, pp. 68–69; Thompson, 1996, pp. 188–189; Weimann, 2000, pp. 176–178; Also in Bianculli, 1996

Ernie Kovacs
Abelman, 1998, p. 312; Adir, 1988, pp. 159–183**; Caldwell, 1995, p. 34; Capsuto, 2000, p. 26; Erickson, 2000, pp. 33–34, 63*; Horton, 2000, p. 75; Monaco, 2000, p. 481; Mott, 2000, pp. 112–113; Putterman, 1995, pp. 128, 136–144**; Rico, 1990, pp. 88–91, 94, 95, 97, 98, 102–112, 118, 142–146, 152, 153, 154–159, 180, 184–189, 191, 193, 194–195, 197, 209, 217, 229, 278–289, 296–298, 300, 303; Stempel, 1992, pp. 111–112; Walley, 1975, whole book**; Weiner, 1992, p. 137; Also in Bianculli, 1996

Escape (1950)
Hawes, 2001, p. 133

Espionage
Gianakos, 1978, p. 424; Williams, 1982, pp. 88–89

Ethel and Albert
Orlik, 1994, pp. 170–171, 188, 252,

254–255, 256, 273–288 (script); Skutch, 1998, pp. 90–91

Ethel Waters Show, The
Bogle, 2001, pp. 9–10

Evening Shade
Craig, 1992, pp. 200–213**; Paietta & Kauppila, 1999, p. 332; Also in Terrace, 1993, Terrace, 2000

Everybody Loves Raymond
Bryant & Bryant, 2001, pp. 187, 190, 195; Horton, 2000, p. 170; Swanson, 2000, pp. 46–47; Wild, 1999, pp. 67–68, 71–75, 155–156, 232–236**

Executive Suite
Coakley, 1977, pp. 196–199; Gianakos, 1981, pp. 203–204; Puette, 1992, pp. 176, 177; Also in Morris, 1997

Exile, The
IN Terrace, 1993

Eye to Eye
Gianakos, 1992, p. 388; Also in Terrace, 1993

Eye to Eye with Connie Chung
Spragens, 1995, pp. 113–116*

Eye Witness
Gianakos, 1980, p. 365

EZ Streets
Swanson, 2000, pp. 131–133

F Troop
Brauer, 1975, p. 21; Castleman & Podrazik, 1982, p. 185; Jackson, 1994, pp. 167–169; Lichter, Lichter, & Rothman, 1991, p. 271; Lichter, Lichter, & Rothman, 1994, pp. 382–383; Pegg, 2002, pp. 321, 324–332*; Yoggy, 1995, pp. 425–432**; Also in Bianculli, 1996, Eisner & Krinsky, 1984, Lentz, 1997, Terrace, 1993

Face the Nation
Bedell, 1981, pp. 238–239; Also in Bianculli, 1996

Facts of Life, The
Cuklanz, 2000, pp. 108, 118, 141–143; Hamamoto, 1989, pp. 128–129; Klobas, 1988, pp. 238–239, 323–324, 457; Owen, 1997, p. 43; Pearl & Pearl, 1999, pp. 28–29, 164; Putterman, 1995, pp. 118–120*; Raymond, 1990, pp. 124–125; Turner, 1994, p. 143; Also in Terrace, 1993

Falcon Crest
Gianakos, 1983, pp. 218–220*; Gianakos, 1987, pp. 280–284*; Gianakos, 1992, pp. 349–351*; Hagen & Wasko, 2000, p. 195; Hamamoto, 1994, p. 7; Lichter, Lichter, & Rothman, 1991, p. 149; Lichter, Lichter, & Rothman, 1994, p. 233; Marc & Thompson, 1992 (Ch. 18 on Lee Rich, i.e. Lorimar), pp. 195–202; Newcomb, 2000, p. 507; Newcomb & Alley, 1983, p. 164; Sackett, 1993, pp. 280–281; U.S. Congress, 1985, p. 157; Vande Berg & Trujillo, 1989, pp. 146–147; Williams, 1992, pp. 179–186 (passim); Also in Morris, 1997

Fall Guy, The
Gianakos, 1983, pp. 211–212; Gianakos, 1987, pp. 240–243*; Gianakos, 1992, pp. 312–315; Klobas,1988, pp. 170–171, 328–329; Marc & Thompson, 1992 (Ch. 16 on Glen Larson), pp. 171–178; Montgomery, 1989, p. 183; Also in Terrace, 1993

Fame
Dates & Barlow, 1990, pp. 279–280; Dates & Barlow, 1993, p. 304; Gianakos, 1987, pp. 253–257*; Gianakos, 1992, pp. 269–273*; Guida, 2000, pp. 216–217; Klobas, 1988, pp. 72–73, 255–256, 325; Lichter, Lichter, & Rothman, 1991, pp. 169, 170; Lichter, Lichter, & Rothman, 1994, pp. 256–257; McDonald, 1983, p. 241; McDonald, 1992, p. 239; Puette, 1992, p. 188; Rowland & Watkins, 1984, p. 261; Turner, 1994, p. 141

Family
Bedell, 1981, pp. 132–134; Capsuto, 2000, pp. 134–135; Castleman & Podrazik, 1982, p. 269; Coakley, 1977, pp. 87, 154; Goethals, 1981, pp. 50–52*; Klobas, 1988, pp. 49–50; Marc & Thompson, 1992 (Ch. 15 on Aaron Spelling), pp. 163–169; Schuth, 1978, pp. 145–148*; Sklar, 1980, pp. 11–12, 59–60, 173–176*; Spelling, 1996, pp. 93–99**; Taylor, 1989, pp. 104–107, 145*; Also in Terrace, 1993

Family Affair
Bennett, 1996, pp. 58–59; Bryant, 1990, p. 42; Castleman & Podrazik, 1982, p. 193; Hamamoto, 1989, pp. 67–68; Jones, 1992, pp. 183–184; Kulzer, 1992, pp. 27–33*; Meehan, 1983, pp. 170–171; Sackett, 1993, p. 149; Also in Eisner & Krinsky, 1984, Terrace, 1993

Family Album
IN Terrace, 2000

Family Feud
Brown, 1990, p. 138; Coakley, 1977, pp. 80–81; DeLong, 1991, pp. 250–251; Fiske, 1987, p. 279; Miller, 1988, pp. 51–59**; Rose, 1985, p. 295; Vane & Gross, 1994, p. 111; Also in Bianculli, 1996

Family for Joe, A
Rafkin, 1998, p. 133; Selnow & Gilbert, 1993, pp. 34–36; Steenland, 1990, pp. 22, 38–39

Family Guy
Johnston, 2000, pp. 1401–141

Family Holvak, The
Gianakos, 1981, pp. 169–170

Family Man, The
IN Terrace, 1993

Family Matters
Bogle, 2001, pp. 330–332; Bryant & Bryant, 2001, pp. 216–217; Gauntlett & Hill, 1999, pp. 35–36; Means Coleman, 2000, pp. 103, 175, 205; Turner, 1994, pp. 136–137*; Ward, 1995 Also in Bianculli, 1996, Terrace, 1993, Terrace, 2000

Family Rules
IN Terrace, 2000

Family Ties
Bryant & Bryant, 2001, pp. 163, 170–171; Crotty, 1995; Davis, 2001, p. 15; Guida, 2000, pp. 213–214; Harris, 1989, pp. 92, 98; Harris, 1994, p. 97; Jones, 1992, pp. 257, 259; Kutulas, 1998; Lembo, 2000, pp. 175, 176, 189, 197; Levinson & Link, 1986, pp. 92–102 (Gary David Goldberg interview)**; Lichter, Lichter, & Rothman, 1991, pp. 53, 93–94; Lichter, Lichter, & Rothman, 1994, p. 165; Marc, 1997, p. 182; McCrohan, 1990, pp. 336–344**; Oskamp, 1988, pp. 108–109; Panati, 1991, pp. 479–480; Putterman, 1995, pp. 102, 103; Roman,

1996, p. 62; Sackett, 1993, pp. 294–295; Selnow & Gilbert, 1993, pp. 3–4, 23–26*; Thomas & Evans, 1990, pp. 292–295*; Tinker & Rukeyser, 1994, pp. 167–170; Also in Bianculli, 1996, Terrace, 1993

Family Tree, The
Gianakos, 1987, p. 311; Klobas, 1988, pp. 233–234

Famous Teddy Z
Guida, 2000, p. 221; Pearl & Pearl, 1999, pp. 34–35*

Fanelli Boys
Cotter, 1997, pp. 392–294*; Also in Terrace, 1993

Fantastic Journey
Gianakos, 1981, pp. 223–224

Fantasy Island
DiMaggio, 1990, pp. 46–51 (script excerpts); Gianakos, 1987, p. 311; Klobas, 1988, pp. 147–149, 163–164, 171–172, 190–192, 228, 393–394, 456*; Marc & Thompson, 1992 (Ch. 15 on Aaron Spelling), pp. 163–169; Newcomb, 1987, p. 459; Newcomb, 1994, pp. 506–507; Rose, 1985, p. 101

Farmer's Daughter, The
Hamamoto, 1989, pp. 74–76*; Lichter, Lichter, & Rothman, 1991, p. 267; Lichter, Lichter, & Rothman, 1994, p. 378; Rafkin, 1998, pp. 46–47; Also in Eisner & Krinsky, 1984

Fast Times
IN Terrace, 1993

Father Dowling Mysteries
Christians, Fackler, & Rotzoll, 1995, pp. 307–309; Steenland, 1990, p. 44; Pearl & Pearl, 1999, p. 52; Also in Terrace, 1993

Father Knows Best
Abelman, 1998, p. 66; Abt & Mustazza, 1997, pp. 43–44; Alley & Brown, 2001, p. 13; Bennett, 1996, pp. 9–12; Bryant & Bryant, 2001, pp. 165–166; Caldwell, 1995, p. 50; Cantor, 2001, p. 91; Cavallo, 1999, pp. 36, 38; Crotty, 1995; Davis, 2001, pp. 5–6; Drummond & Peterson, 1988, pp. 38–42, 50–58**; Frazer & Frazer, 1993; Friedman, 2002, p. 53; Fultz, 1998, p. 147; Gabler, Rich & Antler, 2000, p. 13; Hawes, 2002, pp. 83–84; Himmelstein, 1984, pp. 89–90; Himmelstein, 1994, pp. 125–126; Jones, 1992, pp. 95–102, 123, 233**; Kulzer, 1992, pp. 184–187; Leibman, 1995, pp. 1, 22, 28, 33, 37, 38, 41, 47, 48, 49–50, 52, 59–60, 62, 71, 90–91, 110–112, 124–126, 133, 143–144, 148, 156, 165–168, 175, 180–182, 188–189, 194, 196–197, 199, 225, 228, 235, 236–240, 243–244, 247–248, 267–268**; Lichter, Lichter, & Rothman, 1991, pp. 253–254; Lichter, Lichter, & Rothman, 1994, pp. 173, 360; Marc, 1989, pp. 52, 53, 54–66, 77**; Marc, 1997, pp. 44–55, 64, 177, 178**; Mitz, 1980, pp. 107–111*; Newcomb, 1979, pp. 351–352; Newcomb, 1982, pp. 374–375; Newcomb, 1987, pp. 337, 460–462, 618*; Newcomb, 1994, pp. 507–508; Newcomb, 2000, pp. 502, 565, 566; Nightingale, 1996, p. 127; Panati, 1991, pp. 306–307; Press, 1991, pp. 158, 161–162; Rowland & Watkins, 1984, pp. 63–64; Sackett, 1993, pp. 88–89; Schwartz, 1999, p. 140; Spigel, 1992, pp. 131, 178; Spigel & Curtin, 1997, p. 51; Spigel & Mann, 1992, pp. 112–114, 115–116, 128–137**; Staiger, 2000, p. 50; Also in

Bianculli, 1996, Eisner & Krinsky, 1984, Terrace, 1993

Father Murphy
Gianakos, 1983, pp. 203–204; Gianakos, 1987, p. 229; Klobas, 1988, pp. 293–294; Yoggy, 1995, pp. 543–544; Also in Lentz, 1997

Father of the Bride
Bogle, 2001, p. 94; Jackson, 1982

Fay
Alley & Brown, 2001, p. 159; Castleman & Podrazik, 1982, p. 265; Dow, 1996, p. 60; Erickson, 2000, p. 266; Marc & Thompson, 1992 (Ch. 7 on Susan Harris), pp. 84–92; Also in Terrace, 1993

Faye Emerson Show
Becker, 2001**

FBI, The
Bogle, 2001, p. 107; Buxton, 1990, pp. 41–46, 56*; Carlson, 1985, pp. 32–33; Gianakos, 1978, pp. 478–488**; Kaminsky, 1985, pp. 69–80 (passim), especially pp. 78–80; Lichter, Lichter, & Rothman, 1991, p. 122; Lichter, Lichter, & Rothman, 1994, p. 199; Marc & Thompson, 1992 (Ch. 14 on Martin Quinn), pp. 153–161*; Martindale, 1991, pp. 154–173**; Meyers, 1981, pp. 107–108; Newcomb & Alley, 1983, pp. 53–54; Rovin, 1977b, pp. 97–98; Sackett, 1993, pp. 180–181; Schulman, 2001, p. 81; Stempel, 1992, pp. 85–86; Sumser, 1996, p. 80; Williams, 1982, pp. 125–126

Feather and Father Gang, The
Gianakos, 1981, pp. 221–22

Feds
Jarvis & Joseph, 1998, pp. 222, 224, 234

Felicity
Holtzman, 2000, p 304; Lechner, 2000, pp. 42–43; Wild, 1999, pp. 9, 87

Felony Squad
Gianakos, 1978, pp. 548–551*; Meyers, 1981, pp. 119–120; Williams, 1982, pp. 126–127

Ferris Bueller
IN Terrace, 1993, Terrace, 2000

Fibber McGee and Molly
IN Terrace, 1993

Filthy Rich
IN Morris, 1997

Finder of Lost Loves
Gianakos, 1992, pp. 360–362*; Klobas, 1988, pp. 83, 177–178; White, 1992, pp. 147–157, 167–172 (passim)**

Fireball Fun-For-All
Erickson, 2000, pp. 31–32

Fireside Theatre
Anderson, 1994, pp. 59–60, 64; Carroll, 2000, p. 209; Gianakos, 1980, pp. 207–217**; Lichter, Lichter, & Rothman, 1994, p. 285; Sackett, 1993, pp. 6–7; Seger, 1996, pp. 31–32; Spelling, 1996, pp. 22–23; Spigel, 1992, pp. 62–65*; Spigel, 2001, pp. 196–197; Spigel & Mann, 1992, pp. 28–29

First Hundred Years, The
Matelski, 1999, p. 43

First Impressions
IN Terrace, 1993

First Time Out
IN Terrace, 2000

First Tuesday
Frank, 1991, pp. 308–314

Fish
Newcomb, 1979, pp. 29–30; Newcomb, 1982, pp. 21–22; Newcomb, 1987, pp. 28–30; Also in Eisner & Krinsky, 1984, Terrace, 1993

Fish Police
IN Terrace, 1993

Fitzpatricks, The
Gianakos, 1981, pp. 233–234; Puette, 1992, p. 178

Five Fingers
Gianakos, 1978, p. 231; Also in Terrace, 1993

Five Mrs. Buchanans
Pearl & Pearl, 1999, p. 90; Suman, 1997, p. 4; Also in Terrace, 2000

Flamingo Road
Gianakos, 1983, pp. 187–189*; Also in Morris, 1997

Flash, The
Daniels, 1995, pp. 212–213; Also in Terrace, 1993

Flesh 'n' Blood
IN Terrace, 1993

Flintstones, The
Abelman, 1998, p. 437; Barbera, 1994, pp. 3–15, 136–137, 139–142**; Barnouw, 1990, p. 308; Bendazzi, 1994, p. 235; Bennett, 1996, pp. 92–94; Blanc & Bashe, 1988, pp. 221–222, 242–246*; Castleman & Podrazik, 1982, pp. 143–144; Croteau & Hoynes, 2000, p. 217; Davis, 1995, pp. 59–61; Morris, 1971, pp. 54–55; U.S. Department of Health…, 1982, p. 268; Also in Bianculli, 1996, Eisner & Krinsky, 1984, Terrace, 1993

Flip Wilson Show, The
Acham, 1999*; Adir, 1988, pp. 227–228; Andrews, 1986, p. 134; Bogle, 2001, pp. 175–183**; Dates & Barlow, 1990, pp. 266–267; Dates & Barlow, 1993, pp. 288–290; Haskins, 1984, pp. 77–78; Martin, 1980**; Mayer, 1972, pp. 74–80*; McCrohan, 1990, pp. 197–203**; McDonald, 1983, pp. 172–175*; McDonald, 1992, pp. 177–180*; Miller, 2000, p. 151; Rose, 1985, p. 316; Sackett, 1993, p. 171; Smith, 1997*; Williams, 1982, pp. 98–100*; Woll & Miller, 1987, pp. 79–80; Also in Bianculli, 1996

Flipper
Bennett, 1996, pp. 109–111; Davis, 1995, p. 17; Klobas, 1988, pp. 192–193; Also in Bianculli, 1996

Flo
Lichter, Lichter, & Rothman, 1991, p. 142; Lichter, Lichter, & Rothman, 1994, p. 224; Meehan, 1983, pp. 92–94; Sackett, 1993, p. 263; Williams, 1982, pp. 137–138

Fly by Night
IN Terrace, 1993

Flying Blind
Lichter, Lichter, & Rothman, 1994,

pp. 39, 43; Also in Terrace, 1993, Terrace, 2000

Flying High
Gianakos, 1981, pp. 266–267; Also in Terrace, 1993

Flying Nun, The
Capsuto, 2000, p. 48; Lichter, Lichter, & Rothman, 1991, pp. 141, 222, 278–279; Lichter, Lichter, & Rothman, 1994, pp. 223, 322, 391–392; Pearl & Pearl, 1999, p. 23; Smith, 1989, p. 25; Wylie, 1970, pp. 98–151**; Also in Bianculli, 1996, Eisner & Krinsky, 1984, Terrace, 1993

FM
IN Terrace, 1993

Foley Square
Jarvis & Joseph, 1998, p. 232; Vande Berg & Trujillo, 1989, p. 163

Follow the Sun
Gianakos, 1978, pp. 333–334

Follow Your Heart
Edmondson & Rounds, 1973, pp. 140–158**; Edmondson & Rounds, 1976, pp. 116–132**

For Love and Honor
Gianakos, 1987, p. 338; Also in Morris, 1997

For the People
Gianakos, 1978, pp. 472–473

Ford Star Jubilee
Gianakos, 1980, pp. 444–445; Hawes, 2002

Ford Theatre Hour, The
Gianakos, 1980, pp. 165–168, 343–350*; Hawes, 2001, pp. 78–87, 149**; Skutch, 1998, pp. 48–49, 51

Foreign Intrigue
Daniel, 1996, pp. 7–8

Forever Knight
Muir, 2001a, pp. 320–344**; Also in Terrace, 1993

Fort Apache
Tinker & Rukeyser, 1994, pp. 128–129

Fortune Dane
Gianakos, 1992, p. 414; Lichter, Lichter, & Rothman, 1994, p. 379

48 Hours
Caldwell, 1995, p. 101; Kovach & Rosenstiel, 1999, pp. 113, 134; Murray, 1994, pp. 178–180*; Newcomb, 2000, pp. 389–390; Spragens, 1995, pp. 57–71

Four Seasons
Paietta & Kauppila, 1999, p. 332

Four Star Playhouse
Becker, 2001**; Gianakos, 1980, pp. 350–355*; Hawes, 2002, pp. 134–135; Hewitt, 2001, p. 107

Four Star Revue *see* **Jimmy Durante Show**

413 Hope Street
Bogle, 2001, p. 448; Paietta & Kauppila, 1999, p. 332; Zook, 1999, pp. 104–105

Frank Sinatra Show, The
Hamamoto, 1994, p. 242; Lewis &

Lewis, 1979, pp. 188–197*; Skutch, 1998, pp. 56–57

Frank's Place

Berry & Manning-Miller, 1996, pp. 141, 143–144 (passim); Bogle, 2001, pp. 322–326*; Bryant & Bryant, 2001, pp. 212–213; Dates & Barlow, 1993, pp. 301–303; Ely, 1991, p. 250; Fiske, 1994, p. 40; Kamalipour & Carrilli, 1998, p. 85; Kassel 1993, pp. 108, 117–119*; Lichter, Lichter, & Rothman, 1991, p. 126; Lichter, Lichter, & Rothman, 1994, p. 205; McDonald, 1992, pp. 273, 286–287; Means Coleman, 2000, pp. 99–101, 103, 112–113, 160–162, 254–255**; Newcomb, 2000, pp. 298–299; Pearl & Pearl, 1999, pp. 35–36, 80–81; Rakow, 1992, pp. 193–207**; Swanson, 2000, pp. 53–54, 88–93, 212**; Zook, 1999, p. 9

Frannie's Turn

Lichter, Lichter, & Rothman, 1994, p. 50; Rodriguez, 1997, p. 69

Frasier

Bjorklund, 1997, pp. 58–60; Davis, 2001, pp. 19, Gabler, Rich & Antler, 2000, pp. 61, 70; Grammer, 1995, pp. 211–217, 218–219**; Gross & Woods, 1999, pp. 335–337*; Johnston, 2000, p. 63; Paietta & Kauppila, 1999, pp. 332–333; Pearl & Pearl, 1999, pp. 29, 38; Rafkin, 1998, p. 161; Rannow, 1999, pp. 27–28, 29; Smith, 1999, p. 36; Swanson, 2000, pp. 65–66; Walters, 2001, p. 98; Wolff, 1996, pp. 17–18, 19, 21, 24, 36–38, 39–42, 65–104 (script), 136–137**; Also in Bianculli, 1996, Terrace, 2000

Free Spirit

Muir, 2001a, p. 596**; Also in Terrace, 1993

Freebie and the Bean

Gianakos, 1983, p. 178; Lichter, Lichter, & Rothman, 1991, pp. 152–153; Lichter, Lichter, & Rothman, 1994, p. 237

Freeks and Geeks

Lechner, 2000, pp. 252–253

Fresh Prince of Bel Air

Barker, 1999, p. 127; Bogle, 2001, pp. 383–393**; Bryant & Bryant, 2001, p. 217; Caldwell, 1995, p. 326; Jarvis & Joseph, 1998, p. 176; Lichter, Lichter, & Rothman, 1994, pp. 58, 63; McDonald, 1992, pp. 291–293; Means Coleman, 2000, pp. 108–110, 158–159*; Smith, 1997*; Turner, 1994, p. 137; Ward, 1995; Zook, 1999, pp. 15–24, 29, 91**; Also in Terrace, 1993, Terrace, 2000

Freshman Dorm

Owen, 1997, pp. 82–83

Friday the 13th: The Series

IN Terrace, 1993

Friends

Capsuto, 2000, pp. 348–349, 360, 362–263; Davis, 2001, p. 19; Gabler, Rich & Antler, 2000, pp. 46–47, 61–62; Gross, 2001, p. 92; Gross & Woods, 1999, pp. 294, 338–339; Holtzman, 2000, p 303; Johnston, 2000, pp. 59, 129; Kamalipour & Carrilli, 1998, p. 86; Lechner, 2000, pp. 182–183; Owen, 1997, pp. 7, 19, 61,87, 89, 111–119, 155, 157–159**; Sandell, 1998; Silverblatt, Ferry, & Finan, 1999, p 158; Smith, 1999, pp 16, 29, 44, 50–51, 56–57; Walters, 2001, pp. 183–185; Wild, 1999, pp. 13, 16–18, 56–64, 75, 135, 150–151, 152–155, 221–226, 258–259**; Wolff, 1996, pp. 11, 17, 19;

Zook, 1999, p. 106; Also in Bianculli, 1996, Terrace, 2000

Friends and Lovers
Miles, 1975, pp. 69–70 (Nov. 2, 1974)

Front Page, The
Daniel, 1996, pp. 4–6*

Front Page Detective
Daniel, 1996, p. 8

Front Row Center
Gianakos, 1980, pp. 442–443

Frontier
Gianakos, 1980, pp. 445–446; McDonald, 1987, pp. 52–53; Yoggy, 1995, pp. 82–83; Also in Lentz, 1997, West, 1987

Frontier Circus
Gianakos, 1978, pp. 355–356; Also in Lentz, 1997, West, 1987

Frontier Justice
IN West, 1987

Fugitive, The
Bogle, 2001, pp. 106–107; Caldwell, 1995, p. 40; Capsuto, 2000, p. 49; Castleman & Podrazik, 1982, p. 166, 197; Deane, 1996, whole book**; Gianakos, 1978, pp. 419–423*; Himmelstein, 1984, pp. 176–177; Himmelstein, 1994, pp 216–217; Lichter, Lichter, & Rothman, 1991, pp. 6, 222–223, 279; Lichter, Lichter, & Rothman, 1994, pp. 15, 323, 392; Marc, 1984, pp. 80–81; Marc, 1996, pp. 80–81; Marc & Thompson, 1992 (Ch. 13 on Roy Huggins), pp. 148–149; Martin, 1980**; Meyers, 1981, pp. 88–90*; Newcomb & Alley, 1983, pp. 54–55, 71; Paietta & Kauppila, 1999, p. 333; Robertson, 1993, whole book**; Rovin, 1977b, p. 88; Sackett, 1993, pp. 130–131; Also in Bianculli, 1996, Terrace, 1993

Full House
Caldwell, 1995, p. 18; Kendall, 1989; Lichter, Lichter, & Rothman, 1994, pp. 47, 66; Sackett, 1993, p. 341; Schwartz, 1999, pp. 129, 130–131; Ward, 1995; Also in Bianculli, 1996, Terrace, 1993, Terrace, 2000

Funny Face
Sackett, 1993, p. 191

Fury
Aquila, 1996, p. 163; Davis, 1995, pp. 18–19; Fitzgerald & Magers, 2002, p. 302; Gianakos, 1981, pp. 318–322*; Jackson, 1994, pp. 62–63; Rovin, 1977b, p. 45; Yoggy, 1995, pp. 45–47, 49*; Also in Lentz, 1997

Futurama
Lechner, 2000, pp. 43–44

Gabriel's Fire
Bogle, 2001, pp. 381–382; Also in Terrace, 1993

Gale Storm Show, The
Magers & Fitzgerald, 1999, pp. 231–232; Also in Terrace, 1993

Gallant Men, The
Gianakos, 1978, pp. 402–403

Gangbusters
Hawes, 2002, pp. 106–107; Marc,

1984, pp. 73–74; Marc, 1996, pp. 73–74; Sackett, 1993, p. 38

Garrison's Gorillas
Gianakos, 1978, pp. 590–591

Garroway at Large
Castleman & Podrazik, 1982, p. 44

Garry Moore Show, The
Adir, 1988, pp. 54–55; Castleman & Podrazik, 1982, p. 192; Erickson, 2000, pp. 215–216; Martin, 1980**; Mott, 2000, pp. 56–63, 91–91, 119–120**; Also in Bianculli, 1996

G. E. True
Gianakos, 1978, pp. 368–369

Gemini Man, The
Gianakos, 1981, p. 211; Also in Terrace, 1993

Gene Autry Show, The
Aquila, 1996, p. 163, 164; Brauer, 1975, pp. 25–26, 34; Davis, 1995, pp. 215–216; Fitzgerald & Magers, 2002, pp. 34, 128–129, 222; Gianakos, 1987, pp. 347–350*; Guida, 2000, p. 186; Hawes, 2002, p. 125; Jackson, 1994, pp. 41–43; Magers & Fitzgerald, 1999, pp. 138–139; McDonald, 1987, pp. 25, 26, 28–29, 30, 33; Pearl & Pearl, 1999, p. 18; Rovin, 1977b, pp. 24–25; Yoggy, 1995, pp. 18, 20–24*; Also in Lentz, 1997, West, 1987

General Electric Theater
Gianakos, 1978, pp. 76–83**; Gianakos, 1980, pp. 362–365*; Museum of Television and Radio, 1991, pp. 237, 238, 240; Sackett, 1993, p. 63; Also in Bianculli, 1996

General Hospital
Allen, 1985, pp. 47, 49–50, 57, 63, 87–89; Allen, 1987, pp. 196–204**; Blumenthal, 1997, pp. 54, 56; Brown, 1994, p. 89; Brunsdon, 2000, pp. 170–171; Buckman, 1984, p. 121; Chunovic, 2000, p. 68; Davis, 2001, p. 163; Fiske, 1987, pp. 124–125; Fowles, 1982, pp. 150–151; Fowles, 1992, p. 167; Gitlin, 1986, pp. 43, 44, 51–67**; Greenberg & Busselle, 1996; James, 1991**; Jarvis & Joseph, 1998, p. 186; Jenrette, McIntosh, & Winterberger, 1999; Kalisch, Kalisch, & Scobey, 1983, pp. 160–169, 174**; Kaminsky, 1985, pp. 99, 106; Kaplan, 1983, pp. 85, 104; Lechner, 2000, pp. 74–75, 133; Lembo, 2000, pp. 183, 186; Matelski, 1988, pp. 45, 103–114**; Matelski, 1999, pp. 22–23, 41; Nelson, 1995, p. 61; Newcomb, 1982, pp. 132, 143–147; Newcomb, 1987, pp. 147, 164, 173–177**; Newcomb, 2000, p. 509; Nochimson, 1992, pp. 7, 18–20, 28, 38–39, 77–85, 154–159, 195**; Ornellas, 1987**; Parenti, 1991, p. 99; Rouverol, 1984, pp. 21, 23, 32; Rouverol, 1992, pp. 29, 39–40, 58, 248; Seiter, 1981**; Spigel & Mann, 1992, pp. 218–224; U.S. Department of Health…, 1982, p. 295; Van Fuqua, 1996; Williams, 1992, pp. 4, 11, 31–32, 42, 50, 51–52, 80–81, 84, 87, 89–90, 101, 103, 106–107, 110–111, 116, 133–134, 137, 164, 180**; Also in Bianculli, 1996

Generations
James, 1991**; Matelski, 1999, pp. 43–44; Rouverol, 1992, pp. 252–253; Williams, 1992, pp. 102–103

Gentle Ben
IN Terrace, 1993

George & Leo
Bryant & Bryant, 2001, p. 195

George Burns and Gracie Allen Show, The
Abelman, 1998, pp. 322–323; Blythe & Sackett, 1986, whole book**; Burns, 1980, pp. 163–177**; Burns, 1988, pp. 240–262, 270–281**; Burns, 1990, pp. 276–277; Butler, 1991, pp. 319–324, 328–331**; Caldwell, 1995, pp. 37–38; Castleman & Podrazik, 1982, pp. 56–57; Guida, 2000, p. 181; Heldenfels, 1994, pp. 69–70, 76; Horowitz, 1997, pp. 37, 109–110; Javna, 1985, pp. 218–221*; Jones, 1992, pp. 83–84; Marc, 1989, pp. 19–22*; Marc, 1997, pp. 16–18*; Mellencamp, 1992, p. 315–321*; Mitz, 1980, pp. 33–37*; Modleski, 1986, pp. 82–87, 92–94**; Neale & Krutnik, 1990, p. 230; Nelson & Gaonkar, 1996, pp. 325–326, 335–336; Panati, 1991, pp. 300–302; Putterman, 1995, pp. 23, 32–33, 34, 41, 47; Sochen, 1987, pp. 77–79; Spigel, 1992, pp. 130–131, 155–156, 159–160, 166–167, 170–172, 179*; Spigel, 2001, pp. 280–281; Spigel & Mann, 1992, pp. 10, 16–17, 19–20; Stempel, 1992, pp. 18–19; Taylor, 1989, p. 25; Thompson, 1996, p. 86; Waldrep, 2000, p. 195; Wilk, 1976, pp. 71–72, 182–184; Also in Bianculli, 1996, Eisner & Krinsky, 1984, Terrace, 1993

George Carlin Show, The
IN Terrace, 2000

George Gobel Show, The
Sackett, 1993, p. 53
Also in Bianculli, 1996

George Wendt Show, The
Abelman, 1998, p. 74; Cotter, 1997, pp. 466–467

Geraldo
Abelman, 1998, p. 215; Abt & Mustazza, 1997, pp. 61–64, 70–72, 119–120**; Himmelstein, 1994, pp. 353–355, 362, 363; Keyes, 1997**; Mellencamp, 1992, pp. 213–219*; Munson, 1993, pp. 74–84 (also see index)**; Munson, 1995*; Rivera, 1991, pp. 448–480 (passim)*; Shattuc, 1997, pp. 6–7, 15, 19, 21–22, 25, 31, 40–45, 47, 115, 119, 126, 191–195**; Also in Bianculli, 1996

Gertrude Berg Show, The
IN Eisner & Krinsky, 1984

Get a Life
IN Terrace, 1993, Terrace, 2000

Get Christie Love!
Andrews, 1980, pp. 27–33*; Andrews, 1986, p. 137; D'Acci, 1994, pp. 117–118; Erickson, 2000, pp. 263–264; Gianakos, 1978, pp. 757–758; Lichter, Lichter, & Rothman, 1991, pp. 139–140; Lichter, Lichter, & Rothman, 1994, pp. 221, 279; Martindale, 1991, pp. 175–178; McDonald, 1983, pp. 203–204; McDonald, 1992, pp. 205–206; Meyers, 1981, pp. 207–208; Smith, 1997a; Sochen, 1987, p. 101; Stempel, 1992, pp. 250–251; Sumser, 1996, p. 70; Yearwood, 1979, whole book**; Also in Terrace, 1993

Get Real
Wild, 1999, pp. 272–273

Get Smart
Castleman & Podrazik, 1982, pp. 184–185; Everitt, 2001, p. 187; Green, 1993, whole book**; Hamamoto, 1994, pp. 119–120; Holtzman, 1979, pp. 215–217, 222–223; Javna, 1985,

pp. 50–53*; Jones, 1992, pp. 185–186; Lisanti & Paul, 2002, pp. 27, 126–127, 139, 233; Meyers, 1981, pp. 116–118*; Miller, 2000, pp. 42, 63; Mitz, 1980, pp. 225–229*; Panati, 1991, p. 359; Pearl & Pearl, 1999, p. 192; Putterman, 1995, pp. 86–88*; Rafkin, 1998, pp. 50–51; Smith, 1989, pp. 95–104*; Story, 1993, pp. 198–210*; Wylie, 1970, pp. 153–192**; Also in Bianculli, 1996, Eisner & Krinsky, 1984, Terrace, 1993

Getting Personal
Schwartz, 1999, p. 182

Ghost and Mrs. Muir, The
Gianakos, 1987, pp. 397–399; Guida, 2000, pp. 195–196; Meehan, 1983, pp. 172–173; Also in Eisner & Krinsky, 1984, Terrace, 1993

Ghost Busters, The
Cuklanz, 2000, pp. 46–47; Daniel, 1996, p. 14; Davis, 1995, pp. 109–110; Also in Terrace, 1993

Ghost Story/Circle of Fear
Gianakos, 1978, pp. 729–730; Muir, 2001a, pp. 44–53*

Gibbsville
Daniel, 1996, p. 14; Gianakos, 1981, pp. 213–214; Puette, 1992, pp. 175, 177

Gidget
Bennett, 1996, pp. 105–108; Hamamoto, 1989, pp. 78–81*; Smith, 1989, pp. 24–25; Spigel & Curtin, 1997, pp. 100, 101–102, 103*; Also in Bianculli, 1996, Eisner & Krinsky, 1984, Terrace, 1993

Gillette Cavalcade of Sports
Castleman & Podrazik, 1982, p. 15

Gilligan's Island
Andrews, 1980, pp. 34–43*; Bennett, 1996, pp. 122–124; Cantor, 2001, pp. ix–xvii (passim), xxxviii, 3–33, 41, 45–46, 47, 68, 87–88**; Castleman & Podrazik, 1982, p. 173; Davis, 1995, pp. 110–111; Freeman, 1980, pp. 87–88; Hamamoto, 1989, pp. 81–82; Javna, 1985, pp. 206–209*; Kulzer, 1992, pp. 171–179; Lisanti & Paul, 2002, pp. 191–192; Marc & Thompson, 1992 (Ch. 3 on Sherwood Schwartz), pp. 38–48; Owen, 1997, pp. 29–30; Panati, 1991, p. 357; Press, 1991, pp. 81–83, 136–137*; Putterman, 1995, p. 70; Schwartz, 1988, whole book**; Smith, 1989, pp. 3–11, 107–113**; Stark, 1997, p. 117; Story, 1993, pp. 128–146**; Waldrep, 2000, p. 196; Also in Bianculli, 1996, Eisner & Krinsky, 1984, Terrace, 1993

Gimme a Break
Bryant & Bryant, 2001, p. 169; Dates & Barlow, 1990, pp. 274–277*; Dates & Barlow, 1993, pp. 297–299*; Klobas, 1988, pp. 256–257; McDonald, 1983, p. 247; McDonald, 1992, p. 244; Shales, 1982, pp. 288–289; Turner, 1994, pp. 57–58*; Also in Terrace, 1993

Girl from U.N.C.L.E., The
Gianakos, 1978, pp. 552–554*; Heitland, 1987, pp. 178–187**; Lichter, Lichter, & Rothman, 1991, pp. 172–173; Lichter, Lichter, & Rothman, 1994, p. 261; Lisanti & Paul, 2002, pp. 220, 247–249*; Meyers, 1981, pp. 102–103; Smith, 1989, pp. 155–160; Sochen, 1987, p. 99; Spigel & Curtin, 1997, pp. 87, 89; Story, 1993, p. 103

Girl with Something Extra, The
Miles, 1975, pp. 51–52 (Dec. 7, 1973,

show); Also in Eisner & Krinsky, 1984, Terrace, 1993

Girls, The
Capsuto, 2000, p. 23

Gleason, Jackie *see* **Jackie Gleason Show, Honeymooners**

Glitter
Gianakos, 1992, pp. 372–373

God, the Devil and Bob
Chunovic, 2000, p. 186

Going My Way
Gianakos, 1983, pp. 355–356

Going Places
Also in Terrace, 1993, Terrace, 2000

Going to Extremes
Lichter, Lichter, & Rothman, 1994, p. 42; Paietta & Kauppila, 1999, p. 333

Goldbergs, The
Alley & Brown, 2001, pp. 11–12; Barnouw, 1990, p. 126; Bogle, 2001, p. 41; Butler, 1991, p. 319; Caldwell, 1995, pp. 53, 70: Castleman & Podrazik, 1982, pp. 43, 54–55; Foreman, 1997, pp. 115–116, 144–167**; Gabler, Rich & Antler, 2000, pp. 14–15, 31–32, 34*; Hawes, 2001, p. 33; Hawes, 2002, pp. 70–71; Heldenfels, 1994, p. 76; Holtzman, 2000, p 123; Horowitz, 1997, p. 112; Jones, 1992, pp. 41–43, 44, 45–47*; Lichter, Lichter, & Rothman, 1991, pp. 52, 233; Marc, 1989, p. 51; Marc, 1997, pp. 36, 42–43; Means Coleman, 2000, p. 58; Mitz, 1980, pp. 13–16*; Modleski, 1986, p. 82; O'Dell, 1997, pp. 41, 43–47**; Panati, 1991, pp. 243–244; Pearl & Pearl, 1999, p. 86; Roman, 1996, p. 56; Spigel, 1992, pp. 131, 148–149, 157, 168–170*; Spigel & Mann, 1992, pp. 18, 19, 78–99, 103**; Also in Bianculli, 1996, Eisner & Krinsky, 1984

Golden Girls, The
Alley & Brown, 2001, pp. 159–160; Bell, 1992; Capsuto, 2000, pp. 230–231, 357; Cotter, 1997, pp. 339–355**; Doty, 1993, pp. 15, 41, 44, 122 (note 27), 124 (note 33); Edelman & Kupferberg, 1996, p. 219; Gauntlett & Hill, 1999, pp. 159, 181–182; Gross & Woods, 1999, pp. 322–323, 324, 326*; Hamamoto, 1989, pp. 141–142; Harris, 1989, pp. 57–58; Harris, 1994, pp. 61–62; Jones, 1992, p. 262; Kendall, 1989; Klobas, 1988, pp. 360–362; Lembo, 2000, p. 172; Lichter, Lichter, & Rothman, 1991, p. 34; Lichter, Lichter, & Rothman, 1994, p. 90; Marc & Thompson, 1992 (Ch. 7 on Susan Harris), pp. 84–92, especially pp. 89–91*; O'Dell, 1997, pp. 215–216; Pearl & Pearl, 1999, pp. 104–105, 205–206, 207*; Riggs, 1998, p. 136; Ringer, 1994, pp. 133–134, 136–137; Sackett, 1993, pp. 304–305; Schwartz, 1999, pp. 128–129, 151–152; Seger, 1996, p. 185; Tartikoff, 1992, pp. 145–150*; Vane & Gross, 1994, p. 220; Weimann, 2000, p. 216; Winship, 1988, pp. 69–70; Also in Bianculli, 1996, Terrace, 2000

Golden Palace
Cotter, 1997, pp. 339–340, 355–357*; Also in Terrace, 2000

Gomer Pyle, U.S.M.C.
Castleman & Podrazik, 1982, pp. 172–173; Hamamoto, 1989, pp. 56–59*;

Jones, 1992, pp. 172–174; McCrohan, 1990, pp. 152–157**; Pearl & Pearl, 1999, pp. 56, 87; Pegg, 2002, pp. 304–307*; Sackett, 1993, p. 129; Wittebols, 1998, p. 12; Wylie, 1970, pp. 231–242**; Also in Bianculli, 1996, Eisner & Krinsky, 1984, Terrace, 1993

Good Advice
Bjorklund, 1997, pp. 87–88

Good & Evil
Cotter, 1997, pp. 428–429; Schwartz, 1999, pp. 163–164; Also in Morris, 1997, Terrace, 1993

Good Grief
IN Terrace, 1993

Good Guys, The
IN Terrace, 1993

Good Life, The
Blum & Lindheim, 1987, pp. 64–65; Cotter, 1997, pp. 449–450; Also in Terrace, 1993

Good Morning!
Hack, 1999, pp. 37, 39

Good Morning, America
Alley, 1977, pp. 157–158; Fiske, 1987, pp. 55, 57; Frank, 1991, pp. 377–378; Freeman, 1980, p. 25; Hack, 1999, pp. 1–6, 90–93, 98, 100–102, 103–106, 109, 111–120, 122–124, 127–128, 133–134, 138–142, 145–146, 147, 148–152, 154, 185–186, 193–195, 197, 205–206, 210, 212–213, 215–216, 218–219, 223, 224–226, 227, 238–243, 245–253**; Kaplan, 1983, pp. 16–21*; Kovach & Rosenstiel, 1999, pp. 24, 108–109, 114, 134, 151, 153, 164; Lechner, 2000, pp. 53–54, 55, 56; Newcomb, 1987, p. 576; Rivera, 1991, pp. 256–319*; Schwartz, 1999, p. 163; Scott, 1996, pp. 278–279; U.S. Congress, 1985, pp. 62, 117–118, 136–137; Also in Bianculli, 1996

Good Morning, World
Erickson, 2000, p. 147; Also in Terrace, 1993

Good News
Bogle, 2001, p. 430; Gross & Woods, 1999, p. 11

Good Night America
Rivera, 1991, pp. 215–257**

Good Sports
IN Terrace, 1993, Terrace, 2000

Good Times
Acham, 1999*; Alley, 1977, p. 47; Andrews, 1986, p. 140; Bedell, 1981, pp. 84–85; Berry & Mitchell-Kernan, 1982, p. 125; Bryant & Bryant, 2001, pp. 168, 342–343; Castleman & Podrazik, 1982, pp. 256–257; Craig, 1992, pp. 111–123**; Crotty, 1995; Dates & Barlow, 1990, pp. 269–271, 273; Dates & Barlow, 1993, pp. 291–293, 295; Hamamoto, 1989, pp. 104–108*; Harris, 1994, p. 47; Hiebert & Reuss, 1985, p. 390; Jones, 1992, pp. 218–220; Klobas, 1988, pp. 33–34; Lichter, Lichter, & Rothman, 1991, pp. 54, 227, 241–242, 249, 267; Lichter, Lichter, & Rothman, 1994, pp. 328–329, 377–378; Marc & Thompson, 1992 (Ch. 4 on Norman Lear), pp. 49–60; McDonald, 1983, pp. 185–186; McDonald, 1992, pp. 188–189; Means Coleman, 2000, pp. 89, 91–92, 164–165, 170, 201*; Miller, 2000, p. 157; Mitz, 1980, pp. 317–320*;

Newcomb, 1976, pp. 26–34 (passim); Newcomb, 1979, p. 58; Newcomb & Alley, 1983, pp. 185–186; Pegg, 2002, pp. 346–355**; Rubin, 1980, p. 134; Sackett, 1993, p. 217; Schwartz, 1999, p. 140; Sklar, 1980, pp. 7–8; Stempel, 1992, pp. 148–150; Taylor, 1989, pp. 78–79, 82–84 (passim); Turner, 1994, pp. 130–131, 132, 144; U.S. Department of Health..., 1982, p. 269; Also in Bianculli, 1996, Eisner & Krinsky, 1984, Terrace, 1993

Goode Behavior
Bogle, 2001, p. 430

Goodnight, Beantown
IN Terrace, 1993

Goodtime Girls, The
IN Terrace, 1993

Goodyear Television Playhouse
see **Philco**

Governor and J.J., The
Lichter, Lichter, & Rothman, 1991, p. 268

Grace Under Fire
Alley & Brown, 2001, p. 74; Capsuto, 2000, p. 302; Dow, 1996, p. 208; Horowitz, 1997, pp. 121, 154; Lichter, Lichter, & Rothman, 1994, p. 49; MacDonald, 1995, p. 144; Magers & Fitzgerald, 1999, pp. 130–131; Paietta & Kauppila, 1999, p. 333; Wolff, 1996, pp. 18, 19, 27–29*; Also in Terrace, 2000

Grand
IN Morris, 1997, Terrace, 1993

Grand Slam
IN Terrace, 1993

Grandpa Goes to Washington
Puette, 1992, pp. 182–183

Gray Ghost, The
Fitzgerald & Magers, 2002, pp. 16, 17–18; Gianakos, 1983, pp. 326–328*; Jackson, 1994, pp. 78–79; Rovin, 1977b, p. 54; Also in West, 1987

Great Adventure, The
Gianakos, 1978, pp. 430–432*; Also in Lentz, 1997

Great Ghost Tales
Gianakos, 1978, p. 327

Great Guildersleeve, The
IN Eisner & Krinsky, 1984

Greatest American Hero, The
Gianakos, 1983, pp. 190–192*; Gianakos, 1987, p. 285; Jarvis & Joseph, 1998, pp. 238–239; Marc & Thompson, 1992 (Ch. 19 on Stephen J. Cannell), pp. 205–216; Rose, 1985, pp. 99–100; Thompson, 1990, pp. 38–39, 40–41, 44–46, 98–105**; Vande Berg & Wenner, 1991, pp. 120–121; Also in Terrace, 1993

Greatest Gift, The
Paietta & Kauppila, 1999, p. 333

Greatest Show on Earth, The
Gianakos, 1978, pp. 416–418*

Green Acres
Bennett, 1996, pp. 29–30, 31–34; Himmelstein, 1994, pp. 150–151; Jarvis & Joseph, 1998, pp. 170–171; Jones, 1992, pp. 167–168; Marc, 1984, pp. 59–62*; Marc, 1989, pp. 141–143; Marc, 1996, pp. 59–62*; Marc, 1997, pp. 116–118*; Marc & Thompson,

1992 (Ch. 2 on Paul Henning), pp. 30–37; Penley, et al., 1991, p. 226; Pegg, 2002, pp. 193–194; Putterman, 1995, pp. 38–41, 70*; Sackett, 1993, pp. 140–141; Smith, 1989, pp. 53–54, 57–59; Spigel, 2001, pp. 131–132; Story, 1993, pp. 160–170*; Thompson, 1996, pp. 86, 162; Waldrep, 2000, p. 196; Wittebols, 1998, p. 3; Also in Bianculli, 1996, Eisner & Krinsky, 1984, Terrace, 1993

Green Hornet, The
Gianakos, 1978, pp. 564–565; Harmon, 1992, pp. 48–49; Rovin, 1977b, pp. 101–103; Also in Bianculli, 1996, Terrace, 1993

Griff
Gianakos, 1978, pp. 736–737; Also in Terrace, 1993

Griffin, Merv *see* **Merv Griffin Show**

Grindl
Hamamoto, 1989, p. 73

Grizzly Adams *see* **Life and Times of Grizzly Adams**

Growing Pains
Abelman, 1998, p. 93; Bryant & Bryant, 2001, pp. 170–171; Davies, 1997, pp. 70–72*; Harris, 1989, p. 95; Hiebert, 1999, pp. 248, 249, 250, 252; Jordan, 1995; Kendall, 1989*; Paietta & Kauppila, 1999, pp. 333–334; Sackett, 1993, pp. 312–313; Schwartz, 1999, p. 131; Sumser, 1996, p. 51; Turow, 1989, pp. 260–261; Vane & Gross, 1994, p. 146; Also in Terrace, 1993, Terrace, 2000

Guestward Ho!
Yoggy, 1995, pp. 432–433; Also in Eisner & Krinsky, 1984, Terrace, 1993

Guiding Light
Allen, 1985, pp. 46, 54–57, 71–72, 80–81, 164–170, 204–211**; Allen, 1992, p. 112; Batra, 1987, pp. 87, 96–99*; Bounds, 1996, p. 101; Buckman, 1984, pp. 188–189; Capsuto, 2000, p. 24; Edmondson & Rounds, 1973, pp. 166–167; Edmondson & Rounds, 1976, p. 151; Fowles, 1982, p. 155; Fowles, 1992, p. 173; Gilbert, 1976, pp. 22–37*; Intintoli, 1984, whole book**; James, 1991*; Matelski, 1988, pp. 9, 20, 23, 45, 114–128**; Matelski, 1999, p. 41; Newcomb, 1987, pp. 141–162**; Nochimson, 1992, pp. 57–59; O'Dell, 1997, p. 186; O'Connor, 1983, pp. 306–326**; Parenti, 1991, p. 98; Rouverol, 1992, pp. 59–60; Thompson, 1996, p. 32; Williams, 1992, pp. 24, 85, 108, 115–116, 123–124, 150–151, 161–162, 169–173, 175–178*; Also in Bianculli, 1996

Gun Shy
Yoggy, 1995, pp. 438–439; Also in Lentz, 1997

Gung Ho
Hamamoto, 1989, pp. 145–147; Vande Berg & Trujillo, 1989, pp. 126–127

Guns of Paradise *see* **Paradise**

Guns of Will Sonnett, The
Gianakos, 1978, pp. 606–608*; Jackson, 1994, pp. 183–184; Spelling, 1996, p. 58; Yoggy, 1995, pp. 457–461*; Also in Lentz, 1997, Terrace, 1993, West, 1987

Gunslinger
Gianakos, 1978, pp. 320–321; Also in Lentz, 1997, West, 1987

Gunsmoke

Adler, 1976, pp. 32–34*; Adler, 1981, pp. 70–72*; Aquila, 1996, pp. 169–171*; Arness, 2001, pp. 83, 99–122, 123, 128–132, 134, 137, 146–149, 165–170, 172–177, 182–184, 187–190, 192–194, 196, 201–221**; Barabas & Barabas, 1990, whole book**; Brauer, 1975, pp. 57–58, 61, 67, 140–170, 184, 189–190, 207–215, 223, 225–227**; Broughton, 1986, pp. 24–36 (passim)*; Buscombe & Pearson, 1998, p. 122; Buxton, 1990, p. 31; Castleman & Podrazik, 1982, pp. 104, 200; Cavallo, 1999, pp. 328–39; Davis & Baran, 1981, p. 78; Erickson, 2000, pp. 101–102; Fagen, 1996, pp. 31, 72, 191–193; Field, 1989, p. 255; Fitzgerald & Magers, 2002, p. 135; Freeman, 1980, pp. 79–80; Gianakos, 1981, pp. 322–347**; Gianakos, 1983, pp. 312–317**; Goethals, 1981, pp. 65–66; Hamamoto, 1994, pp. 39–42, 46, 49–52**; Hawes, 2002, pp. 126, 127–129*; Heldenfels, 1994, pp. 210–211; Jackson, 1994, pp. 63–67; Jarvis & Joseph, 1998, pp. 198, 215; Lazere, 1987, p. 253; Lichter, Lichter, & Rothman, 1991, pp. 128, 136, 212–213, 221; Lichter, Lichter, & Rothman, 1994, pp. 207, 310–311, 321, 391; Martin, 1980**; McCrohan, 1990, pp. 104–107*; McDonald, 1987, pp. 54, 65–66, 75, 76, 80–81, 98–100*; Meehan, 1983, pp. 89–91, 164–165; Monaco, 2000, p. 488; Newcomb, 1976, pp. 228, 285; Newcomb, 1979, pp. 294, 425, 432, 532–534*; Newcomb, 1987, pp. 617, 623–624; Newcomb & Alley, 1983, pp. 96–127 (passim)*; Osgerby & Gough-Yates, 2001, pp. 148–149; Paietta & Kauppila, 1999, p. 334; Parks, 1982, pp. 129–139 (passim), 141–146*; Pearl & Pearl, 1999, pp. 71–72*; Peel, 1989, whole book**; Rovin, 1977b, pp. 46, 48; Sackett, 1993, pp. 66–67; Silverblatt, Ferry, & Finan, 1999, p. 42; Spelling, 1996, pp. 18–19; Stark, 1997, pp. 62–64, 67; Stempel, 1992, pp. 20–21; Sturcken, 1990, pp. 104–105; Taylor, 1989, p. 36; Toll, 1982, pp. 92–93; Williams, 1982, pp. 52–54; Yoggy, 1995, pp. 84–126, 129–131, 367–368**; Yoggy, 1998, pp. 180–189**; Also in Bianculli, 1996, Lentz, 1997, Terrace, 1993, West, 1987

Hagen

Gianakos, 1981, p. 288; Goethals, 1981, pp. 67–68

Hail to the Chief

Capsuto, 2000, p. 206; Everitt, 2001, pp. 188–189; Also in Morris, 1997

Hallmark Hall of Fame

Bogle, 2001, pp. 77–79; Gianakos, 1978, pp. 776–783**: Gianakos, 1980, pp. 305–311**; Gianakos, 1981, pp. 162–164*; Gianakos, 1983, pp. 172–173; Gianakos, 1987, pp. 206–207; Gianakos, 1992, pp. 308–309; Hawes, 2001, pp. 121–127; Hawes, 2002, pp. 227–230 (list of shows); Kuney, 1990, pp. 25–40**; O'Dell, 1997, pp. 10–14, 16*; Shales, 1982, pp. 81–83; Skutch, 1998, pp. 113–126, 165–168**; Sturcken, 1990, pp. 57–60, 87–90**; Also in Bianculli, 1996

Hamptons, The

IN Morris, 1997

Hangin' with Mr. Cooper

Bogle, 2001, pp. 409–410; Lichter, Lichter, & Rothman, 1994, pp. 57, 62–63; Means Coleman, 2000, pp. 110–111; Ward, 1995; Also in Terrace, 1993, Terrace, 2000

Happy Days (sitcom)
Alley, 1977, p. 48; Bedell, 1981, pp. 111–113; Bennett, 1996, pp. 87–88; Castleman & Podrazik, 1982, pp. 250–251, 266–267*; Chunovic, 2000, p. 78; Coakley, 1977, pp. 148–151*; Cortes, 2000, p. 67; Craig, 1992, p. 103; Crown, 1999, pp. 39, 40–45, 47–48, 65–66**; Freeman, 1980, p. 43; Hamamoto, 1989, pp. 115–117; Howe, 1983, pp. 109–111*; Jackson, 1997, p. 260; Javna, 1985, p. 19; Jones, 1992, pp. 240–244*; Kaminsky, 1985, pp. 122, 204–210 (passim) (interview with Gary Marshall); Kassel, 1993, p. 43; Klobas, 1988, pp. 54–56, 146–147, 225–227, 412*; Marc, 1989, pp. 212–214*; Marc, 1997, pp. 177–179*; Marc & Thompson, 1992 (Ch. 6 on Gary Marshall), pp. 70–83, especially pp. 74–77*; McCrohan, 1990, pp. 251–261**; Miller, 1980, p. 192; Mitz, 1980, pp. 321–326**; Newcomb, 1982, pp. 77–86 (passim), 395–396*; Newcomb, 1987, p. 478; Newcomb, 2000, p. 65; Newcomb & Alley, 1983, pp. 230–253 (passim)*; Orlik, 1994, p. 120; Orlik, 2001, p. 129; Owen, 1997, pp. 30, 31; Panati, 1991, pp. 424–425; Pegg, 2002, pp. 232, 234–239*; Rannow, 1999, pp. 132–133; Rose, 1985, pp. 113–114; Sackett, 1993, pp. 230–231; Shales, 1982, pp. 13–15; Sklar, 1980, pp. 15–18, 69–70*; Staiger, 2000, pp. 112–113, 114–131, 133, 135–140**; Stempel, 1992, p. 155; Suman & Rossman, 2000, p. 111; Also in Bianculli, 1996, Eisner & Krinsky, 1984, Terrace, 1993

Happy Days (variety)
Erickson, 2000, p. 184

Harbourmaster
Gianakos, 1981, pp. 375–376

Hard Copy
Stark, 1997, p. 252; Vande Berg & Trujillo, 1989, pp. 181–182

Hard Time on Planet Earth
Cotter, 1997, pp. 371–373*

Hardball
Cotter, 1997, pp. 460–461; Also in Terrace, 1993

Hardcastle & McCormick
Gianakos, 1987, pp. 323–325; Gianakos, 1992, pp. 278–281*; Lichter, Lichter, & Rothman, 1991, p. 72; Lichter, Lichter, & Rothman, 1994, p. 139; Marc & Thompson, 1992 (Ch. 19 on Stephen J. Cannell), pp. 205–216; Sumser, 1996, pp. 112, 144; Thompson, 1990, pp. 117–119

Hardy Boys/Nancy Drew
Gianakos, 1981, pp. 218–220*; Heil, 2001, p. 290; Klobas, 1988, pp. 208–210; Marc & Thompson, 1992 (Ch. 16 on Glen Larson), pp. 171–178; Martindale, 1991, pp. 179–184; Meyers, 1981, pp. 239–242

Harper Valley, PTA
Rannow, 1999, pp. 116–121*; Also in Terrace, 1993

Harrigan and Son
Jarvis & Joseph, 1998, pp. 250–251

Harris and Company
Dates & Barlow, 1990, p. 258; Dates & Barlow, 1993, pp. 280–281; McDonald, 1983, p. 228; McDonald, 1992, p. 229; Sklar, 1980, pp. 102–104; Smith, 1997

Harry
Cotter, 1997, pp. 332–335*; Paietta & Kauppila, 1999, p. 334

Harry-O
Capsuto, 2000, p. 109; Collins & Javna, 1989, pp. 17–19; Gianakos, 1978, pp. 763–764; Gianakos, 1981, pp. 140–141; Klobas, 1988, pp. 34–35, 37–38; Martindale, 1991, pp. 184–190; Meyers, 1981, pp. 210–212; Sumser, 1996, p. 69; Also in Terrace, 1993

Hart to Hart
Avery & Eason, 1991, pp. 350–354*; Cross, 1983, pp. 99–100; DiMaggio, 1990, pp. 33–36 (passim), 42, 45, 85–86; Fiske, 1987, pp. 2–4, 16, 21, 25–26, 50–51, 66, 85–86, 90–92, 96, 129–130, 132–135, 139–141, 174**; Gianakos, 1981, pp. 281–283*; Gianakos, 1983, pp. 150–152*; Gianakos, 1987, pp. 237–239; Klobas, 1988, pp. 66–68, 249–250; Lichter, Lichter, & Rothman, 1991, pp. 142–143; Marc, 1984, pp. 89–90; Marc, 1996, pp. 89–90; Marc & Thompson, 1992 (Ch. 15 on Aaron Spelling), pp. 163–169; Marris & Thornham, 2000, pp. 220–229**; Martindale, 1991, pp. 190–200; Meehan, 1983, pp. 82–84, 178–179*; Meyers, 1981, p. 255; Rotan, 1982; Smith, 1989, pp. 160–162; Spelling, 1996, pp. 117–119; Sumser, 1996, p. 15; Surette, 1984, p. 117; Theberge, 1981, pp. 15–17; Also in Bianculli, 1996, Terrace, 1993

Harts of the West
Yoggy, 1995, pp. 625, 629–632*

Hat Squad
Lichter, Lichter, & Rothman, 1994, p. 32; Also in Terrace, 1993

Hathaways, The
Castleman & Podrazik, 1982, p. 151; Also in Eisner & Krinsky, 1984, Terrace, 1993

Have Faith
Suman, 1997, p. 79

Have Gun, Will Travel
Aquila, 1996, pp. 174–175; Brauer, 1975, pp. 55, 61, 71–73; Broughton, 1986, pp. 24–36 (passim); Castleman & Podrazik, 1982, pp. 116–117; Fitzgerald & Magers, 2002, p. 66; Foreman, 1997, pp. 117–119*; Hamamoto, 1994, pp. 7, 59; Himmelstein, 1984, pp. 170–171; Himmelstein, 1994, p. 211; Jackson, 1994, pp. 92–96; Jarvis & Joseph, 1998, pp. 118, 191, 199–203; Lichter, Lichter, & Rothman, 1991, pp. 218–219; Lichter, Lichter, & Rothman, 1994, pp. 317–318*; Magers & Fitzgerald, 1999, pp. 184–185; McDonald, 1987, pp. 62–63, 74–75; Newcomb, 1976, p. 94; Newcomb, 1987, p. 617; O'Dell, 1997, p. 172; Pearl & Pearl, 1999, pp. 24, 47, 59, 68–69, 72*; Rose, 1985, pp. 61–62; Rovin, 1977b, pp. 51–52; Sackett, 1993, p. 74; Spigel & Curtin, 1997, pp. 295, 299–301*; Stempel, 1992, pp. 78–79; Taylor, 1989, pp. 36–37; Yoggy, 1995, pp. 247, 249–256**; Also in Bianculli, 1996, Lentz, 1997, Terrace, 1993, West, 1987

Having Babies *see* Julie Farr, M.D.

Hawaii Five-O
Alley, 1977, pp. 96–98, 107*; Berry & Mitchell-Kernan, 1982, pp. 157–158 (passim); Bodroghkozy, 2001, p. 85; Britos, 2001**; Buxton, 1990, pp. 123–129**; Carlson, 1985, pp. 37–38; Castleman & Podrazik, 1982, p. 207; Cuklanz, 1998; Cuklanz, 2000, pp. 35, 89; Gianakos, 1978, pp. 627–634**; Gianakos, 1981, pp. 141–146**; Hamamoto, 1994, pp. 18–19; Kamalipour &

Carrilli, 1998, p. 126; Klobas, 1988, pp. 22–23, 281–283; Lester, 1996, p. 39; Lichter, Lichter, & Rothman, 1991, pp. 200, 209, 210; Lichter, Lichter, & Rothman, 1994, pp. 219, 294, 307; Martin, 1980**; Martindale, 1991, pp. 201–224; Meyers, 1981, pp. 145–148*; Miles, 1975, pp. 46–48 (Nov. 27, 1973, show); Nelson, 1994, p. 21; Newcomb, 1979, pp. 134–137*; Newcomb, 1982, pp. 105–108*; Newcomb, 1987, pp. 116–117; Osgerby & Gough-Yates, 2001, p. 200; Puette, 1992, p. 181; Rhodes, 1997, whole book**; Rose, 1985, pp. 16–17; Rovin, 1977b, p. 121; Rushkoff, 1994, p. 47; Sackett, 1993, p. 177; Stempel, 1992, p. 142; Suman & Rossman, 2000, pp. 34–35; Sumser, 1996, pp. 80–81, 84, 86–88, 110, 115–117, 127, 137–138, 145–146**; U.S. Congress, 1977b, pp. 363–365, 370–371; Wahl, 1995, p. 59; Wilson & Gutierrez, 1985, p. 102; Also in Bianculli, 1996, Terrace, 1993

Hawaiian Eye
Britos, 2001**; Castleman & Podrazik, 1982, p. 131; Fagen, 1996, p. 191; Gianakos, 1978, pp. 254–258*; Hamamoto, 1994, p. 20; Kulzer, 1992, pp. 145–147; Meyers, 1981, pp. 59–60; Newcomb, 1987, pp. 115–116; Rose, 1985, p. 39; Rovin, 1977b, p. 71; Also in Terrace, 1993

Hawaiian Heat
Gianakos, 1992, p. 377; Hamamoto, 1994, p. 20; Also in Terrace, 1993

Hawk
Bogle, 2001, p. 135; Gianakos, 1978, pp. 563–564; Meyers, 1981, pp. 121–122

Hawkeye
Fagen, 1996, pp. 87–88; Also in Lentz, 1997

Hawkins
Dewey, 1996, pp. 25, 455–458*; Fishgall, 1997, pp. 330–334*; Gianakos, 1978, p. 742; Rovin, 1977b, p. 138

Hazel
Bennett, 1996, pp. 21–24; Jarvis & Joseph, 1998, pp. 169–170; Lichter, Lichter, & Rothman, 1994, p. 192; Sackett, 1993, p. 111; Also in Eisner & Krinsky, 1984, Terrace, 1993

Hazel Scott Show, The
Bogle, 2001, pp. 15–19*

He & She
Castleman & Podrazik, 1982, pp. 200–201; Putterman, 1995, pp. 108–111*; Also in Eisner & Krinsky, 1984, Terrace, 1993

Head of the Class
Kassel 1993, pp. 116–117; Lichter, Lichter, & Rothman, 1994, p. 258; Puette, 1992, pp. 57, 193; Rannow, 1999, pp. 20–21, 32–39, 49–59, 109–110**; Turner, 1994, p. 142; Also in Terrace, 1993, Terrace, 2000

Head Over Heels
IN Terrace, 2000

Headmaster
Castleman & Podrazik, 1982, p. 221

Heart of the City
Lichter, Lichter, & Rothman, 1991, p. 96; Lichter, Lichter, & Rothman, 1994, pp. 168–169; Also in Terrace, 1993

Heartbeat
Lichter, Lichter, & Rothman, 1994, p. 95; Ringer, 1994, pp. 108, 110–119,

127, 130–133, 136, 137–138**; Turow, 1989, pp. 262–263

Heartland
Suman, 1997, p. 78; Also in Terrace, 1993

Hearts Afire
Bogle, 2001, p. 426; Lichter, Lichter, & Rothman, 1994, p. 43; Schultz, 2000, p. 122; Swanson, 2000, pp. 47, 190; Also in Terrace, 1993, Terrace, 2000

Hearts Are Wild
IN Terrace, 1993

Heaven for Betsy
IN Terrace, 1993

Hec Ramsey
Brauer, 1975, pp. 227–228; Jackson, 1994, pp. 194–195; Moyer & Alvarez, 2001, p. 189; Rovin, 1977b, p. 133; Yoggy, 1995, pp. 417–419; Also in Lentz, 1997, West, 1987

Hee Haw
Andrews, 1980, pp. 44–52*; Castleman & Podrazik, 1982, pp. 210–211; Coakley, 1977, p. 54; Erickson, 2000, pp. 184–185; Marc, 1989, p. 153; Marc, 1997, p. 126; Also in Bianculli, 1996

Heights, The
Owen, 1997, pp. 83, 84; Pearl & Pearl, 1999, pp. 198–199; Rapping, 1994, pp. 158–160

Hell Town
Gianakos, 1992, pp. 401–402; Lichter, Lichter, & Rothman, 1991, p. 87; Lichter, Lichter, & Rothman, 1994, p. 157

Hello, Larry
IN Terrace, 1993

Hennesey
Kalisch, Kalisch, & Scobey, 1983, pp. 13–15, 194*; Lichter, Lichter, & Rothman, 1994, pp. 243–244; Paietta & Kauppila, 1999, pp. 334–335; Turow, 1989, pp. 198–201; Also in Eisner & Krinsky, 1984

Hercules: The Legendary Journeys
Lechner, 2000, pp. 25–26, 27

Here and Now
Bogle, 2001, pp. 406–407; Smith, 1997, pp. 212–213

Here Come the Brides
Fagen, 1996, pp. 214–215; Gianakos, 1981, pp. 405–407*; Klobas, 1988, pp. 24–25, 203–204, 457; Pearl & Pearl, 1999, pp. 24, 72–73, 111*; Also in Lentz, 1997

Here We Go Again
IN Terrace, 1993

Here's Lucy (*see also* I Love Lucy, Lucy Show)
Adir, 1988, pp. 22–23; Castleman & Podrazik, 1982, p. 251; Harris, 1991, pp. 286–292, 294–300**; Kulzer, 1992, pp. 41–44; Lichter, Lichter, & Rothman, 1991, pp. 63, 66, 140; Lichter, Lichter, & Rothman, 1994, p. 127; Pegg, 2002, pp. 121–122, 431; Sackett, 1993, p. 161; Sanders & Gilbert, 1993, pp. 316–334, 340–342**; Also in Eisner & Krinsky, 1984

Herman's Head
Capsuto, 2000, p. 347; Cotter, 1997,

pp. 404–410**; Lichter, Lichter, & Rothman, 1994, p. 42; Also in Terrace, 1993

Hero, The
IN Eisner & Krinsky, 1984

He's the Mayor
Hamamoto, 1989, pp. 139–140

Hey Jeannie!
Hamamoto, 1989, pp. 38–39; Spigel & Mann, 1992, pp. 78, 88–89

Hey Landlord!
IN Eisner & Krinsky, 1984, Terrace, 1993

Hey, Mulligan *see* **Mickey Rooney Show, The**

Hi Honey, I'm Home
IN Terrace, 1993

High Chaparral, The
Bogle, 2001, pp. 136–137; Brauer, 1975, pp. 114, 115, 116, 119–120, 187; Gianakos, 1978, pp. 585–588*; Jackson, 1994, pp. 178–180; Lichter, Lichter, & Rothman, 1991, pp. 97, 137, 257; Lichter, Lichter, & Rothman, 1994, pp. 169–170; Rodriguez, 1997, p. 60; Rovin, 1977b, p. 115; Wilson & Gutierrez, 1985, p. 100; Yoggy, 1995, pp. 338–344, 371**; Also in Lentz, 1997, West, 1987

High Mountain Rangers
Yoggy, 1995, pp. 551–552; Also in Terrace, 1993

High Performance
Gianakos, 1987, p. 316

High Society
Gross & Woods, 1999, p. 338; Also in Terrace, 2000

Highway Patrol
D'Acci, 1994, p. 109; Hawes, 2002, p. 108; Magers & Fitzgerald, 1999, pp. 190, 191; Meyers, 1981, pp. 35–36; Also in Bianculli, 1996

Highway to Heaven
Blum & Lindheim, 1987, pp. 7–8; Burks, 1990; Forbes & Mahan, 2000, pp. 45, 53; Gianakos, 1992, pp. 370–372*; Hamamoto, 1994, pp. 154–156; Klobas, 1988, pp. 180–182, 337–338, 423–426, 429–432, 434–435**; Leiby & Leiby, 2001, pp. 239–240; Lichter, Lichter, & Rothman, 1991, pp. 281–282; Lichter, Lichter, & Rothman, 1994, pp. 395–396; Tartikoff, 1992, pp. 36–39*; Thompson, 1996, p. 175; Also in Terrace, 1993

Highwayman
IN Terrace, 1993

Hill Street Blues
Abelman, 1998, pp. 414–419, 427**; Auletta, 1991, pp. 352–356, plus see index*; Avery & Eason, 1991, pp. 80–82, 240–264**; Batra, 1987, pp. 75–80*; Bogle, 2001, pp. 271–278**; Burks, 1990**; Burns & Thompson, 1989, pp. 79–87*; Caldwell, 1995, pp. 63–66*; Capsuto, 2000, pp. 192–193, 195, 237–238; Carey, 1988, pp. 97–99; Chunovic, 2000, pp. 84–87*; Collins & Javna, 1989, pp. 56–60*; Creeber, 2001, p. 23; Cuklanz, 2000, pp. 34, 50–51, 72, 79; Daniel, 1996, pp. 122–123; Davis, 2001, pp. 117–118, 122–123; Dow, 1996, p. 98; Fiske, 1987, pp. 112, 218, 219, 312; Friedman, 2002, pp. 268–269; Gianakos, 1983,

pp. 180–183*; Gianakos, 1987, pp. 271–275*; Gianakos, 1992, pp. 342–345*; Gitlin, 1983, see index, especially pp. 273–324**; Gunter & Wober, 1988, pp. 26–30 (passim); Heil, 2001, pp. 281–282, 295–304, 315–317, 331–432**; Henderson & Mazzeo, 1990, pp. 81–102, especially pp. 90–95*; Himmelstein, 1984, pp. 187–190; Himmelstein, 1994, pp. 228–229; Jarvis & Joseph, 1998, pp. 17–20, 87, 94–95, 98; Javna, 1985, p. 238; Kaminsky, 1985, pp. 23–24; Kidd-Hewitt & Osborne, 1995, pp. 73–74; Klobas, 1988, pp. 167–170, 179–180, 306–307*; Lane, 2001; Lembo, 2000, p. 173; Leonard, 1997, p.p. 65, 151, 153–154; Levinson & Link, 1986, pp. 17–35 (Bochco interview)**; Lichter, Lichter, & Rothman, 1991, pp. 30, 40, 189, 195, 213–214, 216–217, 248–249; Lichter, Lichter, & Rothman, 1994, pp. 84–85, 90, 97–98, 315, 351, 354*; Longworth, 2000, pp. 91, 128, 195–196, 201–202, 205, 206, 207; Marc, 1984, pp. 94–98*; Marc, 1989, p. 166; Marc, 1996, pp. 94–98*; Marc, 1997, p. 137; Marc & Thompson, 1992 (Ch. 20 on Steven Bochco), pp. 218–229, especially pp. 220–226**; Meyers, 1981, pp. 265–266; Miller, 1988, pp. 61–67; Monaco, 2000, p. 494; Moorti, 2001, pp. 116–117; Moyer & Alvarez, 2001, pp. 221–222; Nelson, 1994, p. 23; Newcomb, 1987, pp. 90–93, 108, 193, 577*; Newcomb, 1994, pp. 193–194; Newcomb, 2000, pp. 516–517; Orlik, 1994, pp. 83, 89, 184–185; Orlik, 2001, p. 183; Parenti, 1991, pp. 120–121; Pearl & Pearl, 1999, pp. 200–201; Powers, 1994, pp. 239, 243; Press, 1991, pp. 36, 150–152*; Puette, 1992, pp. 55, 188; Riggs, 1996; Rodriguez, 1997, p. 67; Rose, 1985, pp. 55–80 (passim); Rose, 1999, pp. 102–104, 105–106, 107*; Rowland & Watkins, 1984, pp. 259–261; Rushkoff, 1994, pp. 48–49; Selnow & Gilbert, 1993, pp. 66, 131; Stark, 1997, pp. 237–240, 242, 292–292; Stempel, 1992, pp. 227–236**; Surette, 1984, p. 116; Swanson, 2000, pp. 45, 47; Tartikoff, 1992, pp. 157–167**; Tasker, 1998, p. 97; Taylor, 1989, pp. 164–165; Thompson, 1990, pp. 16–17; Thompson, 1996, pp. 13, 16, 30, 31, 35, 38, 57, 59–74, 80–82, 123–124, 126, 150**; Turow, 1989, pp. 238–240, 269; Vande Berg & Trujillo, 1989, pp. 120–121, 140–141, 171, 197–205, 259–260**; Vane & Gross, 1994, pp. 218–219; Wahl, 1995, p. 8; Winship, 1988, pp. 111–116; Yoggy, 1995, p. 547; Also in Bianculli, 1996

His & Hers

Paietta & Kauppila, 1999, p. 335; Also in Terrace, 1993

Hitchhiker, The

Muir, 2001a, pp. 103–118

Hizzoner

Puette, 1992, p. 182

Hogan Family

IN Terrace, 1993, Terrace, 2000

Hogan's Heroes

Abelman, 1998, p. 69; Andrews, 1980, pp. 53–58*; Bodroghkozy, 2001, pp. 73–74; Bogle, 2001, pp. 113–114; Cantor, 2001, p. 213 (n. 2); Castleman & Podrazik, 1982, pp. 185–186; Jones, 1992, pp. 171–172; Kamalipour & Carrilli, 1998, p. 84; Lichter, Lichter, & Rothman, 1994, p. 383; Lisanti & Paul, 2002, pp. 296–297; Mitz, 1980, pp. 231–232; Royce, 1993, whole book**; Sackett, 1993, pp. 138–139; Stark, 1997, p. 135; Stempel, 1992, p.

99; Also in Bianculli, 1996, Eisner & Krinsky, 1984

Hollywood Beat
Gianakos, 1992, p. 394

Hollywood Opening Night
Gianakos, 1980, pp. 335–336

Hollywood Palace, The
Castleman & Podrazik, 1982, p. 165

Hollywood Squares
IN Bianculli, 1996

Holmes and Yoyo
Meyers, 1981, p. 231

Home Court, The
Jarvis & Joseph, 1998, p. 176

Home Fires
IN Terrace, 1993

Home Free
IN Terrace, 2000

Home Improvement
Abt & Mustazza, 1997, p. 45; Alley & Brown, 2001, pp. 119–120; Blum, 1995, pp. 14–15; Cotter, 1997, pp. 417–428**; Croteau & Hoynes, 2000, pp. 92–93; Davis, 2001, p. 18; Entman & Rojecki, 2000, p. 152; Lichter, Lichter, & Rothman, 1994, pp. 46–47, 64; Meyers, 1999, pp. 153–164**; Sackett, 1993, p. 337; Smith, 1999, pp. 123-139*; Stark, 1997, pp. 283, 285–287; Suman, 1997, pp. 111–112; Ward, 1995; Also in Terrace, 1993, Terrace, 2000

Homeboys from Outer Space
Means Coleman, 2000, pp. 120–121, 124

Homefront
Bogle, 2001, pp. 394–397; Lichter, Lichter, & Rothman, 1994, pp. 50, 60; Owen, 1997, pp. 85–86; Pearl & Pearl, 1999, pp. 203, 204; Puette, 1992, p. 57; Swanson, 2000, pp. 116–122**; Torres, 1998, pp. 6, 118–127, 130–131, 133–134, 136–137**; Also in Morris, 1997

Hometown
Gianakos, 1992, pp. 405–406

Homicide: Life on the Streets
Bignell, 1997, p. 143; Billingham, 2000, pp. 157–178, 180–182**; Bogle, 2001, pp. 439–441; Capsuto, 2000, pp. 303, 410; Cortes, 2000, p. 111; Davis, 2001, p. 111; Friedman, 2002, pp. 277, 279–281, 284*; Jarvis & Joseph, 1998, pp. 100–103*; Kalat, 1998, whole book**; Lane, 2001; Leonard, 1997, pp. 6–7, 160–161*; Longworth, 2000, pp. 41, 45–46, 48–49, 50, 178–179, 183–186*; Orlik, 2001, pp. 164–165; Pearl & Pearl, 1999, pp. 27–28; Rushkoff, 1994, pp. 55–57, 58; Sumser, 1996, pp. 156–158*; Swanson, 2000, pp. 67–68, 131; Thompson, 1996, pp. 186–187, 191; Also in Bianculli, 1996

Hondo
Gianakos, 1978, pp. 605–606; Jackson, 1994, pp. 181–182; Yoggy, 1995, pp. 228–229; Also in Lentz, 1997, West, 1987

Honey West
Edelman & Kupferberg, 1996, p. 219; Gianakos, 1978, pp. 519–521*; Lisanti & Paul, 2002, pp. 25, 27, 128–129; Marc & Thompson, 1992 (Ch. 15 on Aaron Spelling), pp. 163–169; Meyers, 1981, pp. 106–107; Miller, 2000,

pp. 51, 54; Osgerby & Gough-Yates, 2001, pp. 21, 84; Rovin, 1977b, p. 98; Smith, 1989, pp. 150–152; Spelling, 1996, p. 54; Spigel & Curtin, 1997, pp. 73–93**; Also in Terrace, 1993

Honeymooners, The

Adir, 1988, pp. 126–130, 137*; Allen, 1956, pp. 161–163, also see index and index under Gleason; Bacon, 1985, pp. 92–96, 111–115, 123–124, 127–133, 174–176, 194–197**; Barbera, 1994, pp. 3–4; Batra, 1987, pp. 106–107; Bennett, 1996, p. 91; Burns, 1990, p. 280; Caldwell, 1995, p. 37; Cantor & Cantor, 1992, pp. 28–29; Castleman & Podrazik, 1982, pp. 105–106; Craig, 1992, pp. 98–99; Crescent & Columbe, 1990, whole book**; Croteau & Crotty, 1995; Dow, 1996, p. xvii; Hamamoto, 1989, pp. 19–20; Harris, 1989, p. 32; Harris, 1994, p. 37; Hawes, 2002, pp. 97–98; Helford, 2000, p. 1; Henry, 1992, pp. 111–113, 123, 152, 156–167, 170–173, 178–179, 182–183, 296–298, 300–301**; Holtzman, 2000, pp. 123–124; Hoynes, 2000, p. 217; Javna, 1985, pp. 184–187*; Jones, 1992, pp. 108–114, 195, 207**; Lichter, Lichter, & Rothman, 1991, pp. 113–114; Lichter, Lichter, & Rothman, 1994, p. 189; Marc, 1984, pp. 113–118**; Marc, 1989, pp. 24, 135; Marc, 1996, pp. 113–118**; Marc, 1997, pp. 20, 111–112, 148; Mayerle, 1991; McCrohan, 1978, whole book**; McCrohan, 1990, pp. 70–76*; McCrohan & Crescenti, 1986, whole book**; Meadows, 1994, whole book**; Mitz, 1980, pp. 119–124**; Newcomb, 1994, pp. 37–38; Newcomb, 2000, pp. 84–85, 91; Oskamp, 1988, p. 113; Panati, 1991, pp. 307–309; Parenti, 1991, p. 71; Pegg, 2002, pp. 31–32, 36, 38–43, 47**; Press, 1991, pp. 31–33; Putterman, 1995, pp. 31, 74–75; Rose, 1985, pp. 109–110; Rowland & Watkins, 1984, pp. 281–282; Silverblatt, 1995, pp. 85–87; Spigel, 1992, pp. 88, 96, 125–126, 171*; Spigel, 2001, pp. 49–50, 197; Spigel & Mann, 1992, pp. 78, 80, 86, 89, 90–91, 115; Starr, 1997, pp. 67–68, 69–70, 80–81, 144–145, 147–149, 163–166, 188**; U.S. Department of Health…, 1982, pp. 267–268; Weatherby, 1992, pp. 18, 73–80, 82–84, 97–110, 205–207, 212**; Wilk, 1976, pp. 144–149*; Also in Bianculli, 1996, Eisner & Krinsky, 1984, Terrace, 1993

Hong Kong

Daniel, 1996, p. 11; Gianakos, 1978, pp. 304–305; Kamalipour & Carrilli, 1998, p. 126; Also in Terrace, 1993

Hooperman

Capsuto, 2000, pp. 239–240; Lichter, Lichter, & Rothman, 1991, p. 38; Lichter, Lichter, & Rothman, 1994, p. 95; Marc & Thompson, 1992 (Ch. 20 on Steven Bochco), pp. 218–229

Hootenany

Spigel & Curtin, 1997, pp. 308–309

Hopalong Cassidy

Aquila, 1996, p. 161; Buscombe & Pearson, 1998, pp. 120–121, 122; Davis, 1995, pp. 217–219*; Fitzgerald & Magers, 2002, p. 16, 128; Jackson, 1994, p. 33; Jarvis & Joseph, 1998, p. 194; McDonald, 1987, pp. 21–24*; Panati, 1991, pp. 251–252; Rovin, 1977b, p. 17; Sackett, 1993, pp. 20–21; Yoggy, 1995, pp. 6–11*; Also in Bianculli, 1996, Lentz, 1997, West, 1987

Hope & Gloria

Isaacs, 1999, pp. 97–98; Owen, 1997,

p. 120; Rafkin, 1998, pp. 146–148; Also in Terrace, 2000

Hot L Baltimore
Atwan, Orton, & Vesterman, 1978, pp. 385–386; Capsuto, 2000, p. 117; Coakley, 1977, pp. 235–236

Hot Pursuit
Gianakos, 1992, p. 362

Hotel
Capsuto, 2000, pp. 183–184; Cuklanz, 2000, p. 103; Gianakos, 1987, pp. 330–332; Gianakos, 1992, pp. 323–327*; Gross & Woods, 1999, pp. 319–320, 324–326**; Kendall, 1989**; Klobas, 1988, pp. 332, 395–396, 404–406*; Marc & Thompson, 1992 (Ch. 15 on Aaron Spelling), pp. 163–169; Pearl & Pearl, 1999, p. 57; Ringer, 1994, pp. 128–130, 136, 138–139*; Sackett, 1993, p. 289; Spelling, 1996, pp. 130–132 ; Vande Berg & Trujillo, 1989, pp. 143–144, 168, 225–230**

Hotel de Paree
Fitzgerald & Magers, 2002, pp. 91, 214–215; Gianakos, 1978, pp. 267–268; Jackson, 1994, p. 140; Also in Lentz, 1997, Terrace, 1993, West, 1987

Hothouse
Paietta & Kauppila, 1999, p. 335

House Calls
Kalisch, Kalisch, & Scobey, 1983, pp. 135–136; Paietta & Kauppila, 1999, p. 335; Puette, 1992, p. 186; Sackett, 1993, p. 271; Turow, 1989, pp. 221–224; Also in Eisner & Krinsky, 1984

House of Buggin'
Suman, 1997, p. 4

Houston Knights
Ringer, 1994, pp. 101–102

How the West Was Won
Arness, 2001, pp. 151–153, 177–182, 184–187, 196–199**; Hamamoto, 1994, pp. 42–46; Jackson, 1994, pp. 203–204; Yoggy, 1995, pp. 126–129, 372*; Also in Lentz, 1997, West, 1987

How to Marry a Millionaire
IN Eisner & Krinsky, 1984, Terrace, 1993

Howdy Doody
Bodroghkozy, 2001, pp. 21, 35–36; Castleman & Podrazik, 1982, p. 32; Davis, 1987, whole book**; Davis, 1995, pp. 188–192**; Gianakos, 1981, pp. 245–246; Panati, 1991, pp. 246–250*; Putterman, 1995, pp. 129–130; Smith & McCrohan, 1990, whole book**; Spigel, 2001, pp. 203–204, 204–205; Stark, 1997, pp. 2, 14–19**; Weiner, 1992, pp. 135–136; Also in Bianculli, 1996

Hull High
Cotter, 1997, pp. 381–382; Also in Terrace, 1993

Hullabaloo
Jackson, 1997, p. 237; Marc, 1989, pp. 124–125; Marc, 1997, pp. 102–103; Rose, 1999, p. 210; Also in Bianculli, 1996

Human Factor, The
Longworth, 2000, p. 9; Paietta & Kauppila, 1999, pp. 335–336

Human Target, The
IN Terrace, 1993

Hunter
Burks, 1990**; Capsuto, 2000, p. 245; Fiske, 1987, p. 238; Gianakos, 1981, pp. 225–226; Gianakos, 1992, pp. 374–376*; Gross & Woods, 1999, pp. 319, 324, 326; Lembo, 2000, p. 177; Marc & Thompson, 1992 (Ch. 13 on Roy Huggins), pp. 141–151, (Ch. 19 on Stephen J. Cannell), pp. 205–216; Ringer, 1994, pp. 127–128, 137; Steenland, 1990, pp. 43–44; Sumser, 1996, p. 134; Thompson, 1990, pp. 123–125; U.S. Congress, 1977b, pp. 355–359; U.S. Congress, 1985, pp. 47, 111; Also in Terrace, 1993

Husbands, Wives & Lovers
IN Morris, 1997

I Dream of Jeannie
Chunovic, 2000, pp. 56–57; Cox, 2000, whole book**; Erickson, 2000, p. 172; Hamamoto, 1989, pp. 64–65; Helford, 2000, pp. 2–3; Kulzer, 1992, pp. 19–20, 22–26*; Lichter, Lichter, & Rothman, 1991, pp. 69, 271; Lichter, Lichter, & Rothman, 1994, pp. 134, 383; Meehan, 1983, pp. 98–100; Miller, 2000, p. 63; Mitz, 1980, pp. 232–233; Moody, 1980, pp. 114–115; Paietta & Kauppila, 1999, p. 336; Pegg, 2002, pp. 74–76, 79; Penley, et al., 1991, pp. 205–224 (passim), esp. pp. 224–226*; Rafkin, 1998, pp. 48–50; Smith, 1989, pp. 131–141*; Spigel, 2001, pp. 128–131*; Spigel & Curtin, 1997, pp. 58–59; Stark, 1997, p. 118; Story, 1993, pp. 184–197**; Waldrep, 2000, p. 199; Also in Bianculli, 1996, Eisner & Krinsky, 1984, Terrace, 1993

I Had Three Wives
Gianakos, 1992, pp. 403–404; Also in Terrace, 1993

I Led Three Lives
Gianakos, 1987, pp. 365–368*; Hawes, 2002, p. 115; Lichter, Lichter, & Rothman, 1991, pp. 137, 207–208; Lichter, Lichter, & Rothman, 1994, pp. 218, 304; Rovin, 1977b, p. 37; Spigel, 2001, pp. 281–282

I Love Lucy
Adir, 1988, pp. 8–18**; Alley & Brown, 2001, p. 21; Anderson, 1994, pp. 65, 67, 68; Andrews, 1976, whole book**; Andrews, 1985, whole book**; Ball, 1996, pp. 204–224, 231–236, 250–252**; Becker, 2001; Bennett, 1996, pp. 50–57; Berlant, 1997, pp. 133–136*; Brady, 1994, pp. 178–215, 219–220, 222–224, 226–239, 258–259**; Butler, 1991, pp. 320, 324–331**; Caldwell, 1995, p. 52; Castleman & Podrazik, 1982, pp. v, 64–66, 75, 113*; Chunovic, 2000, pp. 33–37*; Crotty, 1995; Davies & Smith, 1998; Davis, 2001, pp. 3–4; Doty, 1993, pp. 39–40, 45–48, 118 (note 4), 121 (note 23)*; Dow, 1996, pp. xvii, 149–150; Fowles, 1982, pp. 100–105, 107–108*; Fowles, 1992, pp. 109–114, 117–118 (same as Fowles 1982); Fox, 2001, p. 29; Hamamoto, 1989, pp. 27–28; Haralovich & Rabinovitz, 1999, pp. 56–64*; Harris, 1991, pp. 20, 89, 91, 160–209, 212, 214–229, 254–255, 324**; Hawes, 2002, pp. 73–76; Heldenfels, 1994, pp. 70–71; Helford, 2000, pp. 1, 48, 56; Horowitz, 1997, pp. 21, 25–43, 60, 76, 111–112, 121**; Javna, 1985, pp. 28–31*; Jones, 1992, pp. 63–75, 76–83 (passim)**; Kuney, 1990, pp. 47–49, 53; Kutulas, 1998; Landay, 1999; Levinson & Link, 1986, pp. 109–111*; Lichter, Lichter, & Rothman, 1991, pp. 51, 63, 236; Lichter, Lichter, & Rothman, 1994, pp. 112, 127, 149, 338–339; Marc, 1984, pp. 16–17, 19; Marc, 1989, pp.

55–56, 92–93; Marc, 1996, pp. 16–17; Marc, 1997, pp. 46, 77, 190; Marling, 1994, pp. 38, 131–312; Martin, 1980**; McClay, 1995, whole book**; McCrohan, 1990, p. 5, 50–61**; Meehan, 1983, pp. 21–26, 162*; Mellencamp, 1992, pp. 322–333, 335–338**; Mitz, 1980, pp. 41–49**; Modleski, 1986, pp. 87–90, 92–94*; Monaco, 2000, p. 483; Newcomb, 1987, pp. 63, 106, 110, 334, 337–338; O'Dell, 1997, pp. 27–30**; Panati, 1991, pp. 302–303; Pegg, 2002, pp. 112–113, 339–341; Penley, et al., 1991, p. 215; Press, 1991, pp. 29–31, 33, 76–77, 124–128, 133–135**; Putterman, 1995, pp. 15–16, 18–19, 96–97*; Rodriguez, 1997, p. 59; Rose, 1985, pp. 108–109; Rose, 1999, p. xiii; Sackett, 1993, pp. 24–25; Sanders & Gilbert, 1993, pp. 33, 35–77, 86–89, 93–96, 99–102, 105–107, 110–111, 123–124, 129–136, 357**; Seger, 1996, pp. 155, 254; Silverblatt, 1995, p. 83; Skutch, 1998, pp. 186–187; Sochen, 1987, p. 85; Sochen, 1999, pp. 20, 152, 154–157*; Spelling, 1996, pp. 16–18; Spigel, 1992, pp. 105–106, 120–121, 130, 141, 151–152, 155, 160, 162–163, 168, 171–176**; Spigel, 2001, pp. 43–44; Spigel & Mann, 1992, pp. 10, 17–18, 20, 31*; Stark, 1997, pp. 2, 26–31**; Stempel, 1992, pp. 27–32**; Tabarlet, 1993; Thomas & Evans, 1990, p. 321; Toll, 1982, pp. 235–237; Tulloch, 2000, p. 175; U.S. Department of Health…, 1982, p. 268; Wilk, 1976, pp. 249–255*; Wilson & Gutierrez, 1985, pp. 99–100; Zook, 1999, p. 55; Also in Bianculli, 1996, Eisner & Krinsky, 1984, Terrace, 1993

I Married Dora
Hamamoto, 1989, pp. 143–144; Kim, 1999; Rodriguez, 1997, pp. 66–67; Also in Terrace, 1993, Terrace, 2000

I Married Joan
Hawes, 2002, pp. 92–93; Jarvis & Joseph, 1998, p. 168; Mitz, 1980, pp. 69–70*; Penley, et al., 1991, p. 215; Putterman, 1995, pp. 17–18; Spigel, 1992, p. 176; Also in Terrace, 1993

I Remember Mama *see* **Mama**

I Spy
Andrews, 1986, pp. 120–122; Barnouw, 1990, pp. 370–372; Bogle, 2001, pp. 115, 117, 119–125**; Castleman & Podrazik, 1982, p. 184; Chunovic, 2000, pp. 49–50; Craig, 1992, p. 101; Dates & Barlow, 1990, pp. 280–281; Dates & Barlow, 1993, p. 305; Fitzgerald & Magers, 2002, p. 216; Gianakos, 1978, pp. 504–508*; Gianakos, 1992, pp. 445–446; Haralovich & Rabinovitz, 1999, pp. 10, 98–119**; Hawes, 2002, p. 199; Heil, 2001, pp. 41–42; Lichter, Lichter, & Rothman, 1991, pp. 70, 237, 238; Lichter, Lichter, & Rothman, 1994, pp. 136, 341; Lisanti & Paul, 2002, pp. 25, 88, 206, 231; McDonald, 1983, pp. 110–112*; McDonald, 1992, pp. 119–121*; Meyers, 1981, pp. 108–109; Miller, 2000, p. 36; Newcomb, 1987, p. 446; Osgerby & Gough-Yates, 2001, pp. 102–104*; Parenti, 1991, p. 133; Rodriguez, 1997, p. 61; Rovin, 1977b, p. 96; Rubin, 1980, pp. 130–131; Schwartz, 1999, p. 140; Smith, 1986, pp. 61–78, 93**; Smith, 1997, pp. 61–76, 111**; Stempel, 1992, pp. 103–104; Torres, 1998, pp. 67–68; Woll & Miller, 1987, p. 77; Worland, 1989; Also in Bianculli, 1996

I Witness Video
Fiske, 1994, p. 224

Ichabod and Me
IN Terrace, 1993

If Not for You
Cotter, 1997, p. 474

I'll Fly Away
Barker, 1999, pp. 82–83; Berry & Manning-Miller, 1996, pp. 172–183**; Bogle, 2001, pp. 397–404, 468**; Jarvis & Joseph, 1998, pp. 245–246; Johnston, 2000, p. 101; Leonard, 1997, pp. 212–214*; Lichter, Lichter, & Rothman, 1994, p. 59; Longworth, 2000, pp. 16, 26; Pearl & Pearl, 1999, pp. 218–219; Spigel & Curtin, 1997, p. 351; Swanson, 2000, pp. 112–116, 146**; Torres, 1998, pp. 6, 118–122, 128–131, 132–137**; Also in Bianculli, 1996

I'm a Big Girl Now
Paietta & Kauppila, 1999, p. 336; Shaner, 1981.

I'm Dickens, He's Fenster
Putterman, 1995, pp. 52–55, 59, 66*; Also in Eisner & Krinsky, 1984, Terrace, 1993

Immortal, The
Gianakos, 1978, pp. 678–679

In Living Color
Berlant, 1997, p. 52; Bernardi, 1998, pp. 1–3*; Bogle, 2001, pp. 376–380*; Caldwell, 1995, p. 196; Capsuto, 2000, pp. 290–293*; Hamamoto, 1994, pp. 9–10, 179–180; Lichter, Lichter, & Rothman, 1994, pp. 28, 56; McDonald, 1992, pp. 289–291*; Moorti, 2001, pp. 1–3; Owen, 1997, p. 116; Pearl & Pearl, 1999, pp. 84–85; Schulman, 1992; Smith, 1997a; Walters, 2001, p. 118; Ward, 1995; Zook, 1999, pp. 4–5; Also in Bianculli, 1996

In the Beginning
Alley & Brown, 2001, pp. 87–88; Lichter, Lichter, & Rothman, 1994, p. 394

In the Heat of the Night
Bell, 1992; Bogle, 2001, pp. 327–329, 330, 468; Bryant & Bryant, 2001, p. 214; Cuklanz, 2000, pp. 36, 39–40, 49–50, 80, 90, 94–97, 110, 117**; Dates & Barlow, 1990, pp. 259–260; Dates & Barlow, 1993, pp. 281–283*; Hamamoto, 1994, pp. 152–154; Moorti, 2001, pp. 130–134*; Pearl & Pearl, 1999, p. 80; Puette, 1992, pp. 192–193; Also in Terrace, 1993

Incredible Hulk, The
Davies, 1997, p. 13; Gianakos, 1981, pp. 252–255; Gianakos, 1983, pp. 165–166; Howe, 1983, pp. 214–215, 216; Kaminsky, 1985, pp. 123–124; Klobas, 1988, pp. 65–66; Puette, 1992, pp. 181, 185; Voort, 1986, pp. 149–150

Inside Edition
Abelman, 1998, p. 34; Kovach & Rosenstiel, 1999, pp. 121, 135; Stark, 1997, p. 252; Vane & Gross, 1994, p. 235

Insiders, The
Gianakos, 1992, pp. 402–403; Also in Terrace, 1993

International Showtime
Davis, 1995, p. 97

Interns, The
Castleman & Podrazik, 1982, p. 221; Gianakos, 1978, pp. 679–680; Kalisch, Kalisch, & Scobey, 1983, pp. 61–63; Paietta & Kauppila, 1999, p. 336; Turow, 1989, pp. 148, 149–152, 177*

Invaders, The
Buxton, 1990, pp. 46–60**; Gerani, 1977, pp. 115–119*; Gianakos, 1978, pp. 570–572*; Rovin, 1977b, p. 116; Also in Terrace, 1993

Investigators, The
Gianakos, 1978, pp. 362–363

Invisible Man (1958), The
Gianakos, 1981, pp. 392–393; Also in Terrace, 1993

Invisible Man (1975) , The
Gianakos, 1981, pp. 171–172; Lichter, Lichter, & Rothman, 1994, p. 260; Also in Terrace, 1993

Iron Horse, The
Gianakos, 1978, pp. 544–546*; Jackson, 1994, pp. 173–175; Yoggy, 1995, pp. 207–208; Also in Lentz, 1997, West, 1987

Ironside
Andrews, 1986, pp. 124–125; Bodroghkozy, 2001, pp. 83–85, 86, 222–225*; Bogle, 2001, pp. 135–136; Bounds, 1996, p. 4; Buxton, 1990, p. 123; Castleman & Podrazik, 1982, p. 202; Edgerton, Marsden & Nachbar, 1997, p. 62; Fiske & Hartley, 1978, pp. 90, 171–177, 181*; Gianakos, 1978, pp. 596–604**; Harris, 1991, p. 301; Klobas, 1988, p. 455; Martin, 1980**; Martindale, 1991, pp. 229–244; Meehan, 1983, pp. 58–59, 74, 76, 172; Meyers, 1981, pp. 134–137, 162*; Newcomb, 1976, p. 276; Newcomb, 1979, pp. 423–424, 432; Newcomb, 1987, pp. 616, 624; Osgerby & Gough-Yates, 2001, pp. 104–106, 201; Pearl & Pearl, 1999, pp. 17, 53, 116; Rose, 1985, p. 16; Rovin, 1977b, p. 116; Sackett, 1993, p. 173; Schwartz, 1999, pp. 157–158; Sumser, 1996, pp. 118, 120, 121–122, 127–128, 137; Toll, 1982, pp. 175–176; Witney & Abels, 1980, pp. 207–208, 212

Island Son
Gianakos, 1978, pp. 291–292; Hamamoto, 1994, p. 20

Islanders, The
Paietta & Kauppila, 1999, p. 336; Also in Terrace, 1993

It Takes a Thief
Gianakos, 1978, pp. 611–613*; Lisanti & Paul, 2002, pp. 28, 88, 164, 192, 202, 204, 312, 316; Marc & Thompson, 1992 (Ch. 16 on Glen Larson), pp. 171–178; Meyers, 1981, pp. 144–145

It Takes Two
Paietta & Kauppila, 1999, p. 336; Also in Terrace, 1993

It's a Living
Hamamoto, 1989, pp. 130–131; Also in Terrace, 1993

It's a Man's World
Erickson, 2000, p. 100; Fagen, 1996, pp. 38, 41; Gianakos, 1978, pp. 369–370; Williams, 1982, pp. 61–64*

It's About Time
IN Eisner & Krinsky, 1984, Terrace, 1993

It's Always Jan
IN Terrace, 1993

It's Like, You Know
Lechner, 2000, pp. 113–114; Wild, 1999, pp. 84–85, 87, 90, 211, 227–230, 252*

It's Your Move
IN Terrace, 1993

Ivanhoe
Gianakos, 1981, pp. 386–387; Rovin, 1977b, p. 57

I've Got a Secret
DeLong, 1991, pp. 174–176; Sackett, 1993, pp. 60–61; Also in Bianculli, 1996

Jack Benny Show, The
Allen, 1956, pp. 60–75, also see index**; Benny, 1990, pp. 90, 92–94, 111–113, 227, 236–249, 278–281**; Benny & Marks, 1978, whole book (passim)**; Blanc & Bashe, 1988, pp. 209–220, 246–247**; Bogle, 2001, pp. 51–55**; Burns, 1990, pp. 230, 277–280, 292–293*; Caldwell, 1995, p. 39; Capsuto, 2000, p. 28; Castleman & Podrazik, 1982, pp. 84–85; Doty, 1993, pp. 63–79**; Entman & Rojecki, 2000, p. 160; Fein, 1976, pp. 142–146, 180–186, 198–218 (passim), 218–224, 238–241*; Gelbart, 1998, pp. 66–70 (passim); Heldenfels, 1994, pp. 68–69; McDonald, 1983, p. 23; McDonald, 1992, p. 24; Museum of Television and Radio, 1991, pp. 18–20, 28–31, 33–39 (passim), 66–77, 184–223, 244–263 (script)**; Putterman, 1995, pp. 22–31, 32–33, 47**; Sackett, 1993, pp. 30–31; Spigel & Curtin, 1997, pp. 279–280; Spigel & Mann, 1992, pp. 51–55*; Stempel, 1992, pp. 17–18; Wilk, 1976, pp. 177–184*; Also in Bianculli, 1996, Eisner & Krinsky, 1984, Terrace, 1993

Jack Paar *see* Tonight Show

Jackie Gleason Show, The
Adir, 1988, pp. 126–137**; Allen, 1956, pp. 145–163, also see index*; Bacon, 1985, pp. 134–135, 169–179**; Henry, 1992, pp. 122–128, 148–151, 183–184, 222–226, 250–253**; Jones, 1992, pp. 108–113 (passim); Lewis & Lewis, 1979, pp. 197–200; Marc, 1984, pp. 102–113**; Marc, 1996, pp. 102–113**; McCrohan, 1990, pp. 67–76**; Mott, 2000, pp. 116–118; Pitrone, 1999, p. 101; Putterman, 1995, pp. 30, 51–52, 72–75*; Sackett, 1993, pp. 44–45; Starr, 1997, pp. 3–5, 69–79, 119–121, 142–145, 147–149, 154–155, 162–166**; Weatherby, 1992, pp. 87–89; 118–119, 147–148, 152–153, 165–166; Also in Bianculli, 1996

Jackie Gleason's American Scene
Marc, 1997, pp. 100–101

Jackie Thomas Show, The
IN Terrace, 1993, Terrace, 2000

Jack's Place
IN Terrace, 1993

JAG
Bryant & Bryant, 2001, p. 191; Jarvis & Joseph, 1998, p. 224; Pearl & Pearl, 1999, p. 190; Suman, 1997, p. 90

Jake and the Fat Man
Bell, 1992; Orlik, 1994, p. 43; Steenland, 1990, pp. 17, 45, 51; Sumser, 1996, p. 73; Also in Terrace, 1993

Jamie
Castleman & Podrazik, 1982, p. 83

Jamie Foxx Show, The
Bogle, 2001, pp. 430–431; Croteau &

Hoynes, 2000, p. 220; Lechner, 2000, p. 222; Means Coleman, 2000, pp. 121–122; Means Coleman, 2002, p. 268

James at 15
Klobas, 1988, pp. 210–211; Montgomery, 1989, pp. 179–180; Shales, 1982, pp. 96–98

Jane Wyman Show *see* **Fireside Theatre**

Jean Arthur Show, The
Lichter, Lichter, & Rothman, 1994, p. 138; Also in Terrace, 1993

Jeff Foxworthy Show, The
Rafkin, 1998, pp. 149–150

Jefferson Drum
Daniel, 1996, p. 10; Jackson, 1994, p. 110; Also in Lentz, 1997, West, 1987

Jeffersons, The
Alley, 1977, p. 47; Andrews, 1986, pp. 140–142, 147; Atwan, Orton, & Vesterman, 1978, p. 386; Bedell, 1981, p. 84; Berry & Mitchell-Kernan, 1982, p. 125; Bryant & Bryant, 2001, pp. 216–217; Castleman & Podrazik, 1982, p. 255; Dates & Barlow, 1990, pp. 271–273; Hamamoto, 1989, pp. 109–112*; Harris, 1989, p. 48; Harris, 1994, p. 51; Jones, 1992, pp. 220–221; Klobas, 1988, pp. 164–165; Lichter, Lichter, & Rothman, 1991, pp. 129, 141, 242; Lichter, Lichter, & Rothman, 1994, p. 208; Marc, 1989, pp. 185, 223; Marc, 1997, pp. 153, 181; Marc & Thompson, 1992 (Ch. 4 on Norman Lear), pp. 49–60; McDonald, 1992, pp. 186–187; Means Coleman, 2000, pp. 89, 92–93, 157–159*; Mitz, 1980, pp. 343–347*; Newcomb, 1976, pp. 26–34*; Newcomb, 1979, p. 58; Panati, 1991, pp. 426–427; Puette, 1992, p. 180; Rotan, 1982; Rubin, 1980, p. 134; Sackett, 1993, pp. 212–213; Schulman, 2001, pp. 53–54*; Schwartz, 1999, p. 140; Sklar, 1980, pp. 8, 72; Sochen, 1987, pp. 82–83; Sochen, 1999, p. 148; Staiger, 2000, p. 154; Taylor, 1989, pp. 80–82, 84; Turner, 1994, pp. 131–132*; Weimann, 2000, p. 222; Woll & Miller, 1987, pp. 82–83; Also in Bianculli, 1996, Eisner & Krinsky, 1984, Terrace, 1993

Jeff's Collie *see* **Lassie**

Jennifer Slept Here
IN Terrace, 1993

Jenny
IN Terrace, 2000

Jeopardy!
Auletta, 1991, pp. 204–206 (passim); Brownlow & Whitener, 1998; Griffin, 1980, pp. 250–251; Also in Bianculli, 1996

Jericho
Gianakos, 1978, pp. 558–559

Jerry Lewis Show, The
Andrews, 1980, pp. 64–70*; Castleman & Podrazik, 1982, pp. 164–165; Levy, 1996, pp. 278–279, 297–307**; Settel, 1958, pp. 215–224 (script)

Jesse
Wild, 1999, pp. 13, 19, 54; Also in Terrace, 2000

Jesse James *see* **Legend of Jesse James**

Jessica Novak
Gianakos, 1983, pp. 213–215; Also in Terrace, 1993

Jessie
Gianakos, 1992, p. 369; Klobas, 1988, pp. 396–397; Paietta & Kauppila, 1999, p. 337; Stempel, 1992, pp. 222–224; Also in Terrace, 1993

Jetsons, The
Barbera, 1994, pp. 149–151; Bennett, 1996, pp. 89–90; Davis, 1995, pp. 65–66; Hendershot, 1998, p. 129; Penley, et al., 1991, pp. 205–224 (passim); Spigel & Curtin, 1997, p. 47; Also in Bianculli, 1996, Eisner & Krinsky, 1984, Terrace, 1993

Jigsaw John
Gianakos, 1981, pp. 191–192; Martindale, 1991, pp. 245–248; Also in Terrace, 1993

Jim Bowie *see* **Adventures of Jim Bowie**

Jimmy Durante Show, The
Bakish, 1995, pp. 129–147**; Burns, 1990, pp. 265–266, 266–267, 272–275*; Everitt, 2001, pp. 61, 63, 64–68*; Pitrone, 1999, p. 82; Robbins, 1991, pp. 135–136, 144–147*; Also in Bianculli, 1996

Jimmy Stewart Show, The
Dewey, 1996, pp. 451–455; Fishgall, 1997, pp. 327–330, 334; Gianakos, 1983, pp. 397–398; Lichter, Lichter, & Rothman, 1991, p. 74; Lichter, Lichter, & Rothman, 1994, p. 141; Molyneaux, 1992, pp. 30, 200–207 (episode guides)*

J. J. Starbuck
Ferre, 1990, pp. 33–34; Yoggy, 1995, p. 208; Also in Terrace, 1993

Joe and Mabel
IN Terrace, 1993

Joe Bash
Lichter, Lichter, & Rothman, 1991, p. 40; Lichter, Lichter, & Rothman, 1994, p. 98

Joe Forrester
Gianakos, 1981, pp. 179–180; Lichter, Lichter, & Rothman, 1991, pp. 43, 194; Lichter, Lichter, & Rothman, 1994, pp. 101–102, 287; Martindale, 1991, pp. 249–251

Joe's Life
IN Terrace, 2000

Joey Bishop Show, The
Crown, 1999, p. 27; Griffin, 1980, pp. 220–221; Also in Eisner & Krinsky, 1984, Terrace, 1993

John Larroqutte Show
Chunovic, 2000, p. 73; Also in Terrace, 2000

Johnny Carson *see* **Tonight Show**

Johnny Jupiter
Davis, 1995, pp. 194–195; Also in Terrace, 1993

Johnny Ringo
Fitzgerald & Magers, 2002, pp. 254–256*; Gianakos, 1983, pp. 345–347*; Jackson, 1994, pp. 132–133; McDonald, 1987, pp. 66, 68, 69; Spelling, 1996, p. 45; Yoggy, 1995, pp. 149–152*;

Also in Lentz, 1997, Terrace, 1993, West, 1987

Johnny Staccato
Gianakos, 1978, pp. 260–261; Meyers, 1981, pp. 60–62; Also in Terrace, 1993

Jonny Quest
Barbera, 1994, pp. 149–151; Davis, 1995, pp. 66–67; Gianakos, 1981, pp. 404–405; Also in Bianculli, 1996

Journey to the Unknown
Gianakos, 1978, pp. 634–635

Judd for the Defense
Gianakos, 1978, pp. 608–611*; Meyers, 1981, p. 134; Rovin, 1977b, p. 119; Wylie, 1970, pp. 298–308**

Judge Roy Bean
Jarvis & Joseph, 1998, p. 196; Also in Lentz, 1997, Terrace, 1993, West, 1987

Judy Garland Show, The
Castleman & Podrazik, 1982, p. 164; Erickson, 2000, pp. 64–65

Julia
Acham, 1999*; Andrews, 1986, pp. 129–131*; Bedell, 1981, p. 84; Berry & Mitchell-Kernan, 1982, p. 76; Bogle, 2001, pp. 140–151, 153–154**; Caldwell, 1995, pp. 53–54, 69; Castleman & Podrazik, 1982, p. 208; Dates & Barlow, 1990, p. 266; Dates & Barlow, 1993, p. 288; Dow, 1996, p. xvii; Hamamoto, 1989, pp. 82, 90–95*; Holtzman, 2000, p. 248; Jones, 1992, pp. 188–189; Kalisch, Kalisch, & Scobey, 1983, pp. 34–36, 194*; Kamalipour & Carrilli, 1998, p. 84; Lichter, Lichter, & Rothman, 1991, pp. 237–238; Lichter, Lichter, & Rothman, 1994, pp. 152, 340; McDonald, 1983, pp. 115–117*; McDonald, 1992, pp. 124–126*; Means, 2000, pp. 84–86, 172–173;*; Paietta & Kauppila, 1999, p. 337; Rodriguez, 1997, p. 61; Sackett, 1993, pp. 158–159; Seger, 1996, p. 155; Smith, 1986, p. 93; Smith, 1997a; Spigel & Mann, 1992, pp. x, 143–164**; Staiger, 2000, p. 98; Thompson, 1996, pp. 54–55; Torres, 1998, pp. 68–69: Wittebols, 1998, pp. 3–4; Turner, 1994, pp. 17, 55–56, 123–125*; Turow, 1989, pp. 201–202; Woll & Miller, 1987, p. 78; Also in Bianculli, 1996, Terrace, 1993

Julie Farr, M.D.
Gianakos, 1981,pp. 249; Kalisch, Kalisch, & Scobey, 1983, pp. 75–77*; Paietta & Kauppila, 1999, p. 337; Turow, 1989, pp. 179–180, 256, 260; Also in Terrace, 1993

June Allyson Show, The
Gianakos, 1978, pp. 242–244*

Just in Time
IN Terrace, 1993

Just Shoot Me
Chunovic, 2000, p. 20; Smith, 1999, pp. 25, 47–48; Also in Terrace, 2000

Just the Ten of Us
Jordan, 1995; Steenland, 1990, pp. 29–30; Also in Terrace, 1993, Terrace, 2000

Justice
Gianakos, 1980, pp. 388–390*; Rovin, 1977b, p. 37

Juvenile Jury
Davis, 1995, pp. 127–129*

Karen's Song
IN Terrace, 1993

Kate & Allie
Burks, 1990; Capsuto, 2000, p. 201; Catron, 1997**; Doty, 1993, pp. 40–41, 43, 45; Dow, 1996, pp. 101–103; Hamamoto, 1989, pp. 131–132; Haralovich & Rabinovitz, 1999, pp. 147–148; Klobas, 1988, pp. 338–340; Lichter, Lichter, & Rothman, 1991, pp. 89, 102, 143; Lichter, Lichter, & Rothman, 1994, p. 160; Newcomb, 1987, pp. 106–107, 109–111*; Oskamp, 1988, p. 116; Press, 1991, pp. 46–47, 123–124; Sackett, 1993, pp. 286–287; Schwartz, 1999, p. 135; Selnow & Gilbert, 1993, pp. 52–53; Sochen, 1987, p. 141; Spigel, 2001, pp. 359–360; Spigel & Mann, 1992, pp. xi, 203–213**; Vane & Gross, 1994, p. 116; Walters, 2001, p. 62; Also in Terrace, 1993

Kate Loves a Mystery
Gianakos, 1981, pp. 275–276; Lichter, Lichter, & Rothman, 1991, pp. 35, 39, 118; Lichter, Lichter, & Rothman, 1994, pp. 42, 96–97, 194; Martindale, 1991, pp. 346–349; Meyers, 1981, p. 173; Also in Terrace, 1993

Kate McShane
Gianakos, 1981, pp. 181–182; Jarvis & Joseph, 1998, p. 164; Lichter, Lichter, & Rothman, 1991, p. 216; Martindale, 1991, pp. 252–254

Kay O'Brien
Paietta & Kauppila, 1999, p. 337; Turow, 1989, pp. 256–257, 260

Kaz
Gianakos, 1981, pp. 259–260; Martindale, 1991, pp. 254–257; Meyers, 1981, p. 249

Kindred: The Embraced
Muir, 2001a, pp. 410–417**; Owen, 1997, p. 155

King of the Hill
Croteau & Hoynes, 2000, p. 220; Smith, 1999, pp. 66–67

King's Crossing
Gianakos, 1983, p. 198; Also in Morris, 1997

Kings Row
Anderson, 1994, pp. 182–183, 186, 192, 201–202, 207–210**; Paietta & Kauppila, 1999, p. 337

Kingston: Confidential
Daniel, 1996, p. 17; Gianakos, 1981, pp. 222–223

Kirk
IN Terrace, 2000

Kit Carson *see* **Adventures of Kit Carson**

Klondike
Gianakos, 1978, pp. 295–296; Also in Lentz, 1997, Terrace, 1993, West, 1987

Knight and Daye
IN Terrace, 1993

Knight Rider
Gianakos, 1987, pp. 304–307*; Gianakos, 1992, pp. 276–278*; Gunter & Wober, 1988, pp. 26–30 (passim), 40–42; Lichter, Lichter, & Rothman, 1991, p. 143; Lichter, Lichter, & Rothman, 1994, p. 226; Marc & Thompson, 1992 (Ch. 16 on Glen Larson), pp. 171–178; Osgerby & Gough-Yates, 2001, pp. 5, 69–80**;

Yoggy, 1995, p. 547; Also in Terrace, 1993

Knots Landing
Allen, 1992, pp. 334–335; Bogle, 2001, p. 264; Gianakos, 1981, pp. 290–291; Gianakos, 1983, pp. 162–165*; Gianakos, 1987, pp. 268–271*; Gianakos, 1992, pp. 340–342*; Joshel, Malamud, & McGuire, 2001, pp. 137–138; Lembo, 2000, pp. 187, 190; Marc & Thompson, 1992 (Ch. 18 on Lee Rich, i.e. Lorimar), pp. 195–202; Marris & Thornham, 2000, pp. 379–380; Moorti, 2001, p. 118; Newcomb & Alley, 1983, pp. 29–31; Press, 1991, pp. 153–154; Sackett, 1993, p. 299; Schultz, 2000, p. 124; U.S. Congress, 1985, pp. 150–151, 158; Williams, 1992, p. 169, 179–180 (passim); Also in Bianculli, 1996, Morris, 1997

Kodiak
Yoggy, 1995, p. 194

Kojak
Adler, 1976, pp. 89–91; Adler, 1981, pp. 85–87*; Alley, 1977, pp. 46–47, 108–111*; Bedell, 1981, p. 75; Buxton, 1990, pp. 134–140**; Carlson, 1985, pp. 37, 42–43; Castleman & Podrazik, 1982, pp. 246–247*; Collins & Javna, 1989, pp. 80–82; Cullingford, 1984, pp. 41–42; Fowles, 1982, pp. 2–3, 7, 131–134*; Fowles, 1992, pp. 2–3, 7, 145–148 (same as Fowles 1982); Gianakos, 1978, pp. 748–750*; Gianakos, 1981, pp. 96–99*; Heil, 2001, p. 292; Himmelstein, 1994, p. 23; Lichter, Lichter, & Rothman, 1991, pp. 145, 189, 193, 228; Lichter, Lichter, & Rothman, 1994, pp. 198, 228, 280, 286, 329*; Martindale, 1991, pp. 261–272; Meyers, 1981, pp. 196–198; Newcomb, 1979, pp. 137–140, 141, 153–155, 550–552*; Newcomb, 1982, pp. 108–111, 543–545 (reprint of Adler, 1976)*; Newcomb, 1987, pp. 640–642*; Newcomb, 1994, pp. 547–548; Newcomb, 2000, pp. 604–606; Osgerby & Gough-Yates, 2001, pp. 5, 53–68**; Root, 1979, pp. 153–154; Rose, 1985, p. 19; Rovin, 1977b, pp. 140, 142; Sackett, 1993, pp. 204–205; Stark, 1997, p. 36; Sumser, 1996, pp. 100–101, 110; U.S. Congress, 1977b, pp. 368–369, 372–375; Wahl, 1995, pp. 8, 59; Witney & Abels, 1980, pp. 253–255; Also in Bianculli, 1996, Terrace, 1993

Kolchak: The Night Stalker
Collins & Javna, 1989, pp. 103–105; Daniel, 1996, p. 13; Gerani, 1977, pp. 135–140; Gianakos, 1978, pp. 768–769; Kaminsky, 1985, pp. 127–132*; Lichter, Lichter, & Rothman, 1991, p. 119; Lichter, Lichter, & Rothman, 1994, p. 195; Martindale, 1991, pp. 272–275; Muir, 2001a, pp. 64–76**; Muir, 2001b, pp. 223–224; Rovin, 1977b, pp. 143–144; Soter, 2002, pp. 113–114, 115; Also in Bianculli, 1996

Kovacs *see* **Ernie Kovacs**

Kraft Mystery Theater
Gianakos, 1978, pp. 325–327*

Kraft Suspense Theater
Gianakos, 1978, pp. 427–430*

Kraft Television Theatre
Barnouw, 1990, pp. 156–164(passim); Bogle, 2001, pp. 61–62; Castleman & Podrazik, 1982, pp. 79, 97; Gianakos, 1980, pp. 171–196**; Gianakos, 1983, pp. 225–226; Guida, 2000, pp. 181–182; Hawes, 2001, pp. 22, 40–55, 148–149**; Jones, 1992, pp. 31, 33, 35;

Krampner, 1997, p. 38; Skutch, 1998, pp. 68–71*; Stempel, 1992, pp. 33–35*; Sturcken, 1990, see index*; Also in Bianculli, 1996

Kukla, Fran, & Ollie
Davis, 1995, pp. 196–197; Panati, 1991, pp. 250–251; Putterman, 1995, p. 130; Rico, 1990, pp. 88–89, 102, 112; Spigel, 2001, p. 201; Weiner, 1992, p. 60; Wilk, 1976, pp. 229–235*; Winship, 1988, pp. 36–43; Also in Bianculli, 1996

Kung Fu
Adler, 1976, pp. 29–31, 118–125**; Adler, 1981, pp. 67–69*; Brauer, 1975, pp. 228–233**; Caldwell, 1995, pp. 54, 55, 70; Castleman & Podrazik, 1982, p. 250; Forbes & Mahan, 2000, pp. 40 (n. 14), 41 (n. 24), 31, 33; Gianakos, 1978, pp. 709–711*; Hamamoto, 1994, pp. 59–63*; Jackson, 1994, pp. 196–198; Jarvis & Joseph, 1998, pp. 105, 113, 215–216; Javna, 1985, p. 20; Lichter, Lichter, & Rothman, 1991, pp. 242–243; Lichter, Lichter, & Rothman, 1994, p. 347; Miles, 1975, pp. 57–59 (Dec. 13, 1973 show); Newcomb, 1976, pp. 105–112**; Newcomb, 1979, pp. 529–532*; Osgerby & Gough-Yates, 2001, pp. 115–126**; Rovin, 1977b, p. 134; Waldrep, 2000, p. 195; Yoggy, 1995, pp. 500–515, 517–525**; Also in Bianculli, 1996, Lentz, 1997, Terrace, 1993, West, 1987

L.A. Doctors
Paietta & Kauppila, 1999, p. 337

L.A. Law
Bignell, 1997, pp. 145, 163; Bogle, 2001, pp. 333–343**; Burks, 1990**; Burns & Thompson, 1989, pp. 79–87 (passim); Caldwell, 1995, pp. 326, 327–330*; Capsuto, 2000, pp. xiii, 232, 272–275, 277–278, 280–281, 305, 333, 358**; Chunovic, 2000, p. 120; Cortes, 2000, p. 67; Cuklanz, 2000, pp. 42, 75–76, 117, 118, 146–151*; Cumberbatch & Negrine, 1992, p. 50; Dow, 1996, p. 98; Gross, 2001, pp. 87–88, 88–89; Gross & Woods, 1999, p. 294; Henderson & Mazzeo, 1990, pp. 27–28, 81–102, especially pp. 95–98*; Himmelstein, 1994, p. 233; Holtzman, 2000, pp 229–231; Jarvis & Joseph, 1998, pp. 21, 24–32, 224–225, 248**; Kendall, 1989; Leonard, 1997, p. 140; Lichter, Lichter, & Rothman, 1991, pp. 149, 217; Lichter, Lichter, & Rothman, 1994, pp. 20, 40, 59, 66, 233, 315–316; Longworth, 2000, pp. 116, 204; Marc & Thompson, 1992 (Ch. 20 on Steven Bochco), pp. 218–229, especially pp. 225–228*; Marris & Thornham, 2000, p. 379; Mayne, 2000, pp. 79–101**; Monaco, 2000, pp. 494, 496; Moorti, 2001, pp. 99, 122, 124, 127–129, 134–144**; Orlik, 1994, pp. 188, 246–247; Pearl & Pearl, 1999, pp. 25, 31, 106, 108, 166–167, 168, 223,226, 227; Powers, 1994, pp. 238–244**; Press, 1991, p. 153; Ringer, 1994, pp. 148, 151–152; Rodriguez, 1997, p. 69; Rushkoff, 1994, pp. 49–51*; Selnow & Gilbert, 1993, pp. 32–33; Simon, 2001; Stark, 1997, p . 246; Steenland, 1990, pp. 14, 49–50; Stempel, 1992, pp. 240–241; Suman, 1997, p. 113; Tabarlet, 1993; Thompson, 1996, pp. 121–130**; Vande Berg & Trujillo, 1989, pp. 122–123, 178, 231–137, 255**; Vande Berg & Wenner, 1991, pp. 144–159**; Wahl, 1995, p. 9; Winship, 1988, pp. 116–117; Also in Bianculli, 1996, Morris, 1997

Ladies' Man
Lechner, 2000, pp. 81–82; Also in Terrace, 1993

Lady Blue
Carey, 1988, pp. 98–99; Gianakos, 1992, pp. 406–407

Lancer
Brauer, 1975, p. 119; Gianakos, 1983, pp. 390–393; Jackson, 1994, pp. 188–190; Klobas, 1988, p. 281; Kulzer, 1992, pp. 136–137; Rovin, 1977b, p. 123; Yoggy, 1995, p. 344; Also in Lentz, 1997, West, 1987

Land of the Giants
Andrews, 1980, pp. 71–76*; Davis, 1995, pp. 21–22; Gerani, 1977, pp. 72, 84–86; Gianakos, 1978, pp. 617–619*; Lisanti & Paul, 2002, pp. 198–199; Rovin, 1977b, pp. 121, 123; Also in Terrace, 1993

Land of the Lost (ABC)
IN Terrace, 1993

Land of the Lost (NBC)
Davis, 1995, pp. 22–23; Also in Terrace, 1993

Lanigan's Rabbi
Meyers, 1981, p. 175; Starr, 1997, p. 197; Also in Terrace, 1993

Laramie
Fitzgerald & Magers, 2002, pp. 213–214; Gianakos, 1978, pp. 245–248*; Jackson, 1994, pp. 137–138; Magers & Fitzgerald, 1999, pp. 194, 244; Also in Lentz, 1997, West, 1987

Laredo
Gianakos, 1978, pp. 509–511; Jackson, 1994, pp. 171–172; McDonald, 1987, p. 76; Yoggy, 1995, pp. 157–160, 415*; Also in Lentz, 1997, West, 1987

Lash of the West
Davis, 1995, p. 221; Jackson, 1994, p. 46; McDonald, 1987, pp. 20–21; Also in Lentz, 1997

Lassie
Castleman & Podrazik, 1982, p. 95; Davis, 1995, pp. 23–25*; Gianakos, 1992, pp. 428–441**; Hawes, 2002, pp. 84–85; Kinder, 1999, pp. 69–71, 81–95**; Rovin, 1977b, p. 39; Also in Bianculli, 1996, Terrace, 1993

Last Resort, The
Lichter, Lichter, & Rothman, 1994, p. 94; Tinker & Rukeyser, 1994, pp. 108–110

Late Night with David Letterman *see* **David Letterman**

Laugh-In
Andrews, 1986, pp. 126–128*; Bodroghkozy, 2001, pp. 112–113, 149–151*; Caldwell, 1995, pp. 54–55; Capsuto, 2000, pp. 54–55, 65–66, 70*; Castleman & Podrazik, 1982, pp. 198–200, 210*; Chunovic, 2000, p. 57; Erickson, 2000, whole book**; Freeman, 1980, p. 43; Helford, 2000, p. 2; Himmelstein, 1984, pp. 149–150; Himmelstein, 1994, pp. 190–191; Horowitz, 1997, pp. 114–117, 140*; Jarvik, 1997, pp. 262–263; Javna, 1985, p. 21; Jones, 1992, p. 187; Kulzer, 1992, pp. 96–102*; Lichter, Lichter, & Rothman, 1994, p. 82; Lisanti & Paul, 2002, p. 90; Marc, 1989, pp. 150–153*; Marc, 1997, pp. 124–127*; McCrohan, 1990, pp. 178–186**; Monaco, 2000, p. 486; Nelson & Gaonkar, 1996, pp. 332–334*; Pegg, 2002, pp. 214–215; Rose, 1985, pp. 315–316; Sackett, 1993, pp. 154–155; Scheider, 1997, p 119–144**;

Smith, 1989, pp. 75, 79–81, 85–89*; Spigel, 2001, pp. 292–294*; Stark, 1997, pp. 142–147**; Starr, 1997, p. 166; Stempel, 1992, pp. 112–115*; Toll, 1982, pp. 239–240; Winship, 1988, pp. 190–196; Also in Bianculli, 1996

Laurie Hill
Cotter, 1997, p. 434; Paietaa & Kauppila, 1999, p. 338

Laverne & Shirley
Bedell, 1981, pp. 127–130*; Bennett, 1996, pp. 117–118; Castleman & Podrazik, 1982, p. 268; Chunovic, 2000, pp. 78–79; Coakley, 1977, pp. 58–59; Crown, 1999, pp. 29, 39–56, 59–66, 71–75, 92–95, 172, 185–219**; Doty, 1993, pp. 41–42, 45, 51–57, 122 (note 27), 124 (note 34)**; Holtzman, 2000, p. 129; Jones, 1992, pp. 243–244; Kaminsky, 1985, pp. 204–210 (passim), interview with Gary Marshall; Kassel, 1993, p. 3; Marc & Thompson, 1992 (Ch. 6 on Gary Marshall), pp. 70–83; McCrohan, 1990, pp. 262–270**; Meehan, 1983, pp. 30–32, 178; Miller, 1980, p. 200; Mitz, 1980, pp. 359–364*; Newcomb, 1976, pp. 72–73; Newcomb, 1982, pp. 78–86 (passim)*; Newcomb, 1987, p. 480; Puette, 1992, pp. 177–178; Putterman, 1995, p. 114; Rafkin, 1998, pp. 91–95*; Sackett, 1993, pp. 220–221; Schwartz, 1999, p. 134; Seger, 1996, p. 155; Sklar, 1980, pp. 15–18, 22–23, 68–69*; Staiger, 2000, pp. 113–114, 116, 131–140, 161, 162, 163, 165; Stempel, 1992, pp. 155–156; Williams, 1982, pp. 136–137; Also in Bianculli, 1996, Eisner & Krinsky, 1984, Terrace, 1993

Law and Harry McGraw, The
Edelman & Kupferberg, 1996, p. 223; Jarvis & Joseph, 1998, p. 237

Law and Mr. Jones, The
Gianakos, 1978, pp. 318–319; Lichter, Lichter, & Rothman, 1991, pp. 138, 148; Lichter, Lichter, & Rothman, 1994, pp. 219, 231–232*; Meyers, 1981, p. 78; Rovin, 1977b, p. 79

Law and Order
Blum, 1995, pp. 11, 36–37, 106–109, 128–129, 182–188*; Bogle, 2001, pp. 435–438*; Bryant & Bryant, 2001, p. 183; Capsuto, 2000, p. 253; Courrier, 1998, whole book**; Davis, 2001, pp. 104, 124, 127–136**; Hamamoto, 1994, p. 231; Holtzman, 2000, pp 229–230; Jarvis & Joseph, 1998, pp. xi, 33–53, 273–274 (n. 16)**; Kalat, 1998, pp. 99, 120, 175–178, 189, 198–202, 277, 282*; Lane, 2001; Leonard, 1997, pp. 7, 159–160; Lichter, Lichter, & Rothman, 1994, pp. 42, 44, 64–65; Lindheim & Blum, 1991, pp. 125–190, 253–322**; Longworth, 2000, pp. 4–5, 11–18, 129, 133**; Monaco, 2000, pp. 497–498; Moorti, 2001, pp. 122, 144–145; Newcomb, 2000, pp. 245–246; Pearl & Pearl, 1999, pp. 84, 119–120, 169*; Schultz, 2000, p. 128; Sharrett, 1999, pp 253–255, 262, 265*; Suman, 1997, pp. 4, 77, 79; Sumser, 1996, p. 155; Swanson, 2000, pp. 45, 60–62*; Thompson, 1996, pp. 183, 185–186

Law and Order: Special Victims Unit
Chunovic, 2000, p. 181; Lechner, 2000, pp. 82–83

Law of the Plainsman
Gianakos, 1978, pp. 259–260; Jackson, 1994, pp. 131–132; Yoggy, 1995, pp. 356–357; Also in Lentz, 1997, Terrace, 1993, West, 1987

Lawless Years, The
Gianakos, 1981, pp. 396–398; Pearl & Pearl, 1999, pp. 77–78; Rovin, 1977b, p. 70

Lawman, The
Brauer, 1975, pp. 57, 61–63, 75, 80–82*; Cavallo, 1999, p. 39; Fitzgerald & Magers, 2002, pp. 266–267; Gianakos, 1978, pp. 210–212*; Jackson, 1994, pp. 111–112; Yoggy, 1995, pp. 163–167*; Also in Lentz, 1997, West, 1987

Lawrence Welk
Castleman & Podrazik, 1982, p. 101; Orlik, 1994, p. 43; Sackett, 1993, pp. 144–145; Sanders & Weissman, 1985, whole book**; Spigel & Curtin, 1997, pp. 265–285**; Stark, 1997, pp. 56–58*; Also in Bianculli, 1996

Lawyers, The
Marc & Thompson, 1992 (Ch. 13 on Roy Huggins), pp. 141–151; Martindale, 1991, pp. 278–281

Lazarus Syndrome, The
Gianakos, 1981, p. 285; Kalisch, Kalisch, & Scobey, 1983, pp. 133–135; Lichter, Lichter, & Rothman, 1994, p. 246; McDonald, 1992, pp. 227–228; Paietta & Kauppila, 1999, p. 338; Turow, 1989, pp. 190–113

League of Their Own
Crown, 1999, pp. 131–132; Also in Terrace, 2000

Leave It to Beaver
Abt & Mustazza, 1997, pp. 43–44: Alley & Brown, 2001, p. 22; Bennett, 1996, pp. 1–8; Bryant & Bryant, 2001, pp. 165–166; Caldwell, 1995, pp. 40, 71; Cantor, 2001, p. 92; Castleman & Podrazik, 1982, pp. 119–120, 193; Cavallo, 1999, p. 36; Crotty, 1995; Davis, 1995, pp. 114–115; Davis, 2001, p. 6; Drummond & Peterson, 1988, pp. 38–42, 50–58**; Friedman, 2002, pp. 262–263; Hamamoto, 1989, pp. 25–26; Hawes, 2002, pp. 86–87; Himmelstein, 1984, pp. 91–97**; Himmelstein, 1994, pp. 125, 127–132**; Inness, 1999, p. 49; Jacobs, 1983, whole book**; Javna, 1985, pp. 134–137*; Jones, 1992, pp. 123–128, 157–159**; Leibman, 1995, pp. 22, 28, 33, 37, 38, 41, 70, 82–84, 125–126, 133, 134–135, 153, 157–158, 175, 185, 207, 224–225, 237, 244–245, 268**; Marc, 1996, pp. 12, 15; Mathers, 1998, whole book (passim); Meyers, 1999, p. 273; Mitz, 1980, pp. 137–140*; Newcomb, 1987, p. 334; Orlik, 2001, p. xvii; Panati, 1991, pp. 309–310; Pegg, 2002, pp. 244–246; Silverblatt, 1995, p. 82; Silverblatt, Ferry, & Finan, 1999, pp. 176, 186; Spigel & Curtin, 1997, p. 125; Spigel & Mann, 1992, pp. 114–115, 128–137**; Stark, 1997, pp. 2, 81–85, 256**; Stempel, 1992, pp. 94–95; Also in Bianculli, 1996, Eisner & Krinsky, 1984, Terrace, 1993

Leg Work
Ringer, 1994, pp. 93–94; Also in Terrace, 1993

Legend
Buscombe & Pearson, 1998, pp. 200, 205; Spigel & Curtin, 1997, p. 343; Also in Lentz, 1997

Legend of Jesse James, The
Gianakos, 1978, pp. 489–490; Jackson, 1994, p. 170; McDonald, 1987, p. 64; Rainey, 1998, p. 99; Also in Lentz, 1997, West, 1987

Legmen
Gianakos, 1987, pp. 341–342

Lenny
Cotter, 1997, pp. 382–383; Also in Terrace, 1993

Leo and Liz in Beverly Hills
IN Terrace, 1993

Leslie Uggams Show
Torres, 1998, pp. 71–72

Let's Make a Deal
Castleman & Podrazik, 1982, pp. 211–212; Himmelstein, 1994, pp. 329–330; Newcomb, 1976, pp. 376–378*; Newcomb, 1979, pp. 353–356*; Also in Bianculli, 1996

Letterman, David *see* **David Letterman**

Liberace Show
Andrews, 1980, pp. 77–83*

Lieutenant, The
Alexander, 1994, pp. 186–188; Bogle, 2001, pp. 103–106*; Gianakos, 1978, pp. 404–405; Lichter, Lichter, & Rothman, 1994, p. 382; Pounds, 1999, pp. 210–211 (n. 35)

Life and Legend of Wyatt Earp, The
Aquila, 1996, pp. 168–169; Brauer, 1975, pp. 53–54, 56, 63; Castleman & Podrazik, 1982, pp. 103–104; Friedman, 2002, p. 65; Gianakos, 1981, pp. 351–361**; Hawes, 2002, p. 130; Jackson, 1994, pp. 59–60; McDonald, 1987, pp. 51, 68; Rainey, 1998, p. 164; Rovin, 1977b, p. 46; Sackett, 1993, p. 76; Yoggy, 1995, pp. 132–143, 144, 297**; Also in Lentz, 1997, West, 1987

Life ... and Stuff
IN Terrace, 2000

Life and Times of Grizzly Adams, The
Goethals, 1981, pp. 62–63; Yoggy, 1995, pp. 229–232*; Also in Lentz, 1997, West, 1987

Life Goes On
Burke & McDaniel, 1991, pp. 192–299 (passim)**; Leonard, 1997, p. 183; Lester, 1996, pp. 124–125; Nelson, 1994, p. 11; Schneider, 2001, p. 86; Steenland, 1990, p. 23; Suman, 1997, p. 77 Also in Terrace, 1993

Life Is Worth Living (Bishop Sheen)
Lynch, 1998, whole book**; Stark, 1997, pp. 37–40*

Life of Riley, The
Adir, 1988, pp. 124–125; Bacon, 1985, pp. 83–85; Castleman & Podrazik, 1982, pp. 51, 77; Hamamoto, 1989, pp. 18–19; Hawes, 2002, p. 80; Henry, 1992, pp. 87–88; Meehan, 1983, p. 163; Mitz, 1980, pp. 71–74*; Parenti, 1991, p. 71; Spigel & Mann, 1992, pp. 79–80, 83, 86, 90; Starr, 1997, p. 58; U.S. Department of Health…, 1982, p. 267; Also in Bianculli, 1996, Eisner & Krinsky, 1984, Terrace, 1993

Life with Father
Hamamoto, 1989, pp. 22–24*; Hawes, 2002, pp. 80–83

Life with Lucy
Harris, 1991, pp. 320–321; O'Dell,

1997, p. 33; Sanders & Gilbert, 1993, pp. 350–353*; Spelling, 1996, pp. 159–160

Life with Luigi
Bogle, 2001, p. 41; Hamamoto, 1989, pp. 36–38*; Hawes, 2002, p. 73; Also in Terrace, 1993

Lifeline
Kalisch, Kalisch, & Scobey, 1983, p. 75

Life's Work
Jarvis & Joseph, 1998, pp. 177, 231

Lights Out
Gianakos, 1980, pp. 219–224*; Krampner, 1997, pp. 32–33

Lime Street
Gianakos, 1992, pp. 394–395

Lineup, The
Gianakos, 1978, pp. 253–254; Gianakos, 1983, pp. 304–310**; Lichter, Lichter, & Rothman, 1991, p. 221; Lichter, Lichter, & Rothman, 1994, pp. 320–321; Rovin, 1977b, pp. 37–38

Little House: A New Beginning
Gianakos, 1987, pp. 219–221; Klobas, 1988, pp. 354–355, 389–390, 422; Yoggy, 1995, pp. 536, 539–543*; Also in Lentz, 1997

Little House on the Prairie
Alley, 1977, pp. 47, 122–124*; Aquila, 1996, p. 180; Castleman & Podrazik, 1982, p. 264; Cuklanz, 2000, pp. 33, 90–94**; Gianakos, 1978, pp. 756–757; Gianakos, 1981, pp. 122–126*; Gianakos, 1983, pp. 137–140*; Goethals, 1981, pp. 68–70*; Guida, 2000, pp. 197–198; Himmelstein, 1984, p. 182; Himmelstein, 1994, pp. 221–222; Jackson, 1994, pp. 198–200; Klobas, 1988, pp. 43–45, 51–54, 74–75, 224–225, 375**; Leiby & Leiby, 2001, pp. 236–239*; Lichter, Lichter, & Rothman, 1991, pp. 32–33, 44; Lichter, Lichter, & Rothman, 1994, pp. 88, 103; Miles, 1975, pp. 49–51 (Nov. 6, 1974, show); Nelson, 1994, p. 1; Newcomb, 1979, pp. 148–150*; Newcomb, 1982, pp. 119–121; Paietta & Kauppila, 1999, p. 338; Pearl & Pearl, 1999, pp. 51, 58, 73, 214; Press, 1991, pp. 163–164; Sackett, 1993, pp. 246–247; Schwartz, 1999, p. 155; Shaner, 1981; U.S. Congress, 1977a, p. 40; Yoggy, 1995, pp. 526–529, 531–544**; Also in Bianculli, 1996, Lentz, 1997, Terrace, 1993

Little People, The (Brian Keith Show)
Kalisch, Kalisch, & Scobey, 1983, pp. 84–85; Marc & Thompson, 1992 (Ch. 6 on Gary Marshall), pp. 70–83; Paietta & Kauppila, 1999, p. 324; Also in Terrace, 1993

Live-in
IN Terrace, 1993

Living Dolls
IN Terrace, 1993, Terrace, 2000

Living Single
Bogle, 2001, pp. 422–426*; Capsuto, 2000, p. 360; Cottle, 2000, p. 122; Kamalipour & Carrilli, 1998, p. 86; Lichter, Lichter, & Rothman, 1994, p. 57; Means Coleman, 2000, pp. 118–119, 127, 134, 202; Owen, 1997, pp. 87–89, 116–117*; Smith, 1997*; Zook, 1999, pp. 65–74, 106**; Also in Terrace, 2000

Lloyd Bridges Show, The
Gianakos, 1978, pp. 378–380*

Logan's Run
Gianakos, 1981, p. 239; Also in Terrace, 1993

Lois and Clark: The New Adventures of Superman
Daniels, 1995, pp. 236–237; Harrison, et al., 1996, p. 236; Helford, 2000, pp. 91–112**; Rose, 1999, p. 107; Wilcox, 1996

Lone Ranger, The
Aquila, 1996, p. 161; Bernardi, 1998, p. 32; Bodroghkozy, 2001, pp. 31–32; Bogle, 2001, pp. 41–42; Brauer, 1975, pp. 36, 37, 39–40, 42, 45–49 (passim)*; Buscombe & Pearson, 1998, p. 13; Castleman & Podrazik, 1982, p. 50; Davis, 1995, pp. 221–225**; Fagen, 1996, pp. 83–85; Fitzgerald & Magers, 2002, pp. 59, 130, 230; Gianakos, 1983, pp. 227–232**; Hanfling, 2001, pp. 159, 215; Harmon, 1992, pp. 139–142*; Hawes, 2002, p. 124; Jackson, 1994, pp. 33–34; Jarvis & Joseph, 1998, pp. 190–191; Magers & Fitzgerald, 1999, p. 138; McDonald, 1987, pp. 26, 27, 31–32, 36–37; Rose, 1985, p. 58; Rovin, 1977b, pp. 17–19*; Sackett, 1993, pp. 16–17; Stempel, 1992, pp. 19–20, 24–25; Weiner, 1992, p. 111; Wilson & Gutierrez, 1985, pp. 95–96; Yoggy, 1995, pp. 11–18, 348–350, 352**; Also in Bianculli, 1996, Lentz, 1997, Terrace, 1993, West, 1987

Loner, The
Engel, 1989, pp. 266–274 (passim); Gianakos, 1978, pp. 477–478; Jackson, 1994, pp. 163–164; McDonald, 1987, p. 69; Rovin, 1977b, p. 94; Yoggy, 1995, pp. 224–227*; Also in Lentz, 1997, West, 1987

Long Hot Summer, The
Alley & Brown, 2001, pp. 100–101; Gianakos, 1978, pp. 511–512; Also in Morris, 1997

Longstreet
Gianakos, 1978, pp. 701–702; Klobas, 1988, p. 454; Martindale, 1991, pp. 281–284; Meyers, 1981, pp. 160, 162; Rovin, 1977b, pp. 130–131; Vane & Gross, 1994, p. 113

Loretta Young Show, The
Alley & Brown, 2001, pp. 14–16; Gianakos, 1978, pp. 184–186; Gianakos, 1980, pp. 375–380*; Hawes, 2002, pp. 95–96; Seger, 1996, pp. 31, 42–45*; Also in Bianculli, 1996

Lost in Space
Alexander, 1994, pp. 255–256; Bennett, 1996, pp. 119–121; Davis, 1995, pp. 26–27; Gerani, 1977, pp. 70, 77–81*; Gianakos, 1978, pp. 496–498; Javna, 1985, pp. 188–191*; Kulzer, 1992, p. 15; Rovin, 1977b, p. 96; Story, 1993, pp. 147–159**; Also in Bianculli, 1996, Terrace, 1993

Lotsa Luck
Miles, 1975, pp. 37–38 (Nov. 12, 1973, show)

Lottery!
Gianakos, 1987, pp. 335–336; Klobas, 1988, pp. 252–254

Lou Grant
Bedell, 1981, pp. 210–212; Berger, 1987, pp. 79–82*; Castleman &

Podrazik, 1982, pp. 289–290*; Cuklanz, 2000, pp. 33, 71, 78, 108; Daniel, 1996, whole book, esp. pp. 19–217**; Davis, 2001, p. 121; Diamond, 1982, pp. 146–159**; Freeman, 1980, pp. 134–135; Gianakos, 1981, pp. 234–237*; Gianakos, 1983, pp. 141–143*; Gitlin, 1983, see index*; Himmelstein, 1984, pp. 188–189; Johnston, 2000, p. 141; Lazere, 1987, pp. 260–261; Lichter, Lichter, & Rothman, 1991, pp. 152, 176, 177, 254–255, 265; Lichter, Lichter, & Rothman, 1994, pp. 237, 361–362, 375–376; Marc & Thompson, 1992 (Ch. 5 on James L. Brooks), pp. 61–69; Martin, 1981; Meyers, 1981, pp. 247–248; Newcomb, 1982, pp. 175–180**; Newcomb, 1987, pp. 67–69, 85–90, 92–93, 101–105**; Newcomb & Alley, 1983, pp. 210, 217–218, 224–229 (passim); Orlik, 1994, pp. 208–209*; Pearl & Pearl, 1999, pp. 29, 121, 122; Puette, 1992, pp. 183, 186, 187, 189; Putterman, 1995, p. 120; Rose, 1999, pp. 92–93; Rowland & Watkins, 1984, p. 259; Shales, 1982, pp. 67–69; Sklar, 1980, pp. 153–157*; Taylor, 1989, pp. 135–136, 137, 142–143, 147–148*; Thompson, 1996, p. 48; Tinker & Rukeyser, 1994, pp. 117–120*; Winship, 1988, pp. 95–96; Also in Bianculli, 1996

Love, American Style (including revival)

Castleman & Podrazik, 1982, p. 215; Crown, 1999, pp. 42–43; Klobas, 1988, pp. 102–104; Lichter, Lichter, & Rothman, 1991, p. 28; Lichter, Lichter, & Rothman, 1994, p. 82; Nelson & Gaonkar, 1996, p. 333; Rafkin, 1998, pp. 58–61*; Rutstein, 1974, p. 101; Also in Eisner & Krinsky, 1984

Love and War

Fiske, 1994, p. 34; Lichter, Lichter, & Rothman, 1994, pp. 38, 48, 60; Suman, 1997, p. 77; Swanson, 2000, p. 47; Also in Terrace, 1993, Terrace, 2000

Love Boat, The

Abelman, 1998, p. 163; Bedell, 1981, pp. 204–205; Caldwell, 1995, pp. 18, 87; Capsuto, 2000, p 200; Carroll, 2000, p. 209; Gottfried, 1999, p. 254; Harrison, et al., 1996, p. 182 (n. 15); Klobas, 1988, pp. 47–48, 63–65, 78–79, 83–85, 129, 144, 160–161, 182–184, 215–216, 239–240, 294–295, 331–332, 349–350, 388–389, 411–412**; Lichter, Lichter, & Rothman, 1991, pp. 38, 255; Lichter, Lichter, & Rothman, 1994, pp. 95–96; Marc & Thompson, 1992 (Ch. 15 on Aaron Spelling), pp. 163–169; Newcomb, 1987, pp. 126–139, 459**; Newcomb, 1994, pp. 506–507; Newcomb, 2000, p. 564; Orlik, 2001, pp. 208–209; Paietta & Kauppila, 1999, p. 338; Pounds, 1999, p. 141; Rafkin, 1998, pp. 88–91, 119*; Sackett, 1993, pp. 268–269; Spelling, 1996, pp. 125–130**; Also in Bianculli, 1996, Terrace, 1993

Love Boat: The New Wave

Wild, 1999, p. 114

Love Connection

Henderson & Mazzeo, 1990, pp. 21–23; White, 1992, pp. 9, 52–68 (passim), 75–81 (passim), 60–61, 64–66*

Love Is a Many-Splendored Thing

Matelski, 1999, p. 44

Love of Life

Allen, 1985, p. 75; Edmondson &

Rounds, 1973, pp. 160, 173, 176–178, 204–214**; Edmondson & Rounds, 1976, pp. 133, 151–157, 161–162, 204–213**; Kuney, 1990, pp. 111–112, 113–114, 123, 126; Matelski, 1999, p. 44; Rose, 1999, pp. 11–14, 24; Williams, 1992, p. 26; Also in Bianculli, 1996

Love on a Rooftop
Castleman & Podrazik, 1982, p. 194; Lisanti & Paul, 2002, p. 90; Smith, 1989, p. 79; Also in Eisner & Krinsky, 1984, Terrace, 1993

Love, Sidney
Abelman, 1998, p. 64; Capsuto, 2000, pp. 160–165**; Chunovic, 2000, p. 90; Gross, 2001, p. 177; Hamamoto, 1989, p. 135; Harris, 1989, p. 59; Harris, 1994, p. 66; Lester, 1996, p. 154; Lichter, Lichter, & Rothman, 1991, pp. 37–38; Lichter, Lichter, & Rothman, 1994, p. 94; Rowland & Watkins, 1984, pp. 154–155; Schwartz, 1999, pp. 129–130; Turow, 1984, p. 95; Also in Terrace, 1993

Love Story
Gianakos, 1978, pp. 747–748

Love That Bob *see* **Bob Cummings Show**

Love That Jill
Kulzer, 1992, p. 72; Also in Terrace, 1993

Love Thy Neighbor
IN Terrace, 1993

Loving
Abelman, 1998, p. 378; James, 1991; Matelski, 1988, pp. 128–132*; Matelski, 1999, p. 44; Rouverol, 1984, pp. 157–158; Rouverol, 1992, pp. 183–220**; Williams, 1992, pp. 57–58, 83–84, 91–92, 121, 132, 163, 169–170*

Lucan
Gianakos, 1981, pp. 248; Also in Terrace, 1993

Lucas Tanner
Gianakos, 1978, pp. 758–759; Gianakos, 1978, pp. 758–759; Lichter, Lichter, & Rothman, 1994, p. 256

Lucie Arnaz Show, The
Paietta & Kauppila, 1999, p. 338; Also in Terrace, 1993

Lucy Show, The *see also* **I Love Lucy, Here's Lucy**
Adir, 1988, pp. 21–22; Ball, 1996, pp. 277–279; Brady, 1994, pp. 278–80, 285–307 (passim)**; Doty, 1993, pp. 45, 120 (note 20); Erickson, 2000, p. 53; Harris, 1991, pp. 268–272, 276–279, 282, 286–287**; Kulzer, 1992, pp. 35, 41–44; Lichter, Lichter, & Rothman, 1991, pp. 63, 109, 140; Lichter, Lichter, & Rothman, 1994, p. 127; McCrohan, 1990, pp. 169–172*; Museum of Television and Radio, 1991, p. 241; Pegg, 2002, pp. 126–127, 341–343; Sackett, 1993, p. 117; Sanders & Gilbert, 1993, pp. 235–237, 253–264, 268, 270–275, 278–279, 285–286, 295, 309–313**; Also in Eisner & Krinsky, 1984

Luigi
Heldenfels, 1994, p. 35

M Squad
Gianakos, 1981, pp. 378–383; Meyers, 1981, pp. 42–43; Rovin, 1977b, p. 57–58

MacGruder & Loud
Cuklanz, 2000, pp. 39, 84, 114; Gianakos, 1992, pp. 384–387; Klobas, 1988, p. 258; Also in Terrace, 1993

MacGyver
Gianakos, 1992, pp. 397–398; Hamamoto, 1994, pp. 187–188; Harris, 1994, p. 232; Lembo, 2000, p. 172; Pearl & Pearl, 1999, pp. 126, 157–158; Vane & Gross, 1994, p. 146; Wahl, 1995, pp 9, 59; Also in Terrace, 1993

Mackenzies of Paradise Cove, The
Hamamoto, 1994, p. 19; Also in Terrace, 1993

Mackenzie's Raiders
Yoggy, 1995, pp. 162–163

Mad About You
Abt & Mustazza, 1997, p. 45; Bryant & Bryant, 2001, pp. 186, 189; Capsuto, 2000, p. 365; Chunovic, 2000, pp. 130–133*; Erickson, 2000, pp. 288–289; Friedman, 2002, pp. 269–270; Gabler, Rich & Antler, 2000, pp. 47, 62, 65–66; Isaacs, 1999, pp. 46–47; Lichter, Lichter, & Rothman, 1994, p. 38; Thompson, 1996, p. 181; Wild, 1999, pp. 123–125; Wolff, 1996, pp. 49–58 (script)**; Also in Terrace, 1993, Terrace, 2000

Madame's Place
IN Terrace, 1993

Maggie Winters
IN Terrace, 2000

Magician, The
Gianakos, 1978, pp. 740–741; Martindale, 1991, pp. 285–288; Rovin, 1977b, p. 138; Also in Terrace, 1993

Magnificent Montague, The
Everitt, 2001, pp. 59–60, 136–139, 177–179*

Magnum, P.I.
Allen, 1987, pp. 52, 54, 61–62, 261–266**; Allen, 1992, pp. 84, 293–297 (passim); Blum & Lindheim, 1987, p. 144; Britos, 2001**; Caldwell, 1995, p. 18; Carey, 1988, pp. 91–95, 96–100 (passim)*; Collins & Javna, 1989, pp. 32–34; Craig, 1992, pp. 105–106; Edelman & Kupferberg, 1996, pp. 236–237; Ferre, 1990, pp. 37–38; Fiske, 1987, pp. 205, 213; Gianakos, 1983, pp. 192–195*; Gianakos, 1987, pp. 249–253*; Gianakos, 1992, pp. 327–329*; Gunter & Wober, 1988, pp. 26–30 (passim), 40–42; Hamamoto, 1994, p. 19; Javna, 1985, p. 241; Klobas, 1988, pp. 267–269, 382–383, 406–407*; Lester, 1996, p. 39; Marc & Thompson, 1992 (Ch. 16 on Glen Larson), pp. 171–178; Marris & Thornham, 2000, p. 411; Meyers, 1981, pp. 266–267; Newcomb, 1987, pp. 112–125**; Pearl & Pearl, 1999, pp. 53–54, 175, 177–178*; Roman, 1996, p. 29; Rose, 1985, p. 47; Sackett, 1993, pp. 274–275; Spigel & Mann, 1992, p. 231; Sumser, 1996, pp. 68–69, 105; Wahl, 1995, p. 59; Also in Bianculli, 1996, Terrace, 1993

Mail Story, The
Gianakos, 1987, pp. 371–372

Major Dad
Mellencamp, 1992, pp. 371–372; Steenland, 1990, p. 13; Also in Terrace, 1993, Terrace, 2000

Major Del Conway of the Flying Tigers
IN Terrace, 1993

Make Room for Daddy
Alley & Brown, 2001, p. 21; Bogle, 2001, pp. 48–50*; Burns, 1990, p 277; Castleman & Podrazik, 1982, pp. 83–84, 118–119*; Foreman, 1997, pp. 121–122; Goldenson, 1991, pp. 119–121; Hamamoto, 1989, pp. 39–41; Hawes, 2002, p. 80; Heldenfels, 1994, pp. 35–36; Jackson, 1982; Jones, 1992, pp. 104–107, 136–137*; Kulzer, 1992, pp. 11–15*; Marling, 1994, p. 155; McCrohan, pp. 117–122**; Mitz, 1980, pp. 87–93**; Panati, 1991, p. 305; Pegg, 2002, p. 148; Putterman, 1995, pp. 96, 105; Rafkin, 1998, pp. 34–35; Sackett, 1993, pp. 70–71; Spigel & Mann, 1992, pp. 10, 20; Spigel, 1992, see index, especially pp. 172–176**; Thomas, 1991, pp. 11–13, 20, 186–199, 206–213, 215, 219–221**; Also in Bianculli, 1996, Eisner & Krinsky, 1984, Terrace, 1993

Makin' It
IN Terrace, 1993

Making a Living
Lichter, Lichter, & Rothman, 1994, p. 92

Making the Grade
Levinson & Link, 1986, pp. 90–92 (Gary David Goldberg interview)

Malcolm and Eddie
Means Coleman, 2000, p. 121; Walters, 2001, pp. 27–28; Also in Terrace, 2000

Malcolm in the Middle
Bryant & Bryant, 2001, pp. 183, 186; Chunovic, 2000, pp. 163–164

Malibu Run
Gianakos, 1978, pp. 302–304; Mehling, 1962, pp. 144–146

Malibu Shores
Owen, 1997, p. 155

Mama
Alley & Brown, 2001, p. 13; Castleman & Podrazik, 1982, p. 43; Hamamoto, 1989, pp. 28–30*; Hawes, 2001, p. 33; Heldenfels, 1994, pp. 8, 38; Jones, 1992, pp. 43–46*; Lichter, Lichter, & Rothman, 1991, pp. 53, 234; Lichter, Lichter, & Rothman, 1994, p. 114; Martin, 1980**; Mitz, 1980, pp. 17–21*; Panati, 1991, pp. 244–245; Press, 1991, pp. 32–33, 156–157; Skutch, 1998, pp. 59–61; Spigel & Mann, 1992, pp. ix–x, 71, 80–83, 89–92, 99–102**; U.S. Department of Health…, 1982, p. 267; Wilk, 1976, pp. 43–51*; Also in Bianculli, 1996

Mama's Boy
Hamamoto, 1989, pp. 135–136

Mama's Family
Hamamoto, 1989, p. 131; Also in Terrace, 1993

Man Against Crime
Barnouw, 1990, pp. 131–134*; Gianakos, 1983, pp. 249–251*; Hawes, 2001, p. 33; Hawes, 2002, p. 110; Jarvis & Joseph, 1998, p. 91; Kulzer, 1992, pp. 7–9; Marc, 1984, pp. 71–72; Marc, 1996, pp. 71–72; Meyers, 1981, pp. 3–4; Rose, 1985, pp. 35–36; Rovin, 1977b, p. 20

Man and the Challenge
Gianakos, 1978, pp. 228–229; Lichter, Lichter, & Rothman, 1994,

pp. 259, 373–374*; Mehling, 1962, pp. 146–147; Paietta & Kauppila, 1999, pp. 338–339

Man and the City, The
Castleman & Podrazik, 1982, p. 231; Gianakos, 1978, pp. 700–701; Lichter, Lichter, & Rothman, 1991, p. 239; Lichter, Lichter, & Rothman, 1994, pp. 342–343; Rodriguez, 1997, pp. 60–61

Man Behind the Badge, The
Gianakos, 1983, pp. 294–297*; Hawes, 2002, p. 107

Man Called Hawk, A
Bogle, 2001, pp. 307–308; Dates & Barlow, 1990, pp. 260–261; Dates & Barlow, 1993, p. 283

Man Called Shenandoah, A
Fagen, 1996, p. 104; Gianakos, 1978, pp. 490–492; Jackson, 1994, p. 171; Rovin, 1977b, pp. 95–96: Yoggy, 1995, pp. 227–228; Also in Lentz, 1997, Terrace, 1993, West, 1987

Man Called Sloane, A
Gianakos, 1981, p. 281; Also in Terrace, 1993

Man from Atlantis
Gianakos, 1981, pp. 230–231; Lichter, Lichter, & Rothman, 1994, p. 260; Also in Terrace, 1993

Man from Blackhawk, The
Gianakos, 1978, pp. 268–269; Jackson, 1994, p. 141; Also in Lentz, 1997, West, 1987

Man from Interpol, The
Gianakos, 1978, pp. 278–279

Man from U.N.C.L.E., The
Buxton, 1990, pp. 107–115**; Castleman & Podrazik, 1982, p. 175; Creeber, 2001, pp. 20–21; Erickson, 2000, pp. 98–99, 101, 102; Gianakos, 1978, pp. 453–460**; Gottfried, 1999, pp. 153–154; Hamamoto, 1994, pp. 118–119; Heitland, 1987, whole book**; Javna, 1985, pp. 36–39*; Lisanti & Paul, 2002, 24, 57–58, 80, 84–85, 86, 89–90, 99, 102, 109–111, 123–124, 126, 128, 139, 150, 152, 153–154, 158–160, 164, 170, 171–172, 196–197, 202, 205–206, 211–212, 216, 218, 220, 229, 231, 238, 265, 270, 272, 285, 293–294, 311–312; Meyers, 1981, pp. 96–104**; Miller, 2000, pp. 34–36*; Newcomb, 1976, p. 229; Newcomb, 1979, p. 295; Newcomb & Alley, 1983, pp. 89–90, 93–94; Osgerby & Gough-Yates, 2001, p. 199; Rovin, 1977b, p. 90; Smith, 1997, p. 73; Stempel, 1992, pp. 102–103; Story, 1993, pp. 98–111**; Worland, 1989; Also in Bianculli, 1996

Man in a Suitcase
Gianakos, 1978, p. 614; Rovin, 1977b, pp. 123–124

Man in the Family, The
IN Terrace, 1993

Man of the People
IN Terrace, 1993

Man Undercover
Gianakos, 1981, p. 266

Man Who Never Was, The
Gianakos, 1978, p. 556

Man with a Camera
Gianakos, 1981, pp. 395–396; Lichter, Lichter, & Rothman, 1991,

pp. 195–196; Lichter, Lichter, & Rothman, 1994, p. 289

Mancuso, FBI
Pearl & Pearl, 1999, p. 191; Also in Terrace, 1993

Manhunt
Gianakos, 1992, pp. 455–457

Manhunter, The
Gianakos, 1978, pp. 760–762; Martindale, 1991, pp. 288–290; Meyers, 1981, p. 206

Manimal
Gianakos, 1987, p. 337

Mann and Machine
IN Terrace, 1993

Mannix
Andrews, 1986, p. 126; Bogle, 2001, pp. 137–139*; Castleman & Podrazik, 1982, p. 202; Collins & Javna, 1989, pp. 41–43; Gianakos, 1978, pp. 577–585**; Klobas, 1988, p. 271; Marc & Thompson, 1992 (Ch. 17 on Richard Levinson and Wm. Link), pp. 180–192; Martindale, 1991, pp. 291–308; Meehan, 1983, p. 173; Meyers, 1981, pp. 137–138; Rovin, 1977b, p. 119; Sackett, 1993, p. 187; Sanders & Gilbert, 1993, pp. 294–295; Sumser, 1996, pp. 66–67, 119–120, 145–146 Also in Bianculli, 1996

Many Happy Returns
IN Eisner & Krinsky, 1984, Terrace, 1993

Many Loves of Dobie Gillis, The
Castleman & Podrazik, 1982, pp. 137–138; Craig, 1992, p. 99; Crotty, 1995; Hamamoto, 1989, pp. 76–78; Javna, 1985, pp. 72–75*; Jones, 1992, pp. 150–155**; Mitz, 1980, pp. 155–158*; Panati, 1991, pp. 310–311; Putterman, 1995, pp. 34–38*; Terrace, 1993; Also in Bianculli, 1996, Eisner & Krinsky, 1984

Marcus Welby, M.D.
Adler, 1976, pp. 99–102*; Adler, 1981, pp. 235–236, 238; Alley, 1977, pp. 63–64, 67–70, 73*; Bodroghkozy, 2001, p. 90; Capsuto, 2000, pp. 5, 91–94, 106–109, 114, 120**; Castleman & Podrazik, 1982, pp. 213–214; Chunovic, 2000, pp. 69–70; Fox, 2001, p. 155; Gianakos, 1978, pp. 649–656**; Gianakos, 1981, pp. 121–122; Gross, 2001, pp. 47–48; Himmelstein, 1994, p. 220; Holtzman, 2000, p. 301; Howe, 1983, p. 106; Kalisch, Kalisch, & Scobey, 1983, pp. 50–58, 193**; Lichter, Lichter, & Rothman, 1991, pp. 36, 159–160; Lichter, Lichter, & Rothman, 1994, pp. 93, 245–246*; Malmsheimer, 1988, pp. 131–132; Martin, 1980**; McCrohan, 1990, pp. 187–197**; Meehan, 1983, pp. 60, 69–71, 173–174*; Montgomery, 1989, pp. 79–85*; Newcomb, 1976, pp. 20–21; Newcomb, 2000, pp. 509–510; Newcomb & Alley, 1983, pp. 74–95 (passim)*; Paietta & Kauppila, 1999, p. 339; Real, 1977, see index, especially pp. 120–124**; Rose, 1985, pp. 79–80; Rovin, 1977b, p. 124; Sackett, 1993, pp. 162–163; Schneider, 2001, p. 95; Stark, 1997, p. 292; Suman & Rossman, 2000, p. 135; Tinker & Rukeyser, 1994, p. 82; Tuchman, Daniels, & Benet, 1978, p. 247; Turow, 1989, pp. 107, 108–133, 138, 158**; Vane & Gross, 1994, p. 176; Also in Bianculli, 1996

Margie
IN Terrace, 1993

Mariah
Paietta & Kauppila, 1999, p. 339

Markham
Gianakos, 1981, pp. 398–401

Married People
IN Terrace, 1993, Terrace, 2000

Married...with Children
Abt & Mustazza, 1997, p. 45; Block, 1990, see index, especially pp. 216–220*; Bryant & Bryant, 2001, pp. 172–173; Capsuto, 2000, pp. 250–251; Chunovic, 2000, pp. 113–116**; Crotty, 1995; Davis, 2001, pp. 16–17; Fiske, 1994, pp. 114–121**; Himmelstein, 1994, pp. 117, 119, 132–134, 137*; Holtzman, 2000, p. 129; Johnston, 2000, p. 59; Jones, 1992, pp. 265–266; Lichter, Lichter, & Rothman, 1991, p. 91; Lichter, Lichter, & Rothman, 1994, pp. 20, 41, 42, 162; Lusane, 1999; Marc, 1997, pp. 191–192, 195; Means Coleman, 2002, pp. 159–160; Newcomb, 1994, pp. 137–138, 212–222**; Nightingale, 1996, pp. 127–129; Owen, 1997, p. 44; Panati, 1991, pp. 482–483; Schneider, 2001, p. 97; Schwartz, 1999, p. 131; Silverblatt, Ferry, & Finan, 1999, p 176; Steenland, 1990, pp. 24–25; Suman, 1997, p. 90; Suman & Rossman, 2000, p. 135; Tabarlet, 1993; Vane & Gross, 1994, pp. 114, 146; Zook, 1999, pp. 37–38; Also in Bianculli, 1996, Terrace, 1993, Terrace, 2000

Marshal of Gunsight Pass, The
Jackson, 1994, p. 36; Also in Lentz, 1997, West, 1987

Marshall Chronicles, The
IN Terrace, 1993

Martha Raye Show, The
Butler, 1991, pp. 348–354*; Everitt, 2001, pp. 78, 86, 89–97**; Horowitz, 1997, pp. 128–129; Pitrone, 1999, pp. 85–86, 91, 93–95, 98, 105–107, 111–112*; Spigel & Mann, 1992, pp. ix, 55–63**

Martial Law
Lechner, 2000, pp. 254–255

Martin
Bogle, 2001, pp. 414–422**; Bryant & Bryant, 2001, pp. 215–216; Davis, 2001, p. 21; Guida, 2000, p. 227; Hiebert, 1999, p. 376; Lichter, Lichter, & Rothman, 1994, p. 57; Martin, 1980**; Means Coleman, 2000, pp. 7, 116–117, 125, 134, 156, 170–171, 175–176*; Smith, 1997*; Ward, 1995; Zook, 1999, pp. 3–62**

Martin Kane, Private Eye
Hawes, 2001, p. 24; Hawes, 2002, p. 110; Marc, 1996, pp. 72–73; Martin, 1980**; Meyers, 1981, pp. 2–4; Rose, 1985, p. 35; Rovin, 1977b, pp. 20, 37; Also in Terrace, 1993

Mary
Newcomb, 1987, pp. 69–71; Also in Terrace, 1993

Mary Hartman, Mary Hartman
Abelman, 1998, p. 376; Buckman, 1984, pp. 147–148; Caldwell, 1995, pp. 43–45*; Castleman & Podrazik, 1982, pp. 277–278*; Coakley, 1977, pp. 24–49 (passim), 93–97, 155–156, 186–187, 192*; Conrad, 1982, pp. 77–78; Edmondson & Rounds, 1976, pp.

168–185, 244**; Gilbert, 1976, pp. 172–184**; Himmelstein, 1984, pp. 140–144*; Himmelstein, 1994, pp. 180–184*; Javna, 1985, pp. 130–133*; Jones, 1992, pp. 234–235; Kaminsky, 1985, pp. 95–96, 108–109; Kellner, 1990, pp. 58–59; Marc & Thompson, 1992 (Ch. 4 on Norman Lear), pp. 49–60; Miller, 1980, p. 191; Newcomb, 1979, pp. 94–95, 97–106, 111–117**; Newcomb, 1982, pp. 68–70, 128–130 (passim), 148–157, 417–421**; Newcomb, 1987, pp. 496–499, 546*; Newcomb & Alley, 1983, p. 195; Putterman, 1995, pp. 152–153; Rose, 1999, pp. 79–81; Taylor, 1989, pp. 93–97*; U.S. Congress, 1977a, p. 28; Williams, 1992, p. 32; Also in Bianculli, 1996, Terrace, 1993

Mary Tyler Moore Hour, The

Newcomb, 1987, pp. 71, 81

Mary Tyler Moore Show, The

Adler, 1976, pp. 27–28, 40–57, especially pp. 40–45**; Adler, 1981, pp. 65–66; Allen, 1987, pp. 128–129; Allen, 1992, p. 156; Alley, 1977, pp. 30–31, 41, 47, 148–150*; Alley & Brown, 1989, whole book**; Alley & Brown, 2001, p. 100; Andrews, 1986, pp. 134–135; Batra, 1987, pp. 112–114*; Bedell, 1981, pp. 63–67*; Bennett, 1996, pp. 115–116; Caldwell, 1995, pp. 56–57; Capsuto, 2000, p. 64; Carey, 1988, pp. 126–144**; Castleman & Podrazik, 1982, pp. 223–226**; Chunovic, 2000, p. 67; Coakley, 1977, pp. 52–53; Crotty, 1995; Daniel, 1996, pp. 19–22 (passim), 31–34*; Daniel, 1996, pp. 20–23, 33; Dates & Barlow, 1990, p. 278; Davis, 2001, pp. 11, 97; Doty, 1993, pp. 41–42, 48–51, 121 (note 25), 122 (note 27)*; Dow, 1996, pp. xii, xvii, xxii, xxiv, 5, 24–58, 64, 118, 209**; Fowles, 1982, pp. 103–104, 110–115*; Fowles, 1992, pp. 121–126 (same as Fowles 1982); Freeman, 1980, pp. 134–135; Gabler, Rich & Antler, 2000, p. 36; Gitlin, 1983, see index*; Gross & Woods, 1999, p. 339; Hamamoto, 1989, pp. 113–115*; Haralovich & Rabinovitz, 1999, p. 146; Himmelstein, 1984, pp. 113–119; Himmelstein, 1994, pp. 157–158; Horowitz, 1997, p. 121; Isaacs, 1999, p. 15; Jarvik, 1997, p. 271; Jarvis & Joseph, 1998, p. 173; Javna, 1985, pp. 160–164*; Jones, 1992, pp. 193–202, 212–213, 230–231**; Kassel, 1993, pp. 9–10; Kutulas, 1998; Leibman, 1995, p. 262; Lichter, Lichter, & Rothman, 1991, pp. 53–54, 60–61, 66, 110–111, 177*; Lichter, Lichter, & Rothman, 1994, pp. 115, 124, 184–185, 254; Marc, 1989, pp. 166–174**; Marc, 1997, pp. 137–142, 143–144**; Marc & Thompson, 1992 (Ch. 5 on James L. Brooks), pp. 61–69, especially pp. 62–63; Meehan, 1983, pp. 51–52, 174–175; Meyers, 1999, p. 274; Miles, 1975, pp. 71–73 (Nov. 2, 1974, show); Miller, 1980, pp. 49–53, 59, 77–78, 127**; Mitz, 1980, pp. 261–268**; Newcomb, 1976, pp. 7, 14–16, 43–53**; Newcomb, 1979, pp. 61–62, 64–73, 528**; Newcomb, 1982, pp. 70–72, 86–87; Newcomb, 1987, pp. 52–57, 64–65, 69–71, 76–78, 81–84, 85–86, 109–110, 340**; Newcomb, 2000, p. 581; Newcomb & Alley, 1983, pp. 197–221 (passim), especially pp. 198–207**; O'Dell, 1997, pp. 212–213; Osgerby & Gough-Yates, 2001, p. 96; Oskamp, 1988, pp. 106–107, 114–115; Owen, 1997, p. 31; Panati, 1991, pp. 422–423; Pearl & Pearl, 1999, pp. 104, 131; Pegg, 2002, pp. 157–167, 292**; Press, 1991, pp. 36–37, 78–80; Putterman, 1995, pp. 44, 107–113**; Rafkin, 1998, pp. 69–70; Rannow,

1999, p. 168; Roman, 1996, p. 29; Root, 1979, p. 158; Rose, 1985, p. 112; Rowland & Watkins, 1984, pp. 256–257; Rubin, 1980, pp. 201–202; Sackett, 1993, pp. 192–193; Schwartz, 1999, pp. 133–134; Seger, 1996, pp. 155, 199; Sklar, 1980, p. 24; Smith, 1989, pp. 48–49; Sochen, 1987, pp. 81–82, 91; Sochen, 1999, pp. 147–148, 166–169, 177–178, 180, 181*; Spigel & Mann, 1992, pp. 207–208; Staiger, 2000, p. 7; Stark, 1997, pp. 118, 167–171, 240**; Stempel, 1992, pp. 157–160; Taylor, 1989, pp. 58, 59, 85, 97, 114–125, 126–127, 141–142, 146**; Thompson, 1996, pp. 29, 49–50, 51, 54, 55–56*; Tinker & Rukeyser, 1994, pp. 87–95, 99, 100–102**; U.S. Department of Health…, 982, p. 280; Vane & Gross, 1994, p. 219; Winship, 1988, pp. 80–86; Wittebols, 1998, pp. 7, 8, 9; Also in Bianculli, 1996, Eisner & Krinsky, 1984, Terrace, 1993

M*A*S*H

Abelman, 1998, p. 131; Adler, 1976, pp. 45–57, especially pp. 45–48**; Alda & Alda, 1983, whole book**; Alley, 1977, pp. 33, 48, 141–147**; Batra, 1987, pp. 108–112*; Bedell, 1981, pp. 67–72*; Bennett, 1996, pp. 125–128; Berger, 1987, pp. 72–77**; Bodroghkozy, 2001, pp. 74, 233–235, 238*; Burks, 1990; Caldwell, 1995, pp. 61–62; Carey, 1988, pp. 128–130; Castleman & Podrazik, 1982, pp. 240–241, 243, 264**; Chunovic, 2000, pp. 73, 74–77*; Craig, 1992, pp. 102–103; Creeber, 2001, p. 25; Croteau & Hoynes, 2000, pp. 251–252; Daniel, 1996, pp. 24–25; Davis, 2001, pp. 11–12, 141; Fiske, 1987, p. 211; Friedman, 2002, pp. 263–266*; Gelbart, 1998, pp. 25–28, 30–61**; Gitlin, 1983, see index*; Hamamoto, 1989, pp. 118–119; Hamamoto, 1994, pp. 23–25*; Harris, 1989, pp. 51, 104; Harris, 1994, pp. 58, 109; Himmelstein, 1984, pp. 132–140**; Himmelstein, 1994, pp. 117, 173–180**; Holtzman, 2000, p. 222; Horton & McDougal, 1998, pp. 310–326**; Javna, 1985, pp. 178–181*; Jones, 1992, pp. 237–241, 244–248**; Kalisch, Kalisch, & Scobey, 1983, pp. 117–130, 195–198**; Kalter, 1988, whole book**; Klobas, 1988, pp. 46–47; Kutulas, 1998; Lembo, 2000, p. 180; Lichter, Lichter, & Rothman, 1991, pp. 21, 121, 164, 256, 272–273, 275, 290, 296*; Lichter, Lichter, & Rothman, 1994, pp. 83, 198, 250–251, 363, 383–385*; Marc, 1989, pp. 188–199**; Marc, 1997, pp. 137, 155–164, 203**; Martin, 1981; Mayerle, 1991; Meehan, 1983, pp. 52–55, 176–177*; Miles, 1975, pp. 67–68 (Nov. 3, 1973, show); Miller, 1980, pp. 74, 114, 192, 193–194; Mitz, 1980, pp. 297–305**; Montgomery, 1989, p. 189; Newcomb, 1979, p. 67; Newcomb, 1982, pp. 75, 158–166**; Newcomb, 1987, pp. 87–91 (passim), 108, 180–193, 462**; Newcomb, 1994, pp. 88–98, 509**; Newcomb, 2000, pp. 170–181**; Owen, 1997, p. 31; Paietta & Kauppila, 1999, pp. 339–340; Panati, 1991, pp. 421–422; Pearl & Pearl, 1999, p. 30; Pegg, 2002, pp. 98, 100–104**; Putterman, 1995, pp. 117, 118–119; Rafkin, 1998, pp. 83–85; Reiss, 1983, whole book**; Rose, 1985, pp. 83, 112–113; Rose, 1999, pp. 91–92; Rowland & Watkins, 1984, pp. 241–245 (passim), 250, 255, 257–259, 284–287**; Rutstein, 1974, pp. 99–100; Sackett, 1993, pp. 202–203; Schrag, 1991; Sison, 1985; Stark, 1997, pp. 209–214**; Stempel, 1992, pp. 160–168**; Strait, 1983, pp. 81, 98, 111–161, 166–197, 204–210, 225–226, 232–233**; Taylor, 1989, pp. 127–130, 140, 143*; Thompson, 1996, pp. 29,

55, 57, 61, 114, 145*; Turow, 1989, pp. 195, 196–197, 205–215, 224–228**; Vane & Gross, 1994, p. 219; Wahl, 1995, pp. 6–7; Williams, 1982, pp. 140–142; Winship, 1988, pp. 72–75; Wittebols, 1998, whole book**; Worland, 1989; Also in Bianculli, 1996, Eisner & Krinsky, 1984, Terrace, 1993

Mask, The
Gianakos, 1980, p. 387

Masquerade
Gianakos, 1987, p. 335

Master, The
Gianakos, 1987, pp. 342–343

Masterpiece Playhouse
Gianakos, 1980, p. 246

Matlock
Bell, 1992; Guida, 2000, p . 221; Jarvis & Joseph, 1998, pp. 55–64, 235–237**; Riggs, 1998, p. 20; Steenland, 1990, p. 45; Also in Terrace, 1993

Matt Helm
Gianakos, 1981, pp. 168–169; Also in Terrace, 1993

Matt Houston
Cuklanz, 2000, pp. 70–71; Gianakos, 1987, pp. 293–296*; Gianakos, 1992, pp. 352–353; Klobas, 1988, pp. 81–82; Lichter, Lichter, & Rothman, 1991, p. 143; Lichter, Lichter, & Rothman, 1994, p. 225; Marc & Thompson, 1992 (Ch. 15 on Aaron Spelling); Spelling, 1996, pp. 139–140; Sumser, 1996, pp. 105, 107; U.S. Congress, 1985, pp. 46–47; Yoggy, 1995, p. 571; Also in Terrace, 1993

Matt Lincoln
Gianakos, 1978, pp. 677–678; Kalisch, Kalisch, & Scobey, 1983, pp. 60–61; Paietta & Kauppila, 1999, p. 340; Turow, 1989, pp. 148–149

Maude
Adler, 1981, pp. 225–229*; Alley, 1977, pp. 35, 46, 129–133, 138–141**; Alley & Brown, 2001, pp. 81–87, 157, 158**; Bedell, 1981, pp. 82–84; Castleman & Podrazik, 1982, p. 255, 239–240*; Coakley, 1977, pp. 47, 67, 103; Crotty, 1995; Crown, 1999, p. 49; Cruz & Lewis, 1994, p. 59; Dow, 1996, pp. 61–63; Haralovich & Rabinovitz, 1999, p. 160; Harris, 1991, p. 298; Hendershot, 1998, p. 19; Himmelstein, 1994, p. 117; Jones, 1992, pp. 228–229; Kutulas, 1998; Leibman, 1995, p. 262; Leonard, 1997, p. 195; Lichter, Lichter, & Rothman, 1991, pp. 28, 73; Lichter, Lichter, & Rothman, 1994, p. 140; Marc, 1989, p. 184; Marc, 1997, p. 152; Marc & Thompson, 1992 (Ch. 4 on Norman Lear), pp. 49–60; Martin, 1980**; Meehan, 1983, pp. 61–63, 176; Miles, 1975, pp. 40–42 (Nov. 27, 1973, show); Miller, 1980, pp. 190, 191; Mitz, 1980, pp. 307–311*; Montgomery, 1989, pp. 27–50**; Newcomb, 1976, pp. 17–19, 26–34**; Newcomb, 1979, pp. 32–35*; Newcomb, 1982, pp. 24–27*; Newcomb, 1987, pp. 30–33, 56*; Panati, 1991, pp. 422–423; Pegg, 2002, pp. 346–355 (passim); Puette, 1992, pp. 54, 180; Sackett, 1993, pp. 194–195; Schwartz, 1999, p. 134; Sklar, 1980, pp. 5–6; Smith, 1997a; Sochen, 1987, pp. 90–91; Sochen, 1999, pp. 161–162; Taylor, 1989, pp. 86–87; Thurer, 1994, p. 266; Waldrep, 2000, p. 195; Also in Bianculli, 1996, Eisner & Krinsky, 1984

Maverick
Anderson, 1994, pp. 229–237, 249, 274–276**; Aquila, 1996, pp. 173–174; Broughton, 1986, pp. 165–178 (passim); Buscombe & Pearson, 1998, p. 129; Castleman & Podrazik, 1982, p. 116; Cavallo, 1999, p. 39; Fitzgerald & Magers, 2002, pp. 60–69, 169–170, 231; Gianakos, 1978, pp. 163–166*; Goldenson, 1991, pp. 155–161*; Hawes, 2002, pp. 132–133; Heil, 2001, pp. 9–14, 26–32, 35–41, 45–50, 56–126**; Jackson, 1994, pp. 89–91, 207–210; Jarvis & Joseph, 1998, pp. 207, 209–212*; Javna, 1985, pp. 94–97*; Lichter, Lichter, & Rothman, 1991, p. 196; Lichter, Lichter, & Rothman, 1994, p. 289; Magers & Fitzgerald, 1999, pp. 16, 18; Marc & Thompson, 1992 (Ch. 13 on Roy Huggins), pp. 141–151, especially pp. 144–146*; McDonald, 1987, p. 63; Meehan, 1983, pp. 85–86, 91–92, 101–102, 165–166; Osgerby & Gough-Yates, 2001, p. 148; Robertson, 1994, whole book**; Rose, 1985, p. 61; Rovin, 1977b, p. 52; Sackett, 1993, pp. 84–85; Stempel, 1992, pp. 64–67*; Strait, 1985, pp. 51, 56–61, 73–92, 95–103, 107–108, 112–118, 122–131, 153–156, 164–165**; Thompson, 1990, pp. 62–69 (passim); Yoggy, 1995, pp. 233–247**; Also in Bianculli, 1996, Lentz, 1997, Terrace, 1993, West, 1987

Max Headroom
Caldwell, 1995, p. 13; Dienst, 1994, p. 92; Friedman, 2002, p. 270; Schultz, 2000, p. 79; Sconce, 2000, pp. 188–191*; Spigel & Mann, 1992, pp. 231–233; Also in Bianculli, 1996, Terrace, 1993

Max Monroe: Loose Cannon
IN Terrace, 1993

Maya
Rovin, 1977b, pp. 116–117

Maybe This Time
Cotter, 1997, pp. 471–472; Also in Terrace, 2000

Mayberry, R.F.D.
Fernandes & Robinson, 1999, whole book**; Sackett, 1993, p. 156; Schultz, 2000, p. 125; Spignelli, 1987 (passim); Story, 1993, pp. 16, 28; Also in Eisner & Krinsky, 1984

McClain's Law
Arness, 2001, pp. 153, 190; Cuklanz, 2000, p. 102; Gianakos, 1983, pp. 216–217

McCloud
Castleman & Podrazik, 1982, p. 232; Marc & Thompson, 1992 (Ch. 16 on Glen Larson), pp. 171–178 (Ch. 17 on Levinson & Link), pp. 180–192; Martindale, 1991, pp. 310–315; Meyers, 1981, pp. 164–165; Miller, 1980, p. 131; Sackett, 1993, pp. 198–199; Stempel, 1992, pp. 175–176

McHale's Navy
Adir, 1988, p. 110; Castleman & Podrazik, 1982, p. 159; Jones, 1992, p. 171; Lichter, Lichter, & Rothman, 1994, pp. 382, 388; Pegg, 2002, pp. 55, 56, 57–60, 63*; Also in Bianculli, 1996, Eisner & Krinsky, 1984, Terrace, 1993

McKeever and the Colonel
IN Eisner & Krinsky, 1984

McMillan and Wife
Castleman & Podrazik, 1982, p. 232; Martindale, 1991, pp. 317–322*;

Meyers, 1981, pp. 165–169; Pitrone, 1999, pp. 173–175; Rovin, 1977b, pp. 129–130; Sackett, 1993, p. 199; Also in Bianculli, 1996

Me and Maxx

IN Terrace, 1993

Me and Mom

Gianakos, 1992, p. 392; Also in Terrace, 1993

Me and Mrs. C

IN Terrace, 1993

Me and the Chimp

Andrews, 1980, pp. 84–89*; Bedell, 1981, pp. 89–90; Crown, 1999, p. 45; Paietta & Kauppila, 1999, p. 340; Rafkin, 1998, pp. 64–66; Thompson, 1996, p. 11

Medic

Adler, 1981, pp. 231–232; Alley, 1977, pp. 58–59, 61; Capsuto, 2000, p. 35; Creeber, 2001, p. 24; Davis, 2001, pp. 140–141; Gianakos, 1980, pp. 393–395; Kalisch, Kalisch, & Scobey, 1983, pp. 9–11, 16–17*; Lichter, Lichter, & Rothman, 1991, pp. 158, 163, 165; Lichter, Lichter, & Rothman, 1994, pp. 243, 249–250, 252*; Paietta & Kauppila, 1999, p. 340; Rose, 1985, pp. 74–75*; Rovin, 1977b, pp. 39–40; Spigel & Curtin, 1997, pp. 186–187, 189–190, 191*; Stark, 1997, p. 294; Turow, 1989, pp. 25–26, 29–45, 47**

Medical Center

Adler, 1976, pp. 84–86, 101–102*; Adler, 1981, pp. 80–81, 237–238; Alley, 1977, pp. 47, 66–68, 73*; Capsuto, 2000, pp. 63–64, 133–134; Cullingford, 1984, pp. 51–52; Fowles, 1982, pp. 123–124; Fowles, 1992, p. 135 (same as Fowles 1982); Gianakos, 1978, pp. 656–661**; Gianakos, 1981, pp. 113–114; Howitt, 1982, pp. 124–125; Kalisch, Kalisch, & Scobey, 1983, pp. 43–50, 58, 192–193**; Klobas, 1988, pp. 415–416; Lichter, Lichter, & Rothman, 1991, pp. 117, 119, 159–160, 164–165; Lichter, Lichter, & Rothman, 1994, pp. 193, 195–196, 245–246, 251*; Meehan, 1983, pp. 59–60, 174; Milgram & Shotland, 1973, pp. 89–180 (model scripts)**; Miller, 1980, p. 77; Newcomb, 1979, pp. 544–546; Newcomb, 1982, pp. 537–539 (reprint of Adler, 1976); Newcomb, 1987, pp. 634–636; Newcomb, 1994, pp. 542–543; Newcomb, 2000, pp. 600–601; Paietta & Kauppila, 1999, p. 340; Pearl & Pearl, 1999, pp. 59, 184, 197, 208; Rovin, 1977b, p. 124; Sackett, 1993, pp. 178–179; Shaheen, 1984, pp. 118–119; Turow, 1989, pp. 134–135, 138, 143–147, 157–158, 177**; U.S. Congress, 1977a, p. 81

Medical Story

Adler, 1976, pp. 104–107*; Adler, 1981, pp. 240–242, 243; Alley, 1977, pp. 71–75*; Gianakos, 1981, p. 189; Himmelstein, 1994, pp. 21–23*; Kalisch, Kalisch, & Scobey, 1983, pp. 64–66; Klobas, 1988, pp. 38–39, 41; Lichter, Lichter, & Rothman, 1994, p. 246; Paietta & Kauppila, 1999, p. 340; Rose, 1985, p. 81; Turow, 1989, pp. 183–184

Medicine Ball

Paietta & Kauppila, 1999, pp. 340–341

Meet Corliss Archer

IN Terrace, 1993

Meet Millie
IN Terrace, 1993

Meet the Press
Ball, 1998, whole book**; Castleman & Podrazik, 1982, pp. 25–26; Cortes, 2000, p. 98; Kovach & Rosenstiel, 1999, pp. 4, 24–25, 29, 30, 108, 115, 140, 167, 169, 170; Lechner, 2000, p. 16; Stark, 1997, pp. 20–24*; Also in Bianculli, 1996

Melba
IN Terrace, 1993

Melrose Place
Abelman, 1998, p. 101; Capsuto, 2000, pp. 282–283, 336–338, 367–368*; Chunovic, 2000, p. 23; Croteau & Hoynes, 2000, p. 224; Gross, 2001, pp. 89, 91, 170; Gross & Woods, 1999, p. 294; Hollows, 2000, pp. 94, 97, 101; Horton & McDougal, 1998, p. 1; Johnston, 2000, p. 74; Lester, 1996, pp. 157–158; Meyers, 1999, pp. 3, 271–285**; Owen, 1997, pp. 10, 59, 60–61, 82, 95–108, 122, 170–174**; Rapping, 1994, pp. 158–160; Silverblatt, Ferry, & Finan, 1999, p 55; Spelling, 1996, pp. 111, 155, 156, 185–194**; Suman, 1997, pp. 76, 77; Thompson, 1996, p. 136; Walters, 2001, pp. 65–68*; Also in Bianculli, 1996

Men Behaving Badly
Gauntlett & Hill, 1999, p. 213

Men from Shiloh *see* **Virginian, The**

Men into Space
Gianakos, 1987, pp. 382–284*; Rovin, 1977b, pp. 74–75

Merv Griffin Show, The
Bodroghkozy, 2001, pp. 119–121; Erickson, 2000, pp. 237–239; Freeman, 1980, pp. 121–128*; Griffin, 1980, pp. 22–40, 57–66, 113–153, 219–269**; Rose, 1985, p. 335; Shanks, 1976, pp. 39, 58–61, 63–64, 193–198**; Also in Bianculli, 1996

Miami Vice
Abelman, 1998, p. 404; Auletta, 1991, pp. 351–360, especially pp. 358–360, plus see index*; Bacon-Smith, 1992, pp. 190–193*; Barker, 1999, pp. 164–165; Barnouw, 1990, pp. 513–514; Batra, 1987, pp. 72–73; Blum & Lindheim, 1987, pp. 8, 79–82, 87, 97–100 (part of script)*; Bogle, 2001, pp. 279–286**; Buxton, 1990, pp. 118, 140–160**; Caldwell, 1995, pp. 66, 87, 88; Chunovic, 2000, pp. 93–99**; Craig, 1992, pp. 31–32, 188–189; Cuklanz, 2000, pp. 41–42, 59–60, 71, 97, 110–111, 150*; Davis, 2001, pp. 108, 123; Fiske, 1987, pp. 112, 205, 221–222, 249–250, 255–262**; Gianakos, 1992, pp. 377–380*; Gitlin, 1986, pp. 151–161**; Gunter & Wober, 1988, pp. 26–30 (passim); Henderson & Mazzeo, 1990, pp. 111–117**; Himmelstein, 1994, p. 229*; Javna, 1985, p. 237; Kellner, 1995, pp. 9, 235, 238–247, 261**; Klobas, 1988, pp. 173–174, 366–367; Lembo, 2000, pp. 177, 197; Leonard, 1997, pp. 155–158, 254*; Lichter, Lichter, & Rothman, 1991, pp. 1–3, 39, 194, 214–215, 245, 250*; Lichter, Lichter, & Rothman, 1994, p. 97; Marc & Thompson, 1992 (Ch. 21 on Michael Mann), pp. 231–240; Marris & Thornham, 2000, pp. 411–412; Mendoza, 1986; Orlik, 1994, p. 62; Osgerby & Gough-Yates, 2001, p. 23; Pearl & Pearl, 1999, pp. 126, 156; Rodriguez, 1997, p. 66; Sackett, 1993, pp. 306–307; Selnow & Gilbert,

1993, pp. 36–37; Spelling, 1996, p. 173; Spigel & Mann, 1992, p. 231; Stark, 1997, pp. 245–246; Stempel, 1992, pp. 241–242; Tartikoff, 1992, pp. 77–80*; Tasker, 1998, p. 94; Tulloch, 2000, pp. 39–41; Turner, 1994, p. 39; Vande Berg & Trujillo, 1989, pp. 138–140, 174, 187–189*; Vande Berg & Wenner, 1991, pp. 273–288**; Winship, 1988, pp. 101–109; Also in Bianculli, 1996

Michael Shayne
Gianakos, 1978, pp. 317–318; Meyers, 1981, pp. 76–77; Also in Terrace, 1993

Mickey
Andrews, 1980, pp. 90–94*

Mickey Rooney Show
IN Terrace, 1993

Midnight Caller
Capsuto, 2000, pp. 223–226*; Hamamoto, 1994, pp. 256–160*; Henderson & Mazzeo, 1990, pp. 67, 69; Leonard, 1997, p. 171; Newcomb, 1994, pp. 117–133**; Ringer, 1994, pp. 95–96, 100, 147; Steenland, 1990, p. 46; White, 1992, pp. 162–167, 167–172 (passim)**; Also in Terrace, 1993

Mike Hammer, Detective
Gianakos, 1987, pp. 339–340; Gianakos, 1992, pp. 275–276; Lembo, 2000, p. 171; Meyers, 1981, p. 51; Rovin, 1977b, p. 65; Also in Terrace, 1993

Mike O'Malley Show, The
Lechner, 2000, p. 116

Millennium
Bryant & Bryant, 2001, p. 190; Muir, 2001a, pp. 467–496**

Millionaire, The
Gianakos, 1980, pp. 425–434**; Hawes, 2002, pp. 192–194; Lichter, Lichter, & Rothman, 1991, p. 149; Lichter, Lichter, & Rothman, 1994, pp. 232–233; Sackett, 1993, p. 59; Also in Bianculli, 1996, Terrace, 1993

Milton Berle ***see*** **Texaco Star Theatre**

Misadventures of Sheriff Lobo, The
Martindale, 1991, pp. 323–327; Meyers, 1981, pp. 253–254

Misery Loves Company
Cotter, 1997, p. 477

Misfits of Science, The
IN Terrace, 1993

Mission: Impossible
Andrews, 1986, p. 123; Barnouw, 1990, pp. 368–373 (passim); Bogle, 2001, pp. 127–130*; Brady, 1994, pp. 291–293; Buxton, 1990, pp. 115–117; Gianakos, 1978, pp. 536–544**; Gianakos, 1992, pp. 411–412; Javna, 1985, pp. 152–155*; Lichter, Lichter, & Rothman, 1991, pp. 116, 200, 237, 258; Lichter, Lichter, & Rothman, 1994, p. 366; Lisanti & Paul, 2002, pp. 27–28, 51–53, 98–100, 107–108, 131, 196, 197, 204, 206, 220, 301–302**; Meehan, 1983, pp. 74, 171; Meyers, 1981, pp. 122–126*; Newcomb, 1979, pp. 155–156, 408–409; Newcomb, 1987, pp. 446–447; Osgerby & Gough-Yates, 2001, pp. 104, 199–200; Pearl & Pearl, 1999, p. 126; Rodriguez, 1997, p. 61; Rovin, 1977b, pp. 109–111; Sanders & Gilbert, 1993, pp. 279–280, 284–285; Stark, 1997,

pp. 2, 133–136; Stempel, 1992, p. 104; White, 1991, whole book**; Worland, 1989; Also in Bianculli, 1996

Mississippi, The
Gianakos, 1987, pp. 318–319

Mr. Adams and Eve
Becker, 2001*; O'Dell, 1997, p. 171

Mr. & Mrs. North
Hawes, 2002, pp. 11–113; Also in Terrace, 1993

Mr. Belvedere
Kendall, 1989; Klobas, 1988, pp. 99–100; Ringer, 1994, pp. 97, 98–99, 100; Also in Terrace, 1993, Terrace, 2000

Mr. Broadway
Gianakos, 1978, p. 442

Mr. District Attorney
Alexander, 1994, pp. 126–128, 131–132, 154–155; Jarvis & Joseph, 1998, p. 7; Magers & Fitzgerald, 1999, pp. 50–51 ; Rovin, 1977b, pp. 32, 38

Mr. Ed
Bennett, 1996, pp. 25–27; Burns, 1990, p. 118; Hamamoto, 1989, pp. 59–60; Javna, 1985, pp. 102–105*; Kulzer, 1992, pp. 206–207; Mitz, 1980, pp. 187–189; Penley, et al., 1991, pp. 205–224 (passim); Stark, 1997, pp. 116–117; Stempel, 1992, pp. 98–99; Story, 1993, pp. 35–44**; Also in Bianculli, 1996, Eisner & Krinsky, 1984, , Terrace, 1993

Mr. Garlund
Hamamoto, 1994, pp. 7–8; Lichter, Lichter, & Rothman, 1991, pp. 120, 137–138, 148; Lichter, Lichter, & Rothman, 1994, pp. 218–219

Mr. I Magination
Davis, 1995, pp. 148–149

Mr. Lucky
Castleman & Podrazik, 1982, p. 136; Meyers, 1981, pp. 62–63; Rovin, 1977b, pp. 71–72; Also in Terrace, 1993

Mr. Merlin
IN Terrace, 1993

Mr. Novak
Bogle, 2001, p. 103; Chunovic, 2000, pp. 48–49; Gianakos, 1978, pp. 414–416; Hawes 2002, p. 211*; Lichter, Lichter, & Rothman, 1991, p. 167; Rovin, 1977b, p. 88; Stempel, 1992, pp. 92–93; Tinker & Rukeyser, 1994, pp. 52–54

Mr. Peepers
Allen, 1956, pp. 131–144 (passim) (about Wally Cox); Castleman & Podrazik, 1982, pp. 66–67; Jones, 1992, pp. 77–78; Kalisch, Kalisch, & Scobey, 1983, pp. 11–12; Krampner, 1997, pp. 78–90*; Lichter, Lichter, & Rothman, 1991, p. 167; Lichter, Lichter, & Rothman, 1994, p. 254; Mitz, 1980, pp. 55–59*; Paietta & Kauppila, 1999, p. 341; Putterman, 1995, p. 55; Skutch, 1998, pp. 92–94*; Stempel, 1992, pp. 41–43*; Wilk, 1976, pp. 74–84**; Also in Bianculli, 1996, Terrace, 1993

Mr. Roberts
Gianakos, 1978, pp. 521–522; Paietta & Kauppila, 1999, p. 341; Also in Eisner & Krinsky, 1984

Mister Rogers Neighborhood
Broughton, 1986, pp. 49–59**; Bryant

& Anderson, 1983, pp. 89–100*; Collins & Kimmel, 1996, whole book**; Comstock, 1991, pp. 108, 114; Davis, 1995, pp. 149–151; Difranco & Difranco, 1983, whole book**; Hendershot, 1998, pp. 148–150; Howitt, 1982, pp. 154–155; Jarvik, 1997, pp. 32–34*; Johnston, 2000, p. 76; Lechner, 2000, pp. 65–66; Mankiewicz & Swerdlow, 1978, pp. 189–192*; Moody, 1980, pp. 57–58; Morris, 1971, pp. 17, 73–74, 143, 191–194*; Palmer & Dorr, 1980, pp. 57–58, 65; Rogers, 1996, whole book**; Rutstein, 1974, pp. 8–10; Tan, 1981, pp. 247–249; Tan, 1985, pp. 291–293; Winn, 1977, pp. 79–80; Winn, 1985, pp. 117–180; Zillmann, Bryant, & Huston, 1994, pp. 79–80; Also in Bianculli, 1996

Mr. Sunshine
Klobas, 1988, pp. 101–102; Vande Berg & Trujillo, 1989, pp. 180–181

Mr. Terrific
Rovin, 1977b, pp. 117–118; Also in Eisner & Krinsky, 1984, Terrace, 1993

Mr. Wizard *see* Watch Mr. Wizard

Mobile One
Meyers, 1981, pp. 216–217; Gianakos, 1981, p. 190; Also in Terrace, 1993

Mod Squad, The
Andrews, 1986, pp. 128–129; Bedell, 1981, pp. 33–34; Bodroghkozy, 2001, pp. 164–198, 209**; Bogle, 2001, pp. 156–159*; Buxton, 1990, p. 123; Caldwell, 1995, p. 53; Carlson, 1985, pp. 34–35; Castleman & Podrazik, 1982, pp. 207–208*; Gianakos, 1978, pp. 620–626**; Himmelstein, 1994, pp. 219–220; Jarvis & Joseph, 1998, p. 15; Javna, 1985, p. 24; Lichter, Lichter, & Rothman, 1991, pp. 124–125, 237; Lichter, Lichter, & Rothman, 1994, pp. 219–220; Marc, 1996, pp. 86–88*; Marc & Thompson, 1992 (Ch. 15 on Aaron Spelling), pp. 163–169, especially pp. 164–166*; Martindale, 1991, pp. 329–341; Meyers, 1981, pp. 142–144; Newcomb, 1987, p. 447; Osgerby & Gough-Yates, 2001, pp. 21–22, 107, 201; Rodriguez, 1997, p. 61; Rovin, 1977b, p. 121; Rushkoff, 1994, p. 47; Sochen, 1987, p. 99; Spelling, 1996, pp. 59–69**; Stark, 1997, p. 99; Turow, 1989, pp. 147–148; Also in Bianculli, 1996

Models, Inc.
Owen, 1997, pp. 106, 108–110*; Spelling, 1996, pp. 194–195

Moesha
Bogle, 2001, pp. 432–433; Davis, 2001, pp. 54–69**; Feinleib, 1999, pp. 28–29; Hiebert, 1999, p. 377; Means Coleman, 2000, pp. 125–126; Zook, 1999, pp. 47–49*; Also in Terrace, 2000

Molloy
IN Terrace, 1993

Molly Dodd *see* Days and Nights of Molly Dodd

Moment of Fear
Gianakos, 1978, p. 282

Mommies, The
IN Terrace, 2000

Monday Night Football
Abelman, 1998, pp. 238–240*; Friedman, 2002, pp. 138–139; Goldenson,

1991, see index, especially pp. 204–213**; Gorman & Calhoun, pp. 57–59, 65–67, 71–72*; Gunther & Carter, 1988, whole book**; Mayer, 1972, pp. 165–187**; Rader, 1984, pp. 107, 113–115, 131–132; Sackett, 1993, p. 285; Winship, 1988, pp. 280–283; Also in Bianculli, 1996

Monkees, The
Bodroghkozy, 2001, pp. 66–75**; Capsuto, 2000, p. 48; Castleman & Podrazik, 1982, pp. 193–194; Hamamoto, 1989, pp. 71–72; Jarvik, 1997, p. 263; Javna, 1985, pp. 196–199*; Lefcowitz, 1989, whole book**; Lichter, Lichter, & Rothman, 1991, pp. 120, 152; Lichter, Lichter, & Rothman, 1994, pp. 197, 236; Putterman, 1995, pp. 66–70*; Stark, 1997, pp. 130–132*; Also in Bianculli, 1996, Eisner & Krinsky, 1984, Terrace, 1993

Monroes, The (Western)
Gianakos, 1978, pp. 554–555; Jackson, 1994, pp. 177–178; Also in Lentz, 1997, Terrace, 1993, West, 1987

Monty
Cotter, 1997, pp. 450–452

Moonlighting
Auletta, 1991, pp. 467–469, plus see index; Brown, 1990, pp. 66–68, 75–76; Burks, 1990**; Caldwell, 1995, pp. 88, 91; Chunovic, 2000, pp. 99–103**; Davies, 1997, p. 70; Field, 1989, pp. 159–161; Fiske, 1987, p. 238; Guida, 2000, pp. 219–222; Henderson & Mazzeo, 1990, pp. 28–35*; Hiebert, 1999, p. 252; Kendall, 1989**; Lichter, Lichter, & Rothman, 1991, pp. 29, 30, 39; Lichter, Lichter, & Rothman, 1994, pp. 84, 85; Puette, 1992, pp. 56, 192; Putterman, 1995, p. 102; Riggs, 1998, p. 20; Rose, 1999, p. 105; Sackett, 1993, pp. 314–315; Schneider, 2001, p. 35; Stark, 1997, pp. 241, 246; Suman, 1997, p. 79; Sumser, 1996, p. 15; Thomas & Evans, 1990, p. 289; Thompson, 1996, pp. 13, 15, 111–121**; Tulloch, 2000, p. 65; Vande Berg & Trujillo, 1989, pp. 178–179; Vande Berg & Wenner, 1991, pp. 88–111**; Wilcox, 1996 ; Williams, 1992, p. 90; Winship, 1988, pp. 124–129; Also in Bianculli, 1996, Terrace, 1993

Morey Amsterdam Show, The
Pegg, 2002, pp. 36–38; Starr, 1997, pp. 48–51

Mork & Mindy
Bedell, 1981, pp. 239–242; Castleman & Podrazik, 1982, pp. 287–288; Field, 1989, pp. 156–158; Freeman, 1980, pp. 41–42; Kaminsky, 1985, pp. 141, 204–211 (passim) (interview with Gary Marshall); Klobas, 1988, pp. 59–60; Lichter, Lichter, & Rothman, 1991, pp. 11, 144, 259; Lichter, Lichter, & Rothman, 1994, pp. 9, 227, 367; Marc & Thompson, 1992 (Ch. 6 on Gary Marshall), pp. 70–83; Miller, 1980, p. 198; Mitz, 1980, pp. 407–410*; Modleski, 1986, p. 181; Newcomb, 1982, pp. 73–74; Newcomb & Alley, 1983, pp. 230–253 (passim); Pegg, 2002, p. 262; Rose, 1985, p. 99; Sackett, 1993, pp. 250–251; Shales, 1982, pp. 121–127*; Sklar, 1980, pp. 73, 161–165*; Weimann, 2000, pp. 241–242; Also in Bianculli, 1996, Eisner & Krinsky, 1984, Terrace, 1993

Morning Show
Castleman & Podrazik, 1982, pp. 86–87; Hack, 1999, pp. 31–33, 34, 35–37*

Morningstar/Eveningstar
Gianakos, 1992, pp. 414–415

Morton and Hayes
IN Terrace, 1993

Morton Downey, Jr. Show, The
Himmelstein, 1994, pp. 353, 363; Munson, 1990*; Munson, 1993, pp. 84–92, also see index**; Newcomb, 1994, p. 277; Newcomb, 2000, p. 364; Powers, 1994, pp. 229–237**; Roman, 1996, p. 71; Shattuc, 1997, pp. 93–94; Twitchell, 1992, pp. 240–242; Also in Bianculli, 1996

Most Deadly Game, The
Gianakos, 1978, p. 666; Meyers, 1981, pp. 152–153; Spelling, 1996, p. 81

Most Wanted
Gianakos, 1981, pp. 201–202; Lichter, Lichter, & Rothman, 1991, p. 189; Lichter, Lichter, & Rothman, 1994, pp. 280–281; Martindale, 1991, pp. 343–346; Meyers, 1981, pp. 231–232

Mothers-in-Law, The
Harris, 1991, p. 281; Kulzer, 1992, pp. 154–156; Sanders & Gilbert, 1993, pp. 298–300, 313–314; Also in Eisner & Krinsky, 1984, Terrace, 1993

Movie of the Week *see* **ABC Movie of the Week**

Movie Stars
IN Terrace, 2000

Movin' On
Gianakos, 1978, pp. 762–763; Gianakos, 1981, pp. 114–116*

Mrs. Columbo *see* **Kate Loves a Mystery**

Mulligan's Stew
IN Terrace, 1993

Munsters, The
Bennett, 1996, pp. 67–70; Capsuto, 2000, p. 48; Castleman & Podrazik, 1982, p. 173; Davis, 1995, pp. 119–120; Jones, 1992, pp. 174–175; Mitz, 1980, pp. 211–215*; Penley, et.al., 1991, p. 220; Skal, 1993, p. 281–282; Spigel, 2001, p. 124; Stark, 1997, p. 117; Stempel, 1992, p. 100; Story, 1993, pp. 112–127**; Wittebols, 1998, p. 4; Also in Bianculli, 1996, Eisner & Krinsky, 1984, Terrace, 1993

Muppet Show, The
Bedell, 1981, pp. 119–120; Davis, 1995, pp. 198–199; Finch, 1981, whole book**; Miller, 2000, p. 76; Tulloch, 2000, pp. 131–133; Also in Bianculli, 1996

Muppets Tonight
Hendershot, 1998, p. 103; Owen, 1997, p. 40

Murder One
Bounds, 1996, p. 100; Jarvis & Joseph, 1998, pp. 65–85**; Leonard, 1997, p. 140; Pearl & Pearl, 1999, pp. 121–122; Tasker, 1998, pp. 97–98

Murder, She Wrote
Bell, 1992; Blum & Lindheim, 1987, pp. 78, 92–95 (part of script); Bounds, 1996, pp. 4, 112–113; Burks, 1990**; Collins & Javna, 1989, pp. 106–108; Delamater & Prigozy, 1998, pp. 113–114, 118–121**; Edelman & Kupferberg, 1996, pp. 47, 77, 208–209, 213, 216–250, 256–257**; Gianakos, 1992, pp. 362–366*; Gottfried, 1999, pp. 265–292, 297**; Gunter & Wober, 1988, pp. 40–42; Hiebert, 1999, p.

251; Isaacs, 1999, p. 130; Klobas, 1988, pp. 258–259; Levinson & Link, 1986, pp. 72–86 (Angela Lansbury interview)**; Lichter, Lichter, & Rothman, 1994, p. 66; Marc & Thompson, 1992 (Ch. 17 on Richard Levinson and Wm. Link), pp. 180–192; Mellencamp, 1992, pp. 302–309**; Owen, 1997, p. 14; Paietta & Kauppila, 1999, p. 341; Riggs, 1996; Riggs, 1998, pp. 2, 15–54**; Sackett, 1993, pp. 296–297; Seger, 1996, p. 155, 183; Steenland, 1990, p. 44; Sumser, 1996, pp. 78, 88–98, 102–104, 107, 108, 109–110, 121, 122, 125–126, 126–127, 128, 130–133, 135, 136, 141–142, 144, 148, 149–151**; Vane & Gross, 1994, pp. 115, 218; Also in Bianculli, 1996, Terrace, 1993

Murphy Brown

Abelman, 1998, pp. 35, 105; Allen, 1992, pp. 156, 194–196*; Alley & Brown, 1990, whole book**; Alley & Brown, 2001, pp. 183–190, 191–196**; Benoit & Anderson, 1996; Blum, 1995, pp. 15, 96–104, 123–126, 160–165, 181–182**; Bryant & Bryant, 2001, p. 247; Capsuto, 2000, p. 285; Chunovic, 2000, p. 121; Cortes, 2000, p. 65; Creeber, 2001, p. 66; Crotty, 1995; Crown, 1999, p. 28; Davies & Smith, 1998; Davis, 2001, p. 16; Dow, 1996, pp. xxiv, 5–6, 118, 135–163, 210, 212**: Fiske, 1994, pp. 1–2, 5, 11, 12, 21–74, 88, 97, 101–106, 113**; Gabler, Rich & Antler, 2000, p. 50; Haralovich & Rabinovitz, 1999, pp. 144–145, 146–147, 148–149, 156–163**; Harris, 1994, p. 102; Harris, 1998, p. 137; Himmelstein, 1994, p. 158; Horowitz, 1997, p. 121; Horton & McDougal, 1998, p. 325; Isaacs, 1999, p. 62; Johnston, 2000, p. 93; Jones, 1992, p. 262; Kutulas, 1998; Leonard, 1997, pp. 65, 67; Lichter, Lichter, & Rothman, 1991, pp. 50, 62, 78, 128; Lichter, Lichter, & Rothman, 1994, pp. 111, 146; Marc, 1997, p. 203; Marc & Thompson, 1992 (Ch. 8 on Diane English), pp. 93–98, especially pp. 95–97*; Mellencamp, 1992, pp. 352–353; Miner, 1996; Morgan, Leggett, & Shanahan, 1999; Orlik, 1994, pp. 35, 244; Parenti, 1991, pp. 82–84; Pearl & Pearl, 1999, pp. 80, 198; Press, 1991, pp. 40–41; Rafkin, 1998, pp. 96–97, 130–131, 137, 141; Rapping, 1994, pp. 111, 161; Riggs, 1998, p. 63; Roman, 1996, p. 62; Rushkoff, 1994, pp. 78–83, 110*; Sackett, 1993, pp. 332–333; Schwartz, 1999, p. 135; Silverblatt, 1995, p. 52; Sochen, 1999, pp. 200, 202, 205–208*; Steenland, 1990, pp. 15–16, 47–48; Stempel, 1992, pp. 256–258; Thurer, 1994, p. 297; Vane & Gross, 1994, pp. 115, 116; Also in Bianculli, 1996, Terrace,1993, Terrace, 2000

Murphy's Law

IN Terrace, 1993

Musical Comedy Time

Gianakos, 1980, pp. 275–276

My Favorite Husband

Lichter, Lichter, & Rothman, 1991, p. 74; Lichter, Lichter, & Rothman, 1994, pp. 141–142; Also in Terrace, 1993

My Favorite Martian

Guida, 2000, pp. 192–193; Kulzer, 1992, pp. 165–169; Lisanti & Paul, 2002, pp. 232–233; Marc, 1989, pp. 131–134*; Marc, 1997, pp. 108–110*; Mitz, 1980, pp. 205–206; Penley, et al., 1991, pp. 205–224 (passim); Rafkin, 1998, pp. 47–48; Rose, 1985, p. 99; Sackett, 1993, pp. 57–63; Sconce,

2000, pp. 120–121; Spigel & Curtin, 1997, p. 59; Stark, 1997, pp. 117–118; Stempel, 1992, p. 98; Story, 1993, pp. 57–63*; Also in Bianculli, 1996, Eisner & Krinsky, 1984, Terrace, 1993

My Friend Flicka
Anderson, 1994, p. 188; Gianakos, 1992, pp. 447–449*; Hawes, 2002, p. 125; Also in Lentz, 1997

My Friend Irma
Hamamoto, 1989, pp. 31–32; Hawes, 2002, p. 92; Also in Terrace, 1993

My Friend Tony
Gianakos, 1978, p. 640

My Hero
IN Eisner & Krinsky, 1984, Terrace, 1993

My Life and Times
IN Terrace, 1993

My Little Margie
Bogle, 2001, pp. 44–45; Castleman & Podrazik, 1982, p. 66; Magers & Fitzgerald, 1999, pp. 230–231; Marc, 1989, pp. 50–51; Marc, 1997, p. 42; Mitz, 1980, pp. 51–53*; Newcomb, 2000, p. 58; Putterman, 1995, pp. 16–17; Also in Eisner & Krinsky, 1984, Terrace, 1993

My Living Doll
Andrews, 1980, pp. 103–108*; Kulzer, 1992, p. 87; Smith, 1989, pp. 119, 122–123; Also in Terrace, 1993

My Mother, the Car
Abelman, 1998, p. 30; Andrews, 1980, pp. 109–115*; Erickson, 2000, p. 157; Jarvis & Joseph, 1998, p. 170; Schultz, 1990, pp. 149–153 (episode guides)*; Waldrep, 2000, p. 196; Also in Bianculli, 1996, Eisner & Krinsky, 1984, Terrace, 1993

My Sister Eileen
IN Eisner & Krinsky, 1984, Terrace, 1993

My Sister Sam
Alley & Brown, 2001, p. 186; Hamamoto, 1989, pp. 133–134; Lichter, Lichter, & Rothman, 1991, p. 65; Marc & Thompson, 1992 (Ch. 8 on Diane English), pp. 93–98; Also in Terrace, 1993

My So-Called Life
Abelman, 1998, p. 440; Capsuto, 2000, pp. 289, 299–301*; Gross, 2001, p. 171; Kinder, 1999, pp. 222–235**; Owen, 1997, pp. 138, 139–143, 167–168, 206–207*; Stark, 1997, pp. 68–69; Thompson, 1996, pp. 139–140; Wild, 1999, p. 42

My Son Jeep
Paietta & Kauppila, 1999, p. 341

My Three Sons
Bennett, 1996, pp. 97–104; Cantor, 2001, pp. 70, 92; Fitzgerald & Magers, 2002, p. 60; Hamamoto, 1989, pp. 66–67; Himmelstein, 1984, pp. 90–91; Himmelstein, 1994, pp. 126–127; Jones, 1992, pp. 159–162*; Kulzer, 1992, pp. 47–54, 75–77*; Leibman, 1995, pp. 11, 22, 28–29, 33–34, 38, 44, 46, 50, 52–55, 63–64, 89–90, 119–120, 123–124, 126, 131–132, 135, 149, 153–154, 156, 157, 165, 169–170, 175, 183–185, 206, 221–222, 223, 227–228, 239, 268**; Mitz, 1980, pp. 169–172*; Pegg, 2002, pp. 113–116*; Thompson, 1996, p. 32; Also in

Bianculli, 1996, Eisner & Krinsky, 1984, Terrace, 1993

My Two Dads
Jarvis & Joseph, 1998, p. 235; Steenland, 1990, p. 22; Also in Terrace, 1993, Terrace, 2000

My World and Welcome to It
Erickson, 2000, p. 212; Also in Bianculli, 1996, Terrace, 1993

Mysteries of Chinatown
IN Terrace, 1993

Naked City
Collins & Javna, 1989, pp. 65–67; Gianakos, 1978, pp. 305–309*; Hawes, 2002, p. 108; Lichter, Lichter, & Rothman, 1991, pp. 192, 211, 221–222, 227; Lichter, Lichter, & Rothman, 1994, pp. 284, 321–322, 328; Meyers, 1981, pp. 51–52; Newcomb, 1976, pp. 78–79, 79–80 (note), 82; Rovin, 1977b, pp. 64–65; Stempel, 1992, pp. 83–84; Williams, 1982, pp. 64–66*; Also in Bianculli, 1996, Terrace, 1993

Naked Truth, The
IN Terrace, 2000

Nakia
Gianakos, 1978, pp. 753–754; Yoggy, 1995, pp. 361–363; Also in Lentz, 1997

Name of the Game, The
Castleman & Podrazik, 1982, p. 207; Gianakos, 1978, pp. 635–639*; Lichter, Lichter, & Rothman, 1991, pp. 175–176, 196–197, 202; Lichter, Lichter, & Rothman, 1994, pp. 290, 297–298; Marc & Thompson, 1992 (Ch. 17 on Richard Levinson and Wm. Link), pp. 180–192; Martindale, 1991, pp. 351–359; McDonald, 1983, pp. 121–122; McDonald, 1992, p. 130; Meyers, 1981, pp. 140–141; Rovin, 1977b, p. 121; Turow, pp. 111–112

Name That Tune
DeLong, 1991, pp. 209–211; Stone & Yohn, 1992, pp. 174–178*; U.S. Congress, 1960, pp. 437–440; Also in Bianculli, 1996

Nancy
Gianakos, 1983, pp. 395–396

Nancy Drew *see* **Hardy Boys/ Nancy Drew**

Nancy Walker Show, The
Capsuto, 2000, pp. 126, 128; Coakley, 1977, pp. 13, 21–22, 42, 48–49; Miller, 1980, pp. 192–193

Nanny, The
Chunovic, 2000, p. 153; Gabler, Rich & Antler, 2000, pp. 55–61; 66, 70**; Meyers, 1999, pp. 305–306, 309–318**; Pearl & Pearl, 1999, pp 88–89, 99; Seger, 1996, p. 262; Also in Terrace, 2000

Nanny and the Professor
IN Eisner & Krinsky, 1984, Terrace, 1993

Nash Airflyte Theatre, The
Gianakos, 1980, pp. 285–286

Nash Bridges
Crown, 1999, pp. 48, 86–87; Davis, 2001, pp. 110–111, 308; Suman & Rossman, 2000, p. 34

Nashville '99
Gianakos, 1981, p. 225

Nat King Cole Show, The
Andrews, 1986, pp. 104–107*; Bogle, 2001, pp. 74–77*; Castleman & Podrazik, 1982, p. 121; Dates & Barlow, 1990, p. 287; Dates & Barlow, 1993, pp. 311–312; Hiebert & Reuss, 1985, p. 386; Jackson, 1982; McDonald, 1983, pp. 57–64**; McDonald, 1992, pp. 64–71**; Newcomb, 1987, p. 347; Newcomb, 2000, pp. 287–288; Turner, 1994, pp. 122–123; Wilson & Gutierrez, 1985, p. 98

National Velvet
Gianakos, 1983, pp. 347–349*; Also in Terrace, 1993

Navy Log
Gianakos, 1980, pp. 475–478*; Hamamoto, 1994, pp. 105–109*; Lichter, Lichter, & Rothman, 1991, pp. 164, 269–270, 274*; Lichter, Lichter, & Rothman, 1994, pp. 251, 380–381, 397*

Ned and Stacey
IN Terrace, 2000

Ned Blessing
Capsuto, 2000, p. 309; Yoggy, 1995, pp. 621–624*; Also in Lentz, 1997

Nero Wolfe
Gianakos, 1983, pp. 196–197; Also in Terrace, 1993

New Adventures of Beans Baxter, The
IN Terrace, 1993

New Adventures of Huck Finn, The
Gianakos, 1983, pp. 389–390

New Attitude
Zook, 1999, p. 38; Also in Terrace, 1993

New Avengers *see* **Avengers**

New Bill Cosby Show, The
Smith, 1997b, pp. 113–117*

New Breed, The
Gianakos, 1978, pp. 347–348; Lichter, Lichter, & Rothman, 1991, pp. 184, 188–189; Lichter, Lichter, & Rothman, 1994, pp. 274, 280

New Dick Van Dyke Show, The
Lichter, Lichter, & Rothman, 1994, p. 83; Williams, 1982, pp. 143–144 (passim); Also in Terrace, 1993

New Doctors, The
Paietta & Kauppila, 1999, p. 342

New Land, The
Gianakos, 1978, p. 753; Also in Lentz, 1997, West, 1987

New Loretta Young Show, The
Gianakos, 1983, pp. 353–354

New Maverick
Robertson, 1994, pp. 171–172, 177–178

New Odd Couple
Means Coleman, 2000, pp 171–172

New People, The
Gianakos, 1978, pp. 648; Spelling, 1996, pp. 69–71

New Perry Mason
Bounds, 1996, pp. 4, 121; Gianakos, 1978, pp. 739–740; Jarvis & Joseph, 1998, p. 60

New Phil Silvers Show, The
Everitt, 2001, pp. 184–185; Also in Terrace, 1993

New Price Is Right *see* **Price Is Right**

New Temperatures Rising *see* **Temperatures Rising**

New York Undercover
Bogle, 2001, pp. 441–442; Leonard, 1997, p. 218; Owen, 1997, pp. 90–91, 117; Pearl & Pearl, 1999, p. 84; Zook, 1999, pp. 88–99**

Newhart
Abelman, 1998, p. 381; Bianculli, 1992, p. 264; Jones, 1992, p. 263; Pegg, 2002, pp. 262–265; Putterman, 1995, pp. 42–43, 46–47*; Stark, 1997, pp. 248–249 (passim); Vande Berg & Trujillo, 1989, pp. 133, 178; Also in Bianculli, 1996, Terrace, 1993

Newlywed Game, The
IN Bianculli, 1996

Newsradio
Wild, 1999, pp. 1, 24, 28–29, 30, 128–129, 132, 177, 180–183, 195–201, 230–231, 248, 275–276**

Next Step Beyond, The
Gianakos, 1981, pp. 269–270; Muir, 2001a, pp. 82–90; Muir, 2001b, pp. 229–258**

Nichols
Gianakos, 1983, pp. 402–404*; Meyers, 1981, p. 158; Montgomery, 1989, pp. 61–62; Rovin, 1977b, p. 132; Strait, 1985, pp. 274–283, 286–290**; Also in Lentz, 1997, Terrace, 1993, West, 1987

Night Court
Capsuto, 2000, p. 202; Carey, 1988, pp. 96–97; Hiebert, 1999, p. 251; Jarvis & Joseph, 1998, pp. 174, 227; Klobas, 1988, pp. 304–306, 359–360; Lester, 1996, pp. 121–122; Nelson, 1994, p. 8; Sackett, 1993, pp. 310–311; Tabarlet, 1993; Vande Berg & Trujillo, 1989, pp. 186–187, 218–221*; Wahl, 1995, pp. 9, 60

Night Editor
Daniel, 1996, p. 9

Night Gallery
Engel, 1989, pp. 323–328*; Gerani, 1977, pp. 127–133*; Gianakos, 1978, pp. 673–676*; Klobas, 1988, pp. 21–22; Lichter, Lichter, & Rothman, 1991, pp. 35–36; Lichter, Lichter, & Rothman, 1994, p. 92; Muir, 2001a, pp. 7–31**; Muir, 2001b, pp. 221–222; Pearl & Pearl, 1999, p. 177; Skelton & Benson, 1999, whole book**

Night Heat
Klobas, 1988, pp. 336–337

Night Stalker *see* **Kolchak**

Nightingales
Auletta, 1991, pp. 451–456, 505–510, 516–523, plus see index**; Lichter, Lichter, & Rothman, 1991, p. 62; Paietta & Kauppila, 1999, p. 342; Selnow & Gilbert, 1993, p. 186; Spelling, 1996, pp. 164–165; Thompson, 1996, p. 42; Also in Terrace, 1993

Nightline
Auletta, 1991, pp. 287–292, 297–298, plus see index**; Barr, 2000, p. 76; Caldwell, 1995, p. 319; Capsuto, 2000, p. 170; Castleman & Podrazik,

1982, p. 293; Craig, 1992, pp. 154–168**; Croteau & Hoynes, 1994, pp. 2–3, 61–114, 117–124, 133–136, 177–181**; Diamond, 1982, pp. 115–116; Goldenson, 1991, pp. 411–412; Hamamoto, 1994, pp. 20–21; Himmelstein, 1994, pp. 268–270, 380–382*; Jarvik, 1997, p. 96; Kanfer, 2000, p. 430; Koppel & Gibson, 1996, whole book**; Kovach & Rosenstiel, 1999, pp. 14, 28, 56–57, 108, 115, 134, 160–161, 164; Lechner, 2000, pp. 154–155; Miller, 1994, pp. 236–237; Modleski, 1986, p. 69; Moorti, 2001, pp. 91–92; Puette, 1992, p. 45; Rapping, 1994, pp. 195–196; Rivera, 1991, pp. 189–190, 377; Scott, 1996, pp. 280–281; Shales, 1982, pp. 239–244*; Smith, 1997a; Winch, 1997, pp. 119–121; Also in Bianculli, 1996

Nightmare Café
Muir, 2001a, pp. 314–319**; Also in Terrace, 1993

9 to 5
IN Terrace, 1993

No Time for Sergeants
IN Eisner & Krinsky, 1984

Noah's Ark
Lichter, Lichter, & Rothman, 1991, p. 278; Lichter, Lichter, & Rothman, 1994, p. 391; Moyer & Alvarez, 2001, pp. 116–117

Norm Show, The
Chunovic, 2000, pp. 20–21; Lechner, 2000, pp. 145–146; Wild, 1999, pp. 41–49, 55–56, 139–140, 159–166, 186–187, 211–212, 236–239**

Normal Life
Steenland, 1990, p. 30

Normal, Ohio
Walters, 2001, p. 220

Northern Exposure
Abelman, 1998, p. 390; Allen, 1992, pp. 332–333; Berry & Asamen, 1993, p. 192; Blum, 1995, pp. 10–11, 83; Caldwell, 1995, pp. vii, x–xi, 166, 251–255**; Capsuto, 2000, pp. 278–279, 308–309, 359–360*; Chunovic, 1993, whole book**; Chunovic, 1995a, whole book**; Chunovic, 2000, pp. 133–137*; Davis, 2001, p. 18; Forbes & Mahan, 2000, p. 54; Gabler, Rich & Antler, 2000, pp. 49, 68, 72–73; Gross, 2001, pp. 89, 90; Gross & Woods, 1999, p. 294; Guida, 2000, pp. 224–225; Himmelstein, 1994, pp. 237–238; Holtzman, 2000, pp 213, 303; Horton, 2000, pp. 4, 77–78, 170; Johnston, 2000, p. 101; Kamalipour & Carrilli, 1998, p. 104; Leonard, 1997, pp. 7, 255–256; Lester, 1996, pp. 52, 157, 158; Lichter, Lichter, & Rothman, 1994, pp. 45–47, 73*; Meyers, 1999, pp. 104–105; Monaco, 2000, p. 497; Nance, 1992, whole book**; Newcomb, 1994, pp. 136–137, 141–145, 147–152**; Orlik, 1994, pp. 264–265*; Paietta & Kauppila, 1999, p. 342; Pearl & Pearl, 1999, pp. 28, 36–37, 41–43, 44, 82, 92, 100, 183, 232–233**; Riggs, 1998, pp. 139, 144; Schultz, 2000, pp. 125–126; Suman, 1997, pp. 77, 78; Swanson, 2000, pp. 59–60, 123; Taylor & Upchurch, 1996; Thompson, 1996, pp. 15, 160–167, 174, 176; Also in Bianculli, 1996, Terrace, 1993

Northwest Passage
IN Lentz, 1997, West, 1987

Not for Publication
Daniel, 1996, pp. 8–9

Nothing Sacred
Cortes, 2000, pp.. 41, 97, 101, 106; Johnston, 2000, pp. 6–7; Suman & Rossman, 2000, pp. 88, 90, 95, 107, 109–110, 128*

Now and Again
Lechner, 2000, pp. 223–225*

Nowhere Man
Cotter, 1997, pp. 467–471*; Muir, 2001a, pp. 589–591*

Number 96
Stempel, 1992, pp. 218–219; Also in Morris, 1997

Nurse
Gianakos, 1983, pp. 195–196; Klobas, 1988, pp. 228–230; Lichter, Lichter, & Rothman, 1991, pp. 47, 162, 203; Lichter, Lichter, & Rothman, 1994, pp. 106, 248, 249, 298; Paietta & Kauppila, 1999, pp. 342–343; Turow, 1989, pp. 255, 258; U.S. Congress, 1985, p. 169

Nurses
Cotter, 1997, pp. 410–415**; Paietta & Kauppila, 1999, p. 343

Nurses, The
Bogle, 2001, pp. 102–103; Capsuto, 2000, p. 49; Gianakos, 1978, pp. 397–402**; Kalisch, Kalisch, & Scobey, 1983, pp. 27–34, 40, 195–198**; Lichter, Lichter, & Rothman, 1991, p. 159; Lichter, Lichter, & Rothman, 1994, p. 245; Paietta & Kauppila, 1999, p. 343; Real, 1977, p. 124; Rose, 1985, p. 78; Rovin, 1977b, p. 84; Spigel & Curtin, 1997, pp. 195–197*; Turow, 1989, pp. 95–103, 105, 106, 221**

Nutt House
Cotter, 1997, pp. 373–374

N.Y.P.D.
Bogle, 2001, p. 136; Capsuto, 2000, pp. 55–56; Gianakos, 1978, pp. 591–593*; Meyers, 1981, p. 134; Rovin, 1977b, p. 119

N.Y.P.D. Blue
Abelman, 1998, pp. 416–417; Bignell, 1997, p. 142; Bogle, 2001, pp. 438–439; Bryant & Bryant, 2001, pp. 183, 188; Capsuto, 2000, pp. 372–273; Carstarphen & Zavoina, 1999, pp. 192, 257; Chunovic, 2000, pp. 145–147*; Davis, 2001, pp. 109–110; Entman & Rojecki, 2000, pp. 149, 150, 152, 154–156, 160*; Forbes & Mahan, 2000, pp. 54, 55; Gauntlett & Hill, 1999, p 213; Hanczor, 1997; Heldenfels, 1994, p. 56; Hollows, 2000, p. 101; Holtzman, 2000, pp 229–230; Jarvis & Joseph, 1998, pp. 88–91, 93–100, 103–104**; Kalat, 1998, pp. 23–25, 53, 80; Kidd-Hewitt & Osborne, 1995, p. 73; Lane, 2001; Leonard, 1997, pp. 162–164*; Lichter, Lichter, & Rothman, 1994, pp. 33–34, 36; Longworth, 2000, pp. xii, 92, 95–97, 100–101*, 202; Miller, 1994, p. 268; Newcomb, 2000, pp. 247–251*; Roman, 1996, p. 64; Rushkoff, 1994, pp. 55, 57–58; Silverblatt, Ferry, & Finan, 1999, p 4; Swanson, 2000, pp. 66–67, 128–130, 198*; Thompson, 1996, pp. 42, 184, 187; Walters, 2001, p. 99; Yeates, 2001; Also in Bianculli, 1996

Occasional Wife
Putterman, 1995, pp. 60–66**; Also in Terrace, 1993

Odd Couple
Bennett, 1996, pp. 60–62; Craig,

1992, pp. 103–104; Crotty, 1995; Crown, 1999, pp. 26–27, 29, 37–38*; Guida, 2000, pp. 196–197; Javna, 1985, pp. 214–217*; Kaminsky, 1985, pp. 204–205, 210 (interview with Gary Marshall); Marc & Thompson, 1992 (Ch. 6 on Gary Marshall), pp. 70–83; Mitz, 1980, pp. 269–273; Newcomb & Alley, 1983, pp. 230–253 (passim); Putterman, 1995, pp. 113–115; Rafkin, 1998, p. 70; Silverblatt, Ferry, & Finan, 1999, p. 108; Stempel, 1992, pp. 153–155; Also in Bianculli, 1996, Eisner & Krinsky, 1984, Terrace, 1993

Off to See the Wizard
Gianakos, 1978, pp. 604–605

Oh Grow up
Keller, 2002, p. 180

Oh, Madeline
IN Terrace, 1993

Oh, Susanna *see* **Gale Storm Show, The**

Oh, Those Bells
IN Terrace, 1993

O'Hara
Kamalipour & Carrilli, 1998, p. 126

O'Hara, U.S. Treasury
Gianakos, 1983, pp. 404–405; Hamamoto, 1994, p. 12; Meyers, 1981, p. 160; Rovin, 1977b, p. 132

O.K. Crackerby
Andrews, 1980, pp. 124–130*

Oldest Rookie
Cotter, 1997, pp. 336–339*

Omnibus
Gianakos, 1980, pp. 323–335; Hawes, 2002, pp. 16–20*; Hewitt, 2001, p. 50; Also in Bianculli, 1996

On Our Own
IN Terrace, 1993

On the Air
Hughes, 2001, pp. 183–192**; Kaleta, 1993, p. 187; Woods, 1997, pp. 159–161; Also in Terrace, 1993

On the Rocks
Greenberg, 1980, p. 10

Once a Hero
IN Terrace, 1993

Once and Again
Lechner, 2000, pp. 118–120*; Longworth, 2000, pp. 76–77, 83–84, 87, 157, 168; Wild, 1999, p. 241

One Big Family
IN Terrace, 1993

One Day at a Time
Allen, 1987, pp. 159–160; Alley, 1977, p. 46; Bryant & Bryant, 2001, p. 157; Crotty, 1995; Dow, 1996, pp. xxiv, 60–85, 108, 209, 210**; Goethals, 1981, pp. 48–50*; Harris, 1989, p. 92; Jones, 1992, pp. 231–234*; Klobas, 1988, pp. 316–317, 380–382; Kutulas, 1998; Lichter, Lichter, & Rothman, 1991, pp. 54, 63, 66, 101–102, 111, 128*; Lichter, Lichter, & Rothman, 1994, pp. 116, 127, 175, 207; Marc, 1997, p. 173; Marc & Thompson, 1992 (Ch. 4 on Norman Lear), pp. 49–60; Mitz, 1980, pp. 365–369*; Pegg, 2002, pp. 149–152*; Rafkin, 1998, pp. 97, 101–110, 111–116**; Rose, 1985, pp.

120–121; Sackett, 1993, pp. 240–241; Schwartz, 1999, p. 128; Shaheen, 1984, pp. 62–64; Sklar, 1980, pp. 7, 71–72; Stempel, 1992, pp. 150, 250; Taylor, 1989, pp. 87–93, 145**; Also in Bianculli, 1996, Eisner & Krinsky, 1984, Terrace, 1993

One in a Million
Puette, 1992, p. 183; Theberge, 1981, pp. 17, 22

One Life to Live
Allen, 1985, pp. 52–54; Allen, 1995, pp. 167, 199–209**; Berry & Manning-Miller, 1996, pp 146, 150; Blumenthal, 1997, p. 53; Buckman, 1984, p. 45; Capsuto, 2000, pp. 297–299*; Gabler, Rich & Antler, 2000, p. 64; Gitlin, 1986, p. 54, 58; Greenberg & Busselle, 1996; Gross, 2001, pp. 216–219*; Gross & Woods, 1999, p. 11; James, 1991*; Jenrette, McIntosh, & Winterberger, 1999; Kaminsky, 1985, pp. 98, 99–100, 106, 108*; Kuney, 1990, pp. 114–119, 121–125**; Lechner, 2000, pp. 71–74*; Lester, 1996, p. 149; Matelski, 1988, pp. 19, 22, 23–24, 26, 46, 132–142**; Matelski, 1999, pp. 41–42; McDonald, 1983, pp. 163–164; McDonald, 1992, p. 169; Nelson, 1995, pp. 61–62; Nochimson, 1992, pp. 64–75, 77, 178–184; Nochimson, 1997a; Schultz, 2000, pp. 110, 117; Van Fuqua, 1996; Williams, 1992, pp. 29–30, 32, 35–38, 50, 57, 73–76, 81–82, 90, 92–94, 97–98, 107, 108, 110, 121, 137–138, 165, 174–175, 181–182, 198–199**; Yoggy, 1995, pp. 556–557; Also in Bianculli, 1996

One Man's Family
Skutch, 1998, pp. 88–89; Williams, 1992, pp. 22–23

One Step Beyond
Gerani, 1977, pp. 25–33**; Muir, 2001b, whole book**

One World
IN Terrace, 2000

Open House
IN Terrace, 1993

Operation Petticoat
Kalisch, Kalisch, & Scobey, 1983, pp. 93–96*; Paietta & Kauppila, 1999, p. 343; Sklar, 1980, pp. 77–78; Also in Terrace, 1993

Oprah Winfrey Show, The
Abelman, 1998, pp. 188, 212–215; Abt & Mustazza, 1997, pp. 58–66**; Abt & Seesholtz, 1994; Acham, 1999*; Alcoff & Gray, 1993; Beaton, 1990, pp. 73–83*; Bignell, 1997, pp. 149–150*; Blumenthal, 1997, pp. 61–62; Bogle, 2001, pp. 357, 358–360, 369–373*; Cloud, 1996; Creeber, 2001, pp. 85–86; Dates & Barlow, 1993, p. 321; Epstein & Steinberg, 1996; Epstein & Steinberg, 1998; Gross, 2001, pp. 159,187; Haag, 1993; Hamamoto, 1994, pp. 235–237; Haralovich & Rabinovitz, 1999, pp. 168–180**; Himmelstein, 1994, pp. 362–363; Hollows, 2000, pp. 199–200; Illouz, 1999; Joyner & Dominick, 1994; Keyes, 1997**; King, 1987, whole book (passim)**; Lechner, 2000, pp. 174–175, 194–195; MacDonald, 1995, p. 51; Mair, 1994, pp. 97–349 (passim)**; Marris & Thornham, 2000, pp. 354–367**; Mellencamp, 1992, pp. 211–219*; Moorti, 1995; Moorti, 2001, pp. 152, 154, 157–176, 179–182, 214–215**; Rakow, 1992, pp. 93–94; Rapping, 1994, pp. 192–196, 224; Rose, 1999, pp. 36–39*; Scott, 1996,

pp. 246–253*; Shattuc, 1997, pp. 39–40, 53–58 (passim), 62, 74, 85–109 passim, esp. pp. 95–109, 111–113, 115–116, 117, 125**; Smith, 1997**; Stark, 1997, pp. 276–277, 278, 279–280; Tulloch, 2000, pp. 238–239; Waldron, 1987, whole book (passim)**; Weimann, 2000, p. 125; Also in Bianculli, 1996

Oregon Trail, The
Gianakos, 1981, pp. 237–238; Jackson, 1994, p. 205; Yoggy, 1995, p. 371; Also in Lentz, 1997, West, 1987

Original Amateur Hour, The
Castleman & Podrazik, 1982, p. 31; Also in Bianculli, 1996

O.S.S.
Gianakos, 1981, pp. 376–377

Otherworld
Gianakos, 1992, p. 380

Our Family Honor
Gianakos, 1992, pp. 400–401; Also in Morris, 1997, Terrace, 1993

Our House
Lembo, 2000, pp. 176, 184–185; Pearl & Pearl, 1999, p. 206; Also in Terrace, 1993

Our Miss Brooks
Alley & Brown, 2001, p. 23; Castleman & Podrazik, 1982, p. 76; Crotty, 1995; Guida, 2000, p. 184; Hamamoto, 1989, pp. 32–33, 35; Hawes, 2002, pp. 89–90; Horowitz, 1997, p. 14; Jones, 1992, p. 85; Kulzer, 1992, pp. 38–40; Lichter, Lichter, & Rothman, 1991, pp. 68, 167; Lichter, Lichter, & Rothman, 1994, p. 254; Mitz, 1980, pp. 75–79*; Panati, 1991, pp. 303–304; Pegg, 2002, pp. 122–125; Putterman, 1995, p. 18; Sanders & Gilbert, 1993, pp. 59, 61–62; Also in Bianculli, 1996, Eisner & Krinsky, 1984, Terrace, 1993

Our Private World
IN Morris, 1997

Our World
Auletta, 1991, see index; Swanson, 2000, pp. xi–xii, 32–43**; Also in Bianculli, 1996

Out All Night
Bogle, 2001, pp. 407–408

Out of the Blue
IN Terrace, 1993

Out of This World
IN Terrace, 1993

Outcasts, The
Andrews, 1986, pp. 125–126; Bogle, 2001, pp.. 159–161; Dates & Barlow, 1990, pp. 255, 257; Dates & Barlow, 1993, pp. 269, 280; Gianakos, 1978, pp. 619–620; Jackson, 1994, pp. 186–187; McDonald, 1983, pp. 124–130; McDonald, 1992, pp. 132–137*; Rovin, 1977b, p. 123; Smith, 1986, p. 77; Yoggy, 1995, pp. 461–465, 467–471**; Also in Lentz, 1997, West, 1987

Outer Limits
Gerani, 1977, pp. 59–67**; Gianakos, 1978, pp. 408–411*; Javna, 1985, pp. 76–79*; Muir, 2001a, pp. 580–585*; Panati, 1991, p. 363; Rovin, 1977a, p. 139; Schow & Frentzen, 1986, whole book**; Schultz, 2000, p. 81; Sconce, 2000, pp. 135–142, 145–147, 149–152,

154–159, 160–163**; Spigel & Curtin, 1997, pp. 21–45, 61**; Worland, 1989; Worland, 1996; Also in Bianculli, 1996

Outlaws, The
Gianakos, 1978, pp. 309–311; Jackson, 1994, pp. 147–148; Yoggy, 1995, pp. 549, 551; Also in Lentz, 1997, West, 1987

Outsider, The
Gianakos, 1978, pp. 626–627; Meyers,1981, pp. 139–140; Also in Terrace, 1993

Over My Dead Body
IN Terrace, 1993

Overland Trail, The
Gianakos, 1978, pp. 279–280; Jackson, 1994, pp. 142–143; Also in Lentz, 1997, West, 1987

Owen Marshall, Counselor at Law
Capsuto, 2000, pp. 78–80*; Castleman & Podrazik, 1982, p. 231; Gianakos, 1978, pp. 702–705*; Martindale, 1991, pp. 364–371; Meyers, 1981, p. 159; Rovin, 1977b, p. 130; Vane & Gross, 1994, p. 176

Ozzie and Harriet *see* **Adventures of Ozzie and Harriet**

Paar, Jack *see* **Tonight Show**

Pacific Station
Cotter, 1997, pp. 415–417; Also in Terrace, 1993

Palace Guard
IN Terrace, 1993

Pall Mall Playhouse
IN West, 1987

Palmerstown, U.S.A.
Dates & Barlow, 1990, p. 259; Dates & Barlow, 1993, p. 281; Gianakos, 1983, p. 149; McDonald, 1983, pp. 228–229; McDonald, 1992, p. 229

Pantomime Quiz
DeLong, 1991, pp. 129–130

Paper Chase, The
Alley & Brown, 2001, pp. 148–149; Carlson, 1985, p. 104; Castleman & Podrazik, 1982, pp. 288–289; Gianakos, 1981, pp. 262–263; Jarvis & Joseph, 1998, pp. 105–113**; Klobas, 1988, pp. 144–146*

Paper Dolls
Gianakos, 1992, pp. 368–369; Also in Morris, 1997, Terrace, 1993

Paper Moon
IN Terrace, 1993

Paradise
Jackson, 1994, pp. 214–216; Yoggy, 1995, pp. 365–367, 568–569, 571–579**; Also in Lentz, 1997, Terrace, 1993

Parent'hood, The
Holtzman, 2000, pp 251–252; Means Coleman, 2000, p. 126; Smith, 1999, pp. 48–49; Also in Terrace, 2000

Paris
Heil, 2001, p. 294; Martindale, 1991, pp. 371–373; McDonald, 1983, p. 227; McDonald, 1992, pp. 227–228; Paietta & Kauppila, 1999, p. 343; Thompson, 1996, pp. 62–63; Tinker & Rukeyser, 1994, p. 128

Paris 7000
Gianakos, 1978, p. 665

Parker Lewis Can't Lose
IN Terrace, 1993, Terrace, 2000

Partners
Andrews, 1986, p. 135; Owen, 1997, pp. 149–152*; Also in Terrace, 1993

Partners in Crime
Gianakos, 1992, pp. 359–360; Also in Terrace, 1993

Partridge Family, The
Bennett, 1996, pp. 112–114; Bryant & Bryant, 2001, p. 168; Jones, 1992, p. 190; Lechner, 2000, pp. 33–35; Mitz, 1980, pp. 275–276; Owen, 1997, p. 29; Pearl & Pearl, 1999, pp. 20, 46, 48, 199–200, 230; Pegg, 2002, pp. 208–209, 216–220; Rafkin, 1998, pp. 68–69; Waldrep, 2000, p. 196; Also in Bianculli, 1996, Eisner & Krinsky, 1984, Terrace, 1993

Party of Five
Cantor, 2001, p. 71; Capsuto, 2000, p. 409; Gross, 2001, pp. 92–93; Lechner, 2000, p. 38; Owen, 1997, pp. 143–148**; Slade, 2002, pp. 67–69, 89–92*; Swanson, 2000, pp. 155, 200; Wild, 1999, pp. 170, 171, 172–174, 246*

Passions
Lechner, 2000, pp. 99–101, 132, 133, 169, 209–211**

Password
IN Bianculli, 1996

Patty Duke Show, The
Bennett, 1996, pp. 17–20; Crotty, 1995; Jones, 1992, pp. 156–157; Mitz, 1980, pp. 208–209; Spigel & Curtin, 1997, pp. 95–116** Also in Bianculli, 1996, Eisner & Krinsky, 1984, Terrace, 1993

Paul Lynde Show, The
Jarvis & Joseph, 1998, p. 172; Also in Eisner & Krinsky, 1984

Peaceable Kingdom
IN Terrace, 1993

Pearl
Suman & Rossman, 2000, p. 34

Pee Wee's Playhouse
Caldwell, 1995, pp. 193, 198–222**; Davis, 1995, pp. 166–168*; Doty, 1993, pp. 81–95**; Putterman, 1995, p. 135; Rushkoff, 1994, pp. 102–108**; Also in Bianculli, 1996

People Are Funny
Munson, 1993, pp. 52–54

People Next Door, The
Paietta & Kauppila, 1999, p. 343

People's Choice, The
Marc, 1989, p. 23; Marc, 1997, p. 19; Putterman, 1995, pp. 91–92, 95*; Schultz, 2000, p. 120; Also in Eisner & Krinsky, 1984, Terrace, 1993

Pepsi Cola Playhouse
Gianakos, 1980, pp. 384–387*

Perfect Strangers
Hamamoto, 1989, p. 143*; Also in Terrace, 1993, Terrace, 2000

Perry Como Show, The
Lewis & Lewis, 1979, pp. 241–248*;

Sackett, 1993, p. 69; Settel, 1958, pp. 147–162 (script); Also in Bianculli, 1996

Perry Mason

Bennett, 1996, pp. 129–131; Bounds, 1996, pp. 1, 3, 11, 17, 39, 98, 101, 105–128, 129–165 (passim)**; Castleman & Podrazik, 1982, p. 122; Collins & Javna, 1989, pp. 29–31; Davis, 2001, p. 118; Delamater & Prigozy, 1998, pp. 123–128**; Edelman & Kupferberg, 1996, pp. 226–227; Fitzgerald & Magers, 2002, p. 106; Gianakos, 1978, pp. 148–161**; Gottfried, 1999, p 276; Hawes, 2002, p. 119–120; Jarvis & Joseph, 1998, pp.x, 5, 7–8, 13, 58, 60, 63–64, 115–128, 279 (n. 1)**; Javna, 1985, pp. 44–47*; Lembo, 2000, p. 173; Lichter, Lichter, & Rothman, 1991, p. 215; Lichter, Lichter, & Rothman, 1994, p. 313; McDonald, 1983, p. 78; McDonald, 1992, p. 88; Meyers, 1981, pp. 44–48*; Miller, 1980, p. 39; Riggs, 1996; Riggs, 1998, pp. 15, 17, 20–27, 49–50**; Rovin, 1977b, pp. 58–59; Sackett, 1993, pp. 96–97; Shales, 1982, pp. 105–106; Stark, 1997, pp. 96–100*Also in Bianculli, 1996; Stempel, 1992, pp. 86–87; Toll, 1982, pp. 172–174

Person to Person

Bogle, 2001, pp. 71–73; Buzenberg & Buzenberg, 1999, p. 30; Hewitt, 2001, p 105; Kanfer, 2000, p. 346; Kendrick, 1969, pp. 31, 35–36, 360–369**; Means Coleman, 2002, pp. 96–97; Merron, 1988, pp. 11–36**; Persico, 1988, pp. 343–354, 403, 404, 430, 437–450 (passim)**; Rico, 1990, pp. 168–169; Scott, 1996, pp. 198–199, 200–201; Sperber, 1986, pp. 424–426, 517–520*; Spigel, 2001, pp. 273–274; Stark, 1997, p. 44; Also in Bianculli, 1996

Persuaders, The

Gianakos, 1978, pp. 690–691; Osgerby & Gough-Yates, 2001, pp. 159–168**; Rovin, 1977b, p. 132; Also in Terrace, 1993

Pete and Gladys

Pegg, 2002, p. 125; Also in Eisner & Krinsky, 1984, Terrace, 1993

Pete Kelly's Blues

Moyer & Alvarez, 2001, pp. 139–140; Also in Terrace, 1993

Peter Gunn

Castleman & Podrazik, 1982, p. 128; Collins & Javna, 1989, pp. 20–22; Gianakos, 1978, pp. 205–207; Hawes, 2002, pp. 115–116; Meyers, 1981, pp. 53–55, 62; Osgerby & Gough-Yates, 2001, pp. 2, 191–194*; Rovin, 1977b, p. 65; U.S. Congress, 1977a, p. 40; Also in Bianculli, 1996, Terrace, 1993

Peter Loves Mary

IN Eisner & Krinsky, 1984, Terrace, 1993

Petrocelli

Cullingford, 1984, pp. 91–92; Gianakos, 1978, pp. 759–760; Gianakos, 1981, pp. 131–132; Klobas, 1988, p. 40; Martindale, 1991, pp. 374–379; Meyers, 1981, p. 210

Petticoat Junction

Bennett, 1996, pp. 29–30; Castleman & Podrazik, 1982, pp. 171–172; Kulzer, 1992, pp. 55–57, 59–63, 78–81*; Lichter, Lichter, & Rothman, 1994, p. 223; Marc, 1984, pp. 58–59; Marc, 1996, pp. 58–59; Marc & Thompson, 1992 (Ch. 2 on Paul Henning), pp. 30–37; Mitz, 1980, p. 209; Paietta & Kauppila, 1999, p. 344; Sackett,

1993, p. 123; Also in Eisner & Krinsky, 1984, Terrace, 1993

Peyton Place
Bogle, 2001, p. 137; Caldwell, 1995, p. 40; Castleman & Podrazik, 1982, pp. 174–175; Chunovic, 2000, pp. 47–48; Goldenson, 1991, pp. 242–243; Haralovich & Rabinovitz, 1999, pp. 10, 75–97**; Kulzer, 1992, pp. 114–117; Paietta & Kauppila, 1999, p. 344; Sackett, 1993, pp. 132–133; Spigel & Curtin, 1997, p. 78; Thompson, 1996, p. 33; Vane & Gross, 1994, pp. 117–118; Also in Bianculli, 1996, Morris, 1997

Phenom
IN Terrace, 2000

Phil Donahue *see* Donahue

Phil Silvers Show, The
Burns, 1990, p. 291; Castleman & Podrazik, 1982, p. 106; Everitt, 2001, pp. xi–xii, 101–117, 119–135**; Field, 1989, p. 150; Freeman, 1980, pp. 45–46; Hamamoto, 1989, pp. 55–56; Javna, 1985, pp. 170–173*; Jones, 1992, pp. 114–119**; Lewis & Lewis, 1979, pp. 216–224*; Lichter, Lichter, & Rothman, 1991, pp. 116, 268–269; Lichter, Lichter, & Rothman, 1994, pp. 379–380; Mitz, 1980, pp. 125–130*; Silvers, 1973, pp. 201–231**; Yoggy, 1995, pp. 431–432; Also in Bianculli, 1996, Eisner & Krinsky, 1984, Terrace, 1993

Philco Television Playhouse
Bogle, 2001, pp. 62–67**; Burns, 1990, p 266; Gianakos, 1980, pp. 123–144**; Hawes, 2001, pp. 55–77, 149**; Hawes, 2002, pp. 190–192; Jackson, 1982; Krampner, 1997, pp. 38–79, 102–104**; Sackett, 1993, pp. 8–9; Skutch, 1998, pp. 73–81**; Also in Bianculli, 1996

Philip Marlowe
Gianakos, 1978, pp. 252–253; Meyers, 1981, pp. 64–65

Phoenix, The
Gianakos, 1983, p. 218

Phyl and Mikhy
IN Terrace, 1993

Phyllis
Alley, 1977, pp. 46, 152–153; Bedell, 1981, p. 86; Chunovic, 2000, pp. 72–73; Coakley, 1977, pp. 53–54; Jarvis & Joseph, 1998, p. 172; Jones, 1992, p. 229; Marc, 1997, p. 176; Mitz, 1980, p. 379; Newcomb, 1987, p. 86; Puette, 1992, p. 53; Sackett, 1993, p. 225; Tinker & Rukeyser, 1994, p. 105; U.S. Congress, 1977a, pp. 91, 325; U.S. Congress, 1977c, p. 25

Picket Fences
Abelman, 1998, p. 74; Capsuto, 2000, pp. 305, 333–334; Forbes & Mahan, 2000, p. 54; Gabler, Rich & Antler, 2000, p. 49; Gross, 2001, p. 93; Jarvis & Joseph, 1998, pp. x, 129–144**; Johnston, 2000, p. 6; Kamalipour & Carrilli, 1998, p. 104; Leonard, 1997, pp. 7, 254; Lichter, Lichter, & Rothman, 1994, pp. 38–39, 41–42, 44, 50, 72–73, 74*; Paietta & Kauppila, 1999, p. 344; Pearl & Pearl, 1999, pp. 84, 106–107*; Schultz, 2000, p. 126; Suman, 1997, p. 77; Swanson, 2000, pp. 45, 62–65*; Thompson, 1996, pp. 13, 42, 167–177**; Walters, 2001, p. 97; Also in Bianculli, 1996, Terrace, 1993

Picture This
Davis, 1995, p. 130

Pinky & the Brain
Owen, 1997, p. 66

Pinky Lee Show, The
Davis, 1995, pp. 168–170*

Pistols 'n' Petticoats
Yoggy, 1995, pp. 433–434; Also in Lentz, 1997, Terrace, 1993

PJ's, The
Bogle, 2001, pp. 451–452; Suman & Rossman, 2000, p. 116.; Also in Terrace, 2000

Planet of the Apes, The
Bedell, 1981, p. 89; Gianakos, 1978, pp. 764–765; Greene, 1996, pp. 153–158, 166–168**; Rovin, 1977b, p. 146; Also in Terrace, 1993

Playhouse, The
Gianakos, 1980, pp. 383–384

Playhouse 90
Becker, 2001**; Burns, 1990, pp. 293–294; Castleman & Podrazik, 1982, pp. 114, 123; Gianakos, 1978, pp. 126–134**; Hawes, 2002, pp. 27–36, 165, 210–211, 231–236**; Krampner, 1997, pp. 121–139**; Skutch, 1998, pp. 129–131, 152–154; Starr, 1997, pp. 87–88, 101–102; Takei, 1994, pp. 145–148; Also in Bianculli, 1996

Please Don't Eat the Daisies
Lichter, Lichter, & Rothman, 1991, p. 53; Lichter, Lichter, & Rothman, 1994, p. 114; Also in Eisner & Krinsky, 1984, Terrace, 1993

Police Squad
Collins & Javna, 1989, pp. 128–130; Also in Bianculli, 1996, Terrace, 1993

Police Story
Alexander, 1994, pp. 233–236; Alley, 1977, pp. 84–88*; Berger, 1987, pp. 63–64; Capsuto, 2000, pp. 100–101*; Christians, Fackler, & Rotzoll, 1995, p. 255; Christians, Rotzoll, & Fackler, 1983, p. 308; Collins & Javna, 1989, pp. 71–73; Condry, 1985, p. 157; Cuklanz, 1998; Gianakos, 1978, pp. 743–745*; Gianakos, 1981, pp. 116–119*; Gitlin, 1983, pp. 242–244; Kaminsky, 1985, pp. 55–83 (passim), especially pp. 78–80; Klobas, 1988, pp. 285–286, 290–291; Lichter, Lichter, & Rothman, 1991, p. 194; Lichter, Lichter, & Rothman, 1994, pp. 286–287; Martindale, 1991, pp. 379–388; Meyers, 1981, pp. 200–201; Newcomb, 1979, pp. 125–128*; Newcomb, 1982, pp. 96–99*; Stempel, 1992, pp. 132–142**; Sumser, 1996, pp. 138–139; Thompson, 1996, p. 61; Turow, 1989, p. 186; U.S. Congress, 1977a, pp. 78, 81, 84–85

Police Story (1952)
Gianakos, 1980, pp. 319–320

Police Woman
Alley, 1977, p. 48; Alley & Brown, 2001, p. 100; Capsuto, 2000, pp. 5, 110–114, 139**; Coakley, 1977, pp. 159, 191; D'Acci, 1994, p. 118; Edelman & Kupferberg, 1996, p. 219; Fiske, 1987, p. 45; Gianakos, 1978, pp. 766–768*; Gianakos, 1981, pp. 158–161*; Gross, 2001, p. 49; Inness, 1999, p. 47; Kidd-Hewitt & Osborne, 1995, p. 166; Lichter, Lichter, & Rothman, 1991, pp. 40–41; Lichter, Lichter, & Rothman, 1994, p. 98; Martindale, 1991, pp. 388–397; Meehan, 1983, pp. 78–79,

177; Meyers, 1981, pp. 201–203; Miller, 2000, p. 158; Montgomery, 1989, p. 90; Newcomb, 2000, p. 106; Osgerby & Gough-Yates, 2001, p. 85; Rubin, 1980, pp. 202–203; Shaheen, 1984, pp. 50–51; Sochen, 1987, p. 100; Sumser, 1996, pp. 110, 119; Also in Terrace, 1993

Pond's Theater
Gianakos, 1980, pp. 437–439*

Port Charles
Fiztgerald & Magers, 2002, p. 64; Matelski, 1999, p. 42

Powers of Matthew Star, The
Gianakos, 1987, pp. 303–304

Powers That Be, The
Schultz, 2000, p. 122; Also in Terrace, 1993

Practice, The (doctors)
Kalisch, Kalisch, & Scobey, 1983, pp. 90–93, 100*; Paietta & Kauppila, 1999, p. 345; Thomas, 1991, p. 271; Turow, 1989, pp. 217–218

Practice, The (lawyers)
Capsuto, 2000, p. 363; Chunovic, 2000, p. 153; Gabler, Rich & Antler, 2000, pp. 49, 64, 74–75*; Jarvis & Joseph, 1998, pp. 27, 31, 233, 273 (n. 9); Johnston, 2000, p. 74; Lechner, 2000, pp. 47–50*; Marek, 1999; Pearl & Pearl, 1999, p. 93; Simon, 2001; Swanson, 2000, pp. 133–134, 211; Walters, 2001, pp. 97, 187–189

Pretender, The
Bryant & Bryant, 2001, pp. 184, 190

Prey, The
Abelman, 1998, p. 282; Lechner, 2000, pp. 64–65, 66, 129; Martin, 1980**; Muir, 2001a, pp. 522–529; Also in Bianculli, 1996

Price Is Right, The
Allen, 1987, p. 151; Allen, 1992, p. 177 (same as Allen 1987); Anderson, 1978, pp. 87, 105–106; Brown, 1990, pp. 135–138*; DeLong, 1991, pp. 224, 227, 238–242*; Fiske, 1987, pp. 276–279*; Lewis, 1991, p. 70; Sackett, 1993, p. 92

Pride & Joy
Cotter, 1997, p. 467

Pride of the Family
IN Eisner & Krinsky, 1984

PrimeTime Live
Auletta, 1991, pp. 533–534; Heil, 2001, p. 154; Kamalipour & Carrilli, 1998, pp. 188–201**; Spragens, 1995, pp. 22, 98–99, 132*

Princesses
IN Terrace, 1993

Prisoner, The
Adler, 1981, pp. 102–106*; Aldgate, 2000, p. 60; Burns & Thompson, 1989, pp. 26–27; Buxton, 1990, pp. 93–96; Cantor, 2001, p. xiv; Castleman & Podrazik, 1982, pp. 202–203*; Davis, 2001, p. 120; Gerani, 1977, pp. 121–125; Gianakos, 1978, pp. 614–615; Himmelstein, 1984, pp. 178–179; Himmelstein, 1994, p. 218; Javna, 1985, pp. 68–71*; Lewis, 1991, p. 57; Meyers, 1981, pp. 111–113*; Miller, 1980, p. 113; Miller, 2000, pp. 43–50**; Osgerby & Gough-Yates, 2001, pp. 25, 200–201; Rakoff, 1998, whole book**; Rovin, 1977a, pp. 142, 146; Rovin, 1977b, p. 120; Soter, 2002, pp. 107–108; White & Ali, 1988, whole book**; Also in Bianculli, 1996, Terrace, 1993

Private Eye
Leonard, 1997, pp. 137–138

Private Benjamin
IN Terrace, 1993

Private Secretary
Alley & Brown, 2001, p. 23; Capsuto, 2000, pp. 25–26; Harris, 1991, p. 229; Hawes, 2002, pp. 94–95; Mitz, 1980, pp. 81–83*; Schultz, 1990, pp. 10–11, 124–136 (episode guides)*; Also in Terrace, 1993

Probe
IN Terrace, 1993

Producers Showcase
Gianakos, 1980, pp. 395–399*; Krampner, 1997, pp. 93–102*

Professional Father
Paietta & Kauppila, 1999, p. 345

Profiler
Bryant & Bryant, 2001, pp. 183, 191; Paietta & Kauppila, 1999, p. 345

Profiles in Courage
Gianakos, 1978, pp. 443–444

Profit
Leonard, 1997, pp. 104–105; Owen, 1997, p. 156*

Project UFO
Gianakos, 1981, pp. 243–245*

Promised Land
Pearl & Pearl, 1999, pp. 116, 169

Pros and Cons *see* **Gabriel's Fire**

Protectors, The
Lichter, Lichter, & Rothman, 1991, pp. 210, 216; Lichter, Lichter, & Rothman, 1994, pp. 314–315; Meyers, 1981, p. 179

Providence
Longworth, 2000, pp. 108–109, 111–116**

Prudential Family Playhouse, The
Gianakos, 1980, p. 286

Pruitts of Southampton
Andrews, 1980, pp. 131–138*

P.S.I. Luv U
IN Terrace, 1993

Psychiatrist, The
Paietta & Kauppila, 1999, p. 345; Turow, 1989, pp. 160–161

Public Prosecutor
Anderson, 1994, pp. 55–56

Pulitzer Prize Playhouse
Gianakos, 1980, pp. 288–290; Hawes, 2001, pp. 131–132

Punky Brewster
Klobas, 1988, pp. 333–335; Lichter, Lichter, & Rothman, 1991, p. 89; Lichter, Lichter, & Rothman, 1994, p. 159; Oskamp, 1988, p. 321; Also in Terrace, 1993

Push
Schwartz, 1999, p. 183

Q. E. D. (1982)
Gianakos, 1983, p. 205

Quantum Leap
Caldwell, 1995, p. 109; Capsuto, 2000, p. 308; Chunovic, 1995b, whole book**; Gross, 2001, p. 170; Harris, 1998, pp. 134–136, 138–139, 140, 142–149**; Means Coleman, 2002, pp. 158, 162; Pearl & Pearl, 1999, p. 165; Swanson, 2000, pp. 103–107**; Wahl, 1995, p. 9; Wiggins, 1993; Williams, 1996; Also in Terrace, 1993

Quark
Castleman & Podrazik, 1982, p. 287; Gianakos, 1981, p. 252; Also in Eisner & Krinsky, 1984, Terrace, 1993

Quest, The (Western)
Coakley, 1977, pp. 112–113; Gianakos, 1981, p. 206; Gianakos, 1987, p. 310; McDonald, 1987, pp. 121–122; Puette, 1992, pp. 176–177; Yoggy, 1995, pp. 484–495**; Also in Lentz, 1997, West, 1987

Quincy, M.E.
Cuklanz, 1998; Cuklanz, 2000, pp. 78, 80–81, 106–107; Fagen, 1996, pp. 87–88; Gianakos, 1981, pp. 226–230**; Gianakos, 1983, pp. 155–158*; Gianakos, 1987, pp. 244–246; Heil, 2001, pp. 320–323; Kalisch, Kalisch, & Scobey, 1983, pp. 69–70; Klobas, 1988, pp. 390–391; Lichter, Lichter, & Rothman, 1991, pp. 118, 121, 123, 149–150, 165–166*; Lichter, Lichter, & Rothman, 1994, pp. 194, 198, 200, 233–234, 253*; Marc & Thompson, 1992 (Ch. 16 on Glen Larson), pp. 171–178; Martindale, 1991, pp. 399–412; Meyers, 1981, pp. 237–239; Paietta & Kauppila, 1999, pp. 345–346; Pearl & Pearl, 1999, pp. 127, 156; Puette, 1992, pp. 49–50, 180–181, 189; Rowland & Watkins, 1984, pp. 259, 272–273; Stempel, 1992, pp. 171–175*; Turow, 1989, pp. 169–174*; Also in Bianculli, 1996, Terrace, 1993

Quiz Kids
DeLong, 1991, pp. 132–133; Himmelstein, 1994, pp. 331–332; Vane & Gross, 1994, pp. 44–46; Also in Bianculli, 1996

Rachel Gunn, R.N.
Paietta & Kauppila, 1999, p. 346; Also in Terrace, 1993

Racket Squad
Gianakos, 1983, pp. 269–274**; Meyers, 1981, pp. 21–22; Rovin, 1977b, pp. 32–33; Stempel, 1992, p. 24

Rafferty
Cuklanz, 1998; Cuklanz, 2000, pp. 33, 115; Gianakos, 1981, pp. 232–233; Kalisch, Kalisch, & Scobey, 1983, pp. 72–75*; Paietta & Kauppila, 1999, p. 346

Rags to Riches
IN Terrace, 1993

Raising Miranda
IN Terrace, 1993

Range Rider, The
Davis, 1995, pp. 225–226; Jarvis & Joseph, 1998, p. 192; Magers & Fitzgerald, 1999, pp. 105–106; Yoggy, 1995, pp. 24–25; Also in Lentz, 1997, West, 1987

Rango
Adir, 1988, p. 116; Pegg, 2002, p. 61; Spelling, 1996, pp. 57–58; Yoggy, 1995, pp. 435–436; Also in Eisner & Krinsky, 1984, Lentz, 1997, Terrace, 1993

Rat Patrol, The
Gianakos, 1978, pp. 546–548*; Rovin, 1977b, pp. 111–112; Worland, 1989

Raven
Hamamoto, 1994, p. 8; Also in Terrace, 1993

Rawhide
Aquila, 1996, p. 176; Bogle, 2001, p. 115; Brauer, 1975, pp. 83–93, 99, 101–103**; Fagen, 1996, p. 34; Fitzgerald & Magers, 2002, pp. 34, 136, 202, 208; Gallafent, 1994, pp. 11–14*; Gianakos, 1978, pp. 190–197**; Hawes, 2002, pp. 143–144; Jackson, 1994, pp. 133–135; Jarvis & Joseph, 1998, pp. 209–212*; Lichter, Lichter, & Rothman, 1991, pp. 117, 137; Lichter, Lichter, & Rothman, 1994, p. 193; Magers & Fitzgerald, 1999, pp. 189–190, 253; McDonald, 1987, p. 112; Newcomb, 1979, p. 424; Newcomb, 1987, p. 617; Pearl & Pearl, 1999, pp. 73–74, 110–111, 196*; Rovin, 1977b, p. 61; Sackett, 1993, pp. 102–103; Stempel, 1992, pp. 80–81; Yoggy, 1995, pp. 263–264, 273–284, 369–370**; Also in Bianculli, 1996, Lentz, 1997, West, 1987

Ray Milland Show, The
IN Eisner & Krinsky, 1984, Terrace, 1993

Raye, Martha *see* **Martha Raye Show**

Real McCoys, The
Castleman & Podrazik, 1982, p. 119; Hawes, 2002, pp. 98–100, 197; Himmelstein, 1984, pp. 98–102*; Himmelstein, 1994, pp. 139–142; Jones, 1992, pp. 130–133*; Marc, 1984, pp. 54–57; Marc, 1989, pp. 77–78; Marc, 1996, pp. 54–57; Marc, 1997, p. 64; Mitz, 1980, pp. 141–144*; Rodriguez, 1997, p. 59; Sackett, 1993, p. 86; Yoggy, 1998, p. 148; Also in Bianculli, 1996, Eisner & Krinsky, 1984, Terrace, 1993

Real People
Bedell, 1981, pp. 267–268; Sklar, 1980, pp. 196–200*

Reasonable Doubts
Jarvis & Joseph, 1998, pp. 224, 305–306 (n. 22); Lester, 1996, p. 124; Lichter, Lichter, & Rothman, 1994, p. 42; Nelson, 1994, p. 11; Pearl & Pearl, 1999, pp. 50, 122–123, 183, 191–192*; Schwartz, 1999, p. 163; Sumser, 1996, pp. 154–155; Also in Terrace, 1993

Rebel, The
Fitzgerald & Magers, 2002, pp. 266, 292–293; Friedman, 2002, pp. 67–72**; Gianakos, 1978, pp. 234–236; Jackson, 1994, p. 136; Jarvis & Joseph, 1998, p. 205; Rovin, 1977b, pp. 72–73; Yoggy, 1995, pp. 214–217*; Also in Lentz, 1997, Terrace, 1993, West, 1987

Rebound
Gianakos, 1980, p. 319

Red Buttons
Allen, 1956, pp. 91–104, also see index*; Lewis & Lewis, 1979, pp. 209–215*

Red Skelton Show, The
Adir, 1988, pp. 205–215**; Allen, 1956, pp. 265–275, also see index*; Castleman & Podrazik, 1982, pp. 75–76; Martin, 1980**; McCrohan, 1990, pp. 157–160*; Mott, 2000, pp.

158–174**; Sackett, 1993, pp. 26–27; U.S. Congress, 1977c, pp. 29–30; Williams, 1982, pp. 114–120**; Also in Bianculli, 1996

Redigo
IN Lentz, 1997, West, 1987

Relativity
Capsuto, 2000, pp. 373–373; Pearl & Pearl, 1999, p. 198

Remington Steele
Fiske, 1987, p. 112; Gianakos, 1987, pp. 307–310*; Gianakos, 1992, pp. 309–312*; Helford, 2000, pp. 92, 93, 111 (n. 5); Klobas, 1988, pp. 172–173, 188–189; Lichter, Lichter, & Rothman, 1991, pp. 29, 56; Lichter, Lichter, & Rothman, 1994, pp. 84, 118; Newcomb, 1987, pp. 71–73*; Press, 1991, pp. 152–153; Rose, 1985, p. 48; Rose, 1999, p. 104; Sumser, 1996, pp. 111–112; Thompson, 1996, p. 112; Vande Berg & Wenner, 1991, pp. 176–177; Wilcox, 1996; Also in Terrace, 1993

Rendezvous
Gianakos, 1992, pp. 454–455

Renegades
Gianakos, 1987, pp. 317–318

Reporter, The
Daniel, 1996, pp. 12–13; Gianakos, 1978, pp. 469–470; Also in Terrace, 1993

Rescue 911
Allen, 1992, pp. 73–74, 82, 85; Diem & Lantos, 1996; Hinton, 1999, pp. 2, 31–32, 219–134**; Newcomb, 2000, pp. 394–396; Roman, 1996, p. 73; Weimann, 2000, pp. 176–178; White, 1992, pp. 181–182; Also in Bianculli, 1996

Restless Gun, The
Gianakos, 1981, pp. 368–371*; Jackson, 1994, pp. 79–80; Leiby & Leiby, 2001, pp. 15, 233; McDonald, 1987, p. 64; Rovin, 1977b, p. 54; Sackett, 1993, p. 79; Yoggy, 1995, pp. 208–211*; Also in Lentz, 1997, West, 1987

Return of the Saint *see* The Saint

Revlon Mirror Theatre
Gianakos, 1980, p. 374

Rhoda
Abelman, 1998, pp. 161–162; Alley, 1977, p. 46; Bedell, 1981, pp. 85–86; Castleman & Podrazik, 1982, p. 258; Coakley, 1977, pp. 55–56, 229–230; Doty, 1993, p. 123 (note 29); Dow, 1996, pp. 59–60; Gabler, Rich & Antler, 2000, pp. 36–37; Jones, 1992, p. 229; Lichter, Lichter, & Rothman, 1991, p. 68; Lichter, Lichter, & Rothman, 1994, p. 134; Marc & Thompson, 1992 (Ch. 5 on James L. Brooks), pp. 61–69; Miles, 1975, pp. 42–44 (Nov. 4, 1974 show); Miller, 1980, pp. 189–190; Mitz, 1980, pp. 349–355**; Newcomb, 1979, p. 527; Newcomb, 1987, pp. 56, 58–64, 65, 81, 86**; Newcomb & Alley, 1983, pp. 196–223 (passim); Pearl & Pearl, 1999, pp. 89, 197; Rafkin, 1998, pp. 97–98; Sackett, 1993, pp. 214–215; Sochen, 1987, pp. 87–88; Sochen, 1999, pp. 158–159; Taylor, 1989, pp. 97–101, 125–126*; Tinker & Rukeyser, 1994, p. 104; Also in Eisner & Krinsky, 1984

Rhythm & Blues
Bogle, 2001, pp. 408–409; Lichter,

Lichter, & Rothman, 1994, p. 63; Also in Terrace, 1993

Rich Man, Poor Man
Broughton, 1986, pp. 274–288 (passim); McCrohan, 1990, pp. 241–247**; Miller, 2000, p. 165; Sackett, 1993, pp. 218–219; Also in Bianculli, 1996

Richard Boone Show, The
Gianakos, 1978, pp. 418–419; Williams, 1982, pp. 82–85*

Richard Diamond, Private Detective
Hawes, 2002, p. 113; Meyers, 1981, pp. 43–44; Rovin, 1977b, p. 58; Smith, 1989, p. 45; Also in Terrace, 1993

Richard Pryor Show, The
Bogle, 2001, p. 117; Haskins, 1984, pp. 139–147**; Himmelstein, 1994, pp. 193–194; Marc, 1989, pp. 218–219; McDonald, 1983, pp. 189–191*; McDonald, 1992, pp. 192–194*; Pryor, 1995, pp. 153–158*; Putterman, 1995, pp. 148–149; Williams & Williams, 1991, pp. 117–121

Richie Brockelman, Private Eye
Collins & Javna, 1989, pp. 35–37; Gianakos, 1981, pp. 255–256; Meyers, 1981, pp. 248–249; Thompson, 1990, pp. 79–82*; Also in Terrace, 1993

Rifleman
Aquila, 1996, pp. 177–178; Castleman & Podrazik, 1982, p. 127; Fagen, 1996, p. 31; Fitzgerald & Magers, 2002, p. 202; Gianakos, 1978, pp. 172–176*; Hawes, 2002, p. 137; Jackson, 1994, pp. 108–110; Lichter, Lichter, & Rothman, 1991, pp. 82, 188; Magers & Fitzgerald, 1999, p. 35; McDonald, 1987, pp. 63, 69–70, 113–114; Meehan, 1983, p. 165; Rovin, 1977b, p. 60; Sackett, 1993, p. 83; Yoggy, 1995, pp. 285–294, 356–357**; Also in Bianculli, 1996, Lentz, 1997, Terrace, 1993, West, 1987

Riker
Gianakos, 1983, p. 183

Rin Tin Tin *see* **Adventures of Rin Tin Tin**

Ripcord
Rovin, 1977b, p. 83; Also in Terrace, 1993

Riptide
Gianakos, 1987, pp. 340–341; Gianakos, 1992, pp. 306–308*; Sumser, 1996, pp. 73, 111, 123, 135, 142–143; Thompson, 1990, pp. 122–123; Also in Terrace, 1993

Riverboat
Gianakos, 1978, pp. 232–233; Jackson, 1994, pp. 138–139; Also in Lentz, 1997, West, 1987

Road of Life
Paietta & Kauppila, 1999, p. 346

Road West, The
Gianakos, 1978, pp. 551–552; Lichter, Lichter, & Rothman, 1991, pp. 71–72; Lichter, Lichter, & Rothman, 1994, p. 138; Also in Lentz, 1997, West, 1987

Roaring Twenties, The
Castleman & Podrazik, 1982, p. 143; Daniel, 1996, p. 11; Gianakos, 1978,

pp. 284–285; Lichter, Lichter, & Rothman, 1991, p. 251; Lichter, Lichter, & Rothman, 1994, pp. 357–358; Rovin, 1977b, pp. 78–79; Also in Terrace, 1993

Robert Montgomery Presents
Gianakos, 1980, pp. 231–245; Hawes, 2001, pp. 111–120, 149–150**; Skutch, 1998, pp. 86–88

Robert Q. Lewis Show, The
Rafkin, 1998, pp. 18–20

Robin Hood
Davis, 1995, pp. 7–8; Gianakos, 1981, pp. 347–351*; Miller, 2000, pp. 21, 22–23; Rovin, 1977b, pp. 42–44

Roc
Bogle, 2001, pp. 412–413; Bryant & Bryant, 2001, pp. 213–214; Caldwell, 1995, p. 70; Capsuto, 2000, pp. 293, 357; Croteau & Hoynes, 2000, pp. 217, 218; Davis, 2001, p. 22; Lichter, Lichter, & Rothman, 1994, pp. 60–61; Means Coleman, 2000, pp. 112–115, 165*; Zook, 1999, pp. 77–87**; Also in Terrace, 1993, Terrace, 2000

Rockford Files, The
Bedell, 1981, pp. 193–194; Bounds, 1996, pp. 119–120; Castleman & Podrazik, 1982, p. 260; Collins & Javna, 1989, pp. 14–16; Cuklanz, 1998; Cuklanz, 2000, pp. 70, 119–121; Cullingford, 1984, p. 43; Delamater & Prigozy, 1998, pp. 126–127; Gianakos, 1978, pp. 765–766; Gianakos, 1981, pp. 147–152**; Jarvis & Joseph, 1998, p. 239; Javna, 1985, pp. 98–101*; Kaminsky, 1985, pp. 148–151, 153–159**; Klobas, 1988, pp. 60–62; Leonard, 1997, pp. 50, 144–145; Lichter, Lichter, & Rothman, 1991, pp. 189, 225; Lichter, Lichter, & Rothman, 1994, p. 280; Marc, 1984, pp. 90–92; Marc, 1996, pp. 90–92; Marc & Thompson, 1992 (Ch. 13 on Roy Huggins), pp. 141–151, (Ch. 19 on Stephen J. Cannell), pp. 205–216; Martindale, 1991, pp. 414–427; Meyers, 1981, pp. 212–214; Miller, 1980, p. 68; Newcomb, 1979, pp. 152–153; Orlik, 2001, p. 28; Osgerby & Gough-Yates, 2001, pp. 201–202; Puette, 1992, p. 182; Robertson, 1995, whole book**; Rose, 1985, pp. 43–44; Rovin, 1977b, p. 145; Shaheen, 1984, pp. 49–50; Shales, 1982, pp. 162–167 (passim); Stempel, 1992, pp. 179–182*; Strait, 1985, pp. 294–319, 321, 323–324, 330–337 (passim)**; Thompson, 1990, pp. 39, 61–74**; Vande Berg & Wenner, 1991, pp. 117–119; Williams, 1982, pp. 145–146; Also in Bianculli, 1996, Terrace, 1993

Rocky and His Friends
Davis, 1995, pp. 52–54*; Also in Bianculli, 1996, Eisner & Krinsky, 1984, Terrace, 1993

Rocky King, Inside Detective
Meyers, 1981, pp. 9–10; Rovin, 1977b, p. 26; Also in Terrace, 1993

Rod Brown of the Rocket Rangers
Gianakos, 1987, pp. 363–365; Also in Terrace, 1993

Rogers, Roy *see* **Roy Rogers Show**

Rogues, The
Castleman & Podrazik, 1982, p. 176; Gianakos, 1978, pp. 444–446; Guida, 2000, p. 193; Meyers, 1981, pp. 104–105

Roll Out
McDonald, 1983, p. 188; McDonald, 1992, p. 191; Tinker & Rukeyser, 1994, p. 100

Roller Girls
IN Terrace, 1993

Rookies, The
Gianakos, 1978, pp. 720–723*; Gianakos, 1981, pp. 119–120; Kalisch, Kalisch, & Scobey, 1983, pp. 101–105, 113*; Lichter, Lichter, & Rothman, 1991, p. 210; Marc, 1984, p. 88; Marc & Thompson, 1992 (Ch. 15 on Aaron Spelling), pp. 163–169; Martindale, 1991, pp. 427–435; McDonald, 1983, p. 201; McDonald, 1992, p. 203; Meyers, 1981, pp. 182–185; Paietta & Kauppila, 1999, p. 346; Rovin, 1977b, pp. 134–135; Schneider, 2001, pp. 103–104; Spelling, 1996, pp. 83–85*

Room for One More
IN Eisner & Krinsky, 1984

Room for Romance
IN Terrace, 1993

Room for Two
IN Terrace, 1993, Terrace, 2000

Room 222
Andrews, 1986, pp. 131–132; Bogle, 2001, pp. 6, 161–164*; Capsuto, 2000, pp. 73–75*; Castleman & Podrazik, 1982, p. 215; Daniel, 1996, p. 24; Gianakos, 1981, pp. 407–411*; Hamamoto, 1989, pp. 97–100*; Jones, 1992, p. 189; Lichter, Lichter, & Rothman, 1991, pp. 167–168; Lichter, Lichter, & Rothman, 1994, p. 255; Marc & Thompson, 1992 (Ch. 5 on James L. Brooks), pp. 61–69; McDonald, 1983, pp. 128–129; McDonald, 1992, pp. 136–137; Rafkin, 1998, pp. 67–68; Rose, 1999, p. 90; Thompson, 1996, pp. 52–53; Tinker & Rukeyser, 1994, p. 86; Torres, 1998, pp. 71, 72–78**; Turner, 1994, pp. 139–140; Also in Eisner & Krinsky, 1984

Roomies
IN Terrace, 1993

Roots (including Next Generation)
Abelman, 1998, pp. 163–164; Atwan, Orton, & Vesterman, 1978, pp. 35–38*; Bedell, 1981, pp. 146, 169–171; Broughton, 1986, pp. 117–128 (passim); Bryant & Bryant, 2001, p. 209; Castleman & Podrazik, 1982, pp. 275–276*; Coakley, 1977, pp. 177–178, 244–245; Cortes, 2000, pp. 81–82; Creeber, 2001, p. 36; Dates & Barlow, 1990, pp. 290–292; Dates & Barlow, 1993, pp. 314–316; Goldenson, 1991, pp. 363–366; Holtzman, 2000, p. 249; Lichter, Lichter, & Rothman, 1991, p. 243; Lichter, Lichter, & Rothman, 1994, pp. 347–348; McDonald, 1983, pp. 214–223**; McDonald, 1992, pp. 216–223**; Miller, 2000, pp. 166–167; Neuman, 1991, p. 109; Newcomb, 1979, pp. 204–230**; Newcomb, 1982, pp. 412–413; Newcomb, 1987, pp. 492–493; Newcomb, 2000, pp. 288–289, 586; O'Connor, 1983, pp. 279–305**; Pearl & Pearl, 1999, pp. 230–231; Rapping, 1987, pp. 154–157*; Rodriguez, 1997, p. 64; Rosenthal, 1999, pp. 271–295**; Schuilman, 2001, p. 77; Sklar, 1980, pp. 169–172*; Stark, 1997, pp. 199–203*; Stempel, 1992, pp. 129–131; U.S. Congress, 1977b, p. 426; Winship, 1988, pp. 141–143; Woll & Miller, 1987, pp. 88–91*; Also in Bianculli, 1996

Ropers, The
Lichter, Lichter, & Rothman, 1991, p. 47; Lichter, Lichter, & Rothman, 1994, p. 106; Sackett, 1993, pp. 254–255

Roseanne
Abelman, 1998, p. 64; Allen, 1992, pp. 74–76, 77, 79*; Alley & Brown, 2001, pp. 73–74, 75–76; Arnold, 1994, pp. 2–20, 91–108, 111–116, 159–163**; Bignell, 1997, p. 143; Blum, 1995, pp. 13, 111–112; Bryant & Bryant, 2001, p. 173; Caldwell, 1995, pp. 3, 59–60; Capsuto, 2000, pp. 275–277, 281, 302–303, 326–329, 360–362**; Chunovic, 2000, pp 13, 107–111; Croteau & Hoynes, 2000, pp. 217, 218; Crotty, 1995; Davies, 1997, p. 70; Davis, 2001, p. 17; Doty, 1993, p. 122 (note 27); Dow, 1996, pp. 99–100, 208; Gottfried, 1999, p 311; Gross, 2001, pp. 89–90; Gross & Woods, 1999, p. 294; Haralovich & Rabinovitz, 1999, pp. 191–192, 192–194; Himmelstein, 1994, pp. 134–135, 137; Hollows, 2000, pp. 198–199; Holtzman, 2000, pp 129–130, 303; Horowitz, 1997, pp. 153–154; Isaacs, 1999, p. 98; Johnston, 2000, p. 58; Jones, 1992, p. 266; Kutulas, 1998; Leonard, 1997, p. 7; Lester, 1996, pp. 157–158; Lewis, 1991, pp. 70–71, 189; Lichter, Lichter, & Rothman, 1991, pp. 65, 78, 90, 114; Lichter, Lichter, & Rothman, 1994, pp. 40, 41, 44, 49–50, 146, 189; MacDonald, 1995, pp. 144–145; Marc, 1997, pp. 195–199, 203*; Marc & Thompson, 1992 (Ch. 9 on Carsey & Werner), pp. 99–107, especially 104–105; Mayerle, 1991; Mellencamp, 1992, pp. 338–350**; Miller, 1994, p. 232; Newcomb, 1994, pp. 101–114, 137, 202–211**; Owen, 1997, pp. 44–46, 123–124*; Parenti, 1991, p. 84; Pearl & Pearl, 1999, p. 21; Press, 1991, pp. 42–44*; Roman, 1996, pp. 26, 62–63; Sackett, 1993, pp. 322–323; Schwartz, 1999, pp. 131, 151; Seger, 1996, pp. 156, 161; Sochen, 1999, pp. 200, 202, 204–205*; Stark, 1997, pp. 26, 28, 262–266*; Steenland, 1990, pp. 29, 48–49; Suman, 1997, pp. 5, 149–151*; Tabarlet, 1993; Tasker, 1998, pp. 167–169; Vane & Gross, 1994, p. 120; Wahl, 1995, p. 52; Walters, 2001, pp. 68–72*; Ward, 1995; Wild, 1999, p. 52; Also in Bianculli, 1996, Terrace, 1993, Terrace, 2000

Rosetti and Ryan
Gianakos, 1981, pp. 238–239; Lichter, Lichter, & Rothman, 1994, p. 92; Meyers, 1981, p. 242

Rough Riders, The
Fitzgerald & Magers, 2002, pp. 168, 292; Gianakos, 1981, pp. 393–394; Jackson, 1994, p. 111; Yoggy, 1995, p. 50; Also in Lentz, 1997, Terrace, 1993, West, 1987

Round Table, The
Owen, 1997, pp. 83–84, 85; Rapping, 1994, pp. 160–161

Rounders, The
Jackson, 1994, pp. 176–177; Yoggy, 1995, pp. 434–435; Also in Lentz, 1997

Rousters, The
Gianakos, 1987, pp. 320–321; Thompson, 1990, pp. 119–122*; Also in Terrace, 1993

Route 66
Bogle, 2001, pp. 95–97; Caldwell, 1995, pp. 34–35; Castleman & Podrazik, 1982, p. 144; Gianakos, 1978,

Lisanti & Paul, 2002, pp. 186–188; Meyers, 1981, pp. 92–95*; Miller, 2000, pp. 27, 42; Osgerby & Gough-Yates, 2001, pp. 32–43, 47–52, 198**; Soter, 2002, p. 10; Also in Terrace, 1993

St. Elsewhere
Abelman, 1998, p. 41; Auletta, 1991, pp. 445–450, plus see index**; Bogle, 2001, pp. 278–279; Burns & Thompson, 1989, pp. 84–85; Capsuto, 2000, pp. 202, 221; Cuklanz, 2000, pp. 86–87, 105, 108–109; Cumberbatch & Negrine, 1992, p. 50; Davis, 2001, p. 142; Ferre, 1990, p. 37; Friedman, 2002, pp. 266–267; Gianakos, 1987, pp. 296–300; Gianakos, 1992, pp. 319–232*; Henderson & Mazzeo, 1990, pp. 110–111; Himmelstein, 1994, pp. 232–233; Kalat, 1998, pp. 93–94; Kendall, 1989**; Klobas, 1988, pp. 250–251, 260, 303–304, 333, 365–366, 457; Lechner, 2000, p. 271; Leonard, 1997, pp. 175–176; Lichter, Lichter, & Rothman, 1991, pp. 30, 34, 47, 87, 100, 163, 165, 189*; Lichter, Lichter, & Rothman, 1994, pp. 85, 157–158, 173, 246, 249*; Longworth, 2000, pp. 40–41, 46, 106–107, 109–110, 127–128; Malmsheimer, 1988, p. 134; Marc, 1989, pp. 166, 202; Marc, 1997, pp. 137, 167; Nelson, 1994, p. 23; Newcomb, 1987, pp. 91–100, 193**; Paietta & Kauppila, 1999, p. 347–348; Pearl & Pearl, 1999, pp. 117, 216–217; Puette, 1992, pp. 54, 55, 56, 190–191; Rose, 1985, p. 82; Stark, 1997, pp. 238–240, 292–293; Stempel, 1992, pp. 237–239, 254–255, 270–271; Swanson, 2000, pp. 50–51; Thompson, 1996, pp. 13, 15, 16, 74–97, 174**; Tinker & Rukeyser, 1994, pp. 170, 172–173; Turow, 1989, pp. 232–234, 238–253, 254–255, 269; Vande Berg & Trujillo, 1989, pp. 123, 135, 142–143, 164, 177, 180, 205–213**; Also in Bianculli, 1996

Saints and Sinners
Daniel, 1996, p. 12; Gianakos, 1978, pp. 370–372*; Lichter, Lichter, & Rothman, 1991, pp. 117–118, 120; Lichter, Lichter, & Rothman, 1994, p. 194; Rovin, 1977b, p. 85

Sally
Pegg, 2002, p. 125

Salvage 1
Gianakos, 1981, pp. 272–273; Also in Terrace, 1993

Sam
Moyer & Alvarez, 2001, pp. 191–193*

Sam Benedict
Gianakos, 1978, pp. 367–368

Sammy Davis, Jr. Show, The
Andrews, 1980, pp. 146–152*; McDonald, 1983, pp. 113–114; McDonald, 1992, pp. 122–123

San Pedro Beach Bums, The
Crown, 1999, p. 30; Spelling, 1996, p. 134

Sandy Duncan Show, The
IN Terrace, 1993

Sanford and Son
Acham, 1999*; Alley, 1977, p. 46; Andrews, 1986, p. 136; Atwan, Orton, & Vesterman, 1978, p. 384; Bedell, 1981, pp. 150–151; Berry & Mitchell-Kernan, 1982, p. 125; Dates & Barlow, 1990, pp. 271, 273; Dates & Barlow, 1993, pp. 293–295*; Davis, 2001, p. 11; Guida, 2000, pp. 198–199; Hamamoto, 1989, pp. 102–103; Haskins,

1984, pp. 79–80; Himmelstein, 1984, pp. 111–112; Himmelstein, 1994, pp. 151–152; Jones, 1992, pp. 214–217*; Lichter, Lichter, & Rothman, 1991, pp. 95, 241, 252*; Lichter, Lichter, & Rothman, 1994, pp. 167–168, 358; Marc, 1989, pp. 184–185; Marc, 1997, p. 152; Marc & Thompson, 1992 (Ch. 4 on Norman Lear), pp. 49–60; McCrohan, 1990, pp. 224–230**; McDonald, 1983, pp. 177, 185; McDonald, 1992, pp. 182, 186; Means Coleman, 2000, pp. 89–90; Miles, 1975, pp. 59–60 (Nov. 2, 1973, show); Miller, 2000, pp. 150–156**; Mitz, 1980, pp. 279–283*; Mott, 2000, pp. 185–186; Pearl & Pearl, 1999, pp. 82–83; Pegg, 2002, pp. 224–227; Rafkin, 1998, pp. 54–57*; Raymond, 1990, pp. 123–124, 125; Sackett, 1993, p. 185; Taylor, 1989, pp. 79–80, 82–84 (passim); Witney & Abels, 1980, pp. 274–279 (passim); Also in Bianculli, 1996, Eisner & Krinsky, 1984, Terrace, 1993

Santa Barbara

James, 1991**; Jenrette, McIntosh, & Winterberger, 1999; Matelski, 1988, pp. 148–152*; Matelski, 1999, p. 44; Nelson, 1995, p. 62; Nochimson, 1992, pp. 7, 8, 105–117, 128–145, 148–153, 184–192, 194, 195, 196–197**; Rouverol, 1992, pp. 107–181**; Suman, 1997, p. 91; Wild, 1999, p. 172; Williams, 1992, pp. 84, 88, 99, 110–112, 122–123, 163*

Sara

Capsuto, 2000, pp. 205–206; Harris, 1989, p. 59; Harris, 1994, p. 66; Jarvis & Joseph, 1998, p. 174; Yoggy, 1995, p. 607; Also in Lentz, 1997, West, 1987

Sarge

Blum & Lindheim, 1987, p. 102; Gianakos, 1978, p. 691; Lichter, Lichter, & Rothman, 1991, p. 280; Lichter, Lichter, & Rothman, 1994, pp. 393–394; Rovin, 1977b, p. 131

Saturday Night Live

Abelman, 1998, p. 314; Beatts, 1977, whole book**; Cader, 1994, whole book**; Caldwell, 1995, pp. 94–96; Carter 1995, pp. 158–159; Castleman & Podrazik, 1982, pp. 271–273*; Chunovic, 2000, pp. 121–123; Crown, 1999, pp. 159–160; Edgerton, Marsden & Nachbar, 1997, pp. 33–42**; Erickson, 2000, pp. 264, 276; Forbes & Mahan, 2000, p. 81; Goethals, 1981, pp. 117–118; Heldenfels, 1994, p. 61; Hill & Weingrad, 1986, whole book **; Himmelstein, 1984, pp. 151–152; Himmelstein, 1994, pp. 192–193; Horton, 2000, p. 74; Jarvik, 1997, pp. 266, 273; Javna, 1985, pp. 166–169*; Kanfer, 2000, p. 411; Leamer, 1989, pp. 259–261; Lechner, 2000, pp. 44–46, 47, 48, 259–264**; Lester, 1996, p. 192; Marc, 1984, pp. 149–160**; Marc, 1996, pp. 149–160**; McDonald, 1983, pp. 240–241; McDonald, 1992, p. 238; Meyers, 1999, p. 305; Miller, 1980, pp. 196, 199; Miller, 2000, pp. 162–163; Modleski, 1986, p. 181; Monaco, 2000, pp. 490–491; Pryor, 1995, pp. 144–146; Putterman, 1995, pp. 112–113, 133–134; Rico, 1990, p. 196; Rose, 1999, pp. 119–122, 136–144**; Shaheen, 1984, pp. 59–60; Shales, 1982, pp. 29–37**; Stark, 1997, pp. 144, 151, 194–199**; Stempel, 1992, pp. 115–118; Suman & Rossman, 2000, p. 111; Tabarlet, 1993; Winship, 1988, pp. 199–203; Zehme, 1999, pp. 4, 153, 160–168, 172–173, 197, 290, 294, 308–309, 328–334**; Also in Bianculli, 1996

Savannah

Owen, 1997, pp. 154–155

Saved by the Bell
IN Bianculli, 1996, Terrace, 1993, Terrace, 2000

Scarecrow and Mrs. King
Fiske, 1987, p. 112; Gianakos, 1987, pp. 325–326; Gianakos, 1992, pp. 290–292*; Lichter, Lichter, & Rothman, 1991, pp. 29, 267; Lichter, Lichter, & Rothman, 1994, pp. 84, 377; Shaheen, 1984, p. 48; Sumser, 1996, pp. 70, 84, 134–135; U.S. Congress, 1985, p. 159; Vande Berg & Trujillo, 1989, pp. 177–178, 179; Also in Terrace, 1993

Scene of the Crime
Gianakos, 1992, pp. 383–384

Schlitz Playhouse of the Stars
Gianakos, 1980, pp. 294–305**

Science Fiction Theatre
Spigel & Curtin, 1997, pp. 60–61

Scorch
IN Terrace, 1993

Screen Directors' Playhouse, The
Gianakos, 1980, pp. 479–480

SCTV
Marc, 1984, pp. 158–166**; Marc, 1996, pp. 158–166**; Newcomb, 1987, pp. 355–356; Rose, 1999, p. 82; Stempel, 1992, pp. 116–118

Sea Hunt
Hawes, 2002, p. 114; Meyers, 1981, p. 53; Rovin, 1977b, pp. 66–67; Also in Bianculli, 1996, Terrace, 1993

Seaquest DSV
Jarvis & Joseph, 1998, p. 277 (n. 22); Kachmar, 2002, pp. 150–161**

Search
Gianakos, 1978, pp. 723–724; Lisanti & Paul, 2002, pp. 88; Also in Terrace, 1993

Search, The
Rovin, 1977b, pp. 135, 137

Search for Tomorrow
Edmondson & Rounds, 1973, pp. 159–160, 191; Edmondson & Rounds, 1976, pp. 132–133, 193; Fowles, 1982, pp. 149–150, 156; Fowles, 1992, pp. 165–166, 173; Gilbert, 1976, pp. 38–57**; Matelski, 1988, pp. 23, 152–164**; Matelski, 1999, pp. 44–45; Newcomb, 1976, pp. 56–57; Newcomb, 1979, pp. 77–78; Newcomb, 1987, p. 146; Rouverol, 1984, pp. 103–106, 134; Rouverol, 1992, p. 253; Also in Bianculli, 1996

Second Hundred Years, The
Paietta & Kauppila, 1999, p. 348

Second Noah
Swanson, 2000, pp. 201–202

Secret Agent
Buxton, 1990, pp. 78–93**; Gianakos, 1978, pp. 323–324; Meyers, 1981, pp. 109–111; Miller, 2000, pp. 26–27; Newcomb, 1976, p. 101; Osgerby & Gough-Yates, 2001, pp. 43–44, 198–199, 200–201; Rovin, 1977b, p. 83; Also in Bianculli, 1996

Secret Diary of Desmond Pfeiffer, The
Bogle, 2001, p. 451; Cortes, 2000, p. 23; Suman & Rossman, 2000, pp. 91, 116, 119; Wild, 1999, pp. 75–76, 142

Secret Storm
Matelski, 1988, p. 7; Matelski, 1999,

pp. 22, 45; Mayer, 1972, pp. 122–124; Williams, 1992, pp. 25–26; Also in Bianculli, 1996

Secrets of Midland Heights
Gianakos, 1983, pp 178–179; Also in Morris, 1997

See It Now
Barnouw, 1990, pp. 171–184, 187, 206, 237, 266**; Batra, 1987, pp. 170–172*; Castleman & Podrazik, 1982, pp. 88–89; Goethals, 1981, pp. 99–102, 107*; Heldenfels, 1994, pp. 32–33, 123–127, 132, 208*; Hewitt, 2001, pp. 49, 56, 104–105; Jarvik, 1997, p. 10; Kendrick, 1969, pp. 24–30, 335–419**; Leonard, 1987, pp. 78–80; Mayer, 1972, pp. 203–205, 250–252; McDonald, 1983, pp. 35–37; McDonald, 1992, pp. 39–41; Merron, 1988, pp. 4–11, 22, 28**; Murray, 1994, pp. 10, 43–54, 57–74, 78–80**; Nelson & Gaonkar, 1996, pp. 320–322, 326–327; O'Connor, 1983, pp. 1–32**; Persico, 1988, pp. 1–3, 301–326, 343–354, 371–374, 392–395, 402–432 (passim)**; Rapping, 1987, pp. 102–104; Rose, 1985, pp. 191, 217, 239, 240*; Rosteck, 1994, whole book**; Sperber, 1986, pp. 351–356, 376–382, 472–473, 478–480, 490–496, 524–535**; Spigel, 2001, pp. 274–276, 282*; Stark, 1997, pp. 42–46*; Streitmatter, 1997, pp. 159–164, 168–169**; Winch, 1997, pp. 50–51; Winship, 1988, pp. 210–214; Also in Bianculli, 1996

Seinfeld
Abelman, 1998, pp. 42, 72–73; Blum, 1995, pp. 14, 83–84, 105; Bogle, 2001, p. 452; Capsuto, 2000, pp. 358, 368–369; Chunovic, 2000, pp. 126–129*; Cortes, 2000, p. 41; Davis, 2001, pp. 18–19, 24–37**; Gabler, Rich & Antler, 2000, pp. 38–40, 43–45, 65, 68, 70**; Gattuso, 1995, whole book**; Gottfried, 1999, pp. 298, 311; Himmelstein, 1994, p. 30; Hirsch & Hirsch, 2000; Horton, 2000, pp. 121–130, 174–175**; Isaacs, 1999, pp. 57, 115; Johnson, 1994; Lichter, Lichter, & Rothman, 1994, pp. 41, 63; Marc, 1997, pp. 199–200, 201–203*; Means Coleman, 2002, pp. 161–163; Owen, 1997, pp. 46–49, 118, 120, 122*; Pearl & Pearl, 1999, pp. 31–32, 57–58, 92–93**; Pegg, 2002, pp. 270, 272–283**; Pierson, 2000; Rannow, 1999, pp. 27, 76, 108; Riggs, 1998, p. 7; Schwartz, 1999, p. 129; Silverblatt, Ferry, & Finan, 1999, p 79; Smith, 1999, pp. 15–16, 32–33, 44, 52–53, 57–59, 150*; Staiger, 2000, pp. 1–2, 141, 203 (n. 28); Stark, 1997, pp. 19, 29, 100, 257, 283–285, 286–287*; Suman & Rossman, 2000, pp. 106, 108, 116; *The Seinfeld Scripts: The First and Second Seasons,* 1998, whole book**; Thompson, 1996, pp. 133, 134, 181; Tracy, 1998, whole book**; Wild, 1999, pp. 64–65, 88–89, 122–123, 138; Wolff, 1996, pp. 11, 13; Also in Bianculli, 1996, Terrace, 1993, Terrace, 2000

Seizure
Turow, 1989, p. 190

Senator, The
Lichter, Lichter, & Rothman, 1991, p. 263; Lichter, Lichter, & Rothman, 1994, p. 373

Sergeant Bilko *see* **Phil Silvers Show**

Sergeant Preston of the Yukon
Davis, 1995, pp. 32–33; Harmon, 1992, pp. 21–23; Hawes, 2002, pp. 108–109; McDonald, 1987, pp. 36, 37;

Rovin, 1977b, p. 44; Yoggy, 1995, pp. 49–50; Also in Lentz, 1997, Terrace, 1993, West, 1987

Serpico
Cuklanz, 1998; Gianakos, 1981, pp. 216–217; Martindale, 1991, pp. 439–441; Meyers, 1981, p. 237; Puette, 1992, pp. 48–49, 175; Sklar, 1980, pp. 32–34

Sesame Street
Barnouw, 1990, pp. 436–438; Berry & Mitchell-Kernan, 1982, pp. 42–44; Bryant & Anderson, 1983, pp. 89–100; Bryant & Bryant, 2001, pp. 416–418, 425, 426–428*; Coakley, 1977, pp. 120, 125, 126; Comstock, 1986, pp. 3–61 (passim), especially pp. 3–6; Comstock, 1991, pp. 95–101, 112*; Coppa, 1979, pp. 119–120; Cullingford, 1984, pp. 26–27, 101–102; Davies, 1997, pp. 35–36, 74–75, 76, 83–92, 184–185, 192–194, 200–201, 208–210, 212, 218–221**; Davis, 1995, pp. 155–157*; Erickson, 2000, p. 186; Fisch & Truglio, 2001, whole book**; Fowles, 1982, pp. 200–201; Fowles, 1992, pp. 219–220 (same as Fowles 1982); Gaunt, 1993, pp. 138–139, 143–144; Greenberg, 1980, p. 14; Harris, 1989, pp. 220–221; Harris, 1994, pp. 228–230; Hendershot, 1998, pp. 137–191**; Howe, 1983, pp. 3–12**; Howitt, 1982, pp. 149–153*; Jarvik, 1997, pp. 34, 49, 51, 52–53**; Johnston, 2000, p. 77; Kinder, 1999, pp. 139–176**; Kuney, 1990, pp. 129–144**; Lesser, 1977, pp. 43–58, 74–82, 87–118, 123–124**; Luke, 1990, pp. 214–225**; Mankiewicz & Swerdlow, 1978, pp. 175–189**; Mayer, 1972, pp. 133–159**; McDonald, 1983, pp. 193–194; McDonald, 1992, pp. 196–197; Miller, 2000, pp. 76–77; Moody, 1980, pp. 20–21, 69–72*; Morris, 1971, pp. 150–173**; Neuman, 1991, pp. 5–7, 94–97*; O'Dell, 1997, pp. 70–74, 76*; Palmer & Dorr, 1980, pp. 9, 12–14, 20–30 (passim), 51–55, 62*; Palmer, 1988, pp. 14–15, 74–77, 91–119**; Postman, 1985, pp. 142–144; Rutstein, 1974, pp. 50, 59; Sklar, 1980, pp. 120–128 (passim); Spigel & Curtin, 1997, p. 17; Stark, 1997, pp. 146, 150–154**; Tan, 1981, pp. 244–247; Tan, 1985, pp. 288–291; Walters, 2001, pp. 97–98; Weimann, 2000, pp. 124, 134; Winn, 1977, pp. 33–36, 55, 127–128*; Winn, 1985, pp. 37–43, 162–163*; Witney & Abels, 1980, pp. 266–267, 273; Zillman, Bryant, & Huston, 1994, pp. 79, 81–82; Also in Bianculli, 1996

Seven Brides for Seven Brothers
Gianakos, 1987, pp. 300–301

Seven Days
Wild, 1999, pp. 9, 76–83, 105–108, 210–211, 241–242, 270**

7th Heaven
Bryant & Bryant, 2001, pp. 187, 190; Johnston, 2000, p. 15; Longworth, 2000, pp. xxiii, 140, 141–151**; Orlik, 2001, p. 138; Wild, 1999, pp. 108, 111–114, 187–190, 262**

77 Sunset Strip
Anderson, 1994, pp. 241–247, 249, 285–286**; Caldwell, 1995, pp. 50–51, 71–72; Castleman & Podrazik, 1982, p. 129; Collins & Javna, 1989, pp. 38–40; Gianakos, 1978, pp. 176–184**; Lichter, Lichter, & Rothman, 1991, pp. 59–60, 67; Marc, 1984, pp. 82–85; Marc, 1996, pp. 82–85; Marc & Thompson, 1992 (Ch. 13 on Roy

Huggins), pp. 141–151, especially pp. 146–148*; Meyers, 1981, pp. 55–58, 62; Osgerby & Gough-Yates, 2001, p. 46; Pearl & Pearl, 1999, pp. 179–180; Rose, 1985, p. 39; Rovin, 1977b, p. 64; Sackett, 1993, pp. 90–91; Stempel, 1992, p. 67; Also in Bianculli, 1996, Terrace, 1993

77th Bengal Lancers *see* **Tales of the 77th Bengal Lancers**

Shadow Chasers
Gianakos, 1992, p. 406; Muir, 2001a, pp. 593–594**

Shaft
Castleman & Podrazik, 1982, p. 247; Gianakos, 1978, pp. 742–743; McDonald, 1983, pp. 202–203; McDonald, 1992, pp. 203–205; Meyers, 1981, p. 186; Osgerby & Gough-Yates, 2001, pp. 108–109; Rovin, 1977b, pp. 137–138; Rubin, 1980, pp. 133–134

Shane
Gianakos, 1978, p. 535; Jackson, 1994, pp. 175–176; Also in Lentz, 1997, West, 1987

Shannon's Deal
Hamamoto, 1994, pp. 178–179; Himmelstein, 1994, pp. 233–235; Leonard, 1997, pp. 140–141; Smith, 1998, pp. 162–173**; Steenland, 1990, p. 13; Also in Terrace, 1993

Shazam!
IN Terrace, 1993

Shell Game
IN Terrace, 1993

Sheriff Lobo *see* **Misadventures of Sheriff Lobo**

Sheriff of Cochise, The
Yoggy, 1995, pp. 172–174; Also in West, 1987

She's the Sheriff
Rafkin, 1998, pp. 122–124; Also in Terrace, 1993

Shindig
Jackson, 1997, p. 237; Also in Bianculli, 1996

Shirley Temple's Storybook
Gianakos, 1978, pp. 161–163

Shirley's World
IN Terrace, 1993

Shore, Dinah *see* **Dinah's Place**

Shotgun Slade
Fitzgerald & Magers, 2002, pp. 293–294; Yoggy, 1995, pp. 213–214; Also in Lentz, 1997, Terrace, 1993, West, 1987

Show, The
Owen, 1997, p. 116; Zook, 1999, p. 7

Sibs
IN Terrace, 1993

Sidekicks
Hamamoto, 1994, p. 14

Sightings
Muir, 2001a, pp. 598–600**

Sigmund and the Sea Monsters
IN Terrace, 1993

Silent Force, The
Gianakos, 1978, p. 669

Silver Spoons
Lichter, Lichter, & Rothman, 1991, p. 90; Lichter, Lichter, & Rothman, 1994, p. 161; Puette, 1992, pp. 53–54, 191; Also in Terrace, 1993

Silver Theater
Gianakos, 1980, pp. 226–227

Silvers, Phil *see* Phil Silvers Show

Simon
IN Terrace, 2000

Simon and Simon
Blum & Lindheim, 1987, pp. 116–120; Cuklanz, 2000, pp. 39, 80, 109, 117; Gianakos, 1983, pp. 204–205; Gianakos, 1987, pp. 257–260*; Gianakos, 1992, pp. 330–332*; Jarvis & Joseph, 1998, p. 239; Kassel 1993, p. 117; Klobas, 1988, pp. 75–77, 164, 174, 362–363; Lechner, 2000, p. 106; Lichter, Lichter, & Rothman, 1991, pp. 154, 200; Lichter, Lichter, & Rothman, 1994, p. 240; Nelson, 1994, pp. 20–21; Puette, 1992, p. 191; Rose, 1985, p. 47; Sackett, 1993, pp. 278–279; Sumser, 1996, pp. 68, 111, 124–125, 125–126, 137, 147*; U.S. Congress, 1985, pp. 32–33, 157–158; Wahl, 1995, p. 60

Simpsons, The
Abelman, 1998, p. 67; Allen, 1992, pp. 335–336; Barker, 1999, p. 165; Bendazzi, 1994, p. 236; Berrlant, 1997, pp. 26–29, 36–52, 158–159**; Bryant & Bryant, 2001, pp. 173–174; Caldwell, 1995, p. 23; Cantor, 1999; Cantor, 2001, pp. ix–xvii (passim), xxvi, xl, 67–109, 181–183, 199–205, 214–215 (n. 7)**; Capsuto, 2000, pp. 312–313, 331, 370; Cartwright, 2000, whole book**; Chunovic, 2000, pp. 117–119*; Creeber, 2001, pp. 74–75; Croteau & Hoynes, 2000, p. 217; Crotty, 1995; Crown, 1999, p. 86; Davis, 2001, pp. xviii, 17, 38–53, 309**; Fiske, 1994, pp. 114–115, 121–123*; Fox, 2001, p. 25; Friedman, 2002, pp. 270–272; Gregory, 2000, p 118; Groening, 1997, whole book**; Himmelstein, 1994, pp. 117, 135–137*; Holtzman, 2000, p. 129; Horton, 2000, pp. 121, 130–135, 174**; Horton & McDougal, 1998, p. 112 (note 5); Hughes, 2001, p. 113; Isaacs, 1999, p. 10; Johnston, 2000, p. 59; Jones, 1992, pp. 266–268; Kassel, 1993, p. 43; Lechner, 2000, pp. 177–178; Leonard, 1997, p. 13; Lichter, Lichter, & Rothman, 1994, pp. 3, 65; Marc, 1997, pp. 192–195*; Marc & Thompson, 1992 (Ch. 5 on James L. Brooks), pp. 61–69; Marris & Thornham, 2000, p. 380; Newcomb, 2000, p. 251; Orlik, 1994, pp. 159, 190–191, 192; Orlik, 2001, pp. 185, 191, 258–259, 353–382 (script); Owen, 1997, pp. 58, 61, 64–66*; Panati, 1991, pp. 483–484; Rushkoff, 1994, pp. 109–116, 242**; Schwartz, 1999, pp. 131, 182; Silverblatt, Ferry, & Finan, 1999, p. 176; Slade, 2002, p. 104; Smith, 1997, pp. 201, 202; Smith, 1999, pp. 51–52, 59–62*; Spigel, 1992, p. 184; Steenland, 1990, p. 28; Vane & Gross, 1994, p. 220; Wahl, 1995, p. 9; Walters, 2001, pp. 72–74*; Ward, 1995; White, 1992, pp. 173–177*; Also in Bianculli, 1996, Terrace, 1993, Terrace, 2000

Sinatra *see* Frank Sinatra Show

Sinbad Show, The
Cotter, 1997, pp. 441–444*; Zook, 1999, pp. 25–35, 42**; Also in Terrace, 2000

Sing Along with Mitch
IN Bianculli, 1996

Singer & Sons
Bogle, 2001, p. 382; Cotter, 1997, pp. 403–404

Single Guy
Torres, 1998, pp. 3, 11 (n. 7)

Sir Lancelot
Rovin, 1977b, pp. 49–50

Sirota's Court
Capsuto, 2000, p. 354; Jarvis & Joseph, 1998, p. 173; Sklar, 1980, p. 9

Sister Kate
IN Terrace, 1993

Sister, Sister
Bogle, 2001, p. 432; James, 1991; Means Coleman, 2000, p. 110; Also in Terrace, 2000

Sisters
Guida, 2000, p. 222; Isaacs, 1999, pp. 98–99; Pearl & Pearl, 1999, pp. 38–39, 49, 202–203**; Rose, 1999, p. 106; Also in Terrace, 1993

Six Million Dollar Man, The
Alley, 1977, p. 46; Castleman & Podrazik, 1982, p. 250; Gianakos, 1978, pp. 735–736; Gianakos, 1981, pp. 92–96*; Marc & Thompson, 1992 (Ch. 16 on Glen Larson), pp. 171–178; Newcomb, 1976, pp. 22–23; Newcomb, 1979, pp. 38, 41; Newcomb, 1982, pp. 30, 33; Newcomb, 1987, pp. 36–37, 523; Newcomb, 1994, p. 529; Paietta & Kauppila, 1999, p. 348; Rovin, 1977b, p. 142; Sackett, 1993, p. 227; Vane & Gross, 1994, p. 111; Witney & Abels, 1980, pp. 207–208, 212; Also in Bianculli, 1996

Six O'Clock Follies
Lichter, Lichter, & Rothman, 1991, p. 176; Lichter, Lichter, & Rothman, 1994, p. 266; Also in Terrace, 1993

Sixth Sense, The
Gianakos, 1978, pp. 706–707; Muir, 2001a, pp. 32–43**; Muir, 2001b, pp. 222–223; Rovin, 1977b, p. 173

$64,000 Challenge, The
Anderson, 1978, pp. 33–34, 80–83, 101–105, 122–124**; DeLong, 1991, pp. 202–206, 216–217*; Stone & Yohn, 1992, pp. 46–58, 61–62, 136–154, 205–207, 240–244, 252–268, 299–301**; U.S. Congress, 1960, pp. 330–331, 434–435, 440–468, 647–648, 654–692, 693–706, 708–927, 980–1000**

$64,000 Question, The
Anderson, 1978, pp. 6–30, 35–37, 40, 83–84, 85–86, 89, 132–133**; Barnouw, 1990, pp. 184–187; Burns, 1990, p 280; Castleman & Podrazik, 1982, pp. 99–101, 114–115, 124–125**; DeLong, 1991, pp. 178–186, 200, 205, 206, 216–217, 219–220**; Frank, 1991, p. 128; Heldenfels, 1994, pp. 207–208; Krampner, 1997, pp. 105–109; McCrohan, 1990, pp. 76–84**; Newcomb, 1976, pp. 184–188*; Rose, 1985, pp. 292–293; Sackett, 1993, pp. 56–57; Stark, 1997, p. 75; Stone & Yohn, 1992, pp. 26–27, 46–58 (passim), 133, 136–154, 183–184, 205–206, 239–244, 252–268, 299–301**; U.S. Congress, 1960, pp. 440–448, 648–667, 748–1006**; Also in Bianculli, 1996

60 Minutes
Agee, Ault, & Emery, 1982, pp. 201-206*; Allen, 1987, pp. 43-46*; Auletta, 1991, see index; Avery & Eason, 1991, pp. 265-293**; Barnouw, 1990, pp. 479-482; Bedell, 1981, pp. 268-273*; Bogle, 2001, p. 358; Broughton, 1986, pp. 75-83*; Buzenberg & Buzenberg, 1999, pp. 59-68, 138-139, 152, 247-248, 269-271**; Campbell, 1991, whole book**; Castleman & Podrazik, 1982, pp. 206, 293-295*; Christians, Fackler, & Rotzoll, 1995, pp. 249-251; Coakley, 1977, pp. 171-172, 175-176; Crossen, 1994, pp. 55-56; Davis, 2001, p. 204; Diamond, 1982, pp. 74-75; Edelman & Kupferberg, 1996, pp. 222, 247; Frank, 1991, pp. 309-311, 314, 345, 348; Friedman & Huttenlocher, 1997; Hewitt, 2001, pp. 1-8, 104-218**; Hiebert & Reuss, 1985, p. 19; Himmelstein, 1984, pp. 204, 210, 221; Johnston, 2000, p. 72; Joyce, 1988, pp. 179-182, 281-282, 456-458, 512-516; Kassel 1993, p. 88; Kolodny, 1996; Kovach & Rosenstiel, 1999, pp. 73, 154, 167; Lechner, 2000, pp. 41-42; Leonard, 1987, pp. 66, 142-154**; Losher, 1982, pp. 31-39, 46-47, 55, 68-78, 111-139, 143-151, 162, 165-181, 189-201, 212-244**; Madsen, 1984, whole book**; Martin, 1981; McCrohan, 1990, pp. 282-290**; Monaco, 2000, pp. 499-500; Murray, 1994, pp. 10, 121, 147-148; Newcomb, 1982, pp. 247-259**; Newcomb, 1987, pp. 292-303**; Newcomb, 1994, pp. 138-139, 303-328**; Owen, 1997, p. 58; Puette, 1992, pp. 42-45; Rapping, 1987, pp. 119-132**; Riggs, 1998, p. 15; Rivera, 1991, pp. 326-327; Rose, 1999, pp. 145-151, 189**; Sackett, 1994, pp. 244-245; Schoenbrun, 1989, pp. 183-188*; Shaheen, 1984, pp. 83-92 (passim), 98-99 (passim); Shales, 1982, pp. 110-114*; Spragens, 1995, pp. 13-56, 104-107, 122-129**; Stark, 1997, pp. 107, 188-194**; Stein, 2001; Thompson, 1996, p. 13; Vande Berg & Wenner, 1991, pp. 331-364**; Westin, 1982, pp. 128-131, 196-197; Winch, 1997, pp. 121-122; Also in Bianculli, 1996

Skag
Gianakos, 1981, pp. 291-292; Goethals, 1981, p. 52; Lichter, Lichter, & Rothman, 1991, pp. 85, 113; Lichter, Lichter, & Rothman, 1994, pp. 188-189; Puette, 1992, p. 146

Sky King
Davis, 1995, pp. 229-230; Gianakos, 1987, pp. 373-374; Harmon, 1992, pp. 191-195*; Jackson, 1994, p. 45; Jarvis & Joseph, 1998, pp. 193-194; Magers & Fitzgerald, 1999, pp. 258, 260-262*; Yoggy, 1995, pp. 41-43*; Also in Lentz, 1997, Terrace, 1993, West, 1987

Slap Maxwell Story, The
Abelman, 1998, p. 342; Himmelstein, 1994, pp. 184-186*

Slattery's People
Gianakos, 1978, pp. 446-448*; Lichter, Lichter, & Rothman, 1991, p. 263; Lichter, Lichter, & Rothman, 1994, p. 373; Rovin, 1977b, pp. 91-92

Sledge Hammer
Lichter, Lichter, & Rothman, 1991, p. 191; Lichter, Lichter, & Rothman, 1994, p. 283; Wahl, 1995, pp. 59-60; Also in Terrace, 1993

Sleepwalkers
Muir, 2001a, pp. 519-521**

Sliders
Jarvis & Joseph, 1998, pp. 164-165

Smart Guy
Bryant & Bryant, 2001, pp. 184, 195; Also in Terrace, 2000

Smilin' Ed McConnell and His Buster Brown Gang
IN Terrace, 1993

Smith Family, The
Gianakos, 1983, pp. 398–400; Lichter, Lichter, & Rothman, 1994, pp. 172–173

Smothers Brothers Comedy Hour, The
Abelman, 1998, pp. 311–313; Barnouw, 1990, pp. 392–393; Bodroghkozy, 2001, pp. 74, 123–138, 140–149, 151–163, 184, 229–230**; Buzenberg & Buzenberg, 1999, pp. 138–139; Capsuto, 2000, p. 54; Castleman & Podrazik, 1982, pp. 192–193, 209–210*; Coakley, 1977, p. 218; Erickson, 2000, pp. 16–18,152–153, 173*; Goethals, 1981, p. 117; Guida, 2000, p. 195; Hamamoto, 1989, pp. 73–74; Himmelstein, 1984, pp. 147–150; Himmelstein, 1994, pp. 188–190; Javna, 1985, p. 25; Marc, 1984, pp. 26–27; Marc, 1989, pp. 143–150**; Marc, 1997, pp. 120–124**; Monaco, 2000, p. 486; O'Connor, 1983, pp. 159–183**; Putterman, 1995, p. 148; Roman, 1996, pp. 58–59; Rose, 1985, p. 315; Spigel & Curtin, 1997, pp. 201–219**; Tabarlet, 1993; U.S. Congress, 1977a, pp. 219–224*; Wittebols, 1998, p. 5; Also in Bianculli, 1996, Terrace, 1993

Smothers Brothers Show, The
Castleman & Podrazik, 1982, p. 192; Marc, 1989, pp. 144–145; Marc, 1997, pp. 118–120; Spelling, 1996, pp. 54–55; Stark, 1997, pp. 137–142**

Snoops
Alley & Brown, 2001, p. 140; Kassel 1993, p. 119; Wild, 1999, pp. 205–208, 264–265; Also in Terrace, 1993

So This Is Hollywood
IN Terrace, 1993

Soap
Alley & Brown, 2001, pp. 157–158; Bedell, 1981, pp. 199–200; Buckman, 1984, pp. 147–148; Capsuto, 2000, pp. 138–144**; Castleman & Podrazik, 1982, pp. 278–280, 282**; Christians, Rotzoll, & Fackler, 1983, pp. 277–280*; Chunovic, 2000, p. 80; Coakley, 1977, pp. 250, 256; Davis, 2001, p. 13; Erickson, 2000, p. 276; Ferre, 1990, pp. 104–106; Goldenson, 1991, pp. 367–368; Gross, 2001, p. 84; Himmelstein, 1984, pp. 121–123; Jones, 1992, pp. 251–253; Joshel, Malamud, & McGuire, 2001, p. 160 (n. 39); Lichter, Lichter, & Rothman, 1991, pp. 34–35; Lichter, Lichter, & Rothman, 1994, p. 91; Marc, 1997, pp. 176–177; Marc & Thompson, 1992 (Ch. 7 on Susan Harris), pp. 84–92; Mitz, 1980, pp. 403–404; Montgomery, 1989, pp. 95–100*; Rodriguez, 1997, p. 66; Schneider, 2001, pp. 36–41, 95–96*; Sklar, 1980, pp. 52–54, 89–94, 96–99**; Suman & Rossman, 2000, pp. 120, 135; Turow, 1984, p. 95; Vane & Gross, 1994, p. 130; Walters, 2001, p. 61; Also in Bianculli, 1996, Morris, 1997

Someone Like Me
Cotter, 1997, p. 460; Also in Terrace, 2000

Somerset
Kaminsky, 1985, p. 108; Matelski, 1999, p. 45

Somerset Maugham TV Theatre
Gianakos, 1980, pp. 287–288

Something Is Out There
IN Terrace, 1993

Sonny and Cher Comedy Hour, The
Bedell, 1981, pp. 76–77, 87; Coakley, 1977, p. 91; Sackett, 1993, pp. 206–207; Scheider, 1997, pp. 153–154; Shaheen, 1984, pp. 57–58; Also in Bianculli, 1996

Sons and Daughters
Gianakos, 1978, p. 755

Soupy Sales Show, The
Davis, 1995, pp. 178–179; Also in Bianculli, 1996

South Central
Bogle, 2001, p. 414; Davis, 2001, p. 57; Means Coleman, 2000, p. 115; Zook, 1999, pp. 36–37, 38–45, 48–49**

South Park
Barker, 1999, p. 165; Chunovic, 2000, pp. 170–172, 176–177*; Creeber, 2001, pp. 74–75; Fox, 2001, p. 31; Gabler, Rich & Antler, 2000, p. 72; Gardiner, 2000; Lechner, 2000, pp. 151–152; Slade, 2002, pp. 27, 95–101, 104–122**; Staiger, 2000, p. 47; Suman & Rossman, 2000, pp. 119–120; Walters, 2001, p. 99; Wild, 1999, pp. 31–32

Space: Above and Beyond
Inness, 1999, pp. 118–119; Schultz, 2000, pp. 86, 90

Space: 1999
Lisanti & Paul, 2002, pp. 52–53; Muir, 1997, whole book**; Muir, 1999, pp. 10–16 (passim), 153; Muir, 2001a, pp. 605–609*; Muir, 2001b, p. 227; Rovin, 1977a, p. 146; Also in Terrace, 1993

Space Patrol
Davis, 1995, pp. 35–37*; Rovin, 1977b, pp. 21, 31; Also in Terrace, 1993

Space Rangers
Leonard, 1997, p. 125

Sparks
Jarvis & Joseph, 1998, pp. 177, 249; Means Coleman, 2000, pp. 119–120

Spencer
IN Terrace, 1993

Spencer's Pilots
Gianakos, 1981, pp. 215–216

Spenser: For Hire
Bogle, 2001, pp. 304–307*; Cortes, 2000, p. 122; Cuklanz, 2000, pp. 40, 82–82, 88–89; Gianakos, 1992, pp. 413–414; Klobas, 1988, pp. 265–266; Lichter, Lichter, & Rothman, 1991, pp. 25, 39, 46, 143, 177, 281; Lichter, Lichter, & Rothman, 1994, pp. 97, 105–106, 267, 394–395*; Spigel & Mann, 1992, p. 231; Sumser, 1996, p. 70; Thomas & Evans, 1990, p. 288

Spin City
Capsuto, 2000, pp. 363, 375–376, 398, 399, 407; Croteau & Hoynes, 2000, p. 224; Gross, 2001, p. 93; Keller, 2002, p. 179; Lechner, 2000, p. 113; Rannow, 1999, pp. 79–83*; Schultz, 2000, pp. 110, 121–122; Suman & Rossman, 2000, p. 24; Walters, 2001, pp. 104–106*

Square Pegs
IN Terrace, 1993

Staccato *see* **Johnny Staccato**

Stage Show
Castleman & Podrazik, 1982, p. 106; Jones, 1992, pp. 111–112

Stage 13
Gianakos, 1980, pp. 260–261

Stagecoach West
Fitzgerald & Magers, 2002, pp. 136, 215, 254; Gianakos, 1978, pp. 298–299; Jackson, 1994, pp. 145–146; Also in Lentz, 1997, West, 1987

Stand by Your Man
IN Terrace, 1993

Star Stage
Gianakos, 1980, pp. 483–484

Star Tonight
Gianakos, 1980, pp. 434–437*

Star Trek [NOTE that general references to more than one series are placed here, as well as references to the original series]
Alexander, 1994, pp. 26, 194–398, 408–410, 420–423, 545–546**; Andreadis, 1998, whole book**; Andrews, 1986, pp. 122–123; Anijar, 2000, whole book**; Bacon-Smith, 1992, pp. 4–5, 11–15, 22–24, 31–34, 37–40, 52–54, 63–65, 82–113, 141–171, 189, 220–231, 240–244, 247**; Barad, 2000, pp. xxi–xvi, 5–8, 12–17, 31–32, 41–50, 53–57, 58–63, 65–70, 79–114, 120–135, 145–147, 154–157, 162–163, 167–169, 180–182, 233–236, 239, 249, 260–263, 271–280, 286–291, 196–297, 304–306, 327–333, 350–358**; Barr, 2000, p. 154; Barrett & Barrett, 2001, pp. 5, 9–13, 16, 18–19, 30, 36, 41–42, 48–51 (passim), 55, 58, 62, 70, 71–73, 77–82, 87, 95–98, 101, 107, 109, 122, 125, 133, 141–142, 156–157, 165–166, 178, 182–183**; Bernardi, 1998, pp. 3, 26–68**; Bodroghkozy, 2001, pp. 87–88; Bogle, 2001, pp. 130–135*; Brady, 1994, pp. 292–297; Brauer, 1975, pp. 18–20; Brown, 1994, pp. 77–78; Buxton, 1990, pp. 60–71**; Byrd, 1998, pp. 3–72, 103–109, 140–152, 174–176, 204–205, 213–235**; Cantor, 2000; Cantor, 2001, pp. ix–xvii (passim), 35, 40–56, 57–58, 64, 179–181, 182–184, 185, 186, 187–188, 223 (n. 38), 228 (n. 34)**; Capsuto, 2000, p. 331; Carroll, 2000, pp. 209–210; Castleman & Podrazik, 1982, pp. 195–197*; Craig, 1992, pp. 101–102; Creeber, 2001, p. 28; Croteau & Hoynes, 2000, pp. 194–195; Doohan, 1996, pp. 33–35, 127–167, 172–185**; Dutta, 1995; Engel, 1994, pp. 5–12, 38–40, 44–137, 149–162**; Farrand, 1994, whole book**; Fiske, 1987, pp. 80, 113; Forbes & Mahan, 2000, pp. 165–179**; Fox, 2001, pp. 31, 161; Franz, 1975, whole book**; Gerani, 1977, pp. 101–112**; Gerrold, 1973a, whole book**; Gerrold, 1973b, whole book**; Gianakos, 1978, pp. 559–563*; Goulding, 1985, whole book**; Greenwald, 1998, whole book**; Gregory, 2000, pp. 6–7, 16–18, 25–37, 106–108, 110, 115–116, 117–118, 119, 121–122, 123, 128, 132, 136–137, 139, 147, 156, 161–167, 181–183, 185, 189–190**; Gresh & Weinberg, 1999, pp. 1–11, 12–13, 39–40, 53–86 (passim), 87, 90, 94, 150–163 (passim)*; Hagen & Wasko, 2000, pp. 72, 83, 84–88*; Hamamoto, 1994, p. 9; Hanley, 1997, pp. 4, 5–7, 9–10, 19–20, 22–23, 24–25, 26–27, 37, 55–58, 66–67, 78, 114, 124–125, 139–140,

142–144, 146–149, 152–154, 185–186, 195, 203–204, 206, 221–222**; Harris, 1998, pp. 10, 19–20, 136, 208, 211; Harrison, et al., 1996, pp. 1–2, 11–31, 69, 70, 71–72, 89 (n. 6), 89 (n. 8), 134 (n. 26), 183 (n. 27), 189–210**; Helford, 2000, pp. 3, 205, 245, 249–250; Heller, 1997; Himmelstein, 1984, pp. 177–178; Himmelstein, 1994, pp. 28–29, 217; Jarvis & Joseph, 1998, p. 295 (n. 15); Javna, 1985, pp. 54–57*; Jindra, 1994; Johason, 1989, whole book**; Kaminsky, 1985, pp. 94–95; Klobas, 1988, pp. 346–347; Kottak, 1990, pp. 104–105; Krauss, 1995, whole book (passim); Kreitzer, 1996; Lagon, 1993; Lichter, Lichter, & Rothman, 1991, pp. 123, 173, 239–240; Lichter, Lichter, & Rothman, 1994, pp. 201, 262, 343; Lisanti & Paul, 2002, p. 99; McDonald, 1983, pp. 123, 157; McDonald, 1992, pp. 131, 163; Muir, 1999, pp. 9–16 (passim), 95; Muir, 2001b, pp. 220–221; Newcomb, 1982, pp. 181–197**; Newcomb, 1994, pp. 448–470**; Newcomb, 2000, pp. 470–493**; Nichols, whole book, (passim)**; Nimoy, 1995, whole book (passim), esp. pp. 30–56, 112–131**; Nochimson, 1997b, p. 126; Okuda, 1993, whole book**; Okuda & Okuda, 1999, whole book**; Orlik, 1994, pp. 58, 184; Orlik, 2001, p. 182; Paietta & Kauppila, 1999, p. 348; Panati, 1991, pp. 364–365; Peel, 1992, whole book**; Penley, 1997, whole book**; Penley, et al., 1991, pp. 171–202**; Porter & McLaren, 1999, whole book**; Pounds, 1999, pp. 7–8, 9, 35–57, 86–87, 91–99, 111–112, 116–121, 132, 134–188**; Reeves-Stevens & Reeves-Stevens, 1995, pp. 5–39**; Richards, 1997, whole book**; Roberts, 1999, pp. 4, 8, 128, 186, 189; Roman, 1996, p. 59; Rose, 1985, pp. 115–122, 124–127**; Rose, 1999, pp. 101–102: Rovin, 1977a, pp. 139–142; Rovin, 1977b, pp. 107, 109; Sanders & Gilbert, 1993, p. 269; Schultz, 2000, pp. 75, 78, 81–82, 84–86, 87–88*; Sconce, 2000, p. 176; Sekuler & Blake, 1998, whole book**; Shatner, 1993, whole book**; Shatner, 1999, whole book**; Silverblatt, Ferry, & Finan, 1999, pp. 28, 159, 171; Solow & Justman, 1996, whole book**; Soter, 2002, pp. 112–113; Spigel & Curtin, 1997, pp. 44–45, 70 (note 33), 114; Stark, 1997, pp. 258–261; Stempel, 1992, pp. 104–107; Story, 1993, p. 156; Takei, 1994, pp. 213–277, 282–284, 294–296**; Tulloch, 2000, pp. 218–224**; Tulloch & Jenkins, 1995, pp. 4–18, 20–30, 35, 38–49, 175–184, 186–265**; U.S. Congress, 1977a, pp. 274–276, 280; Wagner & Lundeen, 1998, pp. 8, 9, 19–21, 22–25, 30–31, 33–34, 36, 39, 40, 41–42, 45–46, 47, 48–49, 50–51, 57, 60–61, 64, 68, 70–71, 75, 79, 81–90, 91, 97–99, 103, 104, 106–108, 109–110, 118, 120–124, 126–129, 130–132, 139–141, 148–150, 154–156, 158–159, 165, 172–173, 174–179, 182, 189, 192, 194, 198–199, 215–217, 222–225, 227–228, 230**; Wahl, 1995, pp. 9, 59; Whitfield & Ruddenberry, 1968, whole book**; Wilcox, 1992; Worland, 1989; Also in Bianculli, 1996

Star Trek: Deep Space Nine

Barad, 2000, pp. 18, 24–27, 30–31, 32–36, 75–78, 136–145, 148–154, 162–163, 169–179, 183–204, 249–260, 339–343**; Barrett & Barrett, 2001, pp. 37–38, 60, 64–69, 70–71, 72, 73–75, 78, 81, 84, 85, 87, 88, 89, 93, 99, 104–105, 107–109, 127, 133, 137–141, 149–156, 157–158, 161–163, 164–165, 172–176, 180–181, 185–189, 191–192, 194, 195, 197, 201, 202, 203–204**; Bernardi, 1998, pp. 3, 24: Byrd, 1998, pp. 87–99, 114–122, 154–156, 207–209**; Capsuto, 2000, pp. 331–332; Erdmann, 2000, whole book**; Gauntlett & Hill, 1999, p 137; Graham, 2000; Gregory, 2000, pp. 10, 23–24, 65, 68–89, 100, 101, 111–112, 116, 120, 130, 133–134, 137–139, 140, 147, 148, 150, 152–153, 172, 173–176, 178–179, 185, 188–189, 190–191, 192, 193–194**; Gresh & Weinberg, 1999, pp. 1, 65, 79–84, 150–163 (passim); Hanley, 1997, pp. 5, 24, 37, 69, 140–142, 144, 145, 158, 164–166, 177–178, 207–208**; Harrison, et al., 1996, pp. 1, 257 (n. 3); Helford, 2000, pp. 249, 251–263**; Isaacs, 1999, p. 131; Jarvis & Joseph, 1998, p. 110; Kapell, 2000; Leonard, 1997, p. 124; Muir, 1999, p. 154; Paietta & Kauppila, 1999, p. 348; Porter & McLaren, 1999, pp. 25–26, 77–100, 209–210**; Pounds, 1999, p. 198; Reeves-Stevens & Reeves-Stevens, 1995, pp. 108–131**; Roberts, 1999, pp. 130–131,183–184; Schultz, 2000, pp. 82, 83, 86, 89, 91; Sekuler & Blake, 1998, whole book**; Wagner & Lundeen, 1998, pp. 9–10, 27–28, 31–32, 35–36, 37, 47–48, 60–61, 64, 71–72, 73, 74, 77, 78, 91–92, 93–94, 96, 101–102, 105, 111–112, 113, 114, 134, 186–188, 190–191, 192–193, 216, 218–220, 223, 228**

Star Trek: The Next Generation
Alexander, 1994, pp. 498–536**; Barad, 2000, pp. 3–5, 9–12, 21, 51–52, 120–125, 208–229, 239, 263–267, 271–276, 280–283, 297–298, 316–317, 319–326, 333–339**; Barr, 2000, pp. 147–156, 160–162*; Barrett & Barrett, 2001, pp. 3–4, 15, 19–22, 26, 37, 55, 57–58, 61, 65, 78, 80, 82–85, 87–88, 90–91, 98–99, 101–102, 106, 111, 117, 125–126, 131, 142–144, 146, 149–150, 156, 164,, 166–169, 177, 181, 192, 200, 201, 202**; Bernardi, 1998, pp. 3, 105–136**; Bignell, 1997, pp. 142, 145; Buhler, 1995; Byrd, 1998, pp. 72–85, 109–114, 153–156, 177–179, 205–207**; Capsuto, 2000, pp. 267, 310–311; Doohan, 1996, pp. 200–202*; Dubek & Tatlow, 1998; Engel, 1994, pp. 219–252**; Gauntlett & Hill, 1999, pp. 131, 135–136, 150, 171–172; Graham, 2000; Gregory, 2000, pp. 19, 21–23, 43–65, 69, 84, 85, 100, 109, 110–111, 118, 120, 122, 123, 126–128, 129, 132–133, 135–136, 137, 139, 140, 146, 147–148, 149–150, 154, 155–157, 158–159, 167–173, 175, 177–178, 182, 183–184, 185–188, 190, 192, 194–195**; Gresh & Weinberg, 1999, pp. 3, 11–12, 16–86, 94–150**; Gross, 1989, whole book**; Hagen & Wasko, 2000, pp. 84–88*; Hamamoto, 1994, p. 247; Hanley, 1997, pp. 4–5, 6, 10–11, 12–15, 16–17, 20–24, 25–26, 27–32, 33–34, 36, 38–39, 43–46, 54–55, 58–59, 62–63, 67–69, 72–78, 80–82, 88, 90–91, 101–114, 115–120, 126–131, 134–135, 139–140, 144–145, 147–149, 155–157, 168–171, 172–173, 177, 178–179, 185, 193, 197, 199, 203, 212–218, 219–221, 223–226, 227–229, 231–234**; Hardy & Kukla, 1999; Harrison, et al., 1996, pp. 1–2, 33–185, 204–220, 231–234, 236–257**; Helford, 2000, pp. 4, 168, 215, 250–251; Jarvis & Joseph, 1998, pp. 157, 159, 161–162, 163, 164, 165–166, 295 (n. 15), 297–298 (n. 36)*; Korzeniowska, 1996; Kottak, 1990, pp. 104–105; Krauss, 1995, whole book (passim); Muir, 1999, pp. 96–97, 151–52, 153; Nichols, 1994, pp. 275–278; Nimoy, 1995, pp. 320–328**; Orlik, 1994, pp. 43, 58; Ott & Aoki; Paietta & Kauppila, 1999, pp. 348–349; Porter & McLaren, 1999, pp. 20–24, 61–76, 85, 203–208**; Pounds, 1999, pp. 9, 68, 71–89, 99–112, 121–132, 134–188, 197–198**; Reeves-Stevens &

Reeves-Stevens, 1995, pp. 66–105**; Reinheimer, 1995; Roberts, 1999, pp. 1–181**; Roberts & Ross, 1995, whole book**; Schultz, 2000, pp. 82–83, 88–89, 91; Sekuler & Blake, 1998, whole book**; Solow & Justman, 1996, pp. 334–337, 432–438*; Soter, 2002, pp. 114–115; Stark, 1997, pp. 260, 261; Stempel, 1992, pp. 106–107; Sternback & Okuda, 1991, whole book**; Takei, 1994, pp. 379–381*; Tulloch & Jenkins, 1995, pp. 184–191, 213–265**; Tulloch, 2000, pp. 223–224; Wagner & Lundeen, 1998, pp. 8, 9, 10–12, 26–27, 31, 34–35, 37–38, 39–40, 51–52, 53–54, 55, 56–57, 57–61, 64, 68, 69, 71, 75, 78, 79, 91–93, 94, 101, 102, 105, 132–234, 135–139, 150–151, 152–153, 158–159, 161–164, 168, 179–180, 186, 190, 193, 194, 195–196, 199–201, 206–207, 211, 216, 223, 225, 230–233**; Wahl, 1995, p. 9; Wilcox, 1992; Winegarden & Fuss-Reineck, 1993; Also in Bianculli, 1996

Star Trek: Voyager

Barad, 2000, pp. 19–20, 57–58, 64, 70–73, 114–118, 230–231, 236–238, 240–248, 284–286, 291–295, 307–316, 318–319, 343–350**; Barr, 2000, pp. 158–159, 160, 277–290**; Barrett & Barrett, 2001, 10–11, 19, 23–24, 26, 37, 38–40, 42, 48, 58–68, 69–70, 72, 73, 75–77, 78, 81–82, 83, 85, 88, 89, 90, 99–101, 105–106, 110–119, 127, 128, 129–132, 146–149, 156, 165, 170–172, 178–180, 181, 183–185, 196, 199–200, 203**; Bernardi, 1998, pp. 3, 24–25, 157–158; Byrd, 1998, pp. 99–101, 156–158, 179–186, 209–210**;. Graham, 2000; Gregory, 2000, pp. 6–7, 65, 90–101, 111, 118, 120, 123, 147, 148, 150–152, 154–155, 156, 157, 172, 176, 183, 192–193**; Gresh & Weinberg, 1999, pp. 41–42, 43–44, 147, 148, 150–163 (passim); Hanley, 1997, pp. 5, 37, 9–70, 118–119, 166–168, 178, 179–180, 183, 208–209, 219, 226–227*; Harrison, et al., 1996, pp. 1, 191; Helford, 2000, pp. 6, 203–221**; Inness, 1999, pp. 103–104, 113–119**; Leonard, 1997, pp. 124–125; Muir, 1999, p. 97; Paietta & Kauppila, 1999, p. 349; Porter & McLaren, 1999, pp. 26–30, 76, 101–116**; Pounds, 1999, p. 198; Reeves-Stevens & Reeves-Stevens, 1995, pp. 134–149**; Roberts, 1999, pp. 183–189*; Schultz, 2000, pp. 83, 89; Sekuler & Blake, 1998, whole book**; Wagner & Lundeen, 1998, pp. 10, 29–30, 32, 37, 38, 41, 54, 55, 60–61, 64, 69, 73–74, 76–77, 91, 94, 95–96, 99, 102, 105, 109–110, 151–152, 153, 177, 180–181, 188–189, 191, 194, 195–196, 199, 216**

Starlight Theatre

Gianakos, 1980, pp. 230–231

Stars of the Family

IN Terrace, 1993

Stars Over Hollywood

Gianakos, 1980, pp. 284–285

Starsky and Hutch

Alley, 1987, p. 47; Andrews, 1986, p. 142; Avery & Eason, 1991, pp. 347–348; Bacon-Smith, 1992, pp. 257–258; Buxton, 1990, pp. 129–134**; Capsuto, 2000, p. 147; Castleman & Podrazik, 1982, pp. 267–268; Coakley, 1977, pp. 115, 241; Cuklanz, 1998; Cuklanz, 2000, pp. 32, 35, 71–72, 89, 104; Cullingford, 1984, pp. 30, 39, 40–42, 54, 68–69, 89–90*; D'Acci, 1994, pp. 113–114; DiMaggio, 1990, pp. 12–13, 43–44, 53–55, 90–116 (script)*; Fiske & Hartley, 1978, pp. 182–183; Fiske, 1987, pp. 88, 213;

Gianakos, 1981, pp. 182–187**; Gunter & Wober, 1988, pp. 26–30 (passim); Klobas, 1988, pp. 207–208, 292–293, 315–316; Marc, 1984, p. 89; Marc, 1996, p. 89; Marc & Thompson, 1992 (Ch. 15 on Aaron Spelling), pp. 163–169; Martindale, 1991, pp. 446–455; Meyers, 1981, p. 226; Moorti, 2001, p. 124; Newcomb, 1987, p. 484; Osgerby & Gough-Yates, 2001, pp. 22, 109–110; Rovin, 1977b, pp. 147–148; Sklar, 1980, pp. 9–11, 48–49; Spelling, 1996, pp. 87–91**; Voort, 1986, pp. 147, 185; Also in Bianculli, 1996

Stat
Cotter, 1997, pp. 396–397

State Trooper
Yoggy, 1995, p. 174

Step by Step
Kutulas, 1998; Owen, 1997, p. 23; Ward, 1995; Also in Terrace, 1993, Terrace, 2000

Stephen King's The Golden Years
Muir, 2001a, pp. 285–291**

Steve Allen Show, The
Bogle, 2001, pp. 431, 433–434; Capsuto, 2000, p. 35; Castleman & Podrazik, 1982, pp. 111–112; Holtzman, 2000, p. 229; Horton, 2000, pp. 75–76; Marc, 1989, pp. 68–74**; Marc, 1997, pp 56–61**; Pegg, 2002, pp. 57, 146–148, 180, 256–258*; Putterman, 1995, pp. 54, 104, 146; Settel, 1958, pp. 211–213 (script); Weiner, 1992, pp. 30–31; Also in Bianculli, 1996

Steve Canyon
Gianakos, 1983, pp. 332–334*; Rovin, 1977b, p. 67; Also in Terrace, 1993

Steve Harvey Show, The
Croteau & Hoynes, 2000, p. 220

Steve Lawrence Show, The
Erickson, 2000, pp. 65–66

Stingray
Gianakos, 1992, pp. 415–416; Lembo, 2000, p. 177; Lichter, Lichter, & Rothman, 1991, pp. 33–34; Lichter, Lichter, & Rothman, 1994, pp. 89–90; Thompson, 1990, pp. 125–126; Also in Terrace, 1993

Stockard Channing Show
IN Terrace, 1993

Stone
Gianakos, 1981, pp. 289–290; Thompson, 1990, pp. 88–94**; Vande Berg & Wenner, 1991, pp. 119–120

Stoney Burke
Gianakos, 1978, pp. 372–373; Jackson, 1994, p. 154; Lichter, Lichter, & Rothman, 1991, p. 31; Lichter, Lichter, & Rothman, 1994, p. 86; Rovin, 1977b, p. 85; Yoggy, 1998, p. 154; Also in Lentz, 1997, West, 1987

Storefront Lawyers
Castleman & Podrazik, 1982, p. 222; Gianakos, 1978, pp. 670–671; Jarvis & Joseph, 1998, pp. 15, 253–254, 255–259, 261–264**; Lichter, Lichter, & Rothman, 1991, pp. 124–125, 216; Martindale, 1991, pp. 455–457; McDonald, 1983, p. 161; McDonald, 1992, pp. 166–167; Meyers, 1981, pp. 151–152; Stark, 1997, p. 99

Straightaway
Gianakos, 1978, pp. 363–364

Strange Report
Gianakos, 1978, pp. 687–688

Strange World
Muir, 2001a, pp. 552–556*

Street, The
Caldwell, 1995, p. 93; Himmelstein, 1994, pp. 230–231

Street Hawk
Gianakos, 1992, pp. 388–389; Also in Terrace, 1993

Street Justice
IN Terrace, 1993

Street Stories
Murray, 1994, pp. 181–183; Spragens, 1995, pp. 74–84, 127–128**

Streets of San Francisco, The
Alley, 1977, pp. 15, 89–90; Capsuto, 2000, p. 107; D'Acci, 1994, pp. 112–113; Gianakos, 1978, pp. 711–715*; Gianakos, 1981, pp. 137–140*; Lichter, Lichter, & Rothman, 1991, pp. 41, 126, 132, 201–202, 211, 297; Lichter, Lichter, & Rothman, 1994, pp. 98–99, 204, 211–212, 296, 308, 427–428*; Marc & Thompson, 1992 (Ch. 14 on Quinn Martin), pp. 153–161; Martindale, 1991, pp. 459–471; Meehan, 1983, pp. 60–61, 66, 175–176; Meyers, 1981, p. 182; Montgomery, 1989, p. 92; Newcomb, 1979, pp. 128–129; Newcomb, 1982, pp. 99–101*; Sumser, 1996, pp. 146, 147

Strike Force
Cuklanz, 2000, pp. 34, 86, 114; Gianakos, 1983, pp. 220–221; Gitlin, 1983, pp. 222–223; McDonald, 1992, pp. 189–190; Mott, 2000, pp. 132–133; Also in Terrace, 1993

Strike It Rich
Castleman & Podrazik, 1982, p. 60; DeLong, 1991, pp. 149–155*

Stu Irwin Show, The
Bogle, 2001, pp. 45–46; Cornes, 2001, pp. 222–224, 227; Hamamoto, 1989, pp. 20–22

Studio 57
Gianakos, 1980, pp. 399–400

Studio One
Bogle, 2001, pp. 79–81; Castleman & Podrazik, 1982, p. 25, 97; Gianakos, 1980, pp. 145–165**; Hawes, 2001, pp. 87–109, 149**; Krampner, 1997, p. 92; Pearl & Pearl, 1999, pp. 75–76; Skutch, 1998, pp. 50–51; Thompson, 1996, p. 26; Also in Bianculli, 1996

Suddenly Susan
Abelman, 1998, p. 131; Gabler, Rich & Antler, 2000, pp. 62–63, 66, 70, 72*; Wild, 1999, p. 231; Also in Terrace, 2000

Sugar and Spice
IN Terrace, 1993

Sugar Hill Times
Andrews, 1986, pp. 64–65

Sugar Time!
IN Terrace, 1993

Sugarfoot
Anderson, 1994, pp. 229, 273; Castleman & Podrazik, 1982, p. 116; Fagen, 1996, pp. 71, 93–94, 107–126, (interview with Will Hutchins), 222**; Gianakos, 1978, pp. 248–249; Jackson, 1994, pp. 85–86; Jarvis & Joseph, 1998, pp. 207–209*; Magers & Fitzgerald,

Swiss Family Robinson
Gianakos, 1981, p. 169

Switch
DiMaggio, 1990, pp. 40–41; Gianakos, 1981, pp. 175–178*; Heil, 2001, pp. 287–288; Marc & Thompson, 1992 (Ch. 16 on Glen Larson), pp. 171–178; Martindale, 1991, pp. 475–483; Meyers, 1981, pp. 226–228; Sklar, 1980, p. 55; U.S. Congress, 1977b, pp. 348–351; Also in Terrace, 1993

Sword of Justice
Gianakos, 1981, pp. 257–258; Meyers, 1981, pp. 249–250; Puette, 1992, p. 182; Also in Terrace, 1993

Sydney
IN Terrace, 1993

Tab Hunter Show
IN Eisner & Krinsky, 1984

Tabitha
Pilato, 1996, pp. 283–289**; Sklar, 1980, pp. 50–51

Talent Scouts *see* **Arthur Godfrey**

Tales from the Crypt
Muir, 2001a, pp. 226–247**; Also in Bianculli, 1996

Tales of the Gold Monkey
Gianakos, 1987, pp. 301–302; Also in Terrace, 1993

Tales of the 77th Bengal Lancers
Gianakos, 1981, pp. 361–362; Rovin, 1977b, p. 50

Tales of the Texas Rangers
Davis, 1995, pp. 230–231; Gianakos, 1983, pp. 310–312*; Jackson, 1994, pp. 68–69; Yoggy, 1995, pp. 154–155; Also in Lentz, 1997, West, 1987

Tales of the Unexpected
Gianakos, 1981, p. 222; Muir, 2001a, pp. 77–81*

Tales of Tomorrow
Gianakos, 1980, pp. 312–313; Spigel & Mann, 1992, pp. 26–27

Tales of Wells Fargo
Fitzgerald & Magers, 2002, p. 213; Gianakos, 1978, pp. 186–190*; Hawes, 2002, p. 138; Jackson, 1994, p. 83; Rovin, 1977b, p. 53; Sackett, 1993, p. 73; Yoggy, 1995, pp. 200–207**; Also in Lentz, 1997, Terrace, 1993, West, 1987

Tall Man, The
Fitzgerald & Magers, 2002, pp. 265–266; Gianakos, 1978, pp. 285–287; Lichter, Lichter, & Rothman, 1991, p. 92; Lichter, Lichter, & Rothman, 1994, p. 163; Magers & Fitzgerald, 1999, pp. 78–79, 159; McDonald, 1987, pp. 64–65; Yoggy, 1995, pp. 148–149; Also in Lentz, 1997, West, 1987

Tammy
IN Terrace, 1993

Tammy Grimes Show, The
Andrews, 1980, pp. 178–185*; Also in Terrace, 1993

Target: The Corrupters
Daniel, 1996, pp. 11–12; Gianakos, 1978, pp. 364–366*; Lichter, Lichter,

& Rothman, 1991, p. 266; Lichter, Lichter, & Rothman, 1994, pp. 376–377

Tarzan
Fury, 1994, pp. 219–228, 231–248**; Gianakos, 1978, pp. 565–567; McDonald, 1983, p. 121; McDonald, 1992, pp. 129–130; Rovin, 1977b, pp. 105–106; Also in Terrace, 1993

Tate
Gianakos, 1978, pp. 565–567; Jackson, 1994, p. 144; Rovin, 1977b, p. 77; Also in Lentz, 1997, Terrace, 1993, West, 1987

Tattingers
Auletta, 1991, pp. 360–362, 445–450, plus see index**

Taxi
Capsuto, 2000, pp. 172–173; Castleman & Podrazik, 1982, p. 291; Field, 1989, pp. 219–220; Javna, 1985, pp. 192–195*; Jones, 1992, p. 247; Klobas, 1988, pp. 112–113, 193–194; Kutulas, 1998; Lichter, Lichter, & Rothman, 1991, pp. 142, 150, 252; Lichter, Lichter, & Rothman, 1994, pp. 224, 234, 358; Lovece, 1988, whole book**; Marc & Thompson, 1992 (Ch. 5 on James L. Brooks), pp. 61–69; Mitz, 1980, pp. 411–415*; Neale & Krutnik, 1990, pp. 239–241; Newcomb, 1987, p. 71; Panati, 1991, p. 428; Puette, 1992, pp. 54, 184; Rose, 1985, p. 121; Sackett, 1993, pp. 256–257; Taylor, 1989, pp. 132–133; Zehme, 1999, pp. 3, 213–218, 221–235, 276–277, 297–298, 338**; Also in Bianculli, 1996, Eisner & Krinsky, 1984, Terrace, 1993

Teachers Only
Kassel 1993, p. 117

Ted Knight Show, The
Puette, 1992, p. 181; Also in Terrace, 1993

Teech
Bogle, 2001, p. 393; Also in Terrace, 1993

Telephone Time
Gianakos, 1980, pp. 484–487

Telltale Clue, The
Gianakos, 1987, p. 370

Temperatures Rising
Kalisch, Kalisch, & Scobey, 1983, pp. 81–84*; Miles, 1975, p. 48 (Nov. 20, 1973, show); Mitz, 1980, pp. 313–314; Paietta & Kauppila, 1999, p. 349; Turow, 1989, pp. 202–205*

Temple Houston
Gianakos, 1978, pp. 426–427; Jarvis & Joseph, 1998, pp. 212–213; Yoggy, 1995, pp. 183–184; Also in Lentz, 1997, West, 1987

Tenafly
Castleman & Podrazik, 1982, p. 248; McDonald, 1983, p. 203; McDonald, 1992, p. 205; Rovin, 1977b, p. 138

Tenspeed and Brown Shoe
Collins & Javna, 1989, pp. 26–28; Thompson, 1990, pp. 94–97*; Vande Berg & Wenner, 1991, p. 120; Also in Terrace, 1993

Tequila and Bonetti
Hamamoto, 1994, pp. 185–187; Also in Terrace, 1993

Texaco Star Theater (Milton Berle)
Abelman, 1998, pp. 309–310; Adir,

1988, pp. 36–44**; Allen, 1956, pp. 76–90, also see index*; Berle, 1974, pp. 1–2, 180–181, 267–309**; Berle, 1988, whole book (passim); Berle, 1999, whole book, (passim); Blanc & Bashe, 1988, pp. 211–212; Burns, 1990, pp. 268–272*; Caldwell, 1995, pp. 38–39; 46–47; Castleman & Podrazik, 1982, pp. 35–36, 37; Erickson, 2000, p. 31; Everitt, 2001, pp. 45–51*; Foreman, 1997, pp. 113–115*; Gabler, Rich & Antler, 2000, pp. 32–33; Gelbart, 1998, pp. 62–66, 112*; Hamamoto, 1994, pp. 238–241*; Jones, 1992, pp. 32–33; Marc, 1984, pp. 25–26; Marc, 1996, pp. 25–26; McCrohan, 1990, pp. 22–33**; McDonald, 1992, pp. 12–13 (same in 1983 ed.); Newcomb, 1987, pp. 344–346; O'Connor, 1983, pp. 59–73**; Panati, 1991, pp. 240–242; Pitrone, 1999, pp. 81–82; Putterman, 1995, p. 10; Rico, 1990, pp. 122, 142; Rose, 1985, p. 309; Sackett, 1993, pp. 4–5; Scheider, 1997, p. 30; Spigel, 1992, pp. 57, 145–146; Stark, 1997, pp. 8–13, 14; Stempel, 1992, pp. 13–17*; Thompson, 1996, pp. 20–21; Toll, 1982, pp. 233–235; Also in Bianculli, 1996

Texan, The
Fitzgerald & Magers, 2002, p. 224; Gianakos, 1983, pp. 334–338*; Hawes 2002, pp. 141, 143; Jackson, 1994, pp. 121–122; Yoggy, 1995, pp. 211–212; Also in Lentz, 1997, West, 1987

Texas
Matelski, 1999, p. 45

Texas Wheelers, The
Tinker & Rukeyser, 1994, pp. 104–105

That Girl
Alley & Brown, 2001, pp. 24–26; Capsuto, 2000, p. 331; Castleman & Podrazik, 1982, pp. 194–195; Crotty, 1995; Davis, 2001, p. 9; Dow, 1996, p. xvii; Jones, 1992, pp. 184–185, 195; Lichter, Lichter, & Rothman, 1991, pp. 49, 60, 66; Lichter, Lichter, & Rothman, 1994, pp. 109, 124; Meehan, 1983, pp. 171–172; Newcomb, 1987, pp. 339–340; Press, 1991, pp. 78, 129–131*; Seger, 1996, p. 155; Smith, 1989, pp. 31–35*; Stark, 1997, p. 118; Also in Bianculli, 1996, Eisner & Krinsky, 1984, Terrace, 1993

That 70's Show
Chunovic, 2000, pp. 22, 165–168**

That Was the Week That Was
Castleman & Podrazik, 1982, pp. 169–170, 178*; Erickson, 2000, pp. 23, 35–37*; Himmelstein, 1994, p. 188; Jarvik, 1997, p. 262; Marc, 1989, pp. 123–124; Marc, 1997, p. 102; Miller, 2000, pp. 115–123, 125**; Wittebols, 1998, pp. 4–5; Also in Bianculli, 1996

That's Hollywood!
Gianakos, 1983, pp. 405–406

That's Incredible!
Sackett, 1993, pp. 258–259; Wild, 1999, p. 41

That's My Boy
IN Terrace, 1993

That's My Mama
Andrews, 1986, p. 139; Means Coleman, 2000, pp. 205–206; Rubin, 1980, p. 134

T.H.E. Cat
Gianakos, 1978, pp. 569–570; Meyers, 1981, pp. 120–121; Rovin, 1977b, p. 103

Thea
Bogle, 2001, p. 410; Means Coleman, 2002, p. 268

Then Came Bronson
Doohan, 1996, pp. 167–168; Gianakos, 1978, pp. 661–662; Himmelstein, 1994, pp. 218–219; Lichter, Lichter, & Rothman, 1991, p. 33; Lichter, Lichter, & Rothman, 1994, p. 89; Rovin, 1977b, pp. 124–125

These Friends of Mine *see* **Ellen**

Thicker Than Water
IN Terrace, 1993

Thin Man, The
Lichter, Lichter, & Rothman, 1991, pp. 136, 142–143; Meyers, 1981, pp. 41–42; Rovin, 1977b, p. 58; Soter, 2002, pp. 155–156; Also in Terrace, 1993

Third Man, The
Rovin, 1977b, p. 79

3rd Rock from the Sun
Barr, 2000, p. 71; Gabler, Rich & Antler, 2000, p. 40; Helford, 2000, pp. 41–59**; Holtzman, 2000, p. 252; Owen, 1997, p. 154; Pearl & Pearl, 1999, pp. 233–234; Rannow, 1999, pp. 19, 28; Smith, 1999, p. 31; Also in Terrace, 2000

Third Watch
Longworth, 2000, pp. 124, 134–135

13 East
Paietta & Kauppila, 1999, p. 349

thirtysomething
Bignell, 1997, p. 163; Brookfield, 1990; Burks, 1990; Caldwell, 1995, pp. 91, 108; Capsuto, 2000, pp. 242–245, 252–253*; Chunovic, 2000, p. 121; Craig, 1992, pp. 34, 108, 192–195*; Croteau & Hoynes, 2000, p. 224; Cruz & Lewis, 1994, p. 29; Dow, 1996, p. 99; Gabler, Rich & Antler, 2000, pp. 61, 63; Gross, 2001, p. 88; Gross & Woods, 1999, p. 294; Harris, 1994, p. 252; Heide, 1995, whole book**; Heil, 2001, pp. 132–147, 162–206, 217–277**; Heldenfels, 1994, p. 84; Hiebert, 1999, p. 251; Himmelstein, 1994, pp. 26, 227; Hollows, 2000, p. 94, 97; Holtzman, 2000, pp. 302–303; Kendall, 1989**; Leonard, 1997, pp. 62–63; Lichter, Lichter, & Rothman, 1991, pp. 87–88; Lichter, Lichter, & Rothman, 1994, p. 158; Longworth, 2000, pp. 75–76, 84–85, 158, 167, 168; Marris & Thornham, 2000, p. 379; Mellencamp, 1992, pp. 31–32, 370–371; Miller, 1994, p. 232; Pearl & Pearl, 1999, pp. 27, 168, 185, 219–222, 226, 227, 231–232**; Powers, 1994, pp. 245–250*; Ringer, 1994, p. 109; Schneider, 2001, pp. 43–45; Stark, 1997, pp. 240–241, 246, 263; Steenland, 1990, pp. 23, 49; Stempel, 1992, pp. 198–201, 260–269**; Thompson, 1996, pp. 130–139**; Vande Berg & Wenner, 1991, pp. 129–142**; Vane & Gross, 1994, p. 144; Wild, 1999, pp. 41–42; Williams, 1992, pp. 106, 177–180 (passim); Also in Bianculli, 1996

This Is Your Life
Hamamoto, 1994, pp. 102–104; Also in Bianculli, 1996

Thomas, Danny *see* **Make Room for Daddy**

Three's Company
Andrews, 1980, pp. 186–192*; Bedell, 1981, pp. 202–203; Burns & Thompson, 1989, pp. 83–85; Capsuto, 2000, pp. 143–144; Castleman & Podrazik, 1982, pp. 280–281; Chunovic, 2000, p. 79; Cross, 1983, pp. 101, 106; DiMaggio, 1990, pp. 120–132 (passim); Erickson, 2000, p. 276; Hamamoto, 1989, pp. 127–128; Jarvik, 1997, p. 266; Jones, 1992, p. 236; Klobas, 1988, pp. 56–57; Lembo, 2000, p. 175; Lichter, Lichter, & Rothman, 1994, p. 57; Marc, 1989, pp. 214–216; Marc, 1997, pp. 179–180*; McCrohan, 1990, pp. 270–278**; Miller, 2000, pp. 159–161*; Mitz, 1980, pp. 395–398*; Newcomb, 1987, p. 483; Pegg, 2002, pp. 174, 183–185; Sackett, 1993, pp. 242–243; Schwartz, 1999, p. 129; Sklar, 1980, pp. 52, 67–68; Toll, 1982, pp. 209–210; Vane & Gross, 1994, pp. 116, 117, 221; Also in Bianculli, 1996, Eisner & Krinsky, 1984, Terrace, 1993

Thriller
Gerani, 1977, pp. 49–55**; Gianakos, 1978, pp. 299–302*; Muir, 2001b, p. 219; O'Dell, 1997, pp. 172, 174; Warren, 1996, whole book**; Also in Bianculli, 1996

Thunder Alley
Cotter, 1997, pp. 452–454; Also in Terrace, 2000

Tic Tac Dough
Anderson, 1978, pp. 44–46, 84–85*; DeLong, 1991, pp. 249–250; Stone & Yohn, 1992, pp. 86–99 (passim), 101–120 (passim), 121–127, 160–164, 186–190, 275–281, 290–292, 294–299*; U.S. Congress, 1960, pp. 304–313, 336–344, 396–397, 405–432, 448–455**

Tightrope
Gianakos, 1978, pp. 250–251; Meyers, 1981, p. 64; Rovin, 1977b, pp. 70–71

Tim Conway Show, The
Adir, 1988, pp. 111–115; Pegg, 2002, pp. 61, 65

Time Express
Gianakos, 1981, p. 275

Time of Your Life
Wild, 1999, pp. 169, 174–176, 242–243, 245–246*

Time Tunnel, The
Gerani, 1977, pp. 71, 82, 84; Gianakos, 1978, pp. 567–569*; Rovin, 1977b, p. 107; Also in Terrace, 1993

T. J. Hooker
Cuklanz, 2000, pp. 33–34, 83–84, 84–85, 87–88, 103–104, 109, 115*; D'Acci, 1994, pp. 111–112, 113; Gianakos, 1983, pp. 198–199; Gianakos, 1987, pp. 203–206*; Gianakos, 1992, pp. 273–275*; Klobas, 1988, pp. 70–72, 87–88, 240–241, 251–252, 391–392, 397–398, 455*; Marc & Thompson, 1992 (Ch. 15 on Aaron Spelling), pp. 163–169; Nelson, 1994, p. 20; Spelling, 1996, pp. 154–155; Wahl, 1995, p. 60; Also in Terrace, 1993

To Rome with Love
IN Eisner & Krinsky, 1984, Terrace, 1993

To Tell the Truth

DeLong, 1991, p. 174; Mott, 2000, pp. 179–180; Skutch, 1998, pp. 154–155; Also in Bianculli, 1996

Toast of the Town

Abelman, 1998, p. 13; Aldgate, 2000, p. 107; Anderson, 1994, p. 160; Andrews, 1986, p. 64; Barnouw, 1990, pp. 117–121*; Becker, 2001; Bowles, 1980, whole book**; Castleman & Podrazik, 1982, pp. 36, 37–38, 111–112; Chunovic, 2000, pp. 40–41; Haralovich & Rabinovitz, 1999, pp. 58–61; Haskins, 1984, pp. 33–35, 38–45 (passim); Heldenfels, 1994, p. 51; Jackson, 1997, pp. 74, 75, 227, 229, 241, 242, 268*; Leonard, 1997, pp. 17–19, 26–47**; Lewis & Lewis, 1979, most of book, especially pp. 54–187, 228–237**; Marling, 1994, p. 180; Martin, 1980**; McCrohan, 1990, pp. 85–92**; McDonald, 1983, pp. 13–14; McDonald, 1992, pp. 13–14; Mott, 2000, pp. 48–56, 65–66, 71**; Moyer & Alvarez, 2001, p. 129; Pryor, 1995, pp. 78–79; Putterman, 1995, pp. 12, 14; Rose, 1985, pp. 309, 318; Sackett, 1993, pp. 48–49; Stark, 1997, pp. 59–62*; Weiner, 1992, pp. 29–31, 139; Wilk, 1976, pp. 26–28; Also in Bianculli, 1996

Today Show, The

Abelman, 1998, pp. 205–206; Auletta, 1991, see index*; Barnouw, 1990, pp. 146–148; Broughton, 1986, pp. 204–221 (passim), especially pp. 204–210*; Castleman & Podrazik, 1982, pp. 69–70, 80; Conrad, 1982, pp. 20–23; Frank, 1991, pp. 47–49, 163–164, 175, 316–319, 354–355, 378, 387–388, 396–399*; Gitlin, 1986, pp. 175–179*; Hack, 1999, pp. 6–31, 33–73, 74–79, 81–90, 93–100, 102–104, 106–109, 113–119, 120–121, 124–127, 128–133, 134–141, 142–143, 146–148, 154, 157–185, 186–192, 195–198, 199–203, 205–206, 210, 211–212, 213–215, 216–218, 219–223, 227–238, 244–245, 249, 250, 251**; Kessler, 1992, whole book**; Kovach & Rosenstiel, 1999, pp. 14, 26, 73, 114, 134, 161; Kuney, 1990, pp. 145–161**; Lechner, 2000, pp. 87–88; Mayer, 1972, pp. 106–110*; Metz, 1977, whole book**; Munson, 1993, pp. 50–51; Newcomb, 1994, pp. 25–26, 28–29; Putterman, 1995, p. 131; Rico, 1990, pp. 124–125, 126, 134, 142, 143,146, 235; Rose, 1999, pp. 1–6**; Schaffer, 1991; Scott, 1996, pp. 196, 241–242, 277–278; Shales, 1982, pp. 42–49 (passim); Stark, 1997, pp. 47–50, 52*; Thompson, 1996, p. 11.; U.S. Congress, 1985, pp. 178–182; Vane & Gross, 1994, pp. 220–221; Wilk, 1976, pp. 196–199, 221–223*; Also in Bianculli, 1996

Today's FBI

Gianakos, 1983, pp. 202–203; Gitlin, 1983, pp. 222–223; Stempel, 1992, p. 141

Together We Stand

IN Terrace, 1993

Tom Corbett, Space Cadet

Alexander, 1994, pp. 119–120; Fagen, 1996, p. 158; Rovin, 1977b, pp. 25–26; Also in Terrace, 1993

Tom, Dick and Mary

Paietta & Kauppila, 1999, p. 349

Tom Ewell Show, The

IN Eisner & Krinsky, 1984, Terrace, 1993

Tom Show, The
Bryant & Bryant, 2001, p. 190

Toma
Castleman & Podrazik, 1982, p. 248; Gianakos, 1978, pp. 750–751; Martindale, 1991, pp. 486–487; Meyers, 1981, pp. 193–194; Rovin, 1977b, p. 139; Thompson, 1990, pp. 56–61*

Tombstone Territory
Gianakos, 1981, pp. 373–375; Jackson, 1994, pp. 103–104; McDonald, 1987, p. 61; Yoggy, 1995, pp. 171–172; Also in Lentz, 1997, West, 1987

Tomorrow
Hack, 1999, pp. 112–113; Also in Bianculli, 1996

Tonight Show, The (general)
Abt & Mustazza, 1997, pp. 57–58, 59; Carter 1995, pp. 13–18, entire book (passim); Carter, 1994, pp. 13–16, entire book (passim); Creeber, 2001, pp. 82–83; Griffin, 1980, pp. 220, 222; Hack, 1999, p. 59; Heldenfels, 1994, p. 72; Himmelstein, 1994, pp. 343–344; Horowitz, 1997, pp. 17, 89, 141; Marc, 1984, pp. 140–148**; Marc, 1996, pp. 140–148**; Metz, 1980, whole book**; Miller, 2000, pp. 113–114; Modleski, 1986, p. 182; Munson, 1993, pp. 50–52; Newcomb, 1994, pp. 274–275; Newcomb, 2000, p. 354; Roman, 1996, pp. 69–70; Rose, 1985, pp. 332–334, 336, 342*; Shattuc, 1997, pp. 35–36; Stark, 1997, pp. 182–188**; Vande Berg & Wenner, 1991, pp. 416–423 (passim)*; White, 1992, p. 276; Wilk, 1976, pp. 222–227; Also in Bianculli, 1996

Tonight Show, The (Steve Allen)
Abelman, 1998, pp. 206–207; Castleman & Podrazik, 1982, pp. 93, 112; Corkery, 1987, pp. 88–91*; Heldenfels, 1994, pp. 66–67; Leamer, 1989, pp. 132–133; Putterman, 1995, p. 131; Rico, 1990, pp. 151–152, 196–205, 217, 227**; Stark, 1997, p. 83

Tonight Show, The (Johnny Carson)
Arnold, 1994, pp. 72–75; Capsuto, 2000, p. 95; Carter 1995, pp. 15–18, 31–32, 86–89; Carter, 1994, pp. 14–15, 31–32, 86–89; Castleman & Podrazik, 1982, pp. 160–161; Chunovic, 2000, pp. 45–46; Conrad, 1982, pp. 59–62; Corkery, 1987, pp. 104–172, 211–234**; De Cordova, 1988, whole book**; Kanfer, 2000, p. 360; Leamer, 1989, pp. 13–16, 135–160, 175–235, 262–273, 326–413**; Leamer, 1989, pp. 67, 88–90, 95–101**; Leno, 1996, pp. 180–195 (passim); Marc, 1984, pp. 145–148; Marc, 1996, pp. 145–148; Mott, 2000, pp. 110–111, 118–119; Newcomb, 1994, pp. 274, 276–277, 279*; Newcomb, 2000, pp. 358–359, 360–365*; Putterman, 1995, p. 73; Rose, 1985, pp. 333–334, 336; Smith, 1987, pp. 41–48, 94–242**; Smith, 1997, pp. 144, 153, 154–155, 159, 162; Stark, 1997, pp. 183–186*; Tartikoff, 1992, pp. 101–104*; Tinker & Rukeyser, 1994, pp. 50–51, 249–251*; U.S. Congress, 1977c, pp. 2, 18, 20–21, 56–57; Vande Berg & Wenner, 1991, pp. 416–423 (passim)*; Zehme, 1999, pp. 155–156, 172, 181–182, 184–185

Tonight Show, The (Jay Leno)
Abelman, 1998, pp. 216–220*; Carter, 1994, pp. 89–92, 107–110, 265–268, 272–276, entire book (passim)**; Carter, 1995, pp. 89–92, 107–110, 265–268, 273–274, 279–280, 283–286, 295–296, 298–299, entire book

(passim)**; Erickson, 2000, p. 266; Kovach & Rosenstiel, 1999, pp. 30, 31, 65, 169, 170; Lechner, 2000, pp. 193–194, 229; Leno, 1996, pp. 196–278**; Rose, 1999, pp. 110–114*; Stark, 1997, pp. 186–188; Tinker & Rukeyser, 1994, pp. 250–251; Torres, 1998, pp. 8, 239–253**

Tonight Show, The (Jack Paar)
Abelman, 1998, pp. 207–208; Castleman & Podrazik, 1982, pp. 112–113, 160; Chunovic, 2000, pp. 45–46; Corkery, 1987, pp. 91–98*; Erickson, 2000, p. 60; Griffin, 1980, pp. 20, 21, 48–57, 219–220, 237, 238**; Leamer, 1989, pp. 118–119, 133–136*; Marc, 1984, pp. 143–145; Marc, 1996, pp. 143–145; Mott, 2000, pp. 151–152; Munson, 1993, pp. 56–57; Paar, 1983, pp. 99–129, 157–165**; Rose, 1985, pp. 332–333; Shanks, 1976, pp. 16–17, 41, 59; Smith, 1987, pp. 70–77**; Stark, 1997, pp. 183, 187; Tabarlet, 1993; Williams, 1982, pp. 48–49

Tony Orlando and Dawn
Scheider, 1997, p. 154

Tony Randall Show, The
DiMaggio, 1990, pp. 39–41; Jarvis & Joseph, 1998, p. 172; Sklar, 1980, p. 9; Tinker & Rukeyser, 1994, pp. 106–108*

Too Close for Comfort
Cross, 1983, pp. 93–94; Pegg, 2002, pp. 17, 21–24, 167–168**; Sackett, 1993, p. 273; Rotan, 1982; Also in Terrace, 1993

Top Cat
Barbera, 1994, pp. 142–147*

Top of the Heap
IN Terrace, 1993

Top of the Hill
Schultz, 2000, p. 125

Topper
Guida, 2000, p. 182; Kulzer, 1992, pp. 65, 68–72; Mitz, 1980, pp. 95–97*; Putterman, 1995, pp. 92–95, 98*; Also in Bianculli, 1996, Eisner & Krinsky, 1984, Terrace, 1993

Torkelsons
Cotter, 1997, pp. 429–431; Also in Terrace, 1993, Terrace, 2000

Tortellis, The
Orlik, 1994, p. 178; Orlik, 2001, p. 174; Also in Terrace, 1993

Touch of Grace, A
IN Terrace, 1993

Touched by an Angel
Bogle, 2001, pp. 426, 428–429; Capsuto, 2000, pp. 376–377; Davis, 2001, pp. 170–183**; Johnston, 2000, p. 15; Longworth, 2000, pp. 107, 110–111; Pearl & Pearl, 1999, pp. 128, 170

Tour of Duty
Ballard-Reisch, 1991; Hamamoto, 1994, pp. 133, 140–144*; Lichter, Lichter, & Rothman, 1991, p. 274; Lichter, Lichter, & Rothman, 1994, pp. 386–387; Thompson, 1996, pp. 141–142*

Tracey Ullman Show, The
Capsuto, 2000, pp. 238–239; Crown, 1999, pp. 85–86; Marc & Thompson, 1992 (Ch. 5 on James L. Brooks), pp. 61–69

Trackdown
Gianakos, 1983, pp. 328–330*; Jackson, 1994, p. 103; Magers & Fitzgerald, 1999, p. 192; Spigel & Curtin, 1997, pp. 296–298*; Yoggy, 1995, pp. 155–157, 258–259*; Also in Lentz, 1997, Terrace, 1993, West, 1987

Trapper John, M.D.
Bogle, 2001, pp. 266–269*; Capsuto, 2000, p. 155; Gianakos, 1981, pp. 283–284; Gianakos, 1983, pp. 135–137*; Gianakos, 1987, pp. 216–219*; Gianakos, 1992, pp. 287–289*; Harris, 1989, p. 100; Harris, 1994, p. 98; Horton & McDougal, 1998, p. 322; Kalisch, Kalisch, & Scobey, 1983, pp. 130–133**; Klobas, 1988, pp. 185–187, 230–231, 243–244, 298–300, 355–357, 401–402, 409–411**; Leiby & Leiby, 2001, p. 212; Lichter, Lichter, & Rothman, 1991, pp. 62, 127–128; Lichter, Lichter, & Rothman, 1994, p. 206; Nelson, 1994, p. 21; Paietta & Kauppila, 1999, pp. 349–350; Pearl & Pearl, 1999, pp. 160–161; Puette, 1992, pp. 184, 189; Rose, 1985, pp. 76, 81–82; Shaheen, 1984, pp. 68–70; Stempel, 1992, pp. 169–170; Turow, 1989, pp. xi–xiii, 232–238, 254–255**; Vande Berg & Trujillo, 1989, pp. 123, 126, 176, 182–183*

Trauma Center
Gianakos, 1987, p. 333; Klobas, 1988, pp. 246–247, 455–456; Paietta & Kauppila, 1999, p. 350

Travels of Jaimie McPheeter, The
Gianakos, 1978, pp. 405–406; Yoggy, 1995, p. 272; Also in Lentz, 1997, West, 1987

Treasury Men in Action
Gianakos, 1983, pp. 251–256**; Hawes, 2002, p. 107; Rovin, 1977b, p. 32

Trial and Error
Rodriguez, 1997, p. 67

Trials of O'Brien, The
Gianakos, 1978, pp. 476–477; Meyers, 1981, pp. 105–106; Rovin, 1977b, pp. 96–97

Trials of Rosie O'Neill, The
Alley & Brown, 2001, pp. 202–203; Swanson, 2000, pp. 179–188**; Vane & Gross, 1994, p. 146; Also in Terrace, 1993

Trouble with Father
IN Terrace, 1993

Troubleshooters
Gianakos, 1978, pp. 266–267

True Blue
IN Terrace, 1993

True Colors
Bogle, 2001, pp. 382–383; Paietta & Kauppila, 1999, p. 350; Also in Terrace, 1993

Truth or Consequences
Munson, 1993, pp. 28–30; Also in Bianculli, 1996

Tucker's Witch
Gianakos, 1987, pp. 302–303; Muir, 2001a, pp. 592–593**; Also in Terrace, 1993

Turn On
Adir, 1988, p. 110; Andrews, 1980, pp. 193–198*; Erickson, 2000, pp. 188–196**; Marc, 1989, pp. 152–153; Marc, 1997, p. 126; Scheider, 1997, p. 141

TV Nation
Caldwell, 1995, p. 245; Moore & Glynn, 1998, whole book**

TV 101
Tinker & Rukeyser, 1994, p. 241

TV Reader's Digest
Gianakos, 1980, pp. 420–425*

Twelve O'Clock High
Gianakos, 1978, pp. 466–469; Lichter, Lichter, & Rothman, 1994, pp. 381–382; Rovin, 1977b, p. 91

Twenty One
Abelman, 1998, pp. 151–153; Anderson, 1978, pp. 38–39, 44–78, 91, 96–101, 119–122, 129–132, 139–143, 185–194, 205–207**; Barnouw, 1990, pp. 243–246; Castleman & Podrazik, 1982, pp. 114–115, 125–126, 133–134*; DeLong, 1991, pp. 213–214, 220–221, 222–224*; Frank, 1991, pp. 128–129; Gabler, Rich & Antler, 2000, pp. 11–12; Hack, 1999, pp. 47–48: Jarvik, 1997, p. 10; Newcomb, 1976, p. 115; Stark, 1997, pp. 76–78; Stone & Yohn, 1992, pp. 26–45, 61–62, 83–120, 127–135, 157–160, 166–173, 178–182, 192–197, 215–224, 232–239, 244–252, 277–278, 292–294, 296–299, 310–317**; U.S. Congress, 1960, pp. 15–262, 401, 459–462, 623–646, 1069–1075**; Also in Bianculli, 1996

21 Beacon Street
Meyers, 1981, p. 59; Story, 1993, p. 48

21 Jump Street
Block, 1990, see index, especially pp. 165–167; Bogle, 2001, p. 333; Capsuto, 2000, pp. 222–223, 235, 337–338; Cuklanz, 2000, pp. 40–41, 46, 51–53, 74–75, 116, 135–139, 143–146**; Hamamoto, 1994, p. 28; Henderson & Mazzeo, 1990, pp. 65–66; Marc & Thompson, 1992 (Ch. 19 on Stephen J. Cannell), pp. 205–216; Moorti, 2001, pp. 125–127, 131–1`32*; Ringer, 1994, pp. 96, 99–100, 100–101*; Steenland, 1990, pp. 42, 44; Also in Terrace, 1993

26 Men
Fagen, 1996, pp. 91–97 (interview with Kelo Henderson), 119*; Fitzgerald & Magers, 2002, p. 224; Gianakos, 1992, pp. 451–453*; Yoggy, 1995, pp. 160–161; Also in Lentz, 1997, West, 1987

20/20
Castleman & Podrazik, 1982, pp. 293–294; Diamond, 1982, pp. 42–43, 51–52; Goldenson, 1991, pp. 397–404 (passim); Lesher, 1982, pp. 151–154, 163–164; Moorti, 2001, p. 198; Rapping, 1987, pp. 119–132**; Rivera, 1991, pp. 320–390, 396–427**; Schultz, 2000, p. 143; Shaheen, 1984, pp. 108–110; Spragens, 1995, pp. 92–98, 131–132**; Westin, 1982, pp. 197–200; Also in Bianculli, 1996

Twilight Zone, The (including revival)
Abelman, 1998, pp. 394–395; Castleman & Podrazik, 1982, p. 137; Davis, 2001, pp. 118–119; Engel, 1989, pp. 178–252**; Everitt, 2001, p. 180; Gerani, 1977, pp. 35–47**; Gianakos, 1978, pp. 272–278**; Gianakos, 1992, pp. 409–411*; Hawes, 2002, p. 122; Javna, 1985, pp. 90–93*; Klobas, 1988, pp. 97–99, 428–429; Lewis & Lewis, 1979, pp. 128–129; Lichter, Lichter, & Rothman, 1991, pp. 283–284; Lichter, Lichter, & Rothman,

1994, pp. 398–399; Miller, 1980, p. 145; Muir, 2001a, pp. 574–580*; O'Dell, 1997, p. 173; Panati, 1991, pp. 361–362; Presnell & McGee, 1998, whole book**; Schultz, 2000, p. 81; Sconce, 2000, pp. 133–135*; Shales, 1982, pp. 107–109; Spigel & Curtin, 1997, pp. 22, 61, 122; Stark, 1997, pp. 85–89**; Starr, 1997, p. 109; Stempel, 1992, pp. 101–102; Wolfe, 1996, whole book**; Worland, 1989; Worland, 1996; Wylie, 1970, pp. 351–379**; Zicree, whole book**; Also in Bianculli, 1996

Twin Peaks
Allen, 1992, pp. 341–349**; Altman, 1990, whole book**; Barker, 1999, p. 57; Berry & Asamen, 1993, p. 192; Bianculli, 1992, pp. 269–271; Bignell, 1997, pp. 159–160, 162*; Birns, 1993; Caldwell, 1995, pp. 286–287; Carrion, 1993; Carroll, 1993; Chunovic, 2000, p. 126; Creeber, 2001, p. 44; Dienst, 1994, pp. 89–99**; Edgerton, Marsden & Nachbar, 1997, p. 133; Himmelstein, 1994, pp. 235–237; Hughes, 2001, pp. 104–138**; Huskey, 1993; Kaleta, 1993, pp. 133–155**; Lafky, 1999/2000; Lavery, 1995, entire book; Ledwon, 1993; Leonard, 1997, pp. 234–245**; Mellencamp, 1992, pp. 236–237; Muir, 2001a, pp. 248–265**; Nelson, 1996; Newcomb, 1994, p. 143; Nickerson, 1993; Nochimson, 1992/1993; Nochimson, 1997b, pp. 72–98**; Orlik, 1994, pp. 264–265; Paietta & Kauppila, 1999, p. 350; Pollard, 1993; Riggs, 1998, p. 20; Rodley, 1997, pp. 155–190**; Soter, 2002, pp. 111–112; Stark, 1997, p. 241; Steenland, 1990, pp. 14, 38; Stempel, 1992, p. 244; Thompson, 1996, pp. 13, 147, 148, 150, 152–160, 170–171, 174, 178; Vane & Gross, 1994, pp. 168, 169, 234–235; Woods, 1997, pp. 94–113, 133–149**; Also in Bianculli, 1996, Morris, 1997, Terrace, 1993

240–Robert
Gianakos, 1981, p. 284; Also in Terrace, 1993

Two Girls Named Smith
IN Terrace, 1993

Two Guys, a Girl and a Pizza Place
Croteau & Hoynes, 2000, p. 218; Also in Terrace, 2000

Two Marriages
Gianakos, 1987, pp. 316–317

Two of a Kind
IN Terrace, 2000

Two of Us, The
IN Terrace, 1993

2000 Malibu Road
Owen, 1997, p. 83; Also in Terrace, 1993

227
Bogle, 2001, pp. 309–312*; Dates & Barlow, 1990, pp. 277–278; Dates & Barlow, 1993, pp. 299–300; James, 1991; Turner, 1994, pp. 137–138; Also in Terrace, 1993

Ugliest Girl in Town, The
IN Eisner & Krinsky, 1984

Uncle Buck
Chunovic, 2000, p. 125; Starr, 1997, p. 218; Also in Terrace, 1993, Terrace, 2000

Under Cover
Gianakos, 1992, pp. 358–359; Also in Terrace, 1993

Under One Roof
Holtzman, 2000, p. 247; Means Coleman, 2000, pp. 1–3; Means Coleman, 2002, p. 277

Under Suspicion
Leonard, 1997, pp. 192–193; Thompson, 1996, p. 185

Underdog
Davis, 1995, pp. 89–90; Also in Bianculli, 1996

Unhappily Ever After
Capsuto, 2000, pp. 301, 349; Cotter, 1997, pp. 463–466* Also in Terrace, 2000

United States
Abelman, 1998, p. 94; Bedell, 1981, pp. 286–287; Gelbart, 1998, pp. 93–103**; Newcomb & Alley, 1983, pp. 38–41*

United States Steel Hour
Gianakos, 1978, pp. 83–105**; Gianakos, 1980, pp. 380–382*; Hawes, 2002, pp. 55–56; Sturcken, 1990, pp. 94–99*; Also in Bianculli, 1996

Unsolved Mysteries
Boylan, 2000, pp. 8–9; Roman, 1996, p. 73; Sackett, 1993, p. 343; Vane & Gross, 1994, p. 234

Unsub
Capsuto, 2000, pp. 245–246; Also in Terrace, 1993

Untouchables, The
Barnouw, 1990, pp. 260–265*; Brady, 1994, pp. 249–250, 308; Buxton, 1990, pp. 36–41, 56, 113*; Collins & Javna, 1989, pp. 74–76; Davis, 2001, pp. 106–107; Fowles, 1982, pp. 16, 18; Gianakos, 1978, pp. 261–266**; Goldenson, 1991, pp. 172–174; Harris, 1991, pp. 240, 251–252, 254–255, 272, 280, 324; Himmelstein, 1994, p. 228; Javna, 1985, pp. 112–115*; Lichter, Lichter, & Rothman, 1991, pp. 190, 209, 213, 235; Lichter, Lichter, & Rothman, 1994, pp. 306, 338; Marc, 1984, pp. 79–80; Marc, 1996, pp. 79–80; Marc & Thompson, 1992 (Ch. 14 on Quinn Martin), pp. 153–161; Mehling, 1962, see index; Meyers, 1981, pp. 60–71; Montgomery, 1989, pp. 20–21; Newcomb, 1976, pp. 229–230; Newcomb, 1979, pp. 295–296, 414; O'Dell, 1997, pp. 172–173; Pearl & Pearl, 1999, p. 26; Rovin, 1977b, pp. 69–70; Sackett, 1993, pp. 106–107; Sanders & Gilbert, 1993, pp. 173–176, 220–223, 230–231, 250–251*; Schneider, 2001, p. 94; Shaheen, 1984, pp. 121–122; Spigel & Curtin, 1997, pp. 162, 167, 171, 175–176, 329–330; Stempel, 1992, pp. 84–85; Toll, 1982, pp. 174–175; Tucker, 2000, pp. 55–130, 147–183**; Vahimagi, 1998, whole book**; Wahl, 1995, p. 8; Also in Bianculli, 1996, Terrace, 1993

U.S. Marshal *see* **Sheriff of Cochise**

V
Gianakos, 1992, pp. 373–374

Valentine's Day
Hamamoto, 1994, p. 8; Putterman, 1995, pp. 58–60, 66*

Valerie
Hamamoto, 1989, p. 133; Also in Terrace, 2000

Van Dyke and Company
Zehme, 1999, 5, 174–175

Vega$
Cuklanz, 2000, pp. 34, 107–108, 109; Gianakos, 1981, pp. 263–265*; Klobas, 1988, pp. 68–69; Marc & Thompson, 1992 (Ch. 15 on Aaron Spelling), pp. 163–169, (Ch. 21 on Michael Mann), pp. 231–240; Martindale, 1991, pp. 488–494; Meyers, 1981, pp. 251–253; Shaheen, 1984, pp. 47–48; Spelling, 1996, pp. 134–138

Verdict Is Yours, The
Rafkin, 1998, pp. 22–23

Veronica's Closet
Capsuto, 2000, pp. 408–409; Keller, 2002, pp. 179–180; Wild, 1999, pp. 18–19, 150–152, 154

Vinnie and Bobby
IN Terrace, 1993, Terrace, 2000

Virginian, The
Brauer, 1975, pp. 118–119, 126–128, 130, 177–179, 184–185, 191–192**; Fagen, 1996, pp. 38–41 (interview with Randy Boone)*; Fitzgerald & Magers, 2002, pp. 137–138; Gianakos, 1978, pp. 382–392**; Jackson, 1994, pp. 150–152; Jarvis & Joseph, 1998, pp. 216–217; Lichter, Lichter, & Rothman, 1991, pp. 82, 257–258; Lichter, Lichter, & Rothman, 1994, pp. 365–366; Magers & Fitzgerald, 1999, pp. 18, 35, 194, 202–204, 205–208, 244*; Marc & Thompson, 1992 (Ch. 13 on Roy Huggins), pp. 141–151; Martin, 1980**; McDonald, 1987, p. 96; Newcomb, 1976, p. 90; O'Dell, 1997, p. 174; Pearl & Pearl, 1999, p. 74; Rovin, 1977b, p. 85; Sackett, 1993, p. 147; Suman & Rossman, 2000, p. 134; Yoggy, 1995, pp. 395–399, 401–416, 424**; Also in Lentz, 1997, West, 1987

Vise, The
Gianakos, 1980, pp. 413–415

Viva Valdez
Rafkin, 1998, pp. 99–100; Stempel, 1992, pp. 151–152

Voyage to the Bottom of the Sea
Alexander, 1994, pp. 297–300; Gerani, 1977, pp. 69–70, 73–77*; Gianakos, 1978, pp. 448–452*; Rovin, 1977b, p. 94; Also in Bianculli, 1996, Terrace, 1993

Voyagers!
Gianakos, 1987, pp. 291–293; Klobas, 1988, pp. 166–167, 244–245; Lichter, Lichter, & Rothman, 1991, p. 257; Lichter, Lichter, & Rothman, 1994, p. 365; Puette, 1992, pp. 189–190; Also in Terrace, 1993

VR.5
Leonard, 1997, p. 126; Owen, 1997, pp. 183–184

Wackiest Ship in the Army, The
Gianakos, 1978, pp. 488–489

Wagon Train
Aquila, 1996, pp. 175–176; Brauer, 1975, pp. 83, 92–101, 105–106**; Buscombe & Pearson, 1998, p. 130; Fagen, 1996, pp. 98–105 (interview with Robert Horton), 212*; Fitzgerald & Magers, 2002, pp. 169, 264, 301, 303–304; Gianakos, 1978, pp. 138–148**; Goethals, 1981, p. 64; Hawes, 2002, pp. 138–139; Jackson,

1994, pp. 104–105; McCrohan, 1990, pp. 108–111*; McDonald, 1987, pp. 78–79; Newcomb, 1976, p. 227; Newcomb, 1979, p. 293; Pearl & Pearl, 1999, pp. 69–70; Rose, 1985, pp. 60–61; Rovin, 1977b, p. 52; Sackett, 1993, p. 81; Stempel, 1992, pp. 79–80; Yoggy, 1995, pp. 263–273, 283–284, 369**; Yoggy, 1998, p. 149; Also in Bianculli, 1996 , Lentz, 1997, West, 1987

Walker, Texas Ranger
Aquila, 1996, p. 183; Pearl & Pearl, 1999, p. 193; Schwartz, 1999, pp. 194–195; Suman, 1997, p. 76; Yoggy, 1995, pp. 617–621*; Also in Lentz, 1997

Walking Tall
Cuklanz, 2000, pp. 34, 70; Gianakos, 1983, pp. 177–178

Walt Disney *see* **Disneyland**

Walter and Emily
Cotter, 1997, pp. 432–433; Also in Terrace, 1993

Waltons, The
Alley, 1977, pp. 117–122**; Bedell, 1981, pp. 72–74; Berger, 1987, p. 216; Broughton, 1986, pp. 192–202**; Davis, 2001, p. 120; Field, 1989, p. 207; Forbes & Mahan, 2000, pp. 45, 49–50; Gianakos, 1978, pp. 724–727*; Gianakos, 1981, pp. 133–137*; Gianakos, 1983, pp. 160–161; Goethals, 1981, pp. 55–56; Haner, 1981; Heil, 2001, pp. 14–18, 50–55**; Himmelstein, 1984, pp. 60, 180; Himmelstein, 1994, p. 220; Kalisch, Kalisch, & Scobey, 1983, pp. 114–117; Klobas, 1988, pp. 36–37, 204–205, 379–380, 457; Marc & Thompson, 1992 (Ch. 18 on Lee Rich, i.e., Lorimar), pp. 195–202; Martin, 1980**; McCrohan, 1990, pp. 231–241**; Miles, 1975, pp. 55–57 (Nov. 8, 1973, show); Newcomb, 1976, pp. 7–8, 66–73, 280–281**; Newcomb, 1979, pp. 8–15, 145–148, 427–428, 433–434**; Newcomb, 1982, pp. 116–119, 198–205*; Newcomb, 1987, pp. 223, 462, 619–620, 625–626; Newcomb, 1994, pp. 195–196, 508–509; Newcomb, 2000, pp. 566–567; Newcomb & Alley, 1983, pp. 28–31, 154–172 (passim)*; Paietta & Kauppila, 1999, p. 351; Pearl & Pearl, 1999, pp. 15, 28, 108–109. 246–247*; Press, 1991, p. 158; Rovin, 1977b, pp. 133–134; Sackett, 1993, pp. 200–201; Schwoch, White, & Reilly, 1992, pp. 12–13; Suman, 1997, pp. 7–8*; Taylor, 1989, pp. 101–104*; U.S. Congress, 1977c, p. 25; Also in Bianculli, 1996, Terrace, 1993

Wanted
Hawes, 2002, p. 107

Wanted: Dead or Alive
Aquila, 1996, p. 175; Caldwell, 1995, p. 51; Fitzgerald & Magers, 2002, pp. 65, 168–169, 223, 230*; Gianakos, 1981, pp. 387–392**; Hawes, 2002, pp. 136–137; Jackson, 1994, pp. 130–131; Magers & Fitzgerald, 1999, pp. 63, 134, 136; McDonald, 1987, pp. 52, 63–64; Newcomb, 1979, p. 542; Sackett, 1993, p. 94; Yoggy, 1995, pp. 256, 258–262*; Yoggy, 1998, pp. 162–166*; Also in Bianculli, 1996, Lentz, 1997, Terrace, 1993, West, 1987

War of the Worlds
Harris, 1998, pp. 179–197**; Also in Terrace, 1993

Warner Brothers Presents
Abelman, 1998, p. 398; Anderson,

1994, pp. 165–173, 179–187, 191–218**; Gianakos, 1980, pp. 468–469

Watch Mr. Wizard
Davis, 1995, pp. 151–153*; Also in Bianculli, 1996

Waterfront
Rovin, 1977b, p. 38; Also in Terrace, 1993

Way Out
Gianakos, 1978, p. 322

Wayans Brothers
Hiebert, 1999, p. 376; Means Coleman, 2000, pp. 122, 136

We Got It Made
Rafkin, 1998, pp. 116–117; Also in Terrace, 1993

W.E.B.
Gianakos, 1981, pp. 265–266; Also in Terrace, 1993

Web, The
Gianakos, 1980, pp. 247–252*; Hawes, 2001, pp. 133–134; Mott, 2000, pp. 66–70*

Webster
Allen, 1987, pp. 147–151*; Allen, 1992, pp. 173–177 (same as Allen 1987)*; Bogle, 2001, pp. 259–261*; Dates & Barlow, 1990, p. 274; Dates & Barlow, 1993, p. 296; Lichter, Lichter, & Rothman, 1991, p. 89; Lichter, Lichter, & Rothman, 1994, pp. 159–160; McDonald, 1992, pp. 258–259; Turner, 1994, pp. 125–130**; Also in Terrace, 1993

Welcome Back, Kotter
Coakley, 1977, pp. 143, 152–153, 179–180; Cuklanz, 2000, pp. 47–48; Greenberg, 1980, p. 10; Jones, 1992, pp. 224–226; Lichter, Lichter, & Rothman, 1991, pp. 44–45, 168; Lichter, Lichter, & Rothman, 1994, pp. 103–104, 256*; Miller, 1980, pp. 190, 198; Mitz, 1980, pp. 371–374*; Pegg, 2002, pp. 249–252*; Rannow, 1999, pp. 17–18, 25–26, 43, 70–71, 84–85, 100–103, 108–109, 110–111, 155–157*; Turner, 1994, pp. 140–141; Also in Bianculli, 1996, Eisner & Krinsky, 1984

Wells Fargo *see* **Tales of Wells Fargo**

Wendy and Me
Kulzer, 1992, pp. 147–148; Lisanti & Paul, 2002, pp. 155; Also in Eisner & Krinsky, 1984, Terrace, 1993

Werewolf
Block, 1990, pp. 210–215*; Muir, 2001a, pp. 161–172**

West 57th
Spragens, 1995, pp. 85–90*; Stark, 1997, p. 246

West Point Story, The
Lichter, Lichter, & Rothman, 1991, p. 276; Lichter, Lichter, & Rothman, 1994, p. 389

West Wing, The
Challen, 2001, whole book**; Chunovic, 2000, p. 152; Lechner, 2000, pp. 146–147, 149–151*; Longworth, 2000, pp. 124–125; Schultz, 2000, p. 130; Sorkin, 2002, whole book**

Westerner, The
Gianakos, 1978, p. 317; Jackson,

1994, pp. 143–144; McDonald, 1987, p. 77; Yoggy, 1995, pp. 218–222*; Also in Lentz, 1997, Terrace, 1993, West, 1987

Westside Medical
Gianakos, 1981, pp. 224–225; Kalisch, Kalisch, & Scobey, 1983, pp. 70–72; Paietta & Kauppila, 1999, p. 351

What a Country!
Hamamoto, 1989, p. 143; Also in Terrace, 1993

What a Dummy
IN Terrace, 1993

What Really Happened to the Class of '65
Klobas, 1988, p. 290

What's Happening!
Andrews, 1986, p. 143; Coakley, 1977, p. 137; Means Coleman, 2000, p. 163; Newcomb, 1982, pp. 83–84; Puette, 1992, p. 179; Rafkin, 1998, pp. 98–99; Rodriguez, 1997, pp. 63, 65; Sklar, 1980, pp. 21–22; Also in Eisner & Krinsky, 1984, Terrace, 1993

What's It All About, World
Erickson, 2000, pp 183–184

What's My Line
Allen, 1956, pp. 39–40; DeLong, 1991, pp. 169–173*; Fates, 1978, whole book**; Rico, 1990, p. 135; Skutch, 1998, pp. 52–56*; Strait, 1983, pp. 96–97; Wilk, 1976, pp. 185–191*; Also in Bianculli, 1996

Wheel of Fortune
Abelman, 1998, p. 266; Caldwell, 1995, pp. 195, 287; Delong, 1991, pp. 244, 251–252; Griffin, 1980, p. 273; Joyce, 1988, p. 180; Lechner, 2000, pp. 181–182; Meinhof, 2000, pp. 98–114**; Newcomb, 2000, pp. 371–381**; Orlik, 1994, p. 205; Riggs, 1998, p. 15; Stark, 1997, pp. 295, 296–300**; Also in Bianculli, 1996

When Things Were Rotten
IN Eisner & Krinsky, 1984

Where I Live
Cotter, 1997, pp. 435–437*

Whirlybirds
Gianakos, 1992, pp. 449–451*

Whispering Smith
Fagen, 1996, p. 159; Gianakos, 1978, pp. 324–325; Jackson, 1994, pp. 148–149; McDonald, 1987, pp. 76–77; Also in Lentz, 1997, West, 1987

White Shadow, The
Dates & Barlow, 1990, p. 274; Dates & Barlow, 1993, pp. 296–297; Gianakos, 1981, pp. 261–262; Gianakos, 1983, pp. 159–160; Klobas, 1988, pp. 216–218; Lichter, Lichter, & Rothman, 1991, pp. 168, 169, 256; Lichter, Lichter, & Rothman, 1994, p. 256; Longworth, 2000, pp. 82–83; McDonald, 1983, pp. 197–198; McDonald, 1992, p. 200; Newcomb, 1987, pp. 74–76*; Thompson, 1996, p. 50; Tinker & Rukeyser, 1994, pp. 127–128; Turner, 1994, pp. 141–142

Whiz Kids
Gianakos, 1987, pp. 329–330; Lichter, Lichter, & Rothman, 1991, p. 155; Lichter, Lichter, & Rothman, 1994, p. 240; Also in Terrace, 1993

Who Wants to Be a Millionaire?
Chunovic, 2000, pp. 161–162; Creeber, 2001, p. 81

Whole New Ballgame, A
Owen, 1997, p. 135

Who's the Boss
Davis, 2001, pp. 15–16; Harris, 1989, pp. 43, 44; Harris, 1994, pp. 45, 47; Hiebert, 1999, p. 250; Jones, 1992, pp. 255–258*; Lichter, Lichter, & Rothman, 1991, p. 90; Lichter, Lichter, & Rothman, 1994, pp. 160–161; Mellencamp, 1992, pp. 350–351; Press, 1991, pp. 120–122; Roman, 1996, p. 29; Sackett, 1993, pp. 308–309; Schwartz, 1999, p. 128; Also in Terrace, 1993

Who's Watching the Kids?
IN Terrace, 1993

Wichita Town
Gianakos, 1978, p. 259; Jackson, 1994, p. 142; Yoggy, 1995, pp. 152–154*; Also in Lentz, 1997, West, 1987

Wide Country, The
Gianakos, 1978, pp. 396–397; Also in Lentz, 1997, West, 1987

Wide World of Sports
Abelman, 1998, pp. 236–238*; Goldenson, 1991, see index, especially pp. 194–198*; Gorman & Calhoun, 1994, pp. 53, 78–79; Leonard, 1997, p. 39; Mayer, 1972, pp. 185–187; Rader, 1984, pp. 107–109, 111, 125, 128; Rose, 1985, pp. 267–268; Rose, 1999, pp. 190–191; Also in Bianculli, 1996

Wild Bill Hickock *see* **Adventures of Wild Bill Hickock**

Wild Oats
Owen, 1997, pp. 133–135*

Wild Wild West, The
Aquila, 1996, pp. 179–180; Bennett, 1996, pp. 47–49; Brauer, 1975, p. 21; Fitzgerald & Magers, 2002, p. 68; Gianakos, 1978, pp. 512–518**; Jackson, 1994, pp. 159–163; Javna, 1985, pp. 138–141*; Klobas, 1988, pp. 279–280, 344–345; Lichter, Lichter, & Rothman, 1991, pp. 144–145; Lichter, Lichter, & Rothman, 1994, p. 227; Lisanti & Paul, 2002, pp. 27, 88, 139, 155–156, 170, 172, 201, 203–204, 210–211, 290–291, 296, 308–309, 314–316*; Meyers, 1981, pp. 113–116*; Miller, 2000, p. 36; Newcomb, 1976, pp. 99–100; Rovin, 1977b, pp. 98–99; Rutstein, 1974, pp. 10, 34–35, 49–50; Story, 1993, pp. 171–183**; Yoggy, 1995, pp. 441–456**; Also in Bianculli, 1996, Lentz, 1997, Terrace, 1993, West, 1987

Wildside
Gianakos, 1992, pp. 387–388; Yoggy, 1995, pp. 547, 549; Also in Lentz, 1997

Will & Grace
Capsuto, 2000, pp. 405–407*; Chunovic, 2000, pp. 22–23; Creeber, 2001, p. 72; Croteau & Hoynes, 2000, p. 224; Davis, 2001, pp. 20, 70–81**; Gabler, Rich & Antler, 2000, p. 66; Gross, 2001, pp. 179–180; Keller, 2002, pp. 121–136**; Lechner, 2000, p. 115; Suman & Rossman, 2000, pp. 24, 86; Walters, 2001, pp. 25, 95, 100–101, 107–111, 208**; Wild,

Sochen, 1987, pp. 100–101; Also in Bianculli, 1996, Terrace, 1993

Wonder Years, The
Gabler, Rich & Antler, 2000, p. 73; Himmelstein, 1994, p. 137; Jones, 1992, pp. 268–269; Lichter, Lichter, & Rothman, 1991, p. 88; Lichter, Lichter, & Rothman, 1994, pp. 158–159; Newcomb, 1994, pp. 137, 194–200**; Orlik, 1994, p. 248; Pearl & Pearl, 1999, p. 21; Sackett, 1993, p. 321; Steenland, 1990, pp. 14–15, 27; Swanson, 2000, pp. 57–59*; Also in Bianculli, 1996, Terrace, 1993, Terrace, 2000

Woops!
Cotter, 1997, pp. 434–435; Also in Terrace, 1993

Work with Me
Lechner, 2000, pp. 144–145

Working Girl
Steenland, 1990, p. 15; Also in Terrace, 1993

Working It Out
IN Terrace, 1993

World War I
Gianakos, 1978, pp. 452–453

Wrangler
Gianakos, 1978, pp. 282–283; Also in Lentz, 1997, West, 1987

Wyatt Earp *see* **Life and Legend of Wyatt Earp**

X-Files, The
Bellon, 2001; Bertsch, 1998; Bignell, 1997, p. 143; Braun, 2000; Campbell, 2001; Cantor, 2001, pp. ix–xvii (passim), xvii–xix, xxiii–xxiv, xxxv–xxxvi, xxxviii, xl, 85, 111–179, 183–211, 215 (n. 7), 228 (n. 33), 228 (n. 35)**; Chunovic, 2000, p. 154; Creeber, 2001, p. 30; Davis, 2001, pp. 184–197**; Delasara, 2000, whole book**; Edwards, 1996, whole book**; Friedman, 2002, pp. 19, 293–312**; Gabler, Rich & Antler, 2000, pp. 49–50; Genge, whole book**; Gregory, 2000, p 149; Helford, 2000, pp. 61–90**; Inness, 1999, pp. 85, 92–101**; Katz, 1997, pp. 101–103*; Lavery, Hague & Cartwright, 1996, whole book**; Kellner, 1999; Lovece, 1996, whole book**; Muir, 2001a, pp. 345–396**; Newcomb, 2000, p. 238, 253–265**; Osgerby & Gough-Yates, 2001, p. 1; *Official Guide to the X-Files,* 1995–2001, whole book**; Owen, 1997, p. 121; Paietta & Kauppila, 1999, p. 351; Pearl & Pearl, 1999, pp. 54–55*; Schultz, 2000, pp. 74–75, 79, 90. 93; Sconce, 2000, pp. 205–206; Sharrett, 1999, pp. 320–339**; Silverblatt, Ferry, & Finan, 1999, pp. 181–182, 202; Simon, 1999, whole book**; Soter, 2002, pp. 98–99, 103, 115–124, 127–148, 190–219**; Suman, 1997, p. 98; Swanson, 2000, p. 70; Tasker, 1998, pp. 98–100*.; Tulloch, 2000, pp. 227–229; Westerfelhaus & Combs, 1998; Wildermuth, 1999; Also in Bianculli, 1996

Xena: Warrior Princess
Calvert, et al., 2001; Helford, 2000, pp. 15, 135–162**; Inness, 1999, pp. 160–176**; Isaacs, 1999, pp. 131–132*; Lechner, 2000, pp. 29–31*; Morreale, 1998; Walters, 2001, p. 101

Yancey Derringer
Fitzgerald & Magers, 2002, pp. 192–193; Gianakos, 1983, pp. 338–339;

Hamamoto, 1994, pp. 48–49; Jackson, 1994, pp. 118–120; Yoggy, 1995, pp. 25, 357–358; Also in Lentz, 1997, Terrace, 1993, West, 1987

Year in the Life
Auletta, 1991, see index; Pearl & Pearl, 1999, pp. 32, 201–202, 227*; Swanson, 2000, pp. 93–96*

Yearbook
Owen, 1997, p. 81

Yellow Rose, The
Gianakos, 1987, pp. 321–323; Also in Morris, 1997

You Are There
Buzenberg & Buzenberg, 1999, p. 39; Gianakos, 1980, pp. 357–361*; Kaminsky, 1985, pp. 79–94**; Lesher, 1982, p. 107; Skutch, 1998, p. 62; Also in Bianculli, 1996

You Bet Your Life (Cosby)
Smith, 1997, pp. 210–211, 214

You Bet Your Life (Marx)
Allen, 1956, pp. 238–243*; Burns, 1990, p. 265; DeLong, 1991, pp. 156–163**; Himmelstein, 1984, p. 293; Himmelstein, 1994, p. 352; Javna, 1985, pp. 80–83*; Kanfer, pp. 319, 325–326, 335, 344–345, 348–349, 350*; Louvish, 1999, pp. 16, 356, 376, 378, 397–398; Marc, 1989, p. 90; Marc, 1997, p. 75; Martin, 1980**; Marx, 1976, pp. 54–216**; Putterman, 1995, p. 126; Sackett, 1993, pp. 32–33; Also in Bianculli, 1996

You Take the Kids
IN Terrace, 1993

You'll Never Get Rich *see* **Phil Silvers Show**

Young and the Restless, The
Allen, 1995, pp. 188–189, 213–232**; Barker, 1999, pp. 114–115; Berry & Manning-Miller, 1996, p. 154; Blumenthal, 1997, p. 95; Buckman, 1984, pp. 55, 69–70; Gilbert, 1976, pp. 152–171*; Greenberg & Busselle, 1996; James, 1991**; Jarvis & Joseph, 1998, pp. 183–186*; Marris & Thornham, 2000, pp. 503–515**; Matelski, 1988, pp. 27–28, 46, 164–175**; Matelski, 1999, pp. 4–5, 42; Mellencamp, 1992, pp. 288–293*; Modleski, 1992, p. 96; Nelson, 1995, pp. 57–58, 63; Nochimson, 1992, p. 7; Ornellas, 1987**; Rose, 1985, p. 142; Rouverol, 1984, pp. 20, 140; Smith, 1997a; Spence, 1990; Suman & Rossman, 2000, p. 16; Williams, 1992, pp. 31, 55–56, 81, 84, 88, 98, 124–126, 136–137, 174–177*; Also in Bianculli, 1996

Young Dan'l Boone
IN Lentz, 1997, West, 1987

Young Lawyers, The
Andrews, 1986, p. 133; Capsuto, 2000, p. 331; Dates & Barlow, 1990, pp. 257–258; Dates & Barlow, 1993, p. 280; Gianakos, 1978, pp. 667–669*; Jarvis & Joseph, 1998, pp. 254, 255–261, 262–264**; Martindale, 1991, pp. 495–498; Means Coleman, 2000, p. 255; Meyers, 1981, p. 152; Stark, 1997, p. 99

Young Maverick
Jackson, 1994, pp. 207–209; Robertson, 1994, pp. 172–173, 179–183*; Also in Lentz, 1997

Young Pioneers, The
IN Lentz, 1997, Terrace, 1993

Young Rebels, The
Gianakos, 1978, pp. 666–667; Mc-

Donald, 1983, pp. 161–163; McDonald, 1992, pp. 167–168; Rovin, 1977b, p. 126

Young Riders, The
Jackson, 1994, pp. 212–214; Rainey, 1998, pp. 218–219; Yoggy, 1995, pp. 367, 594–595, 597–605**

Your Hit Parade
IN Bianculli, 1996

Your Show of Shows
Adir, 1988, pp. 62–88 (passim), especially pp. 67–86, 97–104**; Allen, 1956, pp. 105–118 (passim) (about Sid Caesar), Also index*; Broughton, 1986, pp. 2–15 (passim); Caesar, 1982, pp. 91–116, 135–139**; Edgerton, Marsden & Nachbar, 1997, p. 27; Gelbart, 1998, p. 113; Heldenfels, 1994, pp. 56–57; Horowitz, 1997, pp. 129–130; Hultzman, 1979, pp. 38–39, 51–52, 63–70, 79–98, 111–121 (passim)**; Putterman, 1995, pp. 75–77, 81–82, 83*; Sackett, 1993, pp. 10–11; Sennett, 1977, whole book**; Skutch, 1998, pp. 9–10, 189; Stempel, 1992, pp. 36–39*; Thompson, 1996, p. 21; Wilk, 1976, pp. 57–58, 159–175**; Also in Bianculli, 1996

Your Show Time
Gianakos, 1980, pp. 218–219

You're in the Picture
Andrews, 1980, pp. 199–203*; Henry, 1992, pp. 201, 219–221; Marc, 1996, pp. 121–122; Also in Bianculli, 1996

Zane Grey *see* **Dick Powell's Zane Grey Theater**

Zoe, Duncan, Jack and Jane
IN Terrace, 2000

Zorro
Cotter, 1997, pp. 201–216**; Curtis, 1998, pp. 165–186**; Davis, 1995, pp. 233–234; Jackson, 1994, pp. 102–103; Klobas, 1988, p. 456; Leiby & Leiby, 2001, pp. 287–288; Lichter, Lichter, & Rothman, 1994, p. 339; McDonald, 1987, pp. 38–39; Rovin, 1977b, pp. 55–56; Yoggy, 1995, pp. 61–66, 562–568**; Also in Bianculli, 1996, Lentz, 1997, Terrace, 1993, West, 1987

Zorro and Son
Curtis, 1998, pp. 160–164*; Yoggy, 1995, pp. 438, 439–440; Also in Lentz, 1997

Appendix A: Websites

The television websites listed are megasites that lead to other sites, especially those on television programs.

Cinemedia
(http://www.AFIonline.org)
American Film Institute site. Although emphasis is on films, there is a strong television component.

Internet Movie Database
(http://imdb.com)
The best internet source for information on films and television programs. Much information on credits, summaries, etc.

The Media and Communications Studies Site
(http://www.aber.ac.uk/media)
British-based but much information on academic resources for film and television.

Screensite: Film & TV Studies
(http://www.tcf.ua.edu/screensite)
This is THE site for getting to information of an academic nature related to film and television studies.

TVGuide
(www.tvguide.com)
Links to information on television programs.

Zap2it
(http://www.zap2it.com)
This oddly named site has hundreds of links to television shows. Excellent starting point for finding sites on specific programs.

Two other good sources are directories that lead to information and sites on television programs:

Google web directory to television
(http://directory.google.com/top/arts/television/programs)

Yahoo! TV database
(http://tv.yahoo.com/db)

Appendix B: Index to Groups or Classes of People on Television

African Americans

Abelman, 1998, pp. 38, 329, 371; Alley & Brown, 2001, p. 75; Andrews, 1986, pp. 46–181; Avery & Eason, 1991, pp. 294–305; Barker, 1999, pp. 74–84; Barnouw, 1990, see index under "Blacks"; Barrett & Barrett, 2001, pp. 71–72, 89–90, 91–95 (passim), 137–140; Bernardi, 1998, whole book (passim); Berry, 1993, pp. 155–174, 179–187; Berry & Manning-Miller, 1996, pp. 131–197; 164–165; Berry & Mitchell-Kernan, 1982, pp. 124–126; Bodroghkozy, 2001, pp. 190–197; Bogle, 2001, whole book; Bryant & Bryant, 2001, pp. 157–158, 207–228; Byrd, 1998, pp. 3–122; Caldwell, 1995, pp. 67–72, 302–335; Cantor, 2001, pp. 46–47; Castleman & Podrazik, 1982, pp. 57–59, 77, 121, 208, 247–248, 255–257; Cloud, 1196; Condry, 1985, pp. 71–72; Cortes, 2000, pp. 41–43, 81–82, 85–86; Croteau & Hoynes, 2000, pp. 194–195, 200–202, 204, 207, 208, 224; Cuklanz, 1998; Cumberbatch & Howitt, 1989, pp. 17–18; Dates & Barlow, 1990, pp. 253–340; Dates & Barlow, 1993, pp. 267–366; Davis, 2001, pp. 2–3, 14–15, 21–22, 56–64, 171–183; Diamond, 1982, pp. 55–66; Ely, 1991, whole book (passim), esp. pp. 203–244; Entman & Rojecki, 2000, pp. 39–41, 60–181; Geraghty, 1991, pp. 140–147; Greenberg, 1980, pp. 13–21, 173–181; Gregory, 2000, pp. 18, 181; Hamamoto, 1989, pp. 20–22, 88–95, 97–112, 136–140; Haravolovich & Rabinovitz, 1999, pp. 98–119, 151–153; Harris, 1989, pp. 46–49; Harris, 1994, pp. 49–53; Harrison, et. al., 1996, pp. 55–90 (passim); Helford, 2000, pp. 3, 17, 34, 163–180 passim; Hiebert, 1999, pp. 372–377; Hiebert & Reuss, 1985, pp. 384–393; Holtzman, 2000, pp. 245–252; Howitt, 1982, pp. 58–67; Inness, 1999, p. 175; Innis & Feagin, 1995; Jackson, 1982; whole book; James, 1991; Jarvis, 1998, pp. 8–9, 98–104, 167–168, 176, 214–215, 249; Johnston, 2000, pp. 66–68; Kamalipour & Carilli, 1998, pp. 6–9, 52–53, 79–87; Kassel, 1993, pp. 25–28, 54, 77–78, 92–94, 100–103, 118–119; Kidd-Hewitt, 1995, pp. 67–77; Leonard, 1997, pp. 201–225; Lewis, 1991, pp. 159–202; Lichter, Lichter & Rothman, 1991, pp. 233–253; Lichter,

Aged

American Indians see *Native Americans*

Arabs

Asian Americans

Rothman, 1994, p. 339; Patton, 2001; Riggs, 1998, pp. 124–125; Schwartz, 1999, p. 140; Spigel & Curtin, 1997, pp. 296–298, 349–357; Suman & Rossman, 2000, pp. 116, 119; Torres, 1998, pp. 3, 239–253

Blacks see *African Americans*

Blue Collar (and Labor)

Alley & Brown, 2001, p. 75; Croteau & Hoynes, 2000, pp. 217–218, 220; Diamond, 1982, pp. 91–99; Hamamoto, 1989, pp. 35–38, 41–43; Hiebert, 1999, pp. 397–398; Holtzman, 2000, pp. 119–130; Johnston, 2000, pp. 57–59; Lichter, Lichter, & Rothman, 1991, pp. 111–115; Lichter, Lichter, & Rothman, 1994, pp. 186–191; Marc, 1989, pp. 177–181; Marc, 1997, pp. 146–149, 193–196; Mayerle, 1991; Mosco & Wasko, pp. 131–152, 178–185; Parenti, 1991, pp. 69–90 (passim); Pines, 1994, (passim throughout book), especially pp. 240–259; Puette, 1992, pp. 3–11 (passim), 32–45 (TV news), especially pp. 46–58, 174–193; Stark, 1997, pp. 262–266 (passim); Sumser, 1996, pp. 108–113, 143–145

Business People

Bodroghkozy, 2001, p. 238; Cantor, 2001, pp. 180–182, 183, 186; Hiebert & Reuss, 1985, pp. 296–299; Kidd-Hewitt, 1995, pp. 131–158; Lazere, 1987, pp. 90–92; Leonard, 1997, pp. 104–109; Lichter, Lichter & Rothman, 1991, pp. 130–155; Lichter, Lichter, & Rothman, 1994, pp. 63–69, 209–240, 407–408, 409; Medved, 1992, pp. 220–221; Mosco & Wasko, pp. 167–175, 178–185; Orlik, 2001, pp. 24–25; Pines, 1994, (passim throughout book), especially pp. 240–259; Stein, 1979, pp. 15–28; Sumser, 1996, pp. 93–98; Theberge, 1981, whole book; Van de Berg & Trujillo, 1989, (passim throughout book), especially pp. 111–148

City Dwellers

Johnston, 2000, pp. 97–98; Stein, 1979, pp. 74–80; Wittebols, 1998, p. 2

Clergy (also religion in general)

Abelman, 1998, p. 74; Altheide & Snow, 1979, pp. 199–216; Ferre, 1990, pp. 33–43 (passim); Harris, 1989, pp. 103–107; Harris, 1994, pp. 108–110; Lichter, Lichter, & Rothman, 1991, pp. 266–286; Lichter, Lichter, & Rothman, 1994, pp. 389–399, 412–413; Medved, 1992, pp. 79–84; Stein, 1979, pp. 100–104; Suman, 1997, pp. 4, 28, 125–126

Criminals

Cross, 1983, pp. 115–122; Hiebert & Reuss, 1985, pp. 155–167; Howitt, 1982, pp. 121–140; Kidd-Hewitt, 1995, whole book (passim), esp. pp. 67–77, 131–158; Lichter, Lichter, & Rothman, 1991, pp. 183–230; Lichter, Lichter, & Rothman, 1994, pp. 273–300, 408–409; Medved, 1992, pp. 196–200; Oskamp, 1988, pp. 46–49; Stein, 1979, pp. 29–39; Sumser, 1996, pp. 114–133; Surette, 1992, whole book, especially pp. 30–37

Detectives see *Police*

Disabled

Berry, 1993, pp. 255–267; Cumberbatch & Howitt, 1989, pp. 19–20; Edelman & Kupferberg, 1996, p. 260; Gregory, 2000, pp. 193–194; Harris, 1989, p. 60; Harris, 1994, p. 67; Harrison, et. al., 1996, p. 70; Helford, 2000, pp. 245–264; Kamalipour & Carilli, 1998, pp. 89–98; Klobas, 1988, whole book;

Doctors see *Medical Personnel*

Ethnic Groups (in general)

Family

et. al., 1991, pp. 171–235; Press, 1991, pp. 29–34, 42–46; Rapping, 1994, pp. 148–154, 156–161; Schwartz, 1999, pp. 125–145; Shaner, 1981; Signorielli, 1991, pp. 60–62; Spigel & Curtin, 1997, pp. 119–125; Spigel & Mann, 1992, pp. 71–105; Stark, 1997, pp. 255–256, 264–265; Steenland, 1990, pp. 21–25; Taylor, 1989, whole book; Thomas & Evans, 1990, pp. 291–296; U.S. Department of Health ..., 1982, pp. 220–221, 264–271; Wagner & Lundeen, 1998, pp. 97–103; Wittebols, 1998, pp. 2–4; Zillmann, Bryant & Huston, 1994, pp. 38–49

Farmers see *Rural and Small Town Dwellers*

Gays and Lesbians

Abelman, 1998, pp. 52, 64; Allen, 1995, pp. 199–209; Alley & Brown, 2001, p. 158; Bacon-Smith, 1992, pp. 228–252; Barrett & Barrett, 2001, pp. 188–189, 190–194; Bodroghkozy, 2001, pp. 244–245; Buckman, 1984, pp. 64–65; Capsuto, 2000, whole book; Carstarphen & Zavoina, 1999, pp. 185–197, 211–224; Chunovic, 2000, pp. 69–70, 80, 90, 109; Cortes, 2000, pp. 66–67, 107–109; Craig, 1992, see index under "Homosexuality in television"; Croteau & Hoynes, 2000, pp. 223–225; Davis, 2001, pp. 20, 70–81; Dow, 2001; Gregory, 2000, pp. 187–189; Gross & Woods, 1999, pp. 9, 11, 16–17, 18–19, 293–295, 318–327, 335–340; Hamamoto, 1989, p. 135; Haravolovich & Rabinovitz, 1999, pp. 10–11, 150–151, 160; Harris, 1989, p. 59; Harris, 1994, p. 66; Harris & Alexander, 1998, pp. 9–38, 204–217 (passim), esp. pp. 208–210; Helford, 2000, pp. 18–19, 23–24, 138–158; Holtzman, 2000, pp. 301–305; Hubert, 1999; Huston, 1992, pp. 31–32; Inness, 1999, pp. 168–170; Isaacs, 1999, pp. 130–131; Leonard, 1997, p. 50; Lester, 1996, pp. 149, 153–158; Lichter, Lichter, & Rothman, 1991, pp. 36–39; Lichter, Lichter, & Rothman, 1994, pp. 93–96; Longworth, 2000, pp. 168–169; Marc, 1989, pp. 214–215; Marc, 1997, pp. 179–180; Miller, 1994, p. 232; Montgomery, 1989, pp. 75–100; Nelson & Gaonkar, 1996, pp. 333–334; Newcomb, 1994, pp. 117–133; Osgersby & Gough-Yates, 2001, p. 90; Ott & Aoki, 2001; Riggs, 1998, pp. 136–137, 139, 144; Ringer, 1994, pp. 91–156; Roberts, 1999, pp. 108–124; Rushkoff, 1994, pp. 105–108, 116–122; Schwartz, 1999, pp 129–130, 151; Signorielli, 1985, p. xvii, 166–172 (passim); Spelling, 1996, pp. 153, 154, 156–157; Suman & Rossman, 2000, pp. 23–27, 86, 109–111, 116, 118, 120–121, 135–136; Thompson, 1996, pp. 135–136; Turow, 1984, p. 95; U.S. Congress, 1977a, pp. 93, 254–257; Wagner & Lundeen, 1998, pp. 106–108, 112–114; Waldrep, 2000, pp. 199–201; Walters, 2001, pp. 3–55 (passim), 57–128, 179–209 (passim), 219–224 (passim); Wild, 1999, pp. 246, 260; Wittebols, 1998, pp. 28–29, 57–58

Government see *Politicians*

Hispanics

Berger, 1976, pp. 78–85; Berry, 1993, pp. 215–216, 227; Berry & Mitchell-Kernan, 1982, pp. 205–206; Byrd, 1998, pp. 190–212; Greenberg, 1980, pp. 3–12; Harris, 1989, pp. 49–50; Harris, 1994, pp. 53–55; Holtzman, 2000, pp. 227–230; James, 1991; Jarvis, 1998, pp. 98–100; Jenrette, McIntosh & Winterberger, 1999; Kamalipour & Carilli, 1998, pp. 9–10; Kaminsky, 1985, pp. 184–185; Kim, 1999; Lichter, Lichter, & Rothman, 1991, pp. 236–253; Lichter, Lichter, & Rothman, 1994, pp. 338–339, 346–347, 350, 352–356; Montgomery, 1989, pp. 51–65; Oskamp, 1988, pp. 96–97; Rodriguez, 1997, pp. 13–72, 233–235; Schwartz, 1999, p. 140; Wilson & Gutierrez, 1985, pp. 99–101; Woll & Miller, 1987, pp. 249–251; Zook, 1999, pp. 88–99

(passim); Dow, 1996, whole book; Edelman & Kupferberg, 1996, pp. 218–219; Epstein & Steinberg, 1996; Fiske, 1987, p. 45; Gardiner, 2000; Gauntlett & Hill, 1999, pp. 209–247; Geraghty, 1991, pp. 135–150; Greenberg, 1980, pp. 49–95; Gregory, 2000, pp. 84, 85, 149, 185–189; Haag, 1993; Hamamoto, 1989, pp. 22–24, 27–34, 62–65, 113–117, 130–134; Hanson, 1990; Haravolovich & Rabinovitz, 1999, pp. 56–97, 110–112, 144–200; Harris, 1989, pp. 38–45, 124–127; Harris, 1994, pp. 41–49, 131–133, 231; Harrison, et. al., 1996, pp. 11–50, 62–65, (passim in rest of book); Heldenfels, 1994, pp. 30–42; Helford, 2000, whole book; Heller, 1997; Hiebert, 1999, pp. 390–398; Himmelstein, 1994, pp. 129–131; Hollows, 2000, pp. 23–24, 89–109 (passim), 198–201; Holtzman, 2000, pp. 73–82; Howe, 1983, pp. 83–86; Howitt, 1982, pp. 68–82; Huston, 1992, pp. 26–31; Inness, 1999, whole book; Isaacs, 1999, pp. 45–47, 56, 57, 61–62, 73–74, 78–80, 97–99, 110–112, 115, 129–134; Jarvis, 1998, pp. 168–169, 174, 177–178, 219–248, 256–262; Johnston, 2000, pp. 23–25, 74; Kidd-Hewitt, 1995, pp. 164–183; Korzeniowska, 1996; Kutulas, 1998; Lafley, 1999/2000; Leibman, 1995, pp. 117–127, 129–135, 173–176, 180–188, 190–202, 204–207, 211–212, 217–218; Leonard, 1997, pp. 67–68, 191–200: Lester, 1996, pp. 81–85; Lichter, Lichter, & Rothman, 1991, pp. 34–36, 50–79, 91–96; Lichter, Lichter, & Rothman, 1994, pp. 45–52, 111–147, 405; Longworth, 2000, pp. 108–109; Mankiewicz & Swerdlow, 1978, pp. 131–162; Marc, 1989, pp. 55–59, 62–63, 107–109, 167–172, 182–183, 214–216; Marc, 1997, pp. 46–53, 92–95, 111–116, 138–142, 150–151, 179–180, 194; Marris & Thornham, 2000, pp. 404–413, 663–675; Martin, 1980, whole book; Meyers, 1999, whole book, esp. pp. 99–101, 104–106, 133–149, 153–180, 253–285, 305–318; Miller, 2000, pp. 51–74, 158–162, 178–180; Miner, 1996; Modleski, 1986, pp. 80–94; Moody, 1980, pp. 113–122; Moorti, 2001, whole book; Morreale, 1998; Newcomb, 1994, pp. 19–39; Newcomb, 2000, pp. 100–168, 565, 569; O'Dell, 1997, pp. 34–35; Orlik, 2001, pp. 23–24, 157–158; Osgersby & Gough-Yates, 2001, pp. 83–114, 221–235 (passim); Oskamp, 1988, pp. 88–90, 98–99, 106–117; Patton, 2001; Pearl and Pearl, 1999, pp. 85–90, 195–227; Penley, et. al., 1991, pp. 171–235; Pounds, 1999, pp. 51–53, 110–111, 121, 122–128, 130–131, 168, 178–182; Press, 1991, pp. 27–49; Projansky, 2001, pp. 73, 75–76, 80–81, 82, 88, 108, 110–111, 114–115, 154–195 (passim); Rapping, 1994, pp. 138–173, 282–286; Riggs, 1996; Roberts, 1999, whole book; Rubin, 1980, pp. 190–207; Rutstein, 1974, pp. 94–97; Schwartz, 1999, pp. 132–135; Sconce, 2000, pp. 148–156; Seger, 1996, pp. 155–163 (passim) esp. p. 159, 170–171, 175–180 (passim), 186–188 (passim), 253–254; Shattuc, 1997, pp. 105–109; Signorielli, 1985, pp. xiv–xv, 3–89; Signorielli, 1991, pp. 69–80; Smith, 1997; Sochen, 1987, pp. 99–102, 140–141; Spelling, 1996, pp. 54, 105–106, 164–165: Spigel & Curtin, 1997, pp. 73–135; Spigel & Mann, 1992, pp. 111–138, 143–164, 169–194, 203–213; Stark, 1997, pp. 2, 6–31, 118, 136, 171, 203–209, 262–266 (passim); Sumser, 1996, pp. 139–143; Tasker, 1998, pp. 94–100, 167–174; Taylor, 1989, whole book (passim); Thomas & Evans, 1990, pp. 285–289; Thompson, 1996, pp. 99–100, 105, 107–109, 116, 126, 133, 142–143, 145–146; Thurer, 1994, pp. 249–251, 266, 289–297 (passim); Torres, 1998, pp. 118–139; Tuchman, Daniels & Benet, 1978, pp. 9–17, 30–38, 41–89, 228–299; Turner & Sterk, 1994, pp. 85–97; U.S. Congress, 1977a, pp. 25–29; U.S. Department of Health…, 1982, pp. 179–183, 209–223; Wagner & Lundeen, 1998, pp. 81–115, 162–164; Waldrep, 2000, p. 196; Ward, 1995; Weimann, 2000, pp. 123–127, 138–149 passim; Wilcox, 1996; Williams, 1992, pp. 105–117, 140–157; Williams, 1996; Williams, LaRose, & Frost, 1981, whole book; Wittebols, 1998, pp. 2–3,

Rural and Small Town Dwellers

Cantor, 2001, pp. 67–109 (passim); Harris, 1989, pp. 55–56; Harris, 1994, p. 64; Himmelstein, 1994, pp. 138–152; Johnston, 2000, p. 101; Marc, 1989, pp. 77–78, 141–143; Marc, 1997, pp. 64–65, 116–118; Stein, 1979, pp. 63–73; Wittebols, 1998, p. 3

Scientists

Lichter, Lichter, & Rothman, 1991, pp. 170–174; Lichter, Lichter, & Rothman, 1994, pp. 259–263; Orlik, 1994, p. 165; Sumser, 1996, pp. 133–136

Small Town see *Rural*

Teachers

Lester, 1996, pp. 167–171; Lichter, Lichter, & Rothman, 1991, pp. 166–170; Lichter, Lichter, & Rothman, 1994, pp. 253–258

Urban see *City Dwellers*

Women see *Men and Women in Gender Roles*

Working Class see *Blue Collar and Labor*

Appendix C: Programs Listed by Genre

The assignment of a program to a particular genre is based on its most prominent aspect. All comedies have some drama; all dramas have some comedy. A show too difficult to classify as one or the other is listed as a Dramedy. Westerns are those shows set in the past (the Old West), even if basically comedies (for instance, "Maverick"). Those that are actually Situation Comedies, however, such as "F Troop," are classified as such. Shows set in the West but taking place in modern times are classified as Comedy, Adventure, or Detective. Detective shows include both private eyes and police shows. Shows about lawyers as lawyers are classified as Dramas (e.g., "L.A. Law") but shows about lawyers that investigate and find out the real criminal ("Perry Mason") are classified as Detective. Programs that could not be classified in one of the main genres are in a Miscellaneous category.

Adventure

A-Team, The
Acapulco
Adventures in Paradise
Adventures of Champion, The
Adventures of Sir Francis Drake
Adventures of Sir Lancelot, The
Adventures of Superman, The
Against the Grain
Airwolf
Alaskans, The
Amazing Spider-Man, The
Archer
Asphalt Jungle, The
Assignment: Foreign Legion
Avengers, The
Baa Baa Black Sheep
Baron, The
Batman
Bearcats
Behind Closed Doors
Bert D'Angelo, Superstar
Big Hawaii
Big Shamus, Little Shamus
Bionic Woman, The
B.J. and The Bear
Blacke's Magic
Blue Light
Born Free
Bring 'Em Back Alive
Buccaneers, The

Buffy: The Vampire Slayer
California Fever
Casablanca
Casey Jones
Cassie and Company
Champions, The
Charmed
Circus Boy
Code Red
Combat
Combat Sergeant
Concrete Cowboys, The
Coronet Blue
Court of Last Resort, The
Cowboy in Africa
Crusader
D.A.'s Man, The
Daktari
Dan Raven
Danger Man
Dangerous Assignment
Disney Presents the 100 Lives of Black Jack Savage
Dolphin Cove
E.A.R.T.H. Force
Electra Woman and Dyna Girl
Espionage
Fall Guy, The
Feather and Father Gang, The
Flash, The
Flipper
Fly by Night
Flying High
Follow the Sun
For the People
Foreign Intrigue
Gemini Man, The
Gentle Ben
Girl from U.N.C.L.E., The
Grand Slam
Gray Ghost, The
Greatest American Hero, The
Green Hornet, The
Harbourmaster
Hawkeye
Hercules: The Legendary Journeys
High Mountain Rangers
High Performance
Highwayman, The
Hollywood Beat
Hong Kong
I Led Three Lives
I Spy
Immortal, The
Incredible Hulk
Investigators, The
Islanders, The
It Takes a Thief
Ivanhoe
JAG
Jericho
Kindred: The Embraced
Klondike
Knight Rider
Land of the Lost (ABC)
Land of the Lost (NBC)
Lassie
Life and Times of Grizzly Adams, The
Lime Street
Lois and Clark: The New Adventures of Superman
Lucan
MacGyver
Mackenzies of Paradise Cove
Magician, The
Major Del Conway of the Flying Tigers
Makin' It
Malibu Run
Man and the Challenge
Man from Atlantis
Man from Interpol, The
Man from U.N.C.L.E.
Man Who Never Was, The
Markham
Masquerade
Master, The
Maya
Misfits of Science, The
Mission: Impossible
Mobile One
Movin' On
Mr. Garlund
Mr. Lucky
My Friend Flicka
My Friend Tony
Name of the Game, The
Nashville
National Velvet
NBC Mystery Movie
New Adventures of Beans Baxter, The

New Adventures of Huck Finn, The
New Land, The
Northwest Passage
Nowhere Man
Once a Hero
Paris 7000
Persuaders, The
Prisoner, The
Protectors, The
Q.E.D.
Rat Patrol, The
Raven
Rendezvous
Riker
Ripcord
Riverboat
Robin Hood
Rousters, The
Run for Your Life
Runaways, The
Sable
Salvage 1
Scarecrow & Mrs. King
Sea Hunt
Secret Agent
Seven Brides for Seven Brothers
Shannon
Silent Force, The
Sir Lancelot
Six Million Dollar Man, The
Spencer's Pilots
Steve Canyon
Stingray
Straightaway
Strange Report, The
Street Justice
Superboy
Swamp Thing
Swiss Family Robinson
Sword of Justice
Tales of the 77th Bengal Lancers
Tales of the Gold Monkey
Tarzan
T.H.E. Cat
Then Came Bronson
Third Man, The
Troubleshooters
Twelve O'Clock High
240-Robert
Under Cover
Wackiest Ship in the Army, The
Waterfront
Whirlybirds
Wizard, The
Wizards and Warriors
Wonder Woman
Xena: Warrior Princess
Young Rebels, The

Cartoon

Alvin Show, The
Batman: The Animated Series
Beavis and Butthead
Bullwinkle Show, The
Capitol Critters
Critic, The
Dilbert
Family Dog
Family Guy
Fish Police
Flintstones, The
Futurama
God, the Devil, and Bob
Jetsons, The
Jonny Quest
King of the Hill
Pinky & the Brain
PJ's, The
Simpsons, The
South Park
Top Cat
Underdog

Children's

Captain Kangaroo
Captain Video
Howdy Doody
Johnny Jupiter
Kukla, Fran, & Ollie
Mr. I Magination
Mister Rogers Neighborhood
Off to See the Wizard
Pee Wee's Playhouse
Rocky and His Friends
Sesame Street
Shirley Temple's Storybook
Sigmund and the Sea Monsters
Smilin' Ed's Gang

Soupy Sales Show, The
Watch Mr. Wizard

Comedy

Beautiful Phyliss Diller Show
Burns and Schreiber Comedy Hour
Carol & Company
Dukes of Hazzard, The
Ernie Kovacs
Fireball Fun-for-All
Flip Wilson Show, The
Here Come the Brides
House of Buggin'
In Living Color
Jack Benny Show, The
Jackie Gleason's American Scene
Jerry Lewis Show, The
Jimmy Durante Show, The
Laugh-In
Love, American Style
Love Boat, The
Martha Raye Show, The
Misadventures of Sheriff Lobo, The
Morey Amsterdam Show, The
Muppet Show, The
Muppets Tonight
New Bill Cosby Show, The
Red Buttons
Red Skelton Show, The
Richard Pryor Show, The
Robert Q. Lewis Show, The
Saturday Night Live
SCTV
Shadow Chasers
Six O'Clock Follies
Smothers Brothers Comedy Hour, The
Texaco Star Theater (Milton Berle)
That Was The Week That Was
Tim Conway Show, The
Tracey Ullman Show, The
Turn On
Your Show of Shows

Detective (includes police but not spy, for which see *Adventure)*

Adam-12
Amy Prentiss
Angel Street
Archer
Asphalt Jungle, The
B.A.D. Cats
Banacek
Banyon
Baretta
Barnaby Jones
Beat, The
Big Easy, The
B.L. Stryker
Blacke's Magic
Blue Knight, The
Blue Thunder
Bodies of Evidence
Bourbon Street Beat
Brenner
Broken Badges
Bronk
Brooklyn South
Burke's Law
Cade's County
Cagney & Lacey
Cain's Hundred
Cannon
Caribe
Cases of Eddie Drake, The
Charlie's Angels
Chase
Checkmate
CHiPS
City of Angels
Columbo
Commish, The
Coronet Blue
Cosby Mysteries, The
Cover Up
Cracker
Crazy Like a Fox
Crime and Punishment
Crime Story
D.A., The
Dan August
Dan Raven
Dangerous Curves
Dante's Inferno
Dark Justice
Dear Detective
Decoy
Delphi Bureau
Delvecchio

Detective in the House
Detectives, The
Devlin Connection
Diagnosis: Murder
Diagnosis: Unknown
Dick Tracy
Dog and Cat
Double Dare
Downtown
Dragnet
Due South
Eddie Capra Mysteries, The
87th Precinct
Eischeid
Ellery Queen
Equalizer, The
Exile, The
Eye to Eye
EZ Streets
Father Dowling Mysteries
FBI, The
Feds
Felony Squad
Finder of Lost Loves
Five Fingers
For the People
Forever Knight
Fortune Dane
Freebie and the Bean
Gabriel's Fire
Gangbusters
Get Christie Love!
Griff
Hagen
Half Nelson
Hardball
Hardcastle & McCormick
Hardy Boys/Nancy Drew
Harry-O
Hart to Hart
Hat Squad
Hawaii Five-O
Hawaiian Eye
Hawaiian Heat
Hawk
Hawkins
Heart of the City
Highway Patrol
Hill Street Blues
Hollywood Beat
Homicide: Life on the Streets
Honey West
Houston Knights
Hunter
I Had Three Wives
In the Heat of the Night
Investigators, The
Invisible Man, The
Ironside
Jake and the Fat Man
Jessie
Jigsaw John
J.J. Starbuck
Joe Forrester
Johnny Stacatto
Kate Loves a Mystery
Kaz
Kojak
Lady Blue
Lanigan's Rabbi
Law and Harry McGraw, The
Law and Order
Law and Order: Special Victims Unit
Lawless Years, The
Leg Work
Legmen
Lieutenant, The
Lime Street
Lineup, The
Longstreet
M Squad
MacGruder & Loud
Magnum, P.I.
Man Against Crime
Man Behind the Badge, The
Man Called Hawk, A
Man Called Sloane, A
Man from Interpol, The
Mancuso, FBI
Manhunt
Manhunter, The
Manimal
Mannix
Mariah
Martial Law
Martin Kane, Private Eye
Mask, The
Matlock
Matt Helm
Matt Houston
Max Monroe: Loose Canon

McClain's Law
McCloud
McMillan and Wife
Me and Mom
Meet McGraw
Miami Vice
Michael Shayne
Mike Hammer, Detective
Millenium
Mod Squad, The
Moonlighting
Most Deadly Game, The
Most Wanted
Mr. & Mrs. North
Mr. District Attorney
Mrs. Columbo
Murder, She Wrote
Murphy's Law
My Friend Tony
Naked City
Nakia
Nash Bridges
Nero Wolfe
New Breed, The
New Perry Mason
New York Undercover
Night Heat
N.Y.P.D.
N.Y.P.D. Blue
O'Hara, U.S. Treasury
Oldest Rookie
Outsider, The
Over My Dead Body
Owen Marshall, Couselor at Law
Palace Guard
Partners in Crime
Perry Mason
Peter Gunn
Petrocelli
Philip Marlowe
Police Story
Police Story (1952)
Police Woman
Private Eye
Probe
Profiler
P.S.I. Luv U
Public Prosecutor
Quincy, M.E.
Racket Squad
Reasonable Doubts
Remington Steele
Renegades, The
Richard Diamond, Private Detective
Richie Brockelman, Private Eye
Riptide
Rockford Files, The
Rocky King, Inside Detective
Rookies, The
Saint, The
Sergeant Preston of the Yukon
Serpico
77 Sunset Strip
Shaft
Silent Force, The
Simon and Simon
Snoops
Spenser: For Hire
Starsky and Hutch
State Trooper
Strange Report, The
Strange World
Street, The
Street Hawk
Streets of San Francisco, The
Strike Force
Sunset Beat
Surfside Six
S.W.A.T.
Sweating Bullets
Switch
Telltale Clue, The
Tenafly
Tenspeed and Brown Shoe
Tequila and Bonetti
Thin Man, The
Tightrope
T.J. Hooker
Today's FBI
Toma
Treasury Men in Action
True Blue
Tucker's Witch
21 Beacon Street
21 Jump Street
Twin Peaks
Under Suspicion
Unsub
Untouchables, The
Vega$
Walker, Texas Ranger
Walking Tall

Whiz Kids
Wiseguy
Wolf

Documentary see *Reality & Documentary*

Drama

Academy Theatre
Against the Law
Alcoa Premiere
Alcoa Presents Next Step Beyond
Alcoa Theatre
Alfred Hitchcock Presents
American Girls, The
American Gothic
Americans, The
Andros Targets, The
Angel
Antagonists, The
Apple's Way
Appointment with Adventure
Armstrong Circle Theatre
Arrest and Trial
Barbara Stanwyck Show, The
Bare Essence
Bay City Blues, The
Baywatch
Beacon Hill
Beauty and the Beast
Best Times, The
Big Town
Blue Skies
Bold Ones, The
Boone
Bracken's World
Brewster Place
Bridges to Cross
Brimstone
Bronx Zoo, The
Burning Zone, The
Bus Stop
Byrds of Paradise
Call to Glory
Cameo Theatre
Capital News
Cavalcade of America
Celanese Theatre
Center Stage
Channing
Chevrolet Tele-Theatre, The
Chicago Story
China Beach
Christy
Circle of Fear *see* Ghost Story
Civil Wars
Class of '96
Cliffhanger, The Curse of Dracula
Climax!
Clock, The
Colgate Theatre
Conflict
Convoy
Cosmopolitan Theatre
Court Martial
Covington Cross
Crime Photographer
Crimetime After Primetime
Crossroads
Damon Runyon Theatre
Danger
Dangerous Minds
Darkroom
David Niven Show, The
Dawson's Creek
Defenders, The
Desilu Playhouse
Dick Powell Show, The
Dracula: The Series
Dream Street
East Side/West Side
Eddie Dodd
Eerie, Indiana
Elgin TV Hour, The
Emerald Point, N.A.S.
Emergency
Encounter
Equal Justice
Escape (1956)
Executive Suite
Eye Witness
Fame
Family
Family Holvak, The
Family Tree, The
Fantasy Island
Father Murphy
Felicity
Fireside Theatre

Fitzpatricks, The
For Love and Honor
Ford Theatre
Four Star Playhouse
413 Hope Street
Freaks and Geeks
Freshman Dorm
Friday the 13th: The Series
Front Page, The
Front Page Detective
Front Row Center
Frontier Circus
Fugitive, The
Gallant Men, The
Garrison's Gorillas
General Electric Theater
George Sanders Mystery Theatre, The
Ghost Story
Gibbsville
Glitter
Great Adventure, The
Great Ghost Tales
Greatest Show on Earth, The
Hallmark Hall of Fame
Harris and Company
Headmaster
Hearts Are Wild
Heights, The
Hell Town
Highway to Heaven
Hitch Hiker, The
Hollywood Opening Night
Homefront
Hot Pursuit
Hotel
Hull High
Human Target, The
I'll Fly Away
Insiders, The
Jack's Place
James at 15
Jessica Novak
Joseph Cotten Show
Journey to the Unknown
Judd for the Defense
June Allyson Show, The
Justice
Kate McShane
King's Crossing
Kings Row
Kingston: Confidential
Kolchak: The Night Stalker
Kraft Mystery Theater
Kraft Suspense Theatre
Kraft Television Theatre
L.A. Law
Law and Mr. Jones
Lawyers, The
Life Goes On
Lights Out
Lloyd Bridges Show, The
Long Hot Summer, The
Loretta Young Show, The
Lottery!
Lou Grant
Love Boat: The New Wave
Love Story
Lucas Tanner
Mail Story, The
Man and the City, The
Man in a Suitcase
Man Undercover
Man with a Camera
Masterpiece Playhouse
Midnight Caller
Millionaire, The
Mississippi, The
Mr. Broadway
Mr. Novak
Moment of Fear
Morningstar/Eveningstar
Murder One
My Life and Times
My So-Called Life
Mysteries of Chinatown
Nash Airflyte Theatre, The
New Loretta Young Show, The
New People, The
Next Step Beyond, The
Night Editor
Night Gallery
No Warning
Not For Publication
Nothing Sacred
Now and Again
Number 96
Once and Again
One Step Beyond
O. S. S.
Our Family Honor
Our House
Outer Limits

Palmerstown, U.S.A.
Panic!
Paper Chase, The
Paper Dolls
Party of Five
Peaceable Kingdom
Pepsi Cola Playhouse, The
Pete Kelly's Blues
Philco Television Playhouse
Picket Fences
Playhouse, The
Playhouse 90
Pond's Theater
Practice, The
Producers Showcase
Profit
Project UFO
Promised Land
Providence
Prudential Family Playhouse, The
Pulitzer Prize Playhouse
Push
Rebound
Relativity
Reporter, The
Revlon Mirror Theatre, The
Richard Boone Show, The
Robert Montgomery Presents
Room 222
Room for Romance
Rosetti and Ryan
Round Table, The
Route 66
Safe Harbor
Saints and Sinners
Sam Benedict
Scene of the Crime
Schlitz Playhouse of the Stars, The
Screen Directors' Playhouse, The
Second Noah
Senator, The
7th Heaven
Shannon's deal
Silver Theater
Sixth Sense, The
Skag
Slattery's People
Smith Family, The
Somerset Maugham TV Theatre
Sons and Daughters
Stage 13
Star Stage
Star Tonight
Starlight Theatre
Stars Over Hollywood
Stephen King's The Golden Years
Stone
Storefront Lawyers
Studio 57
Supertrain
Sure as Fate
Survivors, The
Suspicion
Sweet Justice
Tales from the Crypt
Tales of the Unexpected
Target: The Corrupters
Telephone Time
Third Watch
thirtysomething
Thriller
Time Express
Time of Your Life
Top of the Hill
Touched by an Angel
Tour of Duty
Trials of O'Brien, The
Trials of Rosie O'Neill, The
TV 101
TV Reader's Digest
Twilight Zone, The
Two Marriages
Under One Roof
United States Steel Hour
Verdict Is Yours, The
Vise, The
Waltons, The
Way Out
W.E.B.
Web, The
Werewolf
What Really Happened to the Class of '65
White Shadow, The
Willy
Windows
WIOU
Wire Service
Witness, The
Year in the Life, A
Yellow Rose, The
Young Lawyers, The

Dramedy

Ally
Ally McBeal
Brooklyn Bridge
Cupid
Duet
Ed
Harts of the West
Hometown
Mr. Roberts
Mulligan's Stew
Northern Exposure
Rags to Riches
Rogues, The
Shell Game
South Central

Game Shows see *Quiz*

Medical

Ben Casey
Birdland
Breaking Point
Buck James
Chicago Hope
City Hospital
City of Angels
Cutter to Houston
Doc Elliot
Doctor, The
Doctors' Hospital
Doctors' Private Lives
Dr. Kildare
Eleventh Hour, The
ER
Going to Extremes
Greatest Gift, The
Heartbeat
Hothouse
Human Factor, The
Interns, The
Island Son
Julie Farr, M.D.
Kay O'Brien
L.A. Doctors
Lazarus Syndrome, The
Lifeline
Marcus Welby, M.D.
Matt Lincoln
Medic
Medical Center
Medical Story
Medicine Ball
New Doctors, The
Nightingales
Noah's Ark
Nurse
Nurses, The
Psychiatrist, The
Rafferty
Ryan's Four
St. Elsewhere
Seizure
Trapper John, M.D.
Trauma Center
Westside Medical

Miniseries

Centennial
Rich Man, Poor Man
Roots
Winds of War

Miscellaneous

ABC Movie of the Week
A.M. America
Amazing Stories
American Bandstand
Believe It or Not
Big Event, The
CBS Morning News
CBS This Morning
Continental, The
Dating Game, The
Disneyland
Dupont Show of the Week, The
Faye Emerson Show, The
Gillette Cavalcade of Sports
Good Morning!
Good Morning, America
Love Connection
Meet the Press
Monday Night Football
Morning Show
Omnibus
Person to Person

Today Show, The
Tomorrow
Warner Brothers Presents
Wide World of Sports
You Are There

Mystery see *Detective*

News Magazine

American Parade, The
Current Affair, A
Dateline NBC
Entertainment Tonight
Eye to Eye with Connie Chung
Face the Nation
First Tuesday
48 Hours
Hard Copy
Inside Edition
Nightline
PrimeTime Live
See It Now
60 Minutes
Street Stories
20/20
West 57th

Police see *Detective*

Quiz

Beat the Clock
Big Surprise, The
Down You Go
Family Feud
Hollywood Squares
I've Got a Secret
Jeopardy!
Juvenile Jury
Let's Make a deal
Name That Tune
Newlywed Game, The
Pantomime Quiz
People Are Funny
Picture This
Price Is Right, The
Quiz Kids
$64,000 Challenge
$64,000 Question
Strike It Rich
Take a Good Look
Tic Tac Dough
To Tell the Truth
Truth or Consequences
$25,000 Pyramid
Twenty One
What's My Line
Wheel of Fortune
You Bet Your Life
You're in the Picture

Reality & Documentary

Adventure
Air Power
American Chronicles
America's Funniest Home Videos
America's Most Wanted
Big Brother
Big Story, The
Candid Camera
CBS Reports
Cops
Divorce Court
G.E. True
I Witness Video
Navy Log
Our World
Profiles in Courage
Real People
Rescue 911
Survivor
That's Hollywood!
That's Incredible!
This Is Your Life
TV Nation
Unsolved Mysteries
Wanted
West Point Story, The
World War I
Yearbook

Science Fiction

Alien Nation
Automan

Battlestar Galactica
Beyond Westworld
Buck Rogers in the 25th Century
Commando Cody, Sky Marshal
Dark Skies
Earth 2
Fantastic Journey, The
Hard Time on Planet Earth
Invaders, The
Invisible Man, The
Land of the Giants
Logan's Run
Lost in Space
Mann and Machine
Max Headroom
Men Into Space
Nightmare Café
Otherworld
Phoenix, The
Planet of the Apes
Powers of Matthew Star, The
Pretender, The
Quantum Leap
Rod Brown of the Rocket Rangers
Science Fiction Theatre
Seaquest DSV
Seven Days
Shazam
Sightings
Sleepwalkers
Sliders
Something Is Out There
Space: Above and Beyond
Space: 1999
Space Patrol
Space Rangers
Star Trek (original)
Star Trek: Deep Space Nine
Star Trek: The Next Generation
Star Trek: Voyager
Tales of Tomorrow
Time Cop
Time Tunnel, The
Tom Corbett, Space Cadet
V
Voyage to the Bottom of the Sea
Voyagers!
Vr5
War of the Worlds
X-Files, The

Situation Comedy

Abbott and Costello Show, The
Ace Crawford, Private Eye
Adam's Rib
Addams Family, The
Adventures of Ozzie and Harriet, The
A.E.S. Hudson Street
After M.A.S.H
A.K.A. Pablo
Aldrich Family, The
ALF
Alice
Aliens in the Family
All-American Girl
All in the Family
All's Fair
Almost Grown
Almost Home
Aloha Paradise
Alright Already
Amen
American Dreamer
Amos 'n' Andy
Andy Griffith Show, The
Angie
Ann Jillian
Ann Sothern Show, The
Anything But Love
Archie Bunker's Place
Arnie
Babes
Baby Boom
Baby Talk
Baby, I'm Back
Bachelor Father
Baileys of Balboa, The
Bakersfield P.D.
Barefoot in the Park
Barney Miller
Becker
Benson
Best of the West
Better Days
Betty Hutton Show
Betty White Show, The
Between Brothers
Beulah
Beverly Hillbillies, The
Bewitched

Big Eddie
Big Wave Dave's
Bill and Ted's Excellent Adventures
Bill Cosby Show, The
Bill Dana Show, The
Billy
Black Tie Affair
Blansky's Beauties
Bless This House
Blondie
Blossom
Bob Crane Show, The
Bob Cummings Show, The
Bob Newhart Show, The
Bonino
Bosom Buddies
Boy Meets World
Brady Bunch, The
Brand New Life
Breaking Away
Bridget Loves Bernie
Bringing Up Buddy
Brotherly Love
Buddies
Buffalo Bill
Busting Loose
Café Americain
California Dreams
Camp Runamuck
Camp Wilder
Can't Hurry Love
Captain Nice
Car 54, Where Are You?
Cara Williams Show
Caroline in the City
Carter Country
Cavanaughs, The
Charles in Charge
Charlie & Co.
Charlie Hoover
Charmings, The
Cheers
Chicken Soup
Chico and the Man
Cleghorne!
Clueless
Coach
Colonel Humphrey Flack
Coming of Age
Common Law
Corner Bar, The
Cos
Cosby
Cosby Show, The
Courtship of Eddie's Father, The
Crew, The
Cutters
Cybill
Daddy Dearest
Daddy's Girls
Date with Judy, A
Dave's World
Davis Rules
Day by Day
Dear John
Dear Phoebe
December Bride
Delta
Delta House
Dennis the Menace
Designing Women
Detective School
Dharma & Greg
Diana
Dick Van Dyke Show, The
Different World, A
Diff'rent Strokes
Dinosaurs
Doc
Doc Corkle
Doctor, Doctor
Domestic Life
Donna Reed Show, The
Doogie Howser, M.D.
Doris Day Show, The
Double Life of Henry Phyfe, The
Double Trouble
Down and Out in Beverly Hills
Down Home
Down the Shore
Dream On
Drew Carey Show, The
Drexell's Class
Duck Factory, The
Duffy's Tavern
Duke, The
Dumplings, The
Dusty's Trail
Dweebs
Easy Street
Egg and I, The
Eight Is Enough

Ellen
Ellen Burstyn Show
Empire
Empty Nest
Enos
Ensign O'Toole
E/R
Ethel and Albert
Evening Shade
Everybody Loves Raymond
F Troop
Facts of Life, The
Family Affair
Family Album
Family for Joe, A
Family Man, The
Family Matters
Family Rules
Family Ties
Famous Teddy Z, The
Fanelli Boys
Farmer's Daughter, The
Fast Times
Father Knows Best
Father of the Bride
Fay
Ferris Bueller
Fibber McGee and Molly
Filthy Rich
First Impressions
First Time Out
Fish
Five Mrs. Buchanans
Flesh 'n' Blood
Flo
Flying Blind
Flying Nun, The
FM
Foley Square
Four Seasons, The
Frank's Place
Frannie's Turn
Frasier
Free Spirit
Fresh Prince of Bel Air
Friends
Friends and Lovers
Full House
Funny Face
Gale Storm Show, The
George & Leo
George Burns and Gracie Allen Show, The
George Carlin Show, The
George Wendt Show, The
Gertrude Berg Show, The
Get a Life
Get Real
Get Smart
Getting Personal
Ghost and Mrs. Muir, The
Gidget
Gilligan's Island
Gimme a Break
Girl with Something Extra, The
Girls, The
Going My Way
Going Places
Goldbergs, The
Golden Girls, The
Gomer Pyle, U.S.M.C.
Good & Evil
Good Advice
Good Grief
Good Life, The
Good Morning, World
Good News
Good Sports
Good Times
Goode Behavior
Goodnight, Beantown
Goodtime Girls
Governor and J.J., The
Grace Under Fire
Grand
Grandpa Goes to Washington
Great Gildersleeve, The
Green Acres
Grindl
Growing Pains
Guestward Ho
Gun Shy
Gung Ho
Hail to the Chief
Hangin' with Mr. Cooper
Happy Days
Harper Valley, PTA
Harrigan and Son
Harry
Hathaways, The
Have Faith
Hazel

He & She
Head of the Class
Head Over Heels
Heartland
Hearts Afire
Heaven for Betsy
Hello, Larry
Hennesey
Here and Now
Here We Go Again
Here's Lucy
Herman's Head
Hero, The
He's the Mayor
Hey Jeannie!
Hey Landlord!
Hi Honey, I'm Home
High Society
His & Hers
Hizzoner
Hogan Family
Hogan's Heroes
Holmes and Yoyo
Home Court, The
Home Fires
Home Free
Home Improvement
Homeboys from Outer Space
Honeymooners, The
Hooperman
Hope & Gloria
Hot L Baltimore
House Calls
How to Marry a Millionaire
Husbands, Wives & Lovers
I Dream of Jeannie
I Love Lucy
I Married Dora
I Married Joan
I'm a Big Girl Now
Ichabod and Me
If Not for You
I'm Dickens, He's Fenster
In the Beginning
It Takes Two
It's a Living
It's About Time
It's Always Jan
It's Like, You Know
It's Your Move
It's a Living
It's a Man's World
Jackie Thomas Show, The
Jamie
Jamie Foxx Show, The
Jean Arthur Show, The
Jeff Foxworthy Show, The
Jeffersons, The
Jennifer Slept Here
Jenny
Jesse
Jimmy Stewart Show, The
Joe & Mabel
Joe Bash
Joey Bishop Show, The
John Larroquette Show, The
Julia
Julie
Just in Time
Just Shoot Me
Just the Ten of Us
Karen's Song
Kate & Allie
Kirk
Ladies Man
Last Resort, The
Laurie Hill
Laverne & Shirley
League of Their Own, A
Leave It to Beaver
Lenny
Leo and Liz in Beverly Hills
Life…and Stuff
Life of Riley, The
Life with Father
Life with Lucy
Life with Luigi
Life's Work
Little People, The
Live-in
Living Dolls
Living Single
Lotsa Luck
Love and War
Love on a Rooftop
Love That Jill
Love Thy Neighbor
Love, Sidney
Luci Arnaz Show, The
Lucy Show, The
Luigi
Mad About You

Madame's Place
Maggie Winters
Magnificient Montague, The
Major Dad
Make Room for Daddy
Making a Living
Making the Grade
Malcolm and Eddie
Mama
Mama's Boy
Mama's Family
Man in the Family, The
Man of the People
Many Happy Returns
Many Loves of Dobie Gillis, The
Margie
Married People
Married…with Children
Marshall Chronicles, The
Martin
Mary
Mary Tyler Moore Show, The
M*A*S*H
Maude
Mayberry, R.F.D.
McHale's Navy
McKeever and the Colonel
Me and Maxx
Me and Mrs. C
Me and the Chimp
Meet Corliss Archer
Meet Millie
Melba
Men Behaving Badly
Mickey
Mike O'Malley Show, The
Misery Loves Company
Mr. Adams and Eve
Mr. Belvedere
Mr. Ed
Mr. Merlin
Mr. Peepers
Mr. Sunshine
Mr. Terrific
Moesha
Molloy
Mommies, The
Monkees, The
Monty
Mork & Mindy
Morton and Hayes
Mothers-in-Law, The
Movie Stars
Munsters, The
Murphy Brown
My Favorite Husband
My Favorite Martian
My Friend Irma
My Hero
My Little Margie
My Living Doll
My Mother, The Car
My Sister Eileen
My Sister Sam
My Son Jeep
My Three Sons
My Two Dads
Naked Truth, The
Nancy
Nancy Walker Show, The
Nanny, The
Nanny and the Professor
Ned and Stacey
New Attitude
New Dick Van Dyke Show, The
New Phil Silvers Show, The
Newhart
Newsradio
Night Court
9 to 5
No Time for Sergeants
Norm Show, The
Normal Life
Normal, Ohio
Nurses
Nutt House
Occasional Wife
Odd Couple
Oh Grow Up
Oh, Madeline
O.K. Crackerby
On Our Own
On the Air
On the Rocks
One Big Family
One Day at a Time
One in a Million
One World
Open House
Operation Petticoat
Our Miss Brooks
Out All Night

Out of the Blue
Out of This World
Pacific Station
Paper Moon
Parent'Hood
Parker Lewis Can't Lose
Partners
Partridge Family, The
Patty Duke Show, The
Paul Lynde Show, The
Pearl
People Next Door, The
People's Choice, The
Perfect Strangers
Pete and Gladys
Peter Loves Mary
Petticoat Junction
Phenom
Phil Silvers Show, The
Phyl and Mikhy
Phyliss
Pinky Lee Show, The
PJ's, The
Please Don't Eat the Daisies
Police Squad
Powers That Be, The
Practice, The
Pride & Joy
Pride of the Family, The
Princesses
Private Benjamin
Private Secretary
Pruitts of Southampton
Punky Brewster
Quark
Rachel Gunn, R.N.
Raising Miranda
Ray Milland Show, The
Real McCoys, The
Rhoda
Rhythm & Blues
Roc
Roll Out
Roller Girls
Room for One More
Room for Two
Roomies
Ropers, The
Roseanne
Royal Family, The
Ruggles, The
Run, Buddy, Run
Sabrina, the Teenage Witch
Sally
San Pedro Beach Bums, The
Sandy Duncan Show, The
Sanford and Son
Sara
Saved by the Bell
Scorch
Secret Diary of Desmond Pfeiffer, The
Seinfeld
She's the Sheriff
Shirley's World
Show, The
Sibs
Sidekicks
Silver Spoons
Simon
Sinbad Show
Singer & Sons
Sirota's Court
Sister Kate
Sister, Sister
Slap Maxwell Story, The
Sledge Hammer
Smart Guy
Smothers Brothers Show, The
So This Is Hollywood
Someone Like Me
Sparks
Spencer
Spin City
Square Pegs
Stand by Your Man
Stat
Step by Step
Steve Harvey Show, The
Stockard Channing Show, The
Stu Irwin Show, The
Suddenly Susan
Sugar and Spice
Sugar Time!
Sunday Dinner
Suzanne Pleshette Is Maggie Briggs
Sweet Surrender
Sydney
Tab Hunter Show, The
Tabitha
Tammy
Tammy Grimes Show, The
Tattingers

Taxi
Teachers Only
Ted Knight Show, The
Teech
Temperatures Rising
Texas Wheelers, The
That Girl
That 70's Show
That's My Boy
That's My Mama
Thea
Thicker Than Water
3rd Rock From the Sun
13 East
Three Guys, a Girl, and a Pizza Place
Three's Company
Thunder Alley
To Rome with Love
Together We Stand
Tom Ewell Show, The
Tom Show, The
Tony Randall Show, The
Too Close for Comfort
Top of the Heap
Topper
Torkelsons
Tortellis, The
Touch of Grace
Trial and Error
Two Girls Named Smith
Two of a Kind
Two of Us, The
227
Ugliest Girl in Town, The
Uncle Buck
Unhappily Ever After
United States
Valentine's Day
Valerie
Veronica's Closet
Vinnie and Bobby
Viva Valdez
Walter and Emily
Wayans Brothers
We Got It Made
Webster
Welcome Back, Kotter
Wendy and Me
What a Country!
What's Happening!
When Things Were Rotten
Where I Live
Who's Watching the Kids?
Whole New Ballgame, A
Who's the Boss
Wild Oats
Will & Grace
Willy
Wings
WKRP in Cincinatti
Women in Prison
Women of Brewster Place
Women of the House
Wonder Years, The
Woops!
Working Girl
Working It Out
You Take the Kids
Zoe, Duncan, Jack and Jane
Zorro and Son

Soap Opera

All My Children
Another World
As the World Turns
Berrenger's
Beverly Hills 90210
Bold and the Beautiful, The
Bright Promise
Brighter Day
Capitol
Central Park West
City, The
Colbys, The
Dallas
Dark Shadows
Days of Our Lives
Doctors, The
Dynasty
Edge of Night, The
Falcon Crest
Flamingo Road
Follow Your Heart
General Hospital
Generations
Guiding Light
Hamptons, The
Knots Landing
Love Is a Many-Splendored Thing
Love of Life
Loving

Malibu Shores
Mary Hartman, Mary Hartman
Melrose Place
Models, Inc.
One Life to Live
One Man's Family
Our Private World
Passions
Peyton Place
Port Charles
Ryan's Hope
Santa Barbara
Savannah
Search for Tomorrow
Secret Storm
Secrets of Midland Heights
Sisters
Soap
Somerset
Sunset Beach
Texas
2000 Malibu Road
Young and the Restless, The

Spy see *Adventure*

Talk Show

Arsenio Hall Show, The
Chevy Chase Show, The
David Letterman
Dinah's Place
Donahue
Geraldo
Merv Griffin Show, The
Morton Downey, Jr. Show, The
Oprah Winfrey Show, The
Tonight Show, The

Variety

Alan King Show, The
Andy Williams Show, The
Arthur Godfrey
Best of Broadway
Big Party, The
Big Top
Billy Daniels Show, The
Caesar's Hour
Captain and Tennille, The
Carol Burnett Show, The
Cavalcade of Stars
Cher
Chevy Show, The
Circus Time
Colgate Comedy Hour, The
Dana Carvey Show, The
Danny Thomas Hour, The
Dean Martin Show, The
Dean Martin Summer Show, The
Dick Cavett Show, The
Dick Clark Presents the Rock 'n' Roll Years
Dick Clark Show, The
Dick Clark's Live Wednesday
Dick Clark's World of Talent
Dinah Shore Chevy Show, The
Ethel Waters Show, The
Frank Sinatra Show, The
Garroway at Large
Garry Moore Show, The
George Gobel Show, The
Happy Days
Hazel Scott Show, The
Hee Haw
Hollywood Palace, The
Hootenany
Hullabaloo
International Showtime
Jackie Gleason Show, The
Johnny Carson Show, The
Judy Garland Show, The
Lawrence Welk
Leslie Uggams Show, The
Liberace Show
Mary Tyler Moore Hour, The
Musical Comedy Time
Nat King Cole Show, The
Original Amateur Hour, The
Perry Como Show, The
Sammy Davis Jr. Show, The
Shindig
Sing Along with Mitch
Sonny and Cher Comedy Hour, The
Stage Show
Star of the Family
Steve Allen Show, The
Steve Lawrence Show, The
Sugar Hill Times
Sunday Showcase
Super Circus

Toast of the Town
Tony Orlando and Dawn
Van Dyke and Company
What's It All About, World
Window on the World
Your Hit Parade

Western

Adventures of Brisco County, Jr., The
Adventures of Jim Bowie, The
Adventures of Kit Carson, The
Adventures of Rin Tin Tin, The
Adventures of Wild Bill Hickock, The
Alias Smith and Jones
Barbary Coast, The
Bat Masterson
Big Valley, The
Black Saddle
Bonanza
Born to the Wind
Boys of Twilight, The
Branded
Brave Eagle
Bret Maverick
Broken Arrow
Bronco
Buckskin
Buffalo Bill, Jr.
Californians, The
Cheyenne
Chisholms, The
Cimarron City
Cimarron Strip
Cisco Kid, The
Colgate Western Theater
Colt .45
Cowboy G-Men
Cowboy Theater
Cowboys, The
Custer
Dakotas, The
Daniel Boone
Death Valley Days
Deputy, The
Destry
Dick Powell's Zane Grey Theater
Dirty Sally
Dr. Quinn, Medicine Woman
Dr. Six-Gun
Dundee and the Culhane
Fort Apache
Frontier
Frontier Justice
Fury
Gene Autry Show, The
Guns of Will Sonnett, The
Gunslinger, The
Gunsmoke
Have Gun, Will Travel
Hec Ramsey
High Chaparall, The
Hondo
Hopalong Cassidy
Hotel de Paree
How the West Was Won
Iron Horse, The
Jefferson Drum
Johnny Ringo
Judge Roy Bean
Kodiak
Kung Fu
Lancer
Laramie
Laredo
Lash of the West
Law of the Plainsman
Lawman, The
Legend
Legend of Jesse James, The
Life and Legend of Wyatt Earp, The
Little House on the Prairie
Little House: A New Beginning
Lone Ranger, The
Loner, The
Mackenzie's Raiders
Man Called Shenandoah, A
Man from Blackhawk, The
Marshal of Gunsight Pass, The
Maverick
Monroes, The
Ned Blessing
Nichols
Oregon Trail, The
Outcasts, The
Outlaws, The
Overland Trail, The
Pall Mall Playhouse
Paradise
Pistols 'n' Petticoats
Quest, The

Range Rider, The
Rango
Rawhide
Rebel, The
Redigo
Restless Gun
Rifleman
Road West, The
Rough Riders, The
Rounders, The
Roy Rogers Show, The
Shane
Sheriff of Cochise, The
Shotgun Slade
Sky King
Stagecoach West
Stoney Burke
Sugarfoot
Tales of the Texas Rangers
Tales of Wells Fargo
Tall Man, The
Tate
Temple Houston
Texan, The
Tombstone Territory
Trackdown
Travels of Jaimie McPheeter, The
26 Men
Virginian, The
Wagon Train
Wanted: Dead or Alive
Westerner, The
Whispering Smith
Wichita Town
Wide Country, The
Wild Wild West, The
Wildside
Wrangler
Yancey Derringer
Young Dan'l Boone
Young Maverick
Young Pioneers, The
Young Riders, The
Zorro

Sources Used

Abelman, Robert. **1998**. *Reaching a Critical Mass: A Critical Analysis of Television Entertainment.* Mahwah, NJ: Lawrence Erlbaum Associates. "A users guide for the only household appliance that does not come with one." The book describes all aspects of television—the industry, how programs are made, strategies to attract audiences, TV as a social and cultural force. The intended result is to make us all a critical mass audience.

Abt, Vicki, & Leonard **Mustazza**. **1997**. *Coming After Oprah: Cultural Fallout in the Age of the TV Talk Show.* Bowling Green, OH: Bowling Green University Popular Press. Examines talk television as a reflection of an aspect of popular culture. Highly critical of the exploitative aspects of the genre. Discusses shows as seen by viewers but also goes behind the scenes to show the manipulation and deceit involved in producing these shows.

Abt, Vicki, & Mel **Seesholtz**. **1994**. "The Shameless World of Phil, Sally and Oprah: Television Talk Shows and the Deconstructing of Society." *Journal of Popular Culture*, Summer 94, 28(1), p. 171. 21 pages. Criticizes the social influence of talk shows in the United States. Exploitation of the guests' experiences; discussion of the ethical implications of the hosts' techniques to pry into the topic; misrepresentation of problems and issues featured in the talk shows. [Copyright Ebscohost]

Acham, Christine. **1999**. *Peace, Love and Soul: 70's Television and Black Public Space* (Ph.D. Dissertation, University of Southern California). Discusses participation and representation of African Americans on television in the 1970s. Analyzes historical, social, political and economic aspects and compares to contemporary African American programs.

Adams, Mary Jo. **1980**. *An American Soap Opera: As the World Turns, 1956–1978* (Ph.D. Dissertation, University of Michigan). Studies to what effect "As the World Turns" contributed to the development of daytime serial genre. Focuses on history, creation, production ratings and sponsorship rather than an analysis of the show itself.

Adir, Karin. **1988**. *The Great Clowns of American Television.* Jefferson, N.C.: McFarland. Biographical sketches of seventeen comics who had great influence on television comedy.

Adler, Richard. **1979**. *All in the Family: A Critical Appraisal*. New York, NY: Praeger. A collection of three scripts, critical reviews, audience reaction, more sophisticated critiques, and a symposium. Also includes an episode listing from 1971 to 1979.

Adler, Richard, ed. **1976**. *Television as a Cultural Force*. New York, NY: Praeger. A series of critical essays on television's influence on American life and culture. Based on Aspen Program's Workshop on Television. A sequel to *Television as a Social Force* (see Cater 1975).

Adler, Richard, ed. **1981**. *Understanding Television: Essays on Television as a Social and Cultural Force*. New York, NY: Praeger. An anthology of critical essays on several aspects of television. Essays are reprints or original for this collection. The book grew out of two earlier anthologies—see *Television as a Social Force* (Cater 1975) and *Television as a Cultural Force* (Adler 1976).

Agee, Warren K., Phillip H. **Ault**, & Edwin **Emery**. **1982**. *Perspectives on Mass Communications*. New York, NY: Harper & Row. Over one hundred brief essays with editorial comment. Intended as a book of readings for mass communication courses.

Alcoff, Linda, & Laura **Gray**. **1993**. "Survivor Discourse: Transgression or Recuperation?" *Signs: Journal of Women in Culture & Society*, Winter 93, 18(2), p. 260. 31 pages. Discusses the discourse of those who have survived rape, incest and sexual assault. Relatively new, but accessible every day in the US on television talk shows… [Copyright Ebscohost]

Alda, Arlene, & Alan **Alda**. **1983**. *The Last Days of M.A.S.H.* Verona, NJ: Unicorn Publishing House. Heavily illustrated book describes the last shows of this series. Some insights and tidbits might be useful.

Aldgate, Anthony, James **Chapman**, & Arthur **Marwick**, eds. **2000**. *Windows on the Sixties: Exploring Key Texts of Media and Culture*. London, England: I.B. Tauris Publishers. Explores film and television in the 1960s and how they reflect the "cultural revolution" of the 1960s. British emphasis. Mostly film.

Alexander, David. **1994**. *Star Trek Creator: The Authorized Biography of Gene Roddenberry*. New York, NY: Roc. An extensive biography of Roddenberry, authorized by his widow, Majel Barrett.

Allen, Robert C., ed. **1985**. *Speaking of Soap Operas*. Chapel Hill: University of North Carolina Press. A critical examination of the American soap opera and its audiences.

Allen, Robert C., ed. **1987**. *Channels of Discourse: Television and Contemporary Criticism*. Chapel Hill: University of North Carolina Press. Each essay takes a different approach to television criticism (genre study, psychoanalysis, feminist, etc.).

Allen, Robert C., ed. **1992**. *Channels of Discourse, Reassembled*. Chapel Hill: University of North Carolina Press. Revised version of 1987 edition—same approach.

Allen, Robert C., ed. **1995**. *To Be Continued…: Soap Operas Around the World*. London, England: Routledge. A series of essays of a scholarly nature about soap operas around the world, including in the United States.

Allen, Steve. **1956**. *The Funny Men*. New York, NY: Simon & Schuster. A very early look at comedy on television by one of its great practitioners. Most of the book consists of chapters on individual comics that influenced early TV.

Alley, Robert S. **1977**. *Television: Ethics for Hire?* Nashville, TN: Abingdon. A study of the "character of the medium." Claims that television has a negative effect on morality in society and has diminished parental influence.

Alley, Robert S., & Irby B. **Brown**. **1989**. *Love Is All Around: The Making of the Mary Tyler Moore Show.* New York, NY: Delta Books. Tells the story of the show, its creation and evolution. Description of writing, players, production, etc. Includes episode guides.

Alley, Robert S., & Irby B. **Brown**. **1990**. *Murphy Brown: Anatomy of a Sitcom.* New York, NY: Delta Books. A detailed analysis of this show, from concept to execution. Includes information about the cast, the writers, awards, and the look of the show. Has a chapter on "a week on the set." Detailed descriptions of each episode for the first two seasons.

Alley, Robert S., & Irby B. **Brown**. **2001**. *Women Television Producers; Transformation of the Male Medium.* Rochester, NY: University of Rochester Press. Discusses the changes over the years in the participation of women in television and to a lesser extent the portrayal of women in television. Concentrates on women television producers. The main part of book is based on interviews with women from different eras of television and from different types of producing.

Altheide, David L., & Robert P. **Snow**. **1979**. *Media Logic.* Beverly Hills, CA: Sage Publications. A discussion of the logic (perspective, formats, grammar, media personalities) of media, with emphasis on news and politics.

Altman, Mark A. **1990**. *Twin Peaks Behind-the-Scenes: An Unofficial Visitors Guide to "Twin Peaks."* Las Vegas, NV: Pioneer Books. A look at the characters, the production personnel, the themes, etc. Also has episode guides of 1–2 pages.

Anderson, Christopher. **1994**. *Hollywood TV & the Studio System in the Fifties.* Austin: University of Texas Press. A history of how the movie studios, after first resisting and opposing television, became major TV program producers.

Anderson, Kent. **1978**. *Television Fraud: The History and Implications of the Quiz Show Scandals.* Westport, CN: Greenwood Press. A scholarly account of the late 50s scandals. Based on the author's thesis at the University of Washington.

Andreadis, Athena. **1998**. *To Seek Out New Life: The Biology of Star Trek.* New York, NY: Crown Publishers. A medical professor analyzes Star Trek television shows and movies in terms of its biology, including parasites, clones, aliens, symbionts, etc.

Andrews, Bart. **1976**. *Lucy & Ricky & Fred & Ethel: The Story of "I Love Lucy."* New York, NY: E.P. Dutton. A popular writer gives a behind-the-scenes look at this famous sitcom. Includes descriptive episode guide.

Andrews, Bart. **1980**. *The Worst TV Shows Ever* (with Brad Dunning). New York, NY: E.P. Dutton. An amusing book with descriptions and trivia about what the author considers the worst television shows.

Andrews, Bart. **1985**. *The "I Love Lucy" Book.* New York, NY: Doubleday & Company. A revised updated edition of the 1976 work by the same author. Episode guide gives a little more information (such as cast).

Andrews, Bart, & Ahrgus **Julliard**. **1986**. *Holy Mackerel!: The Amos 'n' Andy Story.* New York, NY: E.P. Dutton. Discusses the radio and television show: Its popularity, impact and the controversy surrounding it. Based on interviews with those involved. Also discusses portrayal of African Americans on television.

Ang, Ien. **1985**. *Watching Dallas: Soap Opera and the Melodramatic Imagination.* London, England: Mellon. This work has become a classic study, often cited. Analyzes mythology, cultural values, meaning, audience reaction, and a feminist approach to the show.

Anijar, Karen. **2000**. *Teaching Toward the 24th Century: Star Trek as Social Curriculum* (Pedagogy and Popular Culture, volume 5). New York, NY: Falmer Press. An education professor describes the trekker phenomenon in postmodern terms. Analyzes "Star Trek" as a space western. Shows how to use "Star Trek" for curricula in teaching religion, philosophy, language, and culture.

Aquila, Richard, ed. **1996**. *Wanted, Dead or Alive: The American West in Popular Culture.* Urbana: University of Illinois Press. A series of articles on various types of popular culture and how the West was portrayed in 125 of them. One chapter (written by Gary Yoggy) is devoted to television.

Arness, James. **2001**. *James Arness: An Autobiography.* Jefferson, NC: McFarland. The star of "Gunsmoke" tells about his life.

Arnold, Roseanne. **1994**. *My Lives.* New York, NY: Ballantine Books. An autobiography by one of TV's most powerful women. She gives insights into what that means and into her TV show.

Atwan, Robert, Barry **Orton**, & William **Vesterman**. **1978**. *American Mass Media: Industries and Issues.* New York, NY: Random House. A collection of articles on the interrelationships of corporate media, creative persons, and the mass audience.

Auletta, Ken. **1991**. *Three Blind Mice: How the TV Networks Lost Their Way.* New York, NY: Random House. A thorough account of the decline of the three major networks in the late 1980s. Based on personal interviews. Describes the effects of cable, VCRs, and Fox.

Avery, Robert K., & David **Eason**, eds. **1991**. *Critical Perspectives on Media and Society.* New York, NY: Guilford Press. A selection of articles from a journal (*Critical Studies in Mass Communication*). One part is devoted to describing various theoretical approaches to media criticism. The second part gives some examples of applying these theories.

Bacon, James. **1985**. *How Sweet It Is: The Jackie Gleason Story.* New York, NY: St. Martins Press. A friend of Gleason's writes about his life.

Bacon-Smith, Camille. **1992**. *Enterprising Women: Television Fandom and the Creation of Popular Myth.* Philadelphia, PA: University of Pennsylvania Press. A study of fans of television programs; discusses fan clubs, conventions, etc. Emphasis is on women fans. "Star Trek" is extensively covered.

Baehr, Helen, & Gillian **Dyer**, eds. **1987**. *Boxed In: Women and Television.* New York, NY: Pandora Press. A collection of essays from women about television business, programming, and content on the screen. British emphasis; mostly feminist viewpoint. One chapter devoted to "Cagney and Lacey."

Bakish, David. **1995**. *Jimmy Durante: His Show Business Career with an Annotated*

Filmography and Discography. Jefferson, NC: McFarland. A fairly thorough biography of Jimmy Durante, including his television days. A complete chronology, discography, and listing of appearances in film and television are included.

Ball, Lucille. **1996**. *Love, Lucy*. New York, NY: G.P. Putnam Sons. Based on a manuscript found after her death, this is a personal memoir of Lucille Ball's life into the early 1960s.

Ball, Rick. **1998**. *Meet the Press: Fifty Years of History in the Making*. New York, NY: McGraw-Hill. A guide to the longest running show on television. Includes interviews and selected excerpts from the many shows. Also contains other information about the show and its times.

Ball-Rokeach, Sandra J., & Muriel G. **Cantor**, eds. **1986**. *Media, Audience and Social Structure*. Newbury Park, CA: Sage Publications. Based on the 1984 American Sociological Association meeting, covers mass media from a social science research perspective. Concentrates on audience and content in the media.

Ballard-Reisch, D. **1991**. "China Beach and Tour of Duty: American Television and Revisionist History of the Vietnam War." *Journal of Popular Culture*, Winter 91, 25(3), p. 135. 15 pages. Presents a paper which analyzes the role of American television in both the process of creating and the process of purging the guilt the American people feel towards the realities they witnessed on television of the Vietnam War. Guilt, purgation, and redemption. The American war myth and Vietnam and the role of "China Beach" and "Tour of Duty" in redemption [Copyright Ebscohost]

Barabas, Suzanne, & Gabor **Barabas**. **1990**. *Gunsmoke: A Complete History and Analysis of the Legendary Broadcast Series*. Jefferson, NC: McFarland. A thorough account of the long playing western. Includes radio program as well as television version. Many details, photographs, and quotes. Includes episode guides to both radio and television programs.

Barad, Judith (with Ed Robertson). **2000**. *The Ethics of Star Trek*. New York, NY: Perennial. Uses "Star Trek" shows and movies to teach ethics—religion and culture, virtue, Christian ethics, etc. Explores the ethical makeup of the "Star Trek" universe.

Barbera, Joseph. **1994**. *My Life in 'Toons: From Flatbush to Bedrock in Under a Century*. Atlanta, GA: Turner Publishing Inc. The autobiography of one of the pair who created "The Flintstones," "Jetsons," etc.

Barcus, F. Earle. **1983**. *Images of Life on Children's Television: Sex Roles, Minorities, and Families*. New York, NY: Praeger. A study of how minorities, women, family, etc., are portrayed on television programs aimed at children.

Bare, Richard L. **2001**. *Confessions of a Hollywood Director*. (Filmmakers series No. 89). Lanham, MD: The Scarecrow Press. An autobiographical account from a director of motion pictures and many television shows.

Barer, Burl. **1993**. *The Saint: A Complete History in Print, Radio, Film and Television*. Jefferson, NC: McFarland. A history of the detective series in all formats. Includes episode guides.

Barker, Chris. **1999**. *Television, Globalization, and Cultural Identities*. Buckingham,

England: Open University Press. Examines television and culture in a global context. Emphasizes television's influence on cultural identity.

Barnouw, Erik. **1990**. *Tube of Plenty* (2nd revised edition). New York, NY: Oxford University Press. A history of television broadcasting in the United States by the author who wrote the definitive history (3 volumes) of broadcasting in general.

Barr, Marleen S., ed. **2000**. *Future Females, the Next Generation: New Voices and Velocities in Feminist Science Fiction Criticism*. Lanham, MD.: Rowman and Littlefield Publishers. A collection of scholarly essays on feminist science fiction in all media although books are the main emphasis.

Barrett, Michele, & Duncan **Barrett**. **2001**. *Star Trek: The Human Frontier*. New York, NY: Routledge. A British professor and her teenage son explore "Star Trek" in all its manifestations, concentrating on what it says about being human. Also shows the nautical metaphor of "Star Trek" and discusses how "Voyager" and "Deep Space Nine" are post modern in approach. Much discussion of religion in the shows, esp. DSN.

Batra, N.D. **1987**. *The Hour of Television: Critical Approaches*. Metuchen, NJ: Scarecrow Press. A humanistic and empirical approach to both television programming and its marketplace aspects. Includes chapters on different television genres.

Beaton, Margaret. **1990**. *Oprah Winfrey: TV Talk Show Host*. Chicago, IL: Children's Press. A short biography geared towards young adults.

Beatts, Anne, ed. **1977**. *Saturday Night Live*. New York, NY: Avon Books. A shooting script of one of the shows.

Beck, Ken, & Sim **Clark**. **1985**. *The Andy Griffith Show Book*. New York, NY: St. Martin's Press. A book about Mayberry and its characters. Also has quizzes and an episode summary (brief description.)

Becker, Christine A. **2001**. *An Industrial History of Established Hollywood Film Actors of Fifties Prime Time Television* (Ph.D. Dissertation, University of Wisconsin, Madison). An analysis of how film actors related and reacted to the beginning of television in the 1950s.

Bedell, Sally. **1981**. *Up the Tube: Prime-Time TV and the Silverman Years*. New York, NY: Viking Press. A *TV Guide* reporter writes a biography of one of television's leading executives.

Bell, John. **1992**. "In Search of a Discourse on Aging: The Elderly on Television." *Gerontologist*, June 92, 32(3), p. 305. 7 pages. Analyzes the images of aging presented in five of the prime-time television programs of 1989 most watched by the elderly: "Murder, She Wrote," "The Golden Girls," "Matlock," "Jake and the Fatman," and "In the Heat of the Night," all of which have central elderly characters. Television's portrayal of aging. [Copyright Ebscohost]

Bellon, Joe. **1999**. "The Strange Discourse of The X-Files: What It Is, What It Does, and What Is at Stake." *Critical Studies in Mass Communication*, June 99, 16(2), p. 16. 19 pages. Explores the antecedent genre of the television show "The X-Files" and its effects on modern society. Generic characteristics of science fiction; contention that the show belongs to the ontological detective genre; resignification of the stereotypical relationship between male and female partners in television; depiction of governmental authorities as forces of injustice in the show. [Copyright Ebscohost]

Bendazzi, Gianalberto. **1994**. *Cartoons: One Hundred Years of Cinema Animation*. Bloomington: Indiana University Press. A history of animation worldwide with very little related to television.

Bennett, Mark. **1996**. *TV Sets: Fantasy Blueprints of Classic TV Homes*. New York, NY: TV Books. Drawings of the homes (and sometimes other structures and towns) of various fictional television families, with brief comments on each.

Benny, Jack. **1990**. *Sunday Nights at Seven: The Jack Benny Story*. New York, NY: Warner Books. An unfinished autobiography with editing and extensive commentary by his daughter Joan. Some anecdotes and insights into his show by Jack and those who worked with him.

Benny, Mary Livingston & Hilliard **Marks**. **1978**. *Jack Benny*. Garden City, NY: Doubleday. A biography of Jack by his wife of many years.

Benoit, William L., & K. Kerby **Anderson**. **1996**. "Blending Politics and Entertainment: Dan Quayle versus Murphy Brown." *Southern Communication Journal*, Fall 96, 62(1), p. 73. 12 pages. Analyzes the exchange between Dan Quayle and a character from television program "Murphy Brown," as an example of the intersection between politics and television in the United States. Quayle's accusations of mockery of the importance of fathers; portrayal of single parenting as a lifestyle choice. [Copyright Ebscohost]

Berger, Arthur Asa. **1976**. *The TV-Guided American*. New York, NY: Walker and Company. A discussion of the influence of television on the viewers, with lengthy discussions on specific programs.

Berger, Arthur Asa, ed. **1987**. *Television in Society*. New Brunswick, NJ: Transaction Books. A collection of articles from *Society* magazine. Considers television from broad social perspective and how it reflects and affects society.

Berlant, Lauren. **1997**. *The Queen of America Goes to Washington City: Essays on Sex and Citizenship*. Durham, NC: Duke University Press. Points out how the politics under Reagan led to the idea that the core context of politics is the sphere of private life. There is no longer a "public" aspect to citizenship in U.S. society; everything is related to the private (sex, abortion, family, etc.). Some television shows are discussed.

Berle, Milton. **1974**. *Milton Berle: An Autobiography*. New York, NY: Delacorte Books. Berle writes his own story, revealing much about his private life.

Berle, Milton. **1988**. *B.S. I Love You: Sixty Years with the Famous and the Infamous*. New York, NY: McGraw Hill Book Company. Memoirs of the comedian and television pioneer.

Berle, William (with Bradley Lewis). **1999**. *My Father, Uncle Miltie*. New York, NY: Barricade Books. Milton Berle's son writes about his father.

Bernardi, Daniel. **1998**. *Star Trek and History: Race-ing Toward a White Future*. New Brunswick, NJ: Rutgers University Press. A professor of film and television analyzes the "Star Trek" phenomenon in terms of race. Examines how the meaning of race is influenced by creators, networks, genre, intertextuality, and audience. Also shows how the social and political atmosphere in each era played a part.

Berry, Gordon L., & Joy Keiko **Asamen**, eds. **1993**. *Children & Television: Images in a Changing Sociocultural World.* Newbury Park, CA: Sage Publications. Multidisciplinary approaches to the social effects of television on children. Discusses "the developing child in a multimedia world," how television affects children's world view, and their understanding of diverse cultures.

Berry, Gordon L., & Claudia **Mitchell-Kernan**, eds. **1982**. *Television and the Socialization of the Minority Child.* New York, NY: Academic Press. A collection of scholarly articles on the effects of television on minority children, especially on their socialization.

Berry, Venise T., & Carmen L. **Manning-Miller**, eds. **1996**. *Mediated Messages and African-American Culture: Contemporary Issues.* Thousand Oaks, CA: Sage Publications. Describes how "racialism" affects contemporary media in its portrayal of African-American culture. Covers film, print, radio, and music as well as television.

Bertsch, Charlie. **1998**. "The Personal Is Paranormal: Professional Labor on the X-Files." *American Studies*, Summer 98, 39(2), p. 107. 21 pages. Focuses on the television program "The X-Files." Examination of themes ... success and portrayal of the professional and personal.... Use of contemporary capitalism as a means of understanding the program. [Copyright Ebscohost]

Bianculli, David. **1992**. *Teleliteracy: Taking Television Seriously.* New York, NY: Continuum. A personal positive view of television. Gives a brief history and then describes all the good television has done for our society.

Bianculli, David. **1996**. *Dictionary of Teleliteracy: Television's 500 Biggest Hits, Misses, and Events.* New York, NY: Continuum. As a follow-up to his book on teleliteracy, the author lists 500 television "shows" (some are really events) that had an impact on American culture. Modelled after *The Dictionary of Cultural Literacy.*

Bifulco, Michael, ed. **1998**. *Superman on Television.* Canoga Park, CA: Bifulco Books. Companion to the television series, with behind-the-scenes information, information about the cast, trivia, and episode guides.

Bignell, Jonathan **1997**. *Media Semiotics: An Introduction.* Manchester, England: Manchester University Press. An introductory text to using semiotics as a critical approach to media studies, using many contemporary examples from advertisements, newspapers, magazines, film, and television. Also discusses theory allied to semiotics and challenges to semiotic methods. New media are also considered.

Billingham, Peter. **2000**. *Sensing the City Through Television.* Bristol, UK: Intellect. Using five case studies, analyzes how fictional representations of the city on TV contribute to our sense of identity. Each program is discussed in depth, analyzing structure, content, characterization, narrative, and ideological context.

Birns, Nicholas. **1993**. "Telling Inside from Outside, or, Who Really Killed Laura Palmer." *Literature Film Quarterly*, 21(4), p. 277. 10 pages. Focuses on the killer of Laura Palmer, a character in the television series "Twin Peaks." Separate identity of Leland Palmer; combination of romantic pathos with post-modern pastiche. [Copyright Ebscohost]

Bjorklund, Denais A. **1997**. *Toasting "Cheers."* Jefferson, NC: McFarland. A guide to the show with cast members, background, a chapter on the "Cheers Bar," the characters' "lives," summaries of the episodes.
Blair, Karin. **1977**. *Meaning in Star Trek.* Chambersburg, PA: Anima Books. Analyzes various episodes of the original series in terms of future, past, society, dualities, portrayal of women, etc. Talks in terms of archetypes.
Blanc, Mel, & Philip **Bashe**. **1988**. *That's Not All Folks!* New York, NY: Warner Books. An autobiography by the greatest cartoon voice man, who also appeared with Jack Benny.
Block, Alex Ben. **1990**. *Outfoxed.* New York, NY: St. Martin's Press. The story of the Fox network.
Blum, Richard A. **1995**. *Television and Screen Writing: From Concept to Contract* (3rd edition). Boston, MA: Focal Press. A how-to book with samples from real shows.
Blum, Richard A., & Richard D. **Lindheim**. **1987**. *Prime Time Network Television Programming.* Boston, MA: Focal Press. A behind-the-scenes look at network prime time programming, meant to serve as a textbook. Examples of script fragments.
Blumenthal, Dannielle. **1997**. *Women and Soap Opera: A Cultural Feminist Perspective.* Westport, CN: Praeger. A sociologist looks at soap operas from a feminist cultural perspective. Via an empirical study of viewing habits, she discusses empowerment of women and the differing values of women and men and how they interpret the world. In a patriarchal society, women's values (including soap opera viewing) are devalued.
Blumler, Jay G., Jack M. **McLeod**, & Karl Erik **Rosengren**, eds. **1992**. *Comparatively Speaking: Communication and Culture Across Space.* Newbury Park, CA: Sage Publications. A collection of essays of comparative studies across all types of communication. One essay deals with soap operas.
Blythe, Cheryl, & Susan **Sackett**. **1986**. *Say Goodnight Gracie! The Story of Burns & Allen.* New York, NY: E.P. Dutton. An account of the lives and careers of George Burns and Gracie Allen. Discusses sayings, gags, guest stars, etc. of the television show. Appendices of cast and episodes.
Bodroghkozy, Aniko. **2001**. *Groove Tube: Sixties Television and the Youth Rebellion.* Durham, NC: Duke University Press. A scholarly look at how television responded to the Youth Movement of the 1960s. Attempts were made to appeal to the Baby Boomer market. Also examines how the youth who grew up with television responded to these representations.
Bogle, Donald. **2001**. *Prime Time Blues: African Americans on Network Television.* New York, NY: Farrar, Strauss and Giroux. A comprehensive survey of African Americans in network series. Discusses stereotypes from the blatant early ones to the more subtle recent ones. Analyzes the 90s trend of blacks and whites viewing different programs.
Bounds, J. Dennis. **1996**. *Perry Mason: The Authorship and Reproduction of a Popular Hero* (Contributions to the Study of Popular Culture no. 56). Westport, CN: Greenwood Press. Traces the history of the famous lawyer/detective from its origins in books to television. Uses a neoformalist approach to analyze the various media portrayals of this popular cultural icon.

Bowles, Jerry. **1980**. *A Thousand Sundays: The Story of the Ed Sullivan Show.* New York, NY: G.P. Putnam's Sons. The story of this long-running variety show with behind-the-scenes information, descriptions of key acts that appeared, mishaps, feuds, etc. Also talks about Ed Sullivan himself.

Boylan, Jeanne. **2000**. *Portraits of Guilt: The Woman Who Profiles the Faces of America's Deadliest Criminals.* New York, NY: Pocket Books. The author describes her work as a criminal sketch artist. Some of her works were done for television programs.

Brady, Kathleen. **1994**. *Lucille: The Life of Lucille Ball.* New York, NY: Hyperion. Perhaps the most definitive biography of one of television's pioneering and influential figures.

Brauer, Ralph. **1975**. *The Horse, the Gun, and the Piece of Property: Changing Images of the TV Western* (with Donna Brauer). Bowling Green, OH: Bowling Green University Popular Press. A history of the television western and how the "outside world" influenced its development in terms of portrayal and content.

Braun, Beth. **2000**. "The X-Files" and "Buffy, the Vampire Slayer." *Journal of Popular Film & Television*, Summer 2000, 28(2), p. 88. 7 pages. Focuses on evil in the television programs "The X-Files" and "Buffy, the Vampire Slayer." Description on the characters in both programs; how evil is represented; discussion on the concerns reflected by both programs. [Copyright Ebscohost]

Britos, Peter Joseph Oluloa. **2001**. *Symbols, Myth and TV in Hawaii: "Hawaiian Eye," "Five-O" and "Magnum P.I." The First Cycle* (Ph.D. Dissertation, University of Southern California). A history and analysis of early shows about Hawaii.

Brookfield, S. **1990**. "Using TV Drama to Teach Adults: Realness, Recognition, and Critical Thinking in 'thirtysomething'." *Adult Learning*, Sep. 90, 2(1), p. 20. 3 pages. Examines the way in which TV can sometimes perform an educational function, in this case the author uses "thirtysomething" as an example of a TV show that demonstrates prime-time, network TV can produce drama that connects with many viewers. The show depicts adult life more accurately, naturalistically and realistically than any other show on TV and it invokes critical thinking. [Copyright Ebscohost]

Broughton, Irv, ed. **1986**. *Producers on Producing: The Making of Film and Television.* Jefferson, NC: McFarland. A collection of interviews with 22 producers from almost all television genres. Provides insight into problems and decision-making for TV programs.

Brown, Mary Ellen, ed. **1990**. *Television and Women's Culture: The Politics of the Popular*. London, England: Sage Publications. Feminist television criticism in several aspects (audience, representation, genres, consumption).

Brown, Mary Ellen. **1994**. *Soap Opera and Women's Talk: The Pleasure of Resistance.* Thousand Oaks, CA: Sage Publications. A study of soap opera fans (mostly female). Their network is seen as a form of feminist empowerment.

Brownlow, Sheila, & Rebecca **Whitener**, et al. **1998**. "I'll Take Gender Differences for $1000!: Domain-Specific Intellectual Success on 'Jeopardy'." *Sex Roles,* Feb. 98, 38(3/4), p. 269. 17 pages. Focuses on library research which demonstrated that women underestimate their intellect and abilities, while emphasizing the performance of men and women on the television show "Jeopardy." Significance of perceptions of gender differences in intelligence. [Copyright Ebscohost]

Brunsdon, Charlotte. **2000**. *The Feminist, the Housewife, and the Soap Opera*. (Oxford Television Studies). Oxford, England: Clarendon Press. Traces British and U.S. feminist criticism of television, especially soap opera. British emphasis.

Bryant, Jennings, ed. **1990**. *Television and the American Family*. Hillsdale, NJ: Lawrence Erlbaum Associates. A series of scholarly articles on the use of television by the American family, the effects on the family of television, and (most importantly for this book) the portrayal of the American family on television.

Bryant, Jennings, & Daniel R. **Anderson**, eds. **1983**. *Children's Understanding of Television: Research on Attention and Comprehension*. New York, NY: Academic Press. A collection of studies on the effects of television viewing on children. Emphasis is on attention and comprehension.

Bryant, Jennings, & J. Alison **Bryant**, eds. **2001**. *Television and the American Family* (second edition). Mahwah, NJ: Lawrence Erlbaum Associates. An update of the 1990 edition, this edition includes important developments that occurred in the 1990s, especially relating to technology.

Bryant, Jennings, & Dolf **Zillman**, eds. **1994**. *Media Effects: Advances in Theory and Research*. Hillsdale, NJ: Lawrence Erlbaum Associates, Publishers. Top researchers in the field of the effects of mass media each write a chapter giving the latest research results and theories.

Buckman, Peter. **1984**. *All for Love: A Study in Soap Operas*. London, England: Secker & Warburg. A study of the characters, plots, writers, actors, directors, and critics of soap operas. Also examines soap opera fans and their influence on the shows. Slight British emphasis but much on U.S. soap operas.

Buerkel-Rothfuss, Nancy L., Bradley S. **Greenberg**, & Jane D. **Brown**, eds. **1993**. *Media, Sex and the Adolescent*. Cresskill, NJ: Hampton Press. A collection of studies examining the relationship between sexual content in the media (mostly movies and television) and adolescents.

Buhler, Stephen M. **1995**. "Who Calls Me Villain? Blank Verse and the Black Hat." *Extrapolation*, Spring 95, 36(1), p. 18. 10 pages. Focuses on the television series "Star Trek: The Next Generation's" use of quotations from the villains in William Shakespeare's works to establish a character's status as a villain. Presentation of Shakespeare as a universal cultural resource. [Copyright Ebscohost]

Buresh, Bernice, & Suzanne **Gordon**. **1995**. "Taking on the TV Shows." *American Journal of Nursing*, Nov. 95, 95(11), p. 18. 3 pages. Reports that the television program "ER" has succeeded by creating an illusion of authenticity. Influence of the Emergency Nurses Association on the program; introduction of physicians in to the plots; comparison with "Chicago Hope." [Copyright Ebscohost]

Burke, Chris, & Jo Beth **McDaniel**. **1991**. *A Special Kind of Hero: Chris Burke's Own Story*. New York, NY: Dell Publishing. The actor with Down Syndrome who starred in "Life Goes On" tells about his life.

Burks, Michael Jay. **1990**. *Elements of Visual Style in Television Drama* (Ph.D. Dissertation, University of Kansas). Examines whether certain types of shows use the same visual style and, more broadly, do all fiction storytelling programs look alike.

Burns, Gary, & Robert J. **Thompson**, eds. **1989**. *Television Studies: Textual Analysis*. New York, NY: Praeger. Scholarly essays on television with several chapters devoted to analyzing a specific program.

Burns, George. **1980**. *The Third Time Around*. New York, NY: G.P. Putnam's Sons. A light-hearted autobiography with some anecdotes about his TV show.

Burns, George. **1988**. *Gracie: A Love Story*. New York, NY: G.P. Putnam's Sons. An affectionate biography of Gracie Allen by her husband. Has some autobiographical notes by George as well.

Burns, George. **1990**. *All My Best Friends*. New York, NY: Perigree Book. A memoir by Burns discussing the life and adventures of his show business friends such as Jack Benny, Eddie Cantor, George Jessel, and Milton Berle. There are some brief descriptions of incidents related to their television programs.

Buscombe, Edward, & Roberta E. **Pearson**, eds. **1998**. *Back in the Saddle Again: New Essays on the Western*. London: British Film Institute. A series of essays by scholars about the Western film. Television westerns are also covered by some of the essayists. Because of the book's recency, there is much discussion of ethnic minorities, women and Native Americans as portrayed in film and TV westerns.

Butler, Jeremy G. **1991**. *Star Texts: Image and Performance in Film and Television*. Detroit, MI: Wayne State University Press. Scholarly articles on the star image and acting styles, etc. Concentrates on film but some television stars and shows are included.

Buxton, David. **1990**. *From the Avengers to Miami Vice: Form and Ideology in Television Series*. Manchester, England: Manchester University Press. A structural theoretical critical analysis of television series, with special emphasis on a few.

Buzenberg, Susan, & Bill **Buzenberg**, eds. **1999** [1998] *Salant, CBS, and the Battle for the Soul of Broadcast Journalism: The Memoirs of Richard S. Salant*. Boulder, CO: Westview Press. The story of CBS news during the 1960s and 1970s as told through the eyes of the president of CBS News during that era.

Byrd, Marguita L. **1998**. *Mulitcultural Communication and Popular Culture: Racial and Ethnic Images in Star Trek*. New York, NY: McGraw-Hill. Analyzes all four "Star Trek" series (too early for "Enterprise") in terms of portrayals of various ethnic groups, with emphasis on African Americans but substantial information also on Asians, Native Americans, and Latinos.

Cader, Michael, ed. **1994**. *Saturday Night Live: The First Twenty Years*. Boston, MA: Cader Books. Heavily illustrated "fan type" book with cast, anecdotes, music, behind-the-scenes, list of short sketches, etc.

Caesar, Sid. **1982**. *Where Have I Been? An Autobiography* (with Bill Davidson). New York, NY: Crown Publishers. An autobiography of one of television's early stars, with emphasis on his alcoholism.

Caldwell, John Thornton. **1995**. *Televisuality: Style, Crisis, and Authority in American Television*. New Brunswick, NJ: Rutgers University Press. Emphasizes visual style and image on television. Gives historical perspective and analyzes aesthetic and industrial practice aspects of TV. Also discusses the social symbolism of style and image.

Calvert, Sandra L., et al. **2001**. "Young Adults' Perceptions and Memories of a Televised Woman Hero." *Sex Roles*, July 2001, 45 (1/2), p. 31. 22 pages. Presents a study which examined how young adult males and females perceive and remember televised depictions of a female action hero, Xena, who has a dark side to her personality. [Copyright Ebscohost]

Campbell, John Edward. **2001**. "Alien(ating) Ideology and the American Media." *International Journal of Cultural Studies*, Sept. 2001, 4(3), p. 327. 21 pages. Focuses on the pervasiveness of the alien image in the contemporary American media particularly in television programming. Commentaries on the television series, "The X-Files." Analysis of the utilization of text episodes constituting the progressive government-alien conspiracy. [Copyright Ebscohost]

Campbell, Richard. **1991**. *60 Minutes and the News: A Mythology for Middle America.* Urbana: University of Illinois Press. A communication professor analyzes the stories seen on "60 Minutes" and puts them in a societal frame of upholding middle class values.

Cantor, Muriel G., & Joel M. **Cantor**. **1992**. *Prime Time Television: Content and Control* (2nd edition). Newbury Park, CA: Sage Publications. Through interviews, trade papers, and personal viewing, the authors discuss various aspects of television, including family shows.

Cantor, Paul A. **1999**. "The Simpsons." *Political Theory*, Dec. 99, 27(6), p. 734. 16 pages. Examines how the cartoon series "The Simpsons" affects the youth of the United States politically. Portrayal of the average family in the US by "The Simpsons"; issues taken up in the series; its attitude to both Republicans and Democrats. [Copyright Ebscohost]

Cantor, Paul A. **2000**. "Shakespeare in the Original Klingon: Star Trek and the End of History." *Perspectives on Political Science*, Summer 2000, 29(3), p. 158. 9 pages. Discusses the connection of popular culture with political philosophy in the United States. Review of the political objective of the television series "Star Trek" to viewers in the U.S. Relationship of Shakespeare and his plays to the series. [Copyright Ebscohost]

Cantor, Paul A. **2001**. *Gilligan Unbound: Pop Culture in the Age of Globalization.* Lanham, MD: Rowman & Littlefield Publishers. An English literature scholar analyzes popular culture with an emphasis on television. He shows how it reflects society's beliefs from faith in liberal democracy to more recently global networks. Emphasis is on the 1960s and the 1990s.

Caprio, Betsy. **1978**. *Star Trek: Good News in Modern Images.* Kansas City, KS: Sheed, Andrews and McMeel. Relates the original series to religion, especially Christianity. Written by a fan, argues that, despite the de-emphasis on religion in the show, "Star Trek" is actually a Christian show.

Capsuto, Steven. **2000**. *Alternate Channels: The Uncensored Story of Gay and Lesbian Images on Radio and Television.* New York, NY: Ballantine Books. Traces the growth of gay, lesbian and bisexual images on radio and television. Set against concurrent historical events, the book shows how the images have changed.

Carey, James W., ed. **1988**. *Media, Myths and Narratives: Television and the Press* (Sage Annual Reviews of Communication Research, volume 15). Newbury Park, CA: Sage Publications. "Essays in this volume attempt to elucidate concepts such as myth, ritual, narrative, and story and ... apply them to ... television and the press." A couple of essays deal with specific prime time shows.

Carlson, James M. **1985**. *Prime Time Law Enforcement: Crime Show Viewing and Attitudes Toward the Criminal Justice System*. New York, NY: Praeger. Discusses how television socializes the public. Main focus is on how the attitudes toward crime and the criminal justice system is affected by their portrayal on TV.

Carraze, Alain, & Jean-Luc Putheaud. **1998**. *The Avengers Companion*. San Francisco, CA: Bay Books. This well illustrated guide to the show includes interviews with key people, articles, an episode guide, a behind-the-scenes look, and other miscellanea.

Carrion, Maria M. **1993**. "Twin Peaks and the Circular Ruins of Fiction: Figuring (Out) the Acts of Reading." *Literature Film Quarterly*, 21(4), p. 240. 8 pages. Discusses the narrative structure of the television series "Twin Peaks." [Copyright Ebscohost]

Carroll, Michael. **1993**. "Agent Cooper's Errand in the Wilderness: Twin Peaks and American Mythology." *Literature Film Quarterly*, 21(4), p. 287. 9 pages. Focuses on the television series "Twin Peaks" and its utilization of American cultural mythology. Differences between "Blue Velvet" and "Twin Peaks"; ambivalence of Agent Dale Cooper's role; moral superiority of Dale Cooper; notion of Cooper's law-enforcement companions as surrogate wives; affinities between Cooper and Fenimore Cooper's Leatherstocking. [Copyright Ebscohost]

Carroll, Michael T., & Eddie **Infoya**, eds. **2000**. *Phenomenological Approaches to Popular Culture*. Bowling Green, OH: Bowling Green State University Popular Press. Uses phenomenology, the branch of philosophy concerned with human experience, to study popular culture.

Carstarphen, Meta G., & Susan C. **Zavoina**, eds. **1999**. *Sexual Rhetoric: Media Perspectives on Sexuality, Gender, and Identity* (Contributions to the Study of Mass Media and Communications, no. 57). Westport, CN: Greenwood Press. A series of essays written by scholars analyzing the media (including "new" media and television) in terms of an understanding of popular culture, stereotypical portrayals of men and women and implications for gender roles in society.

Carter, Bill. **1994**. *The Late Shift: Letterman, Leno, and the Network Battle for the Night*. New York, NY: Hyperion. A detailed account of the Letterman vs. Leno (Tonight Show) battle with many insights.

Carter, Bill. **1995**. *The Late Shift: Letterman, Leno, and the Network Battle for the Night* (revised and updated). New York, NY: Hyperion. An update of the 1994 edition.

Cartwright, Nancy. **2000**. *My Life as a 10-Year-Old Boy*. New York, NY: Hyperion.

The voice of Bart Simpson gives anecdotes about the show and talks about her life in this role.
Castleman, Harry, & Walter J. **Podrazik**. **1982**. *Watching TV: Four Decades of American Television*. New York, NY: McGraw-Hill Book Company. A history of television season by season from 1944 through 1981. Shows are discussed in an historical and factual manner—not much critical analysis.
Cater, Douglas, ed. **1975**. *Television as a Social Force: New Approaches to TV Criticism*. New York, NY: Praeger. A series of critical essays on television's influence on American society, stemming from the Aspen Program's Workshop on Television. See also *Television as a Cultural Force* (Adler 1976).
Catron, Rachel Christine. **1997**. *"Kate and Allie": Feminist Criticism, Television, and Social Construction of Reality* (Ph.D. Dissertation, University of Texas at Austin). Examines the way this series portrays women in midlife and divorced. Uses a feminist approach to show how this series challenges a patriarchal perspective.
Cavallo, Dominick. **1999**. *A Fiction of the Past: The Sixties in American History*. New York, NY: St. Martin's Press. An historian looks at the myths of the sixties and shows that much of it was not new. So-called sixties lifestyle had its origins in the forties and fifties. In discussing this background, some mention is made of television and its influence.
Challen, Paul. **2001**. *Inside the West Wing*. Toronto, Canada: ECW Press. A look at the popular presidential drama. Information on cast and characters, production, and episode guides.
Christians, Clifford G., Mark **Fackler**, & Kim B. **Rotzoll**. **1995**. *Media Ethics: Cases and Moral Reasoning* (4th edition). White Plains, NY: Longman. Gives precepts for ethical decisions and then has 78 cases from the media with discussion. A few examples touch on television programs.
Christians, Clifford G., Kim B. **Rotzoll**, & Mark **Fackler**. **1983**. *Media Ethics: Cases and Moral Reasoning*. New York, NY: Longman. Earlier edition—see 1995 (immediately above) for annotation.
Chunovic, Louis. **1993**. *Northern Exposure: The Official Publication of the Television Series*. New York, NY: Citadel Press. Interviews, behind the scenes information, tidbits, and information about the actors and production staff. Includes episode guides.
Chunovic, Louis. **1995**a. *Northern Exposure: The Official Publication of the Television Series*. New York, NY: Citadel Press. An update of the 1993 edition.
Chunovic, Louis. **1995**b. *The Complete Quantum Leap Book*. New York, NY: Citadel Press. "The official publication of the television series." It includes conversations with key personnel, biographies of the characters, and information on production and costume design. The heart of the book is the episode guides; first in airdate order, then in chronological order.
Chunovic, Louis. **2000**. *One Foot on the Floor: The Curious Evolution of Sex on Television From "I Love Lucy" to "South Park."* New York, NY: TV Books. A television reporter and novelist chronicles the way sex was handled on television from the 1950s to the present. Shows how censorship has worked and how much looser standards are now.

Cloud, Dana L. **1996**. "Hegemony or Concordance? The Rhetoric of Tokenism in Oprah Winfrey's Rags-to-Riches Biography." *Critical Studies in Mass Communication*, June 96, 13(2), p. 115. 23 pages. Examines television and print biographies of talk show host and producer Oprah Winfrey. Theories of hegemony, tokenism, star personae and biographical narrative evident in biographies of Winfrey; biographies' representation of Winfrey's rags-to-riches life as a token achievement of the American Dream by an Afro-American. Impact of race and gender on the rhetoric of tokenism. [Copyright Ebscohost]

Coakley, Mary Lewis. **1977**. *Rated X: The Moral Case Against TV*. New Rochelle, NY: Arlington House. An impassioned attack on television as a purveyor of immorality.

Collins, Mark, & Margaret Mary **Kimmel**, eds. **1996**. *Mister Rogers' Neighborhood*. Pittsburgh, PA: University of Pittsburgh Press. A collection of essays by scholars on this famous television show.

Collins, Max Allan, & John **Javna**. **1988**. *The Best of Crime & Detective TV: Perry Mason to Hill Street Blues, The Rockford Files to Murder, She Wrote*. New York, NY: Harmony Books. Brief descriptions of detective-type shows that critics consider the best. Includes cast, quotes from people involved, trivia, etc.

Combs, James, ed. **1993**. *Movies and Politics: The Dynamic Relationship*. New York, NY: Garland Publishing. Essays on the relationship of movies and politics in terms of ideology presented, portrayal of politics, and political history. A couple of essays touch on television.

Comstock, George, ed. **1986**. *Public Communication and Behavior*, volume 1. Orlando, FL: Academic Press, Inc. A social psychology approach to communication, emphasizing experimental approaches. The main focus of the book is on television.

Comstock, George, & Haejung **Paik**. **1991**. *Television and the American Child*. San Diego, CA: Academic Press. A review of research on various aspects of television and children. Includes chapters on time spent, academic achievement effects, knowledge and beliefs, advertising, and behavior.

Condon, Jack, & David **Hofstede**. **2000**. *Charlie's Angels Casebook*. Beverly Hills, CA: Pomegranate Press. Backstage anecdotes, information about the characters and cast, collectible guide and episode guides.

Condry, John. **1989**. *The Psychology of Television*. Hillsdale, NJ: Lawrence Erlbaum Associates. Describes the research on the psychological influence of television. Some discussion on the content of television (how groups are portrayed, for example).

Conrad, Peter. **1982**. *Television: The Medium and Its Manners*. Boston, MA: Routledge & Kegan Paul. A brief account of television from many angles (as furniture, as medium, technology, ads, and different types of shows).

Coppa, Frank, J., ed. **1979**. *Screen and Society: The Impact of Television Upon Aspects of Contemporary Civilization*. Chicago, IL: Nelson Hall. Essays on television by scholars from varied fields, including history, political science, and law.

Corkery, Paul. **1987**. *Carson: The Unauthorized Biography*. Ketchum, ID: Randt & Company. A popular biography of Johnny Carson.

Cornes, Judy. **2001**. *Stuart Erwin: The Invisible Actor*. (Filmmakers series No. 87)

Lanham, MD: Scarecrow Press. A professor of literature writes a biography and critical analysis of this film actor. He was also in some television shows.

Cortes, Carlos E. **2000**. *The Children Are Watching: How the Media Teach about Diversity*. New York, NY: Teachers College Press. Analyzes entertainment and news media to discover how the media frames the issue of diversity and how this influences children's perceptions.

Cotter, Bill. **1997**. *The Wonderful World of Disney Television: A Complete History*. New York: Hyperion. A history of television shows produced by Disney. Includes anecdotes, statistics, schedules of aired episodes, cast, production details, etc.

Cottle, Simon, ed. **2000**. *Ethnic Minorities and the Media* (Issues in Cultural and Media Studies). Buckingham, England: Open University Press. A group of international scholars takes a look at the current state of representation of ethnic minorities in the media. Emphasis is on television and on African Americans. Some bibliographies.

Courrier, Kevin, & Susan **Green**. **1998**. *Law & Order: The Unofficial Companion*. Los Angeles, CA: Renaissance Books. Guide to the show with behind-the-scenes anecdotes, censorship issues, cast and the history of the show. Includes episode guides with critiques.

Cox, Steve. **2000**. *Dreaming of Jeannie: TV's Prime Time in a Bottle*. New York, NY: St. Martin's Griffin. A guide to the show and its cast and crew. Includes trivia, episode guides, some critical analysis, and other miscellanea.

Craig, Steve, ed. **1992**. *Men, Masculinity, and the Media*. Newbury Park, CA: Sage Publications. An anthology of writings on gender in the media with an emphasis on masculine images. Covers music, comic books, commercials, films, and television.

Creeber, Glen, ed. **2001**. *The Television Genre Book*. London, England: BFI Publishing. Introduction to the study of genre on television linking theoretical discussion to analysis of specific programs.

Crescent, Peter, & Bob **Columbe**. **1990**. *The Official Honeymooners Treasury* (new expanded edition). New York, NY: Perigree Books. A fan type book with interviews, behind-the-scenes tidbits, trivia, etc. Episodes are described and analyzed in detail.

Cross, Donna Woolfolk. **1983**. *Mediaspeak: How Television Makes Up Your Mind*. New York, NY: Coward-McCann, Inc. How television influences the way we think and upholds the status quo.

Crossen, Cynthia. **1994**. *Tainted Truth: The Manipulation of Fact in America*. New York, NY: Simon & Schuster. A journalist reveals how sponsored studies, mostly about consumer products, are usually false. Some news magazine shows are mentioned.

Croteau, David, & William **Hoynes**. **1994**. *By Invitation Only: How the Media Limit Political Debate*. Monroe, ME: Common Coverage Press. Shows how television influences political thinking by whom they invite to appear. "Nightline" is the main focus.

Croteau, David, & William **Hoynes**. **2000**. *Media/Society: Industries, Images, and Audiences*. 2nd ed. Thousand Oaks, CA: Pine Forge Press. A textbook on media and American society. Takes a sociological perspective in intertwining all media and all aspects of media and relates it to society.

Crotty, Mark. **1995**. "Murphy Would Probably Also Win the Election: The Effect of Television as Related to the Portrayal of the Family in Situation Comedies." *Journal of Popular Culture*, Winter 95, 29(3), p. 1. 15 pages. Examines how television situation comedies in the United States portray families and family values and analyzes television's impact on viewers' perception of the world. Television's reflection of the changing economic and social tides and Vice President Dan Quayle's labeling of Murphy Brown as an example of declining family values. Impact of television on moral realities. [Copyright Ebscohost]

Crown, Lawrence. **1999**. *Penny Marshall: An Authorized Autobiography of the Director and Comedienne.* Los Angeles, CA: Renaissance Books. A popularized biography of the TV star and movie director, one of the most successful women in show business.

Cruz, Jon, & Justin **Lewis**, eds. **1994**. *Viewing, Reading, Listening: Audiences and Cultural Reception.* Boulder, CO: Westview Press. A collection of scholarly essays on audiences of mass media. Different theories, including feminist, are represented.

Cuklanz, Lisa M. **1998**. "The Masculine Ideal: Rape on Prime-Time Television, 1976–1978." *Critical Studies in Mass Communication*, Dec. 98, 15(4), p. 423. 26 pages. Examines 25 episodes of prime-time television programs in the United States featuring rape as a primary plot element from 1976 through 1978. Hegemonic masculinity; depiction of rapists; attitudes toward rape prior to feminist efforts in the 1960s. [Copyright Ebscohost]

Cuklanz, Lisa M. **2000**. *Race on Prime Time: Television, Masculinity, and Sexual Violence.* Philadelphia, PA: University of Pennsylvania Press. Analyzes the portrayal of rape on prime time television from 1976 through 1990. Notes a change around 1980 to a more sensitive and female perspective. Shows the influence of changes in legal definitions and procedures on television's dealing with the issue of rape.

Cullingford, Cedric. **1984**. *Children and Television.* Hampshire, England: Gower. A study of the effects of television on child development. British emphasis but some American television programs are discussed.

Cumberbatch, Guy, & Dennis **Howitt**. **1989**. *A Measure of Uncertainty: The Effects of the Mass Media.* London, England: John Libbey & Company, Ltd. A "state of the science review of media effects set in the context of the history of mass communications." Discusses portrayals, violence, and pornography. Indexed in groups section only.

Cumberbatch, Guy, & Ralph **Negrine**. **1992**. *Images of Disability on Television.* London, England: Routledge. A study of the way the disabled are portrayed on television. Covers mostly British shows, but there are some references to U.S. shows.

Curtis, Sandra. **1998**. *Zorro Unmasked: The Official History.* New York, NY: Hyperion Books. Traces the character of Zorro in its many manifestations—literature, comic books, toys, film and television.

D'Acci, Julie. **1994**. *Defining Women: Television and the Case of "Cagney and Lacey."* Chapel Hill: University of North Carolina Press. Discusses cultural constructions of gender and femininity vs. feminism. Uses "Cagney and Lacey" as a case study. Includes a script.

Daniel, Douglass K. **1996**. *Lou Grant: The Making of TV's Top Newspaper Drama.* Syracuse, NY: Syracuse University Press. A history of the show, "Lou Grant," from its conception through its run on television to its controversial cancellation. There are chapters on placing the show in context of its depiction of journalism and on the newspaper drama on television. Mentions other television programs.

Daniels, Les. **1995**. *DC Comics: Sixty Years of the World's Favorite Comic Book Heroes*. Boston, MA: Little, Brown and Company. An interesting, heavily illustrated historical account of the leading comic book publisher. Has sections on television programs based on DC characters.

Dates, Jannette L., & William **Barlow**. **1990**. *Split Image: African-Americans in the Mass Media*. Washington, D.C.: Howard University Press. Covers participation and portrayal of African-Americans in music, film, radio, television, news, and advertising.

Dates, Jannette L., & William **Barlow**. **1993**. *Split Image: African-Americans in the Mass Media* (2nd edition). Washington, D.C.: Howard University Press. Revision and update of 1990 edition.

Davies, Jude, & Carol R. **Smith**. **1998**. "Race, Gender, and the American Mother: Political Speech and the Maternity Episodes of I Love Lucy and Murphy Brown." *American Studies*, Summer 98, 39(2), p. 33. 31 pages. Focuses on the issue of maternity in situation comedies on television in the United States. Changes in the representation of gender on television; changes in American life and its representation on television; political debate concerning American life and television. Reference is made to the Murphy Brown program and former vice president Dan Quayle's remarks concerning the show. [Copyright Ebscohost]

Davies, Maire Messenger. **1997**. *Fake, Fact, and Fantasy: Children's Interpretation of Television Reality*. Mahwah, NJ: Lawrence Erlbaum Associates. Examines "media literacy" among children by using children's own words. Describes how children distinguish the real and the unreal.

Davis, Dennis K., & Stanley J. **Baran**. **1981**. *Mass Communication and Everyday Life: A Perspective on Theory and Effects*. Belmont, CA: Wadsworth Publishing Company. Using mass communication theories, analyzes the effect and influence of media on everyday life.

Davis, Jeffery. **1995**. *Children's Television; 1947–1990.* Jefferson, NC: McFarland. Descriptions (about 1 page each—some longer) on children's shows. The book is categorized by types.

Davis, Richard H., & James A. **Davis**. **1985**. *TV's Image of the Elderly*. Lexington, MA: Lexington Books. Discusses television's influence on how the elderly are perceived and provides a guide for those who want to use television to reach the public on issues related to the aging.

Davis, Stephen. **1987**. *Say Kids! What Time Is It? Notes from the Peanut Gallery.*

Boston, MA: Little, Brown and Company. The story of the "Howdy Doody Show" and its cast. Includes many behind-the-scenes tidbits, some not favorable.

Davis, Walter T., et al. **2001**. *Watching What We Watch: Prime-Time Television Through the Lens of Faith.* Louisville, KY: Geneva Press. Posits television as the most dominant storyteller in our culture. Discusses various aspects of reading television in a theological framework. Scholars from religious studies and communication use TV programs to evaluate faith, values, and beliefs.

Dawidziak, Mark. **1989**. *The Columbo Phile: A Case Book.* New York, NY: The Mysterious Press. A behind-the-scenes look at this well known detective show. Includes creation of character, writing, and conflicts between Falk and the producers. There are also detailed synopses of the episodes.

Deane, Bill. **1996** *Following "The Fugitive."* Jefferson, NC: McFarland. A very detailed episode guide to the show. Includes several appendices of trivia.

De Cordova, Fred. **1988.** *Johnny Come Lately.* New York, NY: Simon and Schuster. An autobiography by the producer of the "Tonight Show" with Carson.

Delamater, Jerome H., & Ruth **Prigozy**. **1998**. *The Detective in American Fiction, Film, and Television.* (Contributions to the Study of Popular Culture, no. 63). Westport, CN: Greenwood Press. Under the auspices of Hofstra University, a group of scholars discuss American detectives as portrayed in literature, movies, and television. Television is a minor part of this book.

Delasara, Jan. **2000**. *PopLit, PopCult and the X-Files: A Critical Exploration.* Jefferson, NC: McFarland. A scholarly look at the cult series, discussing style, character, narrative, mythic aspects, and themes. Explains how show fits the times.

DeLong, Thomas A. **1991**. *Quiz Craze: America's Infatuation with Game Shows.* New York, NY: Praeger. A history of quiz shows on television.

Dewey, Donald. **1996.** *James Stewart.* Atlanta, GA: Turner Publishing. An extensive biography of the movie star.

Diamond, Edwin. **1982**. *Sign Off: The Last Days of Television.* Cambridge, MA: MIT Press. A journalist and political scientist views television broadcasting and its future. Topics covered include sex on television, religion, television news (heavy emphasis), and the "myths of television's omnipotence and its liberalism."

Diem, Susan J,. & John D. **Lantos. 1996**. "Cardiopulmonary Resuscitation on Television." *New England Journal of Medicine*, 6/13/96, 134(24), p. 1578. 5 pages. Describes an analysis of how three popular medical programs on television depict cardiopulmonary resuscitation (CPR). Differences between survival rates on television and those in the real world; table showing the causes of cardiac arrest in three television series, "ER," "Chicago Hope" and "Rescue 911." Rates of long-term survival after cardiac arrest as reported in the medical literature; concerns about the impact of representations of CPR on television. [Copyright Ebscohost]

Dienst, Richard. **1994**. *Still Life in Real Time: Theory After Television.* Durham, NC: Duke University Press. Discusses various theoretical approaches to television criticism, particularly the more "radical" (theory-wise, not political) ones.

DiFranco, Joann, & Anthony **DiFranco**. **1983**. *Mister Rogers: Good Neighbor to America's Children*. Minneapolis, MN: Dillon Press. A short biography intended for young people.

Dimaggio, Madeline. **1990**. *How to Write for Television*. New York, NY: Prentice Hall Press. A how-to guide to television scripting with examples from real shows.

Diorio, Al. **1983**. *Barbara Stanwyck*. New York, NY: Coward-McCann, Inc. A popular biography of the star of "Big Valley."

Donahue, Phil. **1979**. *My Own Story: Donahue*. New York, NY: Simon and Schuster. An autobiography by this pioneer talk show host. Gives behind the scenes information on the show and includes many anecdotes.

Doohan, James (with Peter David). **1996**. *Beam Me Up, Scotty*. New York, NY: Pocket Books. Memoirs of the actor who played the engineer, Scotty, on "Star Trek."

Doty, Alexander. **1993**. *Making Things Perfectly Queer: Interpreting Mass Culture*. Minneapolis, MN: University of Minnesota Press. An academic treatise on the "queerness" found in film and television. Although overt homosexuality may not be shown, there are aspects of homosexual culture in TV shows such as "Laverne and Shirley" and "Jack Benny."

Douglas, Susan J. **1994**. *Where the Girls Are: Growing Up Female with the Mass Media*. New York, NY: Times Books. The effects of the media on the self-image of women in the United States, covering the post–World War II era to the present.

Dow, Bonnie J. **1996**. *Prime-Time Feminism: Television, Media Culture, and the Women's Movement since 1970*. Philadelphia, PA.: University of Pennsylvania Press. A scholarly study of the intersection of television entertainment shows and feminism, concentrating on the 1970s, 80s and 90s.

Dow, Bonnie J. **2001**. "Ellen, Television, and the Politics of Gay and Lesbian Visibility." *Critical Studies in Media Communication*, June 2001, 18(2), p. 123. 18 pages. Focuses on the discourses constructing the coming out of Ellen DeGeneres/Ellen Morgan, star of and lead character in the ABC television sitcom "Ellen," illustrating the continuing power of the confessional ritual described by Michele Foucault in "The History of Sexuality." Positive response to the coming-out episodes and DeGeneres sudden media popularity. [Copyright Ebscohost]

Drummond, Phillip, & Richard **Peterson**, eds. **1988**. *Television and Its Audience: International Research Perspectives* (papers from 2nd International Television Studies Conference, 1986). London, England: British Film Institute. Conference papers on media and politics, media and education, history, analysis of content, and audience research. International in scope.

Dubeck, Leroy W., & Rose **Tatlow**. **1998**. "Using Star Trek: The Next Generation Television Episodes to Teach Science." *Journal of College Science Teaching*, March/April 98, 27(5), p. 319. 5 pages. Comments on the use of a science fiction television series to teach science in the classroom, focusing on "Star Trek: The Next Generation." [Copyright Ebscohost]

Duke, Patty, & Kenneth **Turan**. **1987**. *Call Me Anna: The Autobiography of Patty Duke*. Toronto: Bantam Books. A well known autobiography by the actress. Describes her bouts with manic-depressive disorder.

Dutta, Mary Buhl. **1995**. "Very Bad Poetry, Captain: Shakespeare in Star Trek." *Extrapolation*, Spring 95, 36(1), p. 38. 8 pages. Assesses the use of William Shakespeare's works in the entire "Star Trek" television series. Updating of Shakespeare to reflect the values of an enlightened future. [Copyright Ebscohost]

Edelman, Rob, & Audrey E. **Kupferberg**. **1996**. *Angela Lansbury: A Life on Stage and Screen*. New York, NY: Birch Lane Press. A biography of the star of "Murder, She Wrote," including her appearances in film and on Broadway, as well as television.

Edgerton, Gary R., Michael T. **Marsden**, & Jack **Nachbar**, eds. **1997**. *In the Eye of the Beholder: Critical Perspectives in Popular Film and Television*. Bowling Green, OH: Bowling Green State University Popular Press. A collection of essays by scholars from film and television and from communication using a sociocultural perspective. Critically analyzes popular film and television in a cultural context and from many theoretical viewpoints.

Edgerton, Gary R., & Peter C. **Rollins**, eds. **2001**. *Television Histories Shaping Collective Memory in the Media Age*. Lexington, KY: The University Press of Kentucky. This book explores how historical subjects are portrayed on television. Argues that television is the main way most people learn about history. History on TV is personalized, popularized, put in a modern context, and simplified. History topics on TV are also useful as a means of providing history to the general public.

Edmondson, Madeleine, & David **Rounds**. **1973**. *The Soaps: Daytime Serials of Radio and TV*. New York, NY: Stein and Day. A popular approach with descriptions, summaries, and dialog excerpts. Emphasis is on radio.

Edmondson, Madeleine, & David **Rounds**. **1976**. *From Mary Noble to Mary Hartman: The Complete Soap Opera Book*. New York, NY: Stein and Day. Revised and updated edition of *The Soaps*. A little more space devoted to television.

Edwards, Ted. **1996**. *X-Files Confidential: The Unauthorized X-Files Compendium*. New York, NY: Little, Brown and Company. Episode guides for the first three seasons plus other information about the show and its cast. There is also an extensive "encyclopedia" of terms.

Ely, Melvin Patrick. **1991**. *The Adventures of Amos 'n' Andy: A Social History of an American Phenomenon*. New York, NY: The Free Press. A scholar describes the controversy, social implications, stereotyping, etc., surrounding the show, "Amos 'n' Andy."

Engel, Joel. **1989**. *Rod Serling: The Dreams and Nightmares of Life in the Twilight Zone*. Chicago, IL: Contemporary Books. A biography of the writer and television personality.

Engel, Joel. **1994**. *Gene Roddenberry: The Myth and the Man Behind Star Trek*. New York, NY: Hyperion. A journalist writes a biography of the creator of "Star Trek" and a description of how the show got started.

Entman, Robert M., & Andrew **Rojecki**, eds. **2000**. *The Black Image in the White Media: Media and Race in America*. Chicago, IL: The University of Chicago Press. Examines the images of African Americans projected in the media and how this affects society's (especially whites') views of blacks. While there is little overt racism today, there is a subtle pattern that does not advance racial harmony. Emphasis is on news but there is some mention of television entertainment programs. Proposes some guidelines to remedy the situation.

Epstein, Debbie, & Deborah Lynn **Steinberg**. **1996**. "All Het Up!" *Feminist Review*, Autumn 96, issue 54, p. 88. 28 pages. Examines the January 18, 1993, telecast of ... "Oprah Winfrey Show" in an attempt to understand how the program problematizes and normalizes the boundaries of heterosexuality. Format of the program and analysis of the therapeutic and kinship aspects of program discussions. Racialized and class specific dimensions of program discussions. [Copyright Ebscohost]

Epstein, Debbie, & Deborah Lynn **Steinberg**. **1998**. "American Dreamin': Discoursing Liberally on the Oprah Winfrey Show." *Women's Studies International Forum*, Jan./Feb. 98, 21(1), p. 77. 18 pages. Explores competing versions of nation and democracy incorporated into the framework of television program "The Oprah Winfrey Show." Impact of public and educational service; interest to feminist sensibilities; role of host in giving a platform to marginalized groups. [Copyright Ebscohost]

Erdmann, Terry J. (with Paula M. Block). **2000**. *Star Trek: Deep Space Nine Companion*. New York, NY: Pocket Books. The definitive history and official guide to the series. Contains behind-the-scenes information and interviews with the cast and crew. Also detailed synopses of the episodes.

Erickson, Hal. **1995**. *Television Cartoon Shows: An Illustrated Encyclopedia, 1949 through 1993*. Jefferson, NC: McFarland. A directory of cartoon shows with 2–3 pages of information on each one. Most were not prime time and thus are not indexed.

Erickson, Hal. **2000**. *"From Beautiful Downtown Burbank": A Critical History of Rowan and Martin's Laugh-In, 1968–73*. Jefferson, NC: McFarland. A critical history that analyzes the original six seasons and includes background on the show's creation and its creators.

Everitt, David. **2001**. *King of the Half Hour: Nat Hiken and the Golden Age of TV Comedy*. Syracuse, NY: Syracuse University Press. A biography of the creator of Sergeant Bilko and "Car 54, Where Are You?" Also puts his life in the context of 1950s television.

Fagen, Herb. **1996**. *White Hats and Silver Spurs: Interviews with 24 Stars of Film and Television Westerns of the Thirties Through the Sixties*. Jefferson, NC: McFarland. An alphabetically arranged compendium of interviews as outlined in the subtitle.

Fallows, Randall. **2000**. "The Enneagram of Cheers: Where Everybody Knows Your Number." *Journal of Popular Culture*, Fall 2000, 34(2), p. 169. 11 pages. Applies the method of personality analysis called "Enneagram" in the characters of the television program "Cheers." Information on the revisions and expansions undergone by the Enneagram method; advice for using the Enneagram method; how the Enneagram method reveals the wit and humor of the writers of "Cheers." [Copyright Ebscohost]

Farrand, Phil. **1994**. *The Nitpicker's Guide for Classic Trekkers*. New York, NY: Dell Publishing. A detailed description of each episode of the original "Star Trek" series and the movies. In addition to plot summaries, it gives critical comment, great lines and moments, oversights, production information, and lots of trivia.

Fates, Gil. **1978**. *What's My Line?: The Inside Story of TV's Most Famous Panel Show.* Englewood Cliffs, NJ: Prentice-Hall. A behind-the-scenes look at the show.

Fein, Irving A. **1976**. *Jack Benny: An Intimate Biography.* New York, NY: G.P. Putnam's Sons. Jack Benny's personal manager and friend gives "a warm and intimate portrait" of Benny.

Feinleib, David. **1999**. *The Inside Story of Interactive TV and Microsoft WebTV for Windows.* San Diego, CA: Academic Press. This is an account of actually using the web to create interactive TV. A couple of programs are mentioned as examples that were used. The book also has some commentary from producers, advertisers, and others in the television industry. One section is on technical aspects.

Fernandes, David, & Dale **Robinson**. **1999**. *A Guide to Television's "Mayberry R.F.D."* Jefferson, NC: McFarland. A book of extensive (about 2 pages each) episode guides. Also includes information on the cast.

Ferré, John P., ed. **1990**. *Channels of Belief: Religion and American Commercial Television.* Ames, IA: Iowa State University Press. A collection of scholarly articles on the relationship of religion and television.

Field, Syd. **1989**. *Selling a Screenplay: The Screen Writers Guide to Hollywood.* New York, NY: Delacorte Press. A guide to getting a screenplay sold and produced, rather than writing it. Interviews with successful writers include some who wrote for television.

Finch, Christopher. **1981**. *Of Muppets & Men: The Making of the Muppet Show.* New York, NY: Alfred A. Knopf, Inc. A heavily illustrated behind the scenes look at the show and its production personnel. Besides the general information, it takes one through a week of producing the show.

Fisch, Shalom M., & Rosemarie T. **Truglio**, eds. **2001**. *"G" Is for Growing: Thirty Years of Research on Children and "Sesame Street."* Mahwah, NJ: Lawrence Erlbaum Associates. A collection of essays delineating the many years of research on the effects of "Sesame Street." This is a meta-analysis of the research.

Fishgall, Gary **1997**. *Pieces of Time: The Life of James Stewart.* New York, NY: Scribner. A biography following Stewart's death gives an intimate account based on interviews and family cooperation.

Fishman, Jessica M. **1999**. "The Populace and the Police: Models of Social Control in Reality-Based Crime Television." *Critical Studies in Mass Communication*, Sept. 99, 16(3), p. 268. 21 pages. Focuses on the intra-genre diversity of reality-based crime television to the development of ideology on human action in the United States. Means of achieving law and order based on mythological models; interpretation and justification of myths by classic accounts; populist and progressive distinctions between "America's Most Wanted" and "Cops." [Copyright Ebscohost] "Cops" shows police as agents of criminal control while "America's Most Wanted" makes heroes of ordinary citizens [addendum by Dintrone]

Fiske, John, **1987**. *Television Culture.* London, England: Methuen. Discusses television as "bearer of meanings and pleasures" in society. This cultural studies approach talks about audiences, texts, characters, gender, and style.

Fiske, John. **1994**. *Media Matters: Everyday Culture and Political Change*. Minneapolis: University of Minnesota Press. A study of how the media (especially television) helps create the news and influences how the public thinks. Focuses on four stories that became "media events," including "Murphy Brown" and Dan Quayle.

Fiske, John, & John **Hartley**. **1978**. *Reading Television*. London, England: Methuen & Co. Ltd. One of the landmark books in television studies, as a separate discipline (within popular culture studies). Discusses various approaches (content analysis, semiotics, audience research, etc.) British emphasis.

Fitzgerald, Michael G., & Boyd **Magers**. **2002**. *Ladies of the Western: Interviews with Fifty-One More Actresses from Silent Era to the Television Westerns of the 1950s and 1960s*. Jefferson, NC: McFarland. A supplement to their 1999 work (see Magers & Fitzgerald). Arranged alphabetically by actress, these are interviews with women who played in western movies and television shows. Offers interesting insights.

Flower, Joe. **1991**. *Prince of the Magic Kingdom: Michael Eisner and the Re-making of Disney*. New York, NY: John Wiley & Sons. Only a few references to shows put on by the Disney Company.

Forbes, Bruce David, & Jeffrey **Mahan**, eds. **2000**. *Religion and Popular Culture in America*. Berkeley, CA: University of California Press. Discusses relationship of popular culture and religion. Includes essays on film, television, music, sports, and other aspects of pop culture.

Foreman, Joel, ed. **1997**. *The Other Fifties: Interrogating Mid-century American Icons*. Urbana: University of Illinois Press. Various writers discuss aspects of the 1950s to show it was not the innocent and happy era it is often portrayed as being. One section is devoted to television.

Fowles, Jeb. **1982**. *Television Viewers vs. Media Snobs: What TV Does for People*. New York, NY: Stein and Day. The effects of television viewing on audiences; author's outlook is positive (i.e., believes effect is good), opposes "media snobs."

Fowles, Jeb. **1992**. *Why Viewers Watch: A Re-appraisal of Television's Effects*. Newbury Park, CA: Sage Publications. An update of *Television Viewers vs. Media Snobs*.

Fox, Roy F. **2001**. *Mediaspeak: Three American Voices*. Westport, CN: Praeger. Explains three types of communication that dominate in America in recent times. Perpetuated by all types of media, these three are what the author calls doublespeak, salespeak, and sensationspeak. Though the book is not about entertainment television per se, there are some brief references to television programs as examples.

Frank, Reuven. **1991**. *Out of Thin Air: The Brief Wonderful Life of Network News*. New York, NY: Simon & Schuster. A history of NBC News by one of the leading figures in its development.

Frazer, June M., & Timothy C. **Frazer**. **1993**. "'Father Knows Best' and 'The Cosby Show': Nostalgia and the Sitcom Tradition." *Journal of Popular Culture*, Winter 93, 27(3), p. 163. 10 pages. Compares representations of family in the television programs "The Cosby Show" and "Father Knows Best." Portrayal of black and white middle-class families; inhibitions of sexual taboos and fifties decorum in "Father Knows Best"; differences in the representation of gender roles and relationships; reassurance on cooking being a female duty. [Copyright Ebscohost]

Freeman, Don. **1980**. *In a Flea's Navel: A Critic's Love Affair with Television*. San Diego, CA: A.S. Barnes & Company. A collection of short essays written by a well known television critic.

Friar, Ralph E., & Natasha A. **Friar**. **1972**. *The Only Good Indian ... The Hollywood Gospel*. New York, NY: Drama Book Specialties. Mostly devoted to the portrayal of Native Americans in film. There are some references to television programs.

Friedman, James, ed. **2002**. *Reality Squared: Televisual Discourse on the Real*. New Brunswick, NJ: Rutgers University Press. Scholars examine reality shows from several theoretical perspectives. Includes news events, sports, and "reality" shows, as well as analyzing some fictional shows in terms of their portrayal of real events.

Friedman, William J., & Janellen **Huttenlocher**. **1997**. "Memory for the Time of '60 Minutes' Stories and News Events." *Journal of Experimental Psychology/Learning, Memory & Cognition*, May 97, 23(3), p. 560. 10 pages. Examines distance-based memory judgments on long time scales of past and recent events in the "60 Minutes" television show. Comparison of contemporaneous events and news events. [Copyright Ebscohost]

Friendly, Fred W. **1967**. *Due to Circumstances Beyond Our Control*. New York, NY: Random House. Reminiscences of a TV producer most noted for news programs and working with Edward R. Murrow.

Fuller, Linda K. **1992**. *The Cosby Show: Audience, Impact, and Implications*. Westport, CT: Greenwood Press. Based on survey data, this classic study describes audience reaction to the show and what impact it has on beliefs and attitudes.

Fulton, Eileen. **1995**. *As My World Still Turns: The Uncensored Memoirs of America's Soap Opera Queen*. New York, NY: Birch Lane Press Book. An autobiography by the leading player on the soap opera, "As the World Turns."

Fultz, Jay. **1998**. *In Search of Donna Reed*. Iowa City, IA: University of Iowa Press. A biography of actress Donna Reed written by a film historian. Contrasts her private life and her public image.

Gabler, Neal, Frank Rich, & Joyce **Antler**. **2000**. *Television's Changing Image of American Jews*. New York, NY: American Jewish Committee and Norman Lear Center. Papers from a conference on the portrayal of American Jews on television.

Gallafent, Edward. **1994**. *Clint Eastwood: Filmmaker and Star*. New York, NY: Continuum. A biographical and critical account of Clint Eastwood and his films, with brief mention of television.

Gamman, Lorraine, & Margaret **Marshment**, eds. **1988**. *The Female Gaze: Women as Viewers of Popular Culture*. London, England: The Women's Press. A series of essays on how women look at women in popular culture, including television and how it influences them. Includes role, status, and body image issues.

Gardiner, Judith Kegan. **2000**. "South Park, Blue Men, Anality, and Market Masculinity." *Men & Masculinities*, Jan. 2000, 2(3), p. 251. 21 pages. Analyzes the "South Park" television cartoon show and the theatrical performance of The Blue Man Group as symptomatic of a configuration of masculinity in the United States. Theories of anality; how "South Park" and The Blue Man Group reflect market masculinity and consumer resistance; childishness, masculine and passive aggression of "South Park" and The Blue Man Group. [Copyright Ebscohost]

Gattuso, Greg. **1995**. *The Seinfeld Universe: The Entire Domain* (new and updated). Secaucus, NJ: Citadel Press Book. A book of interviews, best episodes, background information about the show, etc.

Gaunt, Philip, ed. **1993**. *Beyond Agendas: New Directions in Communication Research*. Westport, CN: Greenwood Press. A collection of essays from the Wichita Symposium. Includes both descriptions of types of research and some actual studies.

Gauntlett, David, & Annette Hill. **1999**. *TV Living: Television, Culture, and Everyday Life*. London: Routledge/British Film Institute. A study of British viewers experience with television based on a longitudinal diary study. Mostly covers British shows but some American shows are mentioned.

Gelbart, Larry. **1998**. *Laughing Matters: On Writing M*A*S*H, Tootsie, Oh, God!, and a Few Other Funny Things*. New York: Random House. This comedy writer talks about his career writing for television, movies, and theater. More memoir and a collection of some of his writings than a true autobiography.

Genge, N. E. **1995**. *The Unofficial X-Files Companion*. New York, NY: Crown Trade Paperbacks. Very detailed episode guides from the first two seasons. Also has trivia questions.

Gentejohann, Volker. **2000**. *Narratives from the Final Frontier: A Postcolonial Reading of the Original Star Trek Series*. Frankfurt, Germany: Peter Lang. A German scholar analyzes the original series in terms of postcolonial theory—a postmodern ideological reading of elitist vs. "popular."

Geraghty, Christine. **1991**. *Women and Soap Operas: A Study of Prime Time Soaps*. Cambridge, England: Polity Press. Mostly a study of British soap operas but some discussion of "Dallas" and "Dynasty."

Gerani, Gary. **1977**. *Fantastic Television* (with Paul H. Schulman). New York, NY: Harmony Books. A history of fantasy and science fiction on television. Gives facts, credits, summary, and brief episode guides for 13 series.

Gerrold, David. **1973**a. *The Trouble with Tribbles*. New York, NY: Ballantine Books. The writer of one of the most famous episodes of "Star Trek" describes in detail the making of the episode.

Gerrold, David. **1973**b. *The World of Star Trek*. New York, NY: Ballantine Books. The author of "Trouble with Tribbles" tells the story of "Star Trek." Includes information about how the show came about, the characters and cast, the fan culture and phenomenon, and other tidbits. Has a list of episodes of the original series with cast but no other information.

Gianakos, Larry James. **1978**. *Television Drama Series Programming, a Comprehensive Chronicle, 1959–1975*. Metuchen, NJ: Scarecrow Press. The first book in this series, even though not the first chronologically. The main part of the book is a listing by season of titles of episodes in drama series.

Gianakos, Larry James. **1980**. *Television Drama Series Programming, a Comprehensive Chronicle, 1947–1959.* Metuchen, NJ: Scarecrow Press. Following an overview and a schedule listing, this book gives titles of episodes in drama series arranged by season.

Gianakos, Larry James. **1981**. *Television Drama Series Programming, a Comprehensive Chronicle, 1975–1980.* Metuchen, NJ: Scarecrow Press. A supplement to the above two. Starts with some additional shows prior to 1975 and then chronological to 1980.

Gianakos, Larry James. **1983**. *Television Drama Series Programming, a Comprehensive Chronicle, 1980–1982.* Metuchen, NJ: Scarecrow Press. Updates and supplements above. Includes shows from earlier seasons, not previously done as well as 1980–1982.

Gianakos, Larry James. **1987**. *Television Drama Series Programming, a Comprehensive Chronicle, 1982–1984.* Metuchen, NJ: Scarecrow Press. Updates and supplements above titles.

Gianakos, Larry James. **1992**. *Television Drama Series Programming, a Comprehensive Chronicle, 1984–1986.* Metuchen, NJ: Scarecrow Press. Updates and supplements above titles.

Gilbert, Annie. **1976**. *All My Afternoons.* New York, NY: A&W Visual Library. A heavily illustrated descriptive book of major soap operas.

Gitlin, Todd. **1983**. *Inside Prime Time.* New York, NY: Pantheon Books. An often cited landmark study of prime time television with much behind-the-scenes insight into trying to create a hit show.

Gitlin, Todd, ed. **1986**. *Watching Television: A Pantheon Guide to Popular Culture.* New York, NY: Pantheon Books. Essays looking at television as a part of popular culture with emphasis on form and style across different genres.

Glick, Ira O., & Sidney J. **Levy**. **1962**. *Living with Television.* Chicago, IL: Aldine Publishing Company. Analysis of television programs and audiences. Indexed in "groups" appendix only.

Goethals, Gregor T. **1981**. *The TV Ritual: Worship at the Video Altar.* Boston, MA: Beacon Press. Views television as a new form of ritual with church-like attributes.

Goethals, Gregor T. **1990**. *Electronic Golden Calf: Images, Religion and the Making of Meaning.* Cambridge, MA: Cowley Publications. Discusses religious symbols and images. One chapter is devoted to images of religion on television.

Golden, Christopher, & Nancy **Holder**. **1998**. *Buffy, the Vampire Slayer: The Watcher's Guide.* New York, NY: Pocket Books. A guide to the show, giving the mythology, guide to the town, characters, behind-the-scenes information, and tidbits on the music. Also gives first two seasons episode guides.

Goldenson, Leonard. **1991**. *Beating the Odds* (written with Marvin J. Wolf). New York, NY: Charles Scribner's Sons. A history of the American Broadcasting Company by the "man who made it happen."

Gorman, Jerry, & Kirk **Calhoun**. **1994**. *The Name of the Game: The Business of Sports.* New York, NY: John Wiley & Sons. A discussion of how sports has become big business, with some chapters on the influence of television.

Gottfried, Martin. **1999**. *Balancing Act: The Authorized Biography of Angela Lansbury*. Boston, MA: Little, Brown and Company. A fairly extensive biography of this stage, screen, and television star, known by television viewers for her portrayal of Jessica Fletcher on "Murder, She Wrote."

Goulding, Jay. **1985**. *Empire, Aliens, and Conquest*. Toronto, Canada: Sisyphus Press. A sociologist critiques "Star Trek" in terms of societal norms, morality, social relations, political values, etc.

Graham, Jean E. **2000**. "Holodeck Masquing: Early Modern Genre Meets Star Trek." *Journal of Popular Culture*, Fall 2000, 34(2), p. 21. 7 pages. Focuses on the resemblance of the masque "Comus" to the television program "Star Trek." Main features of masques; information on the episodes of "Star Trek"; impact of "Star Trek" on its viewers. [Copyright Ebscohost]

Grammer, Kelsey. **1995**. *So Far....* New York, NY: Dutton. An autobiography of the star of "Frasier," discussing the many painful events in his life, as well as the high points.

Green, Joey. **1993**. *The Get Smart Handbook*. New York, NY: Collier Books. A book of facts, trivia and not, about the show. Includes an episode guide with brief summary, cast, notes, and "gadgets" used. Also rates the episodes.

Greenberg, Bradley S. **1980**. *Life on Television: Content Analysis of U.S. TV Drama*. Norwood, NJ: Ablex Publishing Corporation. A content analysis of the portrayal of ethnic groups, sex roles, families, and behavior on American television.

Greenberg, Bradley S., & Rick W. **Busselle**. **1996**. "Soap Operas and Sexual Activity: A Decade Later." *Journal of Communication*, Autumn 96, 46(4), p. 153. 7 pages. Analyzes sexual content in a sample of five 1994 day-time operas. Reference to a 1985 study of three of the same soap operas. [Copyright Ebscohost]

Greene, Eric. **1996**. *"Planet of the Apes" as American Myth: Race and Politics in the Films and Television Series*. Jefferson, NC: McFarland. Analyzes the movies and television series in terms of race and society. Also discusses the political context in which each movie and the series were made.

Greenwald, Jeff. **1998**. *Future Perfect: How Star Trek Conquered Planet Earth*. New York, NY: Viking. Studies "Star Trek" as a phenomenon, especially its worldwide impact.

Gregory, Chris. **2000**. *Star Trek: Parallel Narratives*. New York, NY: St. Martin's Press. Traces the "Star Trek" phenomenon and its dramatic universe which has become modern mythology. Also examines psychological, social and political themes in the shows.

Gresh, Lois H. & Robert **Weinberg**. **1999**. *The Computers of Star Trek*. New York, NY: Basic Books. A computer scientist and a science fiction writer collaborate on describing the computers on the shows and how they compare to today's computers.

Griffin, Merv. **1980**. *Merv: An Autobiography*. New York, NY: Simon and Schuster. An autobiography by this personality

Gripsrud, Justein. **1995**. *The Dynasty Years: Hollywood Television and Critical Media Studies*. London, England: Routledge. A scholarly study of the show—

origins, life and times, audience reception. Places show in center of media studies.

Groening, Matt. **1997**. *The Simpsons: A Complete Guide to Our Favorite Family.* New York, NY: HarperPerennial. The creator of the show uses cartoons, lots of color, many cross references, and many type faces to guide you through the episodes.

Gross, Edward. **1988**. *The Unofficial Tale of Beauty and the Beast.* Las Vegas, NV: Pioneer Books. A guide to the first season of the show, including cast biographies, interviews, and detailed episode summaries.

Gross, Edward. **1989**. *The Making of The Next Generation.* Las Vegas, NV: Pioneer Books. An early look at the sequel to the original series. Information about the origins and making of the show and interviews with key persons.

Gross, Larry. **2001**. *Up from Invisibility: Lesbians, Gay Men, and the Media in America.* New York, NY: Columbia University Press. Argues there have been advances in portraying gay people in the media. However, there are lingering controversies and stereotypes.

Gross, Larry, & James D. **Woods**, eds. **1999**. *The Columbia Reader on Lesbians and Gay Men in Media, Society, and Politics.* New York, NY: Columbia University Press. Begun as series of readings for a course in gay and lesbian studies. Course (and readings) covers many topics relating to gays and lesbians in society but emphasis is on mass media. Issues of identity and definitions of sexuality are examined. A large section is devoted to the influence of mass media and portrayals of gays and lesbians. Television is included.

Grover, Ron. **1991**. *The Disney Touch: How a Daring Management Team Revived an Entertainment Empire.* Homewood, IL: Business One Irwin. This story of Eisner and the Walt Disney Company includes references to shows Eisner was involved with at Paramount and at Disney.

Guida, Fred. **2000**. *A Christmas Carol and Its Adaptations: A Critical Examination of Dickens' Story and Its Productions on Screen and Television.* Jefferson, NC: McFarland. Although this mostly deals with made for television movies and theatrical films, there are some references to television series which used the theme from "A Christmas Carol."

Gunter, Barrie, & Mallory **Wober**. **1988**. *Violence on Television: What Viewers Think.* London, England: John Libbey & Company. Surveys television viewers on their opinions on violence on television. British emphasis.

Gunther, Marc. **1994**. *The House That Roone Built: The Inside Story of ABC News.* Boston, MA: Little, Brown and Company. The story of Roone Arledge, including sports and news programs on ABC.

Gunther, Marc, & Bill **Carter**. **1988**. *Monday Night Mayhem: The Inside Story of ABC's "Monday Night Football."* New York, NY: Beech Tree Books. A descriptive account of the origins, development and history of MNF to the mid 1980s.

Haag, Laurie L. **1993**. "Oprah Winfrey: The Construction of Intimacy in the Talk Show Setting." *Journal of Popular Culture*, Spring 93, 26(4), p. 115. 8 pages. Analyzes the evolution of television talk show host Oprah Winfrey's star persona. Girl talk and the women's talk show traditions; gender research on female friendship; evolution of the legend of Oprah; and female communication norms and behaviors. [Copyright Ebscohost]

Hack, Richard. **1999**. *Madness in the Morning: Life and Death in TV's Early Morning Ratings War*. Beverly Hills, CA: New Millennium Press. A television critic describes the history of early morning network shows. Behind the scenes information is gathered by interviewing those involved.

Hagen, Ingunn, & Janet **Wasko**, eds. **2000**. *Consuming Audiences: Production and Reception in Media Research*. Creskill, NJ: Hampton Press, Inc. A collection of scholarly essays on the research relating to audiences and the interaction between media production and audience reception. Television shows are mentioned in passing.

Hamamoto, Darell Y. **1989**. *Nervous Laughter: Television Situation Comedy and Liberal Democratic Ideology*. New York, NY: Praeger. An analysis of situation comedy which maintains that the shows espouse liberal democracy (neither right wing nor radical left).

Hamamoto, Darell Y. **1994**. *Monitored Peril: Asian Americans and the Politics of TV Representation*. Minneapolis: University of Minnesota Press. A thorough study of the portrayal of Asian Americans on television. Historical and contemporary; news programs and fiction.

Hanczor, Robert S. **1997**. "Articulation Theory and Public Controversy: Taking sides over NYPD Blue." *Critical Studies in Mass Communication*, March 97, 14(1), p. 1. 30 pages. Suggests a new way of looking at mass media's public controversies. Uses articulation theory to investigate the controversy surrounding "NYPD Blue."

Hanfling, Barrie. **2001**. *Westerns and the Trail of Tradition: A Year-by-Year History 1929–1962*. Jefferson, NC: McFarland. A year-by-year account of westerns from the beginning of the sound era until 1962. Mostly discusses motion pictures but there are some references to television westerns.

Hanley, Richard. **1997**. *The Metaphysics of Star Trek*. New York, NY: Basic Books. A philosopher looks at various aspects of "Star Trek," such as whether artificial life is life; transporting; combinations of beings; aliens; time travel; and other moral and philosophical dilemmas.

Hanson, Cynthia A. **1990**. "The Women of China Beach." *Journal of Popular Film & Television*, Winter 90, 17(4), p. 154. 10 pages. Focuses on the women of the television program "China Beach," a series about the American women in Vietnam during the Vietnam War. Feminist criticism of television and the show's concept as a product of men. [Copyright Ebscohost]

Haralovich, Mary Beth, & Lauren **Rabinovitz**. **1999**. *Television, History, and American Culture: Feminist Critical Essays*. Durham, NC: Duke University Press. Using feminist perspectives, media scholars, in a series of essays, discuss how television reflects and influences American culture and identity. Focus is on women as viewers, producers and images and how television has shaped our understanding of gender, power, race, ethnicity, and sexuality.

Hardy, Sarah, & Rebecca **Kukla**. **1999**. "A Paramount Narrative: Exploring Space on the Starship Enterprise." *Journal of Aesthetics & Art Criticism*, Spring 99, 57(2), p. 177. 15 pages. Explores the active, multiple space that is of "The Enterprise," as it defines and enables the fiction it contains in the television series "Star Trek: The Next Generation." [Copyright Ebscohost]

Harmon, Jim. **1992**. *Radio Mystery and Adventure and Its Appearances in Film, Television and Other Media*. Jefferson, NC: McFarland. Extensive discussion of some famous radio shows; gives brief sketches of these in other media, including television.

Harris, Cheryl, & Alison **Alexander**, eds. **1998**. *Theorizing Fandom: Fans, Subcultures, and Identity* (Hampton Press Communication Series). Creskill, NJ: Hampton Press, Inc. A scholarly multiple theory approach to fans as a subculture of audiences. Discusses the effects of social class and genre on fandom in the context of contemporary society. Many types of fans, including television, are included.

Harris, Richard Jackson. **1989**. *A Cognitive Psychology of Mass Communication*. Hillsdale, NJ: Lawrence Erlbaum Associates. A textbook for a class in mass communication psychology. Has chapter on group portrayals.

Harris, Richard Jackson. **1994**. *A Cognitive Psychology of Mass Communication* (2nd edition). Hillsdale, NJ: Lawrence Erlbaum Associates. Update of 1989 edition emphasizing the many changes in the world (breakup of Soviet Union, South Africa, etc.) and how the media influenced these changes.

Harris, Warren C. **1991**. *Lucy & Desi: The Legendary Love Story of Television's Most Famous Couple*. New York, NY: Simon & Schuster. Based on interviews with friends and colleagues, this is the story of Lucille Ball and Desi Arnaz as a couple.

Harrison, Dan, & Bioll **Habeeb**. **1994**. *Inside Mayberry*. New York, NY: Harper Perennial. Lots of information, mostly useful for trivia buffs about the Andy Griffith Show. Includes information on characters, music, chronology, awards, etc. Also contains an episode guide.

Harrison, Taylor, et al., eds. **1996**. *Enterprise Zones! Critical Positions on Star Trek*. Boulder, CO: Westview Press. Critical essays by scholars in a variety of fields on the "Star Trek" shows, movies, and phenomenon. Studies the text and the intersection between audiences and texts. Analyses include characters in context of race, gender, and sexuality; power relations; and pleasures (sexual, fantasies, other human emotions).

Haskins, Jim. **1984**. *Richard Pryor: A Man and His Madness*. New York, NY: Beaufort Books. A biography of this controversial comedian.

Hawes, William. **2001**. *Live Television Drama, 1946–1951*. Jefferson, NC: McFarland. A professor of communications gives a history and guide to live dramas aired on the networks between 1946 and 1951. Appendices list day by day shows.

Hawes, William. **2002**. *Filmed Television Drama, 1952–1958*. Jefferson, NC: McFarland. Explores the change from live drama to filmed drama. Describes several series and anthologies. Includes several appendices with lists of shows.

Heide, Margaret, J. **1995**. *Television Culture and Women's Lives: Thirtysomething and the Contradictions of Gender*. Philadelphia, PA: University of Pennsylvania Press. A feminist analysis of the show, detailing gender issues portrayed on the show and how women audiences responded to the show.

Heil, Douglas. **2001**. *Prime-Time Authorship: Works About and by Three TV Dramatists*. Syracuse, NY: Syracuse University Press. Analytical essays, interviews, and complete scripts for three successful television writers. This book is meant for students of television scriptwriting.

Heitland, Jon. **1987**. *The Man from U.N.C.L.E. Book: The Behind-the-Scenes Story of a Television Classic.* New York, NY: St. Martin's Press. This book gives information about all aspects of the show. Comments from actors, writers, directors, etc. Also includes an episode guide.

Heldenfels, R. D. **1994**. *Television's Greatest Year: 1954.* New York, NY: Continuum. Concentrates on the year 1954 as being the greatest year in television history, describing such shows as "Caesar's Hour," "Disneyland," "Tonight Show," McCarthy hearings, and "I Love Lucy."

Helford, Elyce Rae, ed. **2000**. *Fantasy Girls; Gender in the New Universe of Science Fiction and Fantasy Television.* Lanham, MD: Rowman & Littlefield Publishers. A collection of scholarly essays about the role of gender in science fiction and fantasy television. Emphasis is on shows of the 90s.

Heller, Lee E. **1997**. "The Persistence of Difference: Postfeminism, Popular Discourse, and Heterosexuality in Star Trek..." *Science Fiction Studies*, July 97, 24(2), p. 226. 19 pages. Discusses sexual relations and differences as well as gender identity, as it relates to "Star Trek." Details on individual cast members on "Star Trek." [Copyright Ebscohost]

Hendershot, Heather. **1998**. *Saturday Morning Censors: Television Regulation Before the V-Chip.* Durham, NC: Duke University Press. A study of children's television in the context of censorship. The theory is that censorship is not just prohibition but is a social process. The television show most extensively discussed is "Sesame Street."

Henderson, Katherine Usher, & Joseph Anthony **Mazzeo**, eds. **1990**. *Meanings of the Medium: Perspectives on the Art of Television.* New York, NY: Praeger. Essays by scholars from traditional humanities, rather than communications. Talks about television and society, television as an art, and television critics.

Henry, William A. **1992**. *The Great One: The Life and Legend of Jackie Gleason.* New York, NY: Doubleday. A journalist writes a fairly extensive biography of Gleason.

Hewitt, Don. **2001**. *Tell Me a Story: Fifty Years and 60 Minutes in Television.* New York, NY: Public Affairs. The producer of one of the most successful shows in television history recounts his experiences as a journalist and news producer.

Hiebert, Ray Eldon, ed. **1999**. *Impact of Mass Media: Current Issues* (fourth edition). New York, NY: Longman. A collection of essays by scholars, journalists and others on various aspects of mass media's impact on our society. Includes sections on power of mass media, First Amendment, business angles, ethics, political aspects, advertising, technology, as well as other topics.

Hiebert, Ray Eldon, & Carol **Reuss**. **1985**. *Impact of Mass Media: Current Issues.* New York, NY: Longman. The latest (as of 1985) thinking on mass media's influence on society. Various authors discuss sex, violence, women, minorities, religion, politics, etc. Heavy emphasis on news and the written press.

Hill, Doug, & Jeff **Weingrad**. **1986**. *Saturday Night: A Backstage History of "Saturday Night Live."* New York, NY: Beech Tree Books. A substantial book (500 pages) about the show and some behind-the-scenes tidbits.

Himmelstein, Hal. **1984**. *Television Myth and the American Mind*. New York, NY: Praeger. A critical history of television, concentrating on its mythic qualities. Covers all aspects of TV, including entertainment, news, sports, and religion. Many shows used as examples of the myth of American life as seen on television.

Himmelstein, Hal. **1994**. *Television Myth and the American Mind* (2nd edition). Westport, CN: Praeger. Update of the 1984 edition with additional newer shows used as examples.

Hinton, Laura. **1999**. *The Perverse Gaze of Sympathy: Sadomasochistic Sentiments from "Clarissa" to "Rescue 911."* Albany, NY: State University of New York. A scholarly look at sentimental novels, films, and television and their relation to male desire with authoritarian, even sadomasochistic, overtones.

Hirsch, Irwin, & Cara **Hirsch**. **2000**. "A Look at Our Dark Side." *Journal of Popular Film & Television*, Fall 2000, 28(3), p. 116. 8 pages. Speculates about the possible factors that led to the success of the television program "Seinfeld." Characters of the show; cross-cultural issues that the show touches; similarities and differences of the characters and description of each character in terms of immaturity, amorality, narcissism, unrelatedness and general ill will toward others. [Copyright Ebscohost]

Hofstede, David. **1998**. *The Dukes of Hazzard: The Unofficial Companion*. Los Angeles, CA: Renaissance Books. Information about the show including cast interviews, production, trivia, and episode guides.

Hollis, Richard, & Brian **Sibley**. **1988**. *The Disney Studio Story*. London, England: Octopus Books. Well illustrated, quite comprehensive account of Disney Studios from its origins. Extensive filmography.

Hollows, Joanne. **2000**. *Feminism, Femininity, and Popular Culture*. Manchester, ENG: Manchester University Press. Identifies key feminist approaches to popular culture from the 1960s to the 1990s. Case studies are used, including soap operas. Feminism is often based on a rejection of both popular culture and femininity.

Holtzman, Linda. **2000**. *Media Messages: What Film, Television, and Popular Music Teach Us about Race, Class, Gender, and Sexual Orientation*. Armonk, NY: M.E. Sharpe. An academic explores issues addressed in the title, admitting that she cannot be completely objective about what is also personal for her. Discusses "the other" as seen in the media.

Holtzman, William. **1979**. *Seesaw: A Dual Biography of Anne Bancroft and Mel Brooks*. Garden City, NY: Doubleday. A back and forth dual biography highlighting the two careers and the relationship of the couple.

Horowitz, Susan. **1997**. *Queens of Comedy: Lucille Ball, Phyllis Diller, Carol Burnett, Joan Rivers, and the New Generation of Funny Women*. Amsterdam, Netherlands: Gordon and Breach Publishers. Using interviews and analysis, an expert in comedy communication discusses comediennes and their impact on the image of women in society.

Horton, Andrew. **2000**. *Laughing Out Loud: Writing the Comedy-Centered Screenplay*. Berkeley, CA: University of California Press. A how-to guide to writing comedy for film and television but with much analysis, theory and history of comedy in general. Examples are given. The author is a professor as well as a screenwriter.

Horton, Andrew, & Stuart Y. **McDougal**, eds. **1998**. *Play It Again, Sam: Retakes on Remakes*. Berkeley: University of California Press. A collection of essays by scholars on remakes of films. Using a variety of film and cultural theories, the remake is discussed from various angles and viewpoints. Included are discussions of remakes in other media, including television.

Howe, Michael J.A., ed. **1983**. *Learning from Television: Psychological and Educational Research*. London, England: Academic Press. Essays and research studies on the educational uses of television.

Howitt, Dennis. **1982**. *The Mass Media and Social Problems* (International Series in Experimental Social Psychology, volume 2). Oxford, England: Pergamon Press. Using models of mass communications research, this book discusses issues such as minority portrayal, sex and violence, and health and education in relation to mass media, including television.

Hubert, Susan J. **1999**. "What's Wrong with This Picture? The Politics of Ellen's Coming Out Party." *Journal of Popular Culture*, Fall 99, 33(2), p. 31. 6 pages. Discusses the controversy regarding an episode of the television program "Ellen" in which actress Ellen DeGeneres portrays a lesbian. Actions taken by various organizations regarding the show; major component behind the complexity of the show; problems behind the politics of the episode. [Copyright Ebscohost]

Hughes, David. **2001**. *The Complete Lynch*. London, England: Virgin Publishing. A companion book to David Lynch's work in motion pictures and on television. Based on interviews, the book attempts to probe the mind of this cult director.

Huskey, Melynda. **1993**. "Twin Peaks: Rewriting the Sensation Novel." *Literature Film Quarterly*, 21(4), p. 248. 7 pages. Focuses on the use of sensational paradigm to understand the complexities and contradictions of the television series "Twin Peaks." Emergence of the sensation novel with the publication of Wilkie Collin's *The Woman in White*; characteristic sensation text for analysis; connection of BOB with all other criminal goings-on in the series; show's reliance on the supernatural. [Copyright Ebscohost]

Huston, Aletha C., et al. **1992**. *Big World, Small Screen: The Role of Television in American Society*. Lincoln: University of Nebraska Press. Based on a study of literature on the effects of television. Study conducted by a task force of the American Psychological Association.

Illouz, Eva. **1999**. "That Shadowy Realm of the Interior: Oprah Winfrey and Hamlet's Glass." *International Journal of Cultural Studies*, April 99, 2(1), p. 109. 23 pages. The purpose of this paper is to address a simple question, obfuscated by the public outrage that is ritually poured over talk shows: what are talk shows about? what makes them such a popular cultural form? what segment of the contemporary imagination do they capture? Conversely, what makes talk shows the target for the elite outcry that they cheapen and threaten cultural values? Argues that the cultural appeal of talk shows resides in the fact that they make sense of the profound transformation of the family in the late modern era... [Copyright Ebscohost]

Innes, Sherrie A. **1999**. *Tough Girls: Women Warriors and Wonder Women in Popular Culture*. Philadelphia: University of Pennsylvania Press. A study of women in mass media that are portrayed as "tough" and how this contrasts with tough men. All media is covered, including television.

Inniss, Leslie B., & Joe R. **Feagin**. **1995**. "The Cosby Show: The View from the Black Middle Class." *Journal of Black Studies*, July 95, 25(6), p. 692. 20 pages. Discusses the views by Afro-American middle class families on the television program "The Cosby Show." Criticisms of the show; image portrayed of Afro-American families in the show; impact of the show on Afro-American audiences; show's failure to address social issues. [Copyright Ebscohost]

Intintoli, Michael James. **1984**. *Taking Soaps Seriously: The World of "Guiding Light."* New York, NY: Praeger. A scholarly study of the soap opera's production, emphasizing cultural and social aspects. Analyzes it more from the production angle than from content.

Isaacs, Susan. **1999**. *Brave Dames and Wimpettes: What Women Are Really Doing on Page and Screen* (The Library of Contemporary Thought). New York, NY: The Ballantine Publishing Group. A best-selling author writes a book length essay on portrayals of women in mass media. Some television shows are included.

Jackson, Harold. **1982**. *From "Amos 'n' Andy" to "I Spy": Chronology of Blacks in Prime Time Network Television Programming, 1950–1964* (Ph.D. Dissertation, University of Michigan). A relatively early study of the portrayal of African Americans on television.

Jackson, John A. **1997**. *American Bandstand: Dick Clark and the Making of a Rock 'n' Roll Empire*. New York, NY: Oxford University Press. Most of the book is a discussion of the "American Bandstand" show, its influences, history, behind-the-scenes, etc. Because Dick Clark's career is so tied in with the show, other shows of his are also mentioned.

Jackson, Ronald. **1994**. *Classic TV Westerns: A Pictorial History*. New York, NY: Citadel Press Books. Very brief descriptions of shows, giving credits and when broadcast. Heavily illustrated.

Jacobs, Will. **1983**. *The Beaver Papers: The Story of the "Lost Season" and Gerold Jones*. New York, NY: Crown Publishers. Parodies of "Leave It to Beaver" script summaries as if they were written by famous authors.

James, Cathy L. **1991**. *Soap Opera Mythology and Racial Ethnic Social Change: An Analysis of African America, Asian/Pacific American and Mexican/Hispanic American Storylines During the 1980s* (Ph.D. Dissertation, University of California San Diego). Focuses on how images of various ethnic groups (see title) have changed in soap operas.

Jankowski, Gene F., & David C. **Fuchs**. **1995**. *Television Today and Tomorrow: It Won't Be What You Think*. New York, NY: Oxford University Press. An overview of programming, business, and technical aspects of television today and a look at future developments.

Jarvik, Laurence. **1997**. *PBS: Behind the Screen*. Rocklin, CA: Prima Publishing. A critical history of public broadcasting from a conservative viewpoint, arguing that PBS has a liberal agenda and should not be subsidized by the government. Favors a "free market" approach to public broadcasting.

Jarvis, Robert M., & Paul R. **Joseph**, eds. **1998**. *Prime Time Law: Fictional Television's Legal Narrative*. Durham, NC: Carolina Academic Press. Describes the portrayal of lawyers and law (including detectives) on television from the 1950s through the 1990s.

Javna, John. **1985**. *Cult TV: A Viewer's Guide to the Shows America Can't Live Without!* New York, NY: St. Martin's Press. A non-scholarly description of television shows that have developed a cult following. Some interesting trivia and anecdotes.

Javna, John. **1988**. *The Best of TV Sitcoms*. New York, NY: Harmony Books. A book full of interesting tidbits with some critical comments and rankings of situation comedies.

Jenkins, Henry. **1992**. *Textual Poachers: Television Fans as Participatory Culture*. New York, NY: Routledge. A study of media fans and their cultures, with emphasis on "Star Trek" and "Beauty and the Beast."

Jenrette, Jerra, Sherrie **McIntosh**, & Suzanne **Winterberger**. **1999**. "Carlotta!: Changing Images of Hispanic-American Women in Daytime Soap Operas." *Journal of Popular Culture*, Fall 99, 33(2), p. 37. 12 pages. Examines the varying roles and changing images of Hispanic-American female characters cast in daytime soap operas. Major breakthrough for Hispanic-Americans. Views on a female character; aspects of ethnic women. Background on several daytime soap operas. [Copyright Ebscohost]

Jhally, Sut, & Justin **Lewis**. **1992**. *Enlightened Racism: "The Cosby Show," Audiences and the Myth of the American Dream*. Boulder, CO: Westview Press. Two scholars discuss how television influences the way we think, especially about race. Uses "The Cosby Show" as the case study. Claims that despite what seems progressive, shows like this actually encourage "enlightened racism."

Jindra, Michael. **1994**. "Star Trek Fandom as a Religious Phenomenon." *Sociology of Religion*, Spring 94, 55(1), p. 27. 25 pages. Presents an ethnographic exploration of "Star Trek" fandom. History and practice of the fans themselves, on computer networks, at conventions and in tourism. [Copyright Ebscohost]

Johason, Shane. **1989**. *Star Trek: The Worlds of the Federation*. New York, NY: Pocket Books. An illustrated guide to the planets and aliens of "Star Trek."

Johnson, Carla. **1994**. "Luckless in New York: The Schlemiel and the Schlimazl in Seinfeld." *Journal of Popular Film & Television*, Fall 94, 22(3), p. 116. 9 pages. Traces the Jewish influences in the storyline and philosophy of the television show "Seinfeld." Similarities between the program's characters and the schlimazl and schlemiel of Yiddish and Jewish folklore; analysis of the show's popularity among the American public. [Copyright Ebscohost]

Johnston, Carla Brooks. **2000**. *Screened Out: How the Media Control Us and What We Can Do About It*. Armonk, NY: M.E. Sharpe. A mass media scholar argues that corporations dictate what we see on television and therefore influence how we think. Media conglomerates screen out the public from genuine communication. Selling is more important than free speech. Urges media literacy as a counter-acting force.

Jones, Gerard. **1992**. *Honey, I'm Home! Sitcoms: Selling the American Dream*. New York, NY: Grove Weidenfeld. An often cited important analysis of situation comedy throughout television history. Discusses how the shows "sell the American dream."

Josefsberg, Milt. **1977**. *The Jack Benny Show.* New Rochelle, NY: Arlington House. An exclusive biography of Jack Benny with much information about the television shows and the people whom Jack worked with.

Joseph, Franz. **1975**. *Star Fleet Technical Manual.* Toronto, Canada: Ballantine Books.

Joshel, Sandra R., Margaret **Malamu**, & Donald T. **McGuire**, Jr., eds. **2001**. *Imperial Projections: Ancient Rome in Modern Popular Culture.* Baltimore, MD: Johns Hopkins Press. Scholars discuss the portrayal of Rome (mainly the empire) in popular culture (film, literature, television, etc). Some prime time shows are mentioned in passing.

Joyce, Ed. **1988**. *Prime Times, Bad Times.* New York, NY: Doubleday. Memoir of an active participant in CBS News, including being president from 1983 to 1986.

Joyner, Patricia, & Joseph R. **Dominick**. **1994**. "Pulp Pulpits: Self-Disclosure on Donahue." *Journal of Communication*, Autumn 94, 44(4), p. 74. 24 pages. Examines the reasons why people choose to self-disclose on the United States television talk show program "Donahue." Examination of the role of television in their lives prior to disclosure; corroboration of decision by evangelical fervor; counter hegemonic struggle. Summary of extensive literature concerning self-disclosure; introduction of research concepts; relationship between disclosure and mental health. [Copyright Ebscohost]

Kachmar, Diane C. **2002**. *Roy Scheider: A Film Biography.* Jefferson, NC: McFarland. Chronicles Scheider's life and career, with filmography.

Kalat, David P. **1998**. *Homicide: Life on the Street, the Unofficial Companion.* Los Angeles, CA: Renaissance Books. A critical guide to the show, including cast, production crew, and a bibliography. Detailed episode guide with commentary, highlights, and notes as well as cast and plot summary.

Kaleta, Kenneth C. **1993**. *David Lynch.* New York, NY: Twayne Publishers. A critical account of Lynch's works with a chapter on "Twin Peaks."

Kalisch, Philip A., Beatrice J. **Kalisch**, & Margaret **Scobey**. **1983**. *Images of Nurses on Television.* New York, NY: Springer Publishing Company. "Chronicles and analyzes the development of the image of nurses and nursing on television."

Kalter, Suzy. **1986**. *The Complete Book of Dallas: Behind the Scenes at the World's Favorite Television Program.* New York, NY: Harry N. Abrams, Inc. This well-illustrated book describes the creation, background, themes and "the making" of this important daytime soap opera. Also includes synopses of the episodes.

Kalter, Suzy. **1988**. *The Complete Book on M*A*S*H.* New York, NY: Abradale Press. After a brief introduction to the origins of the show and the cast, gives summaries, year by year of the episodes.

Kamilipour, Yahya R., & Theresa **Carilli**, eds. **1998**. *Cultural Diversity and the U.S. Media.* Albany, NY: State University of New York Press. A group of scholars explore media portrayals of various racial and ethnic groups.

Kaminsky, Stuart M. **1985**. *American Television Genres* (with Jeffrey M. Mahan).

Chicago, IL: Nelson-Hall Publishers. Investigates ways of classifying television programs by type and shows analytical approaches to these genres.

Kanfer, Stefan. **2000**. *Groucho: The Life and Times of Julius Henry Marx*. New York, NY: Alfred A. Knopf. A biography of the most famous Marx brother.

Kapell, Matthew. **2000**. "Speakers for the Dead: Star Trek, the Holocaust, and the Representation of Atrocity." *Extrapolation*, Summer 2000, 41(2), p. 104. 11 pages. Examines the thematic content of the science fiction television program "Star Trek: Deep Space Nine." Representation of death and atrocity in the TV program; allusions drawn from the period of World War Two. Evocation of the Jewish culture to the characters of the Bajorans and comparison between the Bajoran Holocaust and the Jewish Holocaust. [Copyright Ebscohost]

Kaplan, E. Ann, ed. **1983**. *Regarding Television: Critical Approaches, an Anthology*. Los Angeles, CA: American Film Institute. Critical essays by film and humanities scholars using various theoretical approaches (psychoanalytic, semiotic, feminist, etc.). Soap operas are the focus of three chapters.

Kapsis, Robert E. **1992**. *Hitchcock: The Making of a Reputation*. Chicago, IL: University of Chicago Press. An account of Hitchcock's works and how each added to his growing reputation.

Kassel, Michael B. **1993**. *America's Favorite Radio Station: WKRP in Cincinnati*. Bowling Green, OH: Bowling Green State University Press. A descriptive and critical account of "WKRP" with quotes from personnel involved. Includes some information about other shows they were involved with.

Katz, Jon. **1997**. *Media Rants: Postpolitics in the Digital Nation*. San Francisco, CA: Hardwired. Comments from "the Web's first interactive columnist," a contributing editor for *Wired*, about all aspects of media with emphasis on technology. Some television programs are mentioned.

Kaveney, Roz, ed. **2001**. *Reading the Vampire Slayer: The Unofficial Critical Companion to Buffy and Angel*. London, England: I.B. Tauris & Co. A collection of scholarly essays on various aspects (settings, feminism, characterizations, etc.) of the two shows. Includes episode guides.

Keller, James R. **2002**. *Queer (un) Friendly Film and Television*. Jefferson, NC: McFarland. Studies recent film and television depictions of homosexuality. Takes an issue approach (partnerships, violence, AIDS, etc.).

Kellner, Douglas. **1990**. *Television and the Crisis of Democracy*. Boulder, CO: Westview Press. Discusses the relationship of politics and television. Creates a critical theory of television and shows that there is a need for more democracy in television broadcasting.

Kellner, Douglas. **1995**. *Media Culture: Cultural Studies, Identity, and Politics Between the Modern and the Postmodern*. London: Routledge. Analyzes the nature and effects of contemporary film, television, music, etc. Argues that media culture is the dominant one which socializes us and provides our identity.

Kellner, Douglas. **1999**. "The X-Files and the Aesthetics and Politics of Postmodern Pop." *Journal of Aesthetics & Art Criticism*, Spring 99, 57(2), p. 161. 15 pages. Examines the aesthetics of postmodernism evident in the television program "The X-Files."

Kelly, Richard. **1984**. *The Andy Griffith Show* (revised edition). Winston-Salem,

NC: John F. Blair. A book written by a professor which has some analysis of the show, rather than just descriptions and trivia. Brief description of episodes.

Kendall, Frances Lillian. **1989**. *Gender Differences in the Display of Anger on Prime Time Television* (Ph.D. Dissertation, University of Missouri—Columbia). 1989. Investigates how anger is shown on prime time television and any gender differences. There were many displays of anger but they were unrelated to stereotypes of gender.

Kendrick, Alexander. **1969**. *Prime Time: The Life of Edward R. Murrow*. Boston, MA: Little, Brown and Company. An extensive biography of the newsman.

Kessler, Judy. **1992**. *Inside Today: The Battle for the Morning*. New York, NY: Villard Books. The talent coordinator for "The Today Show" provides an inside look at the show and the war for the morning ratings.

Keyes, Daniel Joseph. **1997**. *The Performance of Testimonial Television on Daytime Talk Shows* (Ph.D. Dissertation, York University, Canada). Considers cultural significances and political implications of discourse on daytime talk shows.

Kidd-Hewitt, David, & Richard **Osborne**, eds. **1995**. *Crime and the Media: The Post-Modern Spectacle*. London: Pluto Press. A series of essays discussing mass media's influence on crime from a post-modern perspective. Emphasis is British. Includes news and entertainment programs.

Kim, L.S. **1999**. "Invisible and Undocumented: The Latina Maid on Network Television." *Aztlan*, Spring 99, 24(1), p. 107. 22 pages. Investigates the representation of Latina maids on network television in the United States. Focus on the programs "I Married Dora," "The Rosa Lopez Hearing," and "Designing Women." Latina maid as a violation of the law and of middle class family values. [Copyright Ebscohost]

Kinder, Marsha, ed. **1999**. *Kids' Media Culture*. Durham, NC: Duke University Press. A series of scholarly chapters on aspects of mass media that is geared towards children. Discusses the conflict between researchers, advocates, and critics versus producers and advertisers. Also addresses other issues, such as violence, gender portrayal and feminist influence. Deals more with traditional media as opposed to digital media.

King, Norman. **1987**. *Everybody Loves Oprah! Her Remarkable Life Story*. New York, NY: William Morrow and Company. A biography of Oprah Winfrey, one of the most successful talk show hosts and African American woman.

Klobas, Laurie. **1988**. *Disability Drama in Television and Film*. Jefferson, NC: McFarland. Describes television programs (movies, episodes from series, etc.) that dealt with various types of disabilities.

Kolodny, Annette. **1996**. "'60 Minutes' at the University of Arizona: The Polemic Against Tenure." *New Literary History*, Autumn 96, 27(4), p. 679. 26 pages. Highlights the attack made by the "60 Minutes" television program against faculty tenure in the University of Arizona. Popularized misconceptions about large research institutions; sensationalization of the necessity of tenure as a safeguard for academic freedom and absence of a real polemic against tenure. [Copyright Ebscohost]

Koppel, Ted, & Kyle **Gibson**. **1996**. *Nightline: History in the Making and the*

Making of Television. New York, NY: Times Books. The emcee and a former producer of the show reveal how the show started and gives backstage insights. Includes excerpts from some of the interviews.

Korzeniowska, Victoria B. **1996**. "Engaging with Gender: Star Trek's 'Next Generation'." *Journal of Gender Studies*, March 96, 5(1), p. 19. 7 pages. Examines the representation of gender roles in the television program "Star Trek: The Next Generation" and explores the concept of gender perpetuated by the series. Series' moves towards androgyny and sexual equality; perpetuation of the prescriptive notion of gender-stereotyped behavior for both sexes. [Copyright Ebscohost]

Kottak, Conrad Phillip. **1990**. *Prime-Time Society: An Anthropological Analysis of Television and Culture.* Belmont, CA: Wadsworth Publishing Company. Examines television from an anthropological perspective. Compares the social context and cultural effects of TV in Brazil and in the United States.

Kovach, Bill, & Tom **Rosenstiel**. **1999**. *Warp Speed: America in the Age of Mixed Media.* New York, NY: Century Foundation Press. Two press experts describe how news gathering has changed—more news but less complete and often unreliable. The speed of getting news out is overwhelming the need to check for accuracy. This leads to the public not knowing what to believe. The Clinton-Lewinsky scandal is the focus of this book but other media stories are also covered.

Krampner, Jon. **1997**. *The Man in the Shadows: Fred Coe and the Golden Age of Television.* Brunswick, NJ: Rutgers University Press. A biography of a man behind the scenes during television's so-called "golden age" (the 1950s) of shows like "Playhouse 90," "Studio One," etc.

Krauss, Lawrence M. **1995**. *The Physics of Star Trek.* New York, NY: Basic Books. Analyzes the "Star Trek" movies and the television programs in light of real physics. Shows what is possible and probable and what is pure fiction.

Kreitzer, Larry. **1996**. "The Cultural Veneer of Star Trek." *Journal of Popular Culture*, Fall 96, 30(2), p. 1. 28 pages. Examines the cultural context of the television series "Star Trek." Indication of the program's literary inheritance. [Copyright Ebscohost]

Kulzer, Dina-Marie. **1992**. *Television Series Regulars of the Fifties and Sixties in Interview.* Jefferson, NC: McFarland. Interviews with 22 actors and actresses who appeared in popular series in the fifties and sixties.

Kuney, Jack. **1990**. *Take One: Television Directors on Directing.* New York, NY: Greenwood Press. Interviews with directors of television programs such as "I Love Lucy," "Sesame Street," and "The Today Show."

Kutulas, Judy. **1998**. "Do I Look Like a Chick?: Men, Women, and Babies on Sitcom Maternity Stories." *American Studies*, Summer 98, 39(2), p. 13. 20 pages. Focuses on the issue of maternity and child birth in situation comedies on television. Description of the changes in the way the issue was handled during the 1950s and the 1990s; Reference to the '"I Love Lucy" show and the "Step by Step" comedies; portrayal of the males in these episodes; reflection of social changes in comedies. [Copyright Ebscohost]

Lafky, Sue. **1999/2000**. "Gender, Power, and Culture in the Televisual World of

Twin Peaks: A Feminist Critique." *Journal of Film & Video*, Fall 99/Winter 2000, 51(3/4), p. 5. 15 pages. Focuses on a feminist criticism on the representation of gender, power and culture in the mystery television series "Twin Peaks" in the United States. Decline of the ratings after the mystery of the death of Laura Palmer was solved; characterization of the heroine; emphasis on a visual style contrasting dark and light; and difference in gender treatment. [Copyright Ebscohost]

Lagon, Mark P. **1993**. "We Owe It to Interfere: Star Trek and U.S. Statecraft in the 1960s and 1990s." *Extrapolation*, Fall 93, 34(3), p. 251. 14 pages. Discusses exploration of metaphors of American foreign policy during the 20th century in the television series, "Star Trek." Star Fleet's interference with internal affairs of other planets; central themes in "Star Trek" reflect American foreign policies. [Copyright Ebscohost]

Landay, Lori. **1999**. "Millions 'Love Lucy': Commodification and the Lucy Phenomenon." *NWSA Journal*. Summer 99, 11(2), p. 25. 23 pages. Examines the conflicts and anxieties about consumption and commodity in the television program "I Love Lucy" in the United States. Impact of the Lucy phenomenon on the mass consumer culture ideology; articulations of gender and middle-class life in the postwar era; presentations of private solutions to public problems in the program. [Copyright Ebscohost]

Lane, Philip J. **2001**. "The Existential Condition of Television Crime Drama." *Journal of Popular Culture*, Spring 2001, 34(4), p. 137. 15 pages. Examines the television crime series "Homicide: Life on the Streets" and "NYPD Blue." Existential themes portrayed by the programs and a review of prior television series which contain existential themes. [Copyright Ebscohost]

Lavery, David, ed. **1995**. *Full of Secrets: Critical Approaches to Twin Peaks*. Detroit, MI: Wayne State University Press. Series of essays giving critical interpretations (post-modern, semiotics, feminist, etc.) of "Twin Peaks." Some mention of other shows.

Lavery, David, Angela **Hague**, & Marla **Cartwright**, eds. **1996**. *"Deny All Knowledge": Reading the X-Files*. Syracuse, NY: Syracuse University Press. A collection of essays by scholars analyzing various aspects of the show—its popularity, its fandom, its mythology, its gender aspects, and how it reflects the times.

Lazere, Donald, ed. **1987**. *American Media and Mass Culture: Left Perspectives*. Berkeley, CA: University of California Press. A series of essays from a leftist viewpoint on various aspects of mass media, including television.

Leamer, Lawrence. **1989**. *King of the Night: The Life of Johnny Carson*. New York, NY: William Morrow & Company. A fairly extensive (over 400 pages) biography of the "Tonight Show" host.

Lechner, Jack. **2000**. *Can't Take My Eyes Off of You*. New York, NY: Crown Publishers. A film producer locked himself at home for a week and watched 12 TVs for 16 hours a day. This repeats an experiment done by Charles Sopkin in the 1960s. This book recounts his experiences.

Ledwon, Lenora. **1993**. "Twin Peaks and the Television Gothic." *Literature Film Quarterly*, 21(4), p. 260. 11 pages. Focuses on the Gothic elements of the television series "Twin Peaks."Gothic literature and film. Television programs with

Gothic elements; combination of television and the Gothic novel; definition of Television Gothic; Gothic devices in "Twin Peaks"; device of the Double. Narrative structure and Television Gothic; use of a domestic technological device; standard Gothic complaints. [Copyright Ebscohost]

Lefcowitz, Eric. **1989**. *The Monkees Tale.* San Francisco, CA: Last Gasp. Description of the show and the group and its members. Includes a list (no details) of episodes, a filmography and a discography; Interviews with key people.

Leibman, Nina C. **1995**. *Living Room Lectures: The Fifties Family in Film and Television.* Austin: University of Texas Press. A study of film and television in the late 1950s and early 1960s in the context of the times. The major part of the book is devoted to analyzing the representation of the American family in film and TV.

Leiby, Bruce R., & Linda F. **Leiby**. **2001**. *A Reference Guide to Television's "Bonanza."* "Jefferson, NC: McFarland. Consists of a history of the show; detailed episode guides, and information about the cast of this long running series.

Lemay, Harding. **2000**. *Eight Years in Another World.* New York, NY: Athenaeum. An account by the writer of the soap opera of his experiences working on it.

Lembo, Ron. **2000**. *Thinking Through Television.* Cambridge, England: Cambridge University Press. Investigates American television viewing habits via interviews, observations, and the literature. Emphasizes social aspects of viewing and shows that TV is not just a powerful influence but that viewers interact with it in different ways. Specific shows are mentioned when discussing reactions of viewers to television.

Leno, Jay. **1996**. *Leading with My Chin.* New York, NY: Harper Collins. An account of his professional life with many anecdotes.

Lentz, Harris M. **1997**. *Television Westerns Episode Guides: All United States Series, 1949–1996.* Jefferson, NC: McFarland. Brief but complete episode guides to westerns during time period in title.

Leonard, Bill. **1987**. *In the Storm of the Eye: A Lifetime at CBS.* New York, NY: G.P. Putnam's Sons. A president of CBS News talks about his experiences.

Leonard, John. **1997**. *Smoke and Mirrors: Violence, Television, and Other American Cultures.* New York, NY: The New Press. A critic takes a balanced view of the social aspects of television, claiming that it is not completely innocent of influence but bemoaning the hysterical recent reaction to violence, etc. He shows that there is much good television, both in quality and in message and that it reflects our society as well as influencing it.

Leonard, Sheldon. **1995**. *And the Show Goes On: Broadway and Hollywood Adventures.* New York, NY: Limelight Editions. An autobiography by one of television's well-known producers, with anecdotes about the shows he was involved with.

Lesher, Stephan. **1982**. *Media Unbound: The Impact of Television Journalism on the Public.* Boston, MA: Houghton Mifflin Company. An analysis of television news and news programs, with greatest attention paid to "60 Minutes."

Lesser, Harvey. **1977**. *Television and the Preschool Child: A Psychological Theory of Instruction and Curriculum Development.* New York, NY: Academic Press. Only show covered is "Sesame Street," but it is covered extensively.

Lester, Paul Martin, ed. **1996**. *Images That Injure: Pictorial Stereotypes in the Media.* Westport, CN: Praeger. A collection of articles by communication experts on portrayals of various groups in the media and how this leads to unfair stereotypes. Emphasizes news and advertising rather than television entertainment programs.

Levinson, Richard, & William **Link**. **1981**. *Stay Tuned: An Inside Look at the Making of Prime-Time Television.* New York, NY: St. Martin's Press. Well-known television writers ("Columbo," "Mannix," "Murder, She Wrote") discuss indepth the creation, production, and writing of shows they were involved with.

Levinson, Richard, & William **Link**. **1986**. *Off Camera: Conversations with the Makers of Prime-Time Television.* New York, NY: New American Library. Two famous television writers and producers interview writers, directors, producers, actors, etc. Gives some insights into how series were created and produced.

Levy, Shawn. **1996**. *King of Comedy: The Life and Art of Jerry Lewis.* New York, NY: St. Martins Press. A film critic explores the life and work of the famous comedian.

Lewis, Justin. **1991**. *The Ideological Octopus: An Exploration of Television and Its Audience.* New York, NY: Routledge. Discussion of audience research and what it shows regarding the influence of television.

Lewis, Marlo, & Mina Bess **Lewis**. **1979**. *Prime Time.* Los Angeles, CA: J.P. Tarcher, Inc. A co-producer of "Toast of the Town" (Ed Sullivan) and his wife describe the early days of television.

Lichter, S. Robert, Linda S. **Lichter**, & Stanley **Rothman**. **1991**. *Watching America.* New York, NY: Prentice Hall Press. Based on an exhaustive survey of prime time shows since the 1950s, describes life as seen on television and compares it with reality.

Lichter, S. Robert, Linda S. **Lichter**, & Stanley **Rothman**. **1994**. *Prime Time: How TV Portrays American Culture.* Washington, DC: Regnery Publishing Co. A comprehensive study of over 1,000 shows to see how life in the U.S. is portrayed on television. Authors claim that this portrayal is not an accurate image of the reality.

Liebes, Tamar. **1992**. "Television, Parents, and the Political Socialization of Children." *Teachers College Record*, Fall 92, 94(1), p. 73. 14 pages. Comments on the impact of television in early, informal learning. Imagining television as a surrogate parent; study of the decoding of the worldwide hit program "Dallas" in the homes of families from different cultural background; work of Elihu Katz. [Copyright Ebscohost]

Liebes, Tamar, & Elihu **Katz**. **1990**. *The Export of Meaning. Cross-Cultural Readings of "Dallas."* New York, NY: Oxford University Press. Describes how "Dallas" is viewed outside of the United States. Through interviews, describes what meaning values and lessons the show conveys.

Lindheim, Richard D., & Richard A. **Blum**. **1991**. *Inside Television Producing.* Boston, MA: Focal Press. Based on interviews with those in the business, this is a how-to on producing. Extensive discussion of "Coach" and "Law and Order."

Lisanti, Tom, & Louis **Paul**. **2002**. *Film Fatales: Women in Espionage Films and Television, 1962–1973.* Jefferson, NC: McFarland. Profiles of 107 women who played roles in film and television spy dramas. Arranged alphabetically, includes filmography, comments by the actresses and anecdotes.

Livingstone, Sonia M. **1990**. *Making Sense of Television: The Psychology of Audience Interpretation.* Oxford, England: Pergamon Press. A social psychological study of how viewers interpret what they watch on television. Following a discussion of theory, reviews several empirical studies. Soap operas are main focus.

Livingstone, Sonia M. **1998**. *Making Sense of Television: The Psychology of Audience Interpretation* (2nd edition). New York, NY: Routledge. Revised and updated edition of 1990 work.

Longworth, James L. Jr. **2000**. *TV Creators: Conversations with America's Top Producers of Television Drama.* Syracuse, NY: Syracuse University Press. A series of interviews with producers of critically acclaimed drama, most of which aired in the 1990s.

Louvish, Simon. **1999**. *Monkey Business: The Lives and Legends of the Marx Brothers.* New York, NY: Thomas Dunne Books. The first comprehensive and fully researched biography of all five Marx Brothers.

Lovece, Frank (with Jules Franco). **1988**. *Hailing Taxi.* New York, NY: Prentice Hall Press. The origins of the show, biographies of cast members, trivia, and other information. Includes a script and outline. Also has episode guides.

Lovece, Frank. **1996**. *The X-Files Declassified: The Unauthorized Guide.* Secaucus, NJ: Citadel Press. Information about the show, including biographies of cast members, awards, "dossiers" on Mulder and Scully, and other miscellany. An annotated episode guide with 2–4 pages on each episode is the heart of the book.

Luke, Carmen. **1990**. *Constructing the Child Viewer: A History of the American discourse on Television and Children, 1950–1980.* New York, NY: Praeger. An historical analysis of the debate over 30 years on television and its effects on children.

Lusane, Clarence. **1999**. "Assessing the Disconnect Between Black & White Television Audiences." *Journal of Popular Film & Television*, Spring 99, 27(1), p. 12. 9 pages. Presents information on a study which focused on the popularity of the television show "Married...With Children" among African-Americans [as an] anti–Cosby show. [Copyright Ebscohost]

Lynch, Christopher Owen. **1998**. *Selling Catholicism: Bishop Sheen and the Power of Television.* Lexington, KY: University Press of Kentucky. A communication professor examines Sheen's message in light of America's postwar society. Uses a textual analysis of the messages from his television program.

MacDonald, Myra. **1995**. *Representing Women: Myths of Femininity in the Popular Media.* London: Edward Arnold. Analyzes the portrayal of women in film, magazines, and advertising with a few references to television programs. Gives definitions of femininity as society and different disciplines see it and then discusses four myths of femininity as seen in popular media.

Madsen, Axel. **1984**. *60 Minutes: The Power & the Politics of America's Most Popular TV News Show.* New York, NY: Dodd, Mead & Company. A journalist writes the story of the show, including key stories, legal problems, personalities, and influence.

Magers, Boyd, & Michael G. **Fitzgerald**. **1999**. *Westerns Women: Interviews with 51 Leading Ladies of Movie and Television Western from the 1930s to the 1960s.* Jefferson, NC: McFarland.

Mair, George. **1994**. *Oprah Winfrey: The Real Story.* New York, NY: Birch Lane Press. A journalist interviewed many people to come up with this revealing portrait of Oprah.

Malmsheimer, Richard. **1988**. *"Doctors Only": The Evolving Image of the American Physician.* New York, NY: Greenwood Press. A history of the image of doctors in American society, with emphasis on popular culture and literature. The final chapter deals with television.

Mankiewicz, Frank, & Joel **Swerdlow**. **1978**. *Remote Control: Television and the Manipulation of American Life.* New York, NY: New York Times Books. The influence of television on American life is discussed. Topics include violence, institutions, behavior, politics, and social change.

Marc, David. **1984**. *Demographic Vistas: Television in American Culture.* Philadelphia: University of Pennsylvania Press. A personal opinion approach to television programming; no analytical theories or quantitative studies are emphasized. Concentrates on comedy.

Marc, David. **1989**. *Comic Visions: Television Comedy and American Culture.* Boston, MA: Unwin Hyman. Analyzes the portrayal of groups and of American society as seen in television situation comedies.

Marc, David. **1996**. *Demographic Vistas: Television in American Culture* (revised edition). Philadelphia: University of Pennsylvania Press. Revision of 1984 edition, which basically only adds a new introduction and conclusion which discusses the decline of network television and the lack of common TV viewing in our society today. Some of the references are also in the 1984 edition but were not included before.

Marc, David. **1997**. *Comic Visions: Television Comedy and American Culture* (2nd ed). Malden, MA: Blackwell Publishing. Update of 1989 edition. Analyzes comedy on television. Includes additional shows.

Marc, David, & Robert **Thompson**. **1992**. *Prime Time, Prime Movers: From I Love Lucy to L.A. Law; America's Greatest TV Shows and the People Who Created Them.* Boston, MA: Little, Brown and Company. Each chapter is devoted to the major producers and writers. Consists of many good quotes giving insight into the creation of some of the most popular television shows.

Marek, Joan Gershen. **1999**. "The Practice and Ally McBeal: A New Image for Women Lawyers on Television?" *Journal of American Culture*, Spring 99, 22(1), p. 77. 8 pages. Explores the image of women lawyers in the television programs "Ally McBeal" and "The Practice." How women lawyers are portrayed in television according to the observations of Christine Alice Corcos. Issues to be considered when assessing female attorneys in "Ally McBeal" and "The Practice." [Copyright Ebscohost]

Marling, Karal Ann. **1994**. *As Seen on TV: The Visual Culture of Everyday Life in the 1950s.* Cambridge, MA: Harvard University Press. A look at popular culture in the 1950s and the profound influence of television on the way people viewed how to live the "good life."

Marris, Paul, & Sue **Thornham**, eds. **2000**. *Media Studies: A Reader* (second edition). Washington Square, NY: New York University Press. An introduction to theoretical perspectives on mass media in the last thirty years. Many key authors (McCluhan, Adorno, etc) are included. British emphasis.

Marsh, Spencer. **1975**. *God, Man, and Archie Bunker.* New York, NY: Harper & Row. Consists of descriptions and quotes which elucidate Archie Bunker's (from "All in the Family") views on religion, Bible, and God.

Marsh, Spencer. **1977**. *Edith the Good: The Transformation of Edith Bunker from Total Woman to Whole Person.* New York, NY: Harper & Row. Using incidents and quotes from "All in the Family" the author shows how the character of Edith Bunker developed.

Martin, Bruce. **1980**. *An Investigation of the Image of American Men as Portrayed in Selected Commercial Prime Time Television Programs, TV Season 1950–51 Through 1975–76* (Ph.D. Dissertation, New York University).

Martin, David, C. **1981**. *Uses and Gratifications Associated with Prime Time Television: Content and Individual Viewer Differences* (Ph.D. Dissertation, University of Oregon). Uses the uses and gratification theory to analyze differences in audience interaction with different types of programs. Five types of use were found: personal utility, societal contact, social utility, escape, and acting. Four TV programs were used in the study.

Martindale, David. **1991**. *Television Detective Shows of the 1970s: Credits, Story Lines, and Episode Guides for 109 Series.* Jefferson, NC: McFarland. As indicated by subtitle, this is mostly a descriptive book with episodes listed. Short-lived shows with a page or less devoted to them were not indexed in this book. Any 1970s detective show can be found in Martindale as the shows are arranged alphabetically.

Marx, Groucho (with Hector Arce). **1976**. *The Secret Word Is Groucho.* New York, NY: G.P. Putnam's Sons. Groucho talks about "You Bet Your Life" on radio and television.

Matelski, Marilyn J. **1988**. *The Soap Opera Evolution: America's Enduring Romance with Daytime Drama.* Jefferson, NC: McFarland. A scholarly study of plots, characters, audience, and trends in soap operas.

Matelski, Marilyn J. **1999**. *Soap Operas Worldwide: Cultural and Serial Realities.* Jefferson, NC: McFarland. A scholarly study similar to her 1988 work but covering the whole world. Some American soap operas are discussed.

Mathers, Jerry. **1998**. *And Jerry Mathers as "The Beaver."* New York, NY: Berkley Boulevard Books. Memoirs of the actor who played the titled role on *Leave It to Beaver.*

Mayer, Martin. **1972**. *About Television.* New York, NY: Harper & Row. A history and analysis of television, with chapters on prime time, children's, and daytime.

Mayerle, J. **1991**. "Roseanne—How Did You Get Inside My House? A Case Study of a Hit Blue-Collar Situation Comedy." *Journal of Popular Culture*, Spring 91, 24(4), p. 71. 18 pages. Discusses the hit TV series "Roseanne" as a blue collar situation comedy, and as a reflection of the growing influence of women in the production of prime time television programming. Marcy Carsey and the Carsey-Werner Company; the integration of two comedic forms; the weekly evolution of an episode of the show. Similarities to "The Honeymooners," "All in the Family," and "M*A*S*H." [Copyright Ebscohost]

Mayne, Judith. **2000**. *Framed: Lesbians, Feminists and Media Culture.* Minneapolis, MN: University of Minnesota Press. A critic and scholar of culture and feminism explores feminist approaches to film and mass culture. Discussion of lesbianism and feminism in film and television.

McAllister, Matthew P. **1992**. "Recombinant Television Genres and Doogie Howser, M.D." *Journal of Popular Film & Television*, Fall 92, 20(3), p. 61. 9 pages. Discusses how the nearly brilliant combination of two established genres, the teen comedy and the medical doctor, have made "Doogie Howser, M.D." such a success. Specific characters, icons, and themes of each genre; cultural perspective, a show about reassurance; reassures viewers about the nature of medicine and the nature of American teenagers. [Copyright Ebscohost]

McCabe, Peter. **1987**. *Bad News at Black Rock: The Sell-Out of CBS News.* New York, NY: Arbor House. An expose of the way "CBS Morning News" was treated by the network and what led to its cancellation.

McCarty, John, & Brian **Kellehv**. **1985**. *Alfred Hitchcock Presents: An Illustrated Guide to the Ten-Year Television Career of the Master of Suspense.* New York, NY: St. Martins Press. Gives the "story behind the series" and then has an episode guide to the 266 shows in the series.

McClay, Michael. **1995**. *I Love Lucy.* New York, NY: Warner Books. A picture history of the show, authorized by the Lucille Ball Estate.

McCrohan, Donna. **1978**. *The Honeymooners Companion: The Kramden's and the Norton's Revisited.* New York, NY: Workman Publishing. Describes the development of the show from its days as a sketch on the "Jackie Gleason Show." Also cast and character information, plot synopses, a timeline, a glossary, and miscellaneous trivia.

McCrohan, Donna. **1990**. *Prime Time, Our Time: America's Life and Times Through the Prism of Television.* Rocklin, CA: Prima Publishing & Communications. Focusing on the top two rated programs each year from 1950/51 through 1988/89, analyzes how these shows reflect our society and influence how we view ourselves.

McCrohan, Donna, & Peter **Crescouti**. **1986**. *The Honeymooners Lost Episodes.* New York, NY: Workman Publishing. A guide to earliest Honeymooners skits, which were hidden away by Jackie Gleason. Shows origins of many of the settings and settings of the show. Includes detailed summaries, interviews, script excerpts and many photos.

McDonald, J. Fred. **1983**. *Blacks and White TV: Afro-Americans in Television Since 1948.* Chicago, IL: Nelson-Hall Publishers. A study of the relationship between television and blacks, the first of book length. Discusses both opportunities for African Americans in TV and the portrayal of them on TV.

McDonald, J. Fred. **1987**. *Who Shot the Sheriff? The Rise and Fall of the Television Western.* New York, NY: Praeger. A critical history of the television western.

McDonald, J. Fred. **1992**. *Blacks and White TV: African Americans in Television Since 1948*. Chicago, IL: Nelson-Hall Publishers. A revised edition of the 1983 work with information on newer shows such as "The Cosby Show."

Meadows, Audrey (with Joe Daley). **1994**. *Love, Alice: My Life as a Honeymooner*. New York, NY: Crown Publishers. The actress who played Alice Kramden describes her experiences working on the "Honeymooners" show.

Means Coleman, Robin R. **2000**. *African American Viewers and the Black Situation Comedy: Situating Racial Humour*. New York, NY: Garland Publishing. Discusses the meanings that African Americans bring to and take away from sitcoms with blacks. Gives a fresh perspective because it presents the viewpoints of the African Americans themselves.

Means Coleman, Robin R., ed. **2002**. *Say It Loud! African-American Audiences, Media, and Identity*. New York, NY: Routledge. A group of scholars write about media representations of blacks and the reactions of the African American community. Based on direct interview research, all types of media, including television, are investigated.

Medved, Michael. **1992**. *Hollywood vs. America: Popular Culture and the War on Traditional Values*. New York, NY: Harper Collins. A critic bemoans the fact that Hollywood producers and writers are not in touch with the "real" America. They promote many values (adultery, drug use, homosexuality, abortion, etc.) that are not in line with the majority. Mostly films are discussed, but there is some mention of TV programs.

Meehan, Diana M. **1983**. *Ladies of the Evening: Women Characters of Prime-Time Television*. Metuchen, NJ: Scarecrow Press. A content analysis of the portrayal of women characters in television. Divides the image of women into ten types (e.g., imp, bitch, matriarch).

Mehling, Harold. **1962**. *The Great Time-Killer*. Cleveland, OH: World Publishing Company. An early analysis of television and its influence. Describes the "degeneration" of TV since the early 1950s.

Meinhof, Ulrike, & Jonathon **Smith**, eds. **2000**. *Intertextuality and the Media: From Genre to Everyday Life*. Manchester, England: Manchester University Press. An international group of scholars shows ways in which meanings are exchanged in social contexts via various media forms. Intertextuality is put in a theoretical framework showing how previous knowledge of the media interacts with other experience to shape understanding of the media.

Mellencamp, Patricia. **1992**. *High Anxiety: Catastrophe, Scandal, Age & Comedy*. Bloomington: Indiana University Press. A feminist semiotic analysis of popular culture and how it leads to anxiety because of its emphasis on negative events. Main focus is on television.

Mendoza, Maria Teresita de Guzman. **1986**. *Television, Ethnicity, and Adolescent Values: Socialization of Filipino and Other Ethnic Youths in the United States* (Ph.D. Dissertation, University of Wisconsin, Madison). Examines the impact of television viewing on values of early teen viewers from several ethnic groups. Emphasis on Filipinos. Programs viewed are mentioned.

Merron, Jeff. **1988**. *Murrow on TV: "See It Now," "Person to Person" and the Making of a Mass Cult Personality."* (Journalism Monographs No. 106). Columbia,

SC: Association For Education in Journalism and Mass Communication. A short scholarly monograph dealing with Murrow's contributions to early television. Emphasis is on mass culture aspects.

Metz, Robert. **1977**. *The Today Show*. Chicago, IL: Playboy Press Books. A look at the show from its inception in 1952 to the date of the book. Describes hosts, guests, intrigue, etc.

Metz, Robert. **1980**. *The Tonight Show*. Chicago, Il: Playboy Press Books. The inside story of the show from its inception in the 1950s to the middle of the Carson era.

Meyers, Marian, ed. **1999**. *Mediated Women: Representations in Popular Culture*. Cresskill, NJ: Hampton Press, Inc. A series of essays by feminist scholars on the meanings behind representations of women in popular culture (films, television, news magazines, music videos, and advertising). Issues addressed are societal, cultural constraint vs. social changes, continued victimization, and the patriarchal world view.

Meyers, Richard. **1981**. *TV Detectives*. San Diego, CA: A. S. Barnes & Company. A narrative history of detective shows on television.

Miles, Betty. **1975**. *Channeling Children: Sex Stereotyping on Prime-Time TV. Analysis by Women on Words and Images*. Princeton, NJ: Women on Words and Images. A short book but valuable because it takes 20 television programs from the 1973 and 1974 seasons and describes the sex role stereotyping on them.

Milgram, Stanley, & R. Lance **Shetland**. **1973**. *Television and Antisocial Behavior: Field Experiments*. New York, NY: Academic Press. A report on experiments to determine the link between viewing television that depicts antisocial behavior and such behavior in real life.

Miller, Frank. **1994**. *Censored Hollywood: Sex, Sin and Violence on Screen*. Atlanta, GA: Turner Publishing, Inc. A teacher and professional analyzes the debate on censorship in the movies. There are some references to television.

Miller, Jeffrey S. **2000**. *Something Completely Different: British Television and American Culture*. Minneapolis: University of Minnesota Press. Examines how British television programs influenced American television and culture in the context of transnational communication theory. Concentrates on the 1960s and 1970s. Shows how Americans made sense of the shows based on a culture different from theirs.

Miller, Mark Crispin. **1988**. *Boxed In: The Culture of TV*. Evanston, IL: Northwestern University Press. A series of essays on the mass media by a professor. Television is the main focus.

Miller, Toby. **1997**. *The Avengers*. London, England: British Film Institute. A professor analyzes the show: its history, place in popular culture, what it says about society and its appeal as a cult classic.

Miller, William. **1980**. *Screen Writing for Narrative Film and Television*. New York, NY: Hastings House. A how-to on screen writing, giving examples from films and television programs.

Miner, Madonne M. **1996**. "Like a Natural Woman: Nature, Technology, and Birthing Bodies in Murphy Brown." *Frontiers: A Journal of Womens Studies*, 16(1), p. 1. 18 pages. Challenges the meanings of "new motherhood" and the "unnatural" technological, patriarchal, and capitalistic dimensions of its creation in the United States based on the television program "Murphy Brown." Situation of Murphy giving birth; ongoing conversation about the place of women within patriarchal, technological, and capitalist culture. [Copyright Ebscohost]

Mitz, Rick. **1980**. *The Great TV Sitcom Book*. New York, NY: Richard Marek Publishers. Fairly lengthy descriptions of situation comedies from the 1950s, 1960s, and 1970s. Selected by the author as "front runners" and "also runs."

Modleski, Tania. **1982**. *Loving with a Vengeance: Mass-Produced Fantasies for Women*. Hamden, CN: Archon Books. A view of popular culture (mostly literature) geared towards the women audience and what messages are being conveyed. There is a chapter on soap operas.

Modleski, Tania, ed. **1986**. *Studies in Entertainment: Critical Approaches to Mass Culture*. Bloomington, IN: Indiana University Press. Essays describing critical approaches to mass media and popular culture. One chapter is devoted to situation comedy emphasizing Gracie Allen and Lucille Ball.

Molyneaux, Gerard. **1992**. *James Stewart: A Bio-Bibliography*. New York, NY: Greenwood Press. A biographical sketch followed by filmography and lists of other appearances (including television), awards, etc.

Monaco, James. **2000**. *How to Read a Film: Movies, Media, Multimedia* (third edition). New York, NY: Oxford University Press. A revised edition of a classic work on film and media. Discusses media as art, craft, technology, etc. Includes new material on multimedia and has a chapter devoted to television.

Montgomery, Kathryn C. **1989**. *Target: Prime Time; Advocacy Groups and the Struggle Over Entertainment Television*. New York, NY: Oxford University Press. Explores the relationship of advocacy groups (from all parts of the political spectrum) and network television. Influences on prime time programs are discussed.

Moody, Kate. **1980**. *Growing Up on Television: The TV Effect*. New York, NY: Times Books. A summary of reports on children's television and its harmful effects, with a "call to action" by parents.

Moore, Michael, & Kathleen **Glynn**. **1998**. *Adventures in a TV Nation*. New York, NY: Harper Collins. The gadfly reporter talks about his short-lived television program.

Moores, Shaun. **2000**. *Media and Everyday Life in Modern Society*. Edinburgh, Scotland: Edinburgh University Press. Investigates the position of media in people's day to day life and how people make sense of time, space and place based on the media. British emphasis.

Moorti, Sujata. **1995**. *Screening Sexuality: Democratic Sphere and Television Representations of Rape* (Ph.D. Dissertation, University of Maryland College Park). Compares discussions of rape on television news and talk shows from a feminist perspective.

Moorti, Sujata. **2001**. *Color of Rape: Gender and Space in Television's Public Spheres*. Albany, NY: State University of New York Press. Analyzes images of rape on television. Discusses public sphere, feminist themes, and ideas of race and gender.

Morgan, Michael, Susan **Leggett**, & James **Shanahan**. **1999**. "Television and Family Values: Was Dan Quayle Right?" *Mass Communication & Society*, Winter/Spring 99, 2(1/2), p. 47. 17 pages. Examines the influence of television on family values and social beliefs in the United States. Controversies regarding the representation of family life in popular culture; criticism of Vice President Dan Quayle on the situational comedy "Murphy Brown"; relations between TV viewing and judgments on single parenthood and illegitimacy. [Copyright Ebscohost]

Morreale, Joanne. **1998**. "Xena: Warrior Princess as Feminist Camp." *Journal of Popular Culture*, Fall 98, 32(2), p. 79. 8 pages. Examines the contradictory representation of Xena's fictitious character by placing her within the historical context of warrior queens. Overview of Xena's representation of women and comments from feminist critics. [Copyright Ebscohost]

Morris, Bruce B. **1997**. *Prime Time Network Serials*. Jefferson, NC: McFarland. Extensive information with episode guide to prime time soap operas.

Morris, Norman S. **1971**. *Television's Child*. Boston, MA: Little, Brown and Company. Based on interviews with psychologists, educators, television personnel, etc. Discusses the effect of television (mostly children's) on children.

Mosco, Vincent, & Janet **Wasko**, eds. **1983**. *The Critical Communications Review. Volume 1: Labor, the Working Class and the Media*. Norwood, NJ: Ablex Publishing Corporation. One of three volumes meant to challenge and change mass media. This volume (only one indexed and only for "groups" section) covers the relationship of labor to media and the portrayal of the working class.

Mott, Robert L. **2000**. *Radio Live! Television Live!* Jefferson, NC: McFarland. A sound effects creator describes behind the scenes activities in the days when radio and television shows were broadcast live. Using his own life as the main focus, he shows the interesting, innovative, and funny events that occurred.

Moyer, Daniel, & Eugene **Alvarez**. **2001**. *Just the Facts, Ma'am: The Authorized Biography of Jack Webb*. Santa Ana, CA: Seven Locks Press. A musician friend of Jack's daughter and a professor collaborated on this biography of a pioneer television personality.

Muir, John Kenneth. **1997**. *Exploring "Space 1999."* Jefferson, NC: McFarland. The history of the show, a summary of critical commentary and some fan and collectible information. However, the main part of the book are extensive (2–3 pages) episode guides.

Muir, John Kenneth. **1999**. *An Analytical Guide to Television's "Battlestar Galactica."* Jefferson, NC: McFarland. A detailed account of each episode in the series. Also includes history of the show and its cast and some analysis of the series as a whole and in comparison to "Star Wars" and "Star Trek."

Muir, John Kenneth. **2001**a. *Terror Television, American Series, 1970–1999*. Jefferson, NC: McFarland. A description, critical review and a list of episodes (episode guides) for television programs of horror shows.

Muir, John Kenneth. **2001**b. *An Analytical Guide to Television's "One Step Beyond," 1959–1961*. Jefferson, NC: McFarland. A detailed account of each episode in the series. Also includes history of the show and the subsequent career of the narrator John Newland. Appendices categorize themes of the show and lists the best episodes and remakes.

Munson, Wayne. **1990**. *Talking About Talk: The Talkshow, Audience Participation, and the Postmodern* (Ph.D. Dissertation, New York University). Looks at audience participation talk shows from a post modern perspective. A critical appreciation from a multiplicity of approaches (aesthetic, institutional, historical, discursive, interpretive, and reception).

Munson, Wayne. **1993**. *All Talk: The Talkshow in Media Culture*. Philadelphia, PA: Temple University Press. A post-modernist analysis of the talk show. Gives its development and its "workings"; i.e., hosts, topics, guests, and audience. Also has a review of current research.

Murray, Michael D. **1994**. *The Political Performers: CBS Broadcasts in the Public Interest*. Westport, CN: Praeger. A professor who once worked for CBS News writes an historical account of the rise of CBS News as "The best."

Muse, Vance. **1994**. *We Bombed in Burbank: A Joyride to Prime Time*. Reading, MA: Addison-Wesley Publishing Co. The story of a failed sit-com, "Black Tie Affair."

Museum of Television and Radio. 1991. *Jack Benny: The Radio and Television Work*. New York, NY: Harper Perennial. A book from an exhibit at the museum on Benny's work.

Nance, Scott. **1992**. *Exposing Northern Exposure*. Las Vegas, NV: Pioneer Books. A popular type book on the show with brief sketches of the cast members. The episode guide, however, is fairly detailed, although it covers only the early episodes. Trivia questions.

Neale, Steve, & Frank **Krutnik**. **1990**. *Popular Film and Television Comedy*. London, England: Routledge. A scholarly account of comedy with a British emphasis. Mostly deals with films but there are references to American television programs.

Negra, Diane. **2001**. *Off-White Hollywood: American Culture and Ethnic Female Stardom*. London, England: Routledge. A professor investigates ethnic white European-American actresses in the media. Using case studies, discusses fantasies and "assimilation myths." Deals mostly with films.

Nelson, Cary, & Dilip Parameshwar **Gaonkar**, eds. **1996**. *Disciplinarity and Dissent in Cultural Studies*. New York, NY: Routledge. A series of essays on cultural studies as an academic discipline and its place in the university (separate, multidisciplinary, politics involved), including its discontents. Broadly based popular culture is being discussed with some references to television.

Nelson, Craig. **1995**. *BAD TV: The Very Best of the Very Worst*. New York, NY: Dell Publishing. A description of shows that were BAD (that is, so bad they are unforgettable and therefore worth watching), not merely bad.

Nelson, Jack A., ed. **1994**. *The Disabled, the Media, and the Information Age*. Westport, CN: Greenwood Press. A collection of essays describing the portrayal of the disabled in media. Emphasis is on news coverage with some references to TV shows.

Nelson, Robin. **1996**. "From Twin Peaks, USA, to Lesser Peaks, UK: Building the Postmodern TV Audience." *Media, Culture & Society*, Oct. 96, 18(4), p. 677. 6 pages. Focuses on the trend of producing and marketing of postmodern television programs in lieu of the audience's preferences. Production of

"Twin Peaks" in the United States; implication of advertising agencies on the production of television programs; approaches of television programming in Great Britain. [Copyright Ebscohost]

Neuman, Susan B. **1991**. *Literacy in the Television Age: The Myth of the TV Effect.* Norwood, NJ: Ablex Publishing Corporation. Looks at studies related to television's effects on literacy and concludes the negative effects are exaggerated.

Newcomb, Horace, ed. **1976**. *Television: The Critical View.* New York, NY: Oxford University Press. Essays giving broad perspectives on different aspects of television (specific program types, TV's meaning in our culture, defining television, and how it differs from other media).

Newcomb, Horace, ed. **1979**. *Television: The Critical View* (2nd edition). New York, NY: Oxford University Press. A revision of the first edition. Some new essays. Themes are the same.

Newcomb, Horace, ed. **1982**. *Television: The Critical View* (3rd edition). New York, NY: Oxford University Press. A revision of previous edition with most of the essays being different ones. Themes are the same.

Newcomb, Horace, ed. **1987**. *Television: The Critical View* (4th edition). New York, NY: Oxford University Press. New essays, updates but same format as previous editions.

Newcomb, Horace, ed. **1994**. *Television: The Critical View* (5th edition). New York, NY: Oxford University Press. A more complete revision than previous editions. Categories are different and only a few essays have the same title and most of these have been updated.

Newcomb, Horace, ed. **2000**. *Television: The Critical View* (6th edition). New York, NY: Oxford University Press. Broadens previous editions to include other than "prime time television fiction" and adds an international perspective.

Newcomb, Horace, & Robert S. **Alley**. **1983**. *The Producer's Medium: Conversations with Creators of American TV.* New York, NY: Oxford University Press. Interviews with several of TV's top name producers. Gives some insights into the programs they produced.

Newitz, Annalee. **1998**. "ER, Professionals, and the Work-Family Disaster." *American Studies*, Summer 98, 39(2), p. 93. 13 pages. Focuses on the television program "ER," highlighting its depiction of personal and professional concerns which affect employees on a daily basis. Description of the program which is based on the work-family unit; conditions in American society that are met through the program; social realms that are mapped in the program. [Copyright Ebscohost]

Nichols, Nichelle. **1994**. *Beyond Uhura: Star Trek and Other Memories.* New York, NY: G.P. Putnam's Sons. Memoirs of the African American actress who played on "Star Trek" and what it meant to her and to other African Americans.

Nickerson, Catherine. **1993**. "Serial Detection and Serial Killers in Twin Peaks." *Literature Film Quarterly*, 21(4), p. 271. 6 pages. Focuses on the television series "Twin Peaks" and its parody and celebration of detective conventions. Subversion of the narrative structures of the detective genre. Gothic elements in the series and use of the double device. [Copyright Ebscohost]

Nightingale, Virginia. **1996**. *Studying Audiences: The Shock of the Real.* London:

Routledge. A critical overview of two decades of television audience research, evaluating five major projects. British emphasis.

Nimoy, Leonard. **1995**. *I Am Spock*. New York, NY: Hyperion. The autobiography of the actor who played Spock on the original "Star Trek" series.

Nochimson, Martha P. **1992**. *No End to Her: Soap Operas and the Female Subject*. Berkeley: University of California Press. The author was a writer and consultant to soap operas, but here takes an academic approach. Treats soap operas as a form of feminist discourse.

Nochimson, Martha P. **1992/93**. "Desire Under the Douglas Firs." *Film Quarterly*, Winter 92/93, 46(2), p. 22. 13 pages. Discusses the different elements David Lynch's television series "Twin Peaks" possesses that make it so interesting to, and watched by, its audience. The dazzled affection that Dale Cooper, hero of the show, inspires; how Lynch asserts that Laura, "Twin Peaks" femme fatale, is not the point of initiation; how Cooper's striking originality is best understood. [Copyright Ebscohost]

Nochimson, Martha P. **1997**a. "Amnesia 'R' Us." *Film Quarterly*, Spring 97, 50(3), p. 27. 19 pages. Discusses the television soap opera "One Life to Live," starred by Erika Slezak. Soap opera's presentation of the collision between reality and melodrama; comparison with Alfred Hitchcock's films *Spellbound* and *Vertigo*; place in the history of amnesia in soap opera; analysis of the main character's behavior; representation of the way soap operas indulge traditional melodramatic fantasies. [Copyright Ebscohost]

Nochimson, Martha P. **1997**b. *The Passion of David Lynch: Wild at Heart in Hollywood*. Austin: University of Texas Press. A critical study of David Lynch and his films, showing the influences on him and one perspective on explaining his work. Included in this index because of "Twin Peaks."

Nochimson, Martha P. **2000**. "Ally McBeal." *Film Quarterly*, Spring 2000, 53(3), p. 25. 8 pages. Presents a critique of "Ally McBeal": regression of Ally to a Production Code mentality that neutralizes most forms of repression. [Copyright Ebscohost]

O'Connor, John E., ed. **1983**. *American History, American Television: Interpreting the Video Past*. New York, NY: Frederick Ungar Publishing Company. Historians view television as a social and cultural force and its meaning for history. Each essayist selects a specific series or genre or phenomenon to discuss.

O'Dell, Cary. **1997**. *Women Pioneers in Television: Biographies of Fifteen Industry Leaders*. Jefferson, NC: McFarland. Short biographical sketches of women who influenced the development of television, particularly its earlier years.

Official Guide to the X-Files. **1995–2001. New York**, NY: Harper Collins. A series of books (six as of 2001) with very detailed descriptions of each episode.

Okuda, Michael, & Denise **Okuda**. **1993**. *Star Trek Chronology: The History of the Future*. New York, NY: Pocket Books. A chronological approach to the "Star Trek" shows and movies, mixed with real events that are mentioned in the show.

Okuda, Michael, & Denise **Okuda**. **1999**. *The Star Trek Encyclopedia: A Reference Guide to the Future* (updated and expanded edition). New York, NY: Pocket Books. The latest edition of this work, which gives information on characters, ships, peoples, episodes, and other terms. Several appendices and indexes to production personnel and to actors and actresses. Includes references to all series and movies up to time of publication.

Ollen, John. **1997**. *Jean Arthur: The Actress Nobody Knew*. New York, NY: Limelight Editions. A biography of a film star of the 1930s and 1940s, famous for screwball comedies.

Orlik, Peter B. **1994**. *Electronic Media Criticism: Applied Perspectives*. Boston, MA: Focal Press. Radio and television criticism is treated like any serious criticism of the arts. Takes a systematic approach in an attempt to refine media criticism.

Orlik, Peter B. **2001**. *Electronic Media Criticism: Applied Perspectives* (second edition). Mahwah, NJ: Lawrence Erlbaum Associates. A revised edition of his 1994 book.

Ornellas, Kriemhild Conee. **1987**. *The Depiction of Sexuality in Daytime Television Melodrama* (Ph.D. Dissertation, Bowling Green University). A content analysis of daytime soap operas looking for how sexuality is portrayed. Finds that a traditional system of values prevails—true sexual satisfaction is only found in marriage; others have consequences.

Osgerby, Bill, & Anna **Gough-Yates**. **2001**. *Action TV: Tough-Guys, Smooth Operators and Foxy Chicks*. London, England: Routledge. A group of scholars contribute essays that describe the history of action series. Institutional, cultural, and societal factors are discussed.

Oskamp, Stuart, ed. **1988**. *Television as a Social Issue (Applied Social Psychology Annual 8)*. Newbury Park, CA: Sage Publications. Essays, most of them presented at a conference in briefer form, on television's influence on social issues. Television defines the public's idea of what a social issue is and influences public behavior.

Ott, Brian L., & Eric **Aoki**. **2001**. "Popular Imagination and Identity Politics: Reading the Future in Star Trek: Next Generation." *Western Journal of Communication*, Fall 2001, 65(4), p. 392. 24 pages. Presents information on a study which analyzed the relationship between collective visions of the future and the identity politics of the present using the syndicated television series "Star Trek: The Next Generation." Role of homosexuality in the United States popular culture; critical reflections on imagining the future. [Copyright Ebscohost]

Owen, A. Susan. **1999**. "Buffy the Vampire Slayer." *Journal of Popular Film & Television*, Summer 99, 27(2), p. 24. 8 pages. Explores the television series "Buffy the Vampire Slayer" through the intersections of postfeminism, postmodernity, and the vampire metanarrative. Appropriation of body rhetorics and narrative agency from masculinist metanarratives; how the characters negotiate the politics of feminism and postmodernity. [Copyright Ebscohost]

Owen, Rob. **1997**. *GenXTV: The Brady Bunch to Melrose Place*. Syracuse, NY: Syracuse University Press. A television critic examines the relationship of so-called Generation X with television. Discusses several shows from all time frames of Generation X's lifespan. Includes comments from Generation X-ers, mostly via e-mail.

Paar, Jack. **1983**. *P.S. Jack Paar*. Garden City, NJ: Doubleday & Company. Memoirs of Jack Paar, describing encounters with celebrities and giving other anecdotes.

Paietta, Ann, & Jean **Kauppila**. **1999**. *Health Professionals on Screen*. Lanham, MD: Scarecrow Press. A listing of films (theatrical and television) and television series that featured health professionals. There is a very brief description of the professional involved. Not much substantive information but useful if trying to find shows that featured doctors, nurses, psychiatrists, etc.

Palmer, Edward L. **1988**. *Television and America's Children: A Crisis of Neglect*. New York, NY: Oxford University Press. A discussion of children's programming with emphasis on public television and "Sesame Street."

Palmer, Edward L., & Aimee **Dorr**, eds. **1980**. *Children and the Faces of Television: Teaching, Violence, Selling*. New York, NY: Academic Press. Describes children's television from three perspectives: the teaching role, violent content, and advertising.

Panati, Charles. **1991**. *Panati's Parade of Fads, Follies, and Manias*. New York, NY: Harper Collins Publishers. Descriptions of twentieth century fads, toys, dances, songs, etc. Includes TV shows for the decades since the 1940s.

Parenti, Michael. **1991**. *Make Believe Media: The Politics of Entertainment*. New York, NY: St. Martin's Press. A view of the media that says it supports militarism, imperialism, racism, etc. The emphasis is on movies but some television shows are mentioned.

Parks, Rita. **1982**. *The Western Hero in Film and Television: Mass Media Mythology*. Ann Arbor, MI: UMI Research Press. The myth of the West and the hero "cowboy," both in film and on television.

Patton, Tracey Owens. **2001**. "Ally McBeal and Her Homies: The Reification of White Stereotypes of the Other." *Journal of Black Studies*, Nov. 2001, 32(2), p. 229. 32 pages. A critical analysis of "Ally McBeal," concentrating on how women and ethnic minorities are portrayed in a negative stereotypical manner.

Payne, Monica A. **1994**. "The 'Ideal' Black Family?" *Journal of Black Studies*, Dec. 94, 25(2), p. 231. 19 pages. Presents an ethnographic and socio-cultural study on the impact of "The Cosby Show" on Caribbean televiewers. "The Cosby Role" as image of "ideal" black family; tendency of "Cosby" to subtly deflect need for greater acceptance of blacks in American mainstream society; general approval of Cosby family as role model; cultural reservations. [Copyright Ebscohost]

Pearl, Jonathan, & Judith **Pearl**. **1999**. *The Chosen Image: Television's Portrayal of Jewish Themes and Characters*. Jefferson, NC: McFarland. A study of the portrayal of Jews and Jewish themes on popular television. Emphasis is on shows with explicit references to Jewish life and customs.

Peel, John. **1989**. *The Gunsmoke Years*. Las Vegas, NV: Pioneer Books. A behind-the-scenes look at this long-running show. Includes interviews and an episode guide.

Peel, John. **1992**. *The Trek Encyclopedia*. Las Vegas, NV: Pioneer Books. One of the early attempts at an encyclopedic guide to the series.

Pegg, Robert. **2002**. *Comical Co-Stars of Television: From Norton to Kramer*. Jefferson, NC: McFarland. Describes the life and careers of "second bananas": those who played in comedies but were not the main stars.

Penley, Constance. **1997**. *NASA/TREK: Popular Science and Sex in America*. New York, NY: Verso. Describes how NASA and "Star Trek" popularize science. Also discusses the internet fans of "Star Trek" and the so-called "slash" stories (gay versions) they write.

Penley, Constance, Elisabeth **Lyon**, Lynn **Spigel**, & Janet **Bergstrom**, eds. **1991**. *Close Encounters: Film, Feminism, and Science Fiction*. Minneapolis, MN: University of Minnesota Press. Based on a special issue of *Camera Obscura*, a collection of essays addressing ways that conventional notions of sexual difference are displaced or reworked in science fiction film.

Persico, Joseph E. **1988**. *Edward R. Murrow: An American Original*. New York, NY: McGraw-Hill Publishing Company. An extensive biography of the famed newscaster.

Pfeiffer, Lee. **1994**. *The Official Andy Griffith Show Scrapbook*. New York, NY: Citadel Press. Heavily illustrated "coffee table" book but contains some insights of the show. Interviews with cast members and episode guide with cast members, critiques, and "Favorite Dialogue."

Phillips, Robert W. **1995**. *Roy Rogers*. Jefferson, NC: McFarland. A chronological type biography and then listings of films, records, memorabilia, and television history.

Pierson, David P. **2000**. "A Show About Nothing: Seinfeld and the Modern Comedy of Manners." *Journal of Popular Culture*, Summer 2000, 34(1), p. 49. 16 pages. Evaluates the type of comedy presented in the television series "Seinfeld." Comparison with other situation comedies; association with comedy of manners dramatic genre. [Copyright Ebscohost]

Pilato, Herbie J. **1996**. *Bewitched Forever: The Immortal Companion to Television's Most Magical Supernatural Situation Comedy*. Arlington, TX: The Summit Publishing Group. A guide to the show with background information, interviews, biographies, a guide to the episodes, and other miscellanea.

Pines, Burton Y. **1994**. *Out of Focus: Network Television and the American Economy*. Washington, D.C.: Regnery. A critical account of how television covers the economy in both its fiction and news. Emphasis is on prime time news magazine programs.

Pitrone, Jean Madden. **1999**. *Take It from the Big Mouth: The Life of Martha Raye*. Lexington, KY: University Press of Kentucky. "First full-fledged biography" of the comedienne who starred in many venues, including TV.

Pollard, Scott. **1993**. "Cooper, Details, and the Patriotic Mission of Twin Peaks." *Literature Film Quarterly*, 21(4), p. 296. 9 pages. Focuses on Special Agent Dale Cooper, a character in the television series "Twin Peaks." First impression of Agent Cooper; epic artistry of Agent Cooper; comparison of Cooper with Walt Whitman; Cooper as an example of Nietzsche's theoretical man; two kinds of contiguous evil; relationship between Leland Palmer and BOB; narrative of redemption. [Copyright Ebscohost]

Porter, Jennifer E., & Darcess L. **McLaren**, eds. **1999**. *Star Trek and Sacred*

Ground. Albany, NY: State University of New York Press. Scholars discuss how "Star Trek" reflects and influences views about society. Emphasis is on religious and mythic themes. Shows how religion is often seen in a negative light (except on "Deep Space Nine"). Scientific humanism is the preferred philosophy on the show.

Postman, Neil. **1985**. *Amusing Ourselves to Death: Public Discourse in the Age of Show Business.* New York, NY: Viking. Examines how "entertainment values" have influenced the way we think. The importance of visual imagery leaves little room for argument or explanation; superficiality takes the place of substance.

Pounds, Michael C. **1999**. *Race in Space: The Representation of Ethnicity in Star Trek and Star Trek: The Next Generation.* Lanham, MD: Scarecrow Press. A scholar looks at how "Star Trek" reflects attitudes toward race and ethnicity.

Pourroy, Jenine. **1995**. *Behind the Scenes at E.R.* New York, NY: Ballantine Books. A description of the development, production and cast of the show in its early years. Includes a glossary of medical and slang terms on the show.

Powers, Ron. **1994**. *The Cruel Radiance: Notes of a Prose Writer in a Visual Age.* Hanover, NH: University Press of New England. A collection of writings by a journalist on many topics related to popular culture. Includes some essays on television.

Presnell, Don, & Marty **McGee**. **1998**. *A Critical History of Television's "The Twilight Zone," 1959–1964.* Jefferson, NC: McFarland. A history of the show is given followed by a fairly extensive list of episode guides (including cast, synopsis, notes and commentary). Appendices cover writers, production personnel, actors, genres, themes, and other information.

Press, Andrea L. **1991**. *Women Watching Television: Gender, Class, and Generation in the American Television Experience.* Philadelphia, PA: University of Pennsylvania Press. Analyzes the role of television in influencing the gender identity of women.

Priest, Patricia J. **1995**. *Public Intimacies: Talk Show Participants and Tell-All TV.* Cresskill, NJ: Hampton Press. A study of the people who appear on talk shows (especially "Donahue") with some insight into the shows themselves.

Projansky, Sarah. **2001**. *Watching Rape: Film and Television in Post Feminist Culture.* New York, NY: New York University Press. Analyzes depictions of rape in U.S. film, television and independent video. Challenges the concept that we are in a post feminist (i.e., equality for women has been achieved) era. Popular culture is viewed as part of our everyday life and practices and must be viewed critically.

Pryor, Richard (with Todd Gold). **1995**. *Pryor Convictions and Other Life Sentences.* New York, NY: Pantheon Books. An autobiography by the comedian.

Puette, William J. **1992**. *Through Jaundiced Eyes: How the Media View Organized Labor.* Ithaca, NY: ILR Press. A discussion of the portrayal of unions in the media, which is described as mostly negative. Written from the viewpoint of Labor.

Putterman, Barry. **1995**. *On Television and Comedy: Essays on Style, Theme,*

Performer and Writer. Jefferson, NC: McFarland. A history and critical account of comedy on television with emphasis on the major influences from the movies and radio.

Rader, Benjamin G. **1984**. *In Its Own Image: How Television Has Transformed Sports.* The Free Press. Shows how sports have changed in response to television.

Rafkin, Alan. **1998**. *Cue the Bunny on the Rainbow: Tales from TV's Most Prolific Sitcom Director.* Syracuse, NY: Syracuse University Press. An autobiographical account from a television director of episodes of many situation comedies, some quite well known. Won an Emmy for an episode of "One Day at a Time."

Rainey, Buck. **1998**. *Western Gunslingers in Fact and on Film: Hollywood's Famous Lawmen and Outlaws.* Jefferson, NC: McFarland. A discussion of famous Western lawmen and outlaws contrasting their real life story with portrayals in film. Includes some television series and episodes.

Rakoff, Ian. **1998**. *Inside the Prisoner: Radical Television and Film in the 1960s.* London, England: B.T. Batsford Ltd. An inside account of this cult show by a writer of the series. Via unpublished material and interviews, the making and significance of the show are described. Includes episode summaries.

Rakow, Lana F., ed. **1992**. *Women Making Meaning: New Feminist Directions in Communication.* New York, NY: Routledge. Feminist essays on the work of women in the field of communication and how this has influenced media portrayals.

Rannow, Jerry. **1999**. *Writing Television Comedy.* New York, NY: Allworth Press. A professional writer gives tips on how to write situation comedy for television. Uses examples from television shows.

Rapping, Elayne. **1987**. *The Looking Glass World of Nonfiction TV.* Boston, MA: South End Press. Analyzes nonfiction (news, talk shows, docudramas) on television and posits that the line between fiction and nonfiction is blurring. Describes social and political influence of television.

Rapping, Elayne. **1994**. *Media-tions: Forays Into the Culture and Gender Wars.* Boston, MA: South End Press. Series of essays on popular culture written from 1973 to 1993 from a leftist feminist perspective. Some contrarian unusual viewpoints on some phenomena such as soap operas.

Raymond, Diane, ed. **1990**. *Sexual Politics and Popular Culture.* Bowling Green, OH: Bowling Green State University Popular Press. A collection of essays discussing power and sexual politics in popular culture. Emphasis is on films but some television is covered.

Real, Michael. **1977**. *Mass-Mediated Culture.* Englewood Cliffs, NJ: Prentice Hall. A cross-cultural study of culture (symbols, beliefs, etc.) available through mass media. Topics covered include education, sports, health, politics, and religion.

Real, Michael. **1989**. *Super Media: A Cultural Studies Approach.* Newbury Parks, CA: Sage Publications. Shows different modes of analyzing the media as a major part of our culture. Film, television, and sports are highlighted.

Reeves-Stevens, Judith, & Garfield **Reeves-Stevens**. **1995**. *The Art of Star Trek.* New York, NY: Pocket Books. Well-illustrated book describing the makeup, costumes, set design and special effects of the "Star Trek" movies and television shows.

Reinheimer, David. **1995**. "Ontological and Ethical Allusion: Shakespeare in The Next Generation." *Extrapolation*, Spring 1995, 36(1), p. 46. 9 pages. Discusses the use of William Shakespeare's texts in the television series "Star Trek: The Next Generation" to define human nature. [Copyright Ebscohost]

Reiss, David S. **1983**. *M*A*S*H*: The Exclusive, Inside Story of TV's Most Popular Show.* Indianapolis, IN: Bobbs-Merrill Company. Interviews with key personnel and description of behind-the-scenes. Also includes episode guides.

Rhodes, Karen. **1997**. *Booking "Hawaii Five-O."* Jefferson, NC: McFarland. Following an introduction to the show's origins and production, there is a detailed episode guide. The last chapter has various tidbits about the show.

Richards, Thomas. **1997**. *The Meaning of Star Trek.* New York, NY: Doubleday. A former professor of literature discusses "Star Trek" in terms of conflict, characters, mythology, and "the sense of wonder."

Rico, Diana. **1990**. *Kovacsland: A Biography of Ernie Kovacs.* San Diego, CA: Harcourt Brace Jovanivich. An extensive biography of this pioneer and innovator in television comedy. His influence is still prevalent.

Riggs, Karen E. **1996**. "The Case of the Mysterious Ritual: Murder Dramas and Older Women Viewers." *Critical Studies in Mass Communication*, Dec. 96, 13(4), p. 309. 15 pages. Analyzes the text of television mystery dramas on how they draw a old female audience to view these programs ritually. Aging detectives as empowering models. [Copyright Ebscohost]

Riggs, Karen E. **1998**. *Mature Audiences: Television in the Lives of Elders.* New Brunswick, NJ: Rutgers University Press. A study of the aged as a television audience: what they watch, why, and its effects. The role of television in their lives is seen as more complex than the usual image of a passive vulnerable audience.

Ringer, R. Jeffrey, ed. **1994**. *Queer Words, Queer Images: Communication and the Construction of Homosexuality.* New York, NY: New York University Press. The portrayal of gays in various media, including television.

Rivera, Geraldo (with Daniel Paisner). **1991**. *Exposing Myself.* New York: Bantam. An autobiography of this colorful and controversial television journalist.

Robbins, Shan. **1991**. *Inka Dinka Doo: The Life of Jimmy Durante.* New York, NY: Paragun House. A popular biography of the famed comedian.

Roberts, Donald. **1993**. "Adolescents and the Mass Media: From 'Leave It to Beaver' to 'Beverly Hills 90210.'" *Teachers College Record*, Spring 93, 94(3), p. 627. 16 pages. Evaluates the influence of mass media on adolescents. Study entitled "The Myth of Massive Media Impact"; examples using "Beverly Hills 90210" and Madonna's video "Papa Don't Preach." [Copyright Ebscohost]

Roberts, Robin. **1999**. *Sexual Generations: "Star Trek: The Next Generation" and Gender.* Urbana: University of Illinois Press. A scholarly look at the portrayal of women and relations between the sexes in "Star Trek: The Next Generation." There is also a chapter devoted to race.

Roberts, Wess, & Bill **Ross**. **1995**. *Make It So: Leadership Lessons from "Star Trek: The Next Generation."* New York, NY: Pocket Books. Two businessmen, one with a doctorate, use examples from "Star Trek: The Next Generation" to illustrate principles of management.

Robertson, Ed. **1993**. *The Fugitive Recaptured: The 30th Anniversary Companion to a Television Classic.* Los Angeles, CA: Pomegranate Press. An episode by episode guide to the series, giving comments and facts about each episode as well as a synopsis. Also includes some background and miscellaneous information.

Robertson, Ed. **1994**. *Maverick: Legend of the West.* Los Angeles, CA: Pomegranate Press. Gives some information about the origins of the show and the personnel involved. Also includes information about spinoffs. The heart of the book is a detailed episode guide with much information about filming of the episodes as well as synopses.

Robertson, Ed. **1995**. *The Rockford Files.* Los Angeles, CA: Pomegranate Press. Some background information on the series, including information on the dispute between Garner and the producers. The majority of the book consists of episode guides.

Robinson, Dale, & David **Fernandes**. **1996**. *The Definitive Andy Griffith Show Reference.* Jefferson, NC: McFarland. Very detailed episode guides followed by brief description of cast and writers and production staff.

Robinson, James D., & Thomas **Skill**. **1995**. "The Invisible Generation: Portrayals of the Elderly on Prime-time Television." *Communication Reports*, Summer 95, 8(2), p. 111. 9 pages. Investigates the portrayal of characters 65 years and older on American prime time television. Random sample of several prime time shows; indication of a decline in role prominence of the elderly; gender differences; public perception of portrayals of the elderly. [Copyright Ebscohost]

Rodley, Chris, ed. **1997**. *Lynch on Lynch.* London: Faber and Faber. A discussion of his films by David Lynch.

Rodriguez, Clara E., ed. **1997**. *Latin Looks: Images of Latinas and Latinos in the U.S. Media.* Boulder, CO: Westview Press. Discusses all media, with major emphasis on film. Says Hispanics are underrepresented and misrepresented, that images have become more negative over time, and that similarities of the portrayals of different types of Hispanics far outweigh differences shown.

Rogers, Fred. **1996**. *Dear Mister Rogers, Does It Ever Rain in Your Neighborhood? Letters to Mister Rogers.* New York, NY: Penguin Books. A collection of letters sent to Mister Rogers.

Roman, James. **1996**. *Love, Light, and a Dream: Television's Past, Present, and Future.* London: Praeger. A survey of the history of television, including technical, programming, regulations, etc. Also predicts the future of the medium.

Root, Wells. **1979**. *Writing the Script: A Practical Guide for Films and Television.* New York, NY: Holt, Rinehart and Winston. Discussion of writing techniques, giving examples from television shows.

Rose, Brian G., ed. **1985**. *TV Genres: A Handbook and Reference Guide.* Westport, CN: Greenwood Press. Examines central elements in a wide variety of television genres.

Rose, Brian G. **1999**. *Directing for Television: Conversations with American TV Directors.* Lanham, MD: The Scarecrow Press. Interviews with television directors about their techniques, how television directing differs from other types, what skills are needed to direct TV, etc. Divided into different genres.

Rosenthal, Alan, ed. **1999**. *Why Docudrama? Fact-Fiction on Film and TV*. Carbondale, IL: Southern Illinois University Press. A series of essays about the dramatization of real events, discussing how accurate they are, the research, and how they are produced. Covers both film and television but only TV movies and miniseries. One chapter, however, is devoted to "Roots," a show which *is* indexed in this book.

Ross, Alan Duncan, & Harlan **Gibbs**. **1996**. *The Medicine of ER or, How We Almost Die*. New York, NY: Basic Books. A writer/producer and a doctor collaborate at this look at the accuracy of the medicine practiced on the show, "ER."

Rosteck, Thomas. **1994**. *"See It Now" Confronts McCarthyism: Television Documentary and the Politics of Representation*. Tuscaloosa: University of Alabama Press. A scholarly account of the attack by Edward R. Murrow on McCarthy, helping lead to his downfall.

Rotan, Gloria H. **1982**. *An Analysis of Supportive Marital Interaction in the Content of Selected Prime Time Commercial Television Programs* (Ph.D. Dissertation, Florida State University). Analyzes and compares three shows on their portrayal of marital interaction and how supportive it is on each show.

Rouverol, Jean. **1984**. *Writing for the Soaps*. Cincinnati, OH: Writer's Digest Books. Advice on writing and insights into the process from a soap opera writer. Includes sample scripts.

Rouverol, Jean. **1992**. *Writing for Daytime Drama*. Boston, MA: Focal Press. Revised edition of *Writing for the Soaps*. Scripts for different shows used as samples.

Rovin, Jeff. **1977**a. *From Jules Verne to Star Trek*. New York, NY: Drake Publishers. A listing with cast and descriptions of science fiction movies with a section on television.

Rovin, Jeff. **1977**b. *The Great Television Series*. Cranbury, NJ: A.S. Barnes and Company. An historical overview of series on television, emphasizing drama and the hero figure.

Rowe, Kathleen. **1995**. *The Unruly Woman*. Austin: University of Texas Press. A study of women in comedy from a feminist perspective. Emphasis is on film but some television is covered.

Rowland, Willard D., & Bruce **Watkins**, eds. **1984**. *Interpreting Television: Current Research Perspectives* (Sage Annual Reviews of Communication Research, v. 12). Beverly Hills, CA: Sage Publications. Theoretical scholarly essays on the study of television in society.

Royce, Brenda Scott. **1993**. *Hogan's Horses: A Comprehensive Reference to the 1965–1971 Television Comedy Series....* Jefferson, NC: McFarland. Describes creation, casting, and production of this series. Lists the cast with brief biography and credits. Contains an episode guide with credits and a fairly substantial plot summary for each episode. Other miscellanies about the show are also included.

Royce, Brenda Scott. **1997**. *Party of Five: The Unofficial Companion*. Los Angeles, CA: Renaissance Books. "A fan's guide," including photos, behind-the-scenes information and episode guides.

Rubin, Bernard, ed. **1980**. *Small Voices & Great Trumpets: Minorities & the Media*.

New York, NY: Praeger. A study of minorities, both behind the scenes and how portrayed in various mass media. Emphasis is on blacks and women.

Rushkoff, Douglas. **1994**. *Media Virus: Hidden Agendas in Popular Culture*. New York, NY: Ballantine Books. Describes the new (late twentieth century) age of information, the "datasphere." Shows how popular media manipulates and is manipulated by those "in the know."

Russell, Maureen. **1995**. *Days of Our Lives: A Complete History of the Long-Running Soap Opera*. Jefferson, NC: McFarland. Based on interviews, newspaper and magazine articles and archives, describes the beginnings, behind the scenes, writers and actors, and storyline of this soap opera.

Rutstein, Nat. **1974**. *"Go Watch TV": What and How Much Should Children Really Watch?* New York, NY: Sheed and Ward, Inc. "Not a traditional piece of scholarship. It is a point of view ... supported by evidence." The author suggests ways parents can deal with children's watching of television.

Sackett, Susan. **1993**. *Prime-Time Hits: Television's Most Popular Network Programs, 1950 to the Present*. New York, NY: Billboard Books. A description with credits, quotes, background, etc., of the top-rated shows over the years. Takes a chronological approach beginning with "Texaco Star Theater" (Milton Berle) from 1950/51 and ending with "Unsolved Mysteries" from 1991/92.

Sandell, Jillian. **1998**. "I'll Be There for You: Friends and the Fantasy of Alternative Families." *American Studies*, Summer 98, 39(2), p. 141. 15 pages. Focuses on the social aspects of the television program "Friends." Description of the program; creation of the alternative family; response of the television audiences to the program; description of the audience that identifies with the program. [Copyright Ebscohost]

Sanders, Coyne Steven, & Tom **Gilbert**. **1993**. *Desilu: The Story of Lucille Ball and Desi Arnaz*. New York, NY: William Morrow and Company, Inc. A "candid, behind the scenes" look at the famous couple with most of the emphasis on the Desilu Studio and on the "I Love Lucy" show.

Sanders, Coyne Steven, & Ginny **Weissman**. **1985**. *Champagne Music: The Lawrence Welk Show*. New York, NY: St. Martin's Press. Highly illustrated account of the show giving much behind the scenes information. Includes a small bibliography and index.

Sanford, Herb. **1976**. *Ladies and Gentlemen: The Garry Moore Show: Behind the Scenes When TV Was New*. New York, NY: Stein and Day. An account of Garry Moore, his show, and 1950s television.

Sautter, Carl. **1988**. *How to Sell Your Screenplay: The Real Rules of Film and Television*. New York, NY: New Chapter Press. This how-to book uses references to real television shows as examples of techniques.

Schaffer, D. **1991**. "Conversing Privately in Public: Patterns of Interaction in Today Show's Co-op Conversations." *Journal of Popular Culture*, Winter 91, 25(3), p. 151. 12 pages. Discusses how the patterns of interaction in NBC's television program the "Today Show"'s co-op conversations, which some believe are public and private conversations, support the usefulness of these interactions for the study of small-group conversations in general. [Copyright Ebscohost]

Scheider, Arthur. **1997**. *Jump Cut! Memoirs of a Pioneer Television Editor*. Jefferson,

NC: McFarland. Reminiscences of one of the off camera pioneers in television. He is most famous for his innovative editing on "Laugh-In."

Schneider, Alfred R. **2001**. *The Gatekeeper: My Thirty Years as a TV Censor.* Syracuse, NY: Syracuse University Press. An attorney who worked in standards and practices at a network discusses his experience.

Schoenbrun, David. **1989**. *On and Off the Air: An Informal History of CBS News.* New York, NY: E.P. Dutton. A television broadcaster's informal thoughts about life at CBS News.

Schow, David J., & Jeffrey **Frentzen**. **1986**. *The Outer Limits: The Official Companion.* New York, NY: Ace Science Fiction Books. A very detailed account of this sci fi/fantasy show. Includes the origins of the show, production information and very detailed description of some of the episodes.

Schrag, R. L. **1991**. "From Yesterday to Today: A Case Study of M*A*S*H's Margaret Houlihan." *Communication Education*, Jan. 91, 40(1), p. 112. 4 pages. Examines how women got from yesterday to today through a look at the evolution of female characters on prime time television that parallels the change in attitude and social status of women in America. Margaret Houlihan, a character from the television series "M*A*S*H," provides a one-character case study that spans much of that evolution. [Copyright Ebscohost]

Schuchman, John S. **1988**. *Hollywood Speaks: Deafness and the Film Entertainment Industry.* Urbana: University of Illinois Press. Emphasis on portrayal of hard of hearing in films, but has a chapter devoted to TV. Also lists episodes from television programs.

Schulman, Bruce J. **2001**. *The Seventies: The Great Shift in American Culture, Society, and Politics.* New York: NY: The Free Press. The author posits that the seventies was a more important decade than is usually assumed. It was a transitional period that transformed the U.S. in politics, society, and culture more profoundly than the 60s. Television is only a small part of this book.

Schulman, Norma Miriam. **1992**. "Laughing Across the Color Barrier: In Living Color." *Journal of Popular Film & Television*, Spring 92, 20(1), p. 2. 6 pages. Discusses how Keenan Ivory Wayans' program "In Living Color" is one of the only prime time television shows that allows both blacks and whites to look at the racial climate of America in the 1990s. What the show's satire depends on; how the happy-go-lucky Negro with a banjo has been replaced by a "boom box"; how the show seeks to rectify racial imbalance; sexism as a correlate for racism. [Copyright Ebscohost]

Schultz, David A., ed. **2000**. *It's Show Time! Media, Politics, and Popular Culture.* New York, NY: Peter Lang. A collection of essays by scholars on the role of media in shaping views on politics. In molding public opinion, reality is often distorted.

Schultz, Margie. **1990**. *Ann Sothern: A Bio-Bibliography.* New York, NY: Greenwood Press. A brief biographical sketch followed by a complete listing of her films, records, television appearances, etc.

Schuth, H. Wayne. **1978**. *Mike Nichols.* Boston, MA: Twayne Publishers. A biography of film director Nichols with one chapter on his TV series "Family."

Schwartz, Lita Linzer, ed. **1999**. *Psychology and the Media: A Second Look.* Washington, DC: American Psychological Association. A collection of scholarly articles on the interaction of psychology and the media. Discusses popular perceptions of various groups and the interactions of psychologists with the media.

Schwartz, Sherwood. **1988**. *Inside Gilligan's Island: From Creation to Syndication.* Jefferson, NC: McFarland. The history of this cult classic, written by its creator. Appendices include an episode guide.

Schwoch, James, Mimi **White**, & Susan **Reilly**. **1992**. *Media Knowledge: Readings in Popular Culture, Pedagogy, and Critical Citizenship*. Albany, NY: State University of New York Press. The role of the media in teaching and how teachers can use it to promote critical thinking.

Sconce, Jeffrey. **2000**. *Haunted Media: Electronic Presence from Telegraphy to Television.* Durham, NC: Duke University Press. A cinema and television professor examines the association of electronic media with paranormal phenomena. Several moments in the history of telecommunications are explored with television being one. Shows such as "Twilight Zone" are used as examples of feeding the fantastical and paranoid imagination of the public.

Scott, Gini Graham. **1996**. *Can We Talk? The Power and Influence of Talk Shows.* New York, NY: Insight Books. A critical analysis of talk shows on both radio and television from social, legal, and psychological points of view.

Seger, Linda. **1996**. *When Women Call the Shots: The Developing Power and Influence of Women in Television and Film.* New York, NY: Henry Holt and Company. A script consultant and author traces the history of women creative artists (mostly behind the scenes) in film and television, with emphasis on film. Much of the book is based on interviews.

The Seinfeld Scripts: The First and Second Seasons. **1998**. New York, NY: Harper Perennial. A collection of some of the scripts from the early shows.

Seiter, Ellen Elizabeth. **1981**. *The Promise of Melodrama: Recent Women's Films and Soap Operas* (Ph.D. Dissertation, Northwestern University). Feminist analysis of popular culture, mostly films and soap operas.

Sekuler, Robert, & Randolph **Blake**. **1998**. *Star Trek on the Brain: Alien Minds, Human Minds.* New York, NY: W.H. Freeman and Company. Professors of psychology use "Star Trek" to describe what we know about psychology and the brain.

Selnow, Gary W., & Richard R. **Gilbert**. **1993**. *Society's Impact on Television: How the Viewing Public Shapes Television Programming.* Westport, CN: Praeger. Describes the influences on those who make television. Interviews with interviewing producers, writers, executives, etc., conclude that the public, interest groups, and advertisers influence TV as much as TV influences society.

Sennett, Ted. **1977**. *Your Show of Shows.* New York, NY: Macmillan Publishing. Well-illustrated account of this pioneering and innovative show. Discusses its origins, gives a behind-the-scenes look, and has information on the stars, Sid Caesar and Imogene Coca.

Settel, Irving, ed. **1958**. *How to Write Television Comedy.* Boston, MA: The Writer, Inc. An early guide from comedy writers on writing for television. Sample scripts are included.

Shaheen, Jack G. **1984**. *The TV Arab.* Bowling Green, OH: Bowling Green State University Popular Press. An analysis of the portrayal of Arabs, Muslims, and Middle Easterners on television news and drama.

Shales, Tom. **1982**. *On the Air!* New York, NY: Summit Books. A collection of brief essays by a well-known television critic (still prominent today).

Shaner, James Michael. **1981**. *Parental Empathy and Family-Role Interactions as Portrayed on Commercial Television* (Ph.D. Dissertation, University of North Carolina at Greensboro).

Shanks, Bob. **1976**. *The Cool Fire: How to Make It in Television*. New York, NY: W. W. Norton & Company. An insider's view on various aspects of the television business.

Sharrett, Christopher, ed. **1999**. *Mythologies of Violence in Postmodern Media*. Detroit, MI: Wayne State University Press. A series of critical essays by scholars on violence in the media. Major emphasis is on film but there is some discussion of television shows.

Shatner, William (with Chris Kreski). **1993**. *Star Trek Memories*. New York, NY: HarperCollins. "Captain Kirk" describes his experiences on the show and in the movies and with the fans.

Shatner, William (with Chris Kreski). **1999**. *Get a Life!* New York, NY: Pocket Books. With a title based on a famous saying by Shatner on "Saturday Night Live," this is a first person account of Shatner's working on Star Trek.

Shattuc, Jane M. **1997**. *The Talking Cure: TV Talk Shows and Women*. New York, NY: Routledge. Argues that talk shows are grounded in feminist politics and need to appeal to women. They provide a public forum for women who are not usually heard.

Shore, Michael (with Dick Clark). **1985**. *The History of American Bandstand: It's Got a Great Beat and You Can Dance to It*. New York, NY: Ballantine Books. A well-illustrated book about the history of the show and its influence. Also discusses fashions, youth culture, and music of the fifties, sixties, seventies, and eighties.

Signorielli, Nancy. **1985**. *Role Portrayal and Stereotyping on Television*. Westport, CN: Greenwood Press. An annotated bibliography to studies of portrayals of groups on television. Indexed in groups appendix only.

Signorielli, Nancy. **1991**. *A Sourcebook on Children and Television*. New York, NY: Greenwood Press. A summary of the many studies on television and children. Has many bibliographical references.

Silj, Alessandro, with others. **1988**. *East of Dallas: The European Challenge to American Television*. Bury St. Edmunds, London England: British Film Institute. Shows how "Dallas" has influenced the production of television shows in Europe.

Silverblatt, Art. **1995**. *Media Literacy: Keys to Interpreting Media Messages*. Westport, CN: Praeger. A guide to critical thinking about all forms of mass communication.

Silverblatt, Art, Jane **Ferry**, & Barbara **Finan**. **1999**. *Approaches to Media Literacy*. Armonk, NY: M.E. Sharpe. A guide to teaching media literacy written by three academics. Discusses different ways of analyzing media content.

Silvers, Phil. **1973**. *This Laugh Is on Me: The Phil Silvers Story*. Englewood Cliffs, NJ: Prentice-Hall. An autobiography by this comedian from stage, screen and television.

Simon, Anne. **1999**. *The Real Science Behind The X-Files: Microbes, Meteorites, and Mutants*. New York, NY: Simon and Schuster. A biology professor investigates the science of "The X-Files," including alien genes, microbes, cloning, nanotechnology, etc.

Simon, William H. **2001**. "Moral Pluck: Legal Ethics in Popular Culture." *Columbia Law Review*, March 2001, 101(2), p. 421. 26 pages. Traces the theme of legal ethics in popular culture through three fictional portrayals of lawyers in the novels of John Grisham and the television series "LA Law" and "The Practice." [Copyright Ebscohost]

Singer, Arthur J. **2000**. *Arthur Godfrey: The Adventures of an American Broadcaster.* Jefferson, NC: McFarland. An account of the life of the radio and television personality and pioneer.

Sison, Gustave F. P., Jr. **1985**. "M*A*S*H: An Illustration of Kohlberg's Stages." *Journal of Humanistic Psychology*, Spring 85, 25(2), p. 83. 8 pages. The main characters of the television show "M*A*S*H" are taken as an illustration of Kohlberg's cognitive-developmental stages of moral development. Physical and verbal samples of the characters' behaviors are given to illustrate each example. Kohlberg's concept of "moral atmosphere" also is considered in relation to the setting of "M*A*S*H." [Abstract from author] [Copyright Ebscohost]

Skal, David J. **1993**. *The Monster Show: A Cultural History of Horror*. New York, NY: W. W. Norton & Company. An analysis of horror in popular culture and how it reflects, in disguised form, the issues in society (Depression, nuclear threat, AIDS, etc.). Mostly about movies but talks about some TV programs.

Skelton, Scott, & Jim **Benson**. **1999**. *Rod Serling's "Night Gallery": An After-Hours Tour.* Syracuse, NY: Syracuse University Press. Following some introductory information, each season and each episode in each season are extensively analyzed. This book is more scholarly and critical than a normal book of episode guides.

Sklar, Robert. **1980**. *Prime-Time America: Life On and Behind the Television Screen*. New York, NY: Oxford University Press. A television critic discusses "the virtues and limitations of television ... in the context of ... American culture." Concludes with twelve reviews of television programs.

Skutch, Ira. **1998**. *The Days of Live: Television's Golden Age as Seen by 21 Directors Guild of America Members* (Directors Guild of America Oral History Series, no. 16). Lanham, MD: Scarecrow Press. Interviews with twenty-one directors of television during the "Golden Age" of live television in the 1950s. The book uses a topical approach, interspersing comments from the interviews throughout the book in subject areas, rather than each interview being printed separately.

Slade, Christina. **2002**. *The Real Thing: Doing Philosophy with Media*. New York, NY: Peter Lang. A scholarly investigation of the philosophically complex world of the media. The book concentrates on television and shows how we connect philosophical principles to what we watch. Coverage is worldwide.

Smith, Beretta Eileen. **1997**a. *Shaded Lives: Objectification and Agency in the Television Representations of African-American Women 1980–1994* (Ph.D. Dissertation, UCLA).

Smith, Buffalo Bob & Donna **McCrohan**. **1990**. *Howdy and Me*. New York, NY: Plume Books. Memoirs of Buffalo Bob, who created Howdy Doody.

Smith, Ella. **1974**. *Starring Miss Barbara Stanwyck*. New York, NY: Crown Publishers Inc. A heavily illustrated review of Barbara Stanwyck's career, mostly in films.

Smith, Evan S. **1999**. *Writing Television Sitcoms*. (A Perigree Book.) New York, NY: Berkley Publishing Group. A practical guide to writing situation comedy for television. It consists of advice from successful producers and is based on a premise driven approach. Gives examples from real sitcoms.

Smith, Gavin, ed. **1998**. *Sayles on Sayles*. London: Farber and Farber. A book length interview with the film director John Sayles. Includes discussion of one television program—"Shannon's Deal."

Smith, Ronald L. **1986**. *Cosby*. New York, NY: St. Martin's Press. A straight narrative (little critical comment) biography of Bill Cosby and his influence on the breakthrough of blacks on television.

Smith, Ronald L. **1987**. *Johnny Carson: An Unauthorized Biography*. New York, NY: St. Martin's Press. A life of the "Tonight Show" host, with anecdotes, little known facts, and insight into his character.

Smith, Ronald L. **1989**. *Sweethearts of 60s TV*. New York, NY: St. Martin's Press. The book is divided into "types" (girls next door, dream wives, comic cuties, fantasy figures, women of action) of female television stars of the 1960s. Each star has a short biographical sketch, information about the show(s) they starred in, and quotes by and about them.

Smith, Ronald L. **1997**. *Cosby: The Life of a Comedy Legend*. Amherst, NY: Prometheus Books. An updated edition of *Cosby* (see above), which includes more information about his later television shows.

Smoodin, Eric, ed. **1994**. *Disney Discourse: Producing the Magic Kingdom*. New York, NY: Routledge. Mostly about Disney Corporation and Disney films. Includes some references to the Disney television shows.

Sochen, June. **1987**. *Enduring Values: Women in Popular Culture* (Media and Society Series). New York, NY: Praeger. A discussion of popular treatment of women, with emphasis on performers and the images they portray.

Sochen, June. **1999**. *From Mae to Madonna: Women Entertainers in Twentieth-Century America*. Lexington, KY: University Press of Kentucky. An historian discusses one aspect of women in popular culture—women movie stars, TV performers and singers. Considered are societal and historical contexts, private vs. public personae, influence of genre, roles, audience, and role models.

Solow, Herbert F., & Robert H. **Justman**. **1996**. *Inside Star Trek: The Real Story*. New York, NY: Pocket Books. Two co-creators (with Roddenberry) of "Star Trek" describe their experiences with the creation and development of the show.

Sorkin, Aaron. **2002**. *The West Wing*. New York, NY: Pocket Books. The producer of the show presents "the official companion." Extensive information on characters and on each episode.

Soter, Tom. **2001**. *Investigating Couples: A Critical Analysis of "The Thin Man," "The Avengers," and "The X-Files."* Jefferson, NC: McFarland. The author (an editor and comedy teacher) discusses male-female detective pairs. Emphasis is on the shows in the title. Episode guides for each series are given in the appendices.

Spelling Aaron (with Jefferson Graham). **1996**. *Aaron Spelling: A Prime-Time Life*. New York, NY: St. Martin's Press. An autobiography by one of television's most successful producers ("Charlie's Angels," "Love Boat," "Beverly Hills 90210," etc.).

Spence, Louise. **1990**. *Life's Little Problems and Pleasures: Watching Soap Operas* (Ph.D. Dissertation, New York University). Studies those who watch soap operas and how they take them seriously and looks at the narrative discourses of soap opera's relating to this audience.

Sperber, A.M. **1986**. *Murrow: His Life and Times*. New York, NY: Freundlich Books. A definitive lengthy biography of Edward R. Murrow.

Spigel, Lynn. **1992**. *Make Room for TV: Television and the Family Ideal in Post-War America*. Chicago, IL: University of Chicago Press. Analyzes the impact of television in its early years (i.e., post-war America) and how it influenced the way we thought about family life.

Spigel, Lynn. **2001**. *Welcome to the Dreamhouse: Popular Media and Post War Suburbs*. Durham, NC: Duke University Press. A feminist scholar explores post-war U.S. media in relation to ideals of home and family life. Many aspects of popular culture (toys, comic books, magazines, television) are explored and analyzed regarding assumptions about class, gender, ethnicity, race, and sexual orientation.

Spigel, Lynn, & Michael **Curtin**, eds. **1997**. *The Revolution Wasn't Televised: Sixties Television and Social Conflict*. New York, NY: Routledge. Looks at television programs in the 1960s in the context of larger social, political, and cultural forces. Unlike earlier and later, this was a time of much standardization; yet some nontraditional voices of the larger society were heard on TV.

Spigel, Lynn, & Denise **Mann**, eds. **1992**. *Private Screenings: Television and the Female Consumer*. Minneapolis: University of Minnesota Press. A collection of essays on the relationship of women, television, and consumer culture.

Spignesi, Stephen J. **1987**. *Mayberry, My Hometown: The Ultimate Guidebook to America's Favorite TV Small Town*. Ann Arbor, MI: Pierian Press. An encyclopedia for fans giving episodes, characters, events, interview, etc.

Spoto, Donald. **1983**. *The Dark Side of Genius: The Life of Alfred Hitchcock*. Boston, MA: Little, Brown and Company. The definitive biography (as opposed to criticism) of Hitchcock.

Spragens, William C. **1995**. *Electronic Magazines: Soft News Programs on Network Television*. Westport, CN: Praeger. An analysis of segments shown on television news magazines such as "60 Minutes."

Staiger, Jane. **2000**. *Blockbuster TV: Must-See Sitcoms in the Network Era*. New York, NY: New York University Press. Discusses four situation comedies the author, a professor, considers true blockbusters. She uses these as case studies to analyze their appeal and what goes into the construction of mass audiences.

Stark, Steven D. **1997**. *Glued to the Set: The 60 Television Shows and Events That Made Us Who We Are Today*. New York, NY: The Free Press. A journalist explores the influence of television on the baby boom generation by discussing specific shows and events covered by television.

Starr, Michael Seth. **1997**. *Art Carney: A Biography*. New York, NY: Fromm International. The life of this famous TV sidekick to Jackie Gleason.

Steenland, Sally. **1990**. *What's Wrong with This Picture? The Status of Women on Screen and Behind the Camera in Entertainment TV*. Washington, D.C.: National Commission on Working Women of Wider Opportunities for Women. A study of women in television, both in terms of employment and on-screen portrayals.

Stein, Ben. **1979**. *The View from Sunset Boulevard*. New York, NY: Basic Books. A key study, often quoted in other books, on how certain groups are portrayed on television.

Stein, Sarah. **2001**. "Legitimating TV Journalism in 60 Minutes: The Ramifications of Subordinating the Visual to the Primacy of the Word." *Critical Studies in Media Communication*, Sept. 2001, 18(3), p. 249. 21 pages. Discusses the implicit bias carried by the television news magazine genre to illustrate this bias in examining several episodes of the TV program "60 Minutes." Negative print media attention generated by the refusal of CBS to air a controversial interview with a former tobacco executive in 1995. [Copyright Ebscohost]

Stempel, Tom. **1992**. *Storytellers to the Nation: A History of American Television Writing*. New York, NY: Continuum. A history of TV writing, highlighting many important writers and many TV shows.

Sternbach, Rick, & Michael **Okuda**. **1991**. *Star Trek: The Next Generation Technical Manual*. New York, NY: Pocket Books.

Stone, Joseph, & Tim **Yohn**. **1992**. *Prime Time and Misdemeanors: Investigating the 1950s TV Quiz Scandal—A D.A.'s Account*. New Brunswick, NJ: Rutgers University Press. An account of the quiz show scandals of the 1950s written by an assistant district attorney who helped uncover it and prosecute those involved.

Storm, Gale. **1981**. *I Ain't Down Yet: The Autobiography of My Little Margie*. Indianapolis, IN: Bobbs-Merrill Company. Autobiography of the movie and television star who played Margie.

Story, David. **1993**. *America on the Rerun: TV Shows That Never Die*. Secaucus, NJ: Citadel Press. Interviews, anecdotes, and general information about shows from the 1960s that are still widely seen as reruns.

Strait, Raymond. **1983**. *Alan Alda: A Biography*. New York, NY: St. Martin's Press. A popular biography of the star of "M*A*S*H" with some early chapters devoted to his father, the actor Robert Alda.

Strait, Raymond. **1985**. *James Garner*. New York, NY: St. Martin's Press. Based on interviews and popular media, a biography of the star of "Maverick" and "The Rockford Files."

Streitmatter, Rodger. **1997**. *Mightier Than the Sword: How the News Media Have Shaped American History*. Boulder, CO: Westview Press. Shows the influence the media had in shaping 14 events in American history. All types of press (newspapers, magazines, radio, TV) are covered depending on the event.

Sturcken, Frank. **1990**. *Live Television: The Golden Age of 1946–1958 in New York*. Jefferson, NC: McFarland. A history of television during its so-called "Golden Age" with emphasis on the live drama anthologies of the era.

Suman, Michael, ed. **1997**. *Religion and Prime Time Television*. Westport, CN: Praeger. Based on a conference at UCLA, religious figures, academics, critics, and industry representatives discuss the portrayal of religion on prime time television.

Suman, Michael, & Gabriel **Rossman**, eds. **2000**. *Advocacy Groups and the Entertainment Industry*. Westport, CN: Praeger. Based on a conference at UCLA in 1997, advocates, lawyers, academics, and industry representatives discuss how advocacy groups affect the entertainment industry. Television shows are sometimes used as examples.

Sumser, John. **1996**. *Morality and Social Order in Television Crime Drama*. Jefferson, NC: McFarland. Explores how television drama (mysteries specifically) views crime and social order. Shows how certain assumptions, stock characters, etc. allow TV to resolve a mystery in 44 minutes.

Surette, Ray, ed. **1984**. *Justice and the Media: Issues and Research*. Springfield, IL: Charles C. Thomas. A series of essays on the state of knowledge (at time of publication) on the relationship of media, crime, and criminal justice. News coverage, violence and its effects, and portrayal of crime and the criminal justice system in the media (including television) are covered.

Surette, Ray. **1992**. *Media, Crime, and Criminal Justice: Images and Realities*. Pacific Grove, CA: Brooks/Cole Publishing Company. Shows how mass media influences the way the public thinks about crime. Compares crime as portrayed in media (news and fiction) and the reality.

Swanson, Dorothy Collins. **2000**. *The Story of Viewers for Quality Television: From Grassroots to Prime Time*. Syracuse, NY: Syracuse University Press. Founder and president of Viewers for Quality Television describes its founding, history and impact and discusses its implications for viewers to have a say in what is on television.

Tabarlet, Joseph Odell. **1993**. *Sexual Incidents on Prime Time Television: Content Analysis and Theories of Effects* (Ph.D. Dissertation, Florida State University). A study of sexual incidents from shows aired in Fall 1990 on networks. Uses two theories (cultivation analysis and sexual socialization) to analyze effects.

Takei, George. **1994**. *To the Stars: The Autobiography of George Takei, Star Trek's Mr. Sulu*. New York, NY: Pocket Books. The autobiography of one of the earliest Asian Americans to be a regular on a primetime network show.

Tan, Alexis S. **1981**. *Mass Communication Theories and Research*. Columbus, OH: Grid Publishing Co. A book intended to be used as a textbook for upper division or graduate courses in mass communication. Treats mass communication as a science.

Tan, Alexis S. **1985**. *Mass Communication Theories and Research* (2nd edition). New York, NY: John Wiley & Sons. A new edition of the 1981 text.

Tartikoff, Brandon. **1992**. *The Last Great Ride*. New York, NY: Turtle Bay Books. An anecdotal account of the "glory days" of NBC television (the 1980s) by the head of programming at the time.

Tasker, Yvonne. **1998**. *Working Girls: Gender and Sexuality in Popular Cinema*. New York, NY: Routledge. This book discusses the portrayal of women, especially as working types, in film of the 70s, 80s, and 90s. Postulates that popular cinema makes a connection between working women and sexual performance. Although the book is essentially about cinema, there is some mention of television shows.

Taylor, Annette M., & David **Upchurch**. **1996**. "Northern Exposure and Mythology of the Global Community." *Journal of Popular Culture*, Fall 96, 30(2), p. 75. 11 pages. Details how the television series "Northern Exposure" addressed the challenge of developing a modern global mythology in a fictional setting. Elements of the mythic early America. [Copyright Ebscohost]

Taylor, Ella. **1989**. *Prime-Time Families: Television Culture in Postwar America*. Berkeley: University of California Press. A history of the portrayal of families on television.

Taylor, John Russell. **1978**. *Hitch: The Life and Work of Alfred Hitchcock*. London, England: Faber and Faber. A biography and critical review of Alfred Hitchcock, with some parts devoted to his television show.

Terrace, Vincent. **1993**. *Television Character and Story Facts*. Jefferson, NC: McFarland. A directory listing characters (cast) and the plotlines of over 1000 shows from 1945 to 1992.

Terrace, Vincent. **2000**. *Television Sitcom Factbook*. Jefferson, NC: McFarland. An alphabetical directory of situation comedies from 1985 to 2000. Brief information (about one page) on each show.

Theberge, Leonard J. **1981**. *Crooks, Conmen, and Clowns: Businessmen in TV Entertainment*. Washington, D.C.: The Media Institute. The author and the Media Institute did a content analysis of the portrayal of business on television. Both status and role were analyzed. Conclusion was that over two-thirds of businessmen on television were portrayed negatively.

Thomas, Danny. **1991**. *Make Room for Danny* (with Bill Davidson). New York, NY: G.P. Putnam's Sons. An autobiography of one of television's early stars and producers.

Thomas, Sari, & William A.C. **Evans**, eds. **1990**. *Communication and Culture: Language Performance, Technology, and Media*. Selected Proceedings from the Sixth International Conference on Culture and Communication, Temple University, 1986 (Studies in Communication, Volume 4). Norwood, NJ: Ablex Publishing Corporation. Scholarly conference papers dealing with language, communication, and mass media. International in scope. Only a few chapters discuss television.

Thompson, Robert J. **1990**. *Adventures on Prime Time: The Television Programs of Stephen J. Cannell*. New York, NY: Praeger. A look at the shows of one of TV's best known producers ("A-Team," "Maverick," "The Rockford Files," etc.). Takes a critical, interpretive approach rather than descriptive.

Thompson, Robert J. **1996**. *Television's Second Golden Age: From Hill Street Blues to ER*. New York, NY: Continuum. Proceeding from the thesis that the best television ever made has been produced since 1980, Thompson discusses several prime time network dramas from this time period.

Thurer, Shari L. **1994**. *The Myths of Motherhood: How Culture Re-invents the Good Mother*. Boston, MA: Houghton-Mifflin. An historical account of the ways motherhood has been portrayed in art, literature, etc.

Tinker, Grant, & Bud **Rukeyser**. **1994**. *Tinker in Television: From General Sarnoff* *to General Electric*. New York, NY: Simon & Schuster. An autobiography of one of television's top executives, the founder of MTM Enterprises. Gives good insight into the workings of television and, of course, concentrates on "The Mary Tyler Moore Show."

Toll, Robert C. **1982**. *The Entertainment Machine: American Show Business in the Twentieth Century*. Oxford, England: Oxford University Press. A history of popular culture, show business, and mass media in the twentieth century, highlighting key people and trends.

Torres, Sasha, ed. **1998**. *Living Color: Race and Television in the United States*. Durham, NC: Duke University Press. Scholarly essays describing race on American television. It covers several genres, historical periods, and racial formations. The book also shows how class, gender, and sexuality interact with images of race. Much of the book covers news events (e.g., Rodney King, O.J. Simpson) as depicted on TV but also includes some discussion of prime time television shows.

Tracy, Kathleen. **1998**. *Jerry Seinfeld: The Entire Domain*. Secaucus, NJ: Birch Lane Press. A biography of the man and a history of the series.

Tuchman, Gaye, Arlene Kaplan **Daniels**, & James **Benet**, eds. **1978**. *Hearth and Home: Images of Women in the Mass Media*. New York, NY: Oxford University Press. Mass media portrayals of women are discussed, with one part devoted to television.

Tucker, Kenneth. **2000**. *Eliot Ness and the Untouchables: The Historical Reality and the Film and Television Adaptations*. Jefferson, NC: McFarland. A scholarly account of the real Eliot Ness and how he was portrayed in films and television. Episode guides to television series.

Tulloch, John. **2000**. *Watching Television Audiences: Cultural Theories and Methods*. New York, NY: Arnold. A professor discusses theories and methods of audience research, surveying works done in a variety of genres. Because author is British, many examples are from British shows.

Tulloch, John, & Henry **Jenkins**. **1995**. *Science Fiction Audiences: Watching Doctor Who and Star Trek*. London, England: Routledge. A study of fans of science fiction shows, especially "Doctor Who" and "Star Trek." Attempts to show the great diversity of sci-fi fans, as opposed to the usual stereotypes.

Turner, Lynn H., & Helen M. **Sterk**. **1994**. *Differences That Make a Difference: Examining the Assumptions in Gender Research*. Westport, CN: Bergin & Garvey. A critical approach to gender research with some discussion of portrayals on television. Indexed in "groups" appendix only.

Turner, Patricia A. **1994**. *Ceramic Uncles & Celluloid Mammies: Black Images and Their Influence on Culture*. New York, NY: Anchor Books. An historical account of black images in toys, film, television, etc.

Turow, Joseph. **1984**. *Media Industries: The Production of News and Entertainment*. New York, NY: Longman. A study of the mass media as an industry and how the public can bring about changes.

Turow, Joseph. **1989**. *Playing Doctor: Television, Storytellers, and Medical Power*. New York, NY: Oxford University Press. Analyzes the TV industry's relationship with the medical system from the viewpoint of social power research.

Much discussion of TV's portrayal of the medical profession and its influence on how society views doctors and nurses.

Twitchell, James B. **1992**. *Carnival Culture: The Trashing of Taste in America*. New York, NY: Columbia University Press. Describes the vulgar (i.e., "trash") in popular culture as an object of scholarly study. Though not favorable towards pop culture, author does not condemn it outright either.

U.S. Congress. 1960. House. Committee on Interstate and Foreign Commerce. *Investigation of Television Quiz Shows*. Hearings before a Subcommittee of the Committee ... October 6–November 6, 1959. Washington, D.C.: U.S. Government Printing Office. Congressional hearings on the quiz show scandals of the late 1950s. Testimony from key players with discussion of the shows themselves.

U.S. Congress. 1977a. House. Committee on Interstate and Foreign Commerce. *Sex and Violence on T.V.* Hearings before the Subcommittee on Communications ... July 9, August 17–18, 1976. Serial No. 94–140. Washington, D.C.: U.S. Government Printing Office. Hearings on the "issue of televised violence and obscenity," with some references to specific shows.

U.S. Congress. 1977b. House. Committee on Interstate and Foreign Commerce. *Sex and Violence on T.V.* Hearings before the Subcommittee on Communications ... March 2, 1977. Serial No. 95–130. Washington, D.C.: U.S. Government Printing Office. Same as above. Also contains some interesting comment sheets from CBS program practices.

U.S. Congress. 1977c. House. Select Committee on Aging. *Age Stereotyping and Television*. Hearing ... September 8, 1977. Washington, D.C.: U.S. Government Printing Office. A Congressional inquiry into the portrayal of the elderly on television. Includes an extensive staff report.

U.S. Congress. 1984. House. Committee on the Judiciary. Subcommittee on Crime. *Crime and Violence in the Media*. Hearings before ... ninety eighth Congress, first session April 13, 1983, Serial No. 83. Washington, D.C.: U.S. Government Printing Office. No mention of specific shows in depth. Indexed for references to groups.

U.S. Congress. 1985. Senate. Committee on Governmental Affairs. *The Role of the Entertainment Industry in Deglamorizing Drug Use*. Hearing before the Permanent Subcommittee on Investigations, March 20, 1985. Washington, D.C.: U.S. Government Printing Office. Testimony and reports dealing with the relationship of television and the "drug culture," including alcoholism. Interesting inserts give drug abuse themes on network programs.

U.S. Department of Health and Human Services, Public Health Service, National Institute of Mental Health. **1982**. *Television and Behavior: Ten Years of Scientific Progress and Implications for the Eighties*, Volume 2: Technical Reviews. Rockville, MD: Author. An update of the famous 1972 Surgeon General's report, this is a collection of scientific studies. Some of the reports give examples of television shows.

Vahimagi, Tise. **1998**. *The Untouchables*. London, England: British Film Institute. A general introduction to gangsters in popular culture, mainly film and television, followed by a description of the television show. There is background on the show, discussion of themes, chapters on each season, and episode guides with very brief information.

Van Fugua, Joy. **1996**. *"Tell the Story:" AIDS in Popular Culture* (Ph.D. Dissertation, University of Pittsburgh). Argues that popular culture is an important outlet for the perception of AIDS in our society. Analyzes stories with no judgment on "truth." Examples are taken from television, film, and video.

Van Hise, James. **1991**. *Addams Family Revealed: An Unauthorized Looks at America's Spookiest Family.* Las Vegas, NV: Pioneer Books. A popular "fan-type" book about the show with descriptions of actors, background, etc. Includes an episode guide.

Van Hise, James. **1992**. *Cheers: Where Everybody Knows Your Name.* Las Vegas, NV: Pioneer Books. Profiles the stars and contains an episode guide. Book was published before show ended.

Vande Berg, Leah R., & Nick **Trujillo**. **1989**. *Organizational Life on Television.* Norwood, NJ: Ablex Publishing Corporation. A thorough analysis of the way organizations, occupations, and industries are shown on television. Also discusses organizational actions, managers, values, and cultures.

Vande Berg, Leah R., & Lawrence A. **Wenner**. **1991**. *Television Criticism: Approaches and Applications.* New York, NY: Longman. Essays on critical viewing of television, meant to serve as a textbook for critical thinking related to watching TV.

Vane, Edwin T., & Lynne S. **Gross**. **1994**. *Programming for TV, Radio, and Cable.* Boston, MA: Focal Press. Intended for use as a textbook for classes in television programming.

Voort, T. H. A. Van Der. **1986**. *Television Violence: A Child's-Eye View.* Amsterdam, Netherlands: Elsevier Science Publishers. A study, from a psychological viewpoint, on television violence and children. Focus is not on effects *per se*, but on what children experience while watching television.

Wagner, Jon, & Jan **Lundeen**. **1998**. *Deep Space and Shared Time: "Star Trek" in the American Mythos.* Westport, CN: Praeger. An anthropologist and a nursing scholar analyze "Star Trek" as a "culturally expressive mythology and a reflection of America's changing social values." Using many examples from the television and movie versions of "Star Trek," this book examines the humanistic optimistic creed of its mythological universe. Shows the tension between liberalism and issues of gender, race and class and considers the ways "Star Trek" explores self, humanity, gender and utopian visions.

Wahl, Otto F. **1995**. *Media Madness: Public Images of Mental Illness.* New Brunswick, NJ: Rutgers University Press. Analyzes depiction of mental illness in the media. Concludes the image is generally unfavorable. Covers all media, with some references to television. One appendix is a useful list of television shows that had episodes about mental illness since 1980.

Wakefield, Dan. **1976**. *All Her Children: The Real Life Story of Americas Favorite Soap Opera.* Garden City, NJ: Double Day & Company. A behind the scenes account of one of TV's leading soap operas.

Waldrep, Shelton, ed. **2000**. *The Seventies: The Age of Glitter in Popular Culture.* New York, NY: Routledge. Explores culture of the nineteen seventies, discussing film, music, fashion, etc. There is some discussion of television programs.

Waldron, Robert. **1987**. *Oprah!* New York, NY: St. Martin's Press.
Waldron, Vince. **1994**. *The Official Dick Van Dyke Show Book.* New York, NY: Hyperion. A detailed account of the show, describing its origins, development, casting, and production. Also has many behind the scenes tidbits and descriptions of some of the most critically acclaimed and popular episodes.
Walley, David G. **1975**. *The Ernie Kovacs Phile.* New York, NY: Bolder Books. A critic writes a light-hearted paean to Ernie Kovacs.
Walsh, John. **1998**. *No Mercy: The Host of "America's Most Wanted" Hunts the Worst Criminals of Our Time in Shattering True Crime Cases.* New York, NY: Pocket Books. A look at the show from many angles including the criminal, the police investigators, and the show itself. Several important cases are discussed.
Walters, Suzanna Danuta. **2001**. *All the Rage: The Story of Gay Visibility in America.* Chicago, IL: University of Chicago Press. Discusses the new gay visibility, especially in popular culture. Is this a sign of social acceptance or window dressing? Walters, a professor of sociology, argues they coexist. While gays are more accepted now, there is still discrimination and stereotyping.
Warner, Gary. **1994**. *All My Children: The Complete Family Scrapbook.* Los Angeles, CA: General Publishing Group. A heavily illustrated "coffee table" book giving background and storylines. Also includes descriptions of the families and other characters and a trivia section.
Warren, Alan. **1996**. *This Is a Thriller.* Jefferson, NC: McFarland. A history and analysis of the show with extensive (2–3 pages) episode guides.
Warrick, Ruth. **1980**. *The Confessions of Phoebe Tyler.* Eaglewood Cliffs, NJ: Prentice-Hall, Inc. The actress who plays Phoebe Tyler, a leading character on "All My Children," takes the reader backstage. She discusses both her life and the character's life and how they intertwine.
Weatherby, W.J. **1992**. *Jackie Gleason: An Intimate Portrait of the Great One.* New York, NY: Pharos Book. A popular sketch biography of the television star.
Weimann, Gabriel. **2000**. *Communicating Unreality: Modern Media and the Reconstruction of Reality.* Thousand Oaks, CA: Sage Publications. A scholarly review of studies on the influence of media, especially in regard to how viewers perceive the real world. The author examines mass-mediated images and the blurring of reality and fiction. All media, including internet, are discussed but television plays a prominent role.
Weiner, Ed. **1992**. *The TV Guide TV Book: 40 Years of All Time Greatest Television Facts, Fads, Hits and History* (with the editors of TV Guide). New York, NY: Harper Collins. A book full of tidbits on various shows, culled from the magazine.
Weisbrot, Robert. **1998**. *Xena, Warrior Princess.* New York, NY: Doubleday. An official guide to the show: its origins, cast profiles and episode guides. There is also a chapter devoted to "heroines of the small screen." Color illustrations are included.
Weissman, Ginny, & Coyne Steven **Sanders**. **1993**. *The Dick Van Dyke Show.* New York, NY: St. Martins Press. Heavily illustrated book about many aspects of the show. Includes short biographies of personnel involved and very brief synopses with cast of the episodes. Also has a trivia quiz and a script for one episode.

West, Richard. **1987**. *Television Westerns: Major and Minor Series, 1946–1978*. Jefferson, NC: McFarland. Short descriptions of westerns on television during period covered in title, alphabetically arranged.

Westerfelhaus, Robert, & Teresa A. **Combs**. **1998**. "Criminal Investigations and Spiritual Quests: The X-Files as an Example of Hegemonic Concordance in a Mass-Mediated society." *Journal of Communication Inquiry*, April 98, 22(2), p. 205. 16 pages. Argues that the television series "The X-Files" is a reflection of contemporary concerns and a new expression of an age-old dialectic between scientific skepticism and a spiritual faith that accepts the mysterious. Use of Celeste Condit's model of hegemony in a mass-mediated society; tension between Western science and nonscientific ways of knowing. [Copyright Ebscohost]

Westin, Av. **1982**. *News Watch: How TV Decides the News*. New York, NY: Simon & Schuster. A former news producer for CBS and ABC discusses how television news has affected the way America votes and thinks.

White, Matthew, & Jaffer **Ali**. **1988**. *The Official Prisoner Companion*. New York, NY: Warner Books. Very detailed episode guides followed by notes, debated issues, themes, etc. Also has some shooting scripts.

White, Mimi. **1992**. *Tele-Advising: Therapeutic Discourse in American Television*. Chapel Hill, NC: University of North Carolina Press. A psychological study of television as a means of therapy, especially as related to conversation, debate, confession, and other means of discourse.

White, Patrick J. **1991**. *The Complete Mission Impossible Dossier*. New York, NY: Avon Books. Information about this show includes origins, cast, production, crew, etc. Also a fairly detailed episode guide.

Whitfield, Stephen E., & Gene **Roddenberry**. **1968**. *The Making of Star Trek*. New York, NY: Ballantine Books. The history of the TV show, describing the concept and creation, the making of the pilot and a close look at the production of the show. Also describes the ship, special effects, characters, aliens, etc.

Wiggins, Kayala McKinney. **1993**. "Epic Heroes, Ethical Issues, and Time Paradoxes in Quantum Leap." *Journal of Popular Film & Television*, Fall 93, 21(3), p. 111. 10 pages. Focuses on the television series "Quantum Leap," which pits an epic hero and an anti-hero against the wrongs that have been done in past lives. The liberal egalitarian ethical stance of the show; how the series deals with issues of race, animal rights, women, the physically disabled, time paradoxes and more. [Copyright Ebscohost]

Wilcox, C. **1992**. "To Boldly Return Where Others Have Gone Before: Cultural Change and the Old and New Star Treks." *Extrapolation*, Spring 92, 33(1), p. 88. 13 pages. Compares the old and new series of Gene Roddenberry's "Star Trek" series, and discusses any cultural changes that it went through over the twenty years between the demise of the original series and the advent of the new one including a changed conception of women's roles, the sharp decline of violence in the show, the growing acceptance of the limitations of American power and how the characters have changed. [Copyright Ebscohost]

Wilcox, Rhonda V. **1996**. "Dominant Female, Superior Male." *Journal of Popular Film & Television*, Spring 96, 24(1), p. 26. 8 pages. Discusses the meaning of gender conflicts between the male and female characters in the television programs "Remington Steele," "Moonlighting," and "Lois & Clark." Patterns of male control in spite of female dominance. Purpose of the programs to illustrate that women underestimate men. [Copyright Ebscohost]

Wilcox, Rhonda V. **1999**. "There Will Never Be a Very Special Buffy." *Journal of Popular Film & Television*, Summer 99, 27(2), p. 16. 8 pages. Analyzes the television series "Buffy the Vampire Slayer," created by Joss Whedon. Context of language and interaction of the series; discussion on the series' symbolism; information on the characters; discussion on the episodes. [Copyright Ebscohost]

Wilcox, Rhonda V., & David **Lavery**, eds. **2002**. *Fighting the Forces.* Lanham, MD: Rowman & Littlefield. An academic analysis of "Buffy, " deconstructing the text. Covers race, gender, religion, etc. A group of scholars analyze the social and cultural issues of the show and place it in a literary context.

Wild, David. **1999**. *The Showrunners: A Season Inside the Billion-Dollar, Death-Defying, Madcap World of Television's Real Stars.* New York, NY: HarperCollins. A journalist colorfully describes a season of television (1998–99), concentrating on the "bankable" writers and producers.

Wildermuth, Mark. **1999**. "The Edge of Chaos: Structural Conspiracy and Epistemology in the X-Files." *Journal of Popular Film & Television*, Winter 99, 26(4), p. 146. 12 pages. Discusses the epistemology in the television program "The X-Files" and the ways in which the program situates itself in the landscape of scientific culture in the late 20th century. [Copyright Ebscohost]

Wilk, Max. **1976**. *The Golden Age of Television: Notes from the Survivors.* New York, NY: Delacorte Press. A man who worked in television interviewed many of those involved in television during the 1950s. Based on these interviews, this is a history of TV's so-called "Golden Age."

Williams, Carol Traynor. **1992**. *"It's Time for My Story": Soap Opera Sources, Structure, and Response* (Media and Society Series). Westport, CN: Praeger. A look at soap operas, the people involved in making them, the audiences, and the archetypes of form and content. Takes a psychological and feminist popular culture approach.

Williams, Frederick, Robert **LaRose**, & Frederica **Frost**. **1981**. *Children, Television, and Sex-Role Stereotyping.* New York, NY: Praeger. Describes the influence of television on children's views on sex roles in our society.

Williams, J.P. **1996**. "Biology and Destiny: The Dynamics of Gender Crossing in Quantum Leap." *Women's Studies in Communication*, Fall 96, 19(3), p. 273. 18 pages. Discusses the inter-relationship of gender as social category and sexuality as a biological factor as portrayed in the television show "Quantum Leap." Innate sense of sexuality; feminism as an aura of artificiality; biological distinction; association of physical violence with traditional masculinity. [Copyright Ebscohost]

Williams, John A., & Dennis A. **Williams**. **1991**. *If I Stop I'll Die: The Comedy and Tragedy of Richard Pryor.* New York, NY: Thunder's Mouth Press.

Williams, Martin. **1982**. *TV: The Casual Art.* New York, NY: Oxford University Press. A collection of essays from a TV critic, most originally published in the

Village Voice. Essays deal with many topics related to television, including reviews of specific programs.

Wilson, Clint C., & Felix **Gutierrez**. **1985**. *Minorities and Media: Diversity and the End of Mass Communication*. Beverly Hills, CA: Sage Publications. Examines the relationship between mass communication media and the four largest racial minorities in the U.S. (Native Americans, Blacks, Latinos, Asians). Discusses both portrayals and "behind the scenes" (employment and control).

Winch, Samuel P. **1997**. *Mapping the Cultural Space of Journalism: How Journalists Distinguish News from Entertainment*. Westport, CN: Praeger. An analysis of "boundary-marking" in the journalistic field. Discusses how journalists try to distinguish hard news from "tabloid" news; news from entertainment; and broadcast journalism from print journalism. Heavy emphasis on television.

Winegarden, Alan D., & Marilyn **Fuss-Reineck**. **1993**. "Using Star Trek: The Next Generation to Teach Concepts in Persuasion, Family Communication and Communication Ethics." *Communication Education*, April 93, 42(2), p. 179. 10 pages. Provides a rationale for the use of popular television in the classroom, and examples and applications from the syndicated television series "Star Trek: the Next Generation." [Copyright Ebscohost]

Winn, Marie. **1977**. *The Plug-In Drug: Television, Children, and the Family*. New York, NY: Viking Press. Discusses the negative effects of television viewing on children and on the family. Likens it to a drug and makes suggestions on how to kick the addiction.

Winn, Marie. **1985**. *The Plug-In Drug: Television, Children, and the Family* (revised edition). New York, NY: Viking Press. A revised edition of the 1977 work.

Winship, Michael. **1988**. *Television*. New York, NY: Random House. A companion volume to a public television series. Concentrates on the people behind the shows and has extensive quotes from them.

Witney, Stephen B., & Ronald P. **Abeles**, eds. **1980**. *Television and Social Behavior: Beyond Violence and Children*. Hillsdale, NJ: Lawrence Erlbaum Associates. Follows up on the Surgeon General's report by giving more emphasis to all aspects of television's influence on social behavior than just to violence and children.

Wittebols, James. **1998**. *Watching M*A*S*H, Watching America: A Social History of the 1972–1983 Television Series*. Jefferson, NC: McFarland. Analyzes "M*A*S*H" in terms of its meaning, impact, and reflection of its times. Discusses the show in the context of societal change in the 1970s. Shows how the series changed to reflect changes in society and politics in the early 1980s.

Wolfe, Peter. **1997**. *In the Zone: The Twilight World of Rod Serling*. Bowling Green, OH: Bowling Green State University Popular Press. A professor analyzes "The Twilight Zone" in terms of themes, artistry, and technical aspects. Discusses how the show tests assumptions about humanity and makes statements about politics, society, and psychology.

Wolff, Jurgen. **1996**. *Successful Sitcom Writing* (with L.P. Ferrante). Revised edition. New York, NY: St. Martin's Press. A guide to how to write situation comedies and how to sell them successfully. Includes examples of scripts from specific shows.

Woll, Allen L., & Randall M. **Miller**. **1987**. *Ethnic and Racial Images in American Film and Television: Historical Essays and Bibliography*. New York, NY: Garland Publishing, Inc. Good overviews of portrayals of various minority groups in film and television. Extensive bibliographies at end of each chapter.

Woods, Paul A. **1997**. *Weirdsville, U.S.A.: The Obsessive Universe of David Lynch*. London: Plexus. An account of Lynch's life and career, emphasizing his obsessive personality.

Worland, Eric J. **1989**. *The Other Living-Room: Evolving Cold War Imagery in Popular TV Programs of the Vietnam Era, 1960–1975* (Ph.D. Dissertation, University of California, Los Angeles). Analyzes prime time representations of the Cold War during the Vietnam era. Several shows are discussed.

Worland, Rick. **1996**. "Sign-posts Up Ahead: The Twilight Zone, The Outer Limits." *Science Fiction Studies*, March 96, 23(1), p. 103. 20 pages. Discusses information on the television science fiction programs "The Twilight Zone" and "The Outer Limits...." [Copyright Ebscohost]

Wylie, Max. **1970**. *Writing for Television*. New York, NY: Cowles Book Company. A basic text on TV writing with several lengthy examples from various types of television shows.

Yearwood, Gladstone Lloyd. **1979**. *Semiology in Television Criticism: A Study of Aesthetics and Ideology in a Television Program—"Get Christie Love!"* (Ph.D. Dissertation, Ohio University). An early attempt to use semantics (meaning) in the study of television and its application to one show.

Yeates, Helen. **2001**. "Ageing Masculinity in NYPD Blue: A Spectacle of Incontinence, Impotence, and Mortality." *Canadian Review of American Studies*, 31(2), p. 47. 10 pages. Explores middle-age masculine problems and crises as portrayed by the character of Sipowicz on "NYPD Blue."

Yoggy, Gary A. **1995**. *Riding the Video Range: The Rise and Fall of the Western on Television*. Jefferson, NC: McFarland. A very thorough and insightful discussion of the history of the western on television.

Yoggy, Gary, ed. **1998**. *Back in the Saddle: Essays on Western Film and Television Actors*. Jefferson, NC: McFarland. Essays on specific actors who made their fame in westerns. Covers both films and television.

Zehme, Bill. **1999**. *Lost in the Funhouse: The Life and Mind of Andy Kaufman*. New York, NY: Delacorte Press. A journalist/biographer writes this biography of the controversial comedian. It is based on his writings and interviews with acquaintances and family.

Zenka, Lorraine. **1995**. *Days of Our Lives: The Complete Family Album* (a 30th anniversary celebration). New York, NY: HarperCollins. Well-illustrated book about this soap opera. Contains interviews, characters and plot descriptions, behind-the-scenes information, and other miscellanea.

Zicree, Marc Scott. **1982**. *The Twilight Zone Companion*. Toronto, Canada: Bantam Books. Following some introductory information on Rod Sterling and the origins of the show, the book is an episode by episode guide with summaries, critical remarks, quotes, and tidbits about the episode.

Zillmann, Dolf, Jennings **Bryant**, & Aletha C. **Huston**, eds. **1994**. *Media, Children, and the Family: Social Scientific, Psychodynamic, and Clinical Perspectives*.

Hillsdale, NJ: Lawrence Erlbaum Associates, Publishers. Papers from a conference which brought together the disciplines in the title to discuss the influence of television on the family.

Zook, Kristal Brent. **1999**. *Color by Fox: The Fox Network and the Revolution in Black Television*. New York, NY: Oxford University Press. A scholarly look at television shows produced by and for African Americans. Explains how the shows reveal complex and contradictory politics of gender, sexuality, and class. Includes interviews.